REA

Historical Dictionary of Afghanistan

Asian/Oceanian Historical Dictionaries
Edited by Jon Woronoff

Historical Dictionary of Afghanistan

Second Edition

Ludwig W. Adamec

Asian/Oceanian Historical Dictionaries, No. 5

The Scarecrow Press, Inc.
Lanham, Md., & London
1997

SCARECROW PRESS, INC.

Published in the United States of America
by Scarecrow Press, Inc.
4720 Boston Way
Lanham, Maryland 20706

4 Pleydell Gardens, Folkestone
Kent CT20 2DN, England

British Library Cataloguing in Publication Information Available

Library of Congress Cataloging-in-Publication Data

Adamec, Ludwig W.
    Historical dictionary of Afghanistan / Ludwig W. Adamec. — 2nd ed.
        p.   cm. — (Asian/Oceanian historical dictionaries ; no. 29)
    Includes bibliographical references.
    ISBN 0-8108-3312-3 (alk. paper)
    1. Afghanistan—History—Dictionaries. I. Title. II. Series.
DS356.A27   1997
958.1'003—dc21   97-2878

ISBN 0-8108-3312-3 (cloth : alk. paper)

♾™ The paper used in this publication meets the minimum requirements of
American National Standard for Information Sciences—Permanence of
Paper for Printed Library Materials, ANSI Z39.48–1984.
Manufactured in the United States of America.

To Rahella

CONTENTS

EDITOR'S FOREWORD

Most Americans are familiar only with the recent, tragic history of Afghanistan since it became embroiled in great power struggles and underwent a long and painful war. But there is much more to Afghanistan than that. As this book shows, it is heir to a tradition of 3,500 years, replete with great kingdoms and celebrated leaders. It would be extremely useful for Americans and others who want to understand the recent past to take a look further back, to see where Afghanistan is coming from and get an inkling of where it may be going.

Thanks to numerous entries on the various periods, prominent figures, and important events, this *Historical Dictionary of Afghanistan* points the way. It makes the transition from one period to another easier with a comprehensive chronology. And it directs those who want to know more toward further literature on subjects that interest them. Even for the recent period, which we think we know best, it helps refresh our memory of "who is who" and what they did. I am therefore certain that this new edition will be particularly welcome.

It was written by Ludwig W. Adamec, professor of Near Eastern studies at the University of Arizona in Tucson. He has considerable familiarity with Afghanistan, having visited it frequently and written on it extensively. He has produced works on Afghanistan's diplomatic history and foreign affairs, an historical gazetteer, a biographical dictionary, and a Who is Who. Of particular interest is his recently published *Dictionary of Afghan Wars, Revolutions, and Insurgencies*. These works have stood him in good stead for this book, which combines many of these facets.

Jon Woronoff
Series Editor

ABBREVIATIONS AND ACRONYMS

A.	Arabic
Af.	Afghani (monetary unit)
AGSA	Afghanistan Security Service
AIG	Afghan Interim Government
AR	Amir Abdul Rahman Biography
ASDP	Afghan Social Democratic Party, also called Afghan Millat
D.	Dari, the Farsi of Afghanistan
DRA	Democratic Republic of Afghanistan, later ROA
Gaz.	Gazetteer, Adamec (vols. 1-6)
Harakat	*Harakat-i Inqilab-i Islami* of Muhammadi
Hizb (H)	*Hizb-i Islami* of Hekmatyar
Hizb (K)	*Hizb-i Islami* of Khales
ISI	Inter-Services Intelligence
Ittihad	*Ittihad-i Islami Barayi Azadi-yi Afghanistan* of Sayyaf
Jabha	*Jabha-yi Milli Najat-i Afghanistan* of Mujaddidi
Jam'iat	*Jam'iat-i Islami* of Rabbani
KAM	Workers' Information Service
KHAD	State Information Service
Khalq	Faction of the PDPA and its newspaper
LCSFA	Limited Contingent of Soviet Forces in Afghanistan
LWA	Ludwig W. Adamec
MAHAZ	*Mahaz-i Milli* of Pir Gilani
MR	Military Report
MRD	Motorized Rifle Division
Nasr	*Sazman-i Nasr* of Shaikh Mir Husain Sadeqi
NFF	National Fatherland Front
NFROA	National Front of the Republic of Afghanistan,

	formerly NFF
NIFA	English Acronym for *Mahaz-i Milli-yi Afghanistan*, National Islamic Front of Afghanistan
NWFP	North-West Frontier Province of India, now Pakistan
OA1,2.3	Official Account, First, Second, and Third Anglo-Afghan War
P.	Pashtu
PP.	Parliamentary Papers Collection
Parcham	Faction of the PDPA and its newspaper
PDPA	Peoples Democratic Party of Afghanistan, later Watan Party
r.	Ruled
R.	Rupee (monetary unit)
ROA	Republic of Afghanistan, formerly DRA
SAZA	*Sazman-i Inqilab-i Zahmatkeshan-i Afghanistan*, Organization of the Revolutionary Toilers of Afghanistan
SCDH	Supreme Council for the Defense of the Homeland
Shu'la	*Shu'la-yi Javid*, name of a newspaper and party
S.o.	Son of
T.	Turkic
WAD	Ministry of State Security, formerly KHAD

USER'S NOTES

Alphabetization and Spellings. Names beginning with "Abdul" (A. *'abd-al*, "servant" or "slave"), followed by one of the names of Allah (God), as for example Abdul Ahad (Servant of the One) or Abdul Hakim (Servant of the Wise), form a unit and should not be taken as first and last names. Abdul Hakim will therefore be found under "A," not "H." Similarly, the name Ghulam (A. slave) and its complement, as for example Ghulam Muhammad, is found under "G," not "M." Compounds with Allah, like Fazlullah (Fazl Allah), Nurullah (Nur Allah), Habibullah (Habib Allah), will be found in alphabetical order under their compound versions. Although not forming a construct, Afghan practice considers names beginning with Muhammad, as for example Muhammad Daud, Muhammad Afzal, etc., one unit; therefore the names will be found be under "M."

The arrangement of entries in alphabetical order treats headings as if they were one word, disregarding punctuation marks; for example, Afghani is preceded by Afghan Hound and followed by Afghan Interim Government. Muhammadi is preceded by Muhammad Hashim and followed by Muhammad Ishaq, and Tanai, Lt. Gen. Shahnawaz, is preceded by Tanai Coup.

Names of individuals are spelled in a modified form of transliteration, even if the person described has his own idiosyncratic spelling; for example Cher Ali, or Scher Ali, is spelled Shir Ali; Kayeum and Kayum are spelled Qayyum; and Abaucy is Abbasi. Variant spellings of names are cross listed. Titles and honorifics are not included in the entry headings.

Statistics. Population statistics are estimates for the pre-war (1979) period, unless otherwise indicated. Estimates of the Afghan population vary from 13 to 15.5 million, this includes about two million nomads. Measurements throughout are in the British, rather than the metric, system. The population of Afghan towns and cities has fluctuated as a result of the war and the movement of internal refugees.

Nomenclature. Afghan rulers of the Sadozai branch of the Durranis (1747-1818) held the title Shah, "king"; but the succeeding Barakzai rulers were known as amirs, which means "chief, prince, commander," as well as "king." Amanullah assumed the title Shah in 1926; in order to avoid referring pedantically to Amanullah's title at a particular time, I have employed the appellation of "king" throughout.

References. References to entries are given in bold characters, but names of towns, provinces, and rivers are not so indicated. All provinces and major towns are listed and it was felt that there was no need to use bold print to refer the reader to those entries.

Scope. The purpose of this volume is to provide a concise reference work on Afghanistan, including entries on major historical events, important places, leading personalities – past and present – and significant aspects of culture, religion, and economy. The focus is on the political history of contemporary Afghanistan. The reader who desires more extensive biographical information may refer to the biographical dictionaries by this author (1975 and 1987). Geographical and tribal information beyond the scope of this work can be found in the gazetteers compiled by this author (1972-85; also see bibliography). Although not definitive in scope, this work should provide a good introduction for the study of Afghanistan and a basis for more extensive study or research.

INTRODUCTION

Afghanistan, the "Land of the Afghans," began as a political entity in 1747 when **Ahmad Shah** (r. 1747-73) was crowned king of a tribal confederation; it is an ancient land with a glorious history of kingdoms dating back some 3,500 years. As part of the nation-building process, Afghan historians in the twentieth century popularized the idea of an organic link existing between modern Afghanistan and its ancient roots. They see a continuum from **Ariana** (1,500 B.C.) of the Indo-Iranians, centered around Balkh, city of Zoroaster, in northern Afghanistan to the Buddhist kingdom of the **Kushanids** (about 50-250 A.D.) with its capital in Peshawar and Bagram. Intermittently Afghanistan was peripheral to empires as a satrapy of the Achaemenid Empire in the sixth century B.C., of Alexander the Great in the fourth century B.C., and the Maurian kingdom of **Asoka** a century later.

Afghanistan's Islamic roots began with the Muslim Arab invasion in the seventh century A.D., but it was not until the tenth century that Islam was firmly established and not until the end of the nineteenth century that the last vestiges of pre-Islamic communities disappeared. The first indigenous Islamic state was the **Ghaznavid** Empire (977-1186), named after its capital Ghazni, a town in eastern Afghanistan. It was destroyed by the **Ghorids** (1150-1217) whose capital was Ghor, a town in central Afghanistan. The domains of both empires included large portions of northern India. The Mongols wreaked destruction in the thirteenth century, as did **Timur-i Lang** almost two centuries later. Timur's descendants rebuilt Herat and made it a great cultural center. By the sixteenth century Afghanistan was again peripheral to powerful neighbors.

Almost simultaneously three empires emerged in the early sixteenth century: the Safavid rulers of Iran (1501-1786) who controlled portions of western Afghanistan; the Moghul rulers of India (1526-1858) who made Kabul their capital in 1504, until **Babur** established himself (1526-1530) and his successors in Delhi and Agra; and the Shaibanid Uzbeks (1500-98) who founded a kingdom that extended from the plains north of the **Hindu Kush** far into Transoxania.

Modern Afghanistan was born as a result of revolt against foreign occupation. **Mir Wais**, founder of the short-lived **Hotaki** dynasty (1709-38), rose in rebellion against Gorgin Khan, the Safavid governor of Kandahar; he defeated the avenging Safavid armies and, encouraged by his success, raided far into Iran. The **Abdali** (later **Durrani**) tribes liberated Herat, and Afghan tribes flocked to the banner of Mahmud (1716-25), son of Mir Wais, who beseiged Isfahan in the Battle of **Gulnabad** in 1722 and ended the rule of the Safavid kings. The Hotaki **Ghilzais** were soldiers, not empire builders. They could not hold on to their conquests, and **Nadir Shah Afshar** reunited Iran (1736-47) under his short-lived empire, which also held Afghanistan and northern India.

Ahmad Shah commanded an Afghan contingent of Nadir Shah's army and, at the sudden death of the latter, was able to intercept a convoy of booty destined for Iran. This gave him the means to augment his forces and consolidate his power. Following the example of previous guardians of the "gateway to India," he led nine invasions into the Indian subcontinent and made himself the undisputed ruler of an empire which Afghans refer to as the "historical" Afghanistan. The boundaries of this state were the **Amu Daria** in the north, the Indus River in the east, the Indian Ocean in the south, and the present Iranian provinces of **Khorasan** and Sistan in the west. Ahmad Shah ruled a heterogeneous population that in addition to the dominant Pashtun element forming the core of his armies included a largely sedentary population of Dari/Farsi speakers, Turkic, and **Baluch** minorities, and a multitude of ethnic and sectarian groups.

The Afghan heartland is a mountain fastness, surrounded by deserts in the north, west, and south, with cultivation supported by five major river systems dependent on melting snow from the mountains. Subsistence agriculture, small-scale mining, and a handicraft industry for domestic consumption did not provide sufficient surplus wealth to support a lavish court. The ruling Durranis and allied tribes depended on a system of military feudalism that allocated agricultural lands to the chiefs in exchange for military service, corresponding to the size of their fiefs (*tiyul*). An alternative was territorial conquest. The Afghans saw it as their manifest destiny to rule the fertile Panjab plains if not all of northern India.

A policy of conquest had definite advantages: it brought prosperity to the Pashtun tribes and kept them united. Ahmad Shah was not an absolute ruler; he was a *primus inter pares* who had to contend with the ambitions of the *khans*, the chiefs of the major tribes. It was for this reason that he also recruited a force of non-Pashtun *qizilbash* soldiers. When Timur, one of Ahmad Shah's six sons, succeeded to the Afghan throne in 1773, he transferred the capital from Kandahar to Kabul, where he was more secure from the intrigues of the Kandahar chiefs. Described as "more a scholar than a soldier," **Timur Shah** faced revolt in the periphery of the empire. **Zaman Shah**, one of Timur's twenty-three sons, ascended the throne in 1793, amid internecine warfare that led to the eventual demise of the Sadozai dynasty. Britain extended her control in India, and the emergence of the Sikh Empire of **Ranjit Singh** (1780-1839) in the Panjab definitively ended Afghan aspirations of eastward expansion.

At the beginning of the nineteenth century, Afghanistan became directly involved in European empire politics. In addition to Russia and Britain, France emerged as a contender in the "Great Game" for imperial conquest. The first contact between a British envoy, **Mountstuart Elphinstone**, and an Afghan ruler (**Shah Shuja**, r. 1803-10 and 1839) took place at Peshawar in February 1809 and led to an alliance against a Franco-Persian invasion that never materialized. The next, more fateful encounter, was the first of three Anglo-Afghan Wars.

In 1600 the British **East India Company** obtained a charter for exploration and commerce in Bengal, India, and a century and a half later, the company was the *de facto* ruler of Bengal. Its Board of Control appointed a governor-general as an executive who conducted the government for the Company until 1858, when the crown ended the charter and appointed a viceroy subject to the control of the London government. At the same time Britain continued its territorial conquests and started to worry about how to protect its new acquisitions from Afghan attacks and Russian expansionism which had reached Persia's borders in the Caucasus.

When **Dost Muhammad** (r. 1835-39 and 1842-63), first of the **Barakzai** amirs, ascended the Kabul throne in 1835, Persia occupied Khorasan with Russian support and beseiged Herat, while Ranjit Singh conquered Multan, Kashmir, Derajat, and Peshawar. Fearing an Afghan alliance with Russia, **Lord Auckland**, governor-general of the British East India Company, decided to restore Shah Shuja to the Afghan throne. The British invasion, though initially successful, resulted in a disastrous defeat in the **First Anglo-Afghan War**. The British government refrained for almost 40 years from conducting a "forward" policy at its northwestern frontier. However, Russian advances in Central Asia continued, and voices in London and Delhi demanded a new policy and consolidation of a "scientific" frontier for the defense of India. In 1876 the British Queen was proclaimed empress of India and in 1878, British-Indian armies again invaded Afghanistan. Amir **Shir Ali** (r. 1863-79), who had negotiated with a Russian envoy at Kabul, was forced to seek refuge in northern Afghanistan where he died shortly afterwards. He was succeeded by his son **Muhammad Yaqub Khan**, who signed the **Treaty of Gandomak** (1879) and permitted a permanent British mission to be established in Kabul. Insurrection and the massacre of the British envoy and his staff led to the demise of Yaqub Khan and recognition of **Abdul Rahman** Khan as the next Afghan ruler in 1880.

With Amir Abdur Rahman (r. 1880-1901), the traditional system of rule came to an end. The "Iron Amir" no longer appointed princes as governors of major provinces, a practice that had led to much strife in the past. He ended the local autonomy of Uzbek khans in the north, Hazaras in the center, and the Kafirs in the east of Afghanistan. Abdur Rahman reconquered the country and expelled or killed any of the notables who could pose a threat to his power. He claimed both the highest secular and spiritual powers and limited the influence of the religious establishment (*ulama*) and the tribes. His reign marked the beginning of centralized rule and the bureaucratization of the government. His regular army gradually replaced feudal and irregular levies, ending the system of military feudalism. An alliance with Britain protected Afghanistan from unprovoked Russian aggression and provided the funds and weapons to eliminate all domestic challenges to his power. In exchange, the Afghan ruler agreed to conduct his relations with neighboring states through the medium of the British government. Abdur Rahman formulated a foreign policy which served Afghanistan well, until King **Amanullah** (r. 1919-29) ended the country's dependence on Britain in the **Third Anglo-Afghan War** (1919). A window to the West, which had begun gradually to open when Amir **Habibullah** (r. 1901-19) received a German mission during World War I, was thrown wide open under King Amanullah. Afghanistan established diplomatic relations with major European and Asian countries.

A contemporary of Kemal Ataturk of Turkey and Reza Shah of Iran, Amanullah ushered in Western reforms and first introduced the institutions of constitutional government. A short period of reaction under **Habibullah Kalakani** (r. 1929) did not end the process of modernization, most visible in the expansion of education during the reigns of **Nadir Shah** in 1929-33 and his son **Zahir Shah** in 1933-73.

The fact that the experiment with democracy in the 1960s ended in failure, war, and foreign intervention should not be surprising. The socioeconomic conditions that favor a trend to a stable, if not democratic, government still did not exist. **Muhammad Daud** felt that strong leadership was required; he rebelled against his cousin, the king, and established a republican form of government, taking direct command of the affairs of the state. He was toppled from power in 1978 by his Marxist supporters who thought they had a cure for the socioeconomic ills of the country. Feeling secure about receiving Soviet support, the Marxist government initiated unpalatable innovations, which resulted in armed resistance and civil war. It evolved into a war of liberation after the Soviets intervened in support of the Kabul government.

During the almost 250 years of its existence, Afghanistan has evolved from empire to state and may be on its way to becoming a nation. It has progressed from rule by a Pashtun warrior caste, followed by civil war, to a more cohesive system established by Amir Abdur Rahman and continued until the 1970s. It was only as a result of the present war in Afghanistan that bureaucratic urban control has given way to autonomy of the countryside. Its inaccessible terrain and the existence of two imperialist neighbors have defined Afghanistan's "natural" borders, and three wars against Britain and one against the Soviet Union have welded a heterogeneous population together.

The departure of Soviet troops from Afghanistan in February 1989 raised hopes that peace would be quickly restored and a popularly elected government could promptly begin the arduous task of political and economic reconstruction. The war has resulted in the emergence of new elites and the politicization of rural Afghanistan but sectarian and ethnic strife has continued as has interference by foreign powers.

After the fall of the Marxist regime in April 1992, Afghanistan was cantonized by hostile forces. Ideology never seemed the determining factor in the civil war and tactical alliances found yesterday's enemies in the same camp. There is no question that the primary motivation in the minds of the combatants is to attain political power. A new force, the *Taliban*, emerged in November 1994 and quickly took control of two-thirds of Afghanistan and is set to capture the rest of the county. The **Pashtun** *Taliban* now face the largely non-Pashtun alliance of **Abdul Rashid Dostum**, **Burnhanuddin Rabbani** and his commander **Mas'ud**, and **Abdul Karim Khalili**, leader of the **shi'i Hizb-i Wahdat**. The *Taliban* seem determined to unify Afghanistan under their own harsh, theocratic rule. Initial hopes for the establishment of a broad-based, liberal government in Afghanistan have been disappointed, and the prognosis is not good for the near future.

THE DICTIONARY

A

ABDALI. The original name of the **Durrani**, the royal Pashtun tribe, located in the Kandahar area. They claim descent from Tarin and his youngest son Bar Tarin, or Abdal, hence their name Abdali. In 1747 Pir Sabir Shah, a sufi shaikh, proclaimed Ahmad Khan of the Abdali tribe *Badshah, Durr-i Dauran* (King, the Pearl of the Age), which Ahmad Shah later changed to *Durr-i Durran* (Pearl of Pearls). His Abdali tribe became henceforth known as the Durrani. *See* AHMAD SHAH and DURRANI.

ABDUL GHANI. An Indian Muslim, born in 1864 and graduated from medical school at Government College, Lahore in 1883. He went to London for further study where he met Sardar **Nasrullah**, son of Amir **Abdur Rahman**, and obtained a scholarship for study in England from the amir. In 1891 he came to Kabul to serve as secretary to Amir Abdur Rahman. Subsequently he served for three years as principal of the Islamia College at Lahore but returned to Afghanistan under Amir **Habibullah** and was appointed chief medical officer, director of public instruction in Afghanistan, and principal of **Habibia School**. He was a champion of political and social reform and attracted a circle of "Young Afghans" who formed a secret organization called *sirr-i milli* (Secret of the Nation). In 1909 he and a number of his followers were arrested for having plotted against the life of Amir Habibullah. He was freed when King **Amanullah** ascended the throne; appointed him a member of the Afghan delegation to the **Rawalpindi Peace Conference** in August 1919. He subsequently returned to India and wrote about Afghanistan and Central Asia. His *A Brief Political History of Afghanistan* was published posthumously by his nephew in 1979. He died in 1945. *See* SIRR-I MILLI.

ABDUL HADI DAWAI. *See* **DAWAI, ABDUL HADI.**

ABDUL HAQ (ABD AL-HAQQ). A *mujahedin* commander affiliated with the *Hizb-i Islami* (Islamic Party) of **Yunus Khales** who had been active in the Kabul area. He is an **Ahmadzai** Pashtun, born about 1958 near Jalalabad, and as a student was affiliated with the Islamic Youth (*jawanan-i musulman*) which opposed the reformist regime of President **Muhammad Daud.** He was imprisoned in 1975 and freed in 1978 after the Saur Revolt. Based in the Shiwaki area, south of Kabul, he was responsible for organizing guerrilla attacks on government posts within Kabul. In 1987 he suffered a crippling injury to his foot that limited his active participation in raids. After the fall of the Marxist regime in April 1992, he was appointed chief of police and security as well as commander of the gendarmerie but resigned from his posts at the beginning of the civil war between the *mujahedin* groups. He and his brother, **Abdul Qadir** who became acting governor of Jalalabad, remained neutral between the *Taliban* and *Jam'iat* forces and engaged in commerce with Pakistan and the Gulf area. On September 11 the *Taliban* captured Jalalabad and forced Abdul Haq and other members of the **shura** to flee the country.

ABDUL KARIM. A **Ghilzai mulla,** the son of Din Muhammad, the famous mulla **Mushk-iAlam.** Amir **Abdul Rahman** gave him the title *Khan-i Ulum* (Chief of [religious] Sciences), but he became disaffected when the amir ended the virtual autonomy enjoyed by the Ghilzai tribes and imposed taxes on hitherto exempt lands. He was one of the leaders of the Ghilzai Rebellion of 1886–87, which was suppressed only with great difficulty. It was the last of three uprisings of this tribe in the 19th century. *See also* GHILZAI.

ABDUL KHALIQ. Son of a **Hazara** servant of **Ghulam Nabi Charkhi** (executed by King Nadir), he avenged the killing of his master by assassinating **Nadir Shah** a year later on November 8, 1933. He was a student at **Najat** (Amani) High School and attended a graduation ceremony in the palace garden where the assassination took place. He was handed over to the King's bodyguard for execution. A number of relatives, students, and teachers of Najat and **Istiqlal** schools were executed in December 1933. This was the last bloodletting in the struggle for power between supporters of King **Amanullah** and the new royal family. *See also* MUHAMMAD AZIM; WALI MUHAMMAD; and GHULAM NABI CHARKHI.

ABDUL QADIR, MAJ. GEN. A *Parchami* member of the **PDPA**. Commander of the Air Defense Forces in 1973, when he supported **Muhammad Daud** in his coup against **Zahir Shah**. Actively participated in the Saur Revolt and was head of the Revolutionary Council until a civilian government was formed under **Nur Muhammad Taraki**. He became minister of Defense for three months in May 1978, but in August he was sentenced to death (commuted to 15 years) for plotting against the **Khalqi** regime. Freed when **Babrak Karmal** came to power, he was restored to his party positions and served again as minister of Defense (September 1982–85). In November 1985 he resigned from the Politburo for "reasons of health" and in November 1986 was appointed ambassador to Warsaw. Recalled two years later and elected a lowly member of Parliament, he is said to have moved to Bulgaria in 1989 and sought asylum in Europe after the fall of the Marxist regime. Born 1944 of a **Tajik** family in Herat Province, he went to military school and attended pilot training and staff college in the Soviet Union.

ABDUL QUDDUS. A nephew of Amir **Dost Muhammad** and general who lived with Amir **Abdul Rahman** in exile in Bukhara and Samarkand. On their return, he assisted the Amir in extending his power over Afghanistan. He captured Herat from **Ayub** Khan, son of Amir **Shir Ali,** in 1881 with a small force of 400 cavalry and 400 infantry soldiers and two machine guns, and during the period 1890–93 he conquered the **Hazarajat** (*See* HAZARA WARS). Amir **Habibullah** gave him the title *Itimad-ud-Daula* (Confidence of the State) and appointed him prime minister, in which position he was confirmed by King **Amanullah**. In the **Third Anglo-Afghan War** Abdul Quddus commanded the Kandahar front. A British officer characterized him as "A Tory of the most crusted type in politics, and an apostle of Afghanistan for the Afghans." His descendants who were prominent in Afghan government adopted his title, **Etemadi**, as their family name.

ABDUL RAHIM. Born about 1886, the son of Abdul Qadir. A Safi from Kuh Daman, north of Kabul, who, from the age of 16, served in various military units and rose from the ranks to become general. At the outbreak of the civil war in 1928 he espoused the cause of **Habibullah Kalakani**. He captured Maimana and Herat for Habibullah and became governor of Herat. Because Abdul Rahim had a powerful base in Herat, the Afghan king was unable to remove him from his post until 1934. In June 1935 he was appointed minister of Public Works and subsequently served as deputy prime minister from 1938 to 1940. He was imprisoned from 1946–48 on suspicion of plotting against the government of Prime Minister **Muhammad Hashim**. Abdur Rahim is the maternal uncle and father-in-law of **Khalilullah Khalili**, the famous poet laureate.

ABDUL RAHMAN, AMIR (ABDUR RAHMAN, r. 1880–1901). Amir of Afghanistan, the oldest son of Amir **Muhammad Afzal** Khan, who assumed the Kabul throne at the end of the **Second Anglo-Afghan War.** He fought his uncle Amir **Shir Ali** in 1864 and was forced to flee to the court of the Amir of Bukhara. Returned to Afghanistan in 1866, he defeated Amir Shir Ali and recognized his father, Afzal Khan, as the new king. Three years later Amir Shir Ali regained the throne and Abdul Rahman was forced into exile, spending some ten years in Bukhara, Tashkent, and Samarkand. After the death of Amir Shir Ali in February 1879, Abdul Rahman Khan returned to Afghanistan and on his way south gathered a large army. The British occupation force feared a repetition of the debacle of the **First Anglo-Afghan War** and, on July 22, 1880, grudgingly recognized Abdul Rahman as "Amir of Kabul and its Dependencies," in spite of the fact that he had come with Russian support. In September 1881 the amir took possession of Kandahar, defeating the forces of **Ayub Khan**, son of Amir Shir Ali. Herat was taken in August, and Abdul Rahman was undisputed ruler of Afghanistan.

Abdul Rahman concluded an agreement with the British government, in which Britain guaranteed him protection from unprovoked Russian aggression, provided he permitted Britain to conduct his foreign relations. He obtained a subsidy in money and materiel to strengthen the defenses of his country. Abdul Rahman considered this treaty an alliance between equals and, having protected his northern borders, he kept the British at arms length, never allowing them to gain any influence in the country under the aegis of their common defense. He formulated a "buffer-state policy" which aimed at playing off Afghanistan's imperialist neighbors against each other. This policy served Afghanistan well until the end of World War II, when changed conditions required new approaches in the conduct of Afghan foreign policy. Afghanistan's northern and eastern boundaries were demarcated during the Amir's tenure, including the Durand Line (1893), which he accepted under "duress" in the **Durand Agreement**. He built the Bagh-i Jahan Noma in Khulm, the Salam Khana castle in Mazar-i Sharif, in Kabul the Masjid-i Idgah, the **Arg**, the Shahrara tower, and the Bagh-i Bala castle. Abdul Rahman died in 1901 and was buried in Bustan Saray in Kabul.

The amir was an impressive personality, being "of middle height, inclined to be fat, and of sound and masculine face and features. He wore a full beard . . . was hard-working . . . in State affairs he consulted none. . . . He had a curious Afghan humour, and a peculiar fascinating attitude towards all his servants, who dreaded him, yet loved him." He had five wives and two concubines. Of his five sons **Habibullah** and **Nasrullah** succeeded to the throne; the latter was amir for only three days.

ABDUL RAHMAN, CAMPAIGNS. The future Afghan king learned his trade as a military commander at an early age. His father, **Muhammad Afzal** Khan, was governor of Balkh and appointed Abdul Rahman, who was then about thirteen years old, subgovernor of Tashqurghan (now called Khulm), a flourishing town and district in Afghan Turkestan. He became a pupil of General Shir Muhammad Khan, a Scotsman named **Campbell** who was captured at the Battle of **Kandahar** and converted to Islam. Abdul Rahman Khan succeeded him as commander of the army of Balkh. He defeated the **Uzbek** chiefs of Qataghan and Badakhshan and forced them to renew their loyalty to Kabul. He helped to place his father on the Kabul throne in 1866 and supported his uncle **Muhammad Azam**'s accession in 1867. He was the most obstinate rival of Amir **Shir Ali** Khan, defeating the amir's superior forces in encounters at Sayyidabad (1866), Qalat (1867), and the Panjshir Pass (1867) but eventually forced into exile.

To capture a fortified position, Abdur Rahman first tried diplomacy, appealing to the defenders to avoid the bloodshed of fellow Muslims and promising leniency. Lured into a trap, when the spiritual leader of the Mirs of Qataghan invited him to dinner, he took his host prisoner and, dividing his cavalry force of some 1,600 *sowars* (cavalry) and two guns into small units, defeated an enemy of 10,000. When he returned from exile, the troops assembled to prevent his crossing into Afghanistan melted away. He proclaimed that "I inform you that I have come to release the country of Faiza from the hands of the English. If I succeed in doing so peacefully, well and good, otherwise we shall have to fight" (AR, 174). As he moved slowly south his forces continued to grow and Sir **Lepel Griffin**, the political officer with the British expeditionary forces at Kabul, initiated negotiations which led to Abdul Rahman's recognition as "Amir of Kabul." A final challenge to his power was **Ayub** Khan's capture of Kandahar in August 1881, when Abdul Rahman took to the field and decisively defeated his rival.

Having eliminated most of his major rivals, Amir Abdul Rahman proceeded to quell local revolts. He defeated Sayyid Mahmud of Kunar in 1881 and took direct control of Maimana in 1883. The **Shinwari** revolt was suppressed in 1883 and the **Ghilzai** Rebellion was crushed during 1886–87. The Iron Amir's last rival, his cousin **Muhammad Ishaq** Khan, was defeated at the Battle of Ghaznigak in 1888. The government control of the **Hazarajat** was achieved by 1893 after a long series of wars (*see* HAZARA WARS), and **Kafiristan** was the last area integrated into the State of Afghanistan (*See* KAFIR WAR). When Amir **Habibullah** ascended to the throne in 1901, the entire country was pacified.

ABDUL WALI. Commander-in-chief of the Central Forces until 1973. Imprisoned as a result of the coup by his cousin **Muhammad Daud** in 1973. Born in 1924, the son of Marshal **Shah Wali** and cousin of ex-King Zahir). Educated in France and England where he attended Sandhurst as well as the Command and General Staff College at Camberley. He is married to Princess Bilqis, daughter of the former King **Muhammad Zahir**, and has been living in Italy since 1976, where he acts as a spokesman for the former king. In August 1995 he went to Pakistan where he was received by large crowds. He talked with high-ranking Pakistani officials and conferred with leading Afghans.

ABI. Irrigated land in Afghanistan (from D. *ab*, water), as distinct from *lalmi*, land which is dependent on "dry-farming" agriculture. Only about 12 percent of Afghanistan's area of 245,000 square miles is cultivable land.

AB-I ISTADA (32-32' N, 67-57' E). "Standing Water," a brackish lake of some 17 miles in length, located astride the border of Ghazni and Paktika Provinces, about 65 miles south-southwest of Ghazni and 44 miles northeast of Kalat-i-Ghilzai. It is a shallow lake and reaches a depth of only 12 feet at its center. The banks of the lake are encrusted with salt, and its major feeder is the Ghazni River. The lake is at an altitude of more than 7,000 feet, and the surrounding land is barren, with few permanent settlements. In spite of the desolate surroundings the lake is populated by multitudes of flamingoes and other birds.

AB-I WAKHAN (37-0' N, 72-40' E). A river that rises southwest of the Wakhjir Pass in the eastern **Wakhan** Corridor and runs in a westerly direction as far as the small town of Ishkashem when its name changes to Ab-i-Panj (or Panja) and forms part of the northeastern boundary with Tajikistan. *See* WAKHAN.

ABU HANIFA (AL-NU'MAN B. THABIT B. ZUTA). A legal scholar and founder of the Hanafite school, one of the four orthodox schools (*madhhab*) of Islamic jurisprudence. His grandfather is said to have been taken prisoner in Kabul and transported to Kufa, an early Arab town on the Euphrates River in present Iraq, where Abu Hanifa was born. He studied at Kufa and gradually gained influence as an authority on legal questions, founding a rationalist school which was named after him. Afghanistan adheres to the Hanafite interpretation of Islamic law which is the largest in number of adherents and the most liberal of the four schools and permits a certain amount of personal reasoning and free judgment in arriving at legal decisions. Abu Hanifa died in 767 A.D.

ACHAKZAI. An important subtribe of the Durranis, located in an area east of Kandahar. The eponymic ancestor of the Achakzai was Achak Khan, a grandson of Barak Khan. Smaller communities of Achakzai are also found in Herat and Farah as well as in Chaman, Pakistan. *See* DURRANI.

ADMINISTRATIVE DIVISIONS. Since the time **Timur Shah** (r. 1773–93) made it his capital, Kabul has been the center of the kingdom, and princes ruled more or less autonomously in the provinces. Major provinces headed by princes included Kandahar, Herat, Afghan Turkestan, and Qataghan and Badakhshan. Amir **Abdul Rahman** (r. 1880–1901) was recognized by Britain as "Amir of Kabul and its Dependencies," and he saw to it that Herat, Afghan Turkestan, the Hazarajat, Nuristan, and Badakhshan were part of his realm. Under **Nadir Shah** (r. 1929–33) Afghanistan was divided into five major and four minor provinces.

Province	Area	Population	Wols.	Alaq.	Center
Badakhshan	48,176	484,000	5	7	Faizabad
Badghis	21,854	247,000	4	1	Qala-i-Nau
Baglan	17,165	486,000	5	4	Baghlan
Balkh	11,833	570,000	7	3	Mazar-i Sharif
Bamian	17,411	285,000	4	2	Bamian
Farah	58,834	356,000	8	2	Farah
Fariab	22,274	547,000	7	5	Maimana
Ghazni	32,797	701,000	10	12	Ghazni
Ghor	38,658	341,000	5	1	Chagh-charan
Helmand	61,816	570,000	8	4	Lashkargah
Herat	50,245	685,000	11	1	Herat
Jozjan	25,548	642,000	5	6	Shiberghan
Kabul	4,583	1,372,000	8	4	Kabul
Kandahar	49,430	699,000	11	4	Kandahar
Kunduz	7,926	575,000	5	1	Kunduz
Laghman	7,227	387,000	4	1	Mehterlam
Logar	4,409	424,000	3	3	Pul-i-Alam
Maidan (1)	9,699	310,000	4	4	Kota-i Ashro
Nangarhar (2)	18,636	786,000	17	14	Jalalabad
Nimruz	41,347	112,000	3	1	Zaranj
Oruzgan	28,756	483,000	8	-	Tirinkot
Paktia (3)	17,772	706,000	11	21	Gardez
Parwan	5,911	418,000	4	4	Charikar
Kapisa	5,358	366,000	4	4	Mahmud Raqi
Samangan	16,640	275,000	3	2	Aibak
Takhar	12,325	528,000	6	5	Taloqan
Zabul	17,298	181,000	5	3	Qalat

(1) Also called Wardak. (2) Including Kunar. (3) Including Paktika.

As a result of the Constitution of 1964, Afghanistan was divided into 26 provinces (*wilayat*,) each with a provincial center (*markaz*) that is graded according to importance into first, second, or third grade; Kabul, Ghazni, Gardez, Jalalabad, Mazar-i Sharif, Herat, and Kandahar are first grade administrative centers. They are headed by a governor, *wali*, who is the executive officer, responsible to the ministry of interior in Kabul. In addition, each province has representatives of various departments who report directly to Kabul at the administrative center. There were also a number of subprovinces, *loy woluswali*, that have since been absorbed into provinces. Each province is subdivided into districts, *woluswali*, with an administrator called *woluswal*, who is responsible to his supervising governor and may himself be in charge of one or more subdistricts, **alaqadari**. The administrator of a subdistrict, *alaqadar*, resides in a major village and is responsible to all his supervising administrators. Districts are divided into four grades, depending on population. Not counting Sar-i Pul, a Hazara province established in the 1980s, the 26 provinces were divided into six subprovinces, 175 districts, and 118 subdistricts in the 1970s. Villages and rural subdivisions or *qarya*, are headed by a village headman (*qaryadar, malik*, or *arbab*) who acts as a link between the rural population and the district chief. Cities are divided into wards, or *nahiya*.

In the 1960s the Afghan government estimated the Afghan population at about 16 million and yearly added 2.6 % to this number, until in the 1970s a demographic survey by a team from New York University arrived at a much lower figure (10,020,600). Hamidullah Amin and Gordon B. Schilz in their *A Geography of Afghanistan* (1976) give an agricultural population of 10,839,870 and 2,500,000 nomads for a total of 13,339,870. The government of **Hafizullah Amin** claimed a population of 15.5 million; Groetzbach's estimate (1990) agrees with this figure.

After the defeat of the Marxist government in April 1992, the central government ceased to exist, and the Afghan countryside was under the control of local commanders and warlords, while the capital under control of **Rabbani** was under siege. A new force, the **Taliban**, emerged in November 1994 and within two years captured two-thirds of Afghanistan, including the capital Kabul. General **Dostum** controls the north-central provinces and his allies, **Abdul Karim Khalili** of the **Hizb-i Wahdat** holds Bamian Province, and Rabani's Commander **Ahmad Shah Mas'ud** holds the northeast.

AFGANTSY (Sing. Afganets). Soviet veterans of the Afghan war
(1980–89) who were mostly conscripts in a war that did not enjoy
popular support. According to a recent study, about 750,000 served in
troop units in Afghanistan from 1979 to 1989. Casualties included about
15,000 dead, 50,000 wounded — of whom about 11,500 remained
invalids — 330 missing in action, and 18 defectors (Galeotti). They felt
neglected and that their needs were ignored. About a quarter of the
veterans are organized in the "afganets movement" with the support of
a Council of Soldiers' Mothers and Widows. Afgantsy in the highest
military posts during 1979–91 include Marshal Sokolov, defense
minister, 1984–87, and first deputy minister, until 1985; Marshal D.
Akhromeev, chief of general staff, 1984–88; General Lobov, chief of
general staff and c-i-c of the Warsaw Pact, 1991; Col. Gen. Grachev, first
deputy minister, 1991; Gen. V. Varennikov, commander of ground
forces, 1989–91; and Gen. Yu Maximov, commander of strategic rocket
forces, 1985– (Galeotti). Some observers see the Afgantsy as a "new
force" of conservative nationalists who may have an impact on the future
political life of Russia. *See also* LIMITED CONTINGENT OF SOVIET
FORCES IN AFGHANISTAN.

AFGHAN. A citizen of Afghanistan. Until the early twentieth century only
Pashtu speakers were referred to as Afghans, whereas other citizens of
Afghanistan were called by their ethnic designations (i.e., **Nuristani** or
Hazara). In the process of nation building, the term gained acceptance
as a designation for all citizen of Afghanistan.

AFGHAN ACADEMY (PASHTU TOLANA). Founded in 1937 as a
national umbrella organization for research in the social sciences and
humanities. It was fashioned initially by combining the Literary Society
(*anjoman-i adabi*) of Kabul, founded in 1930, with the Pashtu Society
(*anjoman-i Pashtu*) of Kandahar, founded in 1931. The Literary Society
promoted research in the social sciences and humanities and conducted
cultural and scientific relations with foreign countries. In 1932 it began
publishing the *Kabul Yearbook,* which appeared without interruption
until 1978 and sporadically thereafter. The Pashtu Society was to
promote Pashtu language and literature with the objective of making it
the official language of Afghanistan to remove Dari from its preeminent
position as the language of the court, the government, and education.
The Pashtu Society office was moved to Kabul in 1935, and two years
later the two societies were merged into one institution, the Pashtu

Tolana. It was headed by **Salahuddin Saljuqi** with Sardar **Muhammad Naim**, a brother of President Daud, as the honorary president. The Academy was under the administrative control of the department of press. It subsequently included the institutes of social sciences, natural sciences, languages and literature, the international center for Pashtu studies, and a number of general directorates for press, encyclopedia, and dictionary production. It finally came under the direction of the ministry of education and was headed by leading scholars and writers such as **Abdul Rahman Pazhwak**, 1941–?; **Abdul Rauf Benawa**, 1946–51; Siddiqullah Rishtin, 1951–56; **Gul Pacha Ulfat**, 1956–?; and Siddiq Ruhi, 1973–79. After the Saur Revolt the Afghan Academy was renamed the Academy of Sciences. **Sulaiman Layeq** was appointed president in 1980, and in 1986 it included, in addition to three vice presidents, eight academicians, 32 candidate academicians, and 22 members who were in charge of various journals and research institutes.

AFGHAN CONSTITUTIONAL DEVELOPMENT. *See* **CONSTITUTIONAL DEVELOPMENT.**

AFGHAN DYNASTIES. *See* **DURRANI** and **MUHAMMADZAI.**

AFGHAN ENCYCLOPEDIA SOCIETY (ARIANA DA'ERAT AL-MA'AREF). An organization within the Pashtu Tolana (**Afghan Academy**) whose principal task was the production of an encyclopedia, in **Dari** and **Pashtu**, published by the Afghan Government Press. The project was started in 1941 under the sponsorship of Sardar **Muhammad Naim**; Mia Husain Mujaddidi, a subsequent finance minister, was its first director. The Dari version comprises six volumes: the first volume was published in 1948 and the last in 1970. The project was overly ambitious, the first five volumes (A-F) each numbering one thousand pages and the sixth covering subjects for the rest of the alphabet in 371 pages. Insufficient funding was given as the reason for ending this monumental project. Leading Afghan scholars contributed articles for this work which was patterned in scope after major Western encyclopedias.

AFGHAN FOREIGN RELATIONS. Afghanistan's relations with her neighbors were always influenced by the fact that the territory inhabited by the Afghans was the "gateway" to the Indian subcontinent. The power that controlled the tribes and the passes leading south and east would not encounter any great physical obstacles in the conquest of the subcontinent and its fabulous riches. **Mahmud of Ghazni** (r. 988–1030), Tamerlane (**Timur-i Lang**, r. 1370–1405), and **Nadir Shah Afshar** (r. 1736–47) crossed the Afghan passes for the propagation of **Islam**, glory, and booty. It is therefore not surprising that **Ahmad Shah** Durrani (r. 1747–73), the founder of the state of Afghanistan, considered it his manifest destiny to create an empire that included a large portion of northern India. He invaded India eight times and defeated the powerful Maratha confederation at the **Battle of Panipat**, north of Delhi, in 1761. But by the turn of the century, the gradual northwest expansion of British influence resulted in a confrontation between Britain and Afghanistan that was to continue into the twentieth century. Afghanistan's foreign relations can be divided into five major periods: first, the expansionist period, which lasted from 1747 to 1800; second, the period of foreign conflict, from 1800 to 1880, which involved Afghanistan in hostilities with Persia and the rising **Sikh** nation in the Panjab as well as with Britain and Russia; third, the period of defensive isolationism and "buffer-state" politics, initiated by Amir **Abdul Rahman** (r. 1880–1901) and continued by Amir **Habibullah** (r. 1901–1919) until his death; and fourth, the period of defensive neutralism which opened Afghanistan to foreign influences and lasted until after World War II when Britain's departure from India ushered in a new era of peaceful coexistence that, nevertheless, ended with the Marxist coup in 1978 and the **Soviet Intervention**. The final period was one of close cooperation with the Soviet Union, ending in the war of the 1980s and the subsequent civil war.

During the expansionist period Afghan rulers conquered territories north of the **Hindu Kush** and east of the Indus River, but internecine fighting among the **Durrani** *sardars* (princes and chiefs) and the emergence of new players in the "**Great Game**" in Central Asia made the Afghan empire a short-lived enterprise. When in 1798 **Zaman Shah** invited the Marquess Wellesley, governor of Bengal (1798–1805), to join him in a campaign against the **Maratha** confederacy of northwestern India, Wellesley sought Persian assistance "to keep Zaman Shah in perpetual check." The period of foreign conflict saw the emergence of the Sikh nation under **Ranjit Singh** who wrested the Panjab from the Afghans. Britain feared the appearance of a French mission in Tehran in 1807 and considered the Russian territorial gains in the Caucasus a serious threat to India. Therefore, in 1808 the British governor-general, Lord Minto, sent **Mountstuart Elphinstone** to Peshawar to conclude a treaty of friendship and common defense against Franco-Persian attacks. **Shah Shuja**, who had ascended the Kabul throne, agreed to prohibit Frenchmen from entering his realm in exchange for military support. This treaty as well as others concluded between Britain and Fath Ali Shah, the ruler of Persia, were "inoperative" almost as soon as they were ratified. Shah Shuja was ousted in 1810 and, after an interval of internecine fighting, the **Muhammadzai** branch of the Durranis replaced the **Sadozai** rulers.

Dost Muhammad, a capable ruler, succeeded to the throne in 1826. He wanted British friendship but also wanted to regain Peshawar from Ranjit Singh, whose forces had conquered Multan in 1810, Kashmir in 1819, and Peshawar in 1823. But Lord **Auckland**, governor-general of the British **East India Company** (1836–42), favored a forward policy; he concluded the Tripartite Agreement of July 1838 with Ranjit Singh and Shah Shuja to restore the shah to the Kabul throne. Dost Muhammad's negotiations with a purported Russian envoy and the amir's hostility to the Sikh ruler were the *casus belli*, and the **Simla Manifesto** of 1838, issued by the British-Indian government, constituted the declaration of war. The **Army of the Indus**, as it was proudly called, invaded Afghanistan in what came to be known as the **First Anglo-Afghan War**. Once installed on the Kabul throne, Shah Shuja was unable to consolidate his power even with British support. Afghan tribal forces attacked isolated outposts, and on November 2, 1841, the British Political Officer **Alexander Burnes** and his staff were assassinated. The British forces were compelled to negotiate an ignominious retreat that resulted in the virtual annihilation of the British-Indian forces. *See* FIRST ANGLO-AFGHAN WAR; CAPITULATION, TREATY OF; and DEATH MARCH.

This extraordinary setback for Britain led to the restoration of Dost Muhammad (r. 1842–63). Like Shah Shuja, he had been in Indian exile, and his return to Kabul began the rule of the **Muhammadzai** dynasty, a collateral branch of the Sadozai, which lasted until 1973. The British-Indian government resigned itself to a period of "masterly inactivity" which left Afghanistan to revert to civil war following the succession of Amir **Shir Ali** in 1863. But the search for a "scientific" frontier and the desire to fill a "power vacuum" in Afghanistan led to a return to a forward policy. Baluchistan came under British control in 1879, and the Indian government had to decide where its boundary with

Afghanistan should be: the crest of the **Hindu Kush**, the **Amu Daria**, or the tribal belt of the northwestern frontier? Lacking any direct control over Afghanistan, Britain wanted envoys stationed at Herat and Kabul who could guard Indian interests in those vital areas. Amir Shir Ali was willing to forge an alliance with Britain, but he wanted protection from Russian aggression, a subsidy in weapons and funds, and British recognition of his son, Abdullah Jan, as his successor (*See* AMBALA CONFERENCE). When he could not obtain a clear commitment from Britain, he listened to the overtures of General **Kaufman**, the Russian governor general of Turkestan Province, and permitted a mission under Major-General **Stolietoff** to proceed to Kabul. The Russians gave the not quite ironclad promise "that if any foreign enemy attacks Afghanistan and the Amir is unable to drive him out ... The Russian Government will repel the enemy either by means of advice or by such other means as it may seem proper."

The British government now insisted that the Amir receive a mission, headed by General **Neville Chamberlain**. Shir Ali asked for a postponement of the mission, but it proceeded in spite of the wishes of the amir. When it was stopped at the Afghan frontier, Britain presented an ultimatum; on January 8, 1879, British troops occupied Kandahar in the start of the **Second Anglo-Afghan War**. The promised Russian support was in the form of "advice," namely that the amir should make his peace with the British. Shir Ali felt betrayed; he was forced to flee and died two months later near Mazar-i Sharif.

His son **Yaqub** Khan succeeded to the throne at the cost of ceding territory to British India in the **Treaty of Gandomak** and permitting **Sir P. Louis Cavagnari** to come to Kabul to head a permanent British mission. History repeated itself when Cavagnari and his staff were massacred in Kabul. General **Frederick Roberts**, son of **Sir Abraham Roberts**, the commander of Shah Shuja's forces during the **First Anglo-Afghan War**, occupied Kabul. In the meantime other contenders for the Kabul throne came to the fore. **Ayub** Khan, another son of Amir Shir Ali, wiped out General Burrows' forces in the **Battle of Maiwand** (1880), and **Abdul Rahman** Khan, a grandson of Amir Dost Muhammad, entered Afghanistan after twelve years in Central Asian exile. To avoid disaster and to extricate their forces from Afghanistan, the British found it advisable to recognize Abdul Rahman as amir of "Kabul and its Dependencies." Amir Abdul Rahman (r. 1880–1901) was quick to eliminate all rivals to his power. He united the country, initiated domestic reforms, and formulated a foreign policy that served

Afghanistan well until World War I. He fashioned a cautious alliance with Britain that obligated Britain to defend Afghanistan from unprovoked Russian aggression and strengthened his power with aid in money and arms. Abdul Rahman agreed to conduct his relations with foreign powers through the intermediary of the British government. Having protected himself from the danger in the north, the amir formulated a policy that was to prevent Britain from gaining influence within his domains under the aegis of their common defense. This policy rested on the following triad: militant assertion of independence, defensive isolationism, and a balancing of the pressures by the two imperialist neighbors.

The "Iron Amir" considered his agreement with Britain an alliance between equals in which the two partners contributed to their common defense. He permitted the establishment in Kabul of a British agency, headed by an Indian Muslim whose sphere of activity was strictly limited, but refused to accept British military advisers and declined an offer of British help in extending the Indian rail system into Afghanistan. Although in 1893 he accepted under "duress" the **Durand** Line which cut large portions of Pashtun territory from the Afghan state, he did not assist in the complete demarcation of the border and continued to lay claim to the free "unadministered" tribal belt, which he saw as a buffer between Afghanistan and India. When Britain made punitive expeditions into this area, the Afghan ruler supported the tribes with shipments of arms and granted fugitives from India shelter in his domains. Amir Abdul Rahman was on a state visit in India in 1885 when Russian troops moved into the Panjdeh oasis (*See* PANJDEH INCIDENT). The fact that Britain did not assist him against Russian aggression convinced him that he could only rely on himself.

Amir **Habibullah** (r. 1901–19) continued the policy of his father. He resisted British demands for modifications of the agreements concluded with Amir Abdul Rahman and succeeded in 1905 in obtaining a treaty that confirmed all the existing provisions (*See* ANGLO-AFGHAN TREATY OF 1905). Two years later, Amir Habibullah visited India for talks with the governor-general, Lord Minto, unaware of the fact that at the same time Russia and Britain had concluded the **Anglo-Russian Convention** of 1907. The amir never permitted Russia the commercial privileges expected under the Convention and made sure that his imperialist neighbors would not solve the "Afghanistan Question" at the cost of his independence. The situation was drastically changed during World War I when both the Central Powers and the

Allies vied for the support of the Afghan ruler. The **Hentig-Nieder-mayer Expedition** (August 1915–May 1916) was able to conclude a treaty with the amir but could not provide any tangible support in funds and weapons. Therefore Habibullah remained neutral, hoping to win rich rewards and complete independence from Britain; when these expectations were not realized he paid for the failure of his policy with his life. Amir Habibullah was assassinated on the night of February 19, 1919, at Kalla Gush in Laghman Province. **Amanullah** Khan ascended the throne over the rival claims of his uncle, **Nasrullah** Khan, and his brother, **Enayatullah** Khan.

King Amanullah (r. 1919-29, he adopted the title of king in 1926) demanded a new treaty from British India that would recognize Afghanistan's absolute independence. When the Indian government was reluctant to comply, he started military action that resulted in the **Third Anglo-Afghan War** of 1919. With India in semi-revolt and British forces demobilized after the European war, the British government did not find this an opportune time to wage war and agreed to a peace treaty at **Rawalpindi** (August 8, 1919, *see* ANGLO-AFGHAN TREATY OF 1919.). It took another three months of negotiations at Mussoorie (Mussoorie Conference, April 17-July 18, 1920.) and almost one year of talks at Kabul, Jan. 1, 1921-Dec. 2, 1921 before normal, neighborly relations were established (*See* ANGLO-AFGHAN TREATY OF 1921). By that time Amanullah had established diplomatic relations with the Soviet Union, Turkey, Persia, and Italy and had modified Abdul Rahman's policy to end the isolation of his country. A contemporary of Reza Shah of Iran and Kemal Ataturk of the young Turkish republic, Amanullah initiated such drastic social reforms that he was ousted in a wave of reaction after a ten-year period of tenuous rule. Next followed the chaotic ten-months rule of a "lowly" Tajik, **Habibullah Kalakani** (Jan. 18-Nov. 3, 1929), called "The Son of a Water Carrier" (*Bacha-i Saqqau*) by his friends and "Amir Habibullah Ghazi, Servant of the Religion of the Messenger of God" (*Khadem-i Din Rasul Allah*), by his followers after his coronation.

The new dynasty of **Nadir Shah** (r. 1929-33) and his son **Zahir Shah** (r. 1933-73) continued Afghanistan's traditional policy of foreign relations but now tried to enlist Germany as a "third power" in obtaining the technical and political support that the Afghan rulers did not dare to accept from their neighbors. Economic and cultural collaboration between Afghanistan and Germany was greatly expanded, and Germans were soon the largest European community in the country.

But the deterioration of the political situation in Europe and the outbreak of World War II ended any possibility that the economic cooperation might evolve into political collaboration. Afghanistan remained neutral during the war.

The end of the war created an entirely new situation: the Soviet Union, although severely battered, acquired nuclear technology and emerged as a superpower, and Britain, in spite of her victory, was forced to relinquish her hold on India in 1947. During the short reign of King Amanullah, Afghanistan's border with the Soviet Union was open to commercial relations, and regular air service to Tashkent existed, but his successors maintained a closed-border policy. Keeping Afghanistan's border to the north closed was criticized in Moscow as inconsistent with friendly "neighborly" relations. Soviet demands for a "normalization" of relations could not be ignored, but it was hoped in Kabul that the United States would fill the vacuum left by the British and serve as a balancing force against the Soviet Union.

The United States formally recognized Afghanistan in August 1934 but did not have an accredited representative in Kabul until 1942, when it appeared possible that the German advance into the Caucasus might make it impossible to maintain a link to the Soviet Union through western Iran. In spite of its status as an independent state, Washington considered Afghanistan within the British sphere of influence and not very important in terms of international trade. With the onset of the cold war during the Truman administration and the policy of containment of Communism under John Foster Dulles, secretary of state under President Eisenhower, the Afghan government might have entered into an alliance with the United States if it would have been given explicit guaranties of protection from Soviet attack.

The United States government had never been willing to give that kind of guarantee; a possible Soviet advance was to be stopped at the **Khaibar Pass**, not north of the **Hindu Kush**. The Baghdad Pact in 1955 (subsequently renamed in 1959 Central Treaty Organization, CENTO) united Turkey, Iraq, Iran, and Pakistan with Britain as the representative of the West and the United States as the sponsor and "paymaster." The alliance inherited the legacy of regional disputes between Middle Eastern neighbors and upset the balance of powers.

A turning point occurred in December 1955, when Nikita Khrushchev and Nikolai Bulganin came to Kabul. The Soviets supported Afghanistan in the **Pashtunistan** dispute and offered massive aid, that the United States was unwilling to match. The government of

Prime Minister **Muhammad Daud,** in spite of its misgivings, turned to the Soviet Union for the weapons it could not obtain from the West.

The weapons arrived with Soviet advisers and experts, and thousands of Afghans went to the Soviet Union for military training. Graduates from Afghan institutes of higher education won fellowships to foreign universities, including those in the USSR, and there emerged a growing cadre of military officers, students, and technocrats with leftist and republican, if not pro-Russian, sympathies. When Sardar Muhammad Daud staged a coup against his cousin, the king, on July 17, 1973, he counted the Left (and *Parchamis*) among his supporters. Five years later a Marxist coup ended the "aristocratic" republic and established the Democratic Republic of Afghanistan. Its alliance with the Soviet Union and the subsequent war, which Soviet intervention in 1979 turned into a war of liberation, resulted in the eventual Soviet withdrawal in 1989 and a "simmering" civil war with no end in sight. *See also* SOVIET-AFGHAN RELATIONS.

AFGHAN HOUND. A hunting dog, called *tazi* (swift, running) in Afghanistan, is greatly valued for its speed and keen eyesight. It hunts by sight rather than by scent. It is long legged, has floppy ears and a silky coat, measures about 24–28 inches tall at the shoulders, and weighs 50–60 pounds. It is a much desired and fashionable pet in Afghanistan. The breed dates back to ancient Egypt.

AFGHANI. Name of the Afghan monetary unit which replaced the Afghan *ropiah* in the period 1925–26. Initially the Afghani was a silver coin subdivided into 100 *puls*, or two *crans*, and 5, 10, and 25 nickel coins, but inflation has since eliminated the use of any change. Paper money was first issued by King **Amanullah** in 1919, but the notes were withdrawn a year later because traders refused to accept them. New banknotes were prepared shortly before the fall of King Amanullah and issued by Amir **Habibullah (Kalakani)**, again with little success.

In November 1935, notes printed in Switzerland in denominations of five, 10, 20, 50, and 100 Afghanis were issued by the **Bank-i Milli** and have continued in circulation since them. In December 1958 coins of two and five Afghanis were put in circulation, as were notes issued by the governments of **Zahir Shah**, President **Daud**, the **PDPA**. In November 1994, notes of afs. 5,000 and 10,000, printed in the Soviet Union, were put in circulation by the Kabul government of **Burhanuddin Rabbani**. In January 1996 the US dollar was traded in the Kabul Bazar at afs. 9,500; it has since risen to 27,000. General **Dostum** issued his own currency.

AFGHAN INTERIM GOVERNMENT. *See* **ISLAMIC ALLIANCE FOR THE LIBERATION OF AFGHANISTAN** and **MUJAHEDIN.**

AFGHANIS/ARABS. Radical Islamists called Afghanis, mostly of Arab nationality, but also from other Muslim countries, who gained fighting experience in the war in Afghanistan and returned to their countries with the intention of toppling their governments and establishing an "Islamic State." They are said to include some 5,000 Saudis, 3,000 Yemenis, 2,000 Egyptians, 2,800 Algerians, 400 Tunisians, 370 Iraqis, 200 Libyans, some Jordanians, as well as citizens of other Muslim countries. They are a serious threat to the military regime in Algeria, have started terrorist activities in Egypt, and are fighting as volunteers in regional wars from Bosnia to Kashmir and in the Philippines. Between 1987 and 1993 as many as 3,340 registered Arabs left Pakistan, but some 2,800 are still in Afghanistan and in the North-West Frontier Province of Pakistan. Most of the Afghanis fought in the ranks of **Hekmatyar**, **Sayyaf**, and **Jamilurrahman**. Osama Bin Laden, a wealthy Saudi citizen, has financed a number of Islamist groups; he and one Islamboli, a relative of the assassin of President Anwar al-Sadat of Egypt, have found shelter in Afghanistan.

AFGHANI, SAYYID JAMALUDDIN. Born in 1838. "Father of the Pan-Islamic movement," Muslim modernist, and political propagandist who advocated unity of the Islamic world and selective borrowing from the West for the purpose of stemming the tide of Western imperialism. He was the adviser of Muslim rulers in many parts of the Islamic world and a political activist in Iran, Afghanistan, Egypt, and the Ottoman empire.

Frequently opposed by the *ulama* (Muslim clergy) and suspected as an intrigant by the temporal powers, he was often on the run. When one of his followers assassinated the Persian ruler Nasruddin Shah (r. 1848–96), Afghani was placed under house arrest by the Ottoman sultan Abdul Hamid II (r. 1876–1907). Afghani died in Istanbul in 1897. Afghans revere his memory and believe him to be a descendant of a family of Sayyids from Asadabad in Kunar Province of Afghanistan. Western scholars agree on his Iranian origin.

AFGHANISTAN. A quarterly journal published by the Afghan Historical Society from 1946 to the early 1990s, with articles in English and French. It is an important source on Afghan history and culture.

AFGHANISTAN BANK. *See* **BANKING** and **DA AFGHANISTAN BANK.**

AFGHANISTAN, THE LAND AND THE PEOPLE. *See* under the provinces and **ADMINISTRATIVE DIVISIONS, ETHNIC GROUPS** and **GEOGRAPHY.**

AFGHAN MILLAT (Afghan Nation). An Afghan weekly newspaper, the organ of the Afghan Social Democratic Party (ASDP — Da Afghanistan Tolanpal Woluswak Gund), first published on April 5, 1966 by **Ghulam Muhammad Farhad** with his brother Qudratullah Haddad and Habibullah Rafi'i as editors. Because of its political activism the newspaper was frequently closed. The newspaper is still published at irregular intervals in Pakistan.

The ASDP was established during a meeting of the 62-member founding congress on March 8, 1966, at the residence of **Qiamuddin Khadem**. Ghulam Muhammad Farhad (one time mayor of Kabul) was elected chairman and held the position until his death in 1984. During his tenure *Afghan Millat*, the popular name of the party, was more nationalist than socialist. It advocated the restoration of "Greater Afghanistan," including the territory of the **North-West Frontier Province** and Baluchistan, which now constitute the western provinces of Pakistan. Because of its irredentist policy, the party contributed to the friction existing between Afghanistan and Pakistan. The party did not support **Muhammad Daud**, even though it agreed with him on the **"Pashtunistan"** question and on the attempt to make Pashtu the national language. In October 1979, the Amin government accused the party of attempting a coup and arrested a number of its members in Kabul.

In the late 1960s, Feda Muhammad Feda'i seceded and formed his own party, called *Millat*, and after the death of Ghulam Muhammad Farhad in 1984, Dr. Muhammad Amin Wakman, who resides in the United States, was elected chairman of *Afghan Millat* at a congress in Peshawar on March 8–9, 1990. It was attended by 390 (out of 500) delegates who also elected a 29-member supreme council and chose Stana Gul Sherzad as its secretary general. Shams al-Huda Shams from

Kunar Province and a number of his supporters did not participate in the election.

The party opposed the **Tanai-Hekmatyar** alliances against the **Najibullah** regime (*see* TANAI, SHAHNAWAZ) and called on its members and sympathizers to continue the struggle to capture political power. The party now emphasizes social democratic policies and, although largely Pashtun in membership, tries to broaden its base to become a national party. The ASDP had a small mujahedin force in the field which was severely mauled by Hekmatyar's forces. The Pakistan government did not give *Afghan Millat* official recognition and material support because of its irredentism. A number of its activists were assassinated by unknown gunmen in Pakistan, including Dr. Ceded Shigawal, Zakir Khan, and in September 1991, Taj Muhammad Khan.

On July 27, 1995, the party convened its fourth congress in Peshawar and elected Dr. Anwar-ul-Haq Ahady as its new president, Abdul Hamid Yaqin Yusufzai as vice president, Stana Gul Sherzad as secretary general, and a supreme council of 35 members. The congress also adopted a new platform which emphasizes the independence, territorial integrity, and national sovereignty of Afghanistan and advocates national unity, democracy, Islam, progress, and social justice.

AFGHAN SECURITY SERVICE. After the **Saur Revolt**, the **Taraki** government established a security service, named AGSA (*Da Afghanistan da Gatay da Satanay Edara* — Afghanistan Security Service Department), which was headed by **Asadullah Sarwari** from May 1978 till August 1979. After his accession to power, **Hafizullah Amin** renamed the service **KAM** (*Da Kargarano Amniyyati Mu'asasa* — Workers' Security Institution). Within a week of their assumption of power on December 27, 1979, the Parchami regime purged the security service of Khalq supporters and renamed it **KHAD** (*Khedamat-i Ettela'at-i Daulati* — State Information Service). It was headed by Dr. **Najibullah** before he succeeded to the position of general secretary of the PDPA in 1986 and president of Afghanistan. Najibullah upgraded KHAD to ministerial status, therefore its acronym WAD (*Wizarat-i Ettela'at-i Daulati* — Ministry of State Security). WAD was subsequently headed by General **Ghulam Faruq Yaqubi.** The organization is said to have controlled from 15 to 30 thousand operatives, organized on the KGB model, with its own military units, including a national guard. Its task appeared to be similar to that of the KGB: detecting and eradicating domestic political opposition, subverting armed resistance, penetrating opposition groups abroad, and providing military intelligence to the armed forces. It is said to have been set up with the assistance of Soviet and East German intelligence officers. Yaqubi did not survive the downfall of the Marxist regime. Former Afghan prisoners have accused WAD and its predecessors of torture, intimidation, and murder. **Rabbani** started his own security service which was also popularly called KHAD.

AFGHAN WOLUS (Afghan Nation). An Afghan weekly newspaper published in 1969 by **Qiamuddin Khadem,** a poet and one time vice president of the **Afghan Academy**. The short-lived paper favored a nationalist, pro-Pashtunistan, policy. Its editors were Muzafar Sadeq and Abdul Qayyum Adramzai.

AFGHAN YEARBOOK. An almanac, or yearbook, published since 1932/1311 by the Afghan Literary Society. It was entitled *Salnama-yi Majalla-yi Kabul* (Kabul Yearbook), until 1940 when it carried the Pashtu name *Da Kabul Kalanai*, and finally *Da Afghanistan Kalanai*. Each volume starts with a general introduction, including an article on the king and the royal family, followed by a section with information on members of all branches of government and the diplomatic community and a record of activities during a particular year. Much space was devoted to aspects of Afghan culture and society, as well as to international news. The almanac was richly illustrated, including photos of leading members of Afghan government and, after elections, of all members of parliament. It is a valuable source for research on Afghanistan. Initially it was written in **Dari** (Farsi) but gradually became a bilingual Dari/**Pashtu** publication. Abridged versions of the yearbook have also appeared in English since 1966. After the Saur Revolt (1978) the yearbook was continued, but it is not clear whether it appeared regularly each year, and after the "victory" of the mujahedin and the ensuing civil war publication came to a halt.

AFKAR-I NAU (New Ideas). A weekly newspaper published by Nurullah Nurzad in 1971 under the editorship of Zia Haidar. The paper supported middle-class, law-and-order causes and an Islamic policy.

AFRIDI. A Pashtu-speaking tribe that is located in the area of the Khaibar Pass, just beyond the Afghan border. Herodotus, the Greek historian, mentions the "Aprytae," the tribe of Osman who called himself "God's Creature" (*afrideh-ye khoda*), whom some Afghan scholars consider the eponymic ancestor of the Afridis. For centuries, the Afridis saw themselves as the "guardians" of the gate to India, and since ancient times invaders have found it preferable to pay for passage rather than fight their way through the **Khaibar**. At times Afridis entered the services of Afghan rulers, primarily as bodyguards and tribal militias, and in conflicts between Afghanistan and British India supported the Afghans; although they could not resist the temptation to loot the Afghan arsenal when the British bombed Jalalabad in 1919.

In the 1960s the Afridis were said to be able to muster an armed force of 50,000 men. A British officer described them as "wiry, shaven-headed, full-bearded, Pashtu-speaking hillmen of uncertain origin" (Ridgway). During the 1980s the Kabul government attempted to enlist Afridis into a militia to attack the supply lines of the *mujahedin*, and the Afridis accepted their pay but did not perform their assigned functions.

At the end of the **Third Anglo-Afghan War**, Sir Hamilton Grant, chief commissioner of the **North-West Frontier**, complained to the viceroy of India that "the constant raiding by Afridi gangs into the Peshawar District is sorely discrediting our administration. It is astounding that such a state of affairs should be possible with the number of troops we have got in the Peshawar Valley and shows how very difficult it would be to make any military operation of trans-frontier area really successful." He added that only subjugation of the Afridis would help, but this would be "a most formidable and undesirable undertaking" (G.C.).

AGSA. *See* AFGHAN SECURITY SERVICE.

AHMAD SHAH. Member of the **Ittihad-i Islami** of **Sayyaf** and, in 1988, prime minister of an interim cabinet founded by the *Ittihad-i Islaimi-yi Mujahedin-i Afghanistan*, an umbrella group of seven *mujahedin* parties headquartered in Pakistan. Born in 1943 in a village in the Bagrami district of Kabul and educated at Ibn Sina School, Kabul Polytechnic Institute, and **Kabul University**, where he obtained an engineering degree in 1958 and started work with the department of agriculture and irrigation. He came to the United States in 1972 and

obtained an M.A. degree in engineering from Colorado State University
in 1974. In 1975 he started a teaching career at King Faisal University
in Saudi Arabia but came to Peshawar after the Soviet intervention in
Afghanistan. He joined the Sayyaf group and became president (*ra'is*)
of the committee for education and later the committee of finance.
When **Hekmatyar** joined the **Rabbani** government in May 1996,
Ahmad Shah became minister of Education. He was forced to flee
when the **Taliban** captured Kabul. He was married to an African
American lady whom he subsequently divorced.

AHMAD SHAH, ABDALI DURRANI. King of Afghanistan, 1747–73,
and founder of the Sadozai dynasty of the **Abdali** (Durrani) tribe. Born
in 1722 in Herat, the son of Muhammad **Zaman** Khan, who was
governor of Herat. After capturing Kandahar, **Nadir Shah** of Iran (r.
1736–47) exiled Ahmad Khan to Mazandaran in northern Iran and
subsequently appointed him governor of that province. At the death of
Nadir Shah, Ahmad Khan was commander of an Afghan contingent of
the Persian army at Kandahar. He was able to capture a caravan with
booty from India which assured his election as king (shah) of
Afghanistan in October 1747 by an assembly of Pashtun chiefs. The
Pashtun tribesmen rallied to his banner, and Ahmad Shah led them on
eight campaigns into India in search of booty and territorial conquest.
He added Kashmir, Sind, and the Western Panjab to his domains and
founded an empire which extended from eastern Persia to northern India
and from the **Amu Daria** to the Indian Ocean. Ahmad Shah appointed
his son Timur (*see* TIMUR SHAH) as his successor and died of a
natural death two months later on April 14, 1772. He was buried in
Kandahar, which became the capital of Afghanistan until Timur Shah
(r. 1773–93) established his capital at Kabul. Sir Percy Sykes in his
History of Afghanistan called Ahmad Shah "a monarch whose high
descent and warlike qualities made him peculiarly acceptable to his
aristocratic and virile Chiefs, as well as to his warlike subjects in
general. In short, he possessed all the qualities that enabled him
successfully to found the kingdom of Afghanistan." (Sykes, I, 367) *See
also* ABDALI.

AHMADZAI. A section of the Sulaiman Khel division of the **Ghilzai** tribe.
They are settled in a "triangle" formed by a line drawn from Kabul to
Jalalabad and Gardez. They are generally wealthy and often employed
as traders, while some have held high positions in the Afghan government and have intermarried with the **Durranis**. Amir **Abdul Rahman**

settled a number of Ahmadzai families in northern Afghanistan to weaken their power and have them serve as Pashtun colonists among the Turkic population. Only a small number of Ahmadzai is nomadic.

AIBAK. Now **SAMANGAN** (36-16' N, 68-1' E). A town, also called Haibak, located at an altitude of 3,000 feet that is the capital of Samangan Province and in 1964 was renamed Samangan. The town is famous for its pre-Islamic archaeological sites. Most important is *Takht-i Rustam* (the Throne of Rustam), a large stupa hewn into solid rock, which is unique for its size, type, and construction. Nearby, at Dara-ye Gaz is a complex of ten Buddhist temples, called by the Chinese pilgrim Hsuan-Tsang (Seventh century A.D.) "Kie Tehe." The town has about 8,000 inhabitants and is located on the main route from Kabul to Mazar-i Sharif. It has a small bazaar, a park in the center of town, and a mosque and administrative center. It was for centuries a major commercial center. Little is known how the present war has affected the town.

AI KHANUM (Moon Lady, 37-8' N, 69-27' E). A small town at the confluence of the Kokcha and Amu Rivers. In November 1964 French archaeologists, headed by Daniel Schlumberger and Paul Bernard, discovered the site of a large Greek town (second to first century B.C.) with an abundance of Greek architecture, ceramics, and inscriptions.

AIMAQ. The name of an ethnic group of some 800,000 Sunni Muslims who speak **Dari** (Afghan Persian) with some Turkic admixture. The word either means "nomad" (in Turkic) or "administrative district" (in Mongol). They are also called Chaha Aimaq and include the **Jamshidis**, **Firuzkuhis**, **Taimanis**, and the Sunni **Hazaras** of Qala-i Nau (*see* HAZARA). They were at times independent or allied with a Durrani prince ruling in Herat. Amir **Abdul Rahman** severely curbed the power of their chiefs and put them under the control of the governor of Herat. The tribes are semi-nomadic and dwell in conical felt yurts. They raise sheep and cattle and are concentrated primarily in Herat, Ghor, and Badghis Provinces.

AIR FORCE, AFGHAN. The Afghan government took the first steps toward creating an air force during the reign of King **Amanullah**. The importance of aerial warfare became apparent during the **Third Anglo-**

Afghan War when British planes bombed Jalalabad and the king's palace and ammunition factory at Kabul. Therefore, in 1921 Amanullah acquired a British fighter plane (which made a forced landing in Katawaz — the Afghans returned the pilot and kept the plane) and subsequently purchased a number of additional planes from Britain and the Soviet Union. By the end of the 1920s, Afghanistan's air force consisted of 22 machines (Bristol Fighters, D.H. 9s, Caprioni Scouts, and a Junkers Monoplane) which were operated by 25 officers, three of them Afghans, four Germans, and the rest Russians. The Soviet Union had donated a number of aircraft on condition that they be operated by Soviet nationals. Young Afghans were sent for training to the Soviet Union, Italy, India, and other countries to create a small cadre of pilots and aircraft mechanics. Amanullah used his aircraft with considerable effect during the **Khost Rebellion** (1924–25) and subsequent tribal revolts. But the conditions for maintaining an effective air force did not yet exist: Afghanistan depended on foreign supplies of spare parts and most of its aircraft were not in proper operating condition when King Amanullah was deposed in the 1929 civil war.

During the reign of **Nadir Shah** (1929–1933) the Russian personnel were gradually eliminated, and in the mid-1930s, **Zahir Shah**'s prime minister negotiated with Britain for the purchase of 24 aircraft and the training of ten pilots, six officers, and 30 mechanics. When the British government wanted assurances that the Afghan government would build up its air force from primarily British sources negotiations came to a halt.

In the mid-1930s, landing strips existed in Herat, Kandahar, Kabul, and Jalalabad, but only Kabul had ground organization and hangar accommodation for 16 aircraft. Aviation fuel had to be imported from India and supplies never exceeded 10,000 gallons. To carry 15,000 gallons required more than 500 camels. Wind, excessive heat, and snow made flying conditions good only in October and November (Handbook, 1933). Because of the war in Europe, development of the air force was limited until the Soviet Union became the major factor in the creation of modern armed forces.

In the mid-1950s, **Ariana Afghan Airlines** was established with technical support provided by Pan American Airways, and the airports of Kabul and Kandahar were modernized for international flights. The Kandahar airport, built with American aid, became one of the military regional headquarters after the Soviet intervention. By 1960 the country's air force included four helicopters and about 100 Soviet combat aircraft, and in 1979 some 140–170 fighters and 45–60 helicopters were organized into a tactical force of seven air regiments, including a strength of 7,000–8,000 men that remained relatively intact throughout the 1980s.

In the present civil war, the air force, just as the army, broke into a number of sections with General **Dostum** and the forces of President **Rabbani** gaining a major part. But, again, a problem of servicing and the provision of spare parts prevented any of the warring parties from gaining aerial superiority.

AKBAR, SARDAR MUHAMMAD (Called GHAZI). The ambitious son of Amir **Dost Muhammad** (r. 1826–38 and 1842–63) and "Hero of Jamrud," who defeated the Sikh army of Hari Singh in April 1837. He was a major figure in the defeat of the British in the **First Anglo-Afghan War**. Akbar was the premier of the Afghan chiefs with whom the British force of occupation sought to negotiate safe passage from Kabul to India (*see* CAPITULATION, TREATY OF). During negotiations with **Sir William Macnaghten**, he killed the British envoy "in a fit of passion." He saved the lives of British women and children as well as a number of officers whom he had taken into "protective" custody during the arduous retreat. Few others survived the massacre of the British expeditionary force of some 16,000 troops and camp followers (*see* DEATH MARCH). Akbar wanted to regain territory lost in the **Panjab**, but his father, Amir Dost Muhammad, who had been restored to the throne in 1842, favored a policy of accommodation with Britain. In 1845 Akbar rebelled, but he died at the age of 29 of poisoning before he could pose a serious challenge to his father. He is revered by Afghans and called **Ghazi** (Victor against Infidels), and a residential area of Kabul and a major hospital, Wazir Akbar Khan, have been named after him.

AKBARI, USTAD MUHAMMAD. Head of the *shi'a Hizb-i Wahdat*'s (Unity Party) political committee who lost in a power struggle with **Abdul Ali Mazari** and joined Rabbani's *Jam'iat-i Islami*. Sayyid Husain Alimi Balkhi, a member of his party, was appointed in July 1996 minister of commerce in Prime Minister Hekmatyar's government until they were evicted from Kabul and Bamian by the *Taliban*.

AKHTAR KHAN, LT. GEN. ABDUL RAHMAN. Director general of the Pakistani military's **Inter-Services Intelligence** organization from 1980–1987, who was said to have coordinated with William Casey, director of the CIA, the operations and supply network for the Afghan *mujahedin*. Brigadier **Muhammad Yousaf**, Akhtar's deputy and head of the Afghan Bureau, controlled the flow of thousands of tons of arms into the hands of the *mujahedin* and directed every aspect of military activities from training of Afghan guerrillas and logistics support to the planning of ambushes, assassinations, and raids and rocket attacks against the Soviet/Kabul forces. Akhtar was promoted to chairman of the Joint Chiefs of Staff Committee and replaced by General Hamid Gul when *mujahedin* started carrying attacks into Soviet Central Asia. Akhtar perished in a plane crash on August 17, 1988, together with Pakistani President Zia-ul-Haq, the American Ambassador Arnold Raphel, Brigadier-General Herbert Wassom, the US defense attache in Islamabad, and eight Pakistani generals. American sources attributed the crash to engine failure, but most Pakistanis believe it was a result of sabotage, variously blaming the KGB, WAD, or CIA.

AKHUND. In Afghan use, a religious instructor (Persian, Dari, and Pashtu); A descendant of an Akhund is called Akhundzada. The term was first used in Timurid times as a honorific for a great scholar, but later denoted a teacher of pupils with a slightly pejorative connotation.

ALAQADARI. Smallest administrative division, a subdistrict of a province (*welayat*) in Afghanistan. It is headed by an *alaqadar*, an administrator appointed by the Kabul government or the governor of a province. He is responsible to a *woluswal*, head of a district, or the *wali*, governor of a province. *See* ADMINISTRATIVE DIVISIONS.

ALI AHMAD. Known as *Wali* (Governor) of Kabul under King **Amanullah** and proclaimed "king" by Afghan tribes in Nangarhar after the abdication of Amanullah in January 1919. Born in 1883, the son of Loinab Khushdil Khan, he was educated in India and served as chamberlain, *shahghasi mulki*, of Amir **Habibullah**. He was president of the Afghan Peace Delegation at **Rawalpindi** in 1919 and successful as a commander in the **Mangal Revolt** (1924) and the **Shinwari** rebellion (1928). He fought **Habibullah Kalakani** and was defeated; brought to Kabul in chains he defiantly kissed the cannon by which he was executed in July 1929.

ALIM. *See* **ULAMA.**

AL-NASR. *See* **NASR, SAZMAN-I.**

AMAN-I AFGHAN (Afghan Peace). A weekly newspaper founded on April 12, 1919 (22. Hammal 1298) as the semiofficial organ of the **Amanullah** era (1919-29). Its motto was to "discuss every kind of scientific and political question and things of interest to the Government and the Nation." The newspaper, named after King Amanullah (*aman Allah* — peace, or protection of God), continued the journalistic tradition began by the *Seraj al-Akhbar Afghaniya*. In order to provide economic support, government officials and courtiers were expected to subscribe. During the first year of its existence there were frequent changes of editors, beginning with **Abdul Hadi Dawai** who was succeeded by Muham-mad Ismail, Faiz Muhammad, and subsequently by Ghulam Nabi (who was assassinated during the Kalakani regime in 1929). The newspaper was printed on excellent paper and was handsomely illustrated; it represents one of the most important examples of early twentieth-century Afghan journalism.

AMANULLAH, KING (AMAN ALLAH, called **GHAZI)**. King of Afghanistan, 1919-29. Born in 1892, the son of Amir **Habibullah** and Sarwar Sultanah, the *Ulya Hazrat* (queen). When Amir Habibullah was assassinated in Jalalabad in February 1919, Amanullah Khan was governor of Kabul and in possession of the arsenal and the treasury. He was crowned in Kabul over the prior claims of his uncle **Nasrullah**, whom he denounced as a usurper and an accomplice in the murder of his father. King Amanullah (he assumed the title of king in 1926) was an ardent reformer and contemporary of like-minded rulers Muhammad Reza in Iran and Kemal Ataturk in Turkey. He demanded a revision of the Anglo-Afghan agreements concluded by Amir **Abdul Rahman** that left Britain in charge of Afghanistan's foreign relations in exchange for protection from unprovoked Russian aggression and a subsidy in money and military materiel (*see* AFGHAN FOREIGN RELATIONS). British reluctance to accept a change in the status quo led to Afghan armed attacks, culminating in the start of the **Third Anglo-Afghan War** on May 3, 1919. Britain was war-weary and in no condition to wage war on the Indian frontier and, after lengthy negotiations in Rawalpindi, Mussoorie, and Kabul, peace was restored, leaving Afghanistan free and independent from British control (*see* ANGLO-AFGHAN WARS; ANGLO-AFGHAN TREATY; and AFGHAN FOREIGN RELA-TIONS). King Amanullah became a national hero and turned his attention to reforming and modernizing his country. He established diplomatic and commercial relations with major European and Asian states, founded schools in which French, German, and English were the major languages of education, and promulgated a constitution which guaranteed the personal freedom and equal rights of all Afghans.

He built a new capital, named **Darulaman** (*Dar al-Aman* — Abode of Peace), which included a monumental parliament and other government buildings as well as villas of prominent Afghans. Social reforms included a new dress code that permitted women in Kabul to go unveiled and encouraged officials to wear Western dress. Modernization proved costly for Afghanistan and was resented by the traditional elements of Afghan society. The **Khost Rebellion**, a tribal revolt in 1924, was suppressed, and Amanullah felt secure enough to travel to Europe in December 1927. Upon his return he faced increasing opposition and, in 1928, an uprising of **Shinwari** tribesmen, followed by attacks of the Kohdamani and Kuhistani forces of **Habibullah Kalakani**, forced the reformer king into exile. After an unsuccessful attempt at regaining the throne, he crossed the Indian border on May 23, 1929, and settled in Italy and Switzerland until his death on April 26, 1960. He was buried in Jalalabad at the side of the tomb of Amir Habibullah.

AMBALA CONFERENCE. A meeting in March 1869 between amir **Shir Ali** and Lord Mayo, the viceroy of India, in which the amir sought an alliance with Britain. Shir Ali had recaptured the Kabul throne and had consolidated his power to the extent that he felt secure enough to accept an invitation by Lord Mayo's predecessor to visit the viceroy at Ambala, a town about 200 miles north of Delhi. Shir Ali was alarmed by the fact that Russian influence had reached Afghanistan's northern boundaries when the Amirate of Buchara became a Tsarist protectorate. The Afghan ruler wanted a promise of British help in case of Russian aggression as well as support against domestic rivals and British recognition of his dynasty and his son, Abdullah Jan, as his immediate successor. Mayo assured the Afghan ruler of his government's sympathies but refused to give any specific promises. As a sign of its friendship, the Indian government presented the amir with 600,000 rupees, 6500 muskets, four 18-pounder siege guns, two 8-inch howitzers, and a mountain battery of six 3-pounder guns. But when an uninvited Russian mission under General **Stolietoff** managed to reached Kabul in the summer of 1878, a British army invaded Afghanistan on November 21, 1878. *See* SECOND ANGLO-AFGHAN WAR.

AMIN, HAFIZULLAH. Born 1929 in Paghman, Kabul Province. President of the **Democratic Republic of Afghanistan** from September 1979 until his assassination on December 27, 1979. He was of the Kharoti (**Ghilzai** Pashtun) tribe whose family came to Paghman in the 19th century. Educated in Afghanistan and the United States, where he was known as a **Pashtun** nationalist, he became a teacher and later principal of Ibn Sina and Teachers Training schools in Kabul. His conversion to Marxism is said to have occurred in 1964. He was elected to the 13th session of Parliament (1969) as a representative from Paghman. During the republican period (1973-78) he successfully recruited followers in the army in competition with *Parchami* efforts. After the Saur Revolt he was appointed vice premier and minister of Foreign Affairs. In April 1979 he became prime minister and, after he ousted **Nur Muhammad Taraki**, he became president on September 16, 1979. He was at odds with **Alexandr Puzanov**, the Soviet ambassador to Kabul, and successfully demanded his recall. Some observers called him the Afghan "Tito" because of his independence and nationalistic inclinations. He was accused of responsibility in the assassination of thousands. Soviet special forces attacked him in a bloody battle with his troops in **Darulaman** and assassinated him on December 27, 1979. He was replaced by **Babrak Karmal** of the *Parchami* faction of the PDPA.

AMIR. Commander, also nobleman, prince, ruler, chief (from A., *amara*, to command). Caliph Omar (r. 634-44) first assumed the title *Amir al-Mu'minin* (Commander of the Believers). In Afghanistan the **Sadozai** rulers carried the title "king" (shah), but the **Muhammadzai** rulers from 1826 assumed the title "amir" until **Amanullah** Khan adopted the title of "king" in 1926. Among some *mujahedin* groups an "amir" is a commander with civil and military powers.

AMU DARIA (34-40' N, 59-1' E, Darya). A river, called Oxus by the ancient Greeks, which forms for about 280 miles the boundary between Uzbekistan and Tajikistan (formerly the Soviet Union) and Afghanistan. Its easternmost sources are the Ab-i **Wakhan** and the Ab-i Pamir, which rise in the Little Pamir Mountains and run into the Ab-i Panj near the village of Qal'a-ye Panjeh. It is fed by the Kukcha and further west the Kunduz Rivers, at which point it is called the Amu Daria. It then flows in a northwesterly direction to run into the Aral Sea. It is navigable only in parts, although its length from the farthest source to

the mouth of the Aral Sea extends some 1,500 miles. A bridge near
Hairatan, completed in 1982, links the Afghan highway from
Mazar-i-Sharif with the **Uzbek** (formerly Soviet) rail terminal at
Termez. Another bridge was constructed at Sherkhan/Qala Kutarma in
Kunduz Province. The bridges were vital links for the supply of Soviet
and Afghan forces during the 1980s.

ANDKHUI (36-56' N, 65-8' E). A town in Fariab Province with about
15,000 inhabitants, located some 45 miles northwest of Shiberghan in
Fariab Province. In Timurid times (late 15th century) and again from
the 17th to the 19th centuries Andkhui was an important commercial
center. It shared the fate of Maimana and Balkh in being part of Uzbek
khanates under Afghan or Bukharan suzereignty until Amir **Abdul
Rahman** took direct control of Afghan Turkestan in the 1880s. It now
has a mixed, but largely **Uzbek**, population and is a market place for
Turkoman rugs, qaraqul skins, sheep, and cattle. Among its important
shrines is the tomb of Baba Wali (a *Sufi Pir*), which is widely known as
a place of pilgrimage. Industrial development, limited to the
establishment of a tannery that employs 250 workers, has been difficult
due to a scarcity of water.

ANGAR, FAIZ MUHAMMAD. A Kandahar businessman and member
of the **Wish Zalmayan** (P., Awakening Youth), a Pashtun political
club. He published the Persian/Pashtu biweekly, *Angar* (1951), which
was critical of the Afghan government and therefore banned after a few
months of existence. **Nur Muhammad Taraki** claimed to have
contributed an article, "What Do We Want?" that was censored and led
to the demise of the paper. Angar died in the 1970's in Kandahar.

ANGLO-AFGHAN TREATY OF 1809. *See* **ELPHINSTONE,
MOUNTSTUART.**

ANGLO-AFGHAN TREATY OF 1905. Renewal in form of a treaty of
agreements signed between Amir **Abdul Rahman** and **Sir Lepel
Griffin**, chief political officer in Afghanistan, in June and July 1880. At
the death of Amir Abdul Rahman on October 3, 1901, the British Indian
government insisted that the agreements with the amir were personal
and therefore subject to renegotiation with his successor. The
government of India sought modifications and concessions including a
more "liberal commercial policy" on the part of Afghanistan,

delimitation of the **Mohmand** border (between Afghanistan and India), and noninterference of Afghanistan in the politics of the transborder (Indian) tribes. Britain exerted great pressure, stopping subsidy payments and prohibiting Afghan imports of arms, but Amir **Habibullah** did not yield. He invited **Louis W. Dane** of the Indian Foreign Department to Kabul and, after three months of negotiations, the "Independent King of Afghanistan and its Dependencies" and Louis W. Dane, "Foreign Secretary of the Mighty Government of India" signed the treaty at Kabul on March 21, 1905. For Amir Habibullah this was a great victory: none of the British objectives was won, the arrears in subsidy were paid, and Britain affirmed that it would not interfere in the internal affairs of Afghanistan. This treaty remained in force until repudiated by Amir **Amanullah** in 1919.

ANGLO-AFGHAN TREATY OF 1919. Peace treaty between the British and the Afghan governments after the **Third Anglo-Afghan War**. It was negotiated at Rawalpindi and signed on August 8, 1919, by A.H. Grant, foreign secretary of the government of India, and **Ali Ahmad Khan**, Afghan commissary for home affairs. The treaty made a return to the "old friendship" between the two states contingent on negotiations started after a six-month waiting period. In the meantime Britain would not permit Afghanistan to import arms and ammunition through India, the payment of a subsidy would be ended, and the arrears in payments would be confiscated. Finally, undefined portions of the **Khaibar** were to be demarcated by a British commission, and Afghanistan was to accept the Indo-Afghan frontier as marked. An annexure stated that "the said Treaty and this letter leave Afghanistan officially free and independent in its internal and external affairs." British hopes that a contrite amir would again conclude an exclusive alliance were soon seen to be unrealistic. Amir **Amanullah** sent a mission to the Soviet Union, Europe, and the United States and acted on his right to establish diplomatic relations with foreign powers. The **Pashtun** tribes on the Indian side of the frontier were made to believe that the treaty represented only a cease-fire after which war was to be resumed if Britain did not agree to various Afghan demands. Indeed it was only after a fruitless, three-month conference at Mussoorie (April 17–July 18, 1920) and at Kabul (Jan. 20–Dec. 2, 1921) that normal neighborly relations between Britain and Afghanistan were established.

ANGLO-AFGHAN TREATY OF 1921. Also called "Treaty of Kabul" because it was negotiated and signed at Kabul by **Henry R. C. Dobbs**, the British envoy, and **Mahmud Tarzi**, chief of the Afghan delegation, after arduous, eleven-month negotiations. The treaty restored "friendly and commercial relations" between the two governments after the **Third Anglo-Afghan War** and negotiations at **Mussoorie** and **Rawalpindi.** The negotiations proceeded in four phases. During the first session, January 20 to April 9, 1921, the Afghan amir unsuccessfully demanded territorial concessions, while Britain wanted the exclusion of Russian consular offices from southeastern Afghanistan. In the second phase, from April 9 to mid-July, 1921, Britain asked Afghanistan to break the newly established diplomatic relations with Russia in exchange for a subsidy of four million rupees and weapons, as well as guarantees from unprovoked Russian aggression. When in the third stage, from mid-July to September 18, the British foreign office informed the Italian government that it was about to conclude an agreement which would "admit the superior and predominant political influence of Britain" in Afghanistan, the Afghans refused to accept an "alliance." An exclusive treaty was impossible after Afghanistan announced ratification of the Russo-Afghan treaty of 1921. In the fourth and final stage of negotiations, from September 18 to December 8, 1921, the British mission twice made preparations to return to India, when finally an agreement was signed at Kabul on November 22, 1921. Ratifications were exchanged on February 6, 1922.

In the treaty both governments "mutually certify and respect each with regard to the other all rights of internal and external independence." Afghanistan reaffirmed its acceptance of the boundary west of the **Khaibar**, subject to minor "re-alignment." Legations were to be opened in London and Kabul, consulates established in various Indian and Afghan towns, and Afghanistan was permitted to import arms and munitions through India. No customs duties were to be charged for goods in transit to Afghanistan, and each party agreed to inform the other of major military operations in the frontier belt. Representatives of both states were to meet in the near future to discuss conclusion of a trade convention, which eventually was signed in June 1923.

ANGLO-AFGHAN WARS. *See* **FIRST, SECOND, AND THIRD ANGLO-AFGHAN WAR.**

ANGLO-RUSSIAN CONVENTION OF 1907. An agreement between Great Britain and Russia concluded on August 31, 1907, that was to "ensure perfect security on their respective frontiers in Central Asia and to maintain in these regions a solid and lasting peace." It divided Iran into spheres of influence between the two powers, permitted Russia to have direct relations of a nonpolitical nature with local Afghan officials in northern Afghanistan, and provided for equal access to "commercial opportunity." Tibet was to be under Chinese sovereignty, but the British were free to deal with Tibetans in commercial matters while Russian Buddhists could deal with the Dalai Lama on religious matters. Although Britain was to continue its treaty obligation of 1905 to protect Afghanistan from unprovoked Russian aggression, and Russia declared Afghanistan outside her sphere of influence, Amir **Habibullah** saw this agreement as an attempt to solve the "Afghanistan Question" over his head. Amir Habibullah was on a state visit to India in January 1907 when Britain and Russia negotiated the treaty, but he was not informed of the Convention until September 10, 1907. He was shocked and felt betrayed by the British and, when he was requested to agree to the Convention, he took a year with his reply refusing to ratify the agreement. Russia never obtained the expected commercial and political benefits, and the Bolshevik government repudiated the Convention in 1918 in an attempt to win the goodwill of its Asian neighbors. As far as Afghanistan was concerned the Convention was a "dead letter" from the beginning.

ANIS, GHULAM MUHYIUDDIN. A supporter of King **Amanullah** and, in 1927, founder of a private newspaper, named *Anis* after him. During the civil war period (1929), he temporarily edited *Habib al-Islam* ("Beloved of Islam") the newspaper of Amir **Habibullah (Kalakani)**. In 1931, *Anis* came under government control and, with the exception of the republican period (1973–75), existed as a national, daily newspaper to the 1980s. A Tajik, Anis was born in Herat and educated in Egypt. Arrested after **Nadir** Shah ascended the throne, he remained in prison until his death in 1938. He is the author of *Crisis and Salvation* (*Buhran wa Nejat*) which describes Nadir's defeat of Habibullah Kalakani.

ANJOMAN-I ADABI (Literary Society). A literary circle founded by Nadir Shah in 1930. Early members included Qari Abdullah the poet laureate; **Mir Ghulam Muhammad Ghobar; Muhammad Sarwar**

Joya; Muhammad Karim Nazihi; **Sarwar Goya Etemadi**; and others. They edited and published the periodical *Kabul* and from 1932 the *Salnamah, Kabul Annual*. The Literary Society and the Historical Society later became part of the **Afghan Academy**.

ANSARI, KHWAJA ABDULLAH (1006–1089). Also called *Pir-i Herat* (Sufi Master of Herat). Brilliant as a youth, he studied in Nishapur under Shafi'ite teachers but later adopted the more severe Hanbali school. He was born in Herat and spent most of his life in that city. A much celebrated Sufi poet and philosopher and "mystic of love," he became a "mystic of *tauhid* (Unity)." He wrote both in Arabic and Persian. His Arabic collection is said to contain more than 6,000 couplets, and his Persian poetry is said to amount to about 14,000 verses. His tomb is in Gazargah, near Herat, amid ruins from the Timurid period.

AQCHA (36-56' N, 66-11' E). A town with about 10,000 inhabitants in Jozjan Province. It is on the road from Shiberghan to Mazar-i Sharif, about 30 miles from the former and 42 miles from the latter. It was an **Uzbek** Khanate until annexed by Amir **Dost Muhammad**. The population is still largely Uzbek. Major enterprises include a carpet industry, tanneries, and the production of vegetable oil. Aqcha is known for its bazaar of silver jewelry.

ARAB. There are some 4,000 Arabs who still speak Arabic (according to Farhadi — but Barfield, in *The Central Asian Arabs of Afghanistan*, has not found any) living in four villages in Jozjan and Balkh Provinces. In addition, there are said to be about 100,000 others who no longer speak Arabic scattered all over northern Afghanistan and Herat Province. They are Sunni Muslims and claim to be the descendants of the Muslim Arab conquerors of **Khorasan**. More likely, they are the descendants of Arabs from Damascus who were settled in Samarkand by **Timur-i Lang** in the 15th century.

ARG or **ARK.** A citadel within a walled city, traditionally the residence of a ruler. After the **Bala Hisar** was destroyed by British forces in 1879, Amir **Abdul Rahman** built the new Arg, located in the center of Kabul. It took five years to build and in addition to the amir and his court housed the major government offices. It was surrounded by a moat and a fifty-foot wall. Later additions and modification radically changed the original plan when modern buildings replaced the earlyresidences. In the *Salam Khana* (Audience Hall) the affairs of government were conducted. The *Del Kusha* (Heart's Delight) Palace was added by Amir **Habibullah** and the *Gul Khana* Palace was built to be the royal office of King **Amanullah**. After the coup by **Muhammad Daud** in July 1973, the president's office was established in the Arg. During the *Khalqi* period (1978–79) **Nur Muhammad Taraki** moved in, and the Arg was renamed the "House of the People" (*Khana-yi Khalq*). In December 1979, **Hafizullah Amin** left the Arg and established himself in the Tapa Taj Beg Palace in **Darulaman**, where he was assassinated by Soviet troops. After the capture of Kabul in April 1992, the Arg became the residence of the president of the **Afghan Interim Government** (AIG), and upon their capture of Kabul, the seat of the *Taliban* governor. In the subsequent battle for supremacy, the contending powers destroyed much of the Arg.

ARGHANDAB (31-27' N, 64-23' E). A major Afghan river that has its source in the Kuh-i Safi (mountain) northwest of Ghazni. It flows in a southwesterly direction north of Kandahar city and, after a course of about 350 miles, runs into the Helmand River. Only the upper part of the stream is perennial. In June 1950, Morrison Knudsen, an American engineering firm, began construction of the 145-foot high Arghandab Dam located about 18 miles above Kandahar city; it was finished in 1952 and greatly increased the land under irrigation in the Kandahar basin. There are also two districts (*woluswali*) named Arghandab: one in Kandahar Province with an area of 214 square miles and a population of 43,000 and the other in Zabul Province with an area of 808 square miles and a population of 18,000 (estimates are for 1978).

ARGHASTAN (31-23' N, 65-46' E). A river which is part of the Helmand-Arghandab system. It is a continuation of the Lori River and runs in a west-southwesterly direction into the Dori, about 25 miles south of Kandahar, and into the Helmand River south of Lashkar Gah. Arghastan is also the name of a district (*woluswali*) with an area of 1,663 square miles and 166 villages, including Arghastan village, the administrative center.

ARIANA (ARYANA). Name of the first territory of the Arians, as mentioned in the *Avesta*, around 1,500 B.C. Afghan historians point with pride to the illustrious roots of the Afghan state, suggesting a direct link between the ancient Arians and the modern Afghans. The name *Ariana* is frequently prefixed to other names to draw attention to Afghanistan's ancient history (for example, **Ariana Afghan Airlines**, and *Ariana*, the name of a journal published monthly since 1942 quarterly from 1973 by the Afghan Historical Society.

ARIANA AFGHAN AIRLINES. The Afghan airline which was started on a small scale in 1955 by Peter Baldwin, an American businessman. At first flights connected major Afghan towns, transported pilgrims to Saudi Arabia, and ran charters to Beirut and Tehran. Baldwin owned 49% of the stock and in 1957 sold out to Pan American Airways for $400,000. Subsequently PAN AM played a key role in operating the airline, maintaining regular service on three routes: Kabul–Tehran–Beirut–Istanbul–Frankfurt–London; Kabul–Tashkent–Moscow; and Kabul–Delhi. During the Republican period (1973–78) the company acquired a DC 10, a wide-body aircraft, that was delivered after the Saur Revolt and operated for a number of years. The company eventually lost landing rights in Western Europe but provided regular services to East Bloc countries. It was subsequently merged with the domestic air service and called Bakhtar Afghan Airlines. In 1988 the company again adopted the former name. In the 1980s the company acquired several Antonov AN-26 turboprops for domestic routes and two Turpolev TU-154s for international flights. *See also* AVIATION IN AFGHANISTAN. In the 1990s a number of private airlines were established, including Balkh Airways, under General **Dostum**'s control, connecting Mazar-i Sharif with Peshawar, Mashhad, and Dubai. Khaibar Airlines connected Jalalabad with neighboring countries. It was controlled by the Jalalabad *Shura* until the city was captured by the *Taliban* in September 1996. Prior to their conquest of Kabul, the *Taliban* had an airline headquartered in Kandahar, and Pamir Airlines, apparently controlled by **Jam'iat**, was centered in northeastern Afghanistan.

ARMS BAZAARS, AFGHAN. Afghanistan depended on foreign imports, smuggled and captured arms, and to a limited extent on local manufacture for its weapons supply. Since most supplies had to enter Afghanistan by way of India, Britain had a monopoly on the sale of weapons and tried to control the supply and quality. Amir **Abdul Rahman** founded the *mashin-khana* factory were guns and ammunition were produced. In addition, numerous workshops existed on the Afghan frontier where guns of all types were manufactured. Because of a lack of electricity, machinery was operated by human or animal power. The tradition of arms manufacture and sales in specialized communities exists to this day. One major weapons bazaar exists in Darra on the Pakistani side of the border that is probably the largest open arms market in the world. In some one hundred shops one can buy anything from rifles to mortars; the price of an AK-47 was $1500 in 1980, which in 1987 was reduced to $750 (Yousaf and Adkin, 135) and in 1994 to $100 in Kabul. The influx of captured Soviet weapons and arms supplied by the supporters of the *mujahedin* produced quite a glut on the market. Even **Stinger** missiles, supplied by the United States to the *mujahedin*, were sold to the highest bidder

ARMY, AFGHAN. Afghanistan's army evolved from its traditional beginnings under Ahmad Shah in a process of gradual modernization throughout the 19th and first half of the 20th century. First efforts at modernization began during the reigns of Amirs **Dost Muhammad** (r. 1826–38 and 1842–63) who mustered a standing army of 15,000 and 45 guns, a force gradually increased. **Shir Ali Khan** (r. 1863–79), after visiting India in 1869, adopted Indian titles: briget (brigadier), karnel (colonel), kaptan (captain), subedar, havildar, etc. Both lacked the type of modern weapons being employed by Afghanistan's neighbors and the nucleus of a modern officers corps. Officers were appointed on the basis of loyalty rather than skill and any Afghan who could ride a horse or carry a gun was considered fit, regardless of age. Military skills were passed on from father to son, and one cannoneer of advanced age had to be carried along on a stretcher to perform his functions. Western military technology came to Afghanistan by means of prisoners of war or foreign mercenaries. One such person, **William Campbell**, alias Shir Muhammad Khan, became commander-in-chief of the Turkestan army. In the 1830s the composition of the Afghan army was described as Pathan, Hindus, Kuzzelbashes, and a few deserters from the Sikh army. Muslims from neighboring countries joined the Afghan forces, including Indian officers of the "Great Sepoy Mutiny" of 1857–58. The reorganized army included a cavalry force of about 15,000 men, divided into two divisions headed by the Amir Dost Muhammad's sons. A specially trained infantry force of about 2,000 men was armed with large muskets and an artillery branch disposed of 50 to 60 serviceable guns. European type uniforms were first used (Gregorian, 76). Military pay was partially in cash and partially in kind, but usually in arrear. Recruitment was often by forcible seizure of able-bodied men, a practice not exclusive to Afghanistan at the time. In addition to the regular army there existed a militia of *jezailchis* (riflemen) and feudal irregular forces. A British military mission headed by Major H. B. Lumsden is said to have contributed advice toward the modernization of the Afghan army. Amir **Shir Ali** continued the modernization process. He obtained a number of artillery pieces and some 5,000 Snider rifles in 1875, but the ensuing civil war in Afghanistan postponed major military reforms to the time of Amir **Abdul Rahman**.

The "Iron Amir" spent most of his subsidy from the British-Indian government on the purchase of arms and expanded the local production of weapons (*See also* INTRODUCTION).

The first attempt to create a modern officers corps was made in 1904 when Amir **Habibullah** (r. 1901–1919) founded the Royal Military College. By 1910 it enrolled 80 cadets, mostly the sons of **Durrani** chiefs, who studied in addition to Islamic topics arithmetic, geometry, and military logistics and underwent a rigorous physical training and drill. In 1907 a Turkish officer, Mahmud Sami, was put in charge of the college, marking the beginning of Turkish influence in the Afghan army.

King **Amanullah** (r. 1919–1929) neglected the army at the cost of his throne. He saw his an "era of the pen — not of the sword" and devoted his resources to the modernization of his country. Turkish advisers were still prominent in the army, including **Jamal Pasha**, one of the triumvirate rulers of the Ottoman war government. Germans, the teachers of the Turks, were also employed, as were members of various other nationalities. The nucleus of an Afghan air force was created in the 1920s with the participation of experts from the Soviet Union. *See* AIR FORCE, AFGHAN.

King Amanullah's army was about 50,000 strong, comprising an infantry of about 38,000 men divided into 78 battalions armed with Martini-Henri and Snider rifles; a cavalry of about 8,000 sabres divided into 21 units; and about 4,000 artillerymen employing some 260 breach-loading guns, mainly German Krupp 75mm and 7-pounders. (O'Ballance, 55) An arsenal at Kabul held 15,000 small-bore rifles and 400,000 Martinis and a few old machine-guns. Heliography had still not replaced telegraph communications.

Nadir Khan, as commander-in-chief, established six army corps headquartered at Kabul, Jalalabad, Matun, Herat, and Mazar-i Sharif. Kandahar was added, and all were headquarters of principal formation. In practice many corps were severely undermanned.

Nadir Shah took power with tribesmen and reconstituted the army in 1930. He faced many insurrections: the Koh Daman revolt (Nov. 29–June 30); the Shinwari Rebellion (Feb. 1930); the Operations against **Ibrahim Bey** (Nov. 1930–Apr. 1931); the **Ghilzai** threat 1931; the Darre Khel revolt Nov. 1932; and the Khost disturbances.

Schools for cavalry, artillery, and infantry were established. German, Italian, and Turkish officers were employed. Pay was increased and clothing and accommodation were improved by 1933.

Astriking improvement occurred in 1936 when the army was about 60,000 strong. It played an important role in internal security, and although regularly paid and housed in better barracks, it was still inferior to British–Indian standards.

"During peacetime the army was organized into two corps (Kabul two, Southern Province three divisions); one division household troops (Guards division); one artillery division; and two independent mixed divisions for a total of 13 divisions and one artillery division" (MR).

King **Muhammad Zahir** (r. 1933–1973), realized that for domestic stability and defense against foreign aggression he needed a strong, modern army. His uncle, **Shah Mahmud**, minister of War and commander-in-chief of the army until 1946, embarked on a project of military reorganization. He purchased weapons from Germany, Britain, Italy, and Czechoslovakia as well as airplanes and tanks and created the first mechanized forces. Additional officers' schools were established in Maimana, Mazar-i Sharif, and those in Kabul and Herat were expanded. Afghan officers were sent abroad for additional training, and Turkish officers replaced foreign advisers at the advent of World War II. A combination of compulsory and voluntary enlistment increased the Afghan army from 70,000 men in 1934 and to 80,000 in 1936. About 50 percent of Afghanistan's revenue of 150 million afghanis was devoted to military expenditures (Gregorian, 371).

After World War II, the Afghan army had reached its traditional size of about 90,000 men, but its weapons and equipment were largely obsolete. The Afghan Prime Minister Shah Mahmud envisaged a "small but well-trained internal security force," reducing the size of the army by half and expanding a central police force to 20,000 men (Bradsher, 18). Formal requests for arms purchases from the United States were repeatedly rebuffed; therefore in early 1955 Prime Minister **Muhammad Daud** turned to the Soviet Union for help. The **Pashtunistan** dispute with Pakistan, a member of the Baghdad Pact and unofficial ally of the United States, was one of the reasons for the growing influence of the Soviet Union in Afghanistan's army. In July 1956 the Soviet Union granted a loan of $32.4 million in military assistance that greatly helped to modernize the Afghan army. But Afghanistan became dependent on Soviet expertise and supplies, and some 3,725 Afghan military personnel went to the Soviet Union for training. On the eve of the Marxist coup in 1978, the Afghan army included all branches of infantry divisions, mechanized, paratroop, commando, and artillery brigades. Equipment included a sizable tank force and an air force of some 140–170 fighter planes and 45 to 60 helicopters. (*See* Introduction and AIR FORCE, AFGHAN.) After the Soviet intervention a Status of Armed Forces Agreement was signed in April 1980, legalizing the presence of the **Limited Contingent of Soviet Forces in Afghanistan**. After the fall of the Marxist regime in April 1992, the army broke into factions that supported various *mujahedin* forces.

ARMY OF THE INDUS. The British-Indian army and **Shah Shuja**'s forces that invaded Afghanistan during the **First Anglo-Afghan War** totalled some 39,000 men. It was composed of three sources, the Bengal army, the Bombay army, and the army of Shah Shuja, most of whose men were transfers from the **British East India Company**'s troops. The Bengal army consisted of the British 16th Dragoons (Lancers), the 13th Foot (Light Infantry), one regiment of Bengal European infantry, two of Light Cavalry, two of Local Horse, and seven Native Infantry. They were complemented with one troop of all-European horse artillery and two all-Indian companies of sappers and miners. From the Bombay army came the 4th Light Dragoons and the 4th and 17th Regiments of Foot (all from British service), one regiment of Light Cavalry and one of Local Horse, two troops of horse, two companies of foot artillery (all European), four regiments of native infantry and one company of sappers and miners.

The British infantry, engineers, and heavy cavalry wore red coats; the light cavalry and artillery wore blue coats. The Indian sepoys in the infantry wore red uniforms, and the cavalry grey, whereas the irregular troops did not wear uniforms. Most were equipped with flintlock muskets (O'Ballance, 10).

Shah Shuja's forces included two regiments of cavalry, four regiments of infantry, and a troop of horse artillery. Two additional infantry regiments were recruited later. Altogether his forces comprised some 6,000 men. Shah Shuja's son Timur commanded a force of 6,000 Sikhs and 4,000 of Shah Shuja's men that invaded Afghanistan from Peshawar.

Because of the lack of roads fit for wheeled traffic, the Army of the Indus depended on animal transport. Some sixty thousand Indian and several thousand Afghan camels were employed, as well as hundreds of bullock carts and a number of baggage elephants. The invasion proceeded without great difficulty. The British forces reached the Kandahar area on April 14, 1839, and on April 25, Shah Shuja entered the city to popular acclaim. Sir John Keane, the commander-in-chief, departed from Kandahar on June 27, 1839 and moved against Ghazni, and on July 23, he succeeded in capturing the city after blowing in the Kabul Gate. The British army took Kabul in the face of little opposition and on August 7 Shah Shuja formally entered the city. In September the Bombay Division returned to India, and a month later parts of the Bengal division left. Most of the remaining troops and camp followers did not survive the invasion. *See* DEATH MARCH and FIRST ANGLO-AFGHAN WAR.

ASOKA (269-232 B.C.). Indian ruler over an empire that extended from southern India into Afghanistan. Tired of the bloodshed he had wreaked, he repented and dedicated himself to propagating Buddhism. He set up rock edicts (Pillars of Morality) throughout his empire, several of which in Greek and Aramaic were found in the area of Kandahar and Laghman. His edicts advocated humanity in government, the abandonment of aggressive wars, and the sanctity of animal life and constitute the "oldest surviving Indian written documents of any historical significance" (Basham, *The Wonder That Was India*).

ATAN. A Pashtun tribal dance performed on festive occasions and as a physical exercise in the army. It is performed to the ever-faster rhythm of drums, the tribesmen's long hair whipping in unison, and is often continued to exhaustion. In some respects it resembles the dance of the "whirling dervishes" of the Ottoman empire. Although Pashtun in origin, it has also been adopted by other ethnic groups as the Afghan national dance.

AUCKLAND, LORD. Governor-General of India (1836–42), who in defiance of the Court of Directors of the **British East India Company** started the disastrous **First Anglo-Afghan War** to replace Amir **Dost Muhammad** with **Shah Shuja**.

He subsequently wrote to the court of directors that "the increase of Russian and Persian influence in Affghanistan, and the impression of the certain fall of Herat to the Persian army, have induced the Ameer Dost Mahomed Khan to avow and to insist upon pretensions for the cession to him, by Maharajah Runjeet Singh, of the Peshawur territory, and to take other steps which are tantamount to the rejection of the friendship and good offices of the British Government; and have in consequence led to the retirement of Captain **Burnes** from the territories of Cabool... The emergency of affairs may compel me to act without awaiting any intimation of your views upon the events which have recently occurred in Persia and Affghanistan" (Auckland to Secret Committee of the Court of Directors of the East India Company, Simla May 22, 1838). The **Simla Manifesto,** issued by Auckland on October 1, 1838, was the declaration of war.

Initially it was decided to give a major role in the task of restoring Shah Shuja to the Kabul throne to **Ranjit Singh** and his army, but the Sikh ruler was not eager; and Auckland subsequently felt that he could not be trusted to successfully carry it out. Therefore, the British **Army of the Indus** was to do the job. Early successes in the war led to one-step promotion toward peerage in 1839. Following the debacle he was denounced and recalled. *See* FIRST ANGLO-AFGHAN WAR.

AVIATION IN AFGHANISTAN. Aviation in Afghanistan began in 1921 when King **Amanullah** acquired a British fighter plane. Additional planes were purchased or acquired as gifts from Britain and the Soviet Union; the latter donated a number of aircraft on condition that they be operated and serviced by Soviet nationals.

By the end of the 1920s, Afghanistan's air force consisted of 22 machines (Bristol Fighters, D.H. 9s, Caprioni Scouts, and a Junker Monoplane) operated by some 25 officers, three of them Afghans, four Germans, and the rest Russians. Young Afghans were sent to Italy, the Soviet Union, India, and other countries for training as pilots and aircraft mechanics.

The air service was largely devoted to transporting the mail, foreign diplomats, and members of the Afghan government. In 1926, average flying times were: Kabul to Kandahar — three hours; Kabul to Jalalabad — 50 minutes; Kabul to Termez (on the Soviet side of the Amu Daria) — two hours and 40 minutes; and Jalalabad to Kandahar — three and a half hours. The flight from Kabul to Moscow took five days, crossing the Hindu Kush at 5,000 meters.

Although half the fleet was out of operation, control of the airspace proved important in suppressing the **Khost Rebellion** and other tribal revolts. After the ouster of King Amanullah, Nadir Shah did not renew the Soviet concession, but Soviet planes continued at an irregular schedule to transport diplomatic personnel to the Soviet Union. In 1937 the Lufthansa Airline established regular air service from Berlin to Kabul, but this was discontinued with the outbreak of World War II. For post-war air service, *see* ARIANA AFGHAN AIRLINES. As a result of the division of Afghanistan into hostile territories, private airlines came into existence to connect Mazar-i Sharif, Kandahar, and Jalalabad with neighboring countries. *See* AIR FORCE, AFGHAN.

AVICENNA. *See* **IBN SINA'.**

AYUB, MUHAMMAD (AYYUB). Son of Amir **Shir Ali** and full brother of **Yaqub Khan**. At the death of his father Yaqub Khan was crowned King at Kabul, and Ayub took over the governorship of Herat. When he learned of the British occupation of Kabul, he incited the Afghan *sardars* to rise and expel the invaders. In June 1880, the *ulama* at Herat proclaimed him amir, and he had coins struck in his name as a sign of his sovereignty. He then marched his army against Kandahar and, on July 27, 1880, he met General Burrows at **Maiwand** and virtually wiped out Burrows's forces (*See* MAIWAND, BATTLE OF). Ayub then proceeded to Kandahar and laid siege to the city, but General **Roberts** came to the rescue, and he was forced to retreat to his base at Herat. He again moved on Kandahar in June 1881, at a time when Britain had recognized **Abdul Rahman** as Amir of Kabul. The "Iron Amir" easily defeated Ayub's forces at Kandahar in September 1881 and at the same time dispatched his general **Abdul Quddus** Khan to capture the lightly garrisoned city of Herat. Being deprived of his base, Ayub was forced to flee to Iran and after a number of years accepted asylum in India for himself and his retinue of 814 individuals.

AZAN (ADHAN). The call to prayer, five times a day, by the *muezzin* from the door of a mosque or a minaret of a large mosque. The muezzin chants the following formula with some repetitions: "Allah is most great. I testify that there is no god but Allah. I testify that Muhammad is the apostle of Allah. Come to prayer. Come to salvation. Allah is most great. There is no god but Allah." At the morning prayer the words "prayer is better than sleep" are added. The *Shi'as* add the words "come to the best work!" And also "I testify that Ali is the *wali* (protected friend) of God."

AZHAR, ABDUL SAMAD. A member of the *Parcham* faction of the PDPA who was appointed ambassador to Belgrade in 1989 and defected in 1990. A Pashtun from Laghman Province who was trained as a police officer in Kabul and Egypt. A member of President Muhammad Daud's investigation team of the **Maiwandwal** "affair" in 1973, he is believed to have been the assassin of the former prime minister. He was arrested in May 1979 by the *Khalqi* government of **Hafizullah Amin** and held until January 1980. The **Karmal** government appointed him commander of police (*Sarandoy*) in January 1980 and alternate member of the central committee; he became a full member in 1986. He served as ambassador at Cuba, 1983–86 and Delhi, 1986–89 and now lives in exile.

B

BABA JAN, LT. GEN. ABDUL WAHED. Member of the *Parcham* faction of the PDPA and chief of General Staff of the Armed Forces, Jan. 1980 — Jan. 1984, and for a short time caretaker at the ministry of national defense. He was elected an alternate member of the PDPA central committee and served as head of the Kabul military academy and as ambassador to Berlin (1985–88). He was educated in military schools in Kabul, Turkey, and the USSR. He is the recipient of the "Order of the Golden Star." After the fall of the Marxist regime, he joined the forces of **Rabbani**.

BABUR, ZAHIR AL-DIN MUHAMMAD (1483–1530). Founder of the Moghul empire, the "greatest soldier of his age," and a talented writer and great poet (Sykes, 1940). He was a Barlas Turk who descended on his mother's side from Genghis Khan and on the male side from Tamerlane (**Timur-i Lang**). He was ousted from his native Ferghana, the Turkic lands north of the **Amu Daria**, and when he could not retake his homeland he settled in Kabul in 1504. Probing expeditions into India led to territorial conquests that became the foundation of the Moghul empire. He loved Kabul and wrote fondly about the town and wanted to be buried in the Bagh-i Babur, a garden he himself had planted on the western slope of Sher Darwaza mountain. He died in

Agra on December 26, 1530, and his body was transported to Kabul where his rather modest tomb is still located.

BACHA-I SAQQAU. *See* **HABIBULLAH KALAKANI.**

BACTRIA. Name of an ancient kingdom, home of Zoroaster, north of the Hindukush and south of the Oxus with the capital at Bactra, near the present Balkh. Bactria was part of the Achaemenid Empire, first conquered by Cyrus the Great (r. 559–530 B.C.), it later became a Greek colony of Alexander (331 B.C.) and his successors. Excavations have revealed numerous examples of Greek sculpture, architecture, and inscriptions from the third to first centuries B.C. The area came under Turkish control in the sixth century and was invaded by the Muslim Arabs a century later. Afghan nationalists seek the historical roots of the present state of Afghanistan in this ancient kingdom. *See also* BALKH and ARIANA.

BADAKHSHAN (36–45' N, 72–0' E). A province in northeastern Afghanistan, comprising an area of 15,786 square miles and a population of about 484,000. The province includes the **Wakhan** Corridor, a narrow valley which extends to the Chinese border and separated Tajikistan from the Indo-Pakistan subcontinent. The province is divided into five districts (*woluswali*) and seven subdistricts (*alaqadari*) with Faizabad as the administrative capital. The province is mountainous, with a number of high valleys and peaks reaching a height of 16,000 feet. It is rich in mineral resources including silver, copper, lead, precious stones, and virtually all the lapis lazuli mined in Afghanistan. Famed for its Marco Polo sheep, ibex, and snow leopards, Badakhshan was becoming an important hunting preserve for wealthy foreigners before the war in Afghanistan interrupted further development. The yak is still used in the Wakhan as a beast of burden. The population is Tajik, with Uzbek communities in the west and Wakhis and Qirghiz in the Wakhan Corridor (most of the latter have fled as a result of Soviet occupation). Much of Badakhshan was ruled by autonomous khans until in 1850 **Dost Muhammad** took it under the direct control of the Kabul government. By the time of Amir **Abdul Rahman**, it had become an integral part of the Afghan state. In 1893 a mission under **Sir Mortimer Durand** demarcated Afghanistan's northern border and allocated the Wakhan Corridor to Afghanistan. Amir Abdul Rahman was reluctant to accept this "arm that could easily be cut by an enemy" but agreed to accept the Wakhan as a buffer between the Russian and British empires when Britain offered to increase his subsidy by 650,000 Indian rupees for his cost of the administration and defense. Badakhshan appears presently to be under control of the *Jam'iat-i Islami* of **Burhanuddin Rabbani**.

BADAKHSHI, TAHIR. With **Babrak Karmal** and **Nur M. Taraki**, one of the founders of the PDPA and member of the central committee in 1965. In 1967 he sided with *Parcham* in the factional dispute but left the party to found the *Setam-i Milli* (National Oppression — a Marxist, anti-Pashtun faction) about 1968. He was born in Faizabad, Badakhshan, and educated in Kabul at **Habibia School** and at the faculty of economics of **Kabul University**. Married to Jamila, a sister of **Sultan Ali Keshtmand**. He was imprisoned in **Pul-i Charkhi** jail, summer 1978, and executed during the rule of **Hafizullah Amin** on September 17, 1979.

BADAL. An aspect of the Pashtun tribal code of honor which requires retaliation for insults and the shedding of blood. It serves as a deterrent to reckless lawlessness but often results in long periods of hostilities between individuals, groups, and entire tribes, causing great suffering for all. Afghan governments have tried to extend Kabul's jurisdiction into the tribal area, and have been unable to eliminate the practice. *See also* PASHTUNWALI.

BADALZAI. *See* **BARECHI.**

BADEZAI. *See* **ACHAKZAI.**

BADGHIS (35–0' N, 63–45' E). Badghis is a province in northwestern Afghanistan and was part of Herat province prior to 1964. The province has an area of 8,438 square miles and an estimated population of 47,000. Major districts include Jowand, Ghormach, Qades, Murghab, Qal'a-i Nau, and Kushk-i Kohna. The province borders on Turkmenistan (formerly the Soviet Union) in the north and Herat in the west. Badghis is a country of beautiful grassy hills but virtually without trees or even bushes in spite of an abundance of good water near the hills. The climate is, as in most parts of Afghanistan, cold in the winter and hot in summer. Barley and wheat are the major crops, and pistachio nuts are harvested in considerable quantities. The area was densely populated until it was devastated by Mongol invaders (13th and 15th centuries) and again by the Safavids under Shah Abbas II (r. 1642–66). Subsequently it was inhabited only by nomadic tribes because of the danger of Turkoman raids from the north. The present population includes **Pashtuns, Jamshidis, Hazaras**, and small com-munities of other ethnic groups.

BADINZAI. *See* **ACHAKZAI.**

BAGH-I BALA. A garden in Kabul, near the present Intercontinental Hotel, where Amir **Abdul Rahman's** palace is located. After his death, the garden and building were closed and fell into neglect. Because of its strategic location on top of a hill overlooking the city, it has become an important command post during wars. **Habibullah Kalakani** made it his base in the 1929 civil war; it was a government post during the Soviet occupation and a valued outpost during the civil war between the *mujahedin* groups.

BAGHLAN (36-11' N, 68-44' E). A province in northeastern Afghanistan with an area of 6,627 square miles and a population of about 486,000. Baghlan is also the name of the administrative capital of the province, having approximately 39,000 inhabitants. The province includes the northern slopes of the Hindu Kush range that are crossed by the Robatak, Barabi, Khawak, and **Salang** Passes. The northern part is largely agricultural, with irrigation from the Baghlan, Qara Batur, Chunghar, and Mar Khana Rivers. Sugar beets and cotton are the major crops, and pomegranates, grapes, and pistachio nuts are important items of export. Qaraqul sheep (*see* QARAQUL) are raised in the northern part of the province. Sugar production, started in 1940 with Czech assistance, has become the most important industry. Coal is extracted in the Karkar valley near **Pul-i Khumri**. A silk industry was started in 1951. Not much is known about the effect of the war on the area.

BAGRAM (BEGRAM) (34–58' N, 69–17' E). Site of an ancient city with an abundance of Buddhist, Graeco-Roman, and Phoenician artifacts. According to some sources, it is the site of *Alexandria ad Caucasum* (Alexandria by the Caucasus, built by Alexander the Great in the period 330–329 B.C.), which flourished for centuries until it was destroyed by the hordes of Genghis Khan in the 13th century. The town is north of Kabul near the confluence of the Panjshir and Ghorband Rivers, about five miles west of Charikar. Bagram is now a small town, the center of the district of the same name in Parwan Province. It is the location of an air base built with Soviet assistance in the 1950s. On July 7, 1979, the first Soviet paratroop battalion deployed there, apparently in preparation for its occupation in December 1979, when one regiment of the 105th Guards Airborne Division landed. Bagram became a primary regional center for independent air regiments as a base for the protection of Kabul and the **Salang** Pass. Although well-fortified, Bagram airbase was frequently attacked. On June 3, 1985, *mujahedin* forces under Commander Abdul Karim led an attack in which he allegedly destroyed 60 to 70 aircraft and killed scores of Soviet soldiers. After the *mujahedin* capture of Kabul, Bagram became an important base of **Rabbani**'s government until it was conquered by the *Taliban.*

BAHES, BAHRUDDIN (BAES). A native of Darwaz, Badakhshan, educated in Islamic studies and law at **Kabul University**. He became an opponent of the Daud government and the subsequent Marxist regime. Said to have been a sympathizer of *Setam-i Milli* and possibly also a member of SAMA (*see* KALAKANI, ABDUL MAJID). He was arrested after the Saur Revolt in 1978 and was secretly executed during the Taraki period. According to unconfirmed reports the kidnappers of the American Ambassador Adolph Dubs wanted to gain Bahes's freedom in exchange for Dubs.

BAHSUD or **BEHSUD.** *See* **HAZARA.**

BAIANZAI. *See* **ACHAKZAI.**

BAIHAQI, ABU'L FAZL (995–1077). Secretary to the **Ghaznawid** court and historian of the dynasty. Of his monumental work the 30-volume *Mujalladat* the extant portion covers the period of Mas'ud (1030–41), called *Tarikh-i Mas'ud* (History of Masud) also called *History of Baihaqi*, and *Tarikh-i Naseri.* Baihaqi was born in 995 in Baihaq, the present Sabzawar in Farah Province of Afghanistan. He studied in Nishapur and became one of the most gifted and graceful writers of Persian prose. He was imprisoned briefly for failure of paying a dowry to a former wife. For 19 years he worked under Abu Nasr Mushkan and was head of the Ghaznawid secretariat for a brief time.

BAIQARA, SULTAN HUSAIN (1469–1506). Timurid ruler at Herat and great sponsor of the arts. At his court were gathered **Kamaluddin Behzad**, the master calligrapher and miniature painter; **Mulla Nur-uddin Abdul Rahman Jami**, mystic, scholar, and one of the great classical Persian poets; and others. Sultan Husain's Wazir Amir Shir Ali Nawa'i was a great statesman who wrote poetry in Turkish.

BAKHTAR AFGHAN AIRLINE. *See* **ARIANA AFGHAN AIRLINE** and **AVIATION IN AFGHANISTAN.**

BALA HISAR. A citadel within a walled town, usually on the crest of a mountain or hill, serving as the residence of an Afghan ruler or governor. The Bala Hisar of Kabul is a huge complex built southwest of the ancient wall on Sher Darwaza mountain. Until the 19th century its high stone walls surrounded a strong citadel that was the residence of the Kabul ruler and his court. **Babur** Shah and **Timur-i Lang** are said to have resided in it. High military and civilian officials were quartered within the outer walls. In the **First Anglo-Afghan War** the British forces built their defenses around a rectangular cantonment in the valley below instead of seeking the security of the Bala Hisar. This turned out to be a fatal mistake. The six-century-old fortress was destroyed on order of the British General **Roberts** after an explosion in the arsenal on October 16, 1879 killed a British officer and a number soldiers of his Gurka unit. The fortress lay in ruins until **Nadir Shah** started the process of reconstruction in the early 1930s. It served as a military college and garrison since 1939. On August 5, 1979, an army regiment at the Bala Hisar revolted against the *Khalqi* regime, and it took a four-hour battle in which MI-24 gun ships and considerable heavy artillery were employed before the revolt was suppressed. Subsequently, the fortress was able to withstand *mujahedin* attacks and fell into their hands only with the capture of Kabul. In the present civil war the Bala Hisar of Kabul was occupied by the **Uzbek** forces of **Dostum**, later by **Rabbani**, who was in turn expelled by the *Taliban*. Aerial warfare and modern weapons technology have made fortresses of this type obsolete.

BALKH (36–46' N, 66–54' E). A province in northcentral Afghanistan with an area of about 4,633 square miles and a population of about 570,000. The administrative capital of the province is Mazar-i Sharif, with about 103,000 inhabitants in 1978, and the location of a shrine Afghans believe to be the burial place of the Caliph Ali (d. 640). The town of Balkh, located on the Balkhab River about 14 miles west of Mazar-i Sharif, derives its name from the ancient city of Bactra amidst the ruins of which it is located. According to local tradition Balkh was founded by Balkh ibn Balakh ibn Saman ibn Salam ibn Ham ibn Nuh (Noah). Zoroastrian tradition holds that it was the birthplace of Zoroaster and was built by the Arian ruler Bakhdi (or Keiomarz?) who founded the Pishdadian dynasty. The city was captured by Alexander the Great (320s B.C.) and became the capital of the Greek satrapy of **Bactria**. In the second century B.C. Bactria was invaded by Turkic nomads who renamed the area Tukharestan. Subsequently the Kushans (*see* KUSHANID KINGDOM) ruled over the area and were followed by other dynasties. The ancestor of the famous Barmakid family of Abbasid wazirs (r. 781–803), Barmak (priest), was a native of Balkh. Genghis Khan (r. 1206–26) destroyed the city, but it was rebuilt during the Timurid period (15th century). In 1480 the tomb of the Caliph Ali was believed to be discovered where Mazar-i Sharif is now located, and Balkh lost its significance. Because of its antiquity, the town is known as "Mother of Cities." *See also* BACTRIA.

BALKHI, JALALUDDIN RUMI (1207–73). Known as Jalaluddin Rumi (from A., *Rum*, Asia Minor), where he spent the greater part of his life. He is acclaimed as the most eminent Sufi poet in Persian, famous for his mystical *mathnawis* (a poetic form in rhyming distichs) which "rank among the great poems of all time" (E. G. Brown, author of *A Literary History of Persia*). Jalaluddin was the founder of the *maulawiyya* order of "whirling dervishes," whose dance was part of their ritual. He was born in 1207 in Balkh and is therefore claimed as a native son by the Afghans and called by the appellation Balkhi (the one from Balkh).

BALKHI, RABI'A. Famous poetess in **Dari** and a contemporary of Rudaki (the first great poet in Persian after the advent of Islam, d. 940 A.D.). She was born in Balkh in the tenth century and therefore called Balkhi by Afghans. Some of her ghazals are extant. Legend has it that she fell in love with a Turkish slave, named Baktash, and had to pay for this illicit love with her life.

BALUCH. One of Afghanistan's ethnic minorities located primarily in Nimruz and scattered in small numbers over Helmand, Farah, Herat, Fariab, Jozjan, Kunduz, and Badakhshan Provinces. Their numbers were estimated in the 1970s between 100,000 and 200,000. Virtually all are *Sunnis* and speakers of the Baluchi language (except for the Dari- speaking Qataghan Baluch). The Baluch are no longer organized into specific tribes and are largely sedentary; their "heartland" lies in the Baluchistan Provinces of Iran and Pakistan, where they are said to number about five million. Small numbers also exist in the Soviet Union. Since the mid-1970s some 2,500 Baluch guerrillas, fighting for autonomy in Pakistan, have found shelter in southern Afghanistan. After the **Saur Revolt**, the **Taraki** government issued Decree No. 4 for the "evolution of literature, education and publication in mother tongues of tribes and nationalities" and declared Baluchi a "national" language whose use was permitted on Afghan media. The **Brahui** who speak a Dravidian language have now largely assimilated with the Baluch.

BAMIAN (34–50' N, 67–50' E). A province in central Afghanistan with an area of about 6,757 square miles and a population of about 285,000 and a town of the same name that is the administrative center of the province. The town lies at an altitude of about 8,200 feet above sea level, about 205 miles by road north of Kabul. Bamian is part of the **Hazarajat**, the mountainous country of central Afghanistan, that is inhabited primarily by **Hazaras**. The province is famous for its two Buddha statues, respectively 120 and 175 feet in height, dating from the fifth and third centuries A.D. The statues are hewn into solid rock and overlaid with stucco, and, although they have suffered from the ravages of time and destruction by man, some of the stucco works and wall paintings are still preserved. The walls of the 300-feet high cliffs are honeycombed with caves that served as living quarters of Buddhist monks and are still inhabited today. The sculptures and paintings are an eclectic hybrid mixing Indian, Central Asian, Iranian, and classical European art styles and ideas.

BAND-I AMIR (34–50' N, 67–12' E). A series of five clear, blue lakes on the north side of the **Koh-i Baba** in Bamian Province. The lakes are formed by the flow of water over a succession of natural dams, running from the higher to the next one below. According to local tradition the dams were the creation of Caliph Ali, and the word *Amir* (Commander) refers to the Caliph, not to any Afghan ruler.

Band-i Amir is also the name of a river which rises in the Band-i Amir lakes and runs through the Yakowlang Valley in a southwesterly direction until it turns northeast, at which point it is known as the

Balkhab; finally it turns north and dissipates in the Turkestan plains. The country on its upper course, especially the Yakowlang Valley, is inhabited by Dai Zangi Hazaras (*see* HAZARA).

BAND-I BABA (34–37'N, 62–40'E). A range of hills north of the **Hari Rud** valley, called by the Turkomans Barkhudung Dagh and known in European sources as the Paropamisus. The **Koh-i Baba** forks into three branches: the Band-i Turkoman in the north, the Band-i Baian in the south, and the central range of the Band-i Baba, which extends east and rises to a height of some 5,000 feet above the Herat Valley.

BAND-I TURKESTAN (35–30' N, 64–0' E). The northern branch of the Koh-i Baba mountain range that runs in a northwestern direction, circling the basin of the upper Murghab River and dividing it from Band-i Amir River. It extends from an area about 45 miles southwest of Maimana and runs for about 125 miles in a generally east-west direction, its northern slopes giving rise to the Sar-i Pul, Maimana, and Kaisar Rivers. The highest peak in the range is the Zangilak, which reaches an altitude of about 11,600 feet.

BANK-I MILLI. *See* **BANKING.**

BANKING. Until the early 1930s there were no banks in Afghanistan, and the banking business was conducted by private individuals and moneylenders. In addition to the Afghan *ropia*, minted in Kabul, silver and gold coins from neighboring countries were also in circulation. It was at times necessary to send caravans of gold and silver bullion to the interior of the country to meet the demand for financial transactions, a risky practice in times of unrest. In 1932 **Abdul Majid Zabuli**, a pioneering Afghan entrepreneur, founded a stock company (*Shirkat-i Ashami-yi Afghanistan*) that was chartered as a commercial bank in 1934. Incorporated with a capital of 35 million Afghanis (£745,500), it was authorized to issue banknotes, import sugar and petroleum products, transact all government purchases and sales, and hold sole option on the exploitation of all mines and the establishment of all industrial institutions in Afghanistan. It became a vital factor in the process of industrialization of Afghanistan and the establishment of a textile industry in the Kunduz and Pul-i Khumri areas. Its monopoly was ended in 1938 with the establishment of the **Da Afghanistan Bank** which performed the functions of a central bank. Its task was to issue currency notes and control the exchange rate of the currency. In 1955 the Afghan Commercial Bank (Pashtanai Tejarati Bank) was established as a joint-stock company for the purpose of developing the commerce of the country. A bank of construction and mortgages existed since 1948 to assist the construction of low-cost houses for government employees as well as hotels and various public buildings. All banks were nationalized during the Daud regime, a policy that was continued after the **Saur Revolt** of 1978. In the 1990s the Bank-i Milli had seven branches in Kabul and ten in the provinces, as well as offices in London, New York, Hamburg, and Karachi. The war in Afghanistan and the occupation of rural areas by *mujahedin* forces has severely restricted banking activities. *See also* AFGHANI and DA AFGHAN-ISTAN BANK. In the ensuing civil war after the fall of the Marxist regime, the Kabul government of **Rabbani** had a monopoly in issuing money, which was printed in Russia under a previous contract. Because of inflation, banknotes in denominations of 5,000 and 10,000 afghanis were issued in 1996.

BARAKATULLAH, MAULAWI. An Indian revolutionary and "prime minister" in 1919 in the "Provisional Government of India in Exile" in which **Mahendra Pratap** was president and **Maulawi Obaidullah** home minister. He met Sardar **Nasrullah** in England during the latter's visit in 1895 and became a news writer (political reporter) for him thereafter, and in 1915 he came to Kabul as a member of the **Hentig-Niedermayer** expedition. Subsequently he is said to have represented **Mahmud Tarzi** as editor of the *Seraj al-Akhbar Afghaniya* while Tarzi was in Europe. In 1927 Barakatullah accompanied Mahendra Pratap to the United States and died shortly thereafter in San Francisco.

BARAKI. A tribe of **Tajiks**, intermarried with **Ghilzais**, and settled in the Logar and Butkhak areas, south and east of Kabul, by **Sultan Mahmud of Ghazni** in the 11th century. The Barakis accompanied the **Ghaznawid** ruler on his invasions of India and were rewarded for their services with a perpetual grant of the lands of Kaniguram in Waziristan. They are divided into the Barakis of Rajan who speak Persian and the Barakis of Barak who speak an idiom of their own.

BARAKZAI. An important section of the Zirak branch of the **Durrani** to which the Barakzai/**Muhammadzai** ruling family belongs. In numbers economic, and political strength they were the paramount tribe of Afghanistan. Their heartland is in the area south of Kandahar, the valley of the Arghastan River, the banks of the Helmand, and the plains bounded by the Helmand River. They were soldiers in the service of **Nadir Shah**, founder of the short-lived Afsharid dynasty in Iran, and were settled on land seized from the **Ghilzai**. They continued to hold *jagirs*, fiefs, in exchange for their military services to **Ahmad Shah Durrani**. When **Painda Khan**, leader of the Barakzais, was assassinated, the Barakzais chiefs under **Dost Muhammad** ousted and replaced the **Sadozai** dynasty. The Barakzai continue to possess large areas of agricultural land and extensive flocks in the area between Herat and Kandahar.

BARECHI. A tribe of Afghans inhabiting the Shorawak region, south of Kandahar. They are divided into the Mandozai, Zakozai, Badalzai, and Shirani, the first three of whom are said to descend from Barech, son of Sharaf-ud-Din and grandson of Saraban, the son of Qais, the putative ancestor of all the **Pashtuns**. The Barechis are cultivators, irrigating their lands from the Lora, which is the lifeline of the Shorawak Valley. They are also known as camel breeders and export their wool to Kandahar. They have been described as peaceful and "fine men...and excellent swordsmen." They intermarry with their Brahui neighbors and, like them, are of the *Sunni* school of Islam.

BAREQ-SHAFI'I, MUHAMMAD HASAN. A leading Afghan poet, writer, and high-ranking member of the **PDPA**. He is a **Pashtun**, born in 1932 in Kabul and educated at Ghazi high school and the theological college in Kabul. He was editor of a number of newspapers and journals, including *Nendari* (Theater), *Zhuandun* (Life), *Pashtun Zhagh*, (Pashtun Voice), and director of *Payam-i Imruz* (Message of the Day). Member of the *Parchami* faction of the PDPA from the beginning, he became editor of *Khalq* in 1966. After the **Saur Revolt** he became minister of Information and Culture in 1978 and minister of Transport in 1979. During the *Khalqi* period he was forced to denounce **Babrak Karmal** and, after the latter succeeded to power, Bareq-Shafi'i was demoted to the status of alternate member of the central committee. He was appointed first vice president of the central council of the **National Fatherland Front** in 1982 and subsequently became governor of Herat province. In 1985 he was appointed second secretary of the Afghan embassy in Libya, and in May 1987 he was appointed the party organ during the presidency of Babrak Karmal, and of *Payam*, its successor, in 1989. He was chairman of the union of journalists but then was unemployed. His daughter is married to Nur Ahmad Nur. Bareq-Shafi'i is said to have sought asylum in Europe.

BARYALAI, MAHMUD. Appointed by Dr. **Najibullah** as first deputy prime minister in May 1990 and member of the executive board of the central council of the *Hizb-i Watan*. Born in 1944 in Kabul and educated at **Habibia School, Kabul University**, and the Soviet Union, he is a half-brother of **Babrak Karmal** and son-in-law of Anahita Ratebzad. A charter member of the **PDPA**, he was imprisoned from 1965–66 for his political activities. He went to the Soviet Union and received an M.A. degree in political economics. After the Saur Revolt he was appointed Afghan ambassador to Pakistan in July 1978 and recalled and purged in October by the *Khalqi* regime but did not return to Kabul. After the ouster of **Hafizullah Amin**, he became head of the international relations department of the PDPA. In 1980 he also became editor of the party organ, *Haqiqat-i Inqilab-i Saur*. He was expelled from the party in July 1991, shortly before the return of Babrak Karmal to Afghanistan. After the fall of the Marxist regime, he lived for a brief time in Microrayon, where he was elected head of the Communist party. Later he moved into the area controlled by General **Dostum** and is said to have sought asylum abroad.

BASHGAL. Or **LANDAI SIND** (Short River, 35–20' N, 71–32' E). A river which rises in the southern slopes of the **Hindu Kush** near the Manual Pass (15,300 feet) in Kunar Province and, running in a south-southwesterly direction, debouches into the Kunar River. The river is also known by its Pashtu name, Landai Sind, and the name Arnawai. The Bashgal Valley of Nuristan is inhabited by the Katir, Madugal, Kashtan, and Kam peoples. They were converted to Islam in 1897.

BASMACHIS. An irregular force, called Basmachis (T., bandits) by the Soviet government, that fought the Bolshevik army in the mountains of Tajikistan and Ferghana in Soviet Central Asia from 1919 until the 1930s. Their leaders included Muhammad Amin Beg, **Ibrahim Beg**, and **Enver Pasha**, the minister of War and leader of the Ottoman war government who fled Turkey after the war. For a time the Basmachis enjoyed a measure of support from King **Amanullah**, who was not averse to becoming the king of a Central Asian confederation.

When the Bolshevik government succeeded in consolidating its power in Central Asia, Ibrahim Beg was forced to use Afghanistan as a sanctuary. After a hot pursuit into Afghan territory by the Red Army, Sardar **Shah Mahmud** expelled Ibrahim Beg, who was captured by Soviet forces and executed in April 1931. *See* IBRAHIM BEG and SOVIET-AFGHAN RELATIONS.

BAZAAR. A traditional marketplace varying in size from a few temporary stalls in a village lane with a minimum of goods for a rural population to a major market place in a large town. The bazaar is often adjacent to the mosque, and in towns and cities it was frequently covered. Shops are usually segregated according to crafts and the types of goods sold. The bazaar is usually in the old town, whereas Western-type shops exist in the "new town" (D., *Shahr-i Nau*).

BEHESHTI, SAYYID ALI. President of the Revolutionary Council of the Islamic Union of Afghanistan (*Shura-yi Inqelabi-yi Ittefaq-i Islami-yi Afghanistan*), which until 1982 controlled large portions of the **Hazarajat**. He is a native of Bamian and was educated in Saudi Arabia and Iraq, where he was a contemporary of Ayatollah Khomeini. He opened a madrasa in Waras to spread his revivalist ideas among **Hazaras** and was speaker in the Takkia Khana at Kabul until the **Saur Revolt**. In September 1979 he was elected president of the **Shura** by a council of elders and *Mirs*. Formed a traditional Islamic resistance group, commanded by **Sayyid Muhammad Hasan "Jagran"** (Major), with headquarters in Waras in Ghor province and became a major force in the Hazarajat until the *Shura* lost ground to the Islamist forces of *Nasr*. The *Shura* recruited its fighters from the Hazara peasantry, officered by **sayyids**. Beheshti appointed governors and mayors of towns, disarmed the population, and created a state apparatus along traditional lines. Torn by factional fighting and pressed by radical Islamists, his domains were greatly reduced. He joined **Rabbani** but was driven from Kabul by the *Taliban*.

BEHZAD, KAMALUDDIN (1450(60?)–1535). Master calligrapher and miniature painter who founded the Herati school of miniature painting. He did the illustrations in the Bustan manuscripts of Sa'di that are at the National Library of Egypt at Cairo. Orphaned as a youth, he was reared and trained by Amir Ruhulla Mirak Naqqash. He became a protege of Shir Ali Nawa'i, Sultan Husain Baiqara's prime minister. After the Safavid ruler Shah Ismail captured Herat in 1510, he took Behzad to

Tabriz. Behzad became director of the royal library there and continued the miniature tradition. He died at age 100 in Tabriz. *See also* HERAT.

BENAWA, ABDUL RAUF. A writer, Pashtun activist, and diplomat. He was born in 1913 in Kandahar and educated in that city. He published the newspaper *Tulu-i Afghan* (Afghan Sunrise), a number of articles, and a book entitled *Pashtana Likwal* (Writers of Pashtu). He became president of the Pashtu Academy (*see* AFGHAN ACADEMY) and later director of Radio Kabul. Served as press attache in New Delhi (1954–55) and Cairo (1964–66) and became minister of information and culture in 1967. He was ambassador to Libya, 1980–84, and came to the United States for medical treatment and died there 1984.

BIRUNI, ABU RAYHAN AL-. (973–1048). Chronicler, astrologer, and scholar at the court of **Mahmud of Ghazni**. He accompanied the **Ghaznawid** ruler on his campaigns to India and he studied Sanskrit and Indian philosophy there. He was one of the most profound and original scholars of medieval Islam. Born about 973 A.D. near Khiva, he was first at the court of the Khwarizm Shahs in Transcaspia and was later called to the court of Mahmud of Ghazni. He was a prolific scholar, said to have 180 works to his name, and as tradition has it his works have "exceeded a camel-load."

BISMIL, MUHAMMAD ANWAR. Poet and director of the Afghan Literary Society (*see* AFGHAN ACADEMY) in the early 1930s. Born in 1908 in Kabul and educated at **Habibia School**, he was imprisoned in 1932 for membership in the secret "Young Afghan Society" (*Jawanan-i Afghanistan*), a reformist social and political movement. In the 1960s he was appointed a member of the senate. Mother tongue Dari.

BITAB, SUFI ABDUL. Poet Laureate (*Malik al-Shu'ara*) of Afghanistan who attained the status of master (*Khalifa*) of the **Naqshbandi** Sufi fraternity. He was born in 1892 in Qasab Kocha (Butcher's Street) in Kabul city and educated under the supervision of his uncle Mulla Abdul Ghafur, after which he embarked on a career of teaching at Habibia School and Kabul University. He was awarded the title of poet laureate in 1951 but was also respected as a commentator of Hadith and author of numerous publications in a variety of fields. He died in 1958.

BOST. *See* **LASHKARGAH.**

BRAHUI. A small ethnic community that speaks a Dravidian language and is located in the southern parts of Nimruz and Kandahar Provinces. They are tenant farmers and hired herders and number about 20,000 (although numbers as high as 200,000 are given). Most Brahui also speak Pashtu and Baluchi and consider themselves akin to the **Baluch.** The majority of Brahui live in the Pakistan province of Baluchistan, where they are divided into two major branches: the Sarawan tribe, claimed to be of Afghan descent, in the area north of Kalat and the Jhalawan to the south. The leading, but by no means largest, section among the Sarawan is the Raisani, whose chief is the sardar of all the Sarawan. Among the Jhalawan the Muhammad Hasanis, or Mamasanis, are the most numerous. They are Sunni Muslims of the Hanafi school.

BRESHNA, ABDUL GHAFUR. Most prominent of Afghan painters, as well as an expert musician, composer, and playwright. Succeeded **Ghulam Muhammad Musawwer Maimanagi** as director of the Kabul School of Fine Arts in 1933 and later became president of all Afghan fine arts schools. He wrote plays for Radio Kabul and was a master cartoonist for the *Anis* newspaper. Composed the national anthem of the Republic of Afghanistan, established in 1973 by **Muhammad Daud.** Born in 1907 of a **Muhammadzai** family, he was educated at **Habibia School** and in Germany. He died on January 4, 1974.

BRYDON, DR. WILLIAM (1811–1873). Assistant surgeon with **Shah Shuja**'s contingent of Hindustani Infantry who was the sole survivor to reach Jalalabad on January 13, 1842 after the disastrous retreat that routed the British **Army of the Indus** and camp followers. Later, hostages and other survivors of the British expeditionary force of some 16,000 reached the safety of India. A painting by Elizabeth, Lady Butler, forcefully depicted the wounded physician on a dying pony at the gates of Jalalabad. A powerful reminder of the extraordinary loss to British prestige and fulfillment of a supposed prediction of **Akbar Khan** that he would annihilate the British army and leave only one man to tell. *See also* DEATH MARCH.

BURNES, ALEXANDER (1805–41). A captain in the Indian Army who was sent by **Lord Auckland**, governor-general of the **British East India Company**, to the court of Amir **Dost Muhammad** in September

1837 for the purpose of concluding an alliance with Britain and establishing peace between the Afghan ruler and **Ranjit Singh**, who had captured Kashmir and occupied Peshawar. Burnes was well received at Kabul, and it appeared that an agreement with the amir was possible; but in spite of Burnes's recommendations Lord Auckland was not willing to make any promises. He recommended that Dost Muhammad waive his claims on Peshawar and make peace with the Sikh ruler. The Afghan amir's correspondence with Russia and the presence of a purported Russian emissary at Kabul, named **Vitkevich**, was India's reason for starting the **First Anglo-Afghan War**. Burnes returned to Kabul with the invading forces to serve as deputy and presumed successor of **Sir William Macnaghten**, the envoy and minister of the British government at Kabul. A revolt in Kabul resulted in the assassination of Sir Alexander (he had been knighted shortly before) on November 2, 1841, and the British debacle in the war (*see* ANGLO-AFGHAN RELATIONS; ANGLO-AFGHAN WARS; and MACNAGHTEN, SIR WILLIAM).

BUZKASHI. An Afghan national game originating in Central Asia and played primarily by **Uzbeks**, **Turkoman**, and **Tajiks** of northern Afghanistan. Buzkashi means "goat-pulling" and is played on horseback by two opposing teams who use the carcass of a calf (a goat was used in former days) as their object of competition. The purpose is to lift up the carcass from the center of a circle, carry it around a point some distance away, and put it again in its original place. All this has to be done on horseback and the *chapandaz*, expert player, must try to keep possession of the headless carcass. Cash prizes are given to the player who scores a goal and to the winning team. Champion teams used to perform each year on major holidays and the king's birthday in Kabul. The tradition of Buzkashi continued even in exile in Pakistan.

C

CALENDAR. Afghanistan reckons time according to the Islamic era that begins with the emigration (*hijra*) of the Prophet Muhammad from Mecca to Medina in 622 A.D. Afghans use two dates, one for Islamic festivities based on the Arabic lunar (*qamari*) year, the other for administrative purposes based on the solar (*shamsi*) year. The lunar year is eleven days shorter than the solar calendar, and the months do not correspond to the seasons. One of King **Amanullah**'s lasting innovation was the introduction of the solar calendar. The Afghan solar year begins on March 21, which is *nauruz*, New Year's day, and in 1990 corresponded to the solar year 1369, or the lunar year 1410. Newspapers in Afghanistan usually carry all three dates. The months are named after the signs of the Zodiac as follows:

Dari	*Pashtu*	*Zodiac*	*English*
Hammal	Wray	Aries (Ram)	March 21
Saur	Ghwayai	Taurus (Bull)	April 21
Jauza	Gargholai	Gemini (Twins)	May 22
Saratan	Chungash	Cancer (Crab)	June 22
Asad	Zmarai	Leo (Lion)	July 23
Sonbola	Wazhay	Virgo (Virgin)	August 23
Mizan	Talah	Libra (Scales)	September 23
Aqrab	Larum	Scorpio (Scorpion)	October 23
Qaus	Lindah	Sagittarius (Archer)	November 22
Jadi	Merghumai	Capricornus (Goat)	December 22
Dalw	Salwagah	Aquarius (Water Carrier)	January 21
Hut	Kab	Pisces (Fish)	February 20

The first six months have 31 days, the next five months have 30 days each, and the last (Hut) has 29 days and 30 days in a leap year. The week ends on Friday, *Jum'a*, which is the day of rest. The four seasons are spring—*bahar*, summer—*tabestan*, fall—*khazan*, and winter—*zemestan*.

According to one author (Poladi, 1989) the *Chagatai*, twelve-year cycle still exists in the **Hazarajat**. The years are named after animals as follows:

Mush	Mouse	Baqar	Ox
Palang	Leopard	Khargush	Rabbit
Nahang	Dragon *	Mar	Snake
Faras	Hare *	Gusfand	Sheep
Shadi	Ape	Murgh	Hen
Kalb	Dog	Khuk	Pig

Winter season, lasting much longer than in most parts of Afghanistan, is divided into eleven *Toghal* (countings). * Translation dubious, LWA.

CALIPH. The word is derived from the Arabic *khalifa*, meaning successor, and was adopted as a title by the leader of the Muslim community after the death of the Prophet Muhammad. The office was first held by the companions of the Prophet, the four Rightly Guided Caliphs (r. 632–750), then by the Abbasids (r. 750–1258) until the Mongol conquest of Baghdad. The rise of military rulers, sultans, ended the importance of the caliphate until Ottoman rulers claimed both the sultanate and the caliphate in an effort to legitimize their rule over the entire Islamic world. Afghanistan and India recognized the legitimacy of the Ottoman claim, but were unable to heed the caliph's call for war (*jihad*) against the Allies in World War I. After the defeat of the Ottoman empire, Mustafa Kemal Ataturk, the founder of modern Turkey, abolished the office of the caliphate in March 1924. Attempts to nominate King **Amanullah** for the position did not succeed.

CAMPBELL. A Scotsman, officer in the **British East India Company** service, who fought in the army of **Ranjit Singh** and during the **Second Anglo-Afghan War** in the service of **Shah Shuja**. He was wounded and captured by forces of **Dost Muhammad** and became military adviser and artillery instructor in the Afghan army. He eventually converted to Islam, assuming the name Shir Muhammad Khan, and rose to the rank of general and commander in chief of the Turkistan army at Balkh. As a youth Amir **Abdul Rahman** learned his military sciences from Campbell and succeeded him at his death in 1866 as commander in chief of the Turkistan army.

CAPITULATION, TREATY OF. On 11 December 1841, the British forces negotiated a surrender with Afghan chiefs, after it was clear that they were unable to defend themselves from increasing Afghan attacks. The treaty was signed by **Eldred Pottinger**, the political agent at Kabul, and Major-General **Elphinstone**, commander of the British forces in Afghanistan, and by Afghan notables including **Muhammad Akbar Khan**. It demanded that the British troops shall speedily quit the territories of Afghanistan and march to India and not return. Two *sardars* were to accompany the army to Afghanistan's border "so that no one should offer molestation on the road." Six English gentlemen were to remain "as our guests [and] shall be treated with courtesy." They would be permitted to leave when Amir **Dost Muhammad** had returned. The British force at Jalalabad was to proceed to Peshawar before the Kabul army arrived, and the troops at Kandahar and other parts of Afghanistan were to depart. All property belonging to Sardar Dost Muhammad Khan was to be returned. If the Afghans needed assistance against foreign invasion, the British government should help; and all detained Englishmen, including the sick and wounded at Kabul, would be permitted to leave. "All muskets and ordnance stores in the magazine shall, as a token of friendship, be made over to our agents." Affixed to the treaty were the seals of 18 chiefs, including Muhammad Akbar Khan, son of Amir Dost Muhammad. (The text of the treaty differs to some extent with the version given by **Lady Sales** in her *Journal of the Disaster in Afghanistan*. This may be due to the fact that the treaty was several times amended before the final version was signed.) The treaty was never implemented, as none of the parties trusted the other. **Sir William Macnaghten** was killed by Sardar Akbar Khan after he tried to make a deal with the sardar's enemies, and the British refused to surrender all their weapons. The British army started its evacuation of Kabul on January 6, 1842 and was routed on its way to the border. (*See* FIRST ANGLO-AFGHAN WAR and DEATH MARCH. For complete text of treaty *see* Sykes, 344-51)

CAVAGNARI, SIR PIERRE LOUIS. A man of mixed British and French ancestry described variously as having "great charm and ability" and being a man "of overbearing temper, consumed by the thirst for personal distinction." He was signatory for the British government of the **Treaty of Gandomak** (1879) with Amir **Yaqub** Khan. As commissioner of Peshawar, he crossed the Afghan border on September 21, 1878 with a small party to prepare the way for the British mission of **Sir Neville Chamberlain** to proceed to Kabul. The party was stopped at Ali Masjid by the Afghan General **Faiz Muhammad**, and the British government made this a *casus belli*. On November 21, an Indian army invaded Afghanistan. Cavagnari was appointed British envoy to the amir's court at Kabul after the conclusion of the **Second Anglo-Afghan War**. He arrived in Kabul in July 1879, but on September 3, mutinous soldiers, joined by Kabuli citizens, attacked the British residence and killed Cavagnari and his staff. The British government feared a debacle similar to the **First Anglo-Afghan War** and extricated its forces from Afghanistan by recognizing **Abdul Rahman Khan** as the new amir. It was not until 1922 that a British envoy was again appointed to Kabul. *See also* ANGLO-AFGHAN WARS.

CAVAGNARI, SIR LOUIS. RECEPTION OF. A Kabul telegram of July 26, 1879 reported that the "Embassy entered city this morning, and received a most brilliant reception. Four miles from city Sirdars

Abdullah Khan, Herati, and Mullah Shah Mahomed, the foreign minister, with some cavalry and two elephants, met us. We proceeded on the elephants with a large escort of cavalry... Large crowd assembled, and was most orderly and respectful." Cavagnari had an audience with the amir, and a news writer reported "that the general opinion in Kabul is that now that the British Envoy has arrived, the arrears of pay due to the troops will be paid; that compulsory enlistment will be discontinued; and that oppressive taxes on the peasantry and on the trading classes will be considerably reduced." But on August 3, it was reported that the amir contemplated a reduction of the allowance hitherto paid to the **Muhammadzai** *sardars*. Three days later it was reported that the "Herati troops move around town in a most disorderly manner, and creating some excitement amongst the rabble of the place." To appease them two Herati regiments were paid, and two regiments were deprived of their ammunition. Eventually all were paid, and their ammunition was taken, but on September 4 the embassy was attacked and all members killed.

A letter dated September 6, from the Amir **Yaqub** to the British government lamented: "Troops, city, and surrounding country have thrown off yoke of allegiance... Workshop and magazines totally gutted: in fact, my kingdom is ruined. After God I look to the Government for aid and advice." (PPCol.)

CHADARI. Chadari (D., *tent*) is a tent-like garment, or veil, worn by women in Afghanistan. It consists of a headpiece with an embroidered eye patch through which a woman can see without revealing her face. The headpiece is attached to a pleated cloak which envelops the entire body. This garment was obligatory for all except nomad and peasant women at work. In the final year of his reign King **Amanullah** encouraged women to discard the veil, and many did, but the civil war of 1929 brought an end to this innovation. It was not until 1959 that Prime Minister **Muhammad Daud** again permitted women to appear in public without the veil, and by the late 1970s women of all walks of life had abandoned the chadari and participated in the economic life of the country. After their conquest of Kabul, the *Taliban* again enforced the wearing of chadaris.

CHAGHCHARAN (34-31' N, 65-15' E). A small town built near a fort (*qasr*) in the early 1960s as the administrative center of Ghor province. It is located on the **Hari Rud** at an altitude of about 7,000 feet, the cause of its severely cold winters. Agriculture, facilitated by irrigation from the Hari Rud and **Murghab** Rivers, and livestock breeding are the major occupations of the inhabitants who are primarily **Taimanis**. Chaghcharan was the heartland of the **Ghorid** sultanate which flourished from the 11th to 13th centuries and ruled over an empire that extended from eastern Iran to Delhi in India and from Marv south to the Persian Gulf. *See also* GHOR and GHORID DYNASTY.

CHAHAR AIMAQ. *See* **AIMAQ.**

CHAI KHANA. The institution of the "tea house," a traditional resting place where travelers stop to eat, listen to bazaar gossip, and find shelter for the night. *Chai khana* (D., *chai* = tea, *khana* = house) exist in every village and along roads leading to towns, but motorized travel on major highways has greatly reduced the traveler's need for the service offered by the tea house.

CHAKHANSUR (31-10' N, 62-4' E). A small town located amid the ruins of the ancient capital of Sistan and an administrative district in Nimruz (until 1968 Chakhansur) Province in the extreme southwest of Afghanistan. The district lies on a high plateau that is seasonally irrigated by the Khashrud and bordered by desert. The inhabitants of the area are listed in order of numerical strength: **Baluch**, **Brahui**, **Tajik** or **Farsivan**, and **Pashtuns**—most of them Sunni Muslims.

CHAMBERLAIN, SIR NEVILLE BOWLES (1820–1902). Commander in chief of the Madras army, selected by Lord Lytton for "his striking presence and address" to lead a mission to Kabul in September 1878. He was refused passage at Ali Masjid by the Afghan General **Faiz Muhammad**. This "insult" was taken as the *casus belli* for the British invasion of Afghanistan. Chamberlain served with General Nott's force during the **First Anglo-Afghan War** at Kandahar, Ghazni, Kabul, and **Istalif** and was many times wounded.

CHAMKANI. Or **TSAMKANI** (33-48' N, 69-49' E). A district in the north of Paktia Province with an area of 102 square miles. The area is inhabited by people who claim to be Sulaiman Khel **Ghilzais** and subsequently adopted the name of the district as their tribal designation, Chamkani and Chakmani. In Pashtu the pronunciation is Tsamkani. Haji Muhammad Chamkani, a member of this tribe, was appointed vice president and adviser to President **Najibullah** and chairman of the nationalities and tribal council, established in May 1988.

CHANDAWOL. *See* **QIZILBASH.**

CHAPAN. A traditional coat for men popular among the Turkic population of northern Afghanistan but also worn by other Afghans. It is a long, buttonless caftan with knee-length sleeves which in warm weather is worn open with a sleeve rakishly thrown over a shoulder. In cold weather fur-lined or quilted chapans are worn, tied around the waist with a cummerbund. It comes in various colors, often striped, and is fashioned of cotton or silk.

CHAPANDAZ. A "master" horseman in the Buzkashi competition. *See* BUZKASHI.

CHARIKAR (35-1' N, 69-11 E). A town with about 22,500 inhabitants located at the mouth of the Ghorband about 40 miles north of Kabul and an administrative district with an area of 73 square miles in Parwan Province. At the turn of the century the town was inhabited by **Tajiks, Uzbeks, Qizilbashs, Hazaras**, and some Hindus (all of the latter traders and shopkeepers). The position of Charikar is of great importance, as the roads over the Hindu Kush unite in its neighborhood. In 1839 Charikar was a major British military outpost that was virtually wiped out by Kuhistani forces who had joined in the general uprising a- gainst the British occupation forces.

CHARKHI. A family from Charkh, a village and administrative district in Logar Province. Prominent members of this family were three brothers: **Ghulam Siddiq, Ghulam Nabi**, and **Ghulam Jilani** (the sons of Amir **Abdul Rahman**'s famous General **Ghulam Haidar**). They were supporters of King **Amanullah** and hostile to the new dynasty established by **Muhammad Nadir**.

CHEHEL ZINA. An archaeological site on the western outskirts of Kandahar. Chehel Zina (D., forty steps), refers to steps hewn into solid rock, leading up to a vaulted chamber with inscriptions describing the conquests of the Moghul Emperor **Babur** (r. 1483-1530) and subsequent rulers.

CHISHT (34-21' N, 63-44' E). A village and subdistrict in Herat Province about 26 miles east of Obeh. It is called Chisht-i Sharif because of the location of Sufi shrines in the village. It is inhabited by a section of **Taimanis** who claim descent from the ancient inhabitants of Ghor and assumed the name Chishtis. It is the birthplace of Muin ud-Din Muhammad (b. 1142), founder of the Chishti Sufi fraternity and much revered in India. Abu Ishaq, also reputed to be a founder of the Chishti, came from Asia Minor and settled in Chisht. There are a number of other Sufi saints who bore the name (*nisba*) Chishti. Members of the local community proclaimed a "Sufi Republic" early in the 1980s.

CLIMATE AND TOPOGRAPHY. The climate in Afghanistan varies with a particular geographic zone. Subarctic conditions exist in the northeast and **Hindu Kush** Mountains, semiarid steppe climate in low lying areas, and mild, moist weather in the areas bordering Pakistan. The estimated annual rainfall is between 11 and 15 inches.

About 83 percent of the *Wakhan-Pamir* area lies at an altitude above 10,000 feet and another 17 percent at an altitude of between 6,000 and 10,000. Therefore, perpetual snow covers mountains above 12,000 feet, and most passes are seasonally closed. The yak and bactrian camel are utilized in the transportation of people and goods.

Similar climatic conditions exists in the *Central Mountains* including most of central and eastern Hazarajat, and the Hindu Kush ranges extending from the Shibar Pass through the Koh-i Baba in the west, which is crossed by the **Salang** Tunnel at an altitude of about 11,000 feet. A limited amount of agriculture exists in the valleys, and nomads seasonally graze their livestock on the foothills.

The *Eastern Mountains* include four major valleys: Kabul, Kuhistan/Panjshir, the Ghorband, and Nuristan, the latter being the most inaccessible. Temperatures reach lows of one degree Fahrenheit, and winter lasts from December until March. Summer temperatures depend on altitude.

In the southwest, stony deserts extend to the Iranian border, and the **Registan**, "Country of Sand," extends south of the Helmand River and eastward as far as Shorawak, forming an almost impregnable boundary with Pakistan. On the edges of the Registan the desert gradually changes into a hilly landscape of sand hills thickly sprinkled with bushes, vegetation, and grass after rains, where **Baluch** and **Brahui** nomads seasonally graze their flocks. The major agricultural areas are confined to the valleys watered by the **Amu Daria** and the "Turkestan" plains, the Hari Rud/Murghab system in the northwest, the Helmand/Arghandab system, and the Kabul River system. The melting snow feeds the dry riverbeds in spring and provides much of the water for irrigation.

CONSTITUTIONAL DEVELOPMENT. Until the late 19th century Afghanistan was governed by a tribal aristocracy, first under the **Sadozai** and later under the **Barakzai** branch of the **Durranis**. Power was decentralized, and members of the royal clan ruled autonomously in the provinces, accepting the suzerainty of the king, or amir, in the capital city.

Although various administrative departments had already existed since the time of **Ahmad Shah**, the king headed all departments and made the influential officers share in the responsibilities of decisions. As his sign of sovereignty his name was mentioned in the Friday sermon (*khutba*), and coins (silver and copper) were struck in his name. The courts were in the hands of the clergy, *ulama*, but the death penalty had to be approved by the King or a governor. Ahmad Shah forbade the mutilation of limbs, and he drafted a code which was, however, not enacted. Little was changed until the time of Amir **Shir Ali**, who was the first Afghan ruler to establish an advisory council to serve as a consultative body.

Amir **Abdul Rahman**, who increasingly centralized all powers in his hand, took the first steps to institutionalize a consultative body. He relied on advice from a council which was composed of three groups: the *sardars*—members of the royal clan; loyal tribal chiefs; and the *ulama*. The "Iron Amir" claimed all temporal and spiritual powers (*imarat* and imamat), and there existed no restraint on his arbitrary rule, except the obligation to conform in his actions to the rules of **Islamic Law**. Amir **Habibullah**, Abdul Rahman's son, continued the tradition of his father. The first written document detailing the prerogatives of the ruler and the rights of the ruled was the Afghan constitution (*nizam-nama- yi tashkilat-i asasiya-yi Afghanistan*) promulgated by King **Amanullah** in October 1923. It consisted of 73 articles that enumerated the rights and prerogatives of the King, presented a "bill of rights" of Afghan citizens, and outlined the duties of ministers and government officials. It authorized the establishment of an advisory committee and provincial councils, half of whose members were to be elected by the people, and established a supreme court (*divan-i ali*). Financial affairs and the activities of provincial departments were defined.

King Amanullah was the chief executive, commander-in-chief, and last court of appeals. He appointed the ministers and presided over cabinet meetings, unless he delegated this task to the prime minister. He was the "Defender of the Faith," having the sole right to issue currency and have his name invoked in the Friday sermons (*khutba*) during noon prayers. His power was absolute, but he established the institutions that could have evolved in representative government and a constitutional monarchy. The constitution promised civil rights to all, abolished slavery, granted non-Muslims religious freedom (but missionary activity was forbidden), and declared the homes of citizens immune from forcible entry. A number of later statutory enactments (*nizam-nama*) further defined the powers and composition of parliament, which was housed in a new building just completed in **Darulaman**. Social reforms, such as the emancipation of women and free compulsory education, were decreed. King Amanullah's constitution was never completely implemented, and his reforms were abandoned in a wave of reaction under a coalition of forces led by **Habibullah Kalakani**. Amir Habibullah (Kalakani) abrogated all constitutional reforms and attempted to rule in the tradition of Amir Abdul Rahman.

A new attempt at constitutional government was made in October 1931 by **Nadir Shah** (r. 1929-33). His fundamental law (*usul-i asasi-yi daulat- i Afghanistan*) was similar to Amanullah's constitution. It included 16 sections with 110 articles that outlined general principles and enumerated the rights of the king, the rights of the people, and the duties of a national council (*Shura-yi Milli*) and provincial advisory committees. Like his predecessor, Nadir Shah enjoyed emergency and veto powers. Non-Muslims had equal rights and were not required to pay a poll tax or be obligated to wear a distinctive type of dress. No legislation was to be contrary to **Islamic law**, but a distinction was made between civil and religious courts. Torture and confiscation of property were prohibited, and publications, including newspapers, and free commercial activity were permitted. As a concession to the religious establishment, two members of the **Mujaddidi** family held the position of minister of Justice until 1935. The important position of prime minister was held by members of the royal family until 1963.

A new, liberal era began with the promulgation of the 1964 constitution (October 1, 1964—*qanun-i asasi-yi Afghanistan*) which limited the participation of members of the royal family in government. Members of the royal family could serve in the foreign service, be advisers (*mushawer*), and hold low-level positions in government departments, but not the positions of prime minister, supreme court justice, and member of Parliament. This was directed against Sardar **Muhammad Daud**, the king's cousin, a strong prime minister (1953–63) whose **Pashtunistan** policy had been a disaster in foreign relations. While **Zahir Shah** (r. 1933–73) continued to hold supreme powers, he permitted an unprecedented degree of democratic government. His constitution, the result of a constitutional drafting committee, included a preamble and eleven titles, comprising 128 articles. Primogeniture was introduced with a provision that "the Throne shall pass to his [Zahir's] eldest son." Freedom of thought, possession of property, unarmed assembly, and education were guaranteed. Afghan citizens were given the right to a free press and to form political parties, subject to the provisions of certain ordinances, provided that no actions were in violation of traditional norms and Islamic law. The provision on formation of political parties was never ratified by the king.

From the time of King Amanullah, constitutional development represented a process of modernization and the gradual introduction of concepts of the division of powers and individual rights. It also brought into being a process where the symbols of democratic government were beginning to gain concrete reality. But socioeconomic factors prevented the rapid implementation of political reforms. Universal education, envisioned by the constitution, remained an aim rather than a reality, and Afghanistan has remained largely illiterate. The introduction of secular schools, in addition to the traditional mosque/**madrasa** system, produced two essentially hostile elites. Afghanistan is still predominantly agricultural, and a great division exists between the urban and rural population. Sectarian and ethnic differences have prevented the forging of a heterogeneous population into a nation. When Sardar Muhammad Daud staged his coup in 1973, the experiment with democracy came to a halt.

Daud wanted one-party government and "democracy based on social justice." His constitution (*qanun-i asasi-yi daulat-i jumhuri-yi Afghanistan*), promulgated on February 14, 1977, aimed at the "exercise of power" by the majority, the "farmers, workers, and enlightened people and the youth." In 13 chapters and 136 articles, the republican government presented its aspirations. It called for the "elimination of exploitation in all its forms," nationalized the mineral resources of the state, large industries, communications, banks, and "important food procurement establishments." Land reforms were to be carried out and cooperatives were to be encouraged. Women were to enjoy equal rights and obligations and every Afghan 18 years or older was to have the right to vote. President Daud enjoyed absolute powers: he could convene and dismiss the national assembly (*Milli Jirgah*), whose members were nominated by his party (*see* NATIONAL REVO-LUTIONARY PARTY), and could veto any law. He felt he had to be strong to fight the evils of "hunger, ignorance, and disease"; but his one-man rule proved to be fatal. His leftist supporters in the army did not permit Daud's shift to the right, and before he could eliminate them from positions of power they staged the **Saur Revolt** of April 27, 1978.

The new regime wanted to establish a government of workers and peasants, with the PDPA as a vanguard to implement its revolutionary objectives. Decrees demanded the emancipation of women, land re-forms, and the introduction of far-reaching social changes. But the provisions of the "Fundamental Principles of the Democratic Republic of Afghanistan" could never be implemented. Armed resistance rose within a few months, turning into a war of liberation after the Soviet intervention.

The government of Dr. **Najibullah** virtually eliminated the trapp-ings of Marxist government in its Constitution of 1987, and the Afghan Interim Government of the seven *mujahedin* groups in Peshawar published the outlines of a constitution that favored the establishment of an Islamic state. The traditional groups, represented by **Sayyid Ahmad Gailani, Sebghatullah Mujaddidi,** and **Muhammad Nabi Muhammadi,** favored the establishment of a democratic Islamic government, not excluding the possibility of a constitutional monarchy; whereas the Islamist groups headed by **Gulbuddin Hekmatyar, Abdul Rasul Sayyaf, Yunus Khales,** and **Burhanuddin Rabbani** tended with some variations to favor an "Islamic state" on a more authoritarian model. They would limit the sphere of activity of women in public life and tend to limit manifestations of westernization. The Shi'a groups appear to favor a federated state in which the interests of the minorities are protected. Some, like the *Pasdaran* (Guardians) and perhaps *Nasr* (Victory) look to Iran as a model of the Islamic state, whereas the *Shura* (Council) appears to prefer a traditional political system. The Shi'as claim to constitute a fifth of the Afghan population and want this to be reflected in parliamentary representation. As long as their claimed popular strength was not reflected in an Afghan interim government, they refused to participate. The civil war, following the demise of the

Marxist regime, has resulted in the division of Afghanistan into two camps. The north and northest is controlled by an alliance of **Dostum**, Rabbani, and **Abdul Karim Khalili**, head of the **Hizb-i Wahdat**. The *Taliban* captured Kabul and two thirds of the country. They favor the establishment of a totalitarian Islamic state, headed by Muhammad Omar, their supreme leader. *See also* ISLAMIC LAW.

CONVENTION OF 1907. *See* **ANGLO-RUSSIAN CONVENTION.**

COURTS. *See* **ISLAMIC LAW.**

CURRENCY. *See* **AFGHANI.**

CUSTOMARY LAW. *See* **ISLAMIC LAW.**

D

DA AFGHANISTAN BANK. Afghanistan's central and major commercial bank, founded by the government in 1939 as a result of the success of the Bank-i Milli. It had sole rights to issue currency and control of foreign exchange. The bank had branches in major Afghan towns, but its impact and operations were confined largely to urban areas. Subsequently a number of specialized banks were established, but all banks were nationalized with the establishment of President **Muhammad Daud**'s republican government. In the 1980s the Da Afghanistan Bank began to be governed by a supreme council, and its director held cabinet rank. The formal banking system is still poorly developed in Afghanistan, and its functions are augmented by the informal money bazaar. Therefore, the traditional system of money-lending has survived all regimes, and foreign exchange dealings have remained a major activity of the bazaar. In the anarchy, following the fall of the Marxist regime, the **Rabbani** government issued banknotes as did his rival General **Dostum** in the north. As a result of inflation, the dollar was traded in January 1997 at afs. 9,500 in Kabul and afs. 27,000 in the north. *See also* BANKING.

DAI KUNDI HAZARAS. *See* **HAZARA.**

DAI ZANGI HAZARAS. *See* **HAZARA.**

DAILY PRAYERS. *See* **ISLAM.**

DANE, SIR LOUIS W. Head of a British mission to Kabul (January 1 to December 2, 1921) that negotiated the Treaty of Kabul. *See* ANGLO-AFGHAN TREATY OF 1921; AFGHAN FOREIGN RELATIONS; and ANGLO-AFGHAN WARS.

DARI. The name of the Farsi spoken in Afghanistan and with **Pashtu** one of the two "official" languages. The name derives from *darbar*, royal court, because it was the language of the Central Asian and Moghul Indian courts. Other etymologies suggested are *darra*, valley, or the language of Darius (522–486 B.C.), the Achaemenid emperor. Afghan scholars claim Dari was the language of **Khorasan** in which some of the oldest Persian poetry was written. In its written form Dari differs very little from the Farsi of Iran, except that it employs a greater amount of Arabic vocabulary and some archaic words no longer used in Farsi. Of the spoken Dari variants the Herati comes closest to Farsi, followed by the educated Kabuli idiom. Hazaragi, spoken by the Hazara, and Tajiki are other major Farsi dialects. All are mutually intelligible. Afghan governments have attempted to make Pashtu the national language and have expended considerable resources to Pashtunize Afghan society, but Dari is still the major language of higher education and serves as a "lingua franca" for all linguistic groups.

DARULAMAN (DAR AL-AMAN) (34-28'N, 69-0'E). The administrative capital of Afghanistan under King **Amanullah** who, in the early 1920s, constructed a number of government buildings, including a monumental parliament and a municipality building. Members of the court and high government officials built villas in the new capital, and a narrow-gauged railroad led to the center of Kabul some six miles away. It is a monument to Amanullah's ten-year reign and ceased being the capital after his downfall. The town was renamed Dar al-Habib (Abode of Habib) after **Habibullah Kalakani** and Dar al-Funun (Abode of the Arts) in 1930, until in 1947 it was again given its original name. The municipality building was subsequently converted into the famous **Kabul Museum**, now largely looted, which housed valuable archaeological and ethnographic collections from the Hellenistic, Greco-Buddhist, and **Ghaznavid** periods. Train service was ended, and the major administrative offices were again located in the old city. The parliament building was gutted by fire in 1969 and restored to house the ministry of defense. It was again severely damaged as a result of the **Tanai** coup of March 1990 and the ensuing civil war between the *"mujahedin"* forces.

DAR UL-ISLAM (DAR AL-ISLAM). The "Abode of Islam," or a country in which the ordinances of Islam are established and is under the rule of a Muslim sovereign. The *Shari'a*, **Islamic law**, prevails in this area, and non-Muslims are subject to their own religious and customary laws, but without the possibility of full citizenship. Hindus and Jews of Afghan citizenship enjoyed equal rights but at certain times had to pay a special poll tax and were exempt from military service. In 1920 the Indian *Hijrat* (or *Khilafat*) movement led to a mass emigration of Muslims from British India, the *dar ul-harb*, to Afghanistan, the *dar ul-Islam* (*see* HIJRAT MOVEMENT).

DAR UL-MU'ALLEMIN (DAR AL-MU'ALLEMIN). A teachers' training college founded in 1914 at Kabul. Initially students entered the school for three years of study after completing six years of primary education. During the reign of King **Amanullah** it was upgraded, and students were required to complete nine grades of education before being admitted. The college was established to train the teachers for the newly-established secular school system. Eventually teachers' training colleges were also established in the major provincial centers.

DARWAZ (38-26' N, 70-47' E). The name of an administrative center in the district of the same name in northern Badakhshan Province. It was part of an independent khanate (headed by a khan, chief) on both sides of the **Amu Daria** but became part of Afghanistan as a result of the settlement of the Russo-Afghan boundary in 1895, when Darwaz became Afghan territory and **Shighnan**, situated across the Amu Daria, was ceded to Russia.

DASHT-I MARGO (30-45' N, 63-10' E). A large desert lying between the **Helmand** and **Khashrud** Rivers about 150 miles in length and some 85 miles in width. It is a plateau, about 2,000 feet above sea level, windswept and barren, visited by **Baluch** herdsmen who alone know the paths leading to occasional water holes. It formed a natural boundary between Afghanistan and British India.

DAUD, MUHAMMAD. *See* **MUHAMMAD DAUD.**

DAWAI, ABDUL HADI (PARESHAN). A **Kakar** Pashtun, famous poet,
diplomat, and government official who published under the pen name
Pareshan (distressed). He was elected senator and became president of
the senate from 1966 to 1973. Born in 1894 in Kabul, he was a
graduate of the first class of **Habibia School** in 1912. In the same year
he became assistant editor of the famous *Seraj al-Akhbar Afghaniya*
and in 1920 of the *Aman-i Afghan*. He entered the foreign service,
participating in the **Rawalpindi** and **Mussoorie** peace conferences. He
was appointed Afghan minister in London in 1922, served as minister
of Commerce from 1925 until his resignation in 1928, and as Afghan
minister in Berlin from December 1929–31. From 1933 until 1946 he
was imprisoned as an **Amanullah** supporter. In 1950 he was elected to
Parliament and became speaker of the House. He served as secretary of
King **Muhammad Zahir** and tutor of the crown prince. He was
appointed ambassador to Cairo (1952–1954) and to Jakarta (1954–58).
He retired from political life and died in 1982 in Kabul.

DEATH MARCH. After signing a treaty of virtual capitulation with
Afghan chiefs in December 1841 (*see* CAPITULATION, TREATY
OF), the British forces of occupation and camp followers, amounting
to about 16,500 persons (690 British fighting men, 2,840 Indian
infantry, 970 cavalry, and over 12,000 camp followers—servants and
merchants in charge of non-weapons logistics and a large number of
women and children), embarked on a march toward the Indian border
in which few survived. The retreat began on January 6, 1842, and only
six miles were covered on the first day. The march quickly turned into
a rout as traffic jams impeded crossing the Logar River, and much of the
baggage was abandoned. On the second day only five miles were
covered to the well-fortified Khurd Kabul Pass. A number of people
froze to death and Amir **Shah Shuja**'s cavalry escort deserted. On the
next day the British rear guard was attacked. British officers tried
unsuccessfully to separate their troops from the camp followers. **Ghilzai**
ghazis attacked the retreating forces, killing some five hundred troops
and twenty-five hundred camp followers. British women and children,
as well as their husbands and a number of officers, were surrendered as
hostages to Sardar **Akbar** Khan and managed to survive. **Eldred
Pottinger** claims that Akbar Khan treacherously shouted "spare them"
in Persian and "kill them" in Pashtu. (George Pottinger, 163) On the
fifth day a last stand was made at Jagdalak, by which time about 12,000
of the retreating force had perished. Sardar Akbar Khan offered to pay

200,000 rupees to the Ghilzai chiefs if they would stop their attacks, but the Ghilzai were out for revenge. By the eighth day two British officers and seven or eight wounded men were taken prisoners, and only one man, Dr. **Brydon**, managed to reach safety at Jalalabad. (Dupree, Retreat) This gave rise to the legend that Akbar Khan had predicted he would wipe out the British army and leave only one man to tell the tale.

DEHGAN. A small tribe settled in the Kunar Valley which speaks the Laghmani or Kohistani language. The tribe is divided into the Dumeh, Chaguni, Kuli, Buzurg, Debazai, and Malikzai sections, the last four of which are found chiefly in the Kunar and Safi Valleys.

DEMOCRATIC REPUBLIC OF AFGHANISTAN (DRA). Name of the Afghan State after the **Saur Revolt**. In the latter part of the Marxist regime, the name was changed to Republic of Afghanistan (ROA).

DEOBAND. A town near Delhi, India, and the location of an Islamic university (*madrasa*) founded in 1867. It is a strictly orthodox institution whose members have traditionally supported pan-Islamic, anti-British, and fundamentalist causes. Graduates of Deoband readily found teaching positions in Afghanistan, where a madrasa of international reputation did not exist. Amir **Abdul Rahman** and King Amanullah at times forbade Deobandis from teaching in Afghanistan. **Muhammad Yunus Khales**, Amir of the Islamist **Hizb**, is a graduate of Deoband.

DHIMMI. Or **ZIMMI.** Also called *ahl al-dhimma*, "people of the covenant or obligation," are non-Muslim monotheists who under Islamic law enjoy freedom of life, liberty, and property provided they are loyal citizens. The dhimmis include Christians, Jews, and in Afghanistan, Hindus, even though they are not considered monotheists. At various times a special tax (*jizya*) was levied on adult male *dhimmis*, and Hindus were obligated to wear a dress distinctive from Muslims but were exempt from serving in the armed forces. Each community was culturally autonomous. As part of the nation-building process in the twentieth century, King **Amanullah** proclaimed all Afghans equal and abolished the separate legal status of *dhimmis*.

DIN. A., religion. Also a name. *Din-i Islam*, the religion of Islam. *See* ISLAM.

DIN MUHAMMAD, MUSHK-I ALAM (1790–1886). Considered a national hero by Afghans because of his implacable hostility to the British. A frontier **mulla** whose grandfather came from India and settled among the Andar Ghilzai near Ghazni. He studied with various ulama and was given the name Mushk-i Alam, "Scent (or Musk) of the World," by one of his teachers because of his excellent mind. He was a militant mulla who opened a madrasa for the training of mullas and gained considerable influence among the **Ghilzais**. He received an allowance from Amir **Shir Ali** and preached *jihad* against the British during the **Second Anglo-Afghan War**. When Amir **Abdul Rahman** tried to restrict his activity he incited the **Mangal** and Ghilzais to rebellion. After his death in 1886, his son, Mulla **Abdul Karim**, led a Ghilzai uprising against Amir Abdul Rahman that was suppressed only with great difficulty.

DOBBS, SIR HENRY. British envoy and chief of the British mission to Kabul that negotiated the **Anglo-Afghan Treaty of 1921** and established "neighborly" relations after the end of the **Third Anglo-Afghan War**. Before that he also headed the British contingent at the **Mussoorie** conference (April 17-July 18, 1920) that failed to normalize Anglo-Afghan relations. He first came to Afghanistan in 1903, when as a political officer he directed a small British contingent whose task was to restore or repair boundary pillars at the Russo-Afghan border. *See* ANGLO-AFGHAN WARS and AFGHAN FOREIGN RELATIONS.

DORAH PASS (36-0' N, 71-15' E). A pass over the eastern **Hindu Kush** range, lying at an elevation of 14,800 feet and crossed by a route leading from Zibak to Chitral in Pakistan. It is located in Zibak district of Badakhshan province and is so named because two roads (D., *do rah*) converge from it to Zibak and to Nuristan.

DORI RIVER (31-29 N, 65-12' E) . A river formed by the junction of the Kadanai and Kushebai Streams south of Shah Pasand and the Lora Stream which originates in Pakistan. It is replenished by the Arghastan, Tarnak, and Arghandab Rivers and numerous streams and finally runs into the Helmand.

DOST MUHAMMAD, AMIR (r. 1826–38 and 1842–63). Afghan ruler, known as the "Great Amir" (*Amir-i Kabir*), who was ousted by the

British in the **First Anglo-Afghan War** but was able to regain the Afghan throne after four years in Indian exile. He was born in 1792 in Kandahar, the son of **Painda Khan**, who was killed by **Zaman Shah** when Dost Muhammad was only eight years old. He became acting governor of Ghazni and, after the death of Muhammad Azam in 1824, established himself as ruler of Kabul. He next defeated his rival **Shah Shuja** at Kandahar and gradually extended his control over the rest of Afghanistan. He defeated the **Sikhs** at the Battle of Jamrud (1837) and assumed the title *Amir-ul-Mu'minin* (Commander of the Faithful). The British-Indian government turned against him when Dost Muhammad made overtures to Russia and Persia and permitted a Russian agent to come to Kabul. Dost Muhammad wanted to regain territory captured by **Ranjit Singh** and was willing to ally himself with the British, but the British government decided to support the Sikh ruler and restore Shah Shuja to the Afghan throne. A British army invaded Afghanistan and sacked Kabul on July 23, 1839. On November 2, 1840, after a few skirmishes, Dost Muhammad gave up; he surrendered to the British who took him as a hostage to India. However, the British occupation of Afghanistan became increasingly tenuous as their lines of communication were disrupted and tribal forces slowly expelled garrisons from outlying areas. Eventually, the army in Kabul was forced to negotiate an ignominious retreat in which most of the British army was eliminated (*see* ANGLO-AFGHAN WARS). Facing a situation of chaos in Afghanistan, the Indian government permitted Dost Muhammad to return and regain his throne. But it took a number of years to consolidate his power: he took Kandahar in 1855 and Herat in 1863. Dost Muhammad died a few days after he entered Herat. Of his 27 sons, **Muhammad Afzal** and **Muhammad Azam** ruled for short periods, followed by **Shir Ali**.

DOSTUM, GEN. ABDUL RASHID. During the 1980s, commander of the Jozjani "Dostum Militia" comprising some 20,000 regular and militia soldiers, most of them **Uzbek**, and entrusted with guarding Jozjan, Fariab, and Sar-i Pol provinces for the Kabul government. He was awarded the distinction of "Hero of the Republic of Afghanistan" and was a member of the central council of the **Watan** (formerly **PDPA**) party. Born in 1954 in Khwaja Dokoh, Jozjan province, of an Uzbek family, he worked for the Oil and Gas Exploration Enterprise of Shiberghan and in 1980 went to the USSR for training. He then joined the ministry of State Security and became commander of Unit 374 in

Jozjan Province. His forces served in various parts of the country and, it is said, one thousand of his soldiers were captured in the *mujahedin* conquest of **Khost**. At the break-up of the Marxist regime, Dostum gained control of the north central provinces of Afghanistan. He and a number of Generals turned against President **Najibullah** and assisted the *mujahedin* in the conquest of Kabul. Dostum's followers are united in a party, called *Junbish-i Milli-yi Islami*, which, at the time of this writing, controls most of Balkh, Fariab, Jozjan, and Samangan Provinces. When President **Rabbani** was unwilling to legitimize the position of Dostum by giving him a cabinet post, the latter joined forces with **Hekmatyar**. In May 1996 Hekmatyar defected and joined the Rabbani government, but both were ejected by the *Taliban;* and Dostum is the last major force to stop the "students" from uniting Afghanistan under their theocratic rule. *See also* MAZAR-I SHARIF, FALL OF.

DRA. Acronym for the Democratic Republic of Afghanistan that has been changed from Democratic Republic of Afghanistan (DRA) under President **Najibullah** to Republic of Afghanistan (ROA).

DURAND AGREEMENT. An agreement signed on November 12, 1893 at Kabul by **Sir Henry Mortimer Durand** and Amir **Abdul Rahman** that defined the boundary between Afghanistan and British India, subsequently called the "Durand Line." This boundary was drawn without regard to the ethnic composition of the population and severed a large portion of Pashtu-speaking Afghans from their brothers in Afghanistan. Amir Abdul Rahman accepted under "duress" a line running from "Chitral and Baroghil Pass up to Peshawar, and thence up to Koh-i Malik Siyah in this way that Wakhan, Kafiristan, Asmar, Mohmand of Lalpura, and one portion of Waziristan" came under his rule. He renounced his claims for "the railway station of New Chaman, Chagai, the rest of Waziri, Biland Khel, Kurram, Afridi, Bajaur, Swat, Buner, Dir, Chilas and Chitral." The Durand Line was never completely demarcated because of the hostility of the tribes, and the tribes on the Indian side of the border never came under the direct administration of the Indian, or subsequently Pakistani, governments. Abdul Rahman obtained an increase in subsidy of 6,000,000 rupees and a letter with the assurance that Britain would continue to protect Afghanistan from unprovoked Russian aggression, provided that the amir "followed unreservedly the advice of the British Government" in regard to his external relations. The Afghan government subsequently claimed that the agreement was forced on Afghanistan in the form of an ultimatum.

After the death of Amir Abdul Rahman, Britain insisted that the treaties with the late ruler were personal, rather than dynastic and therefore subject to renegotiation, but they excluded the Durand Agreement as not subject to this provision. Article 5 of the treaty of peace concluded at **Rawalpindi** on August 8, 1919 stated that "The Afghan Government accept the Indo-Afghan frontier accepted by the late Amir [Habibullah]," and the **Treaty of Kabul** carried a similar provision. When the state of Pakistan was created in 1947, the Afghan government demanded the right of the Pashtuns to decide whether they wanted an independent **Pashtunistan**, union with Afghanistan, or union with Pakistan. The Kabul government did not accept a plebiscite that allowed only a choice for union with Pakistan or India, and in 1979 the Afghan parliament repudiated the Durand Agreement. The Pashtunistan question has remained an issue between Afghanistan and Pakistan and has prevented the establishment of cordial relations between the two Muslim countries. *See also* AFGHAN FOREIGN RELATIONS and PASHTUNISTAN.

DURAND, SIR MORTIMER. (1850-1924). Foreign secretary of the government of India, sent to Kabul in September 1893 for the purpose of negotiating an agreement defining the Indo-Afghan boundary, subsequently called the Durand Line. (*See* DURAND AGREEMENT) Served in the Northwest provinces 1829–38. Political secretary to Sir Frederick Roberts in the Kabul campaign, 1879. Foreign secretary of the government of India, 1884–94.

DURRANI DYNASTY (1747-1973). The Durrani dynasty was founded in 1747 by Ahmad Shah "Durr-i Durran" who ruled Afghanistan until 1978. Ahmad Shah was a direct descendant of Sado, an Abdali chief at the court of the Savafid ruler Shah Abbas the Great (r. 1588-1629). The Durrani are divided into the Sadozai branch (a section of the Popalzai tribe) and the **Muhammadzai** (a section of the Barakzai tribe). The succession from Ahmad Shah to Muhammad Daud, who established a republican government, is as follows:

Sadozai Dynasty 1747–1817

Ahmad Shah	1747–1773
Timur Shah (s.o. Ahmad)	1773–1793
Zaman Shah (s.o. Timur, deposed)	1793–1800
Mahmud Shah (br.o. Zaman, deposed)	1800–1803
Shah Shuja-ul-Mulk (br.o. Zaman, deposed)	1803–1809

Mahmud Shah (br.o. Zaman)	1809–1817
(loses Kabul and Kandahar.)	

Ruling in Herat   1817–1863

Mahmud Shah (Sadozai, assassinated?)	1817–1829
Kamran (s.o. Mahmud, assassinated?)	1829–1841
Yar Muhammad	1841–1851
Said Muhammad Khan (s.o. Yar Muhd.)	1851–1855
Muhammad Yusuf Khan (Sadozai, deposed)	1855
Sirtap Isa Khan (Herati)	1855
Herat conquered by Persians, 1856	
Sultan Ahmad Khan	1855–1863
(Nephew of Dost Muhammad)	
Dost Muhammad Khan	1863

Ruling in Kabul   1817–1863

Muhammad Azim Khan	1817–1822
Habibullah Khan (s.o. Muhammad Azim)	1822–1826
(deposed)	
Dost Muhammad Khan (deposed)	1826–1839
(Uncle of Habibullah Khan)	
Shah Shuja-ul-Mulk (Sadozai)	1839–1841
Zaman Khan (Barakzai)	1841–1842
Fath Jang (Sadozai Contender)	1842?
Dost Muhammad Khan	1842–1863

Ruling in Kandahar 1817–1863

Pur Dil Khan (and bros. Muhdzai.)	1817–1839
Shah Shuja-ul-Mulk (deposed)	1839–1841
Kohan Dil Khan (br.o. Pur Dil)	1842–1855
Dost Muhammad Khan	1855–1863

Ruling Afghanistan   1863–1978

Civil war and anarchy	1863–1868
Shir Ali Khan (br.o. Dost, deposed)	1863–1866
Muhammad Afzal Khan	1866–1867
Muhammad Azam Khan (br.o. M. Afzal)	1867–1868
(deposed)	
Shir Ali Khan	1868–1879
Yaqub Khan (s.o. Shir Ali, abdicated)	1879

Second Anglo-Afghan War 1879–1880

Abdul Rahman Khan (s.o. Muhd. Afzal)	1880–1901
Habibullah Khan (s.o. Abdul Rahman) (assassinated)	1901–1919
Amanullah Khan (s.o. Habibullah, deposed)	1919–1929
Enayatullah Khan (three days, abdic.)	1929
(Habibullah Kalakani, Tajik (Jan. to October) (Son of a Water Carrier)	1929
Nadir Shah (Musahiban Family) (assassinated)	1929–1933
Zahir Shah (deposed)	1933–1973
Muhammad Daud (President) (assassinated)	1973–1978

DURRANI, LAND TENURE. Nadir Shah Afshar gave the Durranis the lands of Kandahar as a military fief. The land had previously been held by a mixed peasantry population that paid taxes to the suzereign ruler since Safavid times. The land of Kandahar had been traditionally divided into divisions called *qulba*, or "plows," which designated the portion of irrigated land cultivated by one person, operating one oxen and one plow, that gave double space for sowing two *kharwar* grain (one *kharwar*, literally a donkey load, amounted to 100 *man* [*maund*]—the exact weight varied in different localities), one half of which was cultivated each year while the other half remained fallow. Nadir Shah's agents ascertained the productivity of the land in various areas as a return of 25 *kharwar* for one *kharwar* of seed. Each *qulba* was assessed a land tax (*kharaj*) of ten percent. As an innovation, every garden, tree, and vine was assessed one copper *pice*.

About 3,000 double *qulba* were distributed to **Durrani** tribes in *tiyul*, fiefs, in exchange for providing 6,000 horsemen, one for each *qulba*. The following table shows the allotment of lands under **Ahmad Shah**:

Durrani Tribes	No. of Qulbas	Quota of Horses
Popalzai	965 ¼	806
Alikozai	1,050	851
Barakzai*	1,018 ½	907
Alizai	661 ¾	819
Nurzai	868 ½	1,169
Ishaqzai	357 ½	635

Khugiani**	163	423
Maku	121 ½	100
Total	5,206	5,710

*These numbers probably include the Achakzai (LWA)
** Spelled Khakwani in some older sources.

The Durranis were estimated at 100,000 families at the time. Six non-Durrani tribes held 110 qulbas but had to provide a much larger contingent of 2,890 horsemen.

Ahmad Shah Durrani greatly increased the land in control of Durrani chiefs, who were paid from 100 to 1,000 *tomans* (one toman was 20 Kandahar rupees) annually. During military service a horseman was paid 25 *tomans* either in money from the royal treasury or in *barat* (written assignment).

DUTANL Or **DOTANL** A tribe of *powindahs*, nomad merchants who used to travel seasonally between India and Afghanistan, selling silk, carpets, and hashish (*chars*). They are also called Lohani and are now settled on the Indian side of the border. *See* POWINDAH.

E

EAST INDIA COMPANY, THE BRITISH. The British East India Company was started in 1600 with a capital of £30,000 and a charter from Queen Elizabeth for 15 years to have a monopoly of trade "together with limited authority to make laws and punish interlopers." The charter was periodically renewed, and by the middle of the 18th century the Company was the de facto ruler of Bengal. Its Board of Control appointed a governor-general as executive who conducted the government for the Company until 1858, when the Crown ended the charter and appointed a viceroy, subject to the control of the London government. The Company concluded treaties with local potentates and waged wars in its attempt to become the paramount power in India, and it bore the responsibility for the debacle of the **First Anglo-Afghan War.** Three presidencies in Bengal, Bombay, and Madras furnished the Company's armies which included both British and Indian branches of cavalry, artillery, and infantry. Vassals and mercenaries were also employed.

ECONOMY. Afghanistan's economy resembles that of other less-developed countries in the sense that agriculture is the largest sector and that the government controlled mining and certain industries, including electric power stations and airlines. After 1977, it took control of all major industries and banking. At that time about 40% of cultivable land was owned by large landowners who made up only two percent of the agricultural population, whereas 80% of farmers each owned less than 11 acres (*Area Handbook for Afghanistan*). About 90% of the population is engaged in agriculture and animal husbandry. In the prewar years about 85% of Afghan agricultural exports consisted of fresh and dried fruit. Qaraqul skins and the Afghan carpet industry (which comprises more than 50% of the handicraft industries) were other important hard currency earners. The Soviet Union was the major trading partner and the only market for Afghan natural gas.

Prime Minister **Muhammad Daud** (r. 1953–63) began a program of development and modernization. Two five-year plans (1956–61 and 1962–67) were to provide the infrastructure of communications while the third (1967–72), initiated by a subsequent government, aimed at agricultural self-sufficiency. About $1.2 billion in foreign aid was expended by the early 1970s, of which the Soviet Union provided 50% and the United States 40%.

Prewar figures given by *The Afghan Statistical Yearbook* (July 1976) show the following values in rounded US dollars of Afghan exports in 1975:

Qaraqul skins	$10 million
Fresh fruit	$27 million
Dried fruit	$50 million
Carpets and kelims	$17 million
Natural gas	$41 million
Exports in barter-trade with neighboring countries:	
Soviet Union	$81 million
India	$29 million
Pakistan	$33 million

Exports and imports with major trading partners:

	Exports	Imports
United States	$10 mil.	$5 mil.
United Kingdom	$15 mil.	$8 mil.
Germany	$21 mil	$10 mil.
Japan	----	$60 mil.

President Daud projected a seven-year plan (1976–83) that emphasized industrial development over the agricultural sector and nationalized large industries, mines, and banks. Aid from the Gulf countries (the Shah of Iran had promised $2 billion) permitted a survey for construction of a railroad, which was to link Iran with the Indian subcontinent. A sudden fall in the price of oil and the downfall of the Iranian and Afghan rulers in the late 1970s ended these ambitious plans. Afghanistan still cannot produce most manufactured goods and processed raw materials. One of the first measures of the Marxist regime was to decree land reforms and to abolish the traditional **bazaar** system of agricultural financing, without providing alternate sources of funds. Since it soon lost control over much of the countryside, the Kabul government could never implement its reforms; nevertheless, in 1983, the Kabul government claimed that it had redistributed about one-fourth of cultivable land. The war in Afghanistan has wreaked enormous damage that cannot be assessed at this time. An agricultural survey conducted under the auspices of the Swedish Committee for Afghanistan examined the decline in agricultural production in Afghanistan between 1978 and 1987 and gave the following statistics:

	Percent growers	Av.area jeribs	Av.yield seers/jerib	Production per farmer
Irrigated wheat	7	-23	-26	-45
Rainfed wheat	-22	-33	-29	-52
Maize	-14	-9	-27	-49
Rice	-14	-20	-19	-40
Barley	-14	-21	-18	-35
Alfalfa	-11	-5	-16	-54
Clover	-25	-5	+3	-58
Bean	-20	-22	-21	-50
Mung Bean	-44	-26	-12	-51
Cotton	-43	-23	-29	-58
Linseed	-8	+30	-39	-14
Melon	-0	-31	-37	-69
Potato	-0	-5	-28	-47
Sesame	-20	-51	-19	-70
Sugar beet	-60	-63	-60	-85
Grape	-4	-3	-21	-36

(Decline in percentages. One hundred *jerib* is twenty hectares, and one *seer* is 7,066 grams.) One cash crop which has been eminently successful in 1996 was opium poppies, making Afghanistan one of the major exporters with a production of some 2,000 ton of opium.

EDUCATION. The modern system of education in Afghanistan dates from the early twentieth century, although attempts at educational reforms were first made under Amir **Shir Ali** (r. 1863–79). In 1868 he opened two schools, a military school, located in the Sherpur district of Kabul and a civil, or royal, school in the **Bala Hisar**. Both schools were directed by Qazi Abdul Qadir, Shir Ali's secretary of the army and publisher of the *Shams al-Nahar*. Education was free, and food and lodging were provided for the students. The schools were for princes and the sons of notables, and the system was adapted from Muslim India and the Ottoman empire. Because of the **Second Anglo-Afghan War**, the experiment was not continued.

Amir **Abdul Rahman** (r. 1880–1901) claimed, with some exaggeration, that he could fill only three clerical positions after advertising all over Afghanistan for 30 positions for literate Afghans. This prompted him to open "various schools for the education of members of my family, my personal attendants, and page boys; for prisoners of war; for the army, and for the children of my officials and other subjects" (Sultan Mahomed Khan, 1901).

The traditional system of education in Afghanistan was the domain of the *ulama* (clergy). It consisted of elementary schools, *maktab*, usually attached to a mosque, where mullas would teach reading, writing and arithmetic, recitation of the Koran (**Qor'an**), and the Islamic duties and prohibitions. There was no uniformity in curriculum, and often students would confine their activities to recitation and memorization of the Koran. The well-to-do would hire tutors for their children.

The secondary system of education was the *madrasa*, in which the *mudares* (teacher), or *alem* (pl. *ulama*), would teach Persian and Arabic literature, poetry, calligraphy, and the Islamic sciences of *tafsir* (exegesis), *ulum-i Illahi* (Islamic theology), *fiqh* (jurisprudence), and *akhlaqiat* (ethics) as well as the "foreign" sciences of logic, philosophy, medicine, mathematics, astronomy, and astrology. The *madrasa* trained the *kazi* (judges), *mufti* (legal experts), and *ulama* (doctors of Islamic sciences) (*see* ISLAMIC LAW). Most *madrasa* were not state institutions, but private enterprises of individual Islamic scholars who would certify completion of a student's course of study. In the late 19th century the most important college of this type was the *Madrasa-yi Shahi* (royal college) at Kabul.

A modern system of education evolved from the time of Amir **Habibullah**. He founded **Habibia School** in 1904, first as a *madrasa*, which later adopted the curriculum of British-Indian secular schools. He appointed his son, Sardar **Enayatullah** as his head of education and allocated an annual budget of 100,000 rupees. Conditions were spartan: the teacher sat on a chair and the students on mats on the floor. In winter open charcoal braziers provided some warmth. In addition to a few Afghan teachers, Indian Muslims were contracted, including the principal, Dr. **Abdul Ghani**.

A school for the children of notables, *maktab-i malikzadaha*, was founded next and eventually developed into the Royal Military College, *madrasa-yi harbi-yi sirajiya*. Its principal was a Turkish officer, Mahmud Sami, who operated under the direction of Sardar Enayatullah, eldest son of Amir Habibullah. The curriculum included Islamic and military sciences as well as gymnastics and drill.

In 1907 an Office of Textbooks (*dar al-ta'lif*) was founded to produce texts for the new secular schools. In 1914 a Teachers' Training School (*dar al-mu'allemin*) was founded, and a year later the primary school system was expanded. Education and textbooks were provided free of charge, and students received a small stipend for living expenses. Primary schools (*ebteda'iya*) included four years of religious education, reading and writing, arithmetic, and geography. Graduates could then enter the military school, continue at Habibia School, or end their education to become lower-level civil servants. Middle schools (*rushdiya*) conducted a three-year program in Persian and Arabic literature and a foreign language. Graduates prepared for government jobs or continued their education in the next cycle of higher education, (*e'dadiya*). Education at this level was in English.

King **Amanullah** further expanded the system of education by founding primary schools in major towns and district centers and, in 1922, the French-language *Amania* School (subsequently renamed by **Nadir Shah** *Istiqlal*—Independence) with a French curriculum and several French teachers. *Amani* School (renamed *Najat* by Nadir Shah, and again *Amani* during the Marxist regime) was founded in 1923 as a German-language school. The top graduates from these schools were sent abroad for higher education. A ministry of education was established in 1919, and Sardar Abdul Rahman was appointed as its first minister. Schools were next opened in the provinces. The *Ghazi* School (Victor—named after Amanullah's title) was founded in 1927, and administrative schools, the *maktab-i hukkam* and *maktab-i usul-i daftari*, were opened to train accountants and administrators.

During the reign of **Zahir Shah** (1933–73) the Afghan system of education was further expanded and extended to the provinces. **Kabul University** was formally established on a separate campus in 1947, but before that the faculty of medicine was founded in 1932, followed by the faculty of law and political science in 1938. Faculties of science and letters were added in 1942 and 1943. In the 1950s theology, agriculture, and economics departments were founded, and in the 1960s home economics, education, engineering, pharmacy, and a polytechnic institute were established. Some departments were affiliated with foreign universities, mostly German, French, and American. The Soviet Union built and directed the operations of the **Polytechnic Institute** from 1967, and the Teachers College of Columbia University reorganized the faculty of education. By 1950, expenditures on education amounted to 40% of the Afghan budget.

Women's education was first sponsored under King Amanullah with the establishment in 1921 of a school in the building of the present Zarghuna High School in Kabul. Afghan and some foreign ladies taught the same curriculum as the boys' schools, as well as cooking, sewing, child care, and readings of the biographies of famous women of the world. Coeducation began in 1928 for the first and second grades at Istiqlal school at Kabul, and some female students were sent to Turkey to continue their education. Coeducation and girls' schools were discontinued for several years after the ouster of King Amanullah. In 1931, under Nadir Shah, women were permitted to take courses at Masturat Hospital in Kabul, and girls' schools were reopened in 1939. Two high schools opened in 1947, and a women's faculty of education was added in 1948. Coeducation was resumed again in the early 1960s at Kabul University. A Women's Institute (*mu'asasa-yi niswan*) was started in 1946 in Kabul under the sponsorship of Queen Humaira, wife of Zahir Shah, which gave classes in handicrafts and became the largest supplier of needlework of various types.

In the years 1936–37 the Afghan government decided to replace Dari with Pashtu as the language of instruction in public schools, but in 1946 this policy was abandoned in favor of Dari/Pashtu bilingualism.

Pashtu-speaking provinces and a few "tribal" schools, like Rahman Baba at Kabul, used Pashtu. In 1963 Nangarhar University was founded in Jalalabad in which Pashtu was the language of instruction, and seven professional and technical schools, existed since 1964 that also use Pashtu for instruction.

By 1970 secondary schools existed in every province except Zabul, and vocational and teachers' training schools, as well as commercial, agricultural, and technical schools, existed in Kabul and a number of provincial towns. The existence of a dual system of education, the traditional system under the ulama and the newly-established secular system, created two elites who competed for government positions. The graduates of the secular system tended to benefit from the process of national development and had little difficulty in finding employment. The state eventually also integrated the madrasa system in the faculty of theology of Kabul University, but an independent, private system of madrasas continued to exist. Thus the ulama had lost its monopoly over education and felt threatened in its position of leadership.

The Marxist government emphasized adult education and literacy programs and printed texts in the newly recognized "national languages" of Baluch, Turkmani, Uzbek, and Nuristani (Kati) as well as in Dari and Pashtu. Universities were established in Balkh and Herat, and primary education was permitted in regional languages. The Afghan ministry of education is responsible for curriculum and educational policy at all levels. War and destruction closed virtually all provincial schools, except for a few *maktab*, operated by *mujahedin* groups and local communities. In Marxist-controlled areas, purges of faculty, the drafting of graduates, and changes in curriculum to conform to Soviet models led to a drastic reduction of students.

The "new education policy" initiated by President **Najibullah** dispensed with most of the Marxist innovations, and after the victory of the *mujahedin*, the campus of Kabul University became a battle ground of one party or another. Local rulers opened universities in Mazar-i Sharif, Bamian, and Herat, but the ongoing civil war and a lack of resources prevented the establishment of viable institutions. The radicals ended coeducation and the *Taliban* closed schools for girls. If peace should one day come to Afghanistan, the establishment of a new educational system should be a priority. *See also* KABUL UNIVERSITY.

ELPHINSTONE, MOUNTSTUART (1779–1859). British envoy to the court of **Shah Shuja** in 1808-9 who negotiated an alliance of "eternal friendship" with the Afghan ruler and called for joint action in case of Franco-Persian aggression. He left Delhi on October 13, 1808 with an escort of 400 Anglo-Indian troops and reached Peshawar on February 25, 1809, where he presented Britain's proposals to the Afghan ruler. This was the first contact between a British official and an Afghan ruler. Elphinstone used the opportunity to learn as much as he could about the "Forbidden Kingdom," and later published a book on Afghanistan, entitled *An Account of the Kingdom of Caubul* (1815), which is one of the first comprehensive accounts of Afghan society. He was rewarded for his services with appointment as governor of Bombay. Elphinstone College in Bombay was named after him. Remarking on the proposed war, Elphinstone said

> If you send 27,000 men up the Bolan Pass to Candahar (as we hear is intended), and can feed them, I have no doubt you will take Candahar and Caubul and set up Soojah [Shuja]; but for maintaining him in a poor, cold, strong, and remote country, among a turbulent people like the Afghans, I own it seems to me hopeless. (Macrory, 94–95)

See also AFGHAN FOREIGN RELATIONS; ANGLO-AFGHAN WARS; and SHAH SHUJA-UL-MULK.

ELPHINSTONE, MAJOR-GENERAL WILLIAM (1782–1842). Commander of the British army in Afghanistan in 1841 and the person held responsible by British historians for the debacle in the **First Anglo-Afghan War**. Gen. Elphinstone was sixty years old and infirm when he accepted the army command. Forbes describes Elphinstone as

> Wrecked in body and impaired in mind by physical ailments and infirmities, he had lost all faculty of energy, and such mind as remained to him was swayed by the opinion of the person with whom he had last spoken. (64)

Elphinstone did not take "decisive" action when **Alexander Burnes**, the assistant to the British envoy at Kabul, was assassinated with members of his mission. He quartered his troops in the vulnerable cantonment, which was commanded from the nearby hills, instead of moving them to the protection of the **Bala Hisar** fortress. Surrounded by Afghan tribal armies, the British had to negotiate a retreat that turned into a rout in which most of the 16,000 troops and camp followers were massacred or died of the freezing cold weather. Elphinstone did not survive the disaster; on April 23, 1842, he died in captivity of exhaustion and various maladies. *See* ANGLO-AFGHAN WARS; AFGHAN-FOREIGN RELATIONS; AKBAR, SARDAR MUHAM-MAD; and CAPITULATION, TREATY OF.

ENAYATULLAH, SARDAR. King of Afghanistan, after King **Amanullah**'s abdication on January 14, 1929, and forced to abdicate three days later, when **Habibullah Kalakani** ascended the throne. He was born on October 20, 1888, the eldest son of Amir **Habibullah**. His father gave him the title "Supporter of the State" (*muin al-sultanat*) and appointed him "Marshal," *sardar-i salar*, in 1905 and minister of education in 1916. He and Sardar **Nasrullah** were on friendly terms with the members of the **Hentig-Niedermayer Expedition** in Kabul. At that time he was believed to be in favor of Afghan intervention in the war against Britain. He married a daughter of Sardar **Mahmud Tarzi**, editor of the *Seraj al-Akhbar Afghaniya* and later foreign minister. After the assassination of Amir Habibullah in Nangarhar Province, Sardar Nasrullah went through the form of offering him the throne in the presence of Nadir Khan and other prominent officials. Enayatullah, however, declined and recognized Nasrullah as the king. But the army revolted and Sardar Amanullah, who was in Kabul, won recognition as the new king. Enayatullah Khan was in virtual retirement during the reign of his brother. On December 14, 1928, when King **Amanullah** was forced to resign, he appointed Enayatullah Khan his successor; three days later Enayatullah was forced to surrender to **Habibullah Kalakani**. On January 18, 1929, he and his immediate family were evacuated to Peshawar, India in an aircraft of the British air force. He lived in Tehran as a guest of the Iranian king until his death on August 12, 1946.

ENGERT, CORNELIUS VAN. American minister plenipotentiary resident at Kabul (1942–43). He first visited Afghanistan unofficially in 1922 and favored early establishment of diplomatic relations with Afghanistan. American diplomats in Tehran or Delhi were accredited to the Kabul government until 1942, when a permanent legation was opened. Van Engert was of Dutch descent born in Austria. *See* UNITED STATES-AFGHAN RELATIONS.

ENVER (ANWAR) PASHA. Minister of War and, with **Jamal Pasha** and Talat Pasha, member of the ruling triumvirate in the Ottoman war government (1913–18). Sentenced to death in 1919, he escaped to Germany after the war and from there to the Soviet Union. He failed to gain Soviet support in replacing Kemal Ataturk as the head of the Turkish government and moved to Central Asia. He apparently intended to seek a safe haven in Afghanistan, where Jamal Pasha had already preceded him and was active as an adviser to King **Amanullah**. He was arrested by **Basmachi** counter revolutionaries but convinced them of his sympathies and became one of their leaders. He fought on their side against the Red Army until he was killed in a skirmish on August 4, 1922.

ERSHAD-UL-NISWAN (IRSHAD AL-NISWAN). Women's weekly magazine first published in Afghanistan in March 1921 by Asma Samia, known as "Bibi Arabi," the wife of **Mahmud Tarzi**. Editor-in-chief was Ruhafza, known as "Munshia," (secretary), wife of Muhammad Zaman Khan and sister of Habibullah Tarzi. The magazine carried domestic and foreign news of interest to women as well as advice on cooking and needlework and touched on problems facing women in society. It was discontinued after the fall of King **Amanullah**.

ESHAQ. *See* **MUHAMMAD ISHAQ.**

ETEHAD. *See* **ITTIHAD.**

ETEMADI, NUR AHMAD (I'TIMADI). A diplomat and government official who served as ambassador to Karachi (1964), prime minister and minister of Foreign Affairs from 1967 to 1971, and subsequently as ambassador to Rome (1971), Moscow (1973), and Islamabad (1976–78). President **Muhammad Daud** summoned him to Kabul for consultation on April 24, 1978, three days before the Saur Revolt. According to some claims, the Soviet government wanted Etemadi to head a "national front" government, which convinced the Taraki government to have him secretly executed in August 1979. He was born in 1921 in Kandahar and educated at Kabul. He was a grandson of **Abdul Quddus** (Etemad ud-Daula).

ETEMADI, SARWAR GOYA. Scholar, historian, and bibliographer who played an important role in cultural relations with Iran. Born in 1909 and privately educated, he became an adviser to the ministry of education. He published documents on the Timurid period of Herat.

ETEMAD UD-DAULA (I'TIMAD AL-DAULA). *See* **ABDUL QUD-DUS.**

ETHNIC GROUPS. The Afghan population is heterogeneous with numerous ethnic groups, speaking various dialects or mutually unintelligible languages. The largest ethnic group are the Pashtuns, followed by the Tajiks, Uzbeks, and Hazara. Orywal (18, 1986) lists the following ethnic groups in Afghanistan:

Pashtun	Tajik	Uzbek
Hazara	Turkoman	Aimaq
Taimani	Tahiri	Baluch
Mauri	Brahui	Arab
Qirghiz	Moghol	Gujar
Qipchaq	Eshkashimi	Munjani
Rushani	Sanglichi	Shighnani
Vakhi	Farsi/Farsiwan	Qarliq
Nuristani	Pashai	Firuzkuhi
Jamshidi	Timuri	Zuri
Maliki	Mishmast	Jat
Jalali	Ghorbat	Pikragh
Shadibaz	Vangavala	Qazaq
Qizilbash	Tatar	Parachi
Tirahi	Gavarbati	Ormuri
Shaikh Muhammadi	Jogi	Kutana
Jews (Yahudi)	Sikh	Hindu

Estimated population figures in millions (Groetzbach, 1990) are

Pashtun	6
Tajik & Farsiwan	4
Uzbek	1.3
Hazara	1.1*
Aimaq	.5
Turkoman	.4
Baluch & Brahui	.16
Arab	.1
Nuristani	.1

Pashai	.1
Tatar	.06
Qizilbash	.04
Hindu & Sikh	.03
Qirghiz & Moghol	.11

* According to Hazara claims, they number as many as two million people in Afghanistan and another two million in Iran and Pakistan.

Virtually all Jews left Afghanistan in the 1970s (of some 600 families, only six individuals remained in Kabul in the late 1980s).

The introduction of state-sponsored education dictated the use of Dari as the language of instruction. Dari has been the language of royal courts since **Ghaznavid** times and was widely used also by the Turkic rulers of Central Asia and the Moghuls of India.

Since the early 20th century Afghan governments have promoted Pashtu as the national language, but any attempts to replace Dari in education have failed. One of the first decrees (No. 4) issued by the Marxist government was to recognize and permit the use of Turkmani, Uzbeki, Baluchi, and Nuristani as "national languages" to ensure the "essential conditions for evolution of the literature, education, and publication in mother tongues of the tribes and nationalities resident in Afghanistan." It ordered the respective ministries to start broadcasting on radio and television and publishing newspapers in these languages. This was an adoption of the Soviet nationalities policy and was seen by some as an attempt to divide and rule. For information on major ethnic groups, see individual entries.

F

FAIZABAD (37-6' N, 70-34' E). Capital of Badakhshan, with about 12,000 inhabitants, the central commercial market of the province, situated on the Kokcha River at an altitude of 3,300 feet. Until the late 17th century the town was called Jauz Gun, or Jauzun, because of the abundance of nuts (*jauz*) in the area. The name of the town was changed to Faizabad (abode of divine bounty, blessing, and charity), when in 1691 Mir Yar Beg brought what was believed to be the Blessed Robe (*khirqa-yi mubarak*) of the Prophet Muhammad to the town. (**Ahmad Shah Durrani** later brought the *khirqa* to Kandahar where it still is today.) In 1821 Murad Beg, the ruler of Kunduz, destroyed the town, but a few years later it again reached a population of 8,000. Many mosques and historical shrines now exist in the area. In 1937 Faizabad became the terminal of a road, connected to the northern highway between Baghlan and Kunduz, which was later extended east toward the **Wakhan** Corridor. The natives speak a number of Badakhshi languages in addition to Dari.

FAIZANI, MAULAWI. An early Islamist activist from Herat and comrade of **Abdul Rasul Sayyaf** and **Ghulam Muhammad Niazi.** Faizani had been a militant anti-Communist since the 1960s. He was arrested in 1975 together with Abdul Rasul Sayyaf and Ghulam Muhammad Niazi and was assassinated in 1978 by the *Khalqi* government in **Pul-i Charkhi** prison. *See* ISLAMIST MOVEMENT IN AFGHANISTAN.

FAIZ MUHAMMAD, AL-HAJJ MULLA. Member of Amir **Abdul Rahman's** secretariat and court secretary (*kateb*) under Amir **Habibullah.** He was a member on the staff of the *Seraj al-Akbar Afghaniya* and held positions in the ministries of education and foreign affairs. He is the author of a number of publications, including the three-volume *Seraj al-Tawarikh* (Torch of Histories), a valuable historical text in Dari. He was born in 1861, the son of Sayyid Muhammad Moghol, a Hazara, and studied Islamic sciences in India and Iran. In 1893 he entered the services of Sardar Habibullah, son of Amir Abdul Rahman, and began work on his monumental three-volume history. A fourth volume is said to exist in manuscript form, extant in the National Archives of Afghanistan in Kabul. Faiz Muhammad died in 1931, purportedly from the complications of a severe beating by **Habibullah Kalakani** who had sent him to bring a document of submission from the Hazarajat.

FAIZ MUHAMMAD, GENERAL. Governor of the Eastern Province who stopped the mission under Neville Chamberlain from entering Afghanistan on the eve of the **Second Anglo-Afghan War. Louis Cavagnari** crossed the border on September 21, 1876 and met Faiz Muhammad at Ali Masjid. He asked whether the Afghan governor would permit Chamberlain to pass and Faiz Muhammad said no, adding "You may take as kindness, and because I remember friendship, that I do not fire upon you for what you have already done" [Crossing the border without permission]. The British chose this "insult" as the *casus belli* for starting the Second Anglo-Afghan War.

FAIZ MUHAMMAD, ZIKRIA (ZAKARIA). Diplomat and high government official, as well as a poet and writer with the pen name "Faizi Kabuli." Born in 1892 and educated at **Habibia School** he entered the foreign service in 1921. He accompanied the Afghan mission under **Muhammad Wali** to Europe and the United States to conclude agreements for establishing diplomatic relations. He became King **Amanullah**'s minister of Education in 1925 and subsequently served as a member of **Habibullah Kalakani**'s "Council for the Maintenance of Order." Appointed foreign minister by **Nadir Shah** in 1929, he served until 1938 and served as ambassador to Turkey (1938–48), Great Britain (1948–50), and Saudi Arabia (1955–60). He retired in 1960 and lived in the United States where he died in 1979. He is buried in Peshawar.

FAMILY. Although great variations exist between and even within groups, the family among most Afghan ethnic groups is patrilineal, patrilocal, and characterized by a low incidence of polygyny, a low divorce rate, and a high birth rate. The extended family is the major economic and social unit. Marriages are arranged by the families of the prospective groom and bride (or an intermediary), and a bride price is paid by the family of the groom. Cousin marriages are often preferred. Afghan rulers since Amir **Abdul Rahman** have tried to limit the bride price (*mahr*) and costly festivities and have forbidden such practices as "child marriage" (contracted long in advance), but these customs still prevail, except among the urban upper classes. While in theory divorce is easy for men (a man can divorce his wife simply by saying "I divorce thee" three times), economic factors and the fact that marriages are often concluded within the clan or are alliances between families make it difficult to divorce. The same factors limit polygyny, in spite of the fact that Islamic law permits a man to have four wives.

The extended family consists of the patriarch, his wife (or wives), and his married sons. Authority descends in the male line, and the Islamic law of inheritance (that allocated a set portion to women) is often ignored in favor of the male members. Afghan law required the registration of marriages, but this was enforced only in the larger urban areas. The Marxist regime of **Nur Muhammad Taraki** tried to limit the bride price to a token amount of 300 afghanis (then six dollars), demanded freedom of choice of the partners, and set a minimum age for marriage at 16 for women and 18 for men. Like previous Afghan rulers, the Marxist government was not able to enforce its marriage laws and eventually rescinded them as well as other unpopular innovations. The victory of the "*mujahedin*" ended all government attempts of control in family affairs.

FAQIR OF IPI, HAJI MIRZA ALI KHAN. A frontier **mulla** residing with the **Waziri** tribe on the Indian side of the Durand Line. He was an implacable foe of the British and incited the tribes to wage *jihad* against India. He collaborated with the Axis powers during World War II and was in touch with their legations in Kabul. The Germans gave him the code name *Feuerfresser* (fire-eater) and supported his efforts by paying him a regular subsidy. The Faqir's activities compelled Britain to keep large forces, that could have been deployed elsewhere, on the Frontier. deployed elsewhere. At one time an army of 40,000 troops was searching for him; he always found shelter among the Waziris and often was forced to hide in a cave. After the creation of Pakistan, the Faqir demanded independence for **Pashtunistan**; he was elected "president" of Pashtunistan by a tribal council and continued his fight against the new state. He received financial support from the Afghan government until his death in 1960.

FARAH (32-22' N, 62-7' E). A province in western Afghanistan with an area of 21,666 square miles; it is the second largest Afghan province, with a population of about 356,000. The province is divided into the districts of Farah, Anardara, Bala Boluk, Purchaman, Bakwa, Shindand, Kala-i-Kah, Gulistan, Khak-i-Safid, and Farsi. The capital of the province is the town of Farah with about 18,800 inhabitants. The province is traversed by the Farah Rud, the Khash Rud, and the Harut Rud (rivers); major mountain ranges include the Khak-i-Safid, Siyah Kuh, Malmand, Kuh-i-Afghan, and the Reg-i-Rawan. The economy of the province depends primarily on agriculture and livestock breeding; barley, cotton, and wheat are the major crops, and livestock includes sheep, **Qaraqul** sheep, goats, cattle, camels, and donkeys. An important junction in Indo-Persian trade in the 17th century, Farah was destroyed in 1837 and remained a small walled town until the early twentieth century when a new town was gradually developed, with a population of about 6,000 in 1934. The town gradually declined when the new Kandahar-Herat Highway, completed in 1965, bypassed the town. In 1972 floods destroyed much of the town, and the provincial administration moved for two years to Farah Rud. The population is largely

Pashtun, but Tajik and other ethnic communities are also represented in Farah.

FARAH RUD (31-29' N, 61-24' E). A river which rises in Ghor Province and flows in a southwesterly direction and runs into the **Hamun-i-Saberi**, a shallow, brackish lake in Nimruz province, which extends across the Iranian border.

FARANGI. Or FRANGI. The **Dari** word is a corruption of "Franks" or French, a name originally applied throughout the Middle East to Italians and Frenchmen, but was later extended to designate all European Christians.

FARHAD, GHULAM MUHAMMAD. Afghan nationalist and founder of the Afghan Social Democrat Party (Jjam'iyat-i susyal demukrat), popularly called *Afghan Millat* (Afghan Nation). Educated in Kabul and Germany, where he obtained an engineering degree, he was president of the Afghan Electric Company (1939–66) and mayor of Kabul (1948–54). He built the *Jada-yi Maiwand* (Maiwand Street), the first major avenue through the old town of Kabul, relocating displaced residents, and changed the traffic from the British Indian system to right-hand driving, which was subsequently adopted throughout Afghanistan. He demanded the restoration of "Greater Afghanistan" with the inclusion of Pakistan's North-West Frontier Province and Baluchistan. Publisher of *Afghan Millat*, 1966–67, a weekly newspaper, which subsequently also became the name of the party. He was pro-German and was accused of giving preference to German technology and experts in the allocation of various developmental contracts. In 1968 he was elected to Parliament but resigned his seat in 1970. In 1978 he was arrested by the *Khalqi* regime, and his party was accused of attempting a coup. He was freed in 1980 in the general amnesty of **Babrak Karmal**. He died in 1984 in Kabul. He was a Pashtun and an ardent supporter of the **Pashtunistan** cause. *See also* AFGHAN MILLAT.

FARHADI, ABDUL GHAFUR RAWAN. Afghan diplomat and scholar who became director general for political affairs in the Foreign Ministry in 1964, secretary to the cabinet (1966–71), and deputy minister for political affairs (1970–73). Born in 1929 in Kabul, he was educated at **Istiqlal Lycée** and in France where he obtained a Ph.D. degree in

Indo-Iranian philology in 1955. He entered service in the foreign ministry in 1955 and was appointed first secretary at the Afghan embassy in Karachi (1958), counselor at Washington, D.C. (1962), and ambassador at Paris (1973) but was recalled by the republican government of **Muhammad Daud**. He was arrested during the *Khalqi* regime, freed in 1980, and employed as an adviser of the ministry of Foreign Affairs until he left for France and the United States. Farhadi was appointed by the **Rabbani** government ambassador of Afghanistan to the United Nations in New York. His mother tongue is Dari.

FARIAB (36-0' N, 65-0' E). A province in north central Afghanistan with an area of 8,226 square miles and a population of about 547,000. The province borders on Turkmenistan in the north, on Badghis province in the south, and Jozjan in the east. The capital of the province is the town of Maimana with about 38,000 inhabitants. Fariab is famous for horse breeding and its *buzkashi* games. Melons, nuts, cereals, and cotton are the major agricultural products. **Qaraqul** sheep are bred for the export of skins, and carpet weaving is an important industry. *See also* MAIMANA.

FARSIWAN. An ethnic group of some 600,000 Farsi-speaking *Shi'a* Muslims living near the Iranian border, in Herat, Kandahar, Ghazni, and scattered over southern and western Afghan towns. They are of Mediterranean stock and are mostly engaged in agriculture. Pashtu-speakers refer to all Dari-speakers as Farsiwan.

FATEH KHAN (FATH). Oldest son of **Painda Khan** (head of the **Muhammadzai** branch of the **Barakzai** tribe), born in 1777 in Kandahar. He was a skillful politician and soldier and helped **Shah Mahmud** (r. 1800–1803 and 1809–18) gain the Afghan throne, capturing Farah and Kandahar from the forces of **Zaman Shah**. He was given the position of grand wazir and established law and order and conducted the government for Mahmud with great skill. When **Shah Shuja** (r. 1803–1809 and 1839–1841) succeeded to the Kabul throne, Fateh Khan was again appointed grand wazir, but he remained loyal to Mahmud and helped restore him to power. Fateh Khan consolidated Afghan control over Kashmir and established order in Herat. **Kamran**, son of Shah Mahmud, was jealous of Fateh Khan's power and had him blinded and, in 1818, killed. The **Barakzai** chiefs rebelled, and the ensuing conflict led to the overthrow of the **Sadozai** dynasty and the assumption of power by the **Barakzai/Muhammadzai** branch of the **Durrani**.

FATWA. A formal legal opinion by a *mufti*, or Sunni canon lawyer, in answer to a question by a judge or private individual. Laws in Afghanistan had to conform to Islamic law, as certified by the *fatwa* of a council of *ulama*. *See* ISLAMIC LAW.

FAZL AHMAD, MUJADDIDI. *See* **MUJADDIDI.**

FAZL OMAR. *See* **MUJADDIDI.**

FIKRI, ABDUL RAUF SALJUQI. *See* **SALJUQI, FIKRI ABDUL RAUF.**

FIQH. The science of law, or jurisprudence, in Islamic law. *See* ISLAMIC LAW.

FIRDAUSI, ABU'L QASIM MANSUR (934?–1020?). Author of the great national epic, the *Shahnama* (Book of Kings), which contains all the legends and history of Persia and ancient Afghanistan known to him. Born in Tus, **Khorasan** he began work on the *Shahnama* there and at age 71 presented it to **Mahmud of Ghazni** (r. 988–1030), at whose court he had completed the work. His work is the most voluminous collection of early Persian poetry and therefore an important source for linguistics and literary studies. He felt not properly rewarded and was forced to flee Mahmud's domain after he made his discontent known.

FIRST ANGLO-AFGHAN WAR (1838–42). In the nineteenth century, European rivalry for commerce and empire quickly extended into the Middle East. In 1798 the Napoleonic invasion of Egypt temporarily established a French foothold in this strategic area, and Britain feared it as an important step in a move against India. Russia moved into Central Asia, and by the end of the 19th century the Czar's influence extended to the **Amu Daria**. Britain was moving into the **Panjab** in search of a "scientific" frontier to make sure that her possessions in India were safe.

In Kabul internecine warfare led to the ouster of **Shah Shuja**, the last of the **Sadozai** rulers, and **Dost Muhammad**, first of the **Muhammadzai rulers**, ascended the throne in 1826. He wanted an alliance with India and hoped to regain Peshawar, which had been lost in 1818 to the emerging **Sikh** nation under **Ranjit Singh**. **Lord Auckland**, the British governor-general of India, chose an alliance with the Sikh ruler instead and decided to restore Shah Shuja to the Afghan throne. The presence of a purported Russian agent at Kabul (*see* VITKEVICH) and Dost Muhammad's hostility to the Sikh ruler were the reasons given for the declaration of war (*see* SIMLA MANIFESTO). A tripartite treaty was signed in July 1838 between Shah Shuja, Ranjit Singh, and Lord Auckland, and the **Army of the Indus** invaded Afghanistan. The invaders met with little resistance, they captured Ghazni on July 23, and occiped Kabul on August 7. Shah Shuja was put on the Kabul throne and Dost Muhammad was forced into Indian exile. The major part of the British army left Kabul on September 18. But it was soon apparent that the Sadozai ruler needed British protection to maintain himself in power, and the army became a force of occupation. The families of British officers came to Kabul, and thousands of Indian camp followers engaged in the lucrative business of importing from India the necessities of colonial life. But all was not well. On November 2, 1841, a Kabuli crowd stormed the British mission and killed its members, including **Alexander Burnes**, its head. The Afghans captured some £17,000 from the treasury in an adjacent house and plundered the commissariat stores located in a number of forts outside the cantonment. **Muhammad Akbar**, a son of Dost Muhammad, together with a number of chiefs, now rallied his forces and increasingly threatened the occupiers. Major General **William Elphinstone** ordered the army to withdraw to the cantonment that was commanded from nearby hills. He commanded seven regiments of horse and foot, with guns and sappers, English and Indian, and decided to recall General **Sale** from **Gandomak** and Nott from Kandahar. But the roads were blocked by the onset of winter and by strong contingents of tribal **lashkars**, preventing a strengthening of the Kabul garrison. A raiding party sent out to silence Afghan guns was badly decimated and had to return, leaving their wounded behind. On December 11, 1841, the British were forced to negotiate a retreat that only few of the 16,000 troops and camp followers survived. (*See* CAPITULATION, TREATY OF and DEATH MARCH.) Britain felt it necessary to have its martial reputation restored, and in September 1842 General George Pollock wreaked vengeance on Kabul, laying torch to the covered **bazaar** and permitting plunder that destroyed much of the rest of the city. The British forces left, and Amir Dost Muhammad returned in December 1842 to rule Afghanistan until he died a natural death twenty years later. The war cost Britain £20 million and some 15,000 lives of all ranks and camp followers.

FIRST ANGLO-AFGHAN WAR: CAUSES. During the siege of Herat in 1838, **Lord Auckland** determined to restore **Shah Shuja** to the throne of Kabul in the hope of establishing a friendly power in Afghanistan that was to form the first line of defense against the threatened advance of Russia on India. A **Tripartite Treaty** was concluded through English pressure, but neither **Ranjit Singh** nor Shah Shuja were happy. The former did not want to send his troops into Afghanistan, and the latter did not want to resign his claim on the **Panjab** and Sind. Lord Auckland informed the directors of the East India Company that

> the increase of Russian and Persian influence in Afghanistan, and the impression of the certain fall of Herat to the Persian army, have induced the Ameer Dost Mahomed Khan to avow and to insist upon pretensions for the cession to him, by Maharaja Runjeet Sing, of the Peshawur territory, and to take other steps which are tantamount to the rejection of the friendship and good offices of the British Government; and have in consequence led to the retirement of Captain Burnes from the territories of Cabool.

The Persian siege of Herat was ended, but Auckland was determined to make war. The resulting disaster was subsequently termed "Auckland's Folly."

FIRUZ KUH (34-30' N, 63-30' E). A mountain range, also called Safid Kuh (White Mountain), extending in a westerly direction from the area of Chaghcharan into eastern Herat Province.

FIRUZKUHI. One of the **Sunni** Chahar Aimaq tribes (*see* AIMAQ), located in eastern Badghis and northern Ghor provinces. They number about 100,000 and are Farsi speakers. Their name, according to one version, comes from Firuz Kuh, a mountain near Semnan in Iran, where they lived until the 14th century when **Timur-i Lang** transferred them to Herat and from where they subsequently migrated further east. According to another version their name derives from an eponymic ancestor, Firuz, who was one of the sons (or slaves?) of Sanzar (progenitor also of Taiman, the eponymic ancestor of the **Taimanis**).

The descendants of Firuz were at first small chiefs under Taimani Khans until they took over most of the Taimani territory southeast of Herat. Major subdivisions are the Mahmudis, including the Zai Murad and the Zai Hakim clans, and the Darazis, all of which are subdivided into a number of sections.

FLAG. Afghanistan's first national flag was the **Abdali** banner, depicting a cluster of wheat, a sword, and stars on a background of red and green. Important chiefs and princes had their own flags. Amir **Shir Ali**'s standard was triangular in shape, red and green, with Koranic inscriptions. **Abdul Rahman** preferred a black banner (Abu Muslim's Abbasid standard) on which was drawn in white a *mihrab* (prayer niche), *minbar* (pulpit), sword, and gun. Amir **Habibullah**'s "national flag" (*bayraq-i daulati*) was similar, except that it omitted the sword and gun. King **Amanullah** introduced the tricolor flag in 1928 with broad horizontal stripes of black, red, and green and an emblem showing the rising sun over snow-capped mountains clothed in wheat. The name Allah was inscribed in the upper left corner.

    Nadir Shah continued the tricolor, but with vertical stripes and an emblem depicting a mosque with pulpit and mihrab (*see* MOSQUE). The mosque was flanked by two banners, and the emblem was framed by a wreath of wheat. A scroll carried the inscription "Afghanistan" above which was the date 1348 (lunar year, corresponding to 1929), the year in which Nadir Shah assumed the throne. The emblem was in the red center portion of the flag.

    President **Muhammad Daud** designed the republican flag in May 1974 retaining the tricolor in horizontal lines. An emblem in the upper left corner consisted of a stylized eagle, *mihrab*, and *minbar*, surrounded by a wreath and a scroll with the inscription *Da Afghanistan Jumhuriat* (Republic of Afghanistan) and the date 26th of Saratan (July 17, 1973), the day he staged his coup. Black was on the top, followed by red, each one-fourth of the width of the flag; the lower half was green.

    In October 1978 the **Taraki** regime introduced the red flag with an emblem in gold in the right hand corner. It consisted of the traditional wreath with the name *Khalq* (People) in the center, a five-cornered star above it, and a scroll with the Pashtu inscription *Da Afghanistan Da Demukratik Jumhuriat* (Democratic Republic of Afghanistan). It carried the date of the Saur Revolt, 7 Saur 1357 (April 27, 1978). The *Khalqi* flag strongly resembled the USSR flag and those of the Soviet

Republics and therefore aroused the ire of many Afghans. When **Babrak Karmal** replaced **Hafizullah Amin** he restored the tricolor but kept the red flag as the banner of the party. After the fall of the Marxist regime, the first *mujahedin* government designed a new tricolor of red, white, and black with a Koranic inscription, and the *Taliban* adopted a white flag. No national flag has been agreed on.

FOREIGN RELATIONS. *See* **AFGHAN FOREIGN RELATIONS.**

FOREIGN TRADE. *See* **ECONOMY.**

FORWARD POLICY. *See* **AFGHAN FOREIGN RELATIONS.**

FRANCO-AFGHAN RELATIONS. Unlike Afghanistan's relations with the Soviet Union/Russia, Britain, and Germany, Franco-Afghan relations were primarily cultural. French was still the language of diplomacy, and Afghanistan needed a cadre of future diplomats conversant in that language. **Muhammad Wali** Khan's mission traveled to Europe and America to establish diplomatic relations with the West, reaching Paris on June 9, 1921. Four months later, a group of 34 young Afghans of the **Muhammadzai** clan were sent to France to enter the Lycee Michelet at Vanves. Relations between the two countries were finally established in 1923 with the exchange of ambassadors, Maurice Foucher at Kabul and **Mahmud Tarzi** at Paris. The Afghan government granted a 30-year monopoly to French archaeologists so that it could refuse concessions to citizens of neighboring powers. But the Afghan government reserved the right of "granting to savants of foreign nations permission to excavate in places where the learned French representatives are not carrying out their operations, and do not intend to start work within a period not exceeding five years," (Adamec, 1974, 76) it refused the Englishman Sir Auriel Stein permission to work in Afghanistan. A similar request in January 1923 from the Soviet legation in Kabul was not granted. The French-language Amania School, later renamed **Istiqlal Lycée**, was opened on February 3, 1923. By the end of King **Amanullah**'s reign some 450 students were enrolled and the French colony in Kabul amounted to 23 persons. The archaeologist Alfred Foucher was soon joined by other French archaeologists, and in the beginning of **Nadir Shah**'s reign the Afghan baccalaureat was recognized as the equivalent of the French exam. The first three graduates went to France for

advanced study in June 1932. A lycee for girls was started in 1939 and
Malalai Lycee in 1942. During the war period, a cadre of Afghan
teachers took over, and in 1946–47 the first four students obtained their
baccalaureat from Malalai High School. A department of French was
opened at **Kabul University** in 1964, and professors participated in the
development of medical and nursing studies. Afghan Kings Amanullah
and **Zahir Shah** visited France in 1928 and 1965 respectively, and
Prime Minister Pompidou came to Kabul in May 1968. Although
smaller than the Russian, German, American, and British colonies in
Afghanistan, the French were a major factor in education and cultural
activities in Afghanistan. After the **Saur Revolt**, cooperation with
France, as with other Western countries, was gradually limited, but
during the ensuing war in Afghanistan, French Méddecins Sans
Frontières provided much needed medical aid in the Afghan
countryside.

G

GAHIZ, MINHAJUDDIN (MINHAJJ AL-DIN). Member of the
Islamist, anti-Communist movement and publisher of the *Jarida-yi
Gahiz* (Newspaper of Gahiz [Dawn in Pashtu]). He was born in 1922
of a Pashtun family in Koh Daman and educated at the teachers' training
high school in Kabul, becoming a teacher at **Ghazi High School**. His
newspaper carried articles on Islamic topics and political attacks
against the emerging Marxist movements. He is said to have been killed
in 1971 by Communist agents who had entered his home as "visitors."

GAILANI, SAYYID AHMAD (AFANDI SAHIB, GILANI).
Descendant of the Muslim Pir Baba Abdul Qadir Gailani (1077–1166)
and hereditary head of the **Qadiria** Sufi fraternity. He succeeded to his
position upon the death of his older brother, **Sayyid Ali**, in 1964. Born
in 1932 in Kabul, the son of **Sayyid Hasan Gailani**, he was educated
at Abu Hanifa College and the faculty of theology of **Kabul University**.
He left Afghanistan after the **Saur Revolt** and founded the National
Islamic Front (NIFA—*Mahaz-i Milli-yi Afghanistan*) in Peshawar. His
movement was part of the seven-member Alliance that formed the
"**Afghan Interim Government**" in 1989. Although Sayyid Gailani did
not want any position in the interim government, he later accepted the
post of supreme justice (*Qadhi al-Qudhat*). Gailani is married to Adela
(daughter of Sardar Abdul Baqi and Aziza—a daughter of Amir

Habibullah) and has three daughters and two sons: Fatima, Mariam, Hamed, Muhammad, and Zahra. *See also* MAHAZ.

GAILANI, SAYYID ALI (GILANI). Born in 1923 in Kabul, the son of **Sayyid Hasan Gailani** and leader of the **Qadiria** religious brotherhood. He died in 1964 and was succeeded by his younger brother **Sayyid Ahmad Gailani**. His son Ishaq Gailani has been a commander of moderate *mujahdin* groups.

GAILANI, SAYYID HASAN (GILANI). Born about 1862 in Baghdad. Sayyid Hasan Gailani is the son of Sayyid Ali Gailani, the son of Sayyid Salman Gailani, descendant of al-Imam Hasan, son of Caliph Ali, son of Abu Taleb. Member of the family of the Naqib al-Ashraf of Baghdad, Sayyid Hasan Gailani came to Afghanistan in 1905. He was welcomed warmly by the king and the *qadirites* of Afghanistan. Amir **Habibullah** paid him an allowance of Rs. 3,500 per month and built him a winter residence at Chaharbagh, near Jalalabad. Thus he became known as the Naqib Sahib of Charharbagh, as well as the Pir Naqib of Baghdad, the place where his ancestor's tomb is located. His reason for leaving Baghdad and coming to Afghanistan was primarily, a disagreement with his older brother, Sayyid Abdul Rahman Gailani, who was the oldest in the family and was Naqib al-Ashraf of Baghdad. He wanted to get married in spite of the wishes of his brother, and Sayyid Hasan Gailani —wherever he would have gone—would have been sent back because of the influence of his brother. So he went to Afghanistan, which was not a part of the Ottoman Empire. Furthermore, Afghanistan is a **Hanafite** Islamic country, having many **Qadiri** followers. Those Afghans who were visiting the Mausoleum of Shaikh Abdul Qadir Gailani in Baghdad had told Sayyid Hasan Gailani about "the Afghan's firm beliefs, their purity of soul and character" and had also familiarized him with their language. And his faithful companion Mahmud Tokhi (an Afghan subject) had told Gailani about the goodwill of the Afghans toward him. Therefore, he decided to make a journey to Afghanistan. "The faith of the people and the insistence of the King induced him to accept Afghan citizenship and to stay in Afghanistan." Sayyid Hasan was respected by the Afghans who took him as an example of the Qadiria life. He was treated with the utmost respect by Amir Habibullah Khan and Sardar **Nasrullah** Khan. He issued a farman in support of King **Nadir Shah** in 1931. Sayyid Hasan Gailani had a daughter, Fatima, from his first wife and two sons, **Sayyid Ali Gailani**

and **Sayyid Ahmad Gailani**, from his fourth wife. In 1941 he died of a brain hemorrhage and was buried in his Chaharbagh garden in Jalalabad.

GANDHARA. A state in the Peshawar Valley, with its capital at Taxila (or Charsada?), that flourished from the late first to the mid-fifth century A.D. It is famous for the fusion of Hellenistic and Buddhist civilization and art styles. The Kabul Museum holds numerous specimens of that art. *See* KABUL MUSEUM.

GANDOMAK (34-18' N, 70-2' E). A village on the Gandomak stream, a tributary of the Surkhab, about 29 miles southwest of Jalalabad. The area was the scene of a number of battles between British and Afghan forces including the massacre of the last remnants of the British army in 1842. It was also the scene of a treaty concluded between Major **Louis Cavagnari** and Amir **Yaqub Khan** signed on May 2, 1879. *See* GANDOMAK, TREATY OF.

GANDOMAK, TREATY OF. A treaty concluded between the British government and Amir **Yaqub Khan**, signed by the amir and Major **Louis Cavagnari** on May 26, 1879 and ratified by Lord Lytton, viceroy of India, on May 30, 1879.

The treaty was to establish "eternal peace and friendship" between the two countries upon conclusion of the **Second Anglo-Afghan War** (Article 1). It provided for amnesty for Afghan collaborators with the British occupation forces (Article 2) and obligated the amir to "conduct his relations with Foreign States, in accordance with the advice and wishes of the British Government." In exchange Britain would support the amir "against any foreign aggression with money, arms, or troops" (Article 3). A British representative was to be stationed at Kabul "with a suitable escort in a place of residence appropriate to his rank and dignity," and an Afghan agent was to be at the court of the viceroy of India (Article 4). A separate commercial agreement was to be signed (Article 7), and a telegraph line from Kurram to Kabul was to be constructed (Article 8). The Khaibar and Michni Passes were to be controlled by Britain (Article 9), Kandahar and Jalalabad were to be "restored" to the amir with the exception of Kurram, Pishin, and Sibi which were to be under British control but were not "considered as permanently severed from the limits of the Afghan kingdom." Afghan historians consider the treaty a sellout to Britain and a treasonable act by Amir Yaqub Khan.

GARDEZ (33-37'N, 69-7'E). Gardez is a town with about 20,000 inhabitants and a district in Paktia Province, located at an altitude of 7,620 feet. The town is inhabited largely by **Ghilzai** Pashtuns and some **Dari**-speakers and is, at the time of this writing, under *Taliban* control. Most of the surrounding villages have been destroyed and the inhabitants have fled to Pakistan. It is a strategically important town because it controls the route north over the Altamur Pass (9,600 feet) to Kabul. It is an ancient town, with a strong citadel and fortress, which for a short time was the seat of the **Kushanid** rulers of Kabul. It was a center of Buddhist culture and, in the early Islamic period, a base of the Kharijite (*Khawarij*—The Seceders) sect of Islam.

GARMSIR. A low-lying, hot country (*garm* = warm), in contrast with *sardsir* (*sard* = cold), a cold place, and therefore summer habitation in high grounds. Nomads would seasonally move from one to the other. Garmsir (or Garmsel) is also the name of a district in Helmand Province.

GAZAR-GAH (34-22' N, 62-14' E). The name of a range of low hills to the north of Herat and the location of the tomb of **Khwaja Abdullah Ansari**, a celebrated eleventh-century philosopher and Sufi poet. The shrine is the residence of the Mir of Gazargah, a man widely revered as the guardian of Ansari's mausoleum.

GENEVA ACCORDS. The result of "proximity" talks between Afghanistan and Pakistan in Geneva, initiated on June 16, 1982 by Diego Cordovez under the auspices of the United Nations and concluded on April 14, 1988. The Accords consisted of four documents and an annex: three between the Republic of Afghanistan and the Islamic Republic of Pakistan; one between the Soviet Union and the United States, promising to "refrain from any form of interference and intervention"; and an annex with a memorandum of understanding, assisting the UN in the implementation of the agreements. The United States and the Soviet Union were the guarantors of the accords. The talks aimed at ending the "external interference" in the war in Afghanistan with a view to establishing peace. The accords resulted in the withdrawal of Soviet troops in mid-February 1989 but failed to end foreign interference or to bring the warring parties closer to peace. One reason for the failure was that the *mujahedin* were not a party to the accords; another was that Washington, and virtually everyone else, expected the Marxist government to disintegrate promptly. When the Soviets departed, they left a considerable amount of war materiel and promised to supply more under the treaty of friendship of December 1978. The United States was obligated to cease military support of the *mujahedin*. The result was a haggling over "symmetry" and "negative symmetry" of arms supplies, not part of the formal agreements. Eventually the Soviets and the US informally agreed on "positive symmetry," that is to say, they reserved themselves the right to send arms in response to shipments by the other. The result was that both powers continued to support their "clients," and Pakistan continued to permit the passage of weapons through its territory. The war continued, and the superpower guarantees of non-interference in the internal affairs of Afghanistan were ignored. In April 1992 the Marxist government fell and the mujahedin began a civil war for control of the Afghan government.

GEOGRAPHY. Afghanistan is a mountainous, land-locked state of some 251,000 square miles (647,500 sq. km), which is approximately the area of Texas, and has a population of about 15.5 million (estimate based on demographic research under the auspices of the Afghan Central Statistics Office).

The climate in Afghanistan varies in accordance with the particular geographic zone: subarctic conditions in the northeast and Hindu Kush mountains (with peaks at 14,000 to 17,000 feet), a semiarid steppe climate in low lying areas, and mild, moist weather in the southeast bordering Pakistan. The estimated annual rainfall is between 11 and 15 inches with great variations—more on the southeastern slopes of mountains exposed to the monsoon rains and much less in the southwestern deserts.

About 83 % of the *Wakhan-Pamir* area lies at an altitude above 10,000 feet and another 17 % at an altitude of between 6,000 and 10,000 feet. Therefore, snow covers mountains above 16,000 feet, and most passes are seasonally closed. The yak and bactrian camel are utilized in the transportation of man and goods.

A similar climate exists in the *Central Mountains* including most of central and eastern **Hazarajat**, and the **Hindu Kush** ranges, extending from the **Shibar Pass** through the **Koh-i Baba** in the west, which is crossed by the **Salang** Tunnel at an altitude of about 11,000 feet. A limited amount of agriculture exists in the valleys, and nomads seasonally graze their livestock on the foothills.

The *Eastern Mountains* include four major regions: Kabul, Kohistan/Panjshir, the Ghorband, and **Nuristan**, the latter being the most inaccessible. Snow exists at altitudes between 10,000 and 12,000 feet. Temperatures reach lows of one degree Fahrenheit, and winter lasts from December till March. Summer temperatures depend on altitude. In the southwest, stony deserts extend to the Iranian border, and the **Registan**, "Country of Sand," extends south of the Helmand River and eastward as far as Shorawak, forming a natural boundary with Pakistan. On the edges of the Registan the desert gradually changes into a hilly landscape of sand hills thickly sprinkled with bushes and vegetation and grass after rains. **Baluch** and **Brahui** nomads seasonally graze their flock in this areas. The major agricultural areas are confined to the valleys watered by the **Amu Daria** and the northern plains, the Hari Rud/Murghab system in the northwest, the Helmand/Arghandab system, and the Kabul River system. The melting snow feeds the dry riverbeds in spring and provides much of the water for irrigation (for specific rivers, see independent entries). About 12% of the land is arable, 46% meadows and pastures, three percent is forests and woodland, and 39% is deserts and mountains.

GERMAN-AFGHAN RELATIONS. German-Afghan relations date from the time of World War I when the **Hentig-Niedermayer Expedition** in August 1915 first established official contact with an Afghan ruler (the claim by one Afghan writer that a secret German mission was sent to the court of Amir **Shir Ali** cannot be substantiated on the basis of British or German archival sources). The first German known to reside in Kabul was Gottlieb Fleischer, an employee of Krupp Steelworks of Essen, Germany, who was contracted by Amir **Abdul Rahman** in 1898 to start manufacture of ammunitions and arms in the newly constructed factory (*mashin-khana*) at Kabul (he was killed in November 1904 near the border while traveling to India). Afghanistan existed in self-imposed isolation and the British-Indian government refused to permit passage to Afghanistan to other than their own nationals. It was not until World War I that Germans again appeared in Kabul. A number of Austrian and German prisoners of war, held in Russian Central Asia, escaped and made their way to Kabul, where they were "interned" but enjoyed freedom of movement and contributed their skills to various public works projects.

The first official contact was the Hentig-Niedermayer mission that included also Turkish and Indian members and was charged with establishing diplomatic relations between the Central Powers and Afghanistan. The Germans hoped that Amir **Habibullah** would heed the Caliph's call to holy war and, together with the Pashtun Frontier tribes, attack India. The mission caused considerable anxiety in India, but although Amir Habibullah wanted to rid himself of British control, he was not to be drawn into a conflict whose outcome seemed at best dubious (*see* AFGHAN FOREIGN RELATIONS). Nevertheless, the mission was not a complete failure, as it forced Britain to maintain troops on its northwest frontier which could have been used in the European theater of war. Habibullah appeared to be willing to act but demanded assistance in funds and arms that only a victorious Germany could have provided. When it became apparent that no such victory was in sight, he informed Britain that he would remain neutral in the war in exchange for a financial reward and British recognition of Afghanistan's independence (*see* HABIBULLAH, AMIR).

Germany rendered Afghanistan a potentially important service by insisting on Russian recognition of Afghan independence in Article VII of the Treaty of Brest-Litovsk (March 3, 1918), which ended Russian participation in World War I.

German influence became solidly established during the reign of King **Amanullah** (r. 1919–29). The "Reformer King" won the independence of his country in a short, undeclared war (*see* ANGLO-AFGHAN WARS) and quickly established relations with the major powers of the world.

In 1923 **Fritz Grobba**, the German minister plenipotentiary, joined the diplomatic representatives of the Soviet Union, Persia, Britain, Turkey, and Italy in Kabul, and it was soon clear that there existed a community of interest between Germany and Afghanistan. King Amanullah needed Western expertise for his modernization projects and felt that nationals from states, other than his powerful neighbors, should be engaged. The United States was reluctant to move into an area that it considered within the British sphere of influence (*see* UNITED STATES-AFGHAN RELATIONS); Italy was willing to assist, but the execution of an Italian who killed an Afghan policeman soured relations between the two countries. France was seen as a colonial power that had acquired large portions of the Ottoman empire, whose ruling sultan/caliph Afghans recognized as the spiritual head of the Islamic world. Germany had been an ally of the Ottomans and offered Afghanistan industrial hardware and skilled technicians at competitive rates. A consortium of German enterprises formed the Deutsch-Afghanische Companie (DACOM), which established an office in Kabul. In 1923, King Amanullah founded the German-language high school, *Amani* (called *Najat* under **Nadir Shah**), in addition to French- and English-language secondary schools, and German influence was growing. By 1926 the German colony was second only to the Russians and soon became the largest of all foreign groups. Relations developed to the extent that major incidents that might have had a serious impact on German-Afghan relations were amicably resolved. In November 1926, a German national killed an Afghan nomad, and in June 1933 an Afghan student, and supporter of the deposed King **Amanullah**, shot **Sardar Muhammad Aziz**, a half brother of Nadir Shah and his minister at Berlin. In September 1933, **Muhammad Azim**, a teacher at the German high school, wanted to provoke an international incident by shooting the British minister at Kabul (he killed an Englishman, an Afghan, and an Indian employee instead). The last two incidents were seen as the manifestation of a power struggle between the followers of King Amanullah and the new ruling family, and there existed some worries in Kabul that Germany was supporting the ex-King. These incidents had no lasting effect on German-Afghan relations.

In October 1936 the two countries agreed in a "confidential protocol" on the delivery 15 million marks of war materiel on credit to be repaid in half with Afghan products. By that time Germany had become an important economic and political factor in Kabul, and the way seemed clear for even closer cooperation. In 1937 Lufthansa Airline established regular service from Berlin to Kabul with the intention of eventually extending service to China. And in summer 1939, shortly before the outbreak of World War II, a German commercial delegation arrived in Kabul to expand German-Afghan trade; but the political situation precluded any desire of the Kabul government to tie itself even closer to Nazi Germany. German annexation of Austria in March 1938 and the annexation of Czechoslovakia a year later, and above all the conclusion of a non-aggression pact between Germany and the Soviet Union in August 1939, made it appear likely that Europe would be engulfed in war. Germany could no longer be a "third force" in Afghanistan's attempt to balance the influences of her powerful neighbors.

On the outbreak of World War II, **Zahir Shah** proclaimed Afghanistan's neutrality and was determined to stay out of the war. For Germany, Afghanistan's strategic location gained a priority over commercial consideration. The German foreign ministry and its political counterpart, the *Aussenpolitische Amt*, toyed with the idea of supporting a pro-Amanullah coup to establish an allied government in Kabul. It sent Peter Kleist, a German diplomat, and **Ghulam Siddiq Charkhi**, a former Afghan ambassador and supporter of King Amanullah, to Moscow to query Vyacheslav Molotov, the Soviet foreign minister, as to whether the Soviets would support such a move. The Soviets were noncommittal, and nothing came of the project. When Germany invaded the Soviet Union in June 1941, Afghanistan's neighbors were allied for the second time since the **Anglo-Russian Convention** of 1907, and they were soon to take a common stand in Kabul: in separate diplomatic notes of October 9 and 11, 1941, the Soviet Union and Britain demanded the evacuation of all Axis nationals from Afghanistan. Prime Minister **Muhammad Hashim** was forced to comply, even though the Afghan government considered it an infringement of its sovereign rights. A *Loya Jirga*, national council, convened on November 5 and 6 and approved the decision after the Axis nationals had left for India and traveled under a promise of free passage to a neutral country. Axis diplomats were permitted to stay, and their contacts with Pashtun tribes on the Indian side of the border did not achieve any tangible results. In spite of sympathies for the enemy of Afghanistan's traditional enemies, there was no question of armed cooperation with Germany.

After its defeat in World War II, the German "phoenix" rose from its ashes again, and soon German expertise again found a ready demand in Kabul. Although Germany was unable for a while to deliver industrial products, her nationals would again be a major factor in Afghanistan's development projects. A dam and hydroelectric power station at Sarobi became one of the first major German projects after the war. American funds and German contractors built the new campus of **Kabul University**. German teachers served on the faculties of science and economics of Kabul University, and by the 1970s, German economic aid ranked third after Soviet and American assistance.

Najat **School** became a model institution, rivaling the French-supported *Istiqlal Lycée*, and the English-language schools in Kabul. The *Deutsche Entwicklungsdienst* (German Development Service), a volunteer organization, brought Germans with attractive skills to Afghanistan. The Goethe Institute for the promotion of German language and culture was opened in Kabul, and a consortium of German universities offered Afghans opportunities to study in Germany. East Germany, not recognized by the Afghans, eventually also appeared on the scene, vying with its Western "brothers" to win friends and influence people. West German influence lasted long after the Soviet intervention in Afghanistan, although East Germans gradually replaced Germans from the West. Because of its long and fruitful association with Afghanistan, its nationals have enjoyed a good reputation in Kabul and may well continue to have an important cultural and economic role in Afghanistan. In July 1996, Norbert Holl, a German, replaced Mahmud Mestiri as special UN envoy for Afghanistan, to continue the so far futile task of bringing peace to Afghanistan.

GHAFFAR KHAN. *See* **KHAN, KHAN ABDUL GHAFFAR KHAN.**

GHAUSUDDIN KHAN, GEN. Commander of Afghan forces during the **Panjdeh Incident** in March 1885. He confronted Col. Alikhanov, commander of the Russian forces, but was defeated by the superior power of the Russians. A British officer called him "a very superior Afghan... he selected his position at Ak Teppe with a great deal of judgements. He. . . has shown much tact in his dealings with the Sarikhs [a Turkoman tribe], among whom he is as popular as an Afghan [Pashtun] can be." He is buried in Caliph Ali's Mausoleum in Mazar-i Sharif. *See* PANJDEH INCIDENT.

GHAZI. Originally the designation for Arab beduin raiders who would strike from their desert refuge (*ghazw*), seeking booty in enemy territory. (The European term *razzia* for a predatory raid or police raid is a corruption of *ghazw*.) After the advent of Islam a *ghazi* was a holy warrior fighting against a non-Muslim enemy, synonymous to the term *mujahed* (pl. *mujahedin*) used by the Afghan resistance in the 1980s. *Ghazis* during the Anglo-Afghan wars were irregular fighters who took vows to die in battle against the unbelievers and staged suicidal attacks against superior forces, for Paradise was assured to the martyr. They were often poorly armed, but their reckless bravery made them a dangerous enemy. A British military historian said

> A true ghazi counts no odds too great to face, no danger too menacing to be braved; the certainty of death only adds to his exaltation... If every Afghan were a ghazi ... our defenses would

have been carried, and enormous slaughter would have followed on
both sides. (Hensman, 333–34)

The term became a title given to a victorious commander. **Mahmud
of Ghazni**, King **Amanullah**, **Habibullah Kalakani**, **Nadir Shah**,
and others claimed this title. The sons of Sardar Shah Mahmud adopted
his title as a family name.

GHAZI HIGH SCHOOL. Founded at Kabul in 1928 by King **Amanullah**.
It received its name from the king's title *Ghazi*, "Victor" in the **Third
Anglo-Afghan War**. Like **Habibia School**, it is a 12-grade English-
language preparatory school, most of whose graduates continued their
higher education at Kabul or abroad.

GHAZI, SHAH MAHMUD. War minister and commander-in-chief from
1929 until 1946, when he became prime minister until 1953. Born in
1886, the youngest son of Muhammad Yusuf, he embarked on a military
career. He served as military commander and governor in various
provinces and was appointed deputy Interior minister in 1928. Assisted
his brother Nadir Khan in defeating **Habibullah Kalakani** and served
Nadir Shah and his successor **Zahir Shah** as prime minister until
1953, when he resigned in favor of Sardar **Muhammad Daud**. He
allowed substantial freedom of speech and of the press but reverted to
more authoritarian measures when the political liberalization led to
increasing attacks on his government. He died in December 1959.

GHAZNAVID DYNASTY (977–1186). A dynasty of Turkic origin
founded by Nasir al-Daula Sebuktegin (r. 977– 97) with its administrative capital in the city of Ghazni. During the reign of Sultan
Mahmud Ghazni (r. 998–1030) the Ghaznavid Empire extended from
the Tigris to the Ganges River and from the Indian Ocean to the **Amu
Daria**. The city of Ghazni experienced a period of enormous wealth,
most of it amassed by Mahmud during some seventeen campaigns into
the Indian subcontinent. He attracted some 400 scholars and poets to his
capital, including **Abu'l Qasim Firdausi** and **Abu Rayhan al-Biruni**.
Although the dynasty counted nineteen rulers over a period of two
centuries, the empire began to disintegrate after Mahmud's death.
Under Mahmud's son, Mas'ud, the Seljuks took possession of
Khorasan, and during the reign of Bahram Shah (1117–57) Ghazni
was sacked by Ala-ud-Din of Ghor. Ogadai, son of Genghis Khan,

seized the city in 1221, and it became part of the Ilkhanid Empire. *See* MAHMUD OF GHAZNI.

GHAZNI (33-33' N, 68-26' E). The name of a province and town in eastern Afghanistan. The town had about 30,000 inhabitants in 1978 and is located at an elevation of some 7,000 feet on the road from Kabul to Kandahar, about 80 miles southeast of Kabul. The old town on the left bank of the river is walled and guarded by a citadel that was garrisoned by Afghan army units until it was taken by the *mujahedin*. Ghazni derives its fame from the fact that it was the capital of the **Ghaznavid dynasty** (977–1186). It is strategically located and was the scene of severe fighting between Afghan and British forces during the first two Afghan wars. A British garrison stationed in the town during the **First Anglo-Afghan War** was wiped out in December 1841. The population of the town is largely Tajik with some Ghilzais, Durranis, Hazaras, and a few Hindu shopkeepers.

GHILZAI. A major Pashtu-speaking tribe inhabiting an area roughly bounded by Kalat-i-Ghilzai in the south, the Gul Kuh range in the west, the Sulaiman range in the east, and the Kabul River on the north. The Ghilzai call themselves Ghaljai (pl. Ghalji) and count themselves the descendants of Ghalzoe, son of Shah Husain, said to have been a Tajik or Turk, and of Bibi Mato, who descended from Shaikh Baitan (the second son of Qais—progenitor of the Afghan nationality). The origin of the name Ghilzai comes either from "Ghal Zoe" (thief's son), "Khilji" the Turkic word for swordsman, or the name of Khilji Turks who came into the area in the tenth century. From Ghalzoe the tribe divided into the Turan and Burhan Ibrahim divisions.

The Sulaiman Khel are the most important of all, and the Ali Khel are the most important of the Burhan. In the 19th century they were said to number about 100,000 families with 30,000 to 50,000 fighters. They were largely nomadic and called *Powindahs* in India and often traveled far into India, making a living as merchant nomads.

The Hotaki Ghilzais achieved their fame in Afghan history as the liberators of Kandahar from Safavid control and the leading tribe in the invasion of Iran and the destruction of the Persian empire in 1722. **Mir Wais**, a descendant of Malakhi, a leading chief at Kandahar, was taken by the Safavid governor to Isfahan but was later permitted to return. He raised a revolt against the Kandahar governor and ruled over the province for some years (1709–15). His son Mahmud raised an army and invaded Persia, defeating the Safavid armies at the **Battle of Gulnabad** in 1722. However, Mahmud was unable to hold on to his conquest. **Nadir Khan**, founder of the short-lived Afsharite dynasty, reunited the Persian empire and in turn invaded Afghan lands. After the death of Nadir Shah, the Ghilzai were weakened to such an extent that they could not prevent the emergence of the **Durrani** dynasty. The Ghilzai fought the British when they invaded Afghanistan and subsequently became the major rivals of the Durranis. They rebelled repeatedly against **Muhammadzai** rule and were suppressed only with difficulty in 1801, 1883, 1886, and 1937. Urban Ghilzai have since intermarried with Muhammadzai. The Ghilzai were well represented in the Marxist leadership (**Taraki, Najibullah, Hafizullah Amin, Watanjar**, Layeq, **Muhammad Rafi'i** and many others) but also among the resistance (**Hekmatyar** and **Sayyaf**), which prompted one expert to remark that for the first time power has passed from the Durrani to the Ghilzai. *See also* ABDUL KARIM.

GHOBAR, MIR GHULAM MUHAMMAD. A historian, writer, and poet who was widely known for his critical analyses of Afghan history in his book *Afghanistan dar Masir-i Tarikh* (Afghanistan in the Path of History), published in 1967. Born in 1897 in Kabul of a Sayyid family, he entered the services of King **Amanullah**. He was editor of *Sitare-yi-Afghan*, 1919–20; chief of police, 1920–21; and served as secretary at the Afghan embassies in Paris, 1926 and Berlin, 1930. In the final days of King Amanullah he participated in the Paghman *Loya Jirga*. He became a prominent member of the Afghan literary society, 1931–32, the historical society, 1943–48, and a literary adviser to the department of press, 1948. Imprisoned from 1933–35 and again from 1952–56, he served intermittently as representative of Kabul in parliament in 1948 and again from 1949–51. He was a founding member of the *Watan* party and editor of *Watan* (Homeland), its newspaper in 1951. He died at age 81 on February 5, 1978, in Germany.

GHOR (GHUR) (34-0'N, 65-0'E). A west-central province of Afghanistan with an area of 13,808 square miles and a population of about 341,000. The capital of the province is the town of Chaghcharan. The province is mountainous with some wheat and barley cultivation in the Farah, Hari Rud, and Murghab Valleys. Major mountain ranges include the Firuzkoh (Safidkoh), Siyahkoh, and Band-i Bayan. The population is primarily of **Taimani** (Chahar **Aimaq**) origin. *See also* GHORID DYNASTY.

GHORID DYNASTY (1150-1217). The Ghorid dynasty derived its name from Ghor, its capital near the present Qala-i-Ghor (Taiwara). At the height of their power, the Ghorids ruled over an area from eastern Iran to Bengal in India. In the early 11th century, Ghor was conquered by **Mahmud of Ghazni** and forced to pay tribute to the **Ghaznavids**, but in 1151 the Ghorid Ala ud-Din in turn sacked and destroyed Ghazni. In 1176 the Ghorids, under Ghias ud-Din, took Herat, in 1198 Balkh, in 1200 Nishapur, Merv, Sarakhs, and Tus and moved far into India. The empire quickly disintegrated after the death of Ghias ud-Din in 1202, and subsequent invasions by the hordes of Genghis Khan and **Timur-i Lang** ended the brief glory of Ghor. In 1958 a French archaeologist discovered a minaret from the time of Ghias ud-Din.

GHULAM HAIDAR CHARKHI. Commander in chief of the Afghan army in the **Second Anglo-Afghan War** and an implacable foe of the British. When General **Sir Frederick Roberts** proclaimed a general amnesty on December 20, 1880, he was one of four Afghan sardars excluded. He served Amir **Abdul Rahman**, subduing the tribes in the Eastern province and in 1882 was again appointed commander-in-chief. In 1888, the Amir gave him the title *Wazir* (minister). He died in 1898.

GHULAM JILANI CHARKHI. Major general of Amir **Habibullah**, he led successful campaigns against rebellious tribes. He was born in 1886, the son of **Ghulam Haidar**. In 1912, he was appointed superintendent of the military college in Kabul. He served King **Amanullah** as governor and commander of troops in various provinces and was appointed minister at Ankara in 1925. Recalled to Kandahar by King Amanullah in April 1929, he was unable to defeat the forces of **Habibullah Kalakani** and fled to India with the King and also accompanied him to Rome. He returned to Afghanistan in August 1930 but was arrested and executed in 1933.

GHULAM NABI CHARKHI. A general in the service of Amir **Habibullah**. A native of Charkh and son of **Ghulam Haidar**. King **Amanullah** appointed him minister to Moscow, 1922–24 and later deputy minister of Foreign Affairs. He continued to direct pacification campaigns and served in the Logar Valley during the **Mangal**

Rebellion, 1924–25. Toward the end of King Amanullah's reign he served short assignments as minister at Paris and Moscow. In 1929 he led an army officered by Afghan cadets who had been studying in Turkey in an attempt to return Amanullah to power. But he was unable to defeat the forces of **Habibullah Kalakani** and was forced to withdraw to the Soviet Union. In 1932 he returned to Afghanistan under a pardon, but was executed because of "subversive activities" against **Nadir Shah**.

GHULAM SIDDIQ CHARKHI. A diplomat and high government official of King **Amanullah** who with his brothers, **Ghulam Jilani** and **Ghulam Nabi**, was a foe of the Yahya Khel dynasty. Born in 1894, the son of **Ghulam Haidar**, he entered the service of King Amanullah. Ghulam Siddiq was second counselor to the Afghan mission of **Muhammad Wali** Khan, which visited European capitals and the United States for the purpose of establishing diplomatic relations after the end of the **Third Anglo-Afghan War**. He was Afghan minister at Berlin, 1922–26, first private secretary to King Amanullah and minister of court, 1927, and Foreign minister in 1928. He left Afghanistan with King Amanullah and served shortly as minister in Berlin but was dismissed as a supporter of the deposed king. He married a sister of Queen Suraya and remained in Berlin until the end of World War II. He died in 1962 and is buried in Afghanistan.

GHURID. *See* **GHORID DYNASTY.**

GILANI. *See* **GAILANI.**

GIRISHK (31-48' N, 64-34' E). A town on the Helmand River in Helmand (formerly Girishk) Province. It lies on the road from Kandahar to Herat, about 78 miles from Kandahar. The town, located at a strategic position and protected by a strong citadel and high walls, was destroyed by **Nadir Shah Afshar**, and rebuilt by Sardar Kohan Dil. In 1839 it was captured by General **Sir Robert Sale** but besieged during the entire war and finally abandoned by the British. A British officer visited Girishk in 1879 and described the town as "a fort with half a dozen small villages scattered round it, and a bazaar outside the gate." He said the fort was almost useless, but the position of great strategic importance. Reconstruction of the area was begun in 1937, and the Helmand project produced some growth; but in 1957 the state capital was transferred from Girishk to Lashkargah (Bost) and the town lost some of its earlier importance.

GOD-I ZIRREH (GOWD or **GAUD)** (30-5'N, 61-45'E). A large depression in southwestern Afghanistan, extending close to the Iran/Pakistan border. About once every decade water from the Hamun-I Helmand overflows and runs down the Shelag channel, creating a shallow lake. The water has a high salt content, and when dry the God-i Zirreh is covered with a thick deposit of salt.

GOLDSMID AWARD. Was the result of the Sistan boundary arbitration in 1872 made by Sir Frederic Goldsmid in which the boundary between Iran and Afghanistan was drawn. Persian forces had occupied portions of Sistan claimed by Afghanistan, and the British government offered its good offices to resolve the dispute. Gen. Goldsmid made the following award: "That Sistan proper, by which is meant the tract of country which the Hamun on three of its sides and the Helmand on the fourth cause to resemble an island, should be included by a special boundary line within the limits of Persia; that Persia should not possess land in the right of the Helmand...." It was also stipulated that no works should be carried out to interfere with the supply of water from the Helmand. Neither Iran nor Afghanistan was satisfied with the award, and the question of the distribution of the Helmand waters remained a potential conflict. It was not until 1973 that the Helmand Water Treaty was concluded; it was ratified by the Afghan government in 1977.

GORCHAKOFF. *See* **GRANVILLE GORCHAKOFF AGREEMENT.**

GRANVILLE-GORCHAKOFF AGREEMENT. An Anglo-Russian agreement based on assurances given in the years 1868–69 and confirmed several times later in an exchange of letters between the foreign ministers, Lord Granville and Prince Gorchakoff, which stipulated that "Badakhshan with its dependent district of Wakhan from Sar-i-Kul on the east to the junction of the Kokcha River with the Oxus (or Panja) forming the northern boundary of this Afghan Province throughout its entire length." Further west, however, the border was not clearly defined, eventually enabling Russia to annex **Panjdeh**. Russia agreed that Afghanistan was outside its sphere of influence and, except for the territorial changes of **Shignan** and **Roshan** and the Panjdeh oasis, the Afghan border has remained as it is today. The agreement is also known as the Clarendon-Gortchakoff Agreement.

GREAT GAME. A term attributed to Rudyard Kipling describing the competition between Russia and Great Britain in the conquest of the territories lying between their colonial possessions. Russia was aiming at gaining access to the warm water ports of the Persian Gulf, if not to the riches of India, and Britain wanted to prevent it. Afghanistan was a major player and desired by both as an ally. Afghan rulers realized that Russia needed to take Afghanistan to realize their objectives and therefore concluded a cautious alliance with Britain. Twice during the 19th century British armies invaded Afghanistan for the purpose of finding a "scientific frontier" on the crests of the **Hindu Kush** or the **Amu Daria** (Oxus) River. When direct control failed, Britain resigned itself to concluding an alliance with the Afghan ruler and to support him against the eventuality of Russian aggression. When Britain left India in 1947, the "Great Game" seemed to be over, because the United States was unwilling to guarantee Afghanistan's territorial integrity from Soviet aggression. Therefore, the Soviet Union seemed to have won the game when in 1978 it intervened militarily in support of the Marxist government of Afghanistan. As during previous invasions, the Afghan people eventually prevailed.

GRIFFIN, SIR LEPEL Chief political officer at Kabul during the **Second Anglo-Afghan War** whose negotiations with Sardar **Abdul Rahman** led to the recognition of the latter as amir of Afghanistan.

GROBBA, FRITZ. First German minister in Afghanistan, who came to Kabul in December 1923 and left the country under a cloud of suspicion in summer 1926. The incident which clouded the hitherto cordial German-Afghan relations was an attempt by Grobba to smuggle a German, Gustav Stratil-Sauer, out of the country. Stratil-Sauer, who came to Afghanistan on a motorcycle, got into a scuffle with a tribesman when crossing the Lataband Pass. He shot the man, purportedly in self-defense, and fled to Kabul where he sought the protection of the German legation. Stratil-Sauer was sentenced to four years imprisonment but was pardoned in July August 1926 by King **Amanullah**. An Italian engineer, named Piperno, was hanged in 1925 in a similar case. Grobba was replaced, and Germany upgraded its legation to the level of embassy. Grobba later published his memoirs, *Männer und Mächte im Orient*, avoiding any discussion of this incident.

GROMOV, GENERAL LIEUTENANT BORIS V. Commander of the 40th Army, comprising the **Limited Contingent of Soviet Forces in Afghanistan**, who spent three tours in Afghanistan. The 45–year-old general led a combined Soviet/Afghan force of some 10,000 troops from Gardez against Khost, temporarily lifting the siege of this strategic town in January 1988. It was the last major Soviet operation facing considerable *mujahedin* opposition, and the type of action not originally considered his task. Gromov stated that Soviet forces were intended to establish garrisons, stabilize the situation, and refrain from significant combat operations, leaving counter insurgency to the DRA forces (McMichael, 10). Eventually only about 30 to 35 % of Soviet forces were devoted to security and defense of fixed sites, and it was inevitable that defense also required counter insurgency operations. McMichael quotes Gromov as saying "The war in Afghanistan demonstrated a large rupture between theory and practice." Gromov felt it was unavoidable. He was assigned the task of evacuating the last contingent of 450 armored vehicles and about 1,400 Soviet troops from Afghanistan. On February 14, 1989, he was the last Soviet soldier to cross the "Friendship Bridge" into Soviet territory. He announced to the assembled reporters that "We have fulfilled our international duty to the end" (O'Ballance, 196). He became minister of interior in 1990 and commander of all Russian ground troops in 1992.

GUERRILLA WARFARE. Military operations conducted by informal forces during foreign invasion or civil war, mainly of the hit-and-run type, against a superior enemy. It was the typical warfare of the *ghazis* and *mujahedin* against British and Soviet forces. Temporary concentration of forces go on the offensive and quickly disperse, before counter measures can be taken. Counter insurgency measures, therefore, included the destruction of entire villages, crops, fruit trees, livestock, channels of irrigation (*karez*), and other sources to deprive the guerrillas of their support. Although the Afghan *ghazis*, or *mujahedin*, fought under the banner of Islam, tribalism and nationalism, as well as sectarian allegiance, may in fact have been the dominant motivation.

GULBAHAR (35-9'N, 69-17'E). A town on the west bank of the **Panjshir** River and the site of an important industrial center. In 1960 a textile industry was established with German financial assistance, eventually employing some 5,000 people. A new town was built apart from the old village to house the employees of the new industrial enterprise.

GULNABAD, BATTLE OF. An important victory of Afghan forces under Mahmud, son of the Ghilzai chief **Mir Wais**, which marked the end of the Safavid empire of Iran. On March 8, 1722, Mahmud met and decisively defeated a superior Iranian army and then besieged Isfahan for six months before taking the capital of the empire. The Ghilzais proved to be better soldiers than empire-builders; they were forced to yield power to **Nadir Shah Afshar** and withdrew to their Afghan homeland where they were superseded by the **Durranis**. *See also* NADIR SHAH AFSHAR; MIR WAIS, and GHILZAI.

GUMAL (GOMAL) (31-56'N, 70-22'E). A river in southeastern Afghanistan that rises in the Sulaiman range and run

H

HABIB, ASADULLAH. A poet and writer who joined the **PDPA** and was president of the writers' union in 1980 and rector of **Kabul University**, 1982–88. In 1986 he was elected a candidate academician of the Academy of Sciences (*see* AFGHAN ACADEMY) and member of the central committee of the PDPA. He was born in 1941 in Maimana of an Uzbek family and educated in Maimana, Kabul, the United States, and the Soviet Union, where he obtained a Ph.D. degree.

HABIBI, ABDUL HAI. Educator, historian, and representative of Kandahar in parliament. Self educated, he started as a teacher and became editor of the **Pashtu** daily *Tulu-ye-Afghan* (Afghan Sunrise) in 1931. He was a Pashtun nationalist and a member of *Wish Zalmayan* (Awakened Youth). In 1940 he was appointed president of the **Afghan Academy** and in 1941 dean of the faculty of literature of **Kabul University**. He was forced to live in exile because of his opposition to the government of **Shah Mahmud** and in Pakistan published *Azad Afghanistan* (Free Afghanistan), a political journal in which he advocated the replacement of the monarchy by a republic. In 1961 he was permitted to return to Afghanistan and became professor on the faculty of letters of Kabul University. He was appointed president of the **Afghan Historical Society** in 1966 and published a number of books on Afghan history as well as a purported Pashtu record of early poetry, the *Pata Khazana* (Hidden Treasure). An adviser to the ministry of information and culture during the Daud and Marxist periods, and a member of the Academy of Sciences, he refused to join the "Fatherland Front." Shortly before he died in Kabul in 1984, he published a book on the constitutionalist movement in Afghanistan (Junbesh-i Mashruti-yat dar Afghanistan) which described the movement as nationalist, rather than socialist.

HABIBIA SCHOOL (or **COLLEGE**). A preparatory school of higher education, established in 1904 and named after its founder Amir **Habibullah**. It started as a *madrasa* (Islamic school of higher education) but was gradually transformed into a school with a British-Indian curriculum. The language of instruction was English, and the most successful students would win scholarships for study abroad. The school eventually adopted a modified American curriculum. *See also* EDUCATION.

HABIB-UL ISLAM (HABIB AL-ISLAM). A weekly newspaper published during the short-lived reign of **Habibullah Kalakani** to legitimize the government of the "outlaw turned king" and to propagate a return to "orthodox" Islamic principles. It was founded in January 1929 (17th of Ramadhan 1348/9) and edited by Ghulam Muhyi ud-Din (succeeded by Sayyid Muhammad Husain and **Burhanuddin Kushkaki**). *See* HABIBULLAH KALAKANI.

HABIBULLAH, AMIR (1901–19). Amir of Afghanistan who kept his state neutral in World War I but wanted to end Britain's quasi protectorate over his country. He was born in Samarkand on April 21, 1871, the son of Amir **Abdul Rahman** and an **Uzbek** lady from Badakhshan. During his father's life he took an active part in the administration and was generally popular. He succeeded to the throne on October 3, 1901 and assumed the title of *Siraj al-Millat wa'd-Din* (Torch of the Nation and Religion). He increased the pay of the army, permitted exiles to return, including many sardars (nobles) and their families, released prisoners, and promised reforms.

The British government was not satisfied with some of the provisions of the agreements concluded with Amir Abdul Rahman and therefore wanted to force certain changes before it recognized the new amir. London maintained that the agreements were with the *person* of the amir, not the State of Afghanistan, and therefore had to be renegotiated with his successor. In spite of severe pressures, Habibullah did not yield. Two years later, he finally agreed to meet in Kabul with **Louis W. Dane**, foreign secretary of the government of India (India was ruled by a viceroy who was responsible to the British government in London). The result was a complete victory for Habibullah when Britain was forced to renew the agreements concluded with Amir Abdul Rahman in the form of a treaty that recognized Habibullah's title as "Independent King of the State of Afghanistan and its Dependencies."

Amir Habibullah showed great interest in Western technology, and he embarked on a process of modernization. He imported automobiles and built roads, founded **Habibia School** in 1904, the first modern school in Afghanistan, and brought electricity to Kabul. In January 1907 Amir Habibullah traveled to India and was cordially received by the Viceroy, Lord Minto. A crisis in relations with British India occurred when Habibullah learned that Afghanistan's powerful neighbors had concluded the **Anglo-Russian Convention** of 1907. This agreement divided Afghanistan (and Iran) into spheres of influence with provisions for "equality of commercial opportunity" in Afghanistan for Russian and British traders and the appointment of commercial agents in Kabul. The amir was invited to ratify the agreement, but he refused, and the Convention was never implemented.

The outbreak of World War I posed another crisis in foreign relations: in spite of warnings not to do so from the viceroy of India, Amir Habibullah received a German mission at Kabul. He met with members of the **Hentig-Niedermayer Expedition** (that included a Turk and several Indians) and initialed the draft of a secret treaty of friendship and military assistance with Germany to provide for the eventuality of an Allied defeat. Germany could not deliver, and Britain promised a handsome reward for Afghan neutrality; therefore a realistic appraisal of the situation prompted the Afghan ruler to stay out of the war.

Britain showed itself miserly and, once the crisis was over, wanted to reestablish its exclusive control over Afghanistan. The "war party" at his court felt that the amir had failed to take advantage of a unique opportunity of winning independence from Britain, and his enemies conspired to depose him. He was assassinated on February 20, 1919, while he was on a hunting trip at Kala Gosh in Laghman.

Amir Habibullah was about five feet four inches in height, very powerfully built. He had a speech impediment, a slight stammer that he was, however, able to control. He was the father of Sardar **Amanullah**, who succeeded him to the throne.

HABIBULLAH KALAKANI, AMIR. (r. January 18–October 1929). A Tajik of humble origins who was a leader of the anti-reformist reaction that swept King **Amanullah** from power and him to the throne. He was known as *Bacha-i-Saqqao* (son of a water carrier—the occupation of his father, Aminullah, a Tajik from the village of Kalakan in the Koh Daman district north of Kabul). With the support of a loose coalition of Kohistani forces, he took advantage of a tribal revolt by **Shinwari**, Sulaiman Khel, and other **Pashtun** tribes in the east to capture Kabul and have himself proclaimed Amir Habibullah, *Ghazi* (Victor). Following the custom of Afghan rulers, Habibullah adopted the title "Servant of the Religion of the Messenger of God," (*Khadem- i Din-i Rasulullah*) and set about to consolidate his power.

Two factors militated against his royal aspirations: he was of **Tajik**, rather than the dominant Pashtun ethnic background; and he was known as a brigand, albeit of a Robin Hood nature, as seen from the perspective of his Kohistani brothers. British archival sources provide the following composite regarding Habibullah's background:

Born about 1890 at Kala Kan village near Sarai Khwaja in Kohdaman, the son of Aminullah, a water carrier (*saqqao*). Said to have held various menial positions, including work as a servant of an Afghan official (**Muhammad Wali**), until he joined **Jamal Pasha**'s (a head of the Ottoman war government) regiment (the Qita Namuna) in Kabul in 1919. Deserted with his rifle because of sympathy with the **Mangals** in the rebellion of 1924. Later fled to Peshawar where he worked for some time as a tea seller, after which he went to Parachinar, where he was sentenced to eleven months' imprisonment for house breaking. After the Mangal Revolt he became a highwayman and "showed considerable generosity to the poor, but was merciless to Afghan officials and wealthy travelers."

Habibullah was a natural leader and charismatic personality, but his assumption of the throne was challenged from the beginning. A British officer reported from Peshawar that "Bacha-i-Saqao's accession has come as a profound shock to the tribes on both sides of the Durand Line" (Adamec, 1974). Even the Shinwaris, whose revolt started the civil war, were not willing to submit to the new king. The fact that Habibullah had found some 750,000 British pounds at the conquest of the **Arg** (royal palace) permitted him to pay his troops and win some tribal support.

The *Habib al-Islam* (his name of Islam) depicted Habibullah as a pious Muslim, a brave fighter, and a wise ruler. He issued a proclamation that all sectors of Afghan society had recognized his rule, including the Shinwaris, **Khugianis**, **Ghilzais**, and Amanullah's own **Durranis**.

Attempts by forces loyal to King Amanullah were unable to recapture the throne, but **Muhammad Nadir** and his brothers succeeded. **Shah Wali** Khan, brother of Nadir and brother-in-law of King Amanullah, captured the Arg in October 1929, and Habibullah was forced to surrender. On November 1, Habibullah, his brother Hamidullah, and Sayyid Husain, together with nine leaders of their turbulent regime, were executed. Habibullah's purported autobiography *My Life: From Brigand to King* describes his career as bandit and king, and a recent book in Persian, entitled *A Hero from Khorasan*, by **Khalilullah Khalili** also a Kohistani and poet laureate, depicts him as a *mujahed*, a holy warrior, against an infidel king. Khalili's maternal uncle was **Abdul Rahim**, the general who contributed to Kalakani's conquests and served as his governor at Herat.

HABIBURRAHMAN, ENG. (HABIB AL-RAHMAN). One of the four leaders of the Organization of Muslim Youth (*Sazman-i Jawanan-i Musulman*), called *Ikhwanis* by their opponents, who was secretary of the council (*Shura*) until 1975 when he was replaced by **Gulbudin Hekmatyar**. He recruited **Ahmad Shah Mas'ud**, the **Jam'iat** commander, as his deputy. He was arrested in 1973 and executed during the Daud regime. *See* ISLAMIST MOVEMENT.

HADDA (34-22'N, 70-29'E). A village in the Chapriar (Chaparhar) District about six miles south of Jalalabad, inhabited largely by Mohmands. In the fourth century Hadda was a great center of Buddhism and the location of numerous shrines. The name Hadda means "bone" and refers to the belief that Buddha's head was enshrined there. The village is famous for the archaeological excavations nearby that yielded an abundance of stupas, Buddhas, and various statuary. The village is also known for the "Hadda Mulla," one Najm-ud-Din, who preached jihad against the British and was a leader of numerous hostile actions against British India. At present there is an important madrasa in this village, called *Najm al-Madares* (Star of Madrasas). The stupas discovered at

Hadda were partially destroyed in military operations and looted during the present war.

HAFIZ. Title of honor given to one who has memorized the Qor'an in its entirety.

HAIBAK. See AIBAK.

HAJ Properly spelled **HAJJ.** See HAJJ.

HAJIGAK (34-40' N, 68-6' E). A village located near the pass of the same name in Bamian Province (The name comes from the **Hazara** *aja-gak*, meaning "Dear Grandmother"). Foreign experts from a number of countries have found high grade iron ore in the area, with estimated reserves amounting to almost two billion tons. The area is inaccessible, and the development of infrastructure and construction of a furnace complex, planned under President **Muhammad Daud**'s seven-year plan (1976-83), was never begun.

HAJJ. Pilgrimage to Mecca. A legal obligation of every adult Muslim of either sex to travel at least once in a lifetime to Mecca, provided the person is economically able to do so. Thousand of Afghans perform this obligation each year, and special **Ariana Afghan Airline** flights are chartered for this purpose.

HAJJI. Title of honor of a person who has performed the pilgrimage to Mecca.

HAJJI MIRZA ALI KHAN. See FAQIR OF IPI.

HAKIM. A wise man, philosopher, doctor, or practitioner of traditional "Greek medicine," *tebb-i-yunani* (pronounced hakeem). A governor of a sub-province, commander (pronounced haakem).

HAMUN. A term used for a shallow depression or morass, usually of high salt content in southern and western Afghanistan. The hamuns are seasonally filled with water and become shallow lakes. The Hamun-i Sabari in Nimruz Province extends into Iran, and the Hamun-i Lora in Kandahar Province extends across the border into Baluchistan Province of Pakistan. The **God-i Zirreh**, another large hamun in Nimruz Province, is located near the Pakistani border.

HANAFI SCHOOL. *See* **ISLAM.**

HAQANI, MAULAWI JALALUDDIN (JALAL AL-DIN HAQQANI). Deputy chief of **Hizb-i Islami** who joined **Muhammad Yunus Khales** after the break with **Hekmatyar**'s faction in 1979. Born in 1930, a Jadran (Zadran) from Paktia Province, he was educated at a private *madrasa* and finished his studies at Peshawar. He became a major commander who had the support of his own Jadran tribe and in 1979 held large areas of Urgun in Paktia Province under his administration. He and his brothers Abdul Haq and Abdul Qadir were major leaders in the Jalalabad *Shura* that ruled Nangarhar Province until the capture of Jalalabad by the *Taliban* and then joined the *Taliban*.

HARAKAT-I INQILAB-I ISLAMI. The Islamic Revolutionary Movement, *Harakat*, is one of the earliest *mujahedin* movements, which arose from the merger of Islamist factions of the 1960s, represented in the *Jam'iat*, *Hizb-i Islami*, and others. It was headed by **Maulawi Muhammad Nabi Muhammadi**. In the early 1980s it was the largest *mujahedin* movement but lost some of its influence when the Islamists under **Rabbani** and **Hekmatyar** seceded and formed their own parties. *Harakat* is based on a network of clergy and *madrasa* students with some Pashtun tribal support in the south. The movement is traditional in outlook and was among the moderate forces represented in the **Mahaz** of **Gailani** and **Jabha** of **Mujaddidi;** but in March 1995 Muhammadi joined the radical Islamist *Taliban*, many of whom were his students. *See also* MUHAMMADI, MAULAWI MUHAMMAD NABI.

HARAKAT-I ISLAMI. A Shi'a *mujahedin* group headed by **Ayatollah Muhammad Asef Muhsini** which is not a member of the Shi'a Unity Party, *Hizb-i Wahdat*. It allied itself with the Kabul government of **Rabbani** and was represented in **Hekmatyar**'s cabinet by Sayyid Husain Anwari who held the portfolio of minister of works and social affairs. For further details *see* MUHSINI, AYATOLLAH MUHAMMAD ASEF.

HARI RUD (37-24' N, 60-38' E). A river in western Afghanistan that is formed by the confluence of the Sar-i Jangal and Lal Streams. It runs in a westerly direction past the city of Herat and then turns north, forming the boundary between Iran and Afghanistan, and crosses into Turkmenistan at Zulfiqar and dissipates in the desert.

HARUT RUD (31-35' N, 61-18' E). A river, also called Adraskan in its northern portion, which rises southeast of Herat and runs in a southwestern direction, eventually turning south and running into the Hamun-i Sabari.

HASHIM KHAN, MUHAMMAD. Prime minister of Afghanistan from 1929 to 1946 and de facto regent of **Zahir Shah**. Born in 1886, the son of Sardar Yusuf Khan (and half-uncle of ex-King Zahir), he was described as "austere and tough in his dealings with the people." He underwent military training and became commander of Amir Habibullah's body guard. He served as governor of the Eastern Province and officiated as minister of war in 1922. He served as minister in Moscow, 1924–26 and there acquired a considerable dislike of the Soviet government. He took a fatherly attitude to the young king and was the de facto ruler during his tenure. He was never married and seemed to have groomed his nephews **Muhammad Daud** and **Muhammad Na'im** as his successors. He died on October 26, 1953.

HASHT-NAFARI. A system of recruitment imposed on the frontier tribes by which they were to provide one able-bodied man out of eight (D., *hasht*—eight, *nafar*—persons). Amir **Abdul Rahman** introduced this system in 1896; similar to previous feudal levies, the notables and chiefs of tribes had to make the selection and provide the enlistee with all his needs. The tribes were willing to perform military service but wanted to do so only during emergencies; therefore there were occasional rebellions protesting the *hasht-nafari* recruitment during peacetime. Discontinued, and reintroduced in 1922 on advise of **Jamal Pasha**, the *hasht-nafari* system contributed to the growing opposition to King **Amanullah**.

HAYATULLAH KHAN. Born in 1888, the second son of Amir **Habibullah** Khan. He served as governor of Kataghan (now Kunduz Province) in 1905 and after the death of his father became minister of Education (1923) and minister of Justice (1925). Although a brother of

King Amanullah and a minister, he did not take a very active part in public life. Arrested in January 1929 by **Habibullah Kalakani** and accused of planning a coup, he was executed on October 17, 1929.

HAZARA. Hazaras are a people with predominantly Mongoloid features, mostly *imami* **Shi'a.** Small numbers are **Isma'ilis**, and those in the Darra-yi Hazara in Panjshir are Sunnis. Their number has been estimated at about one million, but Hazaras claim a population of about two million with up to two million more in neighboring countries. All the Hazaras were originally Sunni Muslims until the 16th century when they were converted to Shi'ism under the Safavid dynasty of Iran (1501–1786). Their heartland is the **Hazarajat**, but they are also found in the major cities of Afghanistan where they are employed as day laborers or seasonal workers. They speak a Farsi dialect, called Hazaragi, which also includes some Turkic and Mongol vocabulary (a dictionary of the Hazara dialect, *Qamus-i Lahja-yi Dari-yi Hazaragi*, by Ali Akbar Shahrestani, published in Kabul in 1982, lists some 1,200 words, which according to Dr. Ravan Farhadi are 90% of eastern Turkic origin, rather than Mongol).

The Hazara are no longer organized along tribal lines and are largely sedentary. They are divided into groups as follows:

Dai Kundi	Dai Zangi	Behsud	Dai Mirdad
Ghazni Hazara	Jaghuri	Polada	Oruzgani
Shaikh Ali	Walang (Olang)	Kala Nau Hazara	

Kala Nau Hazaras (formerly also Dai Zangi and Dai Kundi) are mostly Sunnis and inhabit an area of about 2,300 square miles. They claim descent from the hordes of Genghis Khan that settled in Kala Nau (now Badghis Province) and were moved into the area under the Persian ruler **Nadir Shah Afshar**. Their first chief was Mir Kush Sultan whose son, Aghai Sultan, was the founder of Kala Nau. The tribe was involved in the struggle for control of Herat Province, collaborating with the rulers of Herat. **Yar Muhammad**, Shah **Kamran**'s *wazir*, destroyed the power of the Hazaras in 1847. When in 1856 the Persians besieged and took Heart, they removed the tribe to **Khorasan**. Most of them returned 14 years later, but about 2,000 families remained in the Isfarayin area, south of Bujnurd in present Iran. They supported the governor of Herat against Amir **Dost Muhammad** and were in constant conflict with the **Jamshidis** and **Firuzkuhis**.

The Dai Mirdad Hazaras inhabit the area of Dara-i Suf (now Samangan Province) and at the turn of the century amounted to about 1,000 families. They resemble **Pashtuns** more than Hazaras and dress like **Tajiks** or **Uzbeks**.

The Dai Kundi and Dai Zangi are two different groups but have been closely connected in regards to location and administration.

The Ghazni Hazaras comprise the Jaghatu, Muhammad Khwaja, and the Chahar Dasta Hazaras.

Since the founding of modern Afghanistan in 1747, the Hazaras came increasingly under the under jurisdiction of the Kabul government, paying taxes but living under the independent or autonomous control of their Mirs (chiefs). **Yazdan-Bakhsh** was undisputed chief of the Hazaras in the mid-19th century but was eventually assassinated. Amir **Abdul Rahman** fought the Hazaras piecemeal, and his general Sardar **Abdul Quddus** completed the conquest of the Hazarajat in a war that lasted from 1890 to 1893. The war caused considerable destruction in the Hazarajat, annexation of territory by Pashtun tribes, and the flight and enslavement of many. Amir **Habibullah** proclaimed an amnesty and asked the Hazara refugees to return to Afghanistan; but many remained in India and a large community now exists in Quetta, Pakistan. King **Amanullah** abolished slavery and won Hazara support in his fight with **Habibullah Kalakani** in 1929.

From 1979 the Hazarajat has enjoyed virtual independence, at first under an elected **shura** (council) headed by **Sayyid Ali Beheshti**, who took over all the functions of the pre-war Afghan government. He levied taxes, recruited men into his *mujahedin* forces, and set up his own bureaucratic establishment. But his authority was soon challenged by a combined force of **Nasr** and **Pasdaran** Islamists who conquered most of the Hazarajat. In spring 1988, the Kabul government created the Hazara Province of Sar-i Pul by adding the districts of Shulgara, Charkent, and Keshendeh from Balkh Province, combining it with the districts of Sar-i-Pul, Balkhab, Sozma Kala, and Kohestanat from Jozjan Province. This appears to have been a political move to appeal to Hazara nationalism. In 1996 part of the Hazarajat is controlled by the **Hizb-i Wahdat**, which had allied itself with the opponents of Rabbani before the latter was expelled from Kabul by the *Taliban*.

HAZARAJAT (33-45' N, 66-0' E). The name of a mountainous area in central Afghanistan in which the **Hazara** people predominate. Its heartland includes Ghor, Oruzgan, and Bamian Provinces, and portions of the adjoining provinces.

The Hazarajat is dominated by the **Koh-i Baba** range and its branches whose peaks are at altitudes from 9,000 to 16,500 feet. The mountain ranges are crossed by passes at altitudes of 8,000 to some 10,000 feet. Few roads for motorized transportation exist, and the modern highway from Kabul to Herat skirts the Hazarajat. The central route from Kabul to Bamian and east to Chaghcharan can be taken with great difficulty by four-wheel drive vehicles during the few summer months. Because of the high altitude, the climate of the Hazarajat is characterized by long and cold winters, lasting from late September to April. Heavy snowfall from December until spring provides the reservoir that feeds the major rivers that take their origin in the Hazarajat and irrigate the rest of the country. July and August are hot and dry. The area is rich in mineral deposits, most of which are too inaccessible to be profitably mined. For people and history, *see* HAZARA.

HAZARA WARS. When in July 1880 Britain recognized Amir **Abdul Rahman** as "Amir of Kabul and its Dependencies," it was not certain what the "dependencies" would be. Britain had toyed with the idea of severing Herat and Kandahar from Kabul control, and Russia coveted Turkestan territory, finally annexing a section of northwestern Afghanistan in 1885 in the **Panjdeh Incident**. Afghanistan's boundaries were not clearly defined, and the "Iron Amir" found it necessary to extend his authority to every corner of his realm lest his powerful neighbors continue their forward policies. In a series of wars he eliminated rivals to his power and gained control of Kandahar, Herat, Afghan Turkistan, the **Hazarajat**, and **Kafiristan** (now **Nuristan**).

This extraordinary achievement of nation-building proved to be a calamity for the Hazara community. Amir Abdul Rahman stated his reasons for the war, saying

> the Hazara people had been for centuries past the terror of the rulers of Kabul, even the great Nadir who conquered Afghanistan, India, and Persia being unable to subdue the turbulent Hazaras;
> the Hazaras were always molesting travelers in the south, north, and western provinces of Afghanistan;
> they were always ready to join the first foreign aggressor who attacked Afghanistan. . . . (AR, I, 276)

And, indeed, the Hazaras shared the inclination for raiding with other ethnic communities. As a religious minority they were willing to collaborate with the enemies of the Kabul regime.

Initially, Amir Abdul Rahman embarked on a gradual process of reconquest. After three campaigns in 1881, 1882, and 1883 and attempts at peaceful penetration, the Shaikh Ali Hazaras northwest of Bamian were the first to be pacified in 1886. Shortly thereafter all Hazara tribes with the exception of those of Pas-i Koh in Oruzgan Province were forced to pay taxes on land and livestock. In 1890 Abdul Rahman appointed Sardar **Abdul Quddus** governor of Bamian and ordered him to win the submission of the Oruzgan Hazaras. The latter accepted a deal in which they were to retain their internal autonomy and pay no taxes for a number of years.

When a year later Abdul Quddus again entered Hazara territory with a 10,000–man force, he claimed to have met armed resistance and began to disarm Hazara communities and collect taxes from them. Thereupon the Sultan Muhammad Hazaras, headed by Mir Husain Beg, rose in rebellion and defeated the forces of Abdul Quddus as well as a relief force under Faiz Muhammad sent by the amir. Their success encouraged other Hazara sections to join the general revolt, and the amir realized that the situation required a large scale campaign to suppress the rebellion.

Amir Abdul Rahman felt that an all-out effort including psychological warfare was needed. The amir claimed that Iranian publications in the possession of Afghan **Shi'as** had insulted the **Sunni caliphs** as usurpers and urged the Shi'i community to rise against Sunni control. The amir's chief *mufti* (canon lawyer) issued a legal opinion, *fatwa*, declaring Shi'as infidels and proclaiming holy war on the Hazara. A council of Hazaras countered that instead of obeying a temporal ruler they relied on their spiritual ruler "the Master of the sword of Zulfikar" (Hazrat Ali, the Shi'a *imam* and fourth of the Sunni caliphs).

In addition to regular forces, tribal levies were called up with great success as there was considerable promise of booty. *Mullas* accompanied the troops to keep passions high and incite them to heroic feats of bravery. Pashtuns flocked to the colors in considerable numbers and according to a British observer "the Ghilzays...showed more zeal than the Durranis." In spite of the holy war *fatwa*, levies of Hazaras of the Dai Kundi, Behsud, and Jaghori sections were enlisted, but most of those who survived defected during the war.

In spring 1891 Amir Abdul Rahman ordered a concerted attack by Sardar Abdul Quddus from Bamian, Shir Muhammad from Kabul, and Brigadier Zabardast from Herat that led to the occupation of Oruzgan. Hazara chiefs were brought to Kabul in an attempt to win their submission. But in spring 1892 the Hazara chiefs Muhammad Azim and Muhammad Husain, supported by their chief *mujtahid* (legal expert) Kazi Asghar, turned against Amir Abdul Rahman. Rebellion rose with new fury, and it was only when concerteds attack from Turkestan, Kabul, Ghazni, Herat, and Kandahar was renewed that the Hazara uprising was quelled. It was not until September 1893 that all Hazara sections were subdued. The Amir had given permission that "everybody would be allowed to go and help in the punishment of the rebels," and punishment was indeed severe. Forts were demolished and governors, judges, and *muftis* were appointed in every district. About 16,000 **Durrani** and **Ahmadzai Ghilzai** tribesmen were ordered to settle in Oruzgan Province, and large numbers of Hazaras emigrated to Mashhad (Iran) and Quetta (India—now Pakistan) where they are still living today. In accordance with an old tradition, conquest by force ('anwatan) permitted the enslavement of prisoners, and thousands of Hazaras were taken to Kabul.

HAZRAT OF SHOR BAZAAR. A title given the head of the family of Sirhind spiritual leaders who adopted the family name of **Mujaddidi**. They were among the most important and influential religious leaders in Afghanistan in the years following King **Amanullah**'s accession. Their residence was in the area of Shor Bazaar in Kabul, hence the head's designation "Excellency" (*Hazrat*) of Shor Bazaar. For members of the family, *see* MUJADDIDI.

HEKMATYAR, GULBUDDIN. Amir (chief) of the *Hizb-i Islami-yi Afghanistan* (Islamic Party of Afghanistan), one of the seven *mujahedin* groups formed in Peshawar. His party is radical Islamist and fights for the establishment of an Islamic republic, to be governed according to its interpretation of Islamic law. Born in 1947 in Imam Sahib, Kunduz, a **Ghilzai Pashtun**, Hekmatyar attended the faculty of engineering at **Kabul University** for two years and became involved in campus politics. He became a member of the "Muslim Youth" movement in 1970 and was elected to its executive council (*Shura*). He was imprisoned in Dehmazang jail in Kabul, 1972-73 and, after the Daud coup of 1973, fled to Pakistan. In 1975 he became leader of the

Hizb-i Islami and began armed attacks from bases in Pakistan with clandestine support from the Bhutto government. Isolated raids developed into modern guerrilla warfare after the **Saur Revolt** of April 1978. The party adopted from the **Muslim Brotherhood** such features as centralized command structure, secrecy of membership, organization in cells, infiltration of government and social institutions, and the concept of the party as an Islamist "vanguard" in Afghan society.

Being Islamist rather than nationalist, the party enjoyed considerable support from like-minded groups in Pakistan and the Gulf. His party received most of its armed support from the West and Gulf sources and apparently was able to hoard a vast amount of weapons that served him well in the subsequent battle for Kabul. He surprised friends and foes alike when he allied himself with General **Shahnawaz Tanai**, a radical *Khalqi*, in a coup against the Kabul government of Dr. **Najibullah**. After the downfall of the Marxist regime, many of the *Khalqi* military officers joined Hekmatyar's forces, as did General **Dostum**, a former *Parchami*, who controls large portions of northern Afghanistan. The Hizb-i Islami of Gulbuddin Hekmatyar and the **Jam'iat-i Islami** of **Burhanuddin Rabbani** were the major protagonists in the war for the conquest of Kabul until a new force, the *Taliban*, expelled Hekmatyar from his headquarters in Charasia and portions of Kabul. Hekmatyar fled to Sarobi where his party had another base. In May 1996 he concluded an alliance with Rabbani and assumed the position of prime minister in Kabul. One of his first measures was to prohibit the broadcast of music from Kabul Radio and television and ordered women to wear "Islamic" dress. He and Rabbani were expelled from Kabul by the *Taliban. See also* ISLAMIST MOVEMENT.

HELMAND (31-0' N, 64-0' E). A province in southwestern Afghanistan with a population of about 570,000 and an area of 23,058 square miles — the largest of Afghan provinces. The capital of the province (Girishk until 1957) is Lashkargah (Bost) with about 21,600 inhabitants. The population is largely **Pashtun** with some **Hazara** in the north and **Baluch** in the south. The economy of the province is based primarily on agriculture: barley, cotton, wheat, and a great variety of fruit. Livestock raised include sheep, goats, cattle, camels, horses, and donkeys. The province is irrigated by the Helmand River, which also provides hydroelectric power. The river rises near the Unai Pass and with its five tributaries — the Kaj Rud, Tirin, Arghandab, Tarnak, and Arghastan — drains all of southwestern Afghanistan. After running in a southwestern direction as far as Khwaja Ali, the Helmand runs due west to Band-i-Kamal Khan and then north to the Lash Juwain hamuns. The river formed part of the border with Iran, and when it changed channels the **Goldsmid** boundary arbitration was again called into question. *See also* LASHKARGAH and HELMAND VALLEY AUTHORITY.

HELMAND VALLEY AUTHORITY. An Afghan organization that was created to oversee an irrigation and electrification project in the Helmand Valley. It was fashioned after the American Tennessee Valley Authority to implement work in conjunction with the Morrison-Knudsen Afghanistan construction company of Boise, Idaho. From 1946 to 1959 the American firm built the Arghandab and Kajakai Dams and a network of canals to bring additional land in the Helmand Valley under cultivation. The project soon drained the hard currency resources of the country to the extent that the Afghan government was forced to apply for loans to the U.S. Import-Export Bank (21 million in 1951 and 18 million in 1953) and for Point Four assistance (an assistance program which pre-dates USAID). When the project was finished in 1959 some 100 million dollars (40% of the state budget) had been expended for rather modest gains. The failure of the Afghan government to conduct adequate soil studies was responsible for waterlogging in some areas and excessive salination in others. Cultural factors, such as the inclinations and interests of the people in the area, were ignored and many of the 1,300 nomad and peasant families settled in the Nad-i-Ali area eventually left their lands. When high expectations turned into disappointment, American prestige suffered. Remedial measures where eventually taken with American financial support.

HENTIG-NIEDERMAYER EXPEDITION. An expedition conceived in August 1914 by the German general staff for the purpose of "revolutionizing India, inducing Afghanistan to attack India, and securing Iran as a bridge from the Ottoman empire to Afghanistan." The leading members were Werner Otto von Hentig, a young German diplomat who had served in Iran, and **Oskar von Niedermayer**, a captain in the German army. They were accompanied by **Kazim Bey,** a Turkish officer, **Maulawi Barakatullah** and **Mahendra Pratap**, two Indian revolutionaries, and a number of **Afridi** Pashtuns who had been taken from a prisoner of war camp. Hentig carried an unsigned letter purported to be from the German Kaiser and a message from von Bethmann-Hollweg, the chancellor, for Amir **Habibullah**. He was to establish diplomatic relations and conclude a treaty of friendship or, if possible, an alliance, with Afghanistan. Niedermayer was to discuss matters of a military nature, and the Indians were to appeal to Amir Habibullah for support in the fight against the British in India. Kazim Bey was to convey special messages from the sultan-caliph and the leaders of the Ottoman war government. The expedition crossed Iran and entered Afghanistan in August 1915 and five weeks later reached Kabul.

Amir Habibullah was well aware of the power of Britain and, although his heart and ultimate loyalty was with the Ottoman sultan-caliph, he was not willing to rush into a risky adventure. He initialed the draft of a treaty which was so extravagant in its demands, that only a victorious Germany could have provided the financial and military support requested. The expedition disbanded in May 1916, and Hentig returned to Germany by way of the **Wakhan** Corridor to China and from there to the United States. Niedermayer went through Russian Central Asia to Iran and the Ottoman Empire. The expedition was the first diplomatic contact with Germany and marked the beginning of the end of the British monopoly over the conduct of Afghan foreign relations. In 1970, von Hentig visited Afghanistan as guest of **Zahir Shah**. Hentig published a book, entitled *Mein Leben eine Dienstreise*. *See also* NIEDERMAYER.

HERAT (34-20'N, 62-12'E). Herat is a province in northwestern Afghanistan with an area of 16,107 square miles and a population of about 685,000 in 1979. The capital of the province is the city of Herat, with about 140,000 inhabitants the third largest city in Afghanistan.

The economy of Herat is based primarily on agriculture, the planting of cotton, rice, and wheat. Pistachios are an important item of export. Also important is livestock breeding, including the Qaraqul sheep. Local industries produce cement, edible oil, and textiles. Home industries produce carpets, silk materials, pustins (fur jackets and coats), and products of camel hair.

The province is drained by the Murghab, Harirud, Farah Rud, and Adraskan Rivers, permitting extensive irrigation. **Kariz**, subterranean water channels, are also widely used to bring water from the foothills to villages and fields.

The city of Herat, located at an altitude of 2,600 feet, is the major commercial center of western Afghanistan. The old town was surrounded by a wall built in 1885 and mostly destroyed in the 1950s.

It is crossed by two streets that divide the old town into four districts, named the Bazar-i Kushk in the east, the Bazar-i Iraq in the west, the Bazar-i Malik in the north, and the Bazar-i Kandahar in the south. The new town, *shahr-i nau*, was largely constructed in the period after World War II and has been considerably expanded since.

Herat is of great strategic importance and has therefore been the site of fortified towns since antiquity. It is an ancient city, first mentioned in the *Avesta* (the holy book of Zoroastrianism) as *Hairava*, which Afghan historians conjecture to be derived from Aria, or Ariana, the first "Afghan" kingdom flourishing about 1,500 B.C. The town was on the route of the Achaemenid armies of Cyrus and Darius and two centuries later of Alexander the Great, who in 330 B.C. built *Alexandria Ariorum* on the site of Herat. In the 11th century Herat became a famous urban center in Islamic **Khorasan**, where scholars like **Khwaja Abdullah Ansari** and others flourished. The city had been destroyed numerous times—by Turkomans in the 12th century and a century later by the hordes of Genghis Khan, when only a handful of the population survived a general massacre. In the 14th century **Timur-i Lang**'s forces devastated the city. Rebuilt by Timur's son Shah Rukh the city experienced a period of glory. Again in the early 16th century, **Sultan Husain Mirza Baiqara** made Herat "the most renowned center of literature, culture, and art in all Central and Western Asia." The city and its vicinity has numerous archaeological remains. The principal buildings are the Jum'a Masjid, built under the **Ghorids** in about 1200 A.D., which measured 465 feet in length by 275 feet width and had 408 cupolas, 130 windows, 444 pillars, 1300 arches, and six entrances. Minarets of the Timurid theological colleges, the Mosalla, and the shrine of the Sufi poet Abdullah Ansari are located near the city. The tomb of Amir **Dost Muhammad** is located nearby. A building of more recent date is the Arg-i Nau, the citadel.

In 1509 the city came under Safavid rule until the **Abdalis** took control of the city around 1715. In 1730 it was captured by **Nadir Shah Afshar** and in 1750 by **Ahmad Shah Durrani**. Next Herat was ruled by various princes whose internecine fighting invited Persian attack. In December 1837, the Safavid ruler, Muhammad Shah, besieged the city, but the endurance of the Heratis and British intervention in the Persian Gulf forced him to give up after a nine-month long effort. Amir **Abdul Rahman** ended Herat's semi-independence. About 70 years ago the city was still confined to the walled town and had about 20,000 inhabitants. In 1925 **King Amanullah** began the construction of the new town, *shahr-i nau*, which quickly grew in population to about 73,000 by 1970 and 140,000 ten years later. The present war in Afghanistan has lead to considerable destruction, which began with a popular revolt against the Kabul government in March 1979. The Kabul government regained the city, but the *mujahedin* controlled much of the countryside. In April 1988, some 3,000 government forces defected to the *mujahedin* when they were offered an amnesty. After the fall of the **Najibullah** government, **Isma'il Khan** became the paramount chief of Herat Province until dislodged in September 1995 by the newly emerging forces of the *Taliban*.

HERAT, SIEGE OF. Persia, encouraged by Russia, laid siege to Herat for three years (1835–38) but was unable to capture the city. A British officer, **Eldred Pottinger**, claimed an important role in the defense of the city. When Britain could not induce the Shah to desist, Indian troops landed on June 19, 1838 on the island of Kharak in the Persian Gulf. It was only then that Persia lifted the siege and withdrew in September 1838.

HERAT UPRISING. On March 21, 1979, demonstrators against the Marxist regime seized control of the city and liberated political prisoners. They proceeded to attack government officials and killed many of the Soviet advisers and their families, carrying the heads of some through the city on pikes. When the Marxist government sent troops to quell the uprising, the entire Afghan 17th Division mutinied, and a powerful resistance organization was born, headed by Captain **Isma'il Khan**. The Kabul government brought in air strikes that eventually broke the resistance at the cost of some 5000 deaths.

HEZB. *See* **HIZB.**

HIJRAT MOVEMENT. "Emigration Movement," also called *Khilafat* movement (of 1920), which originated in the **North-West Frontier Province** of India in protest of the destruction of the Ottoman Empire by Britain and her allies. Indian Muslims recognized the Ottoman claims to the caliphate and spiritual leadership of the (Sunni) Islamic world. Muhammad Ali and other leaders of the movement proclaimed it the "Islamic duty" of Indian Muslims "to abandon a country ruled by a sacrilegious government," the *dar al-harb* (Abode of War), and migrate to the *dar al-salam* (Abode of Peace—Islamic state). Encouraged by King **Amanullah**, who had just won the independence of his country, some 18,000 Muslims came to Afghanistan. The Afghan king hoped to attract professional and skilled manpower, but most of the immigrants (*muhajerun*) were unskilled and poor and could not adapt to the new environment. Some Pashtuns from Peshawar were settled in the area of Kunduz and some Sindhis in the area of Balkh, and a few went on to the Soviet Union and Europe, but most of the *muhajerun* eventually returned to India.

HINDKI (HINDUS). The name of Hindus living in Afghanistan who speak a Panjabi dialect (except for those in Kandahar who speak Sindhi and Riasti) and number about 15,000. They are scattered all over Afghanistan, but are primarily in Kabul, Kandahar, Kunduz, Nangarhar, and Paktia Provinces, where they are occupied in trade. They once transacted most of the banking business in the country. As non-Muslims they were at times subjected to the *jizya*, poll tax, and were restricted in their religious observances to the privacy of their homes. Since the days of Amir **Habibullah**, the Hindkis have gradually gained full citizen status. One Hindki, **Naranjan Das**, received the title of civil colonel in 1906 and was appointed chief revenue officer and finally civil brigadier under King **Amanullah**. This gained the Afghan ruler a positive image in India. There are also about 7,000 **Sikhs** in Afghanistan, all of them Panjabi-speakers. Most Hindkis fled as a result of the civil war.

HINDU KUSH. The major mountain massif that originates in the southwestern corner of the Pamirs and with its extension, the **Koh-i Baba**, runs the entire length of central Afghanistan, constituting a formidable barrier to north-south communication. Its general elevation is between 14,500 and 17,000 feet, with numerous peaks over 20,000 feet high. Several passes leading across the massif lie at altitudes above 12,000 feet.

The name Hindu Kush is of uncertain origin and is not used generally by Afghans, who have local names for the range in their area. In the West the name has been interpreted as "Killer of Hindus"; but the name may be derived, according to some sources, from Hindu Kuh, marking the most northern extent of pre-Muslim Hindu control. The range is divided into three major sections: the eastern from the Pamirs to the Dorah Pass, the central from the Dorah to the Khawak passes, and the western from the Khawak Pass to the termination of the range near the Shibar Pass.

During the winter months, the mountain range seals off northern Afghanistan from the rest of the country, and the rugged terrain has allowed small, non-martial populations to survive in remote, economically marginal valleys. Poor lines of communication fostered a measure of autonomy and extensive linguistic and cultural diversity. The construction of the **Salang** Tunnel and an all-weather road in 1964 has contributed to the strengthening of central control over the northern part of the state. In the 1980s the Salang Highway became an important artery for supplying the Kabul government with Soviet materiel and therefore was a frequent object of attacks by *mujahedin* forces, especially those of Commander **Mas'ud**.

HISTORICAL SOCIETY OF AFGHANISTAN (ANJOMAN-I TARIKH-I AFGHANISTAN). Founded in 1941 at the suggestion of **Zahir Shah** for the purpose of research and study of Afghanistan's historical heritage. It was part of the Afghan Literary Society since 1933 and under the administrative control of the department of press and later the ministry of education and developed into a research and translation institute. It produced numerous publications, including the journals *Aryana* (1942) and *Afghanistan* (1945). Ahmad Ali Kohzad held the position of president of the Historical Society for many years. During the 1980s it was part of the Afghan Academy of Sciences. *See* AFGHAN ACADEMY.

HIZB. The word *hizb* (from Arabic) means "party" and is used in the name of various parties and movements, as for example *Hizb-i Demukrat-i Khalq-i Afghanistan,* People's Democratic Party of Afghanistan (PDPA). For parties see individual entries.

HIZB-I INQILAB-I MILLI. Party of President Daud; *see* NATIONAL REVOLUTIONARY PARTY.

HIZB-I ISLAMI (HEKMATYAR). The larger of two Islamist *mujahedin* movements with the same name, headed by Gulbuddin Hekmatyar. It has its origin in the "Muslim Youth" movement of the 1960s (*see* ISLAMIST MOVEMENT) that opposed the secularization of Afghan society and the emergence of Marxist groups on the campus of **Kabul University**. The movement was forced underground during the republican government of President **Muhammad Daud** (r. 1973–78). Hekmatyar fled to Pakistan and from there carried out raids into

Afghanistan. Isolated raids developed into modern guerrilla warfare after the **Saur Revolt** in April 1978. The party adopted from the **Muslim Brotherhood** (or Leninist model?) such features as centralized command structure, secrecy of membership, organization in cells, infiltration of government and social institutions, and the concept of the party as an Islamist "vanguard" in Afghan society.

The party is said to have three degrees of membership: those who were members before 1975; those who joined between 1975 and 1978; and those who joined after the Marxist coup. Only those in the first category are said to have the right to vote. Three-fourths of the members are **Pashtuns**, and **Hekmatyar**'s "Army of Sacrifice" was recruited from schools established by *Hizb-i Islami.*

Being Islamist rather than nationalist, the party enjoyed considerable support from the Pakistan government and from like-minded groups in Pakistan and the Gulf. Specifics regarding the type of government desired by the Hizb are not clear. Hekmatyar has at times rejected such traditional Afghan bodies as the *Loya Jirga* (national council), because its decisions may be subject to manipulation by his opponents. He accepts a *shura*, council of Islamic legal experts (*ahl-i hal wa-aqd*), that is to advise the *amir*, leader of the community of Muslims (*umma*). The amir is elected by a council (*Shura*) which delegates considerable powers to its leader. How the *Shura* is to be chosen is not clear. The people swear *bay'a*, loyalty, to the chosen amir and, by definition, are bound in obedience to him. The incumbent may nominate his successor.

The Hizb favors the establishment of an Islamic state in which the *Shari'a* (**Islamic law**) prevails and Islamic obligations are enforced. The participation of women in public life is to be restricted; the consumption of alcohol prohibited; and innovations adopted from the West eliminated. In May 1996 Hekmatyar made peace with the Kabul government of Rabbani and assumed the position of prime minister. But in September the Kabul government was ousted by the *Taliban.*

HIZB-I ISLAMI (KHALES). An Islamist party, headed by the *mujahedin* leader **Yunus Khales**, that split from the more radical group headed by **Gulbuddin Hekmatyar** in 1979. It is represented primarily in Pashtun regions, especially in Nangarhar, Kabul (Commander **Abdul Haq**), and Paktia (Commander **Jalaluddin Haqani**) provinces. His group enjoys some tribal support, especially among Khales' own **Khugiani** and the **Jadran** tribes.

Ideologically, the party of Khales differs little from the other Islamist groups (*see* HIZB), but, unlike Hekmatyar's group, favors cooperation with all *mujahedin* parties. After the fall of the Marxist regime in April 1992, Khales and his commanders became the dominant power in a **Shura** which ruled Jalalabad and most of Nangarhar Province, until Jalalabad fell to the *Taliban* in September 1996. *See also* ISLAMIST MOVEMENT.

HIZB-I WAHDAT. A coalition of eight Hazara **Shi'a** parties led by **Abdul Ali Mazari** and centered in the area of Bamian and Wardak. It forged an alliance with **Hekmatyar**'s *Hizb-i Islami* in August 1993 and controlled parts of Kabul west of the **Darulaman** road and south of Sarak-i Say-i Aqrab, as well as parts of **Kabul University** and all of the **Kabul Polytechnic** compound. Mazari prevailed in a power struggle with **Ustad Muhammad Akbari,** who was head of the Wahdat's political committee (Akbari was forced to flee and joined the forces of **Rabbani**.). In January 1995 *Hizb-i Wahdat* was fighting for turf with the Shi'a *Harakat-i Islami* of **Ayatollah Muhsini**. When Hekmatyar's forces were driven from Kabul in February 1995, *Jam'iat* captured the territory of the weakened *Wahdat,* and Mazari joined, or surrendered, to the *Taliban* and was killed while in captivity on March 13, 1995. He is succeeded by **Abdul Karim Khalili** who allied himself with Rabbani and Dostum against the *Taliban*.

HIZBULLAH (HIZB ALLAH). The "Party of Allah," headed by one Shaikh Ali Wusuki, is a small **Shi'a** group of *mujahedin* in Herat and a few scattered areas with ties to the Iranian Pasdaran (Guardians of the Revolution). In 1990 the Kabul government gave permission for the formation of political parties, one of which carries the name Hizbullah. It is headed by Shaikh Yusufi of Ghazni, but no details are known regarding the program or members of this Shi'a group.

HOTAKIS. Or **OHTAKS.** A main division of the **Ghilzai** tribe located in the Kushrud and Tarnak Valleys. The Hotakis numbered about 7,000 families at the turn of the century.

The Hotaki Ghilzais made their mark in Afghan history when they liberated Kandahar from Persian control and then proceeded to invade Iran, thus ending the reign of the Safavid dynasty (*see* GHILZAI). Hotaki rulers include the following:

Mir Wais Khan	in Kandahar	1709-15
Mir Abdul Aziz	in Kandahar	1715-16
Mir Mahmud	in Persia	1716-25
Mir Ashram	in Persia	1725-30
Mir Husain	in Kandahar	1730-38

HUDUD AL-'ALAM. Title of a 10th century anonymous Persian geography that is one of the first sources mentioning the name Afghanistan.

HUMAIRA, QUEEN. Wife of ex-King Muhammad Zahir and daughter of Ahmad Shah by his first wife Zarin. She encouraged the emancipation of women and accompanied the king on many trips abroad. She now lives in Italy with her husband.

HUSAIN KHAN. Ruler of Maimana. *See* MAIMANA.

I

IBN SINA, ABU ALI (AVICENNA). The great philosopher-physician, "Prince of Physicians," known as Avicenna in the West, was born near Bukhara (now Uzbekistan) in 980 A.D. and died in Hamadan (or Isfahan?), Iran in 1037. He wrote in Arabic and Persian and continued the traditions of Aristotle in philosophy and Hippocrates and Galen in medicine and was dominant in both fields. His *Kitab al-Qanun fi Tibb*, Book of Medicine, and *Kitab al-Shifa*, Book of Healing, were valued in Europe until the 17th century. Afghans claim him as a native son because his father was a native of Balkh. A hospital and a high school in Kabul are named after him.

IBRAHIM BEG. An **Uzbek Basmachi** leader who fought the Bolshevik government in Central Asia, at times using Afghan territory as a safe haven. He visited Kabul in 1926 and was entertained as a state guest by King **Amanullah**, who was not averse to the idea of becoming ruler of a Central Asian confederation of Muslim states. In May 1929, Ibrahim Beg supported **Habibullah Kalakani** and fought King Amanullah's general, **Ghulam Nabi Charkhi**, taking a prominent part in the capture of Mazar-i Sharif. In 1930, after repeated representations by the Soviet Union, the government of **Nadir Shah** took steps to prevent Ibrahim Beg from raiding across the border, with the consequence that he started raiding in Afghanistan as well. He was finally driven from Afghan territory and captured by Soviet troops. The battles between Afghan troops and Ibrahim Beg's supporters are called by Afghans *jang-i Laqay* (War of the Laqai, an Uzbek tribe.). He was executed in April 1931. *See also* BASMACHIS.

IKHWAN AL-MUSLIMIN. *See* **MUSLIM BROTHERHOOD.**

IMAMI SHI'AS. *See* **SHI'ISM** and **ITHNA ASHARIYA.**

INAYATULLAH KHAN. *See* **ENAYATULLAH.**

INTER-SERVICES INTELLIGENCE (ISI). A Pakistani military intelligence organization, headed by General **Abdul Rahman Akhtar** from 1979 to 1987, and subsequently by General Hamid Gul, that was heavily involved in the war against Soviet/Kabul government forces in Afghanistan. Brigadier Muhammad Yousaf, head of the Afghan Bureau of the ISI, claims the credit for coordinating the logistics, recruitment, training, assignment of missions, including raids into the Soviet Union. The ISI distributed the weapons and funds provided by friendly countries, while the government of Pakistan maintained an increasingly "implausible deniability" of involvement in the war. Muhammad Yousaf detailed ISI activities in a book entitled *The Bear Trap: Afghanistan's Untold Story,* edited by the military historian Mark Adkin.

ISHAQ KHAN, MUHAMMAD. *See* **MUHAMMAD ISHAQ.**

ISHAQZAI. A section of the Durrani tribe. The majority of the Ishaqzai inhabit the Pusht-i Rud area, where they amounted to about 7,000 families at the turn of the century. Smaller groups of Ishaqzai are established near Sar-i Pol in Jozjan Province.

ISLAH (RECONSTRUCTION). A national Dari newspaper, first published in 1923 under the editorship of Muhammad Bashir in Khanabad, Badakhshan, when **Nadir** Khan, the subsequent king, visited the province. In 1929 Nadir Khan founded another Dari/Pashtu newspaper with this name as part of his campaign against **Habibullah Kalakani**. It continued as a daily Kabul newspaper until 1973, when Sardar **Muhammad Daud** took power and proclaimed the republic. Among the first editors were **Burhanuddin Kushkaki, Abdul Rahman Pazhwak**, and **Qiamuddin Khadem**.

ISLAM. A monotheistic religion which continues the prophetic Judeo-Christian tradition and recognizes Muhammad as the last of the prophets. It is the religion of virtually all Afghans. The word is Arabic and means submission, the obligation to "submit" to the commands of Allah, the omniscient and omnipotent God. Islam can be summarized under a code of rituals called the "Five Pillars of Islam," as follows:

1. *Shahadat*, the profession of faith. A Muslim says: "I testify that there is no god but Allah and I testify that Muhammad is the Messenger of Allah." Anyone who sincerely testifies to that fact is a Muslim.

2. *Salat*, prayer, which is to be performed five times a day, facing the *qibla*, prayer direction, the location of the *Ka'ba*, a cube-like building in Mecca (built by Abraham, according to the Qor'an). Prayers include recitation of the Arabic text accompanied by rhythmical bowings, *rak'ah*, and can be performed in public or private. A ritual washing, *wudhu*, is required before prayer. If there is a congregation, one person is the leader, *imam*, and the rest perform their prayers in unison. The muezzin, *mu'adhdhin*, sounds the *azan*, call to prayer, often from top of a minaret. The Friday sermon, *khutbah*, may have political significance because the name of the ruler is invoked, indicating the political loyalty of the congregation.

3. *Zakat*, almsgiving, is the requirement to give either a percentage of one's wealth or of one's yearly income to the poor. This obligation is not uniformly enforced in the Islamic world.

4. *Sawm*, fasting (ruza in Dari), is enjoined during the Muslim month of Ramazan (Ramadhan), "the month during which the Koran was sent down." From sunrise to sundown the believer is to abstain from food or drink, which poses considerable hardship when Ramazan occurs during the long, hot, summer months. Children, the ill, pregnant mothers, travelers, and soldiers in war are exempt, but those prevented must make up this obligation at a later time.

5. *Hajj*, pilgrimage, is a legal obligation of every adult Muslim of either sex to travel at least once in a lifetime to Mecca, provided he/she is economically able to do so. Thousands of Afghans now travel yearly

in special flights to Saudi Arabia, and one who has performed pilgrimage carries the honorific title of "hajji."

Minor differences exist in the performance of these obligations within the four orthodox Sunni schools. In Afghanistan the Hanifi school, named after **Abu Hanifa** (d. 767) is the prevalent one; it is the most liberal in the interpretation of Islamic law, *Shari'a*.

In addition to acts of devotion and rituals (*ibadat*), Islam also involves a creed of beliefs (*iman*): Muslims believe in one God, Allah, who is the Creator, Supreme Power, Judge, and Avenger but is also the Compassionate and Merciful One. Angels are Allah's messengers and, like humans, his creatures and servants. They record men's actions and bear witness against them on the Day of Judgment. The Angel Gabriel is God's chief messenger. There are also *jinn*, spirits, who are good or evil like men. The fallen or evil jinn are called *shaitans*, devils, whose leader is the *Shaitan* or *Iblis* (Satan). He is given "authority over those who should be seduced by him." God sends his prophets to bring his message. The major messengers include Adam, Noah, Abraham, Moses, and Jesus but Muhammad is the last of the prophets, and the Koran is the last message, superseding the Torah of Moses, the Zabur (Psalms) of David, and the Injil (Gospel) of Jesus. Muslims believe in a Day of Judgment, when the good will enter Paradise, and the evil will be condemned to eternal hellfire. Personal responsibility before God is important in Islam, and there is no belief in atonement.

Jihad, "Striving in the Way of God," is not one of the Five Pillars of Islam. Jihad is a war in defense of Islam, securing immediate salvation and heaven for the fallen martyr; but jihad is any effort in a good cause. *See also* SHI'ISM.

ISLAMIC ALLIANCE FOR THE LIBERATION OF AFGHANISTAN. A loose coalition founded on January 27, 1980 by five *mujahedin* groups with headquarters in Pakistan. It was headed by **Abdul Rasul Sayyaf**, who at that time did not have a force of his own. The sixth group, **Hekmatyar**'s *Hizb-i Islami*, did not participate because it was not given preeminent status. The Alliance was formed for the purpose of gaining recognition as a government in exile and to secure support from the Islamic Foreign Ministers Conference, held in Islamabad in May 1980. The Alliance disintegrated in December of the same year. In early 1981, the Pakistan government announced that it would henceforth recognize only six groups (later seven) and that all refugees in the country must register as members of one of these groups.

Refugee aid as well as *mujahedin* support would be channeled through these groups. Thus in 1985 the Alliance reconstituted itself under the label of *Islamic Unity of Afghan Mujahedin* with the moderates in the "Unity of Three" (**Gailani, Mujaddidi,** and **Muhammadi**) and the radicals organized in the "Unity of Seven" of whom only four (**Rabbani,** Hekmatyar, Sayyaf, and **Khales**) represented viable groups. While the moderates were reasonably united, the radicals were constantly at odds, especially the groups headed by Rabbani and Hekmatyar. In May 1983, the Alliance elected Sayyaf chairman for a term of two years, but when, in 1985, he attempted to remain in this position the Alliance members objected. Subsequently a chairman of the Alliance served on a rotating basis for three months. There was otherwise little coordination between the groups.

Upon becoming spokesman in February 1988, Pir Sayyid Ahmad Gailani announced the formation of an Afghan Interim Government (AIG). Eng. **Ahmad Shah,** an American-educated Afghan and member of Sayyaf's party, was chosen as prime minister, and the cabinet included the following:

> Dr. Zabihullah Mujaddidi (Jabha)   deputy prime minister
> Maulawi Muhammad Shah Fazli (Harakat) deputy prime minister
> Haji Din Muhammad (Hizb Khales) Defense
> Sayyid Nurullah Ahmad (Jam'iat) Interior
> Qazi Najibullah (Hizb Hekmatyar) Foreign Affairs
> Muhammad Ismail Siddiqi (Harakat) Finance
> Faruq Azam (Mahaz) Rehabilitation and Reconstruction
> Maulana Mir Hamza (Jam'iat) Education
> Mutiullah Muti (Hizb Khales) Agriculture and Livestock
> Din Muhammad Gran (Mahaz) Scientific Research
> Ali Ansari (Hizb Hekmatyar) Justice
> Yasser (Ittihad Sayyaf) Publicity and Islamic Guidance
> Abdul Aziz Faruq (independent) Planning
> Wasiq Wayezzada (Jabha) Health

Elections were to be held among the *mujahedin* and refugees within three months. The government was short-lived: it did not hold a valid election as planned, because of disagreement regarding representation in a 520 man assembly (*Shura*). Each of the seven groups was to delegate sixty members. Twenty "good Muslims" (Afghans under Marxist control, but not supporters of the regime) from Kabul were to be included, and sixty seats were allocated to the **Shi'a** groups in Iran. The Shi'a groups wanted 120 seats and refused to participate; Sebghatullah Mujaddidi's offer of 100 seats and seven of 28 ministerial positions was not acceptable to some Peshawar groups.

On February 20, 1989, the *Shura* (at Madinat-ul Hajjaj, a town near Rawalpindi) elected an Afghan Interim Government (AIG), naming Sibghatullah Mujaddidi president and Abdul Rasul Sayyaf prime minister. The first meeting of the new cabinet was held on March 10, 1989 in the village of Shiwa in Khost Province of south-eastern Afghanistan. Leaders of the alliance held major portfolios:

Maulawi Muhammad Nabi Muhammadi	Defense
Muhammad Shah Fazli (Harakat)	Scientific research
Maulawi Islamuddin (Harakat)	Agriculture
Gulbuddin Hekmatyar	Foreign Affairs
Ali Ansari (Hizb Hekmatyar)	Frontier Affairs
Qazi Najibullah (Hizb Hekmatyar)	Justice
Yunus Khales	Interior
Haji Dean Muhammad (Hizb Khales)	National Security
Maulawi Abdul Razzaq (Hizb Khales)	Religious Affairs
Burhanuddin Rabbani	Reconstruction
Najibullah Lafra'i (Jam'iat)	Islamic Guidance
Ishan Jan (Jam'iat)	Mining and Industries
Ahmad Shah (Ittihad)	Communications
Sayyid Nadir Khurram (Jabha)	Health

Additional portfolios were reserved for Iran-based *mujahedin* and representatives from Kabul. In May 1989, Pir Sayyid Ahmad Gailani challenged the legitimacy of the government, and in August of the same year Gulbuddin Hekmatyar again withdrew.

Disagreement as to the type of a future Afghan government and ethnic and sectarian divisions prevented the AIG from becoming a viable institution. Gulbuddin Hekmatyar took independent action in disregard of the cost to Afghan unity. On July 9, 1990 Sayyid Jamal, one of his commanders in Takhar Province, ambushed and killed a number of commanders, most of them from *Jam'iat*; the deed was eventually avenged. This was only one in a long series of incidents in which Hekmatyar's Hizb was the culprit. Such actions lend credence to the suspicion that Hekmatyar did not want unity but intended to gain sole control of the Afghan government. He was responsible for the merciless bombing of Kabul that left much of the city in ruins. But in May 1996, after he was ousted by the *Taliban* from his stronghold south of Kabul, Hekmatyar made peace with Rabbani and assumed the post of prime minister in Kabul. The Islamic Alliance, never really allied, found a new challenge in the *Taliban* who in September 1996 captured Kabul and control about two-thirds of Afghanistan.

ISLAMIC LAW. Islamic law (*Shari'a*, A. from *shar'*, the path) is God-given and a prescription for the believer to the right life in this world and for salvation in the world to come. During lifetime, the Prophet Muhammad transmitted Allah's commands. These were eventually collected in the book of readings or recitations, the Qor'an (Koran). The Qor'an was the basis of law for all Muslims, although various sects and schools differed in its interpretation. When no conclusive guidance was found in the Qor'an, the *sunna*, practice of the Prophet and his companions, was consulted. Four schools of law eventually developed in *Sunni* Islam named after early legal scholars, the *Malikite*—named after Malik ibn Anas (d. 795), the *Shafi- 'ite*—named after ibn Idris al-Shafi'i (d.819), the *Hanbalite*—named after Ahmad ibn Hanbal (d. 855), and the Hanifite—named after **Abu Hanifa** (d.767). The Hanifite school has the largest number of adherents and is dominant in Afghanistan. It recognizes as a basis of jurisprudence, in addition to the Qor'an, the *sunna*, *ijma* (consensus of the Muslim community), and *qiyas* (reasoning by analogy). Legal reasoning is called *ijtihad*, the struggle or effort, in arriving at a legal decision. By the 10th century Muslim jurists decided by consensus that Islamic law was complete and that independent interpretation, *ijtihad*, was no longer permissible. Henceforth, Muslims were to follow, or imitate (*taqlid*), God's law. Islamic modernists want to reopen the "Gate of Ijtihad" to permit a reinterpretation of Islamic law in order to meet new, modern requirements.

Judges (*qadis*) in Shari'a courts are to apply the law, subject to consultation with legal experts (*muftis*) who issue legal decisions (*fatwas*). A jurist (*faqih*) is trained in an Islamic college (*madrasa*) to serve as lawyer, teacher, judge, and mufti.

Punishments include the penalties for major offenses prescribed in the Qor'an (*hadd*, pl. *hudud*), discretionary and variable punishments (*ta'zir*), and retaliation (*qisas*).

Although the shari'a has been the law of Afghanistan, there has always existed a dichotomy of "God's law" and the "King's law."

During the time of **Ahmad Shah** (r. 1747–73) there were central and provincial courts with administration in the hands of the *qadis*, all of whom were appointed by the ruler on the recommendation of the court *imam*. The death penalty could not be exacted without the king, or governor's, approval. Ahmad Shah forbade mutilation of limbs and drafted a legal code that was, however, not enacted. Tribal courts existed in the Pashtun frontier areas where cases were decided by council (**jirga**). **Timur Shah** first appointed a minister of justice, *amir-i dar al-qaza,* and a chief justice, *qazi al-quzat*, to whom all courts were subordinated. All legal functionaries were appointed by Kabul. Amir **Abdul Rahman** established a court of appeals with twelve members, headed by the *khan-i ulum* (chief of [religious] sciences). Under Amir **Habibullah** there existed courts headed by his brother **Nasrullah** Khan and his son **Inayatullah** Khan, the *shari'at*, and the *kotwali*, police court. Appeals against decisions of governors and high officials were made to the Amir. The Ottoman codification of Hanafi law (*majalla*) was translated into Dari (*siraj al-ahkam*).

The sphere of the "king's law" was considerably expanded during the period of King **Amanullah** (r. 1919–29). He drafted the first constitution in 1923 and initiated judicial reforms, *nizam-namah*, that aimed at reducing the influence of the *ulama* (clergy), and a guide for judges in civil and criminal law was published (*tamasuk al-quzzat*). The introduction of administrative courts for civil servants, commercial courts, and reconciliation courts took over many functions of the Shari'a courts. A number of statutes restricted the powers of the *qazis* (judges). These innovations were abolished after the fall of King Amanullah but were resumed as a result of **Nadir Shah**'s constitution of 1931. The *usul-namah*, a code of statutory legislation, replaced the *nizam-namah*. It was more conservative in nature and merely supplementary to Islamic law. A hierarchy of primary and appellate courts existed, with the court of cassation (*tamyiz*) at the highest level. The mufti played a role only on the primary level.

The constitution of 1964 (*qanun-i asasi*) established an independent judiciary with the supreme court as the highest official organ. In March 1967 the office of public prosecutor was established, and the offices of minister of justice and attorney general were combined. Penal and civil codes were enacted, and criminal procedure was divided into customary law (Islamic law) and statutory law (*qanun*). The supreme court was temporarily replaced with a high judicial council, after **Muhammad Daud** established a republican form of government. The gap between statutory law and the shari'a widened. The sovereignty of God was gradually replaced by sovereignty of the nation or the people.

President Daud's constitution of 1977 centralized the legal establishment, and the vestiges of separation of powers were abolished, as the minister of justice took over the functions of the chief justice. The *Milli Jirga* (National Council) replaced parliament, and the Revolutionary Council was the highest authority in the state. The Marxist government set up a higher council of the judiciary that was responsible to the revolutionary council. Revolutionary and extraordinary courts that were responsible for the executions of many existed for some time. In spite of the trend toward secularization of law, the lower courts in the provinces and small towns continued to operate in the traditional manner. The *Shari'a* has remained dominant in matters of family law, inheritance, property, and contracts and is now rigorously enforce since the *Taliban* captured Kabul in September 1996. *See also* CONSTI-TUTIONAL DEVELOPMENT.

ISLAMIC UNITY OF AFGHAN MUJAHEDIN. *See* **ISLAMIC ALLIANCE FOR THE LIBERATION OF AFGHANISTAN.**

ISLAMIST MOVEMENT. The movement was born in large measure as a reaction to the process of Westernization in Afghanistan and the growth of secular, liberal ideologies among Afghan youth. The movement owes much of its organization and ideology to the influence of the **Muslim Brotherhood** of Egypt (*Al-Ikhwan Al-Muslimin*), and its adherents were therefore dubbed *Ikhwanis* by their opponents. The party originated in religious, intellectual circles in the late 1950s and had as its chief ideologues and mentors **Ghulam Muhammad Niazi**, **Burhanuddin Rabbani, Sayyid Musa Tawana**, and others who had studied at al-Azhar University in Egypt and taught at the faculty of theology of **Kabul University**. They soon gathered a circle of like-minded students, who organized themselves in 1970 in the Islamic Youth (*Jawanan-i Muslimin*) movement. At first they went through a process of ideological development when members studied the works of Islamic thinkers Hasan al-Banna' (1906–49), the "Supreme Guide" of the Ikhwanis; Sayyid Qutb, executed in Cairo in 1966; and Abu'l Ala Maududi (died 1979), founder of the Pakistani *Jama'at-i Islami* and author of religio-political treatises. The movement took a political turn during the premiership of Sardar **Muhammad Daud** (1953–63) and the subsequent liberal period. Islamist students staged demonstrations, protesting government policies and such international issues as Zionism and the war in Vietnam. By 1970 Islamists won a majority in student elections, a fact that alarmed the Marxists and their supporters. In 1971 the movement began to formally organize at a meeting in Kabul at the house of Professor Rabbani. A leadership council was formed with Rabbani as the chairman. **Abdul Rasul Sayyaf** his deputy and **Habiburrahman** was secretary. Council members were assigned responsibility for financial, cultural, and political tasks. Some leaders, like Niazi, refrained from open participation, others, like **Hekmatyar**, were jailed. The organization selected the name *Jam'iat-i-Islami* (Islamic Society), but the student faction, operating quite openly, was known as the *Jawanan Musulman* (Muslim Youth) and popularly called *Ikhwanis*. Other Islamist individuals and circles, not affiliated with the Jam'iat were **Minhajuddin Gahiz**, who in 1968 published his newspaper *Jarida Gahiz*, (Dawn); *Khuddam al-Qur'an* (Servants of the Koran) founded by the **Mujaddidi** family; and the *Jam'iat-i Ulama-i Muhammadi* (Society of Muslim Ulama) founded by **Sebghatullah Mujaddidi.**

After the coup of Muhammad Daud (July 17, 1973), the movement was forced to go underground. Rabbani raised the question of armed struggle, and weapons were collected; but before any action could begin, the government police arrested many of the members, including Ghulam Muhammad Niazi. Rabbani and Hekmatyar fled to Pakistan, where they sought help from the Pakistan government and the Islamist *Jama'at-i Islami*. In 1975, Hekmatyar staged sporadic raids into Afghanistan, and when the attacks failed, the differences between Rabbani and Hekmatyar became public.

After the Saur Revolt of April 1978 an attempt at reconciliation was made. Each party nominated seven members to a 21-member reconciliation committee including the mediators. The *Jami'at* members voted for Rabbani to be president of the party, and Hekmatyar's party voted for Qazi Muhammad Amin as deputy president. The mediators voted for Maulawi Fayez who became the compromise president. But the Islamists were also divided on ethnic and ideological lines. The largely Tajik supporters of Rabbani favored preparation rather than precipitous armed activity. Hekmatyar aspired to leadership of the Islamists and advocated immediate struggle. In April 1978, **Maulawi Muhammad Nabi Muhammadi** was chosen as a compromise leader, but the movement broke up over the distribution of funds provided by foreign donors. Hekmatyar organized the *Hizb-i Islami*, and the tradi-

tionalist Muhammadi founded his own *Harakat-i Inqilab-i Islami* party. Rabbani worked with Mujaddidi and his *Jabha-yi Milli-yi Beraye
Najat-i Afghanistan* (National Liberation Front), and continued to lead
his own Jam'iat. **Muhammad Yunus Khales** formed his own Hizb
party in 1979.

The Islamists were puritanical moralists who perceived moral laxity,
lack of respect for traditional values, and an infatuation with Western
secular culture among the Afghan youth and were determined to impose
the laws of Islam on the social and political life of the state. They were
not fundamentalist, but reformist, and supported a political activism first
seen in the great Pan-Islamist, **Jamaluddin Afghani**. They were
critical of the fundamentalist views of the *ulama'* and were themselves
the object of criticism by the clergy. They went underground and organized in cells, were accused of resorting to political assassinations, and
were themselves the objects of assassinations. They rejected aspects of
both Communism and democracy although they copied from both.

A new movement, the *Taliban*, emerged in November 1994 and
within two years captured more than half of Afghanistan. They oppose
the *mujahedin* groups and want to establish their concept of an
"Islamic State." For additional information, see individual party entries
and ISLAMIC ALLIANCE FOR THE LIBERATION OF AFGHAN-
ISTAN, TAWANA, and MUSLIM BROTHERHOOD.

ISMA'IL KHAN. *See* **MUHAMMAD ISMA'IL.**

ISMA'ILIS (ISMA'ILIYA). A **Shi'a** Islamic sect begun when the Shi'a
Imam Isma'il (son of Ja'far al-Sadeq) died in 765 A.D. and was thought
by his followers to be the final, Seventh Imam, who was to return on the
Day of Judgment. The present leader of the Isma'ili community is
Karim, Agha Khan IV, who administers to some 300,000 people
residing in Africa, Syria, Iran, Tajikistan, India, and Pakistan, as well as
northeastern Afghanistan. Isma'ilis pay a tax that goes to the support of
the needy in their community. The Isma'ilis believe in an esoteric interpretation of the *Qor'an* with stages of initiation, depending on the
comprehension of the believer. The head of the Isma'ili community in
Afghanistan was Nadir Shah Kayani, known as **Sayyid-i Kayan**. As a
small sectarian community, the Isma'ilis refused to cooperate with the
mujahedin groups operating in their territory, but allied themselves
with Dostum against the *Taliban*, after the latter captured Kabul. *See
also* SHI'A and SAYYID-I KAYAN.

ISTALIF (34-50' N, 69-0'E). A small town in the Koh Daman area, located about 20 miles northnorthwest of Kabul, which is famous for its scenic beauty and blue-colored pottery. The village is "built on the side of the hills in the form of a pyramid, the houses rising one above the other by terraces, and the whole being crowned by the magnificent chinars which denote the shrine of Hazrat Eshan, whilst far below in a deep glen rushes a foaming yet clear brook" (Gaz. 6). The name, Istalif, has been linked to the Greek *istafel*, grapes, which are grown there in great abundance.

Istalif was captured and destroyed by British troops in the **First Anglo-Afghan War**. During the present war it has been held by various *mujahedin* groups and is said to have suffered considerable destruction.

ISTIQLAL LYCEE. An academic high school in Kabul with a French curriculum, founded by King **Amanullah** in 1922, hence its name *Amaniya*. After the accession of **Nadir Shah** it was renamed *Istiqlal* (Independence) Lycée. It began with five French and twelve Afghan teachers and in 1926 had 33 teachers and 350 students. Subsequently it was greatly expanded and became one of the most prestigious preparatory schools in the country. *See also* EDUCATION.

ITHNA ASHARIYA (TWELVER). A *Shi'a* sect believing that the Twelfth Imam (A. *ithna 'ashariya*) Muhammad al-Mahdi is the last imam (leader of the *Shi'a* community) who went into occultation and will return at the end of time "to announce the last judgment and to fill the earth with justice." The Safavid rulers of Iran made Twelver Shi'ism the state religion and forcefully converted much of its Sunni population. In Afghanistan most of the **Hazara**, the **Qizilbash,** and about half of the population of Herat belong to this sect. The Twelvers are also called *Imami* Shi'as and constitute a religious minority in Afghanistan. *See also* SHI'A.

ITTIHAD-I-ISLAMI BARAYE AZADI-YE AFGHANISTAN. "Islamic Union for the Liberation of Afghanistan," founded by **Abdul Rasul Sayyaf** after he served as chairman of the **Islamic Alliance,** 1980-81. It is a small **Islamist** group that favors the establishment of an Islamic state in Afghanistan. Sayyaf has been able to gain considerable financial support from the Arab Gulf states which helped him to found his own organization. It was part of the loose federation of the Islamic

Unity of the Afghan *Mujahedin* and was expelled from Kabul with the
Rabbani government. *See* SAYYAF, ABDUL RASUL; ISLAMIC
ALLIANCE FOR THE LIBERATION OF AFGHANISTAN; and
ISLAMIST MOVEMENT.

J

JABAL-US-SIRAJ (JABAL AL-SIRAJ) (35-1' N, 69-14' E). A town and
administrative district in Parwan Province that has become a center of
Afghanistan's textile industry. Built by Amir **Habibullah** in 1906, the
town got its name from the amir's title *Siraj al-Millat wa'l Din* (Torch
of the Nation and Religion). It included a fortress and **Arg** (palace) and
a cantonment, housing some 12,000 men. Between 1910 and 1913 a
hydroelectric plant was constructed by a Scottish engineer, James
Miller, to provide electricity for Kabul. For a long time this was the only
plant of its type in Afghanistan. Subsequently the industrial base was
further expanded with the construction of a textile mill in the 1930s and
a cement factory in the early 1960s.

JABBAR KHEL. A section of the **Ghilzai** tribe occupying the area of
Hisarak-i Ghilzai in Nangarhar, between the Siah Koh range and the
Surkhab River, and scattered over the greater part of Laghman
Province.

JABHA-YI MILLI BERAYE NAJAT-I AFGHANISTAN. National
Liberation Front, one of the seven *mujahedin* groups headquartered in
Pakistan, founded by **Sibghatullah Mujaddidi** in 1978. It advocated
the overthrow of the Marxist regime in Kabul and the establishment of
a traditional Islamic state with a parliamentary democracy. Members of
the Naqshbandi Sufi fraternity predominate in this group. The *Jabha* is
ideologically close to the moderate groups of **Gailani** and **Muhammadi** and cooperated with them. Mujaddidi has actively participated in
Afghan politics, and after the capture of Kabul by the *Taliban* recognized their government. *See also* MUJADDIDI, SEBGHATULLAH.

JADRAN (DZADRAN or ZADRAN). A tribe related to the Khostwal
Pashtuns, inhabiting the eastern slope of the Sulaiman range in Paktia
Province. They are excellent fighters and entered the war against the
Kabul government in 1979. Under the able command of **Jalaluddin
Haqani**, they have been able to expel government troops from the area

of Urgun. The Jadran are loosely affiliated with the party of **Yunus Khales**.

JAGIR. A feudal, military fiefdom, such as granted by **Ahmad Shah Durrani** to chiefs of his tribe. It was an allotment of land that was tax-free but required its holder to provide a number of troops and arms corresponding to the size of the *jagir* (also called *tiyul* and A. *iqta'*). Land was divided into divisions called *qulba*, or "plows," that designated the portion of irrigated land cultivated by one person, employing one oxen and one plow. The area was divided into two sections for sowing of two *kharwar* grain (one *kharwar*, literally a donkey load, amounted to 100 *man*, up to 160 pounds); one section was cultivated each year while the other half remained fallow. About 3,000 double *qulba* were distributed to Durrani tribes in Kandahar for which they had to provide 6,000 horsemen for the amir's army.

JAGRAN, SAYYID MUHAMMAD HASAN (JAGLAN). Jagran (major) is the nom de guerre under which Sayyid Hasan, the 50-year-old commander of the Hazara front in Behsud, Ghazni Province, is known. Successful in various military engagements against government forces, he reportedly administered his area autonomously during the 1980s. He is affiliated with the *shura-yi ittifaq-i Islami* of **Sayyid Ali Beheshti** which is the only **Shi'a *mujahedin*** movement attending the consultative council of commanders in Rawalpindi, Pakistan in February 1989. Jagran has fought **Nasr** and **Pasdaran** and does not enjoy good relations with the other *Shi'a* groups. *See also* BEHESHTI, SAYYID ALI and SHI'A MUJAHEDIN GROUPS.

JAJI. A tribe in Paktia Province, estimated to number about 5,000 families. They are Sunnis and have engaged in occasional blood feuds with the neighboring **Shi'a Turis**. They have a reputation as good fighters. They supported the **Sulaiman Khel** in ousting King **Amanullah**, and sided with **Nadir Shah** against **Habibullah Kalakani**. After 1930 many Jaji chiefs came to Kabul and, encouraged by **Shah Mahmud Ghazi**, established themselves in the trucking business. In the present war in Afghanistan the Jajis eventually allied themselves with the Mahaz of **Gailani**.

JALALABAD (36-46' N, 65-52' E). The capital of Nangarhar Province that had an estimated 54,000 inhabitants in the 1970s, reportedly increased by 1988, as a result of the influx of internal refugees, to about 200,000. When the *mujahedin* besieged the city in March 1989, this number was again considerably reduced. The population is largely **Pashtun** of **Khugiani, Shinwari, Tirahi** (Tira'i), **Mohmand,** and **Ghilzai** tribal backgrounds, in addition to **Sikhs,** Hindus, and some **Tajiks** and **Sayyids.** It had the largest community of Sikh and Hindu merchants (about 4,000) of any Afghan city. Situated at an altitude of 1950 feet in a fertile valley watered by the Kabul and Kunar Rivers some 90 miles east of Kabul, Jalalabad lies on the trade route to the Indo-Pakistani subcontinent. Invaders passed through the Jalalabad Valley, including Alexander the Great (330 B.C.), **Babur Shah** (1504), and the British who occupied the town in two **Anglo-Afghan wars.**

Babur Shah, the founder of the Moghul Empire of India, first planted beautiful gardens in the area, and in 1560 A.D. his grandson Jalaluddin Akbar founded the town, hence its name Jalalabad. In the 19th century it was a walled town with about 2,000 inhabitants, swelling during the winter to some 20,000.

Because of its beauty and mild climate it was the winter capital of Afghan kings. Amir **Habibullah** was assassinated in the vicinity of the town on February 20, 1919 during one of his visits. He and his son **Amanullah** are buried in the city. A dam on the Kabul River and a hydro electric power station at Darunta, north of Jalalabad, have made possible the irrigation of additional land, providing the city with electricity. Mechanized farms produced large quantities of citrus and olive fruits, wheat and alfalfa. The area is famous for its orchards and gardens. Virtually all the citrus fruit in Afghanistan is grown here. The civil war caused considerable destruction in 1929, and the present war has forced many to flee the town and surrounding area. In March 1989, *mujahedin* forces attacked the city but were unable to take it. After the fall of the **Najibullah** regime in April 1992, the *mujahedin* also took Jalalabad, and the city was ruled by a council of commanders and military officials until it was captured by the *Taliban* in September 1996.

JALALABAD, ATTACK ON. Soviet forces left in February 1989, and Kunar was taken by the *mujahedin*; the time seemed ripe for the insurgents to progress from the stage of guerrilla to conventional warfare. Jalalabad seemed a suitable target for the first capture of a major Afghan city. It was located only about 37 miles from the Pakistani border and within easy access of reinforcement in men and munitions.

If taken, the city could have served as the capital of the Afghan Interim Government (AIG), there to be recognized and openly assisted by its foreign supporters. Hamid Gul, director of Pakistani military intelligence (**ISI**), was heavily involved in various stages of the campaign. In March the *mujahedin* had gathered some 7,000 men in the area amid great publicity about their intended target. The men came primarily from **Hekmatyar**'s, **Khales**'s, **Sayyaf**'s and **Gailani**'s forces although other groups also participated. The garrison was estimated at about 4,500, and the defenses were under the command of General Delawar, the Afghan chief of staff. Mine fields provided a secure perimeter, and munitions had been collected in anticipation of the attack. The *mujahedin* seemed to be well-supplied with heavy artillery and surface-to-air missiles, including the dreaded **stinger**, and began their attack on March 6, 1989, proclaiming an amnesty for enemy soldiers in the hope of achieving massive defections. They quickly captured Samarkhel, an important post in the defense of the city, and rocketed the airport to prevent supplies from being brought in. But the fighting quickly bogged down. The *mujahedin* fought only during the daylight hours and returned to rear bases for the night. Commanders did not always coordinate their actions, Hekmatyar being the major culprit, and they failed to maintain the blockade of the road from Kabul, permitting convoys to supply the city. High-altitude bombing and close air support by MIG-21s, as well as SCUD missiles with 1,700-lb warheads, exacted a heavy toll on the *mujahedin*. In April the defenders were able to recapture the airport and, after a ten week long siege, the Kabul government prevailed. On May 10, foreign journalists were permitted to visit Jalalabad to see that the *mujahedin* had been defeated with heavy losses. One source claims that some 5,000 casualties resulted on all sides, and most of the *mujahedin* casualties were caused by bombing and mines. On July 4 the Kabul government launched a surprise attack and consolidated its control of Samarkhel and the surrounding area, achieving a badly-needed boost in morale of the Afghan army and permitting the Kabul regime to continue in power for another three years. It was only after the fall of Kabul in April 1992 that Jalalabad was taken by a council of *mujahedin* commanders and in 1996 by the *Taliban*.

JALALABAD, SIEGE OF. During the siege of the Kabul cantonment in the **First Anglo-Afghan War**, Jalalabad became an important base for British-Indian troops. **Sir Robert Sale**, the commanding general, was unable to come to the rescue of the Kabul forces; therefore he decided to remain and took possession of the town on November 13, 1841. He worked on reinforcing the walls and fortifications, having only some 1,600 troops and six guns to defend a perimeter of about 2,200 yards. On November 15, an Afghan force, estimated by British officers at about 5,000 tribesmen, surrounded the town but was initially dispersed; however, the Afghans eventually captured the town, forcing the British brigade to withdraw into the citadel. On January 6, 1842, the Afghan commander demanded the British brigade to depart with honor to India in fulfillment of the Kabul **Treaty of Capitulation**, but General Sale refused, not trusting the promise of safe conduct. On February 19, 1842 an earthquake destroyed the parapets, making a considerable breach in the ramparts which had to be restored. Two days later, Sardar **Akbar Khan** attacked British foraging parties and established a rigorous blockade which lasted until April 7. Various sallies succeeded in capturing livestock for provisions, but the native troops were put on half rations and the camp followers on quarter rations. Starvation was averted when the British were able to capture a flock of 500 sheep and goats which were grazing a little too close to the wall of the town. On April 7, General Sale sallied out with virtually all his forces and defeated Muhammad Akbar's army of some 6,000 men. According to British accounts only 31 officers and men were killed and 131 wounded. On April 16, **General Pollock** reached the city practically unmolested. Before the British departed they destroyed the defenses of Jalalabad.

JAM (34-21'N, 64-30'E). A village in Ghor Province west of Chaghcharan. Near the village stands a 190-foot-high minaret which was discovered by the governor of Herat and studied by a French archaeologist in 1958. The minaret was constructed in the 12th century under the **Ghorid** ruler Ghias ud-Din and is located in a desolated area. The geometric design of the brickwork can still be recognized, and kufic inscriptions from the Qor'an give the *sura* (verse) of Mary, mother of Jesus.

JAMA'AT-I-ISLAMI. Name of a Pakistani political organization founded by Maulana Abu'l- Ala Maududi (1903–79) in 1940 that advocates the establishment of an Islamic state patterned after the early Islamic community. Olivier Roy (1986) characterized the Jama'at as an elite religio-political society, similar to the Opus Dei. It is Pan-Islamic in nature and looks at the Muslim community as one nation (*umma*) and rejects nationalism and ethnicity as contrary to the concept of Islamic brotherhood. The Jama'at opposed the creation of Pakistan and favors union with Afghanistan as a first step in reestablishing the Islamic Umma. Zia-ul-Haq, the Pakistani president, tried to implement some of Maududi's ideas. The Jama'at has strongly supported the forces of **Gulbuddin Hekmatyar** and other **Islamist** *mujahedin* groups in Afghanistan, in preference to the nationalist and traditionalist groups.

JAMAL PASHA (JEMAL). Member of the Ottoman ruling triumvirate, serving as minister of the navy and governor of Syria during World War I. He came with a small staff to Afghanistan on October 27, 1920 to escape extradition for "war crimes." He took charge of the reorganization of the Afghan army and founded the "Qita Namuna," an elite force, comprising a battalion of infantry and a regiment of cavalry. He was responsible for reinstituting and expanding the hated *hasht-nafari* recruitment system and other unpopular reforms. He left Afghanistan with some members of his staff in September 1921 and was assassinated by an Armenian near Tiflis on July 21, 1922.

JAMALUDDIN AFGHANI. *See* **AFGHANI, SAYYID JAMAL-UDDIN.**

JAMI, MULLA NUR-UD-DIN ABDUL RAHMAN. The last great poet of classical Persian, scholar, and mystic who was born in Jam (now **Khorasan** Province of Iran) in 1414 (which was then under the political control of Herat) and died in Herat in 1492. Afghans consider Jami a native son because he lived in Herat at the court of **Sultan Baiqara** where he enjoyed the friendship and support of the wazir Ali-Shir Nawa'i (1469–1506). Afghan historians therefore call him Abdul Rahman *Harawi*, the Herati. *See* HERAT and BAIQARA, SULTAN HUSAIN MIRZA.

JAM'IAT-I ISLAMI-YI AFGHANISTAN. Islamic Society of Afghanistan, headed since 1971 by Professor **Burhanuddin Rabbani** and since 1978 a *mujahedin* force that fought the Marxist government in Kabul. It was one of the seven *mujahedin* groups accorded recognition by Pakistan and was headquartered in Peshawar, and is largely non-Pashtun in membership. Affiliated commanders controlled areas in northeastern, northern, and western Afghanistan. They include **Ahmad Shah Mas'ud**, in the Panjshir Valley, and **Isma'il Khan**, who operated in Herat Province. The party is Islamist (*see* ISLAMIST MOVEMENT) in orientation and favors the establishment of an Islamic state. In spite of their common ideological origin, the *Jam'iat* was in a virtual state of war with **Gulbuddin Hekmatyar**'s *Hizb-i Islami*. On July 9, 1989 a group of mostly Jam'iat commanders returning from a strategy meeting with Commander Mas'ud in Takhar Province were attacked and killed, some of them after they were captured alive. In October 1990, Commander Mas'ud came to Peshawar and approved a reconciliation between *Jam'iat* and *Hizb*, but it was not until May 1996 that an agreement was signed, and Hekmatyar came to Kabul to assume the position of prime minister. The barely formed government was expelled from Kabul in September by *Taliban* forces who instituted a severe interpretation of Islam.

JAM'IAT-I 'ULAMA'. A consultative body of *ulama* (scholars of Islamic sciences) founded by Nadir Shah in 1931 to judge the constitutionality of laws. For a time this council had considerable powers as all new laws had to be submitted to it; but its powers waned after **Muhammad Daud** became prime minister in 1953, and it became a rubber stamp legitimizing body of Afghan governments. It published a journal called *Al-Falah* (Salvation). After the **Saur Revolt**, remaining members of the council issued *fatwas* (legal decisions) that recognized **Nur Muhammad Taraki** as the legitimate ruler of Afghanistan and authorized "jihad" against the "Ikhwanis," Islamist *mujahedin* groups.

JAMILURRAHMAN, MAULAWI HUSAIN (JAMIL AL-RAHMAN). Amir of the *Jama'at-i Da'wa*, an Islamic revivalist movement whose members call themselves *Salafis* or *ahl-i hadith* and are popularly called "Wahhabis." He captured most of Kunar Province and proclaimed an "Islamic Amirate," which he ruled for a time to the exclusion of other *mujahedin* groups. Born in 1933 in Pech district of Kunar Province of a Safi tribal family, he received a traditional education. In the early 1970s he became a member *Jam'iat-i Islami* and took part in armed attacks against the government of President Daud. After the **Saur Revolt** he joined the *Hizb-i Islami* of **Hekmatyar** and was until 1982 his amir in Kunar Province. Eventually he broke with Hekmatyar and ousted other *mujahedin* groups from his area. He issued decrees allowing only bearded men to enter his territory and prohibited the consumption of tobacco in all its forms.

In February 1991 he announced his cabinet including, among others, the following portfolios:

Defense	Maulawi Rahmatullah
Interior	Haji Rozi
Foreign Affairs	Mir Muhd. Majidi (of Hizb H)
Justice	Maulawi Ihsan
Information	Shurish
Finance	Rahman Gul
Education	Qari Din Muhammad

On April 20, 1991, an explosion at his Asadabad headquarters so decimated the ranks of his followers (including numerous Pakistanis and Arabs) that Hekmatyar's forces, supported by commanders of other groups, were able to capture Asadabad and expel most of the "Wahhabis" from Kunar Province. Muhammad Husain, alias Jamilur-rahman, was assassinated by an Egyptian in Pakistan. One Maulawi Sami'ullah succeeded as leader of the remnant of the party until it was ousted from power in September 1996 by the *Taliban*. *See also* KUNAR.

JAMSHIDI. One of the Chahar Aimaq communities, variously estimated to number from 40 to 80 thousand people, concentrated in western Badghis and in smaller groups in Herat Province, northwestern Badghis, and southern Fariab Provinces. They trace their name to Jamshid, their purported eponymic ancestor, and call themselves Kayanis, claiming descent from the legendary pre- Islamic Kayan kings of Sistan. According to some sources their name is a corruption of *jam-shoda*, which means "collected together." A member of the Jam-shidi clan was put in charge of the district of Badghis by Shah Abbas (r. 1642–68), and Khushi Khan, contemporary of **Nadir Shah Afshar**, was the first chief of the Jamshidi tribe. The Jamshidis are Hanafi Sunnis and speak Dari.

JAT. Gypsy-like groups of Sunni itinerants who call themselves *Ghorbat* (travelers) and make a living as musicians, dancers, fortune-tellers and therefore are considered to be of low status. Their women engage in door-to-door selling of small bazaar items. They belong to six different ethnic groups and speak various dialects, some of Iranian and others of Indian origin. Their number has been estimated as from nine to 12 thousand, scattered all over the country.

JEZAIL. A long-barreled musket with a thin, curved butt that was the major Afghan firearm during the 19th century and can still be seen in the bazaars of the country. It was muzzle loaded and therefore required several minutes to prepare, but it is said to have had greater accuracy and range than the British muskets (Sir Charles Napier claimed the musket was on balance the better weapon, Macrory, 170). A *jezailchi*, rifleman, would carry several *jezail* on his horse and fire them in rapid succession, after which he would retire or join the enemy in hand-to-hand combat. It was the major Afghan firearm during the Anglo-Afghan wars, and was eventually replaced by the breech-loading Martini-Henry and other rifles of foreign and domestic manufacture.

JIHAD. Jihad, holy war (A., literally "great effort," but generally "holy war"), is the obligation to fight against "unbelievers" until they accept Islam or submit to Islamic rule. Monotheists with a sacred book, like Christians and Jews, are not forced to convert and enjoy the status of protected subjects (**dhimmis**). A Muslim who dies in *jihad* is a martyr, *shahid*, and is assured of Paradise. Technically Muslims constitute one community, *umma*, and war between them is forbidden; therefore an enemy is proclaimed sinful or apostate before he can be legally fought. Although the **PDPA** in Afghanistan did not officially adopt the atheism of Marxist ideology, it was accused by the **mujahedin** (fighters in *Jihad*) as apostate and therefore subject to be eliminated. On the other hand, the council of Afghan clergy (*jami'at-i ulama'*) in 1978 issued a **fatwa**, legal decision, legitimizing the Kabul government and proclaiming "Jihad" against the Islamist *mujahedin*. During Jihad, all tribal hostilities must temporarily stop. Muslim modernists quote a ranic passage that says: "Fight in the Way of God against those who fight against you, but do not commit aggression...", maintaining that the obligation of jihad was binding only for the early Islamic period and that Jihad also means fighting political and social war and inwardly waging war against the carnal soul—a kind of moral imperative.

JIRGA. A tribal council that has legislative and juridical authority in the name of the tribal community. Although the Afghan government claims exclusive jurisdiction, it permits Pashtun tribes in the border areas to resolve internal disputes in their traditional manner. *Jirgas* can be composed of chiefs and notables or of all adult male members of a tribe. A chief, or respected greybeard, leads the discussion, and votes are weighed according to the importance of the individual rather than counted. The decision of a *jirga* is binding on all members of the tribe. *Jirgas* also resolve intra-tribal disputes, often with the mediation of a respected member of the *ulama* (clergy) or *pirs* (leaders of mystical orders).

In times of national emergency Afghan rulers have convened a *Loya Jirga*, Great Council, which includes representatives from all parts of the country. Its decisions thus become an expression of the national will. *See* LOYA JIRGA.

JIZYA. A tax levied on monotheistic non-Muslims who are possessors of a scripture, the *ahl al-kitab*, or Peoples of the Book (such as Christians, Jews). Only adult males of sound mind and body and financial means were to be so taxed. In exchange, they enjoyed freedom of life, liberty, and property and were not drafted into the military. In Afghanistan this tax was levied largely on Indians. Afghan constitutions since the time of King **Amanullah** declared all Afghan citizens equal and abolished the *jizya*. *See also* DHIMMIS.

JOYA, MUHAMMAD SARWAR. A poet, writer, and social critic who was a supporter of King **Amanullah**'s reforms and opposed to the regime of **Nadir Shah**. Founded the Danesh printing press in Herat, and served as editor of the daily newspaper *Ittifaq-i-Islam* (Consensus of Islam) in Herat, 1928–30, the daily *Anis*, and the bi-weekly *Watan*. He was jailed repeatedly and died in prison in 1961.

JOZJAN (JOWZJAN) (36-30' N, 66-0' E). A province in north central Afghanistan with an area of 10,126 square miles and an estimated population of about 642,000. The administrative capital of the province is Shiberghan with some 19,000 inhabitants. The province is rich in mineral resources; oil and natural gas have been discovered at Khwaja Gugirdak and Jarquduq, near Shiberghan, and reserves of natural gas have been estimated at 500 trillion cubic feet. A pipeline transporting natural gas to the Soviet Union was completed in 1968, and except for a limited amount of local use in the production of fertilizer, all was delivered to the Soviet Union below the world market rates. One reason for this was, no doubt, the fact that the Soviet Union was the only feasible trading partner.

JOZJANIS. A militia composed largely of **Uzbeks** from Jozjan Province, numbering about 3,000–4,000 men in the 1980s, who served the Kabul government as a reliable and effective force in southern and western Afghanistan. It replaced the Soviet troops in Kandahar, where it protected the airport. After the fall of Kabul to the *mujahedin*, the Jozjanis seemed to have merged with the Uzbek forces of General **Dostum** and became one of the contenders for control of portions of Kabul. They first helped *Jam'iat* to capture Kabul and subsequently pulled out of the city at the insistence of **Hekmatyar** in a deal with **Rabbani**. Later they joined Hekmatyar when Rabbani was unwilling to include Dostum in his government. The Jozjanis have been feared as a fierce and unruly mercenary army and appear to be the defenders of Uzbek ethnic interests in present Afghanistan. They are now part of General Dostum's army in north central Afghanistan.

JUNBESH-I MILLI-YI ISLAMI. *See* **DOSTUM, ABDUL RASHID.**

JUDICIARY. *See* **ISLAMIC LAW.**

JUM'A. The day of "general assembly," Friday, and the Islamic Sabbath, when Muslims attend religious services, preferably in a major mosque, often referred to as the *Jum'a* (or Friday) Mosque. A sermon, *khutba*, is read on Fridays in the name of the ruler. After the sermon, those in attendance often discuss matters of importance to the community and to the congregation. The *khutba* has political significance because it indicates the loyalty of the congregation. It is a sign of rebellion if the ruler's name is omitted or if it is replaced by another name. In the civil war of 1929, the governor of Herat had the *khutba* read in the name of the "Islamic King" to avoid making a choice between King **Amanullah** and **Habibullah Kalakani**.

JUMHURIAT (REPUBLIC). A daily newspaper that temporarily replaced *Anis* and *Islah* after President **Muhammad Daud** proclaimed the Republic in 1973. It was the official organ of the republican government and ceased to exist after the Marxist coup of 1978.

K

KABUL (34-31' N, 69-12' E). The capital and largest city in Afghanistan, situated at an altitude of almost 6,000 feet above sea level, and a province with an area of 1,822 square miles and a population of 1,372,000. In 1978 the city had some 500,000 inhabitants, but this number had in the 1980s increased to about one million and a half as a result of the influx of refugees from the war-ravaged areas. Kabul is strategically located in a valley surrounded by high mountains at the cross roads of north-south and east-west trade routes. Therefore it has been the site of towns since antiquity, called Kubha in the Rigveda (about 1,500 B.C.) and Kabura by Ptolemy (second century A.D.). Muslim Arabs under Abdul Rahman Samurah captured Kabul in the middle of the seventh century A.D., but it took the Islamic invaders another 200 years before the Hindu rulers of Kabul were finally ousted. Kabul continued to be disputed, resulting in much destruction until Islam was definitely established under the Saffarids (nineth century A.D.). The city was part of the **Ghaznavid** Empire to suffer again from Genghis Khan's hordes (13th century A.D.). Kabul became the capital of a province of the Moghul Empire, whose founder, **Babur Shah**, is buried on the eastern slope of the Sher Darwaza Mountain. In the period 1775–76 **Timur Shah** made Kabul his capital, and Afghan amirs ruled henceforth from that city. In the 19th century Kabul endured British occupation during the two Anglo-Afghan wars and the destruction of its covered bazaar as a punitive measure.

The city includes the old town, between the northern slope of the Sher Darwaza Mountain and Kabul River, and a new town (*shahr-i nau*) begun in 1935. A large wall, twenty feet high and twelve feet thick, parts of which archaeologists believe to date from the fifth century A.D., still stands. It extends to the **Bala Hisar**, the citadel, an imposing fortress that was destroyed by the British in 1878 and rebuilt to serve as a garrison and military college in 1939. Afghan amirs resided in the Bala Hisar until in 1888 Amir **Abdul Rahman** constructed the **Arg**, a citadel and walled palace, in the center of town. At the beginning of this century Amir **Habibullah** further modernized the town, providing electricity for the Arg and eventually also for other parts of the town. In the 1920s the city had 60,000 inhabitants. King **Amanullah** constructed his own capital in **Darulaman**, about six miles from the center of town, with several government buildings and an imposing parliament building. Members of the royal court and high government officials built their villas in the new capital, but after Amanullah's fall from power the center of government moved back into town.

The city grew rapidly after World War II with the addition of new quarters. *Karta-yi Chahar* (Fourth District) was developed in 1942, followed by Khairkhana in the northwest, Nur Muhammad Shah Mina east of the old town, Nadir Shah Mina to the northeast, Wazir Akbar Khan east of *Shahr-i Nau*, and Khushhal Khan Mina. In 1953 the *Jada-yi Maiwand* (Maiwand Street) was drawn through the old city, followed by paved avenues, villas, high-rise buildings, and prefabricated apartment complexes that have replaced much of the old town. The streets were paved with Soviet assistance, and a grain silo and bakery were constructed.

A network of paved roads connects Kabul via the **Salang** Pass Tunnel to the north, via the Tang-i Gharu (Gharu Gorge) to Pakistan, via Kandahar and Herat to Iran. Hydroelectric power stations in Sarobi (1957), Mahipar, and Naghlu (1966) provided electricity for the city. Soviet style city planning and the construction of pre-fabricated apartment complexes have given parts of the town the appearance of a Soviet Central Asian town. Since the late 18th century Kabul has been the seat of political power, and to be recognized as ruler of Afghanistan, one had to be in possession of the town. Kabul is still the preeminent city in Afghanistan and the seat of a government that exerts a tenuous control over the major towns and arteries of transportation. The city has been under siege for years and subject to destructive missile attacks, first by **Hekmatyar**'s forces and subsequently by the *Taliban*, who finally captured it on September 27, 1996.

KABUL MUSEUM. An important repository of archaeological and ethnographic collections of the Hellenistic, Graeco-Buddhist, **Ghaznavid**, and subsequent periods. Its main collection, workshop, and offices were housed in the former municipality building, constructed under King **Amanullah** in **Darulaman**. The museum was unique in scope, housing among others some 20,000 artifacts of the Gandharan school, about 40,000 coins from the eighth century B.C. to the 19th century—the largest collection in the world, and priceless manuscripts. During the regime of **Hafizullah Amin** some of the contents were removed but later returned to the museum. In 1989, some of the most valuable items were on display in a small building in the **Arg**, and portions of the ethnographic materials were relocated to a separate museum. It was feared that as a result of the war in Afghanistan some of the treasures may be lost, but the Kabul government claimed that all the contents have been preserved. It was only after the *mujahedin* conquest that much was destroyed or plundered. In May 1993 rockets pounded the museum and destroyed parts of the upper floor, and subsequently the museum was on the front line of *mujahedin* fighting. Soon thereafter artifacts appeared in Peshawar and on the international antique market. A collection of 21,000 Bactrian gold objects, discovered by Russian archaeologists in 1978, was kept in the Palace in control of President **Rabbani**. It is not clear if the collection is still intact and in *Taliban* hands.

KABUL RIVER (33-55' N, 72-14' E). A river that rises on the eastern slopes of the Sanglakh range near the Unai pass, about 45 miles west of Kabul. It flows in an easterly direction past Kabul and through the Tang-i Gharu to Dargai, Jalalabad and on to Dakka where it enters Pakistan territory and finally runs into the Indus at Attock after a course of about 350 miles. It is the only Afghan river system that flows into an ocean. Major tributaries in Afghanistan include the Panjshir, Logar, Surkhab, Laghman, and Kunar Rivers. Much of the upper part of the river is used for irrigation; therefore it is almost dry during the summer months. It becomes a sizable river only below the confluence, east of Kabul, of its four major tributaries.

KABUL TIMES, THE. An English language, daily newspaper published under the auspices of the ministry of information and culture in Kabul since 1962. Before that time diplomats and foreign residents depended on newsletters in various languages, published by embassies and the ministry of information and culture. The ministry subsidizes the paper and provides the physical plant but at times permitted the paper a measure of autonomy. After the **Saur Revolt** (April 1978) it became a mouthpiece of the Marxist government. President **Nur Muhammad Taraki** changed the name of the paper to *The Kabul New Times* to reflect the new ideology in Kabul. In the process of discarding ideological trappings, the *Parchami* regime restored the paper's former title. Since the capture of Kabul by *mujahedin* forces the newspaper has ceased to exist.

KABUL TREATY OF 1921. *See* **ANGLO-AFGHAN TREATY OF 1921.**

KABUL UNIVERSITY. Kabul University is the major educational institution in Afghanistan. It was founded in 1932 with the establishment of the school of medicine with French and Turkish professors. Faculties of law and political science (1938), natural sciences (1941), economics (1957), home economics (1962), education (1962), engineering (1963), and pharmacy (1963) were eventually added. The University was officially inaugurated in 1946, when a president was appointed by the ministry of education and an academic senate was formed. In 1965, a university law was passed that provided for autonomous governance under an elected president.

A new campus was constructed with American financial assistance in 1964, and two years later the Soviet-directed **Polytechnic Institute** was completed. Foreign countries participated in the development of education. The departments of agriculture, education, and engineering were affiliated with American universities; law and political science enjoyed French support; and a consortium of German institutions was affiliated with the faculties of science and economics. The faculty of theology established links with al-Azhar University of Egypt. Outstanding graduates of Kabul University often won fellowships to continue their studies at affiliated institutions. In the 1960s, Kabul University became a center of political discourse and a training ground for cadres of the entire political spectrum. About half the student body lived in dormitories on campus. The leadership of the Islamist, Marxist, and nationalist parties emerged from its campus, where they would hone their oratorical skills and engage in verbal abuse and often physical violence. Therefore, the Afghan government in 1968 banned political activities on campus.

After the **Saur Revolt**, the curriculum of Kabul University was changed to conform to Soviet models, and Russian became the favored foreign language. Because of the need for manpower in the 1980s, graduates were at times recruited directly from campus. Therefore, the student body was greatly reduced in numbers (from 8,500 in 1976) and, in 1990, was said to be seventy percent female. Of 800 teachers in the 1970s only 350 remained in the late 1980s. Politics interfered in admissions and academic policies; nevertheless, the university campus continued to be a volatile center of student protest. After the fall of the capital to the *mujahedin*, the university grounds became a battlefield of rivaling groups, and sporadic attempts to open the University were unsuccessful until *Jam'iat* established control over the city in 1994. Under the new regime of Prime Minister **Hekmatyar** and his *Taliban* successors coeducation is no longer permitted. Local rulers established universities in Herat, Mazar-i Sharif, and Bamian, but the ongoing civil war and lack of funds has prevented the creation of viable educational institutions. *See also* EDUCATION.

KAFIR. Arabic, for an "unbeliever" or "infidel," a name popularly given to non-Muslims, but technically referring only to polytheist and "worshipers of idols" who do not have a "Book," or scripture. In

Afghanistan Kafirs were the inhabitants of **Kafiristan** who remained pagans until they were converted to Islam in 1896. Kafirs are destined for hell, whereas "Peoples of the Book" (*ahl al-kitab*), such as Christians and Jews, are monotheists and not condemned to eternal hellfire.

KAFIRISTAN (35-30' N, 70-45' E). "The Land of the Infidels," was an area in eastern Afghanistan now called **Nuristan**, the "Land of Light," meaning the light of the Islamic religion that was brought into the area by conquest in 1896. Kafirs and now Nuristanis are generally divided into two categories: free men who can own pasture for their animals, and former slaves and craftsmen who did not own goats or sheep. These lower classes served as cowherds or craftsmen, making all the tools and structures in the communities.

There were no chiefs as such, but free men who demonstrated superior capabilities and generosity could gain leadership status and a corresponding influence in community affairs. Because the Kafirs inhabited valleys with dense forests, their material culture varied significantly from neighboring peoples. Kafirs sat on chairs and stools, unlike neighboring peoples who sat on carpets. Their idols, houses, furniture, and other implements are wooden carved with intricate patterns. There existed little or no ceremony in marriage, as long as the bride price was paid, and men could divorce their women at will. Polygamy was practiced. There is a considerable incidence of blond or red hair and blue or light eye color, which gave rise to legends that they were the descendants of the armies of Alexander the Great. Physical anthropologists speculate that Kafirs were contemporaries of the Arian migrations that moved south into India.

The Kafirs had a reputation as excellent fighters, and their mountainous, forested country had given them a refuge from their Islamic neighbors. When the **Durand** Line included the larger part of Kafiristan within Afghan territory, Amir **Abdul Rahman** lost little time in taking control. He ordered his army to invade the country from all directions, and within forty days controlled much of the area, although it took years to stamp out all resistance. Some Kafirs were deported to the Kuhdaman area, and others converted when offered gifts and protection from their traditional enemies. In 1906, Amir **Habibullah** changed the name of the country to Nuristan, and today all Nuristanis are Muslims. *See also* NURISTAN.

KAFIR WAR. In his biography (AR 238–92) Amir **Abdul Rahman** gave the reasons for his action as necessitated by Russian penetration of the Pamir region and British control of eastern **Kafiristan**. If Kafiristan remained independent, the Russians (or British) might want to annex it and, since Panjshir, Laghman, and Jalalabad once belonged to the Kafirs, the Russians "might persuade them to reclaim their old possessions." Furthermore, the warlike Kafirs would always pose a threat when the amir was engaged in fighting an enemy elsewhere. The Kafirs had continuously raided into Afghan provinces and had to be stopped once and for all.

The amir decided to start his campaign in winter, when snow cover would prevent the Kafirs from seeking the safety of their mountain retreats. If the passes were open the Kafirs could retreat into Russian territory and seek the support of that power. The war had to be short, before the neighboring powers could react and the Christian missionaries could make "unnecessary trouble."

In fall 1895, Abdul Rahman organized an army under Captain Muhammad Ali Khan whose main force proceeded through Panjshir to Kulam; another force under General **Ghulam Haidar Charkhi** approached Kafiristan from the direction of Asmar and Chitral; and a third force under General Katal Khan approached the area from Badakhshan. A smaller, fourth force proceeded from Laghman under its Governor Faiz Muhammad Charkhi. Since all four bases were near the Afghan border, the movement of troops did not raise any suspicions of what was to come; and suddenly in winter of 1895 the four armies, supplemented by tribal levies, attacked simultaneously and conquered Kafiristan within forty days. The Kafirs did not have a chance. Their weapons consisted primarily of spears, bows and arrows, and only a few rifles, and their numbers, about 60,000, were no match against the amir's army divided into well-equipped artillery, cavalry, and infantry branches. Some Kafir prisoners were settled in Paghman, and after conversion to Islam a large number of their youth was trained for military service. Within a few years all Kafirs were converted to Islam, and in 1906 Amir Habibullah changed the name of the country to **Nuristan**, the "Country Enlightened by the Light of Islam." This conquest greatly increased the reputation of the amir as the Islamic king of a unified and solidly Muslim state.

In commemoration of this victory, Abdul Rahman's general left behind the following inscription: "In the reign of Amir Abdul Rahman Ghazi, in 1896, the whole of Kafiristan, including Kullum, was conquered by him, and the inhabitants embraced the true and holy religion of Islam." A Qor'anic inscription added "Righteousness and virtue have come, and untruth has disappeared."

KAJAKAI DAM (32-22' N, 65-11' E). A dam built as part of the Helmand Valley irrigation and electrification project by the Idaho-based Morrison-Knudsen Company. The dam is 300 feet high, 887 feet long, and stores a reservoir that is 32 miles long and has a capacity of 1,495,000 acre-feet of water. It was completed in April 1953 and it partially destroyed as a result of the civil war. *See also* HELMAND VALLEY AUTHORITY.

KAKAR. A Pashtun tribe, that claims descent from Kak or Kakar. It is loosely organized into four divisions, all located across the Afghan border in Pakistan, south and southeast of Kandahar: the Sanzar Khel — located in the Zhob Valley as well as in Pishin and Loralai; the Sanatia—who live primarily in the Quetta-Pishin district; the Targhara — in Pishin district; and the Sarghara—also in Pishin. The Kakars were merchant nomads (*see* POWINDAH) and traveled seasonally far into India.

KALA-I-NAO HAZARA. *See* **HAZARA.**

KALAKANI, ABDUL MAJID. A poet and writer and one of the founders of the Marxist *Shu'la-yi Javid* (Eternal Flame) party. He was born in 1939 at Kalakan in Kuhdaman district (north of Kabul). A biography, published by his organization, states that his father and grandfather were hanged, but does not give any details. He went with members of his family into exile in Kandahar. After the Marxist takeover, he was one of the founders of the Organization for the Liberation of the Afghan People (*SAMA — Sazman-i Azadibakhsh-i Mardum-i Afghanistan*) and the United National Front of Afghanistan. SAMA was an underground movement whose aim was the formation of a working class party, a united front with like-minded groups, and the creation of a "people's army." It opposed the **Pashtun**-dominated **PDPA**. On February 27, 1980 Kalakani was arrested and was executed on June 8. His brother Abdul Qayyum Rahbar (born in 1942 and educated at al-Azhar) succeeded to the leadership of SAMA but was killed by unknown assailants on January 27, 1990 in Peshawar. A number of other members of this family have been assassinated since the beginning of the war. According to recent declarations, SAMA advocates the establishment of a "national democratic" government with universal suffrage, the protection of human rights, and freedom of worship. It favors a federated state and the protection of minorities and denies that it is a Maoist party. It split and appears now to be a party of exiles.

KALAKANI, AMIR HABIBULLAH. *See* **HABIBULLAH, KALAK-ANI, AMIR.**

KALANTAR. The term for an official, during the reign of Amir **Abdul Rahman**, who was to preserve law and order in urban areas. He was (similar to the official known as *muhtasib*) responsible for dealing with minor offenses and had powers of arresting an offender. He was also in charge of producing lists of names of all males age sixteen to twenty-eight in his district for the purpose of establishing a pool of possible recruits for the police force. The *kalantar* was chosen by the community, unlike the *muhtasib*, who was chosen by a *qazi*.

KAM. Workers Intelligence Institute (*Da Kargarano Amniyyati Mu'assasa*) of President **Hafizullah Amin** which succeeded AGSA, the security service of President **Nur Muhammad Taraki**, with minor changes in personnel. It was headed by Aziz Ahmad Akbari for two months (August-September 1979) and then by Hafizullah's nephew, Asadullah Amin, who was killed with Hafizullah on December 27, 1979. Akbari is the nephew of **Asadullah Sarwari** and joined him in virtual exile as first secretary at the Afghan embassy at Ulan Bator, Mongolia. For further details *see also* KHAD and AFGHAN SECURITY SERVICE.

KAMRAN, PRINCE. The son of **Mahmud Shah** (r. 1800–1803 and 1809–17) and "King of Herat" after the death of his father in 1830. During the wars of succession, following the ouster of **Zaman Shah**, Kamran supported his father, who became Afghan king in 1800. Kamran recovered Peshawar for his father and was appointed governor of Kandahar. When his father was defeated by **Shah Shuja** in 1803, Kamran was driven from the city by Qaisar, son of Zaman Shah, and forced to seek safety in Herat. During the second reign of Mahmud Shah he established himself in Herat where **Fateh** (Fath) **Khan**, the oldest son of **Painda Khan,** was wazir. Kamran was ambitious and resented the power of the wazir; therefore, he had him blinded and subsequently killed. This started a struggle for power between the **Sadozai** and **Muhammadzai** branches of the **Durrani** clan, resulting in the fall the

Sadozai dynasty. In 1818 **Dost Muhammad** captured the Kabul throne, and in 1819, Mahmud Shah proclaimed himself king at Herat and made Kamran his wazir. Mahmud Shah died in 1829 under mysterious circumstances and was succeeded by Kamran. Kamran had the reputation of being a cruel and power-hungry man; he eventually ignored the conduct of the affairs of state and delegated much authority to his wazir, **Yar Muhammad** Alekozai. Trying to reassert his power, he made preparations to rid himself of the wazir but was captured and killed in 1842, after ruling Herat for twelve years. He was the last of the Sadozai rulers.

KANDAHAR (QANDAHAR, 31-35'N, 64-45'E). A province in south central Afghanistan with an area of 19,062 square miles and a population of 699,000. The province borders on Pakistan in the south, Helmand Province in the west, Oruzgan in the north, and Zabul in the east. Kandahar is the second largest town in Afghanistan, lying at an elevation of 3,050 feet and comprising an area of 15 square miles. In the late 1970s the city had about 178,000 inhabitants. Its strategic location has made it a desirable spot for settlements since ancient times. It was the capital of Afghanistan until 1775, when **Timur Shah** established his capital at Kabul. It is one of the major **Pashtun** cities and is inhabited mostly by **Durranis** but also has a **Hazara** population and Afghans of other ethnic groups. The old, walled town, of which only traces remain, was built by Timur Shah. The mausoleum of **Ahmad Shah**, founder of modern Afghanistan, is one of the major architectural features, as is the mosque of the *Khirqa Sharif*, where the cloak of the Prophet Muhammad is believed to be kept under lock and key. In the garden of the citadel overlooking the town is the shrine of Baba Wali, frequently visited by pilgrims. On the same hill, carved into the rock, are the "Forty Steps," *Chel Zina*, leading to a niche with 16th-century inscriptions from the days of the Moghol rulers Babur and Akbar Shah.

The city was part of the Achaemenid Empire of Darius I (r. 521–485 B.C.). It was rebuilt by Alexander the Great in 329 B.C., hence the name Kandahar, a corruption of "Iskander," the Eastern name for Alexander. Muslim Arabs conquered Kandahar in the seventh century. Thereafter Kandahar formed part of various Islamic kingdoms. In the 16th century the city was disputed between the rulers of the Safavid and Moghol Empires until **Mir Wais**, the **Ghilzai** governor of Kandahar, rebelled against Safavid control and began the process that led to the establishment of Afghanistan in 1747. British forces occupied the city in two Anglo-Afghan wars and suffered one of their severest defeats nearby at the **Battle of Maiwand** (July 27, 1880), when Sardar **Muhammad Ayub** wiped out a British Brigade under General Burrows.

Kandahar is surrounded by fertile land, covered with orchards, and famous for its grapes and pomegranates. The city is connected by a paved highway with Kabul, Herat, and Chaman, which lies on the Pakistan border. It has a major airport that the Afghan government had planned as a link in international travel. Its location made Kandahar an important trade and commercial center and key route to Iran and south into Pakistan, where a train link connects it with Karachi. Kandahar is dominated by Durranis who are rivals of the Ghilzai and tend to support ex-King **Muhammad Zahir**. When Russian troops evacuated the city, the Kabul government installed Nur-ul-Haq Ulumi, a Durrani, as governor. On November 5, 1994 the *Taliban* captured Kandahar and made it their provisional capital.

KAPISA (34-45' N, 69-30' E). A province created in 1964 with its capital at Mahmud Raqi and subsequently merged with Parwan Province. It is named after the ancient town of Kapisa, located at the present Bagram, which was said to have been founded by Alexander the Great (fourth century B.C.), the summer capital of Kanishka, the ruler of the Kushanid kingdom (second century A.D.). The city was destroyed in the eighth century.

The province is watered by the Nijrab, Panjshir, and Tagab Rivers. It is known for an abundance of mulberries and pomegranates. Major industries include the Gulbahar textile mills and cement production in **Jabal-us-Siraj**. For further details *see* PARWAN.

KARAKUL. *See* **QARAQUL.**

KARIZ. Or **QANAT.** An underground water channel used widely in southern and western Afghanistan for the purpose of irrigation in areas where electricity and pumps are not available. Well-like shafts are dug into the water table as much as 50 feet deep and connected by a channel that conducts water to fields some distance away. The channels are kept in working condition by dredging, a dangerous and difficult job, since a channel may collapse and bury the person working in it. As a result of the war in Afghanistan many kariz have fallen into disuse or have been destroyed, and formerly irrigated land has been lost.

KARMAL, BABRAK. President and secretary general of the **PDPA** from January 1980 until May 1986, when Dr. **Najibullah** took over control of the Afghan government. Born in 1929 in Kabul, the son of Major General Muhammad Husain (one-time governor of Paktia Province). He adopted the pen name Karmal (friend of labor) in about 1954. A founding member of the PDPA, he was a student activist at **Kabul University** and known as a Communist. Jailed from 1953 to 1956, he then worked in departments of the ministries of education and planning. In 1965 and 1969 he was elected to Parliament as representative of Kabul. He was a member of the central committee and subsequently secretary of the central committee of the PDPA. As a result of a dispute with **Nur Muhammad Taraki** over leadership of the party in 1965, he led the *Parcham* faction until it reunited with the *Khalqis* in 1977 and became a member of the secretariat and the politburo. In 1978 he was imprisoned after the funeral of **Mir Muhammad Akbar Khaibar**, but liberated as a result of the Saur Revolt. He was then elected vice-chairman of the revolutionary council and deputy prime minister of Afghanistan. In July 1978, the *Khalqi* regime purged the *Parchami* leadership, appointing Karmal Afghan ambassador to Czechoslovakia. In August, 1978, he was accused of plotting against the *Khalqi* government and stripped of party membership and all his positions. Restored to power with Soviet assistance, he succeeded **Hafizullah Amin** on Dec. 27, 1979. Karmal was described as an idealist, rather than a revolutionary. He was an eloquent orator in **Dari** and, with Anahita Ratebzad, an expert propagandist and the best known of the Marxist leadership. Having been restored to power with Soviet support, he was unable to consolidate his power and, in 1986, he was replaced by Najibullah and left Afghanistan for Moscow. After the fall of the Marxist regime in April 1992, many *Parchamis* joined **Jam'iat** and Babrak eventually moved to Mazar-i Sharif where his comrade, **Abdul Rashid Dostum** is the dominant political leader, and finally again to Moscow, where he died in December 1996.

KAUFMAN, GENERAL CONSTANTIN P. Conqueror of Samarkand in 1868 and Khiva in 1873, he became the first governor general of Russian Turkestan and subsequently *aide de camp* to the Tsar. He corresponded with Amir **Shir Ali** and his foreign minister and sent **General Stolietoff** to Kabul to conclude an alliance with the amir.

A treaty signed by the amir offered Russian support "either by means of advice or by such other means as it may consider proper."

When Britain made war, Russia did not send any assistance but advised Amir Shir Ali to make his peace with Britain. *See* SHIR ALI, AMIR; STOLIETOFF; and FIRST ANGLO-AFGHAN WAR.

KAZI. Or **KADHI** *See* **QAZI.**

KAZIM BEY, CAPT. Delegated by **Enver Pasha**, the Ottoman minister of War, to accompany the **Hentig-Niedermayer Expedition** to Afghanistan for the purpose of winning Afghan support in World War I. When the group disbanded in May 1916, Kazim Bey remained in Herat until the end of the war and then proceeded to Russian Central Asia. Together with **Barakatullah**, a Muslim-Indian member of the Hentig expedition, he conducted Pan-Islamic propaganda in Russian Turkestan. In September 1919 he accompanied the Afghan mission of **Muhammad Wali** to Moscow before he returned to Turkey.

KESHTMAND, SULTAN ALI. Member of the *Parcham* faction of the **PDPA** and at one time second in command in the government of **Babrak Karmal**. Born in 1935 in Kabul Province of a **Hazara** family and educated in economics at **Kabul University**, he took a position in the ministry of Mines and Industries. He was elected to the PDPA central committee at its founding congress, siding with Babrak Karmal in his disputed with **Nur Muhammad Taraki**. After the Saur Revolt he was purged with other leading *Parchamis* and sentenced to death, but his sentence was commuted to 15 years imprisonment. At the return to power of Babrak Karmal he became a member of the politburo and a year later was appointed prime minister (1981–88). After 1988 he held the positions of secretary of the central committee and chairman of the executive committee of the council of ministers. In May 1990 he was appointed first vice president of the Republic of Afghanistan, the highest ranking Hazara in the PDPA, but in February 1991 he was ousted from all his positions and went to Moscow until July. As a private individual he began to attack Pashtun chauvinism and demanded equal representation for the Afghan **Shi'a** community. After the fall of Kabul he left Afghanistan and now resides in England. His sister is married to **Tahir Badakhshi**.

KHAD. Later **WAD.** The State Security Service (*Khedamat-i Ittila'at-i Daulati*) of **Babrak Karmal** that evolved with some replacements in leadership out of AGSA, established by **Nur Muhammad Taraki**, and

KAM of **Hafizullah Amin**. It was headed by Dr. **Najibullah** before he succeeded to the position of general secretary of the **PDPA** and president of Afghanistan. Najibullah upgraded KHAD to ministerial status hence its new acronym WAD (*Wezarat-i Ittila'at-i Daulati*). General **Ghulam Faruq Yaqubi** succeeded Najibullah. The organization was reputed to control thousands of operatives and informers, as well as the National Guard and other fighting units. They were the best trained and disciplined forces and were well paid and provisioned and a major source of Dr. Najibullah's power. WAD was *Parchami* controlled and a balancing factor to the *Khalqi* strength in the military, which WAD had effectively penetrated. After the capture of Kabul by the *mujahedin*, President **Rabbani** set up his own security service which was also popularly called KHAD. *See also* AFGHAN SECU-RITY SERVICE.

KHADEM, QIAMUDDIN. A poet and writer who was vice president of the Pashtu Academy (1941) and in 1943 director of the Pashtu encyclopedia project (*see* AFGHAN ENCYCLOPEDIA SOCIETY). He served as editor of the *Ittihad-i Mashriqi* (1942), *Tulu-ye Afghan* (1950), *Kabul Majalla* (1951), *Islah* (1953), *Zeri* (1955), *Haywad* (1963), and as publisher of *Afghan Wolus* (1969). He was born in 1907 in Kama, Nangarhar Province, and educated under the supervision of his father. He began his career as a teacher but then turned to journalism. A founding member of *Afghan Millat*. He was appointed a senator in 1965 and died in 1979.

KHAIBAR, MIR MUHAMMAD AKBAR. Chief *Parchami* party ideologue whose assassination sparked the **Saur Revolt** of 27th April 1978. Born in 1925 in Logar Province, he attended Kabul Military School and became an instructor in the Police Academy. Arrested in 1950 as a leftist agitator, he met **Babrak Karmal** in prison and became his ally and a founding member of the **People's Democratic Party of Afghanistan**. He was called "Ustad," Master, by his *Parchami* comrades and was for a time editor of *Parcham*, the party newspaper. His major activity was to recruit army officers for his party. He was assassinated on April 17, 1978, a day after he visited the air force base at Bagram, according to *Parchami* claims, by *Khalqis*, his Communist rivals. The Marxists blamed the Daud government for the assassination and staged mass demonstrations in Kabul that led to the arrest of some party leaders. A few days later, members of the armed forces started the Saur coup that brought a Marxist government to power.

KHAIBAR PASS (34-1' N, 71-10' E). A historic pass, through a gorge and barren hills, from the Afghan border to Peshawar, Pakistan. It starts about ten miles from Peshawar, at Ali Masjid village, narrows to about 200 yards, and reaches its highest point at 3,518 feet. Eventually the pass widens and ends at Torkham, the Afghan frontier post. The population within the area of the pass is largely **Afridi**. A narrow-gauge railroad, built by the British in the late 19th century, connects the pass with the Peshawar rail terminal. Britain gained control of the pass in the **Treaty of Gandomak**, and this Afghan "gateway to India" is now on the Pakistani side of the **Durand** Line. Landi Kotal, located a few miles within the pass, is one of the smugglers' markets of the Frontier where one can buy foreign-made goods found only in the tribal area of Pakistan. The Pakistan government has tried to curb this lucrative trade but will probably never succeed.

KHALES, MUHAMMAD YUNUS. Leader (amir) of the *Hizb-i Islami*, one of two groups with the same name headquartered in Pakistan. Born in 1919 in Gandomak, Khugiani, he was educated in **Islamic law** and theology. He is a radical Islamist and fervent anti-Communist and in the 1960s contributed articles to the conservative *Gahis* newspaper. After the Daud coup in 1973 he was forced to flee to Pakistan, because he had made many enemies among **Muhammad Daud**'s supporters. A member with **Hekmatyar** of Hizb-i-Islami, he seceded and formed his own group with the same name which fought the Kabul government in the **Khugiani** area. He often accompanied **Jalaluddin Haqani**, his deputy, on raids inside Afghanistan. Other commanders of his forces include **Abdul Haq**, who operated in the Kabul area, and Haji Qadir in Nangarhar. Khales is opposed to universal suffrage, the emancipation of women, and **Shi'a** participation in the Afghan Interim Government, although he was a strong supporter of the AIG. Khales and his commanders were the major force in a council that ruled Nangarhar Province until it was captured by the *Taliban* in September 1996. *See also* ISLAMIC ALLIANCE FOR THE LIBERATION OF AFGHAN-ISTAN; ISLAMIST MOVEMENT; and HEKMATYAR.

KHALIFA . *See* **CALIPHATE.**

KHALILI, ABDUL KARIM. Succeeded **Abdul Ali Mazari** as head of the *Shi'a* **Hizb-i Wahdat** that controls the **Hazarajat**. He evicted his *Shi'a* rivals Ustad **Akbari** and **Muhammad Asef Muhsini** from Bamian in October 1995. Khalili is allied with **Abdur Rashid Dostum** against the government of President **Rabbani**, but joined the latter to fight the *Taliban* movement. *See also* HIZB-I WAHDAT.

KHALILI, KHALILULLAH. Afghan "Poet Laureate" whose collected works (*diwan*) have been published in three parts in 1960, 1975, and 1984. He was born in Kabul the son of Muhammad Husain Khan (financial secretary of Amirs **Abdul Rahman** and **Habibullah**). His father was executed in the early **Amanullah** period and Khalili moved with members of his family to Kohistan (now in Parwan Province) until the rise of **Habibullah Kalakani** in 1929. He held various offices under the **Tajik** king, but then lived as a refugee in Tashkent and later with his uncle **Abdul Rahim Khan** in Herat. At Herat he wrote his first work, History of Herat, which attracted wide acclaim. In 1944 Khalili and members of his family were imprisoned as supporters of the Safi revolt. After a period of exile in Kandahar, Khalili became lecturer at **Kabul University** (1948) and secretary of the **Shah Mahmud** cabinet (1949). In 1951 he became minister of press and information and chief adviser for press and information to King **Zahir** (1953). In 1965 he was elected a member of parliament from Jabal-us Siraj and founded the centrist *Wahdat-i-Milli* (National Unity) party. He was appointed Afghan ambassador to Saudi Arabia and Iraq from 1969–78. In 1985 he left Afghanistan and died in Pakistan two years later. He published a historical biography of **Habibullah Kalakani**, called *A Hero from Khorasan*, in which he depicts the Tajik king as a noble *mujahed* and sensitive man. *See* HABIBULLAH KALAKANI.

KHALIS. *See* **KHALES, MUHAMMAD YUNUS.**

KHALQ. Meaning "people," is the name of a weekly newspaper first published on April 11, 1966 by **Nur Muhammad Taraki** and edited by **Bareq-Shafi'i.** The name of the paper was subsequently given to the Taraki/**Amin** faction of the **PDPA**, in distinction to the *Parchamis* (also named after their party organ) headed by **Babrak Karmal**. The newspaper was banned by the Afghan government six weeks after its first appearance. *See also* PEOPLES DEMOCRATIC PARTY OF AFGHANISTAN and KHALQ (PARTY).

KHALQ (PARTY). One faction of the **PDPA** headed by **Nur Muhammad Taraki** (April 1978 to September 1979) and **Hafizullah Amin** (September to December 1979), popularly named so after its newspaper, *Khalq*. The party split into two major factions in 1965. *Khalq* continued under the leadership of Taraki until 1977 when it reunited with the *Parcham* faction, led by **Babrak Karmal**. Together they staged the **Saur Revolt** (April 27, 1978), but Taraki's faction captured the government and purged the leadership of *Parcham*. In December 1979 Karmal returned to power with Soviet support and *Parcham* became the dominant faction of the PDPA. Only two of six party members in President **Najibullah**'s government (May 1990) were *Khalqis*: **Muhammad A. Watanjar** and Raz Muhammad Paktin. The factions never stopped fighting for supremacy, the latest manifestation of which was the attempted coup by the *Khalqi* minister of defense, **Shahnawaz Tanai**. After the fall of the Marxist regime in April 1992, many *Khalqis* joined **Hekmatyar**, and *Parchamis* sided with **Rabbani**. Because of their **Pashtun** background, many of the *Khalqi* officers joined the *Taliban* after they conquered Kabul and two-thirds of Afghanistan. For information on the PDPA, *see* PEOPLES DEMO-CRATIC PARTY OF AFGHANISTAN.

KHAN. Title of tribal chiefs, landed proprietors, and heads of communities. Feudal khans were given honorary military ranks in exchange for providing levies for the Afghan army in case of national emergency. The title was also used in designating the tribe of the ruling family, *khan khel*, and in positions like *khan-i ulum*, chief justice. Now khan is used like "mister" and placed after the name of a person.

KHAN, KHAN ABDUL GHAFFAR. Pashtun nationalist, acclaimed as the "Frontier Gandhi" because he advocated non-violent means for gaining independence from Britain for the Frontier Afghans. He was born in 1890 in Utmanzai village in the **North-West Frontier Province** (NWFP) of India and educated in village schools and in high schools in Peshawar. He founded various organizations, including the *Khuda-i Khidmatgaran* (Servants of God), also called "**Red Shirts**," and attracted many followers in the NWFP and Afghanistan. He was imprisoned many times by the British Indian and Pakistan governments and was always an honored guest at Kabul, where the **Pashtunistan** issue was strongly supported. King **Amanullah** gave him the title *Fakhr-i Afghan* (Pride of the Afghans) and he lived intermittently in

Kabul as guest of the royal, republican, and Marxist governments. He died in Peshawar in the late 1980s and is buried in Jalalabad.

KHASADAR. A tribal militia supplementing the regular Afghan army, usually under the direct command of provincial governors or district chiefs. They were employed in various duties, including collecting fines and serving as border guards. They were stationed throughout the country and only during campaigns did they come under the direct command of the of the army commanders. Many were recruited from **Waziri** and **Mahsud** tribes from the British side of the border, in spite of British protests.

KHASHRUD (31-11' N, 62-1' E). A river which rises in the Siahband range, running in a southwesterly direction past Dilaram and the village of Khash. From there it continues to Chakhansur in Nimruz Province, circles Zaranj, and after a course of about 250 miles dissipates in the **Hamun** on the Iranian side of the border.

KHATAK, KHUSHHAL KHAN (1613–89). A famous Afghan warrior, poet, and tribal chief of the Khatak tribe who called on the Afghans to fight the Moghuls then occupying their land. He admonished Afghans to forsake their anarchistic tendencies and unite to regain the strength and glory they once possessed. But he was pessimistic, saying "The day the Pashtuns unite, old Khushhal will arise from the grave." Khushhal Khan was born near Peshawar, the son of Shahbaz Khan, a chief of the Khatak tribe. By appointment of the Moghul emperor, Shah Jehan, Khushhal succeeded his father in 1641, but Aurangzeb, Shah Jehan's successor, kept him a prisoner in the Gwaliar fortress in Delhi. After Khushhal was permitted to return to Peshawar he incited the Pashtuns to rebel. His grave carries the inscription: "I have taken up the sword to defend the pride of the Afghan, I am Khushhal Khattak, the honorable man of the age." The Khatak tribe of Khushhal Khan now lives in the areas of Kohat, Peshawar, and Mardan in the **North-West Frontier Province** of Pakistan and numbers between 100,000 and 160,000 people.

KHILAFAT MOVEMENT. *See* **HIJRAT MOVEMENT.**

KHORASAN. The word means the East or "Land of the Rising Sun," the name of a province in northeastern Iran and the historical name of an

area that roughly corresponds to eastern Iran and Afghanistan at the
time of **Ahmad Shah** (r. 1747–73). It was part of the Achaemenid and
Sasanian Empires, then conquered by the Muslim Arabs in A.D.
651–52. Abu Muslim raised the "Black Banner" of the house of Abbas
and with his Khorasanian army defeated the Umayyads, bringing the
Abbasid caliphs to power. Khorasan was virtually independent under
the Tahirid, Saffarid, and Samanid dynasties (821–999) and part of
Ghaznavid, Seljuk, and Khwarizm Empires. The Mongols controlled
the area, and the Safavids fought the **Uzbeks** over Khorasan before it
became the heartland of Ahmad Shah's empire. Khorasan was called
the "cradle of classical Persian culture."

KHOST (33-22' N, 69-52' E). A town (also called Matun) and district in
Paktia Province, with a population of about 50,000 people. The area
saw some of the fiercest fighting during the war against the Marxist
government (*see* KHOST, FALL OF and ZHAWAR, BATTLE OF).
The district is inhabited by Khostwals in the north and **Waziris** in the
south, which impinges on Waziristan, a district in Pakistan.

  In addition to a limited amount of agriculture and livestock breeding,
Khost supports a timber industry. It is one of few wooded areas in
Afghanistan, and timber is smuggled to Pakistan where it fetches a good
price. Because of the present civil war, government prohibitions of
timber export to Pakistan are ignored, and deforestation is resulting in
irreparable harm. The *Taliban* captured the area in September 1996
prior to their conquest of Jalalabad and Kabul.

KHOST, FALL OF (33-22' N, 69-52' E). A town and district in Paktia
Province, which had seen severe fighting because it was a major
government base for cutting the line of *mujahedin* forces. The town
was commonly called "Little Moscow" because of the fact that many of
the Marxist leaders were native to this area and therefore enjoyed the
support of the population. Located only about 18 miles from the
Pakistan border, the town was under siege since 1986 and had to be
supplied mostly by air. The town was protected by a 3,000-man
garrison, supported by militia units, and fortified with a mined perimeter
that could not be easily breached. In March 1991 a unified *mujahedin*
force headed by a 23-member council in which **Jalaluddin Haqani** had
a prominent role began to close in on the town. The Kabul government
may have had information of *mujahedin* plans and had airlifted
reinforcements into the besieged town. High-ranking officers had

arrived, among them Colonel-General Muhammad Zahir Solamal, a deputy minister of defense. On March 13, a few days before the beginning of Ramadhan (the month of fasting), the *mujahedin* started with a three-day rocket barrage followed by ground attacks from all sides, but it was not until March 30 that the airport was captured; a day later the garrison surrendered. Bad weather and surface-to-air missiles, including **stingers**, did not permit close aerial support, but some 40 SCUD missiles were fired. It appears that the surrender was achieved largely as a result of negotiations, and the militia units are said to have changed sides in time to permit their escape. About 2,200 Kabul soldiers were taken, and 500 wounded were transported to receive medical assistance. About 300 were killed. Among the prisoners were Colonel-General Solamal; Major-General Ghulam Mustafa, chief of political affairs of the armed forces; Major-General Muhammad Qasim, commander of artillery; Major Muhammad Azam, an air force commander; and Lt.-Gen. Shirin, commander of the Khost militia units. For the *mujahedin* this was a major morale booster; the Kabul government announced a "day of mourning" and accused the *mujahedin* of violating the "sanctity of Ramadhan." It blamed the defeat on *Khalqi* betrayal and claimed that Pakistani forces had participated in the assault. The relatively lenient treatment of the prisoners, some 2,000 (1,200 according to AFGHANews) families of Kabul supporters were permitted to find shelter in Pakistan, may be explained by the surrender and the fact that the battle was primarily between Pashtuns who did not want to incite tribal feuds. The town suffered from reprisal bombing and *mujahedin* plunder. The *mujahedin* obtained large quantities of arms and ammunition, including tanks, armored cars, helicopters, and light and heavy guns. **Hekmatyar**'s forces were blamed of having snatched more than their "allotment." No numbers were given as to *mujahedin* casualties.

KHOST REBELLION. A rebellion led by the **Mangal** tribe that seriously threatened the rule of King **Amanullah**. The revolt started in March 1924 in response to the king's reforms. The Mangals, under Abdullah Khan and Mulla-i Lang (the Lame Mulla), were able to establish a base in Khost and were about to advance on Kabul. At the same time Abdul Karim, son by a slave girl of ex-Amir **Yaqub Khan**, escaped from British-Indian exile and joined the rebels. In April 1924, the rebels were beaten but not yet defeated. **Sulaiman Khel** and Ali Khel tribes (*see* GHILZAI) joined the revolt. In August, King Amanullah dramatically proclaimed holy war against them. But it was not until January 1925 that the rebels were defeated. Abdullah Khan and the Mulla-i Lang were captured and executed together with 53 prisoners. The citizens of Kabul were treated to a victory parade, headed by **Muhammad Wali Khan**, which carried the booty, followed by almost 2,000 prisoners, including women and children, organized according to tribal affiliation. The prisoners were, in the words of the German representative in Kabul, "wild men with sullen, taciturn faces who did not take the least notice of the amir" (Adamec, 1974). The revolt slowed down the amir's process of reform until 1928, when King Amanullah again forced the process of Westernization.

KHUGIANI. A Durrani tribe settled primarily in the Jalalabad area but also in Laghman and Kandahar. It is divided into three major clans: the Wazir, Kharbun, and Sherzad. They are neighbors of the **Shinwaris** and **Ghilzais**. In 1928 they joined the Shinwaris and other tribes in a rebellion that led to the ouster of King **Amanullah**. In the war against the Marxist government, the Khugianis made up the majority of the *mujahedin* forces of the **Hizb** of **Yunus Khales**.

KHULM. *See* **TASHQURGHAN.**

KHURAM. *See* **KHURRAM, ALI AHMAD.**

KHURD KABUL PASS (34-23' N, 69-23' E). A pass about twenty miles east of Kabul, extending for a length of about six miles and only about 100 to 200 yards wide, through which passes a road, crossing the Kabul River twenty-three times. On the third day of their **Death March** during the British retreat on January 8, 1842, **Ghilzai** forces blocked the pass and opened fire on the British troops and camp followers, causing panic of the "frightened mass, abandoning baggage, arms, ammunition, women and children, regardless of all but their lives." (GAZ5) Some 3,000 soldiers and camp followers perished.

KHURRAM, ALI AHMAD. Minister of Planning from 1974 until his assassination on November 17, 1977. According to an article by Zalmai Popal, an official in the ministry of planning, Ali Ahmad Khurram fell victim to President **Muhammad Daud**'s change of policy. Daud wanted to broaden economic ties with the West and discontinue "excessive reliance" on Soviet support in the process of developing the country. Arab and Iranian funds were expected to become available, and Khurram had instructions to speedily complete projects started with Soviet technical and financial assistance and not accept any new ones. The assassin, one Muhammad Marjan, is said to have had *Khalqi* connections but claimed to have acted "in the name of the Islamic Revolution." He was sentenced to imprisonment for life but was later freed in a general amnesty. Khurram was born in 1931 in Kabul and educated at **Kabul University** and in the United States and began work in the ministry of planning in 1956.

KHUTBA. Friday sermon delivered at a congregational mosque. It has political significance because the *Khateb* (preacher) traditionally invokes the name of the recognized ruler. When Afghanistan was in rebellion against King **Amanullah**, preachers in disputed areas read the sermon "in the name of the Islamic king," in order to avoid indicating their loyalty. *See also* ISLAM and MOSQUE.

KHYBER. *See* **KHAIBAR.**

KIRGHIZ. *See* **QIRGHIZ.**

KISHTMAND. *See* **KESHTMAND, SULTAN ALI.**

KIZILBASH. *See* **QIZILBASH.**

KOH-I BABA (34-41' N, 67-30' E). A mountain range extending from east to west across the center of Afghanistan and forming part of the **Hindu Kush** mountain massif. The range includes peaks rising over 16,000 feet and difficult passes reaching altitudes of 12,000 and 13,000 feet. North of the Koh-i Baba the Turkestan plateau extends to the **Amu Daria**.

KOH-I NUR. A diamond measured at 191 carats (subsequently cut in London to 108 carats) that was part of **Nadir Shah Afshar**'s booty from the Moghul treasure of Delhi in 1739. After Nadir's assassination in 1747, the Koh-i Nur (Mountain of Light) came into the possession of **Ahmad Shah**, founder of the **Durrani** Empire, who passed it on to his sons. As a result of internecine fighting between Afghan princes, **Shah Shuja** was forced to flee and seek the hospitality of the Sikh ruler **Ranjit Singh**. The latter took possession of the precious stone in 1813.

When in 1849 the British defeated their erstwhile ally they took the Koh-i Nur from the Sikhs. The viceroy of India subsequently presented it to Queen Victoria, and it has since been worn in the crowns of British queens (superstition has it that it brings misfortune if worn by men).

KOHISTAN (35-1' N, 69-18' E). A district in Parwan Province north of Kabul. It includes the valleys of Tagao, Nijrao, Panjshir, Ghorband, and Charikar as well as collateral valleys. The population is largely Tajik and Sunni Muslim. **Habibullah Kalakani**, Afghan king for nine months, and Ahmad Shah Mas'ud were natives of this district.

KUCHI. Kuchi (T.) literally means a person who migrates. In Afghanistan the term is applied to all nomads. In India the term **Powindah** is used for Kuchi. *See also* POWINDAH.

KUNAR (35-15' N, 71-0' E). A province in northeastern Afghanistan with an area of 3,742 square miles and a population of about 250,000, which is composed principally of **Nuristanis** in the north and west and **Pashtuns** in the south and east. The two ethnic groups have long been at odds because of infringement by the Pashtuns on Nuristani land. The province is traversed by the Kunar River which is fed by the Pech, Waigal, and Chitral Streams and runs in a southwesterly direction into the Kabul River near Jalalabad. It provides irrigation for corn, rice, and wheat cultivation, largely on a subsistence level. Kunar and Paktia Provinces are the major forested areas in Afghanistan. Kunar borders on Pakistan in the east, Nangarhar Province in the south, Laghman in the west, and Badakhshan in the north. The administrative center of the province is Asadabad (near Chegha Sarai), which Afghans believe to be the birth place of **Sayyid Jamaluddin Afghani**. In the 1970s Kunar Province was absorbed into Nangarhar Province, with Asadabad the administrative center of the sub-province (Loya Woluswali); but in 1977 it was again designated a province. After the withdrawal of Soviet forces in 1988, the Kabul government created Nuristan Province from portions of Kunar and Laghman Provinces. The remainder of Kunar was once again consolidated into Nangarhar Province.

The *mujahedin* revolt began in 1978 in Kunar Province. Within a year government bases were captured. Virtually all *mujahedin* groups operated in the province, but in Asadabad the "Wahhabi Republic" (or *Salafia*, Islamic revival movement, also called *ahl-i hadith* people of the traditions) headed by **Maulawi Jamilurrahman** and **Hekmat-**

yar's **Hizb** were the major contenders. Based on Saudi and Kuwaiti support, Jamilurrahman was able to win a large following, which adopted the alien Hanbali school as its religious authority. Radical **Islamist** volunteers from Arab countries provided both military and financial support to the Wahhabi forces. *Daulat* (State), another Wahhabi group headed by one Maulawi Afzal, had some strength in the areas of Kamdesh and Bargamatal. The Wahhabis were accused of killing their prisoners and enslaving women and have therefore come under criticism from other *mujahedin* groups. The Iraqi invasion of Kuwait led to a cut in funds and greatly limited the activities of Jamilurrahman's forces. In February 1991 he announced his cabinet (*See* JAMILURRAHMAN, MAULAWI HUSAIN) and proclaimed his area an "Islamic Amirate."

Elections were held in the Kunar Valley in which the victory of the "Arabs" was disputed by Hekmatyar. Armed clashes between the Wahhabis and members of Hekmatyar's forces increased. After Hekmatyar made peace with the **Rabbani** government in May 1996, one member of the Wahhabis was represented in Hekmatyar's cabinet of July 1996. But the independent enclave was ended when the *Taliban* captured Asadabad in September 1996.

KUNDUZ (QONDUZ) (36-45'N, 68-51'E). A province in northern Afghanistan with an area of 2,876 square miles and an estimated population of 575,000. The province borders on Tajikistan in the north, Takhar Province in the east, Baghlan in the south, and Samangan in the west. The administrative capital of the state is the town of Kunduz, with about 53,000 inhabitants. Kunduz River, called Surkhab at its source in the **Koh-i Baba** range, meanders through Kunduz Province and runs in a northwesterly direction into the **Amu Daria**. Afghanistan's cotton industry began in Kunduz in the 1940s. An industrial complex, the Spin Zar Company, grows and gins cotton and produces edible oil and soap. Sericulture was started at about the same time, and silk weavers produce colorful fabrics for local use and export. **Uzbek** garments, like the long-sleeved *japan* (caftans), soft-soled boots, and embroidered caps, constitute an important home industry. The population is largely Uzbek, but Pashtuns and Persian-speakers as well as other ethnic communities can also be found.

KUSHANID KINGDOM. A kingdom that flourished during the first two centuries A.D. and included parts of the Indus Valley, eastern

Afghanistan, and Central Asia north to the Aral Sea. It was founded by Kajula Kadphises (40–78 A.D.) and enjoyed its cultural greatness under his successor Kanishka (d. 123 or 173 A.D.), whose capitals were located at Peshawar and Kapisa (now the site of **Bagram**) as well as in Mathura, south of Delhi. The empire brought about a cultural renaissance and the spread of Buddhism into China. A hundred temples were built in Kapisa, supporting some 6,000 monks. Gandharan art, representing a fusion of Hellenistic and Buddhist civilizations and art forms, testify to the splendor of the Kushanid court. The kingdom was destroyed by Hephtalite invaders in the fifth century.

KUSHKAKI, BURHANUDDIN. Educator, journalist, and scholar of Islamic law, born in 1894 in Kushkak, Nangarhar Province. He served as editor or director of many important Afghan newspapers, including *Ittihad-i Mashriqi* (Eastern Union) in Jalalabad, *Aman-i Afghan* (Afghan Peace), *Habibul Islam* (Friend of Islam), and *Islah* (Reconstruction) in Kabul. He is the author of *Rahnama-yi Qataghan wa Badakhshan* (Guide to Qataghan and Badakhshan) and *Nadir-i Afghan*; he translated the **Qor'an** into Pashtu. He died in 1953.

L

LAGHMAN (35-0' N, 70-15' E). A province in eastern Afghanistan that comprises an area of 2,790 square miles and a population of about 387,000. Laghman borders on Kapisa in the west, Badakhshan in the north, Kunar in the east, Nangarhar in the south, and Kabul Province in the southwest. The administrative center is the village of Mehterlam. According to local mythology, Laghman got its name from Lamech, father of Noah, whose ark is supposed to have landed on Kund Mountain, part of the Kafiristan mountain range. From Lamech the name changed to Lamakan and Laghman. Lamech was supposed to have taken the country from the Kafirs but was killed in the battle. **Sultan Mahmud of Ghazni**, inspired by a dream, went to Mehtarlam and built a tomb over the presumed grave of Lamech. Originally occupied by Kafirs, the area was subsequently taken over by Jabbar Khel and Abu Bakar Khel **Ghilzais**.

LALMI. Land cultivated without the benefit of irrigation.

LANGUAGE GROUPS. Three languages predominate in Afghanistan—**Pashtu, Dari** (or Farsi), and Turki (including **Uzbek,** Turkoman, Qirghiz). No reliable statistics exist, but Pashtu is said to be the language of about six and one half-million Afghans. Pashtu speakers are the dominant group and were until recently the only ones called Afghans, whereas the others were known by their ethnic appellation (**Tajik, Baluch,** etc.). The Pashtuns predominate in the south of Afghanistan and in the cities of Kandahar and Jalalabad, although they can be found in smaller communities in most parts of the country.

Second in numbers are the speakers of Dari and its dialects, including Hazaragi, spoken by the **Hazara.** They number about five million and predominate in the center, northwest, and northeast of Afghanistan as well as in urban areas. Dari is still the predominant language in education, although the Afghan government has made a great effort to make Pashtu the national language. The Afghan constitution of 1964 recognized both Pashtu and Dari as official languages of Afghanistan. Turkic languages include Uzbek, with one million speakers the largest of this group of languages, followed by Turkoman, Moghol, and Qirghiz, spoken by about 150 thousand people. The Baluch, Brahui, and Nuristani languages are spoken by fewer than 500,000. Although there exist groups of Arab descent, none of them presently speaks Arabic or an Arabic dialect. Indian languages were spoken by small groups, including Hindu and **Sikh** citizens of Afghanistan, most of whom left the country as a result of the civil war. Most Afghans are bilingual, and most newspapers carry articles in both Pashtu and Dari. Only since the **Saur Revolt** was an effort made to cultivate other minority languages. The "homogenizing" effort at creating an Afghan nation out of many nationalities gave way to a policy of cultural autonomy when the Marxist government recognized Uzbek, Turkmani, Baluchi, Pashai, and one Nuristani dialect as "national languages." Newspapers appeared in these languages, and radio and television offered programs in minority languages. The present civil war and the division of the country have ended the existence of a national press and language policy. *See also* ETHNIC GROUPS.

LASH JUWAIN (31-43' N, 61-37' E). A small town and administrative district in the southwestern corner of Farah Province. The name is a combination of Lash, a fort on the Farah River, and Juwain, the surrounding plain, and is also written Lash-o-Juwain or Lash-i Juwain. The country surrounding the town is scattered with ruins testifying to a prosperous past that ended with Mongol invasions. The land is fertile and in the 1970s supported an agricultural population of some 15,000.

LASHKAR. Afghan tribal armies, recruited during emergencies in support of the regular army. They fought under their own chiefs, often in competition with other *lashkars*, and therefore not always cooperating in joint operations. The **Sulaiman Khel Ghilzais** were able to muster some 20,000 fighters and, all together, the Afghan nomads, traveling yearly to India, could muster as many as 100,000 fighters. For a long time they were superior to the regular army, considered brave to recklessness, but out for plunder and of limited staying power. They would be reluctant to operate far from their tribal areas. Feuds, temporarily ended to face a foreign invader, were quickly resumed. During the war of the 1980s, both the Kabul government and the *mujahedin* engaged tribal forces to protect their lines of supply. With the growth and modernization of the Afghan army, the *lashkars* lost much of their importance.

LASHKARGAH (31-35' N, 64-21' E). Capital of Helmand Province with about 21,600 inhabitants in the 1970s and also the site of an ancient town built by **Sultan Mahmud of Ghazni** in the tenth century. It is located on the Helmand River, a few miles south of the main road linking Kandahar and Herat. The Ghorids sacked the town in 1150 A.D. but rebuilt it in new splendor. It was irreparably destroyed by the hordes of Genghis Khan (1226). Because of its strategic location, Afghan rulers constructed a number of forts on the site. A visitor to the area at the turn of the century observed the fortified plateau "covered thickly with the remains of towers, forts, and palatial buildings, which exhibit traces of great architectural skill, and afford evidence of the existence at one time on this site of a large and important city, fortified with unusual skill and strength, and inhabited by a people who combined a knowledge of military art with considerable taste and culture" (Gaz. 2).

The town was called Lashkari Bazaar by the local population as well as Kala-i Bist or Bost. *See also* HELMAND.

LAW. *See* **ISLAMIC LAW.**

LAWRENCE, COLONEL T. E. The Englishman of "Lawrence of Arabia" fame is suspected by many Afghans to have been a link in a conspiracy to topple King **Amanullah** from his throne. The Afghan government learned from reports in the London *Sunday Express* of September 13, 1928, that Lawrence was on the Afghan border on a "secret" mission. He was indeed there under the alias of "Shaw." The *Aman-i-Afghan* of December 12, 1928 commented that it was certain that the man who had "gathered the miserable Arabs in a revolt against the Turks" was up to mischief in Afghanistan. But the paper debunked his effectiveness on the Afghan Frontier, for after all "he is only an Englishman." The London *Daily News* of December 5, 1929 reported that Lawrence was in India, busily learning Pashtu, and "inferred he intends to move into Afghanistan." Much of the non-British press was convinced that this was a conspiracy in support of **Habibullah Kalakani**. No sources have been found in British archives to support this conspiratorial theory, and the British government denied all charges. In a letter to Edward Marsh, dated June 10, 1927, Lawrence reported "... do you know that I nearly went there [Kabul], last week? The British Attache at Kabul is entitled to an airman clerk, and the Depot would have put my name forward, if I had been a bit nippier on a typewriter." Lawrence spent eighteen months in India, most of this time in Karachi but a short time also in Miranshah (across the border from Paktia Province) as well as one weekend in Peshawar. After the British minister at Kabul, Sir Francis Humphrys, frantically appealed to London, Lawrence was finally sent back to Britain.

LAYEQ, SULAIMAN. A poet and writer in **Pashtu** and **Dari** who was a founding member of the **PDPA**, member of the politburo, the party secretariat, and president of the **Afghan Academy** of Sciences. He is the author of the Marxist national anthem. Born on October 7, 1930 of the **Sulaiman Khel** tribe, he studied Islamic sciences but was expelled from school because of his leftist activism. He was employed with *Haiwad* newspaper and Radio Kabul and in 1968 became publisher and editor of the Marxist newspaper *Parcham*. After the Saur Revolt he became minister of Radio and Television, but was purged by the *Khalqi* regime and imprisoned. After the *Parchami* faction of the PDPA came to power, Layeq was appointed president of the Academy of Sciences (April 1980) and minister of Frontier Affairs (1981). In the **Najibullah** government he remained a member of the politburo and the secretariat of the central committee. After the fall of the Marxist regime in April 1992, Layeq went abroad and is said to have sought asylum in Europe.

LIMITED CONTINGENT OF SOVIET FORCES IN AFGHAN-ISTAN (LCSFA). Soviet term for its forces in Afghanistan that included, according to McMichael (14), 85,000 ground troops, 25,000 support troops, and 10,000 air force troops. To this should be added some 30,000 soldiers and airmen who operated from Soviet territory. The ground units were made up of the 40th Army Headquarters, five motorized rifle divisions, four to five separate motorized rifle brigades or regiments, three to four air assault or airmobile brigades, one to three brigades or special operations troops (*spetsnaz*), one engineer regiment/brigade, and one army artillery brigade. About one-third of the force was concentrated in the Kabul area, and the rest were deployed in Jalalabad, Kunduz/Mazar-i Sharif, Herat/Farah, Shindand, and Kandahar. Smaller garrisons were stationed in other towns. *See also* AFGANTSY and GROMOV, GEN. LT. BORIS V.

LOGAR (33-50' N, 69-0' E). A province south of Kabul with an area of 1,702 square miles and a population estimated in the late 1970s at 424,000 (in 1989 about 176,000 of this number were refugees in Pakistan). The province is bounded in the west by Wardak Province, in the north by Kabul, in the east by Nangarhar, in the south by Paktia, and in the southwest by Ghazni Province. The administrative center is the town of Pul-i-Alam, located about 50 kilometers south of Kabul. The population is largely **Pashtun** of the **Ahmadzai** tribe and some **Tajik** in the Khoshi area. In 1979, about 80 % of the population were farmers, and the area was called the "granary of Kabul." Fruit, specifically grapes and apples, and vegetables are the major cash crops. This is supplemented with animal husbandry and trading. Continuous war has caused considerable damage to the economy of the province.

LOHANI. Or **LOWANA.** Nomadic tribes, also called **Powindahs**, who conducted cross-border trade with India. They are **Ghilzai** Pashtuns and claim descent from Ibrahim, second son of Ghalzoe, whose mother called him "Loeday," meaning he is the "greater son." They are now located in the **NWFP** of Pakistan in the areas of Kohat, Bannu, and Peshawar. The 16th-century Afghan Lodi dynasty of India is named after the Lohanis. *See also* POWINDAH.

LOINAB. *See* **ALI AHMAD.**

LOYA JIRGA. Great (or national) council, it is the highest organ of state power that Afghan rulers convened to decide matters of national importance. It was first held by **Mir Wais** (r. 1709–15), the Hotaki Ghilzai chief who rebelled against the Persian occupation of Kandahar. **Ahmad Shah**'s assumption of the throne was legitimized by a Loya Jirga of tribal chiefs, as were the constitutions of King **Amanullah** (1923) and **Zahir Shah** (1964). When in October 1941 the Allies forced the Afghan government to expel all Axis nationals, the Loya Jirga reluctantly gave its approval but insisted that they be given free passage through Allied territory.

Amir **Abdul Rahman**'s Loya Jirga was composed of *sardars*, the heads of the royal families; important *khans*; and high religious leaders. The 1964 Loya Jirga was composed of 455 members representing the following sectors:

Elected members	176
National assembly	176
Appointed by the King	34
Senate members	19
Cabinet members	14
Supreme court members	5
Constitutional committee	7
Constitutional advisory commission	24 (L. Dupree, 1973)

Some jirgas were easily manipulated and no more than rubber stamps of the decisions of the Afghan ruler, but at times jirgas defied the monarch. A jirga convened by King Amanullah in Paghman in August 1928 forced the king to compromise and rescind some of his reforms. Both the ***mujahedin*** and the Marxist governments have convened Loya Jirgas in support of their cause. However, the validity of the jirgas was disputed because they were not representative of the Afghan population and, in the case of the *mujahedin*, were convened outside Afghan territory. President **Rabbani** convened a *Shura*, council, of "the people with power to loose and bind" (*ahl al-hall wa-al-'aqd*), trying to legitimize his position, but it is not clear whether he intended to Islamize the institution of the *Loya Jirga*.

M

MACNAGHTEN, SIR WILLIAM (1793–1841). British chief secretary to the Indian government, appointed envoy and minister to the court of

Shah Shuja after the occupation of Kabul on August 7, 1839 in the **First Anglo-Afghan War**. With the benefit of hindsight, historians gave him a good measure of the blame for the British debacle that also cost Sir William his life. Soon after the invasion it became apparent that Shah Shuja would not be able to maintain himself on the throne without the protection of a British garrison. Therefore Macnaghten was prepared for an indefinite occupation of Afghanistan. He became the power behind an insecure throne, paying subsidies to tribal chiefs and directing the affairs of the country to safeguard British imperial interests. Deceived by the apparent quiescence of the Afghan chiefs, he permitted the families of British officers to come to Kabul to join a colony of some 4,500 soldiers and 11,500 camp followers. All seemed well and, as a reward for his services, Macnaghten was to receive the much coveted governorship of Bombay; **Alexander Burnes** was to succeed him in Kabul. But Afghan forces began to harass the British lines of communication and, eventually, mutinous soldiers in Kabul attacked Burnes's residence and killed the members of the mission. Realizing the danger of his situation, Macnaghten concluded a treaty with the dominant tribal chiefs that provided for the withdrawal of the British army to India. But he had still not given up hope. Trying a divide-and-rule tactic, the envoy bribed some of the sardars after contracting with Sardar **Muhammad Akbar**, the ambitious son of Amir **Dost Muhammad**. When the latter discovered the duplicity, he killed Macnaghten in a fit of rage. Only a few survived the retreat of the Army of the Indus (*see* ANGLO-AFGHAN WARS; SIMLA MANIFESTO; and AFGHAN FOREIGN RELATIONS).

MADRASA. A school of higher education in Islamic sciences, usually attached to a principal mosque. In Afghanistan, as elsewhere in the Islamic world, education was the domain of the Islamic clergy. **Mullas** taught the basics, reading and recitation of the Qor'an. The *ulama*, doctors of Islamic sciences, trained the judges (*qazis*), *muftis*, and other members of the religious establishment. In the 15th century, Timurid rulers (*see* TIMUR-I LANG) established famous madrasas in Herat, some of which continued as major centers of education until the early 19th century; but invasions and civil wars led to a general decline of the educational system. After Amir **Abdul Rahman** ascended the throne in 1880, he founded the Royal Madrasa at Kabul which became the foremost institution of its type. When Amir **Habibullah** founded **Habibia School** in 1904 as a secular school, he established a dual system of education that has continued to this day. *See also* EDU-CATION.

MAHAZ-I MILLI-YI AFGHANISTAN. The National Islamic Front of Afghanistan (NIFA) was founded in 1979 in Peshawar as an armed resistance movement by **Sayyid Ahmad Gailani**. It is a liberal, nationalist, Islamic party and, according to its manifesto, advocates both the protection of the national sovereignty and territorial integrity of Afghanistan and the establishment of an interim government that would draft a national and Islamic constitution with the separation of executive, legislative, and judicial powers. It demands an elected and free government that would guarantee such fundamental rights as free speech, freedom of movement, the protection of private property, and social justice, including medical care and education for all Afghans. Until establishment of a democratically elected government in Afghanistan, NIFA aims to strengthen the unity and solidarity of the *mujahedin* movements and its Afghan Interim Government (AIG) and to prepare the draft of a national Islamic constitution and its eventual implementation. In its foreign relations, NIFA wants good relations with its neighbors and supports the principles of the Charter of the United Nations, the Declaration of Human Rights, and the Islamic Organization Conference. NIFA favors a policy of non-alignment, respect for the rights of all nations, and condemns expansionistic and hegemonistic policies. It was part of a loose coalition of traditional, or moderate, *mujahedin* groups. *See also* GAILANI, SAYYID AHMAD.

MAHMUD OF GHAZNI (r. 998–1030). Son of Sebuktigin and founder of the **Ghaznavid** Empire that had its capital at **Ghazni**, southwest of Kabul, and controlled an empire extending from eastern Iran to the Indus River and from the **Amu Daria** to the Persian Gulf. Muslims see him as the epitome of the Ghazi warrior, the "Breaker of Idols" as he called himself, and Hindus remember him as the plunderer of Hindustan. He lavished the treasures he amassed in India on a court that was famous for its wealth and splendor and for being a center of intellectual life where poets like **Firdausi**, author of the *Shahnama* (Book of Kings), the historian **Baihaqi** (d. 1077), the philosopher al-Farabi (d. 950), and the scholar **Biruni** (973–1048) flourished. The British historian, Sir Percy Sykes called Mahmud "a great general who carefully thought out the plan of each campaign that he engaged in," who was not a fanatic and "whose encouragement of literature and science and art was as remarkable as his genius for war and for government." Mahmud's tomb was spared **Ghorid** destruction and can still be seen in the outskirts of Ghazni. *See* GHAZNAVID DYNASTY and GHORID DYNASTY.

MAHMUD PACHA, SAYYID. Also called Babu Jan, a spiritual leader to whom Amir **Shir Ali** gave some territory in the Kunar Valley as endowment. In 1868 Mahmud Pacha revolted against **Azam Khan** (r. 1867–69) who was then nominally amir. On the return of Amir Shir Ali to power, Mahmud Pacha was appointed a member of the newly formed advisory council at Kabul, but for a time was deprived of his chiefship. Amir **Abdul Rahman** confirmed him in his position but gradually deprived him of his independence and forced him to remit revenues to Kabul. He rebelled against the amir but was forced to accept exile in India. His descendants, called the Sayyids of Kunar, have held important positions in 20th century Afghanistan. Afghan historians claim that the great Pan-Islamist **Sayyid Jamaluddin Afghani** is a descendant of the Kunari sayyids. *See* AFGHANI, SAYYID JAMALUDDIN.

MAHMUD SHAH (r. 1800–03 and 1809–17). One of the twenty-three sons of **Timur Shah** who were engaged in an internecine struggle for power. He was governor of Herat and from this base successfully fought his brother **Zaman Shah** for the Kabul throne. He became Afghan king in 1800 but did not show great interest in the conduct of state affairs and delegated much authority to his **Barakzai** ministers **Fateh Khan** and Shir Muhammad. However, internecine warfare continued and, in 1803, **Shah Shuja**, the seventh son of Timur Shah, captured Kabul and made Mahmud his prisoner. Mahmud managed to escape and, with the help of Fateh Khan, moved against Kandahar and subsequently on Kabul, regaining the throne in 1809, where he ruled until 1817 when he was again driven from Kabul. He fled to Herat where he enjoyed all the "honors of sovereignty" while his son **Kamran** held all real power. Mahmud was poisoned by his ambitious son in 1829.

MAHMUDI, ABDUL RAHIM. Founder and publisher of *Shu'la-yi Javid* (Eternal Flame), a leftist weekly newspaper in **Pashtu** and **Dari**, which was banned after nine issues in July 1969 because it advocated armed struggle to achieve power. In the 1970s, his brothers founded the New Democratic Organization of Afghanistan (*Sazman-i Demokratik-i Navin-i Afghanistan*, commonly called after its newspaper *Shula-yi*

Javid party). He was imprisoned from 1969 to 1972 and went underground in 1973 when **Muhammad Daud** proclaimed the republic. Several members of his family were killed during the *Khalqi* period, and he was forced to flee abroad.

MAHMUDI, ABDUL RAHMAN. Founder of *Nida-yi Khalq* (Voice of the People), a biweekly **Dari/Pashtu** language newspaper in 1951 that was banned after 29 issues. Born in 1909 and educated in Kabul, Mahmudi was one of the first graduates of the faculty of medicine of **Kabul University**. Elected to Parliament in 1949, he was later jailed for ten years; he died a few months after he was freed in 1963. His brothers, Hadi and Rahim (see above), founded the *Shu'la-yi Javid* party.

MAHSUD. A Pashtun tribe in Waziristan in the **North-West Frontier Province** of Pakistan, counting about 70,000 members. The *British Handbook of the Indian Army* describes them as "democratic," permitting any tribesman the opportunity to rise to the position of chief "if he distinguishes himself in bravery or wisdom," and says approvingly that their "physique and stamina are good, and they are highly spoken of as soldiers." The Mahsuds have frequently been involved in border wars and supported the forces of **Nadir Khan** in the **Third Anglo-Afghan War** and during his conquest of Kabul in 1929.

MAIDAN (NOW WARDAK) (34-15'N, 68-0'E). A province in east central Afghanistan that is now called Wardak. *See* WARDAK.

MAIMANA (35-55' N, 64-47' E). A town in northern Afghanistan with about 38,000 inhabitants, mostly Uzbeks, and the capital of Fariab Province. Maimana was at one time the capital of a semi-independent *khanate* (chief ship, from *khan*, chief) and a dependency of the ruler of Kabul.

When the Persian ruler **Nadir Shah** died in 1747, a soldier of fortune and comrade-in-arms of **Ahmad Shah**, the first Afghan king, was appointed *wali*, governor, of Maimana and Balkh on the condition that he provide a certain number troops upon request. He was an **Uzbek** named Haji Khan, and upon his death his fiefdom was passed on to his son Jan Khan. But **Timur Shah** reduced the size of the fiefdom by taking Balkh and Akcha under the direct control of Kabul. Jan Khan's son fought over the succession, and one son, Ahmad Khan, was able to rule from 1798 to 1810. Because of his misrule, he was assassinated by the people of Maimana and replaced by his nephew Allah Yar Khan, who ruled until his death in 1826. Nizrab Khan, the oldest son of Ahmad Khan, succeeded but was involved in numerous wars and was eventually poisoned in 1845. Wazir **Yar Muhammad**, ruler of Herat, made war against Maimana in 1846 and kept the province under the control of Herat. The *khans* of Maimana tried to stay in power by playing off one force against another, including the Shah of Iran and the Amir of Bukhara, but in 1861 they had to resubmit to control by Herat, and in the 1880s Amir **Abdul Rahman** took direct control of the *khanate*.

Maimana was said to have had from 15 to 18 thousand inhabitants in 1845, but its population was greatly reduced as a result of protracted warfare and there were no more than about 16 to 17 thousand inhabitants in 1973. More recently, the town and surrounding districts have greatly increased in population as a result of industrial development and internal migration. The town now has a modern grid system of streets with bungalow-style housing. Little is known of recent developments or of the social and economic impact of the present war in Afghanistan. Since the fall of the Marxist regime in April 1992, Maimana is part of General **Dostum**'s domain.

MAIMANAGI, GHULAM MUHAMMAD MUSAWWER. Founder and director of the Kabul School of Fine Arts. Born in 1873 in Maimana Province, he moved to Kabul when he was eight years old and studied painting and techniques of enameling. After advanced study in Berlin he embarked on a career of teaching, training an entire generation of Afghan artists. He died at the age of 62 in Kabul. The Kabul Institute of Fine Arts was named after him.

MAIWAND, BATTLE OF. A battle on July 27, 1880, in which a force of 2,600 men under Brigadier-General G. R. S. Burrows was totally defeated. At the end of the **Second Anglo-Afghan War**, Britain had decided to dismember Afghanistan, severing Kandahar Province under Wali Shir Ali Khan, who was to be a vassal of Britain. Sardar **Abdul Rahman** was recognized as "Amir of Kabul and its Dependencies," but his cousin **Ayub** also had aspiration to the throne and had himself proclaimed amir at Herat. Kandahar was held by a garrison of some 4,700 British troops of all ranks to which were added the Afghan forces of the newly appointed "hereditary" ruler, Shir Ali Khan, when it was learned that Ayub Khan's army was moving south. Shir Ali felt he could not rely on his forces against Ayub and requested the assistance of a British brigade. General Primrose, the commander of Kandahar, dispatched Brigadier-General Burrows with a brigade, about 2,300 strong, consisting of a troop of horse artillery, six companies of the 66th, two Bombay native infantry, and 500 native troopers. At the approach of Ayub Khan, Shir Ali Khan's forces deserted en masse, taking most of their weapons with them. According to British estimates, Ayub Khan's regular forces numbered about 4,000 cavalry and between 4,000 and 5,000 infantry, as well as about 2,000 deserters and an unknown number of irregular *ghazis*. Burrows's forces fell back to the vicinity of Kushk-i Nakhud, about 30 miles from Girishk and 40 miles from Kandahar, to block Ayub's approaches to these towns; but Ayub succeeded in moving his army around Burrows's forces, interposing himself between the British forces and Kandahar. The British brigade thereupon moved toward Maiwand in anticipation of Ayub's advance and to secure the provisions available at that village. On July 27, 1880 at about 10:00 a.m., the British Brigade, replenished to 2,600 men, made contact with the Afghan forces that had moved toward Maiwand on their left flank. At a ravine, the 66th Foot was on the right, its flank thrown back to prevent it from being turned. On the left were four companies of Jacob's Rifles (30th Native Infantry) and a company of sappers, while the center was held by the horse artillery and smooth bore guns. The cavalry was in the rear to prevent the Afghans from encircling the British forces. The baggage was about 1,000 yards in the rear, only lightly guarded. In an artillery duel lasting about two hours the Afghans with thirty guns proved to be superior against the brigade's twelve. By two in the afternoon, the British cavalry had lost about 14 % of its men and 149 horses (out of 460), and the Afghan horsemen had succeeded in surrounding the brigade. Now swarms of *ghazis* went on the attack, quickly demoralizing the British troops. The 66th regiment was overwhelmed: "The slaughter of the sepoys was appalling—so utterly cowed were they that they scarcely attempted to defend themselves" (Forbes, 301). Afghan sharpshooters began to pick off British officers, who could be recognized by their helmets. A call for counter attack was ignored, and the British forces were in full flight, except for several attempts at a last stand that no British eyewitness survived. The British lost seven guns, 2,424 baggage animals and their loads, and about 1,000 dead; only 168 wounded survived. The rest fled to Kandahar where many were ambushed on the way by Afghan villagers. British estimates of Afghan casualties were 1,250 regular troops and some 600 tribesmen (1,500 regulars and 3,000 according to Heathcote, 151). General Primrose, the commander of Kandahar, panicked and called for a British retreat into the walls of the city, where they soon came under siege. Legend has it that Malalai, a tribal maiden, used her veil as a banner to incite the Afghan forces to heroic deeds. The defeat at Maiwand was a factor in convincing the British occupation forces that Afghanistan could not be held at a tolerable cost.

MAIWANDWAL, MUHAMMAD HASHIM. Prime Minister (1965–67) and founder of the Progressive Democratic Movement (*jami'at-dimukrat-i mutaraqi*), whose mission he announced on Radio Afghanistan in August 1966. It recognized **Zahir Shah** as the "personification of national unity" and advocated a program of action "in accordance with the principles of Islam, constitutional monarchy, nationalism, democracy and socialism" and aimed at reforms in the "economic, social, cultural, civic, moral and spiritual spheres" of Afghan national life. He published the weekly **Dari/Pashtu** newspaper *Musawat* in January 1967 to propagate his ideas. He resigned in 1967 because of ill health. Born in 1919 and educated at **Habibia High School** in Kabul, he embarked on a career as editor of *Itifaq-i Islam* (Agreement of Islam, 1942–45) in Herat and subsequently as editor of the daily newspaper *Anis*. President of the press department, 1951. He served as deputy minister of Foreign Affairs in 1955 and as ambassador to Britain (1956), Pakistan (1957–58), the United States (1958–63), and again Pakistan (1963). He was imprisoned when **Muhammad Daud** took power in 1973 and was killed in jail, reputedly under torture. The government announced that he had committed suicide but sentenced him posthumously to death in December 1973.

MAJLIS. Originally the name of a tribal council (from A. *jalasa*, to sit with someone) in pre-Islamic Arabia which conducted the affairs of a tribe. Thus, the name was used for a parliament or similar representative body. In Afghanistan the term was used for the senate (*majlis-i ayan*); the **Pashtu** equivalent of *majlis* is the *jirga*. *See* JIRGA and LOYA JIRGA.

MAJRUH, SAYYID BAHA'UDDIN. Professor of philosophy and sociology at **Kabul University** and president of the Afghan Historical Society (1972) who fled Afghanistan after the **Saur Revolt** and founded the Afghan Information Centre in Peshawar. He published the *Monthly Bulletin*, which was an independent newsletter reporting on the events in the Afghan war. He was assassinated in Peshawar in February 1988 by unknown assailants who did not share his moderate views. Born in 1928 in Kunar Province, the son of Sayyid Shamsuddin, he was educated at **Istiqlal Lycée** and studied in Britain, Germany, and France where he obtained a Ph.D. degree. He was the author of numerous publications, including *Azhdaha-yi Khudi* (Dragon of Selfishness), which was translated from **Dari** into French and published under the title *Voyageur de Minuit.*

MALIK. A "big man" or "petty chief" among the **Pashtuns** who possesses influence rather than power. He is a leader in war and an agent in dealings with representatives of the government. The term is synony- mous with *arbab* in the west and *beg* and *mir* in the north of Afghan- istan. In non-Pashtun areas, a malik is elected from among local landowners and acts as middleman in the collection of taxes and other services demanded by the central government.

MANGAL. A Pashtun tribe that inhabits parts of the Kurram Valley and Zurmat in Paktia Province. The Mangals have always been jealous of their independence and fought Afghan rulers and British alike. In 1924 they were the major force behind the **Khost Rebellion**, which seriously threatened the government of King **Amanullah**. In the 1980s they had supported the *mujahedin. See* KHOST REBELLION.

MANGAL REVOLT. *See* **KHOST REBELIION.**

MARATHAS. *See* **PANIPAT, BATTLE OF.**

MARGO, DASHT-I (30-45' N, 63-10' E). An extensive, almost waterless desert lying between the Helmand and Khash Rivers, extending from eastern Nimruz Province to western Helmand Province. The highway from Kandahar to Herat passes to the north of it. The desert was frequented by Baluch herders during certain times of the year, but it was impassable for anyone who did not know the scant sources of water.

MASJID. *See* **MOSQUE.**

MAS'UD, AHMAD SHAH (MASSOUD). One of the most successful, and most publicized, active *mujahedin* leaders in the Panjshir valley of Parwan Province, north of Kabul. He withstood numerous Russian invasions into his territory but in 1983 concluded a temporary truce with Soviet forces, which was described as a tactical measure and did not prevent him from carrying out attacks elsewhere. He organized a supervisory council and is one of few commanders who sought to set up a civil administration, instill discipline in his troops, and use modern military principles of tactical warfare. He is a member of the *Jam'iat-i Islami-yi Afghanistan*, headed by Professor **Burhanuddin Rabbani**, which is largely of non-Pashtun background. After the withdrawal of the Soviet troops from Afghanistan he was able to extend his territorial control, establishing his headquarters at Taluqan. His group was involved in bloody clashes with **Gulbuddin Hekmatyar**'s *Hizb-i Islami* which resulted in considerable casualties on both sides. In October 1990 Mas'ud participated in a meeting to coordinate the efforts of *mujahedin* commanders from many parts of Afghanistan and subsequently came to Pakistan where he and Hekmatyar appeared to have reconciled their differences. Because of his successes, Mas'ud is called "The Lion of Panjshir" by his admirers. Born in 1956, he was educated at **Istiqlal Lycee** and the Military Academy, where he graduated in 1973. He was a member of the radical Islamist movement (*See* ISLAMIST MOVEMENT). Mas'ud captured Kabul with the help of the Uzbeki forces of General **Dostum**, but other groups, including the *Shi'a Wahdat*, carved out areas under their influence and fighting continued over the control of the city. Mas'ud was elected minister of Defense, a post he relinquished in an attempt to compromise with the *hizb-i Islami* of Gulbuddin Hekmatyar. Nevertheless, Mas'ud continued to control the armed wing of the *Jam'iat-i Islami*, and he gained control of the entire city of Kabul after defeating the other *mujahedin* groups. When Rabbani made peace with Hekmatyar in May 1996, the latter came to Kabul to resume his position as prime minister. He is now engaged in a struggle for survival against the *Taliban*, who have captured Kabul and most of Afghanistan.

MATUN See **KHOST.**

MAULAWI (MAWLAWI). A graduate from a *madrasa*, college of Islamic studies; also an *alim* (pl. *ulama*), doctor of Islamic sciences.

MAZARI, ABDUL ALI. Chief of the radical **Nasr** (Victory) party that succeeded in capturing most of the **Hazarajat** from traditional groups. In 1989 he joined the *Hizb-i Wahdat*, a coalition of seven *Shi'a* parties, and subsequently became its head. He collaborated with **Rabbani**, but eventually allied himself with **Hekmatyar**. A hard liner, accused of having liquidated some of his opponents, he was himself killed in *Taliban* captivity, after he surrendered to this new force. He was buried in Mazar-i Sharif. *See also* HIZB-I WAHDAT.

MAZAR-I SHARIF (36-42' N, 67-6' E). Capital of Balkh Province with an estimated population of 70,000 and at one time also the name of a province that included the present Jozjan, Balkh, and Samangan Provinces. Mazar-i Sharif, located about 13 miles east of Balkh village, is named "The Noble Tomb" because of a local claim that the **Caliph** Ali (r. 656–61) is buried in the city (Najaf in present Iraq is generally accepted as the burial place). According to that claim, Ali's body was placed on the back of a white camel that was permitted to wander about. It was decided to bury the caliph on the spot where the camel eventually halted. Two cupolas were constructed over the tomb by Sultan Ali Mirza in the early fifteenth century. Subsequently a great mosque and shrine were built in its location, and Mazar-i-Sharif became an important place of pilgrimage. As the town grew it eventually superseded Balkh in importance and became the capital of the province.

In the late 19th century the town had some 20,000 inhabitants, and by the 1930s it had become the major commercial center in northern Afghanistan. In the 1970s the new part of the town was built according to principles of modern town planning, with avenues intersecting at right angles and modern shops rather than the traditional bazaar. The town is an important commercial center famous for its **Qaraqul** skins, carpets, and melons and is developing into a major industrial town for fertilizer and textile production. Because of its proximity to the former Soviet border and its flat terrain, the area was easily defended from *mujahedin* attacks and became a stronghold of the Marxist regime. It lies about 270 miles northwest of Kabul on the paved road that connects the capital with northern Afghanistan. After the fall of the Marxist government in Kabul, General **Dostum** made Mazar-i Sharif his capital. He founded a university in Mazar which enrolled 6000 students, about 35 percent women.

MAZAR-I SHARIF, FALL OF. The fall of Mazar-i Sharif precipitated the fall of President **Najibullah** and his Kabul government. It occurred in March 1992, not as a result of military conquest but rather as the consequence of a power struggle within the Marxist leadership. Najibullah wanted to replace the Tajik General Mumin, commander of the Hairatan garrison and guardian of the major weapons depot in the northern province, with the Pashtun General Rasul. Mumin refused to go and allied himself with General **Dostum**, commander of the Jozjani militia, and Sayyid Mansur Nadiri, head of the **Isma'ili** forces which control the area north of the **Salang** Pass. They cooperated with **Mas'ud** and assisted the latter in the capture of Kabul on April 25. Dostum then founded the National Islamic Movement, *Junbesh-i milli-yi Islami,* with Nadiri and others and has since controlled the north-central area of Afghanistan. *See also* DOSTUM, ABDUL RASHID.

MELMASTIA. *See* **PASHTUNWALI.**

MESHRANO JIRGAH. Pashtu name for the Upper House (or House of Notables) of the bicameral Parliament established by the 1931 and 1964 constitutions. According to the 1931 constitution, its members were appointed by the king; in 1964 a third of the members were appointed, and the rest were elected. Its minimum membership was 20 but was subsequently increased. The upper house was also called by the **Dari** name *majlis-i a'yan,* which also means House of Notables.

MILITIA. *See* **ARMY, AFGHAN.**

MILLER, JAMES. A Scottish engineer engaged by Amir **Habibullah** during his Indian tour in 1907. He set up a furniture factory and, having accomplished this, built a clock tower in the garden of the Dilkusha (**Arg**) palace. Subsequently he was employed on various irrigation schemes and built the Darunta Bridge over the Kabul River northwest of Jalalabad.

MINBAR. *See* **MOSQUE.**

MIR KHWAJA JAN. A Kohistani, belonging to the Sahibzada family of religious leaders. He was exiled to India by Amir **Abdul Rahman**, but Amir **Habibullah** permitted him to return to Kabul. He served on the amir's advisory council and later on the staff of the amir's son, Sardar

Enayatullah. He had three sons who became important members of Amir **Habibullah Kalakani**'s government: Ata-ul Haqq, his foreign minister; Shir Jan, minister of court; and Muhammad Siddiq, who commanded the Gardez forces and fought General Nadir Khan in 1929. Mir Khwaja Jan died in 1971. *See* HABIBULLAH KALAKANI.

MIR SAYYID JAN PACHA. Known also as the "Badshah (ruler) of Islampur" in Kunar Province, where he had his home. A sayyid (descendant of the Prophet Muhammad) and pupil and successor of the Hadda Mulla, whose tradition of militant hostility to the British government in India he continued. Probably the most powerful mulla in Afghanistan in 1913. He operated a mosque and a *langar*, or charitable kitchen, at **Hadda**, six miles south of Jalalabad, which was built for his predecessor by Amir **Abdul Rahman**. Said to have received Rs. 12,000 per annum from Amir **Habibullah**. Crowned Sardar **Nasrullah** Khan in 1919 but later submitted to King **Amanullah**.

MIR WAIS KHAN HOTAKI (r. 1709–15). A **Ghilzai Pashtun** and founder of the short-lived **Hotaki** Dynasty (1709–38). Leader of the Afghan tribal revolt against Persian domination that led to the foundation of modern Afghanistan. He was a Ghilzai chief who lived as a hostage at the court of the Safavid ruler in Isfahan while Kandahar was ruled by Gorgin Khan, a Georgian governor. Mir Wais got permission to go on a pilgrimage to Mecca where he obtained a **fatwa** (legal decision) authorizing revolt against the *Shi'a* domination of western Afghanistan (which is largely *Sunni*). Upon his return to Kandahar he used the *fatwa* to win the support of tribal chieftains and, in 1709, staged a successful revolt against Gorgin Khan's troops. Mir Wais and his Afghan forces defeated all attempts by the Safavid armies to recapture Kandahar and laid the basis for the Afghan invasion of Persia and the defeat of the Safavids at **Gulnabad** in 1722. *See also* HOTAKI and GHILZAI.

MOGHOLS (MONGOLS). A small ethnic group southeast of Herat who speak **Dari** with a small amount of Mongolian vocabulary and claim to be the descendants of 13th-century Mongolian soldiers who intermarried with local people. They belong to the *Sunni* school of Islam and numbered about 800 families at the turn of the century. In recent years they were estimated at from one to five thousand persons.

MOHMAND. A powerful tribe of eastern **Pashtun** origin that migrated from the area north of Kandahar to the Peshawar area. Their territory was dissected by the Durand Line in 1893 (*see* DURAND AGREEMENT), but they continued to be a factor in the politics of both states. In the early 20th century they were estimated to comprise some 40,000 families and could raise 18,000 fighters. They supported Prince **Kamran** in the early 19th century and joined the **Shinwaris** in their revolt against King **Amanullah** in November 1928. In 1930 the Haji of Turangzai, a tribal mulla, led them against British forces on the frontier. The Mohmand area was always autonomous, and the British Indian, as well as later the Pakistan government, controlled the Mohmand Agency indirectly by means of an agent who acted as the representative of the government. In September 1935, they staged a major uprising against the British government. During the1980s civil war, the Mohmands generally remained neutral.

MOSQUE (MASJID). The Islamic place of worship, where Muslims assemble for prayer, especially on Fridays when communal prayers are obligatory and the traditional sermon (*khutba*) is delivered. Masjids vary in size from one-room buildings to monumental structures, but all mosques have a prayer niche (*mihrab*) that indicates the direction of the **Ka'ba**, the Islamic shrine in Mecca. Before prayer Muslims must perform a ceremonial washing, *wudhu'*, and enter the prayer room without their shoes. Prayer includes repeated bowings (*ruku'*) whereby one touches the ground with the forehead. Prayers are usually performed in unison with one person leading in prayer. Larger mosques have a pulpit, *minbar*, and minarets from which the "crier," *muezzin*, gives the call to prayer. Cathedral mosques usually have a large courtyard with fountains, high minarets, and buildings for schools and colleges.

On special holidays Afghan kings attend prayers at the Idgah Mosque in Kabul, and high government officials attend prayers in provincial capitals. The Friday sermon is read in the name of the ruler and, therefore, has political significance (*see* ISLAM and KHUTBA). Until the government took over these functions, mosques were centers of education, public welfare, and social or political gatherings. Mosques are supported by the state or local communities, as well as by pious endowments administered by the *ulama* (the doctors of Islamic sciences). *See also* ISLAM.

MUFTI. A canon lawyer of reputation who gives a formal, legal opinion, *fatwa*, in answer to a question submitted to him either by a judge or a private individual. All laws passed by Afghan legislatures are required to be in conformance with Islamic law and it is (or was) the duty of a high member of the *ulama* or a council of the *ulama* (**jam'iat-i ulama**) to pass on the constitutionality of laws. The 1957 law on the administration of justice by **Shari'a** relegated the function of the *mufti* to primary courts, and the constitution of 1964 dispensed with the services of a *mufti* and established a supreme court. The *Taliban* rulers restored the function of the mufti. *See also* ISLAM and ISLAMIC LAW.

MUHAMMAD AFZAL, AMIR (r. 1866–67). Eldest son of Amir **Dost Muhammad** who served as governor of northern Afghanistan in the 1850s. He fought his half brother, **Shir Ali**, for the throne and was proclaimed amir in 1866. He died a year later in Kabul of cholera and was succeeded by his brother **Muhammad Azam**. Muhammad Afzal was the father of the subsequent Amir **Abdul Rahman**.

MUHAMMAD AZAM (r. 1867). Son of Amir **Dost Muhammad** Khan; succeeded his brother **Muhammad Afzal** to the Kabul throne in 1867 but was defeated by his half brother **Shir Ali** and forced to flee to Iran, where he died in October 1869 on his way to Tehran. British authors spell the name Azim.

MUHAMMAD AZIM, AMIR. *See* **MUHAMMAD AZAM.**

MUHAMMAD AZIM. A teacher at the German-language Amani (later **Najat**) high school in Kabul who entered the British legation in Kabul on September 6, 1933 with the intention of assassinating the minister, Sir Richard Maconachie. He wanted to precipitate war between Britain and Afghanistan. Instead of killing the minister he shot an English mechanic and two employees of the legation. This act was seen as a continuation of the struggle between the followers of King **Amanullah** and **Nadir Shah**. Muhammad Azim was executed on September 13, as were six prominent prisoners and high officials of King Amanullah, including **Muhammad Wali** and **Ghulam Jilani Charkhi**.

MUHAMMAD AZIZ. Half brother of **Nadir Shah** and father of **Muhammad Daud** (r. 1973–75). He was born in 1877, the son of

Sardar Muhammad Yusuf, and entered service as assistant private secretary of Amir **Habibullah** and supervisor of Afghan students in France in the 1920s. Nadir Shah appointed him ambassador to Moscow in 1929 and in 1933 to Berlin where he was assassinated on June 6, 1933 by one Sayyid Kemal, apparently in retaliation for the killing of **Ghulam Jilani Charkhi**.

MUHAMMAD DAUD, SARDAR. President of the Republic of Afghanistan from July 1973 until his assassination in April 1978 as a result of the **Saur Revolt**. Born in 1909 in Kabul, the son of Sardar **Muhammad Aziz**, and educated in Kabul and France. He embarked on a military career and was governor and general officer commanding of the Eastern Province (1934), Kandahar (1935), and commander of Central Forces (1939–47) stationed in Kabul and minister of Defense in 1946. A minister of Interior (1949–50) and prime minister (1953–63), he encouraged social reforms and in 1959 permitted women to abandon the veil, thus contributing to their emancipation and participation in the economic life of Afghanistan. He initiated two five-year plans (1956–61 and 1962–67) and a seven-year plan in 1976 and relied for military and development aid on the Soviet Union. He demanded the independence of **Pashtunistan**, the **North-West Frontier Province** of Pakistan, which led to repeated crises with Pakistan and ended with his resignation in 1963. Ten years later Muhammad Daud staged a coup against his cousin, King **Muhammad Zahir**, and in July 1973 proclaimed Afghanistan a republic. Whether he just wanted power or felt that the political liberalization during the democratic decade (1963–73) had failed to remedy the social and economic problems of Afghanistan is not clear. He relied on the support of leftists to consolidate his power, crushed the emerging **Islamist movement**, and in 1975 established his own **National Revolutionary Party** as an umbrella organization for all political movements. Thus he wanted to limit the power of the left and create a left-of-center movement loyal to himself. Toward the end of his rule he attempted to purge his leftist supporters from positions of power and sought to reduce Soviet influence in Afghanistan. Financial support from Iran and the Arab Gulf states was to enable him to repay Soviet loans and improve his relations with the West. He and members of his family were assassinated on April 27, 1978 as a result of the **Saur Revolt** that brought Marxist parties to power in Kabul.

MUHAMMAD HASANI Or **MAMASANI**. A Brahui tribe located in the area of Shorawak. *See* BRAHUI.

MUHAMMAD HASHIM, SARDAR. Prime minister of Afghanistan (1929–46), said to have been a good administrator but austere and harsh in his dealing with the Afghan people. He groomed his nephew, **Muhammad Daud**, for the position of prime minister. Born in 1886, the son of Sardar Yusuf Khan, he embarked on a military career and commanded Amir **Habibullah**'s bodyguard. He became King **Amanullah**'s governor of the Eastern Province (1919) and served as Afghan minister in Moscow (1924–26) before joining his half-brother **Muhammad Nadir** in France. When Nadir Khan ascended the throne in December 1929, Muhammad Hashim became his prime minister and ruled with a strong hand until his retirement in 1946. He died on October 26, 1953.

MUHAMMADI, MAULAWI MUHAMMAD NABI. Leader of the *harakat-i inqilab-i Islami* (Islamic Revolutionary Movement), a traditional Islamic *mujahedin* group headquartered in Pakistan. He was born in 1921 in Logar, the son of Haji Abdul Wahhab, and educated in *madrasas* (religious colleges) in Logar Province. In the 1950s he was one of the first members of the religious establishment to agitate against "Communist influence" in the Afghan educational system. Elected to Parliament in 1964 as a representative of Logar Province. After the Marxist coup, he fled to Pakistan and utilized a network of *maulawis* (graduates of madrasas) to organize armed resistance against Kabul. In the early 1980s his **Harakat** was the largest of *mujahedin* groups, but it lost members to the more radical Islamist parties of **Sayyaf** and **Rabbani**. It has **Pashtun** support in Kandahar, Ghazni, Logar, Kabul, and Baghlan Provinces. In 1992 Muhammadi became vice president in Rabbani's government, but in March 1995 he recognized the *Taliban* movement. *See also* HARAKAT-I INQILAB-I ISLAMI.

MUHAMMAD ISHAQ (ESHAQ). Since 1982, political officer of **Jam'iat** and frequent contributor to its fortnightly *AFGHANews*. Born in 1952 in Panjshir and a graduate of the faculty of engineering of **Kabul University**, he became a member of the *Jawanan-i Musulman* (*see* ISLAMIST MOVEMENT). He cooperated in 1975 with **Commander Mas'ud** in raids against military posts of the Daud government and after the **Saur Revolt** joined **Mas'ud** against the Kabul government.

MUHAMMAD ISHAQ. Son of Amir **Muhammad Azam** Khan and cousin of Amir **Abdul Rahman**, he proclaimed himself amir in June 1888 and unsuccessfully fought Abdul Rahman for the throne. Born about 1851 of an Armenian mother, he was in command of Abdul Rahman Khan's forces in Afghan Turkestan at age 18. He was defeated by Amir **Shir Ali** and lived with Abdul Rahman in exile at Samarkand. In 1879 he returned with Abdul Rahman Khan to Afghanistan. When the latter assumed the Kabul throne, he appointed Muhammad Ishaq governor of Turkestan, as the northern provinces were then called. Ishaq Khan was ambitious; he demanded autonomy amounting to virtual independence, subject to token allegiance to the Kabul throne. He next extended his control over Herat Province, and when Amir Abdul Rahman was ill in 1888, proclaimed himself amir. Amir Abdul Rahman quickly recovered and raised an army under General **Ghulam Haidar** that decisively defeated the rebellious cousin in the Battle of Gaznigak on September 19, 1888. Ishaq Khan was forced to flee to Russian Turkestan where he died shortly thereafter.

MUHAMMAD ISMA'IL. *Mujahedin* commander affiliated with the *Jam'iat-i Islami*. He was the "Amir" of Herat, Badghis, Ghor, and Farah Provinces and built a good military organization. He was born in 1946 in Shindand (now Farah Province), the son of Muhammad Aslam. After completing his elementary education in Shindand, he continued his education at Kabul Military School and the Military Academy. He was a second lieutenant in the 17th Division stationed in Herat when he defected and participated in the uprising of March 1979. When the uprising was suppressed, he fled to Iran and made his way to Pakistan, where he joined the forces of **Burhanuddin Rabbani**. In 1987 he was said to have received **stinger** missiles that helped him to secure control of much of Herat Province. He called himself "Amir" and seemed to have ambitions for autonomous rule but was defeated by *Taliban* forces and fled to Iran on September 5, 1995.

MUHAMMAD NADIR SHAH. King of Afghanistan, 1929–33. Born in 1883, the son of Sardar Muhammad Yusuf Khan, he embarked on a military career. Appointed a brigadier in 1906, he was promoted to lieutenant general, *naib salar*, for his services in suppressing the

Mangal Revolt in December 1912. Appointed general, *sipah salar*, 1914. He and other members of the Afghan court had accompanied Amir **Habibullah** to Jalalabad, the winter capital, and when the amir was assassinated while on a hunting trip, he was arrested. Amir **Amanullah** exonerated him of any involvement and sent him to command the troops in Khost Province. During the **Third Anglo-Afghan War**, Nadir Khan led an army across the Afghan border into Waziristan and besieged the British base at Thal. This prevented a British offensive in the east and threatened to cause a general uprising among the "British" Afghans which was one of the factors forcing Britain to accept Afghan independence. Amir Amanullah appointed him minister of war in 1919, in which post he served until 1924, when he was appointed Afghan minister at Paris. He resigned two years later because of illness (or because he disagreed with King Amanullah's policies). Nevertheless, he remained in France, where he was joined by his half brother **Muhammad Hashim** Khan and his brother **Shah Wali** Khan. After the abdication of King Amanullah in January 1929, Nadir left France for India and established himself at the Afghan frontier. He collected tribal support, including **Waziri** tribal forces from the Indian side of the border, and, after initial setbacks, defeated **Habibullah Kalakani** and captured Kabul on October 13, 1929. Nadir Khan was proclaimed king two days later. He made great efforts to reorganize the country and reopen schools and founded the faculty of medicine in 1932 that ten years later merged with a number of faculties to become **Kabul University**. He drafted a new constitution (1931) that provided for a bicameral parliament, the national council (*shura-i milli*), the senate (*majlis-i a'yan*), and an advisory council (*jam'iat-i ulama*). He fought those who aimed at restoring King Amanullah to the throne and executed **Ghulam Nabi**, one of his chief opponents, in 1932. He was assassinated in 1933 by a **Hazara** student who was an adopted son of Ghulam Nabi's family.

MUHAMMAD NAIM, SARDAR. Minister of Foreign Affairs and deputy prime minister (1953–63) and foreign policy adviser of President Daud (1973–78). Born in 1912, the son of **Muhammad Aziz** and brother of **Muhammad Daud**, he embarked on a diplomatic career and served as Afghan minister in Rome (1932), London (1946–47), and the United States (1948–50). He was assassinated together with President Daud and members of their family as a result of the **Saur Revolt** of April 27, 1978.

MUHAMMAD RAFI'I, COL. GENERAL. Member of the *Parchami* faction of the **PDPA** who was minister of Public Works in the first *Khalqi* cabinet (May to August 1978) and was purged with other *Parchamis* and arrested and sentenced to twenty years for plotting against the **Taraki** government. Appointed minister of Defense by the **Karmal** government (1980–82 and 1986–88), he became a member of the politburo in 1981. In 1988 he was one of four vice presidents of the **Najibullah** government. Born in 1946 of a Kharoti **Ghilzai** family of Paghman, he was educated at the Kabul Military Academy and the Academy of General Staff in the Soviet Union. When he became a member of the PDPA in 1973, he was the highest ranking party member in the Afghan army.

MUHAMMAD WALI. *See* **WALI MUHAMMAD.**

MUHAMMAD YUSUF. Appointed Afghan prime minister in 1963, succeeding Sardar **Muhammad Daud** as the first commoner in this position. He served during the process of drafting and ratification of the Constitution of 1964. The newly elected, bicameral Parliament was soon bogged down in recriminations and political infighting. When the lower house, *wolesi jirgah* (P., People's Council), decided to hold closed meetings, demonstrations, largely by students, led to police repression in which two persons were killed and a number of others wounded. Thereupon Dr. Yusuf resigned. The *Sewwum-i Aqrab* (the third of the month Aqrab, corresponding to October 25, 1965) was subsequently a day of protest and demonstrations of the Left. Born in 1917 in Kabul, Muhammad Yusuf was educated at **Najat** school and in Germany, where he received a Ph.D. degree in physics. He became a professor at **Kabul University** and deputy minister of Education in 1949. He held the position of minister of Mines and Industry for ten years (1953–63) before his appointment as prime minister. After his resignation he served as Afghan ambassador to Bonn (1966–73) and Moscow (1973) but was recalled after the Daud coup. He presently lives in Germany and continues to be active in Afghan affairs.

MUHAMMAD ZAHIR SHAH. *See* **ZAHIR SHAH.**

MUHAMMADZAI. The Muhammadzai (a branch of the **Barakzai** of the **Durrani** tribe) are the descendants of **Sardar Painda Khan**. They captured the Kabul throne in 1826 under Amir **Dost Muhammad** and continued in power (with the exception of the nine-month rule of the Tajik **Habibullah Kalakani**) until the Marxist coup in 1978 deposed President **Daud**. For Muhammadzai rulers, see individual entries. *See also* DURRANI DYNASTY.

MUHSINI, AYATOLLAH MUHAMMAD ASEF. A Hazara, born in 1935 in Kandahar Province and educated at *Shi'a* universities in Iraq. He is called Ayatollah by his supporters. Upon his return to Afghanistan he founded a cultural organization called "Dawn of Science" (*sobh-i danesh*) that became the nucleus of the rural-based *mujahedin* group *Harakat-i Islami-yi Afghanistan* (Islamic Movement of Afghanistan). In 1980 he was elected chairman of the Afghan Shi'a Alliance, a *mujahedin* umbrella group headquartered in Iran, but subsequently he left the alliance and moved to Quetta. His group once rivaled **Nasr** in importance and collaborated with Nasr in expelling the *Shura* of **Ayatollah Beheshti** from most of the **Hazarajat**. In June 1990, the Shi'a groups announced formation of a new organization, called Unity Party (*hizb-i wahdat*), but Muhsini presented a number of conditions for joining the coalition. Muhsini is known as a moderate who receives no support from Iran. After the fall of the Marxist regime, his party supported the government of President **Rabbani**, and two members of his group were represented in Prime Minister **Hekmatyar**'s short-lived cabinet of July 1996.

MUHTASIB. An overseer of public morality, common in Afghanistan before local police forces were established. He was to discourage sinful behavior, encourage attendance at prayers, check measures and weights in the bazaars, and ascertain that foodstuffs were not adulterated. He was appointed by a *qazi* (judge), paid from the public treasury, and was empowered to administer whippings for minor offenses. With the establishment of regular police forces in towns in the early 1920s, the position of *muhtasib* began to disappear. *See also* KALANTAR.

MUJADDIDI. The name of a family of religious leaders who are the descendants of the Sufi reformer Shaikh Ahmad Sirhindi (purported to be born in Kabul Province in 1564 and buried in Sirhind, India, 1624), called *Mujaddid Alf-I Thani* (Renewer of the Second Millennium). Qayyum Jan Agha (descendant in seven generations of the Shaikh) came to Afghanistan in the early 19th century and founded a *madrasa* (Islamic college) and *khanaqa* (Sufi center) in the Shor Bazaar area of

Kabul, and his successor therefore assumed the title Hazrat Sahib of Shor Bazaar. Succession went from Qayyum Jan Agha to Fazl Muhammad (Shams al-Mashayekh—the Sun of Shaikhs, assumed title in 1925), Fazl Omar (Nur al-Mashayekh—the Light of Shaikhs), Muhammad Ibrahim (Zia al-Mashayekh—the Light of Shaikhs, assumed title in 1956). Members of the family also established themselves in Herat (the Hazrat Sahib of Jaghatan) and other towns in Afghanistan. They are leaders of the **Naqshbandi** Sufi order in southern Afghanistan and have long played an important political role. They preached **jihad** (holy war) against Britain, opposed the secular reforms instituted by King **Amanullah** and **Muhammad Daud**, and encouraged tribal revolts to restore their concept of Islamic orthodoxy. Some members held government positions, and some lived in exile. In January 1979, Muhammad Ibrahim and some 96 male members of the Mujaddidi family were arrested and executed during the *Khalqi* regime.

MUJADDIDI, SEBGHATULLAH. Elected president in February 1989 of an "Afghan Interim Government" made up of members of the seven-party alliance of *mujahedin* headquartered in Pakistan (*see* MUJAHEDIN). He founded and leads the National Liberation Front of Afghanistan (*jabha-yi milli beraye najat-i Afghanistan*) that conducted armed attacks on Soviet and Afghan government forces from about 1980. Born in 1925 in Kabul, the son of Muhammad Masum, he was educated in Kabul and at al-Azhar University in Egypt and subsequently taught Islamic studies at high schools and colleges in Kabul. He publicly denounced "unbelievers" and communists and was imprisoned (1959–64) for involvement in a purported plot to assassinate the Soviet premier, Nikita Khrushchev. When he was freed, he traveled abroad for two years and upon his return founded the *Jam'iat-i Ulama-i Muhammadi* (1972, Organization of Muslim Clergy). He was again politically active and participated in anti-reformist demonstrations in Kabul in the 1970s and was forced to flee abroad in order to escape arrest. He was head of the Islamic Center in Copenhagen, Denmark (1974–78); and after the **Saur Revolt** he went to Pakistan where he led the armed resistance of the National Liberation Front. His supporters are primarily Pashtun members of the **Naqshbandi** Sufi order in Paktia and Kunar Provinces. In spite of his radical background, he was counted among the moderates who did not rule out the establishment of a constitutional monarchy. After the fall of the Marxist government in April 1992, Mujaddidi served as interim president for two months (April 28–June 28) in which capacity he amnestied his communist opponents and promoted **Abdul Rashid Dostum** to the rank of general. In the subsequent power struggle, Mujaddidi supported **Hekmatyar** against **Rabbani**, when the latter refused to step down at the end of his two year appointment. He resigned from the **Supreme Coordination Council of the Islamic Revolution in Afghanistan** (SCCIRA) in November 1995, when Hekmatyar unilaterally negotiated with Rabbani. The constellation of forces changed again, when in May 1996 Hekmatyar made peace with Rabbani and established himself in Kabul as the new prime minister.

When the *Taliban* captured Kabul in September 1996, Mujaddidi recognized their regime.

MUJAHEDIN (MUJAHEDUN). Fighters in a holy war, *jihad*. (A., sing. *mujahed*; pl. *mujahedun, mujahedin*). Afghan resistance fighters adopted this designation to indicate that they are waging a lawful war against an "infidel" government (according to Islamic law, a *jihad* can be fought only against non-Muslims and apostates). The *mujahedin* were organized in a tenuous alliance of seven Sunni groups stationed in Peshawar, including the moderate leaders **Muhammad Nabi Muhammadi, Sebghatullah Mujaddidi**, and **Sayyid Ahmad Gailani** and the Islamist radicals **Burhanuddin Rabbani, Muhammad Yunus Khales, Gulbuddin Hekmatyar**, and **Abdul Rasul Sayyaf**. In 1989, these groups formed an Afghan Interim Government (AIG) with Sebghatullah Mujaddidi as the president. In 1989 a *Shi'a* alliance of eight groups (some of them small or inactive) in Iran united in an umbrella organization called *Hizb-i Wahdat* (Unity Party) that, however, refused to join the AIG of the Sunni groups because of what they considered insufficient representation. Refugees in Pakistan and commanders in the field were required to be affiliated with one of the seven groups if they wanted to receive outside assistance. The Pakistani government recognized only six (later seven) Sunni groups, preventing the proliferation of parties. The Pakistani military **Inter-Services Intelligence** (ISI) took an active part in planning and executing attacks and favored Islamist (rather than nationalist or moderate) groups, especially **Gulbuddin Hekmatyar**'s *Hizb-i Islami*, in the supply of funds and war materials. Many of the commanders did not necessarily share the ideology of their leader and some switched "allegiance," when it helped in obtaining supplies. *Mujahedin* were also grouped according to regional, tribal, and ethnic origin; the *Jam'iat* of Rabbani, largely

non-Pashtun in ethnic composition, is active in north eastern Afghanistan. Although Rabbani is Islamist (*see* ISLAMIST MOVEMENT), the
Jam'iat was in conflict with its ideological brother, the *Hizb* of
Gulbuddin Hekmatyar. Ideological purity (never precisely defined) also
suffered as a result of the "tactical alliance" in March 1990 between
Shahnawaz Tanai, a *Khalqi* hard liner, and Hekmatyar, one of the
most vocal radical Islamists. In the ever-changing constellation of
forces, Hekmatyar made his peace with Rabbani in May 1996 and
established himself in Kabul as prime minister. The *Taliban* ended the
dream of the allies at Kabul, when they captured the city and chased its
leaders into the Panjshir Valley. The major actors in the struggle for
political power at the time of this writing are General **Dostum**, a former
communist, in the north; the *Taliban,* controlling two-thirds of
Afghanistan; the *Jam'iat–i Islami,* in flight to northeastern Afghanistan; and the *Hizb-i wahdat,* which control part of the Hazarajat. See
also JIHAD and individual entries for *mujahedin* groups.

MUJTABA KHAN. In charge of a school of accounting in Kabul, the
Maktab-i Usul-i Daftari, opened by Amir **Amanullah** in 1919. It had
100 students who were trained to be tax collectors. Mujtaba Khan was
active in the financial administration and held the positions of financial
secretary (*mustaufi*) of Kabul, 1920-24; deputy finance minister, 1929
(under **Habibullah Kalakani**) and 1932; and inspector general of the
tribunal at the prime ministry, 1945. He became a member of the senate
in 1952. He died in the late 1950s. His descendants have adopted the
family name Mustamandi.

MULLA. A preacher and spiritual adviser as well as a teacher in elementary mosque schools (*maktab-see* EDUCATION). There is no clergy in
Sunni Islam, no need for an intermediary between God and man, no
ordination or strict hierarchy. Educational preparation ranges from
informal study to rigorous training at a faculty of theology or well-
known Islamic university. A mulla performs such religious activities as
recitation of the *adhan* (call to prayer) in the ear of the newborn and
presides at marriage and burial ceremonies. He is paid for his services
by donations from his parish and often needs to supplement his income
by pursuing a trade or agricultural work. Mullas vary considerably in
educational background, from the barely literate to those with some
madrasa education. They never have held political power on a national
scale, but some have had great influence on a grass-roots level. They

sometimes mediate in tribal disputes (not being members of the tribe) and have been active in mobilizing the masses against a foreign invader or an "infidel" ruler. Famous mullas include Mushk-i Alam (*see* DIN MUHAMMAD) who proclaimed *jihad* against the British in the **Second Anglo-Afghan War** and subsequently led **Mangal** and **Ghilzai** forces against Amir **Abdul Rahman**, as well as Mulla-i-Lang (the Lame Mullah) who led a tribal army against King **Amanullah** (*see* KHOST REBELLION). Amir Abdul Rahman first tried to keep mullas under state control by requiring tests for certification and made attempts at improving the quality of religious education in Afghanistan. Since the time of King Amanullah (1920s) the Afghan government established state-sponsored *madrasas* and in 1951 a faculty of theology affiliated with Al-Azhar University in Cairo, but the informal, private system of religious education has continued to exist to this day. Most mullas are either self-described or recognized by others as such. For the higher religious functionaries, *see* ULAMA.

MUNJANI. A small ethnic group of **Isma'ili** Muslims living in twelve villages in the Munjan Valley of Badakhshan Province. They are engaged in agriculture and speak Munjani (a northeastern Iranian language of the Pamir group) as well as Farsi.

MURGHAB (38-18' N, 61-12' E). A river formed by the confluence of the Chiras and Wajan Streams, rising in the eastern ranges of the **Band-i Baba** and **Band-i Turkestan** Mountains. It flows in a westerly direction and turns northwest about eleven miles below Bala Murghab in Badghis Province, where it receives the waters of the Karawal Khana. It then crosses into Turkmenistan and, running in a northerly direction, dissipates in the plains of Merv. The river is some 500 miles in length; about half of its course is in Afghanistan.

MURSHID. Master, or head, of a mystic order.

MUSAHEBAN. A family also called Yahya Khel, because of its members descent from Muhammad Yahya and Muhammad Yusuf who were companions, *musahiban*, of Amir **Habibullah**. Prominent members of the family were **Muhammad Nadir**, the Afghan king (1929–33), and his brothers and half brothers **Muhammad Aziz**, **Muhammad Hashim**, **Shah Wali**, and **Shah Mahmud** who held high positions in

Zahir Shah's government. They were exiled in India until 1901 when Amir Habibullah permitted them to return to Afghanistan.

MUSA SHAFIQ. *See* **SHAFIQ, MUHAMMAD MUSA.**

MUSAZAI. *See* **MOHMAND.**

MUSHK-I ALAM. *See* **DIN MUHAMMAD (MASHK).**

MUSLIM BROTHERHOOD. The Society of Muslim Brethren (*Jam'iat-i Ikhwan al-Muslimin*), founded in 1929 in Isma'iliyya, Egypt by Hasan al-Banna (1906–49), was a religio-political organization that eventually spread to other parts of the Islamic world. Al-Banna, an ascetic and charismatic teacher, was the "Supreme Guide," *murshid al-'amm*, who advocated social and economic reforms, expulsion of the British from Egypt, and establishment of an Islamic state. The movement is Pan-Islamic in outlook and aims at imposing Islamic law on all aspects of the social and political life of the Muslim nation (*umma*). As a political party it was never very successful, but it was able to mobilize considerable support among the masses of the lower urban and rural classes. The Ikhwan was accused of political assassinations, and Hasan al-Banna was himself assassinated in 1949 (reputedly by government agents). The Ikhwan was represented in the Egyptian Parliament, and other, more radical groups, have taken over the Islamist cause.

A number of founders of the **Islamist movement** (**Rabbani, Sayyaf, Niazi**) in Afghanistan became members or sympathizers of the Ikhwanis while residing in Egypt for study and upon returning to Afghanistan contributed to the spread of the movement's ideology. They were the teachers of young radicals recruited from Afghan government schools who formed the nucleus of the Islamist movement. The Islamists are popularly called "Ikhwanis" in Afghanistan. *See* ISLAMIST MOVEMENT.

MUSSOORIE CONFERENCE. A conference at Mussoorie (April 17–July 18, 1920) north of Delhi in India, that was to restore "friendly" relations between the governments of Afghanistan and British India after the **Third Anglo-Afghan War**. It was a sequel to the peace treaty at Rawalpindi (August 8, 1919, *see* AFGHAN FOREIGN RELATIONS and ANGLO-AFGHAN TREATY, 1921) and pitted the Afghan foreign minister, **Mahmud Tarzi**, against the foreign secretary to the government of India, **Sir Henry Dobbs**, in a fruitless attempt to conclude a treaty of friendship between the two states. A British *aide-memoire* provided for some economic assistance but postponed the establishment of normal, "neighborly" relations for another conference at Kabul in 1921.

N

NADIM, ABDUL GHAFUR. Dari poet and traditional scholar. Born about 1880 at Kabul, the son of Rajab Ali Khan. Although he died at 37, he wrote some 3,500 verses, consisting mainly of odes and other lyrical poetry. His poems are still greatly appreciated. He taught **Dari** literature at **Habibia School** for several years and in 1915 published the first modern Dari grammar, entitled *Sarf-i Nadim* (the Grammar of Nadim). He also published a newspaper called *Iksar*. He died in 1918 in Kabul.

NADIRI, SAYYID SHAH NASIR. *See* **SAYYID-I KAYAN.**

NADIR SHAH. King of Afghanistan (1929–33). *See* MUHAMMAD NADIR SHAH.

NADIR SHAH AFSHAR. Ruler of Iran (1736–47) and founder of the short-lived Afsharid Dynasty (1736–95). Born in 1688 as Nadir Quli in northern **Khurasan**, the son of Imam Quli of a clan affiliated with the Afshar tribe, he started life as a raider for booty and became one of the last great nomadic conquerors of Asia. He ended the **Ghilzai** dream of ruling an empire after Mahmud, son of **Mir Wais**, captured Isfahan in 1722. Nadir defeated the Afghans and drove them out of Iran. He attacked Herat and invaded India, where he defeated the Moghul army at Karnal, near Delhi, in 1739. Rather than fighting the Afghan tribes he enlisted them into his army, making Ahmad Khan Abdali (the subsequent **Ahmad Shah**) one of his military commanders. He moved the **Abdali** tribe from Herat to their original home in the Kandahar area and settled them on Ghilzai lands. This led to the ascendancy of the Abdalis (**Durrani**) over the Ghilzais and contributed to the long-standing rivalry between these two **Pashtun** tribes. Nadir Shah also settled Jewish and Armenian traders from Iran in Afghan towns to encourage trade with India. Ruling over a heterogeneous population, he wanted to unite his subjects by proclaiming *Shi'ism* the fifth (Ja'farite) orthodox school of Sunni Islam. The Shi'a clergy objected to this. Nadir became increasingly tyrannical and was eventually killed by one of his own tribesmen. Some of Nadir's **Qizilbash** soldiers settled in Afghanistan where their descendants had successful careers in the army (until the end of **Dost Muhammad**'s rule), government, the trades, and crafts. The last Armenian merchants were expelled from Afghanistan in 1897, and virtually all Jewish residents and immigrants from Central Asia had emigrated to Israel by the late-1980s. At the time of Nadir Shah's death, Ahmad Khan, Abdali, was able to fill the political vacuum and become the first Durrani ruler of Afghanistan.

NAGHLU (34-38' N, 69-43' E). A village in the southern part of Laghman Province on the left bank of the Kabul River, opposite Sarobi. It is the site of a 350-foot high dam for irrigation and generation of electricity. The project was financed by the Soviet Union, started in January 1960, and completed in 1968. Long controlled by **Hekmatyar**'s militia, the power plant was frequently shut down to deprive Kabul of electricity. In September 1996 the **Taliban** were able to capture the area prior to the conquest of Kabul.

NAIM MUHAMMAD. *See* **MUHAMMAD NAIM, SARDAR.**

NAJAT SCHOOL (NEJAT). A comprehensive elementary and secondary school founded in Kabul by King **Amanullah** in 1923. The school had a German curriculum, and German was the language of instruction. Many of the graduates were sent by the Afghan government to German-speaking countries for higher education. The school was first named Amani after King Amanullah (Aman Allah) but was renamed Najat (also spelled Nejat—Liberation) School after **Nadir Shah** defeated **Habibullah Kalakani** in 1929 and ascended the throne. Nadir Shah was assassinated by a student of this school. The school was renamed Amani by the Marxist regime in the 1980s as part of its effort to establish links between it and the progressive policies of King Amanullah. *See also* EDUCATION.

NAJIBULLAH. President of the Republic of Afghanistan and general secretary of the **PDPA** from May 1986 to April 1992. Born in 1947 in Kabul of an **Ahmadzai** family (his father, a **Ghilzai Pashtun**, was Afghan trade agent in Peshawar), he was educated at **Habibia School** and **Kabul University**, graduating from the College of Medicine in 1975. He became a member of the *Parcham* faction of the PDPA in 1965 and was repeatedly arrested for his political activities. After the **Saur Revolt** he was appointed Afghan ambassador in Tehran

(July–October 1978), in a move to get leading *Parchamis* out of the country but was quickly dismissed with other *Parchamis* by the **Taraki** government when they were suspected of plotting a coup. He remained abroad and returned to Kabul with **Babrak Karmal** after the ouster of **Hafizullah Amin** in the final days of December 1979. He next held the position of general president of **KHAD** (1980–86) and in 1986 replaced Babrak Karmal as secretary general of the PDPA. He purged the central committee and brought in new members and reorganized government in 1988 and 1990. In March 1990, he successfully withstood a *Khalqi* coup, headed by **Shahnawaz Tanai**, his defense minister. He downplayed Marxist ideology and annulled most of the early reforms. When he agreed to step down in April 1992, members of his party deserted him, and the *mujahedin* were able to capture Kabul. He remained in a building of the United Nations in Kabul and was not permitted to go into exile, as was arranged through the United Nations. When the *Taliban* captured Kabul in September 1996, they tortured and brutally killed Najibullah. He was married to a Muhammadzai. *See also* PEOPLES DEMOCRATIC PARTY OF AFGHANISTAN.

NANAWATI. Nanawati (mediation or protection) is a vital element of the Pashtun code, *pashtunwali*. It is the obligation to afford protection or asylum to anyone in need or assist in mediation to help the weaker in a feud who seeks peace with someone he has injured. *See* PASHTUNWALI.

NANGARHAR (34-45' N, 70-50' E). A province in eastern Afghanistan with an area of 7,195 square miles and a population of about 740,000 of which almost 400,000 are settled in refugee camps in Pakistan. The capital of the province is Jalalabad, with a peacetime population of about 56,000 (presently increased to 200,000). The population is largely Pashtun of the Khugiani, Mohmand, Shinwari, and Tirahi tribes, but other major ethnic groups are also represented in Jalalabad.

Local tradition associates the name, Nangarhar, with *nuh*—nine, and *nahar*—river, or, according to another version, with the Sanskrit "nau vihara"—meaning "nine monasteries." The Nangarhar area was a flourishing center of Buddhism until the fifth century. Because of its mild climate, Jalalabad was the winter capital of Afghan kings after they were established in Kabul. The eastern part of the province is well irrigated, producing two or three crops a year. Wheat, corn, and some rice are the major crops, and Soviet-developed mechanized state farms produce olive and citrus fruits, much of which were formerly exported to the Soviet Union. Timber is cut on the upper slopes of the **Safid Kuh** and smuggled to Pakistan where it fetches a better price. The Darunta Dam on the Kabul River provides hydroelectric power and makes possible large irrigation projects. In March 1989 a *mujahedin* assault on Jalalabad failed to dislodge the forces of the Kabul regime. This demonstrated the fact that the *mujahedin* were as yet unable to switch from guerrilla warfare to conventional war, which led to a lull in large-scale operation. After the capture of Jalalabad by the **mujahedin**, a council of *mujahedin* ruled Nangarhar for four years until Jalalabad was taken by the **Taliban** in September 1996. **See also** JALALABAD.

NAQIB OF BAGHDAD. Title of Sayyid Abdul Rahman in the late 19th century, Naqib al-Ashraf (Representative of the Sayyids) and custodian of the Baghdad Shrine of the Sufi saint Abdul Qadir Gailani (1077–1166 A.D.), founder of the **Qadiri** Sufi fraternity. He was in contact with Amir **Habibullah** through his brother **Sayyid Hasan Gailani**, a man of great importance and influence in Afghanistan. Was often visited by Afghans going on Haj via the Hijaz railway. He was the brother of Sayyid Hasan Gailani who came to Afghanistan in 1905 and the uncle of Sayyid **Ahmad Gailani**, head of **Mahaz-i Milli-yi Afghanistan**. *See* GAILANI.

NAQSHBANDI (NAQSHBANDIYYA). A Sufi fraternity named after its founder, Muhammad ibn Muhammad Baha' al-Din al-Bukhari Naqshband (1317–89 A.D.), which has many devotees in Afghanistan. The **Hazrat of Shor Bazaar** of the **Mujaddidi** family is the leader of the Kandahar and eastern branches of the order by virtue of his descent from the Naqshbandi reformer Shaikh Ahmad Sirhindi. Among the *mujahedin* forces of **Sebghatullah Mujaddidi** are many devotees of the Naqshbandi order, whereas northern (non-Pashtun) Naqshbandis are affiliated with the *Jam'iat* of **Rabbani**.

NARANJAN DAS. An Afghan Hindu who held high offices during the reigns of Amir **Habibullah** and King **Amanullah**. Born in Kabul about 1853, he was accountant-general (a kind of finance minister) at Kabul and was granted the rank of civil (not military) colonel in 1906. He was a member of the Afghan delegations to the peace conference at Rawalpindi in 1919 (*see* ANGLO-AFGHAN TREATY OF 1919) and the **Mussoorie Conference** in 1920. His participation in the Afghan delegation had an excellent propaganda effect among the Hindu population of India, who saw King Amanullah as a potential ally in their struggle for independence.

NASIR Or **NASAR.** One of the wealthiest and strongest of the **Kuchi Pashtun** tribes which dwells in black tents and formerly traveled into the Indian subcontinent in the winter. They have a reputation of being democratic and not dominated by their chiefs. They have long feuded with the **Waziris**, who attacked the Nasir when they passed through their territory. At such time the Nasir stopped all feuds and united in obedience under a chief. Amir **Abdul Rahman** wanted to settle the tribe in Herat Province; they refused and agreed to pay taxes to continue their nomadic way of life. For further details, *see* POWINDAH.

NASR, SAZMAN-I. "Victory Organization," a **Hazara** *mujahedin* party, founded by Shaikh **Mir Husain Sadeqi**, after the Saur Revolt. It recruited its followers from Hazaras living in Iran and obtained some material support from Iran. It eventually succeeded in becoming a major force in the **Hazarajat** and allied with the **Pasdaran** in expelling the traditionalist **Shura** (headed by **Beheshti**) from much of the area. It is radical Islamist in outlook and is said to govern with the assistance of Islamic *komites*, ideological committees. Nasr is now part of the **Hizb-I Wahdat**. *See also* SADEQI, HOJJAT AL-ISLAM MIR HUSAIN.

NASRULLAH KHAN. Second son of Amir **Abdul Rahman** and viceroy, *na'eb al-saltana*, in charge of most of the government administration while his brother Amir **Habibullah** was amir. He was commander in chief of the army and president of the amir's advisory council. He was conservative in outlook, a sponsor and supporter of the religious establishment and militant foe of the British. Was sent by his father to London in 1895 to win Queen Victoria's consent to establish an Afghan embassy in London. London was not willing to grant this, and the failure of his mission was one of the reason for Nasrullah's hostility to Britain. When Amir Habibullah was assassinated in February 1919, Nasrullah Khan was proclaimed king in Peshawar, but the army supported **Amanullah** Khan, who was in control of the Kabul palace and the treasury. Nasrullah was arrested and assassinated while in confinement. He is buried in Qot-i Chakan in Kabul.

NATIONAL FATHERLAND FRONT (NFF). A national umbrella organization (*jabha-yi milli-yi pader-watan*) established by **Babrak Karmal** in 1980 to "unite all progressive forces." Dr. Saleh

Muhammad Zirai (Zeary) was appointed chairman, and the **PDPA** was the vanguard or "guiding force" in an organization that included all unions, guilds, women's and professional organizations. The NFF was said to have had 55,000 members in 1984, but it never succeeded in mobilizing the masses under party control. (Similar "national front" governments, set up in East-bloc countries, remained under Communist party control.) In 1987 the Afghan government renamed the organization the National Front of the Republic of Afghanistan (NFROA), headed by Abdul Rahim Hatef, but it did not outlast the fall of the Najibullah government.

NATIONAL ISLAMIC FRONT (NIFA). *See* **MAHAZ-I MILLI-YI AFGHANISTAN** and **GAILANI, SAYYID AHMAD.**

NATIONAL LIBERATION FRONT OF AFGHANISTAN. Name of the *Jabha-yi Najat-i Milli-yi Afghanistan*, one of seven resistance organizations sanctioned by Pakistan after the Saur Revolt. It is headed by Sebghatullah Mujaddidi. *See* JABHA-YI MILLI BERAYE NAJAT-I AFGHANISTAN and MUJADDIDI, SEBGHATULLAH.

NATIONAL RESCUE FRONT. A short-lived *mujahedin* organization founded in June 1978 by **Burhanuddin Rabbani**. It was a forerunner of the *Jam'iat*. *See* JAM'IAT-I SLAMI-YI AFGHANISTAN and ISLAMIC ALLIANCE FOR THE LIBERATION OF AFGHANISTAN.

NATIONAL REVOLUTIONARY PARTY (NRP). *Hizb-i Inqilab-i Milli*, name of a party founded in 1975 by President **Muhammad Daud** to support his republican regime. It was headed by a central council that Dr. Abdul Majid, Gen. Ghulam Haidar Rasuli (the minister of defense), Sayyid Abdullah (minister of finance), and Prof. Abdul Qayyum. Only one political party was to be permitted, and the NRP was to be an umbrella organization for "all progressive forces." It represented an attempt by Muhammad Daud to limit the influence of his erstwhile Communist supporters and gain grassroots support.

NAURUZ. New year (D., *nau*— new, *ruz*—day), the first day of the Afghan and Iranian solar calendar, coinciding with the vernal equinox on March 21 (1. *Hamal*). Nauruz is an important holiday, going back to pre-Islamic times, which is celebrated throughout Afghanistan and Iran. *See* CALENDAR.

NEJAT SCHOOL. *See* **NAJAT SCHOOL.**

NEW DEMOCRATIC PARTY. *Jam'iat-i Demukrati-yi Nawin*, official name of the *Shu'la-yi Javid*.

NEWSPAPERS. *See* **PRESS AND JOURNALISM.**

NIAZI, ABDUL RAHMAN (NIYAZI ABD AL-RAHMAN). One of the leaders of the Islamist youth movement. *See* ISLAMIST MOVEMENT.

NIAZI, DR. GHULAM MUHAMMAD (1932–1978). One of the founders of the *Sazman-i jawanan-i musulman* (Organization of Muslim Youth), which was affiliated with the *Jama'at-i islami* (Islamic Society) in Pakistan and formed the nucleus of the subsequent Islamist movement (*see* ISLAMIST MOVEMENT). He was born in the village of Rahim Khel in Ghazni Province and educated at Abu Hanifa Theological School in Kabul and al-Azhar University at Cairo, where he was exposed to the teachings of the *Ikhwan al-Muslimin* (**Muslim Brotherhood**) and the writings of Sayyid Qutb. He returned to Afghanistan and became a teacher and later dean at the faculty of theology of **Kabul University**. The *mujahedin* leaders **Burhanuddin Rabbani** and **Abdul Rasul Sayyaf** were his students, and Rabbani succeeded him in 1972 as amir (leader) of the youth movement. Niazi was arrested in 1974 and executed during the *Khalqi* regime in 1978.

NIDA-I-KHALQ. A biweekly **Dari/Pashtu** newspaper with a circulation of about 1500. It was published by **Abdul Rahman Mahmudi** and edited by Wali Ahmad Ata'i and represented the views of *Khalq*, a liberal group (unrelated to the *Khalqi* faction of the PDPA). Its first edition appeared on September 15, 1971 (*du shanba*, 12. *hamal* 1330 q.) and ceased publication in January 1972.

NIEDERMAYER, OSKAR VON. A German officer from Bavaria and in the years 1915–16 coleader, with Werner Otto von Hentig, of an expedition to Afghanistan for the purpose of winning Amir **Habibullah**'s support for military action against British India during the First World War. The expedition did not achieve its objectives (*see* HENTIG- NIEDERMAYER EXPEDITION). After the defeat of Germany, Niedermayer was in the Soviet Union under provisions of the secret Treaty of Rapollo of 1922, where he and other German military officers participated in the modernization of the Red Army. At the end of World War II, Niedermayer was arrested by Soviet forces in eastern Europe and died in Moscow's Lubjanka prison in about 1945.

NIFA. The English-language acronym for the National Islamic Front of Afghanistan, the *mujahedin* party of Pir Sayyid Ahmad Gailani. For details *see* MAHAZ-I MILLI-YI AFGHANISTAN and GAILANI, SAYYID AHMAD.

NIGHT LETTERS. Clandestine leaflets, attacking Afghan rulers and government officials, which became a potent propaganda tool in the war of the *mujahedin* with the Soviet/Kabul forces. Night letters, protesting the secular policies of Afghan government, were handwritten and copied and distributed by Islamist groups since the 1960s. President **Muhammad Daud** was the target of such leaflets, as were the Marxist and Soviet governments after 1978. Letters, written in **Dari** and **Pashtu**, called for resistance against government policies, urging Afghans not to "accept the orders of the infidels, wage jihad against them" (Bradsher, 208). Soviet soldiers were addressed in Russian, telling them to resist the policies of their dictatorial regime. On February 21, 1980 one successful campaign summoned the citizens of Kabul to shout "Allahu Akbar" (God is Great) from their rooftops. This was followed by rioting and a general strike which was severely repressed. The letters were distributed at night, hence the name, *shab-nama* (D., *shab* night, *nama* letter).

NIMRUZ (30-30' N, 62-00' E). A province in southwestern Afghanistan with an area of 20,980 square miles and a population of 112,000. The capital of the province is Zaranj, a small town built in the 1960s. The province was called Chakhansur until 1968 and is part of ancient Sistan. Although the second largest in area, it is the smallest province in population. The economy is based primarily on agriculture in the Helmand Valley and animal husbandry. **Baluch** nomads graze their herds in the deserts. A strong wind prevails for about 120 days and is harvested by countless windmills. Nimruz is watered by the Helmand, Khashrud, and Farah Rivers which dissipate in the **hamuns** east of Zaranj.

A multitude of *tepe*, mounds, indicating ancient settlements, as well as mud brick and baked brick ruins can be found throughout the province, testifying to a flourishing civilization before its destruction as a result of Mongol invasions. *See also* CHAKHANSUR.

NIZAMNAMA. A code of regulations enacted in the 1920s by King **Amanullah** that embodies his reforms, such as the Constitution of 1923 (*nizam-nama-yi asasi*—basic law). Nizamnama included regulations as to the organization of the state and the payment of taxes, as well as rules concerning engagements and marriages and the establishment of schools for women. Traditional elements strongly opposed these innovations, which they considered contrary to **Islamic law**, and with tribal support succeeded in ousting King Amanullah. *See also* ISLAMIC LAW and CONSTITUTIONAL DEVELOPMENT.

NOMADS. *See* **POWINDAH.**

NORTH-WEST FRONTIER PROVINCE (NWFP). The North-West Frontier Province of India (now Pakistan) is inhabited largely by Pashtuns, the same ethnic group that is politically dominant in Afghanistan. Because of the inaccessibility of the Frontier area and the martial reputation of its people, the British and Pakistani governments found it preferable to rule the area indirectly, leaving it politically and culturally autonomous under their tribal chiefs. The province had been part of Afghanistan since 1747 but gradually came under British control as Britain was searching for a "scientific frontier" to protect India. In 1893 **Sir Mortimer Durand**, foreign secretary of the government of India, drew a boundary line, subsequently called the Durand Line, in disregard of ethnic and cultural considerations, which Amir **Abdul Rahman** accepted under "duress." The 1893 agreement was reconfirmed in subsequent Anglo-Afghan treaties. When the state of Pakistan came into existence, the Afghan government wanted the Pashtuns of the NWFP to be given the choice of reunion with Afghanistan or independence in addition to the option of union with Pakistan or India. These choices were not given, and a minority of Pashtuns of the NWFP opted for union with Pakistan. The **Pashtunistan** Question subsequently had a deleterious effect on Afghan-Pakistani relations. Pashtun nationalists of the NWFP demand the right to call their province by its ethnic designation Pakhtunkhwa, Land of the Pashtuns. *See* PASHTUNISTAN and DURAND AGREEMENT.

NURISTAN (34-57' N, 70-24' E). A district in Laghman Province that comprises an area of 1,404 square miles and is part of ancient Kafiristan. *See* KAFIRISTAN.

The Nuristanis are **Sunni** Muslims, estimated at numbering 90 to 100 thousand. They predominate in Kunar and Laghman Provinces and speak several languages and dialects of languages which have intrigued historical linguists, since they have elements of both Indian and Iranian languages. This suggests that these languages (and populations) became isolated at a time when Indo-Iranian populations had not differentiated. Their country was called by Afghans **Kafiristan** (Land of Unbelievers) until 1895–6 when Amir **Abdul Rahman** conquered it and converted the Kafirs to Islam. Henceforth the country was called *Nuristan* (Land of Light—meaning the enlightenment of Islam). The Nuristanis and their neighboring **Safi Pashtuns** were among the first people to rise in October 1978 in rebellion against the **PDPA** regime. After attempts to pacify Nuristan failed, the area remained largely autonomous and was an important base for *mujahedin* operations. As part of its nationalities policy, the Kabul government elevated Kati (not a lingua franca for all Nuristani communities) to the status of a "national" language and permitted the publication of radio broadcasts and newspapers in that language. *See also* KUNAR and LAGHMAN.

NURISTANI, ABDUL QADIR. Commandant general of the police and gendarmerie, 1973–75 and minister of Interior, 1975–78. He participated in the Daud coup in 1973 and was responsible for the arrest of Marxist leaders. He was loyal to President **Muhammad Daud** and remained with him in the palace when Daud and his family were killed by Marxists who stormed the palace on April 27, 1978.

NURZAI. A large and prosperous tribe of **Durranis** located primarily in the Rabat and Kadanai districts of Kandahar Province and in Farah and Herat Provinces. In the early 1930s they were estimated to number about 30,000 fighting men. They are largely cultivators and live in mud brick villages as well as in the traditional black tents.

NWFP. *See* **NORTH-WEST FRONTIER PROVINCE.**

O

OBAIDULLAH, MAULAWI. An Indian Nationalist and revolutionary, exiled to Kabul in 1915. He was an associate of **Mahendra Pratap** and with him established the "Free Government of India" in exile with himself as "Home Secretary." He was a **Sikh** who had converted to Islam and was educated at the Deoband Islamic School in India and subsequently was prominent in the Wahhabi (fundamentalist, anti-British) movement. He fled India in February 1915 and arrived in

Kabul, October 1915, where he was a leader of the Pan-Islamic Party of Muslim Indians in Kabul. He eventually returned to India where he founded a political party in the 1940s, known as Jamna Narbada Sind Sagar Party, and died shortly thereafter.

OBEH (34-22' N, 63-10' E). A small town and administrative district in eastern Herat Province that lies on the **Hari Rud**. The inhabitants are primarily Qipchak (Turks) as well as some **Taimanis, Ghilzais**, and **Sayyids** (see individual entries). About 26 miles east of Obeh is the village of Chisht, the birthplace of Muinuddin Muhammad (b. 1142), founder of the Chishti Sufi fraternity and one of the great Sufi masters of India.

OJHIRI CAMP EXPLOSION. Ojhiri Camp was the **Inter-Servises Intelligence** command post for the war in Afghanistan. It comprised an area of some 70–80 acres, located on the northern outskirts of Rawalpindi, about eight miles from Islamabad. The camp included a training area, a psychological warfare unit, a stinger training school, and mess halls for some 500 men. Most importantly, it contained the warehouses where some 70–80 % of all arms and ammunition for the *mujahedin* were held. On April 10, 1988, the entire stock was lost in a giant explosion. According to Yousaf and Adkin (220) "Some 30,000 rockets, thousands of mortar bombs, millions of rounds of small-arms ammunition, countless anti-tank mines, recoilless rifle ammunition and **stinger** missiles were sucked into the most devastating and spectacular firework display that Pakistan is ever likely to see." About 100 persons died and over 1,000 were wounded as people as far away as eight miles were hit by falling rockets. The depot was stocked to capacity with four months worth of supplies needed by the *mujahedin* for their spring offensive. The cause of the explosion was never examined in a public inquiry, and Zia-ul Haq dismissed the government that wanted to blame the ISI and the Pakistani army for this disaster. Conspiracy theorists saw it as a result of KGB or CIA sabotage, while others called it an accident. Fire was supposed to have started in a box of Egyptian rockets that had not been defused before shipping. A box was dropped and wounded several people, and the fire was permitted to burn for several minutes while the wounded were carried away. Ten minutes later, the entire depot went up, and secondary explosions occurred for the following two days.

OMAR, MAULAWI MUHAMMAD. Supreme leader of the *Taliban* movement and virtual ruler over much of western, southern, and eastern Afghanistan. He led his **madrasa** students in a spectacular campaign of two years to capture Kabul, the seat of the Afghan government, and is positioned to capture and unify the rest of the country. The 37-year-old mulla was a *mujahed* in the **Harakat** of **Muhammad Nabi Muhammadi** and rose to the rank of deputy chief commander. He is an expert marksman and is reputed to have destroyed several tanks in the battle with Soviet and Marxist forces. He was wounded and lost one eye. How this force of students was able to achieve such conquests is still not clear, but observers agree that it must have received considerable assistance from Pakistan. Omar is said to be of Nurzai **Durrani** background from Oruzgan Province. He was unable to finish his education; nevertheless, in April 1996 a **shura** of about 1000 members of the **ulama** recognized him as *Amir al-Mu'minin*, (Commander of the Faithful). He established himself in Kandahar from where he directs the organization. The closing of girls' schools, the restriction of women, and often brutal punishment of enemies and "sinners" have struck fear in those who do not accept his interpretation of Islam. *See also* TALIBAN.

ORAKZAI. Pashtun tribe located at the Pakistani side of the Afghan border and is divided into seven clans: the Sultanzai, Bahramzai, Ismailzai, Massuzai, Alizai (or Sturi Khel), Lashkarzai, and Daulatzai. There are various traditions as to its origin: according to one, they are the descendants of a Persian prince, Sikander Shah, who was exiled ("Wrukzai") in the Kohat area a thousand years ago; another tradition claims its origin from Abdul Aziz a, descendant of Warak, one of three brothers who came from Afghanistan to the Orakzai hills. Western scholars speculate that they are of Indian stock with some infusion of Turkic blood, and are now reckoned to be Ghurghusht Pashtuns (Ridgway, *Pathans*, 1910).

ORMURI. A group of perhaps 300 families who speak Ormuri, one of a number of almost extinct eastern Iranian languages. They are **Sunni** Muslims and also speak **Pashtu** and **Dari** and are located primarily in the Logar Valley as well as in Peshawar and Waziristan on the Pakistani side of the border.

ORUZGAN (33-15' N, 66-0' E). A province in central Afghanistan with an area of 11,169 square miles and about 483,000 inhabitants and also the name of a village and its surrounding district. The population is largely **Hazara** with some **Pashtuns** and other ethnic communities in the south. The administrative center of the province is Tirinkot. The province is part of the **Hazarajat** and in the late 19th century was incorporated into Kandahar Province. In 1964 Oruzgan became a province and elected representatives to the Afghan parliament.

It is a mountainous area, easily accessible only from the south, through valleys at altitudes at of 3,000 to 7,600 feet. It is traversed by the Helmand River and its tributaries. The province is largely agricultural with the cultivation of cereal grains. Major handicrafts include the production of woven carpets, called *gelim*.

OXUS. Greek name of the **Amu Daria**, still used in the West. *See* AMU DARIA.

P

PAGHMAN (34-36'N, 68-57'E). A foothill town about 12 miles northwest of Kabul, where King **Amanullah** built a modern town, including a royal palace. Members of the upper class also built beautiful villas. A triumphal arch (*taq-i zafar*) was built in honor of the martyrs in the **Anglo-Afghan wars**. An open-air theater was constructed for the entertainment of Kabuli citizens who would visit the town on weekends during the hot summer months.

The town lies at an altitude of about 8,000 feet on the eastern slope of the Paghman range. A reservoir and water line from the area supplies Kabul with potable water. Although it is near Kabul, it is surrounded by woods and high mountains and was a shelter for *mujahedin* groups. Much of the town has been destroyed. Paghman is the birthplace of several prominent political leaders, including the *Khalqi* President **Hafizullah Amin** and the radical Islamist *mujahedin* leader **Abdul Rasul Sayyaf**. Paghman was controlled by **Rabbani** until the surprise victory of the **Taliban** in September 1996.

PAINDA KHAN (PAYANDA). Chief of the **Muhammadzai** section of the **Durranis** and ancestor of the families of both King **Amanullah** and ex-King **Zahir Shah**. He was the son of Haji Jamal Khan (1719–1805), who helped **Ahmad Shah** gain the throne in 1747. Painda Khan backed **Zaman Shah** in his struggle for the throne against other sons of **Timur Shah** but subsequently plotted against him and was executed at the direction of Zaman Shah. Painda Khan's sons avenged this deed and thus contributed to the downfall of the **Sadozai** dynasty. His son **Dost Muhammad** (r. 1826–39 and 1842–63) became the founder of the Muhammadzai dynasty.

PAKHTUN. Another form of Pashtun, as pronounced in the eastern Pashtun dialect. *See* PASHTUN.

PAKTIA (33-35'N, 69-35'E). A province in eastern Afghanistan comprising an area of almost 3,860 square miles and a population of about 484,000. The capital of the province is Gardez, with a pre-1978 population of about 10,000. Until the early 1970s Paktia also included Paktika Province and southeastern parts of Ghazni Province. The province is largely mountainous, but well watered and cultivated and shares an almost 125 mile-long border with Pakistan. The population is largely **Ghilzai Pashtun**, but in the south and west are found Jadran and in the east Jaji, Mangal, Tani, and Waziri tribes (for tribes, see individual entries).

The economy depends largely on agriculture with wheat, maize, barley, and rice being the principal crops. Land holdings are generally small, and animal husbandry and illegal timber cutting supplement agricultural activities.

Paktia was an area of strategic importance for the *mujahedin* because it has a common border with Pakistan and lies on the route to Kabul. There has been considerable fighting in the area because many of the PDPA leadership were Ghilzais from Paktia, where the Kabul government also enjoyed some support. A *mujahedin* offensive finally led to the capture of Khost on March 31, 1991 (*see* KHOST). According to UN estimates a large portion of the population lived as refugees in Pakistan, more than from any other province. The area was controlled by various *mujahedin* groups until it was conquered by the **Taliban** in summer 1996.

PAKTIKA (32-25' N, 68-45' E). Paktika Province was created during the tenure of President **Muhammad Daud** (r. 1973–78) from the southeastern districts of Paktia and Ghazni Provinces. It comprises an area of about 7,336 square miles and has an estimated population of about 245,000. The population is largely **Ghilzai** of the **Sulaiman Khel**, Kharoti, and **Jadran** tribes but also includes **Tajiks** and **Waziri Pashtuns**. About 31 % of the population had settled as refugees in Pakistan.

Paktika suffered greatly from the war, and the destruction of the ancient system of irrigation in the Katawaz plain has greatly reduced the amount of cultivated land. Unrestricted cutting of timber has denuded formerly forested areas. From 1990 the province was in *mujahedin* control until captured by the *Taliban* in summer 1996.

PAMIRS (38-0' N, 73-0' E). A mountain range running in a north-south direction and dividing the Oxus basin from the plains of Kashgar, Sinkiang Province of China. There is a series of valleys forming plateaus at altitudes of from 11,000 to 13,000 feet. Located in the **Wakhan** Corridor, which extends to the Chinese border, the plateaus were inhabited by **Qirghiz** hunters and herders, most of whom fled to Pakistan and emigrated to Turkey.

PANIPAT, BATTLE OF. A battle on January 14, 1761 in which **Ahmad Shah Durrani** decisively defeated the Maratha tribal confederation near the town of Panipat some 50 miles north of Delhi. The Maratha Empire, founded in 1680 by Shivaji in the present Maharashtra Province, gradually grew in size and in a successful guerrilla war supplanted the Moghuls in a wide area of India. They were warriors and champions of Hinduism and became a serious threat to the Afghans when they occupied the **Panjab**. Ahmad Shah was able to cross the Jumna River unopposed and took up a position near the Maratha army, commanded by Sadashiv Bhau. For two months the two armies engaged in skirmishes with varying success, but eventually the Afghan forces were able to block the supply routes of the Indians. Both armies were organized in the traditional left and right wings with large center divisions; the Afghans had the advantage in numbers, about 60,000 against 45,000 Indian troops. The Marathas were handicapped with most of their camp followers, families, and supplies located in Panipat, making it impossible for them to retreat quickly. Sadashiv Bhau therefore tried to negotiate, but when the Afghans refused to deal, he was forced into combat. The artillery of the Afghans was lighter and more mobile than the heavy guns of the Marathas; nevertheless, in a desperate move, the Marathas seemed to be able to penetrate the Afghan center. But the Afghans were able to bring in reinforcements and enveloped the Marathas from three sides. One squadron after another discharged their muskets, leaving the Indians little opportunity to compose themselves. Wishwas Rao, the nominal head of the Marathas, and Sadashiv were killed, and the Marathas were routed. The battle ended the dreams of both the Marathas and Afghans to become the rulers of India. Ahmad Shah's troops hated the heat of the Indian plains and wanted to return home with their plunder, forcing the Afghan ruler to return.

PANJA. The name given to the **Wakhan** branch of the **Amu Daria**. *See* AMU DARIA.

PANJAB Or **PUNJAB**. An area watered by five rivers (D., *panj*—five, water—*ab*), the Beas Jhelum, Chenab, Rawi, and Sutlej in northern India. It is now divided into the western Panjab of Pakistan and the eastern Panjab of India. It is a rich and fertile area and has been the scene of numerous battles.

PANJDEH INCIDENT. A military encounter in 1885 in which a Russian force under General Alikhanov annexed the Panjdeh district north of Herat Province (now part of Turkmenistan). The military action pitted superior Russian troops against about 500 defending Afghan soldiers headed by the Afghan General **Ghausuddin**. Afghan rulers claimed the area by virtue of the fact that the Turkomans of Panjdeh had been their occasional tributaries, but the Russians insisted that they were part of the Turkoman nation of Khiva and Merv, which Russia had annexed in 1881 and 1884.

An Anglo-Russian commission was to meet and resolve the dispute, but military action began on March 30, 1885 before Sir Peter Lumsden, a British-Indian general, and his Russian counterpart had arrived on the scene. Amir **Abdul Rahman** learned of the incident while he was on a state visit in Rawalpindi, India and accepted the fait accompli at the urging of Lord Dufferin, the viceroy of India. The fact that Britain did not come to Afghanistan's defense, as she was obligated to do in case of unprovoked Russian aggression, confirmed the Afghan ruler in his belief that he could not rely on British promises of support.

Before the beginning of armed action, the commanding officers hurled insults at each other. Alikhanoff sent a letter to General Ghaus-uddin saying:

> Be it known to Ghaus-ud-din. I thought you were a wise man and were a General of an army, and I therefore wanted to come and see you. As you are such a bad man I do not want to see you, and I consider it a disgrace to meet you. But you must know that the order of our General is that, so long as the frontier dispute is not settled, your sowars should not come to this side of Arsh Doshan, nor will our sowars go beyond that place towards Panjdeh.

Ghausuddin replied:

> From General Ghaus-ud-din Khan, Ghazi. Be it known to Ali
> Circasion [sic]. You write that, until the surveyors of the two
> Governments come, Arsh Doshan should be the frontier. You are
> mistaken. If God please, through the blessings of the Prophet, I will
> turn you out of Kara Bolan. All the servants who are in Panjdeh were
> glad to think that to-morrow they would be called Ghazis.

In a telegram of April 1, it was reported that Captain Yate and all
British officers at Panjdeh had left and "Russians attacked and defeated
Afghans, and occupied Panjdeh on the 30th. [March]. Afghans are said
to have fought gallantly, and have lost heavily, two companies being
killed to a man in entrenchments. Survivors retreated along Maruchak
road. British officers, who were neutral, left, as Colonel Alikhanoff was
reported to have urged Sariks to attack them, and have offered 1,000
krans a head."

On May 4, the Panjdeh question was solved; the secretary of state
reported "We propose to accept in principle this arrangement, which
would leave to the Amir the three points, viz., Zulfikar, Gulran, and
Meruchak.... The whole agreement to be ultimately embodied in a
Convention between us and Russia (S. Pol.& Sec. Memo).

PANJSHIR (34-38' N, 69-42' E). An administrative district in northern
Parwan (now Kapisa) Province with an area of about 273 square miles
and an agricultural population of about 30,000. The district is traversed
by the Panjshir River, which rises on the southern slopes of the Hindu
Kush in the vicinity of the Khawak Pass.

The population is largely **Tajik**, converted to Sunni Islam as late as
the 16th century. The area was often independent or autonomous and,
although the Panjshiris acknowledged the Afghan amir as their ruler,
they rarely paid taxes to the Kabul government. It was only since the
time of Amir **Abdul Rahman** that the Kabul government asserted its
sovereignty over the area.

The Panjshir Valley is quite inaccessible; therefore, the Soviet and
Kabul forces never succeeded in bringing it under full government
control. Its location, impinging on the strategic **Salang** road that
connects Kabul with the northern provinces, made the Panjshir Valley
an ideal base for *mujahedin* activity. **Ahmad Shah Mas'ud**, called
"The Lion of Panjshir" by his admirers, was able to withstand numerous
Soviet incursions and was not evicted from the valley, making him one

of the most successful *mujahedin* commanders. As irony would have it, when the *Taliban* captured Kabul in September 1996, Mas'ud was forced to flee to the Panjshir Valley, where he is now under siege.

PANJSHIR, SOVIET OFFENSIVE. Of about nine offensives, the seventh Soviet Panjshir offensive of April–May 1984 has been cited by military historians as the typical example of Soviet frustration in fighting a counter insurgency war in this area. It began in response to **Ahmad Shah Mas'ud's** refusal to renew his 1983 cease-fire with Soviet forces and involved some 10,000 Soviet and 5,000 Afghan troops (20,000 Soviet and 6,000 Afghans according to Isby, 1989, 32). According to Brigadier Yousaf and Adkin (71–73) Mas'ud had learned of the planned offensive and organized the evacuation of hundreds of villages in the lower portion of the Panjshir Valley. He laid mines along the road up the valley and in one successful ambush was able to destroy 70 fuel tankers and two important bridges. He then pulled back his forces before the start of aerial bombardment. Mountain ridges, rising to 19,000 feet, border the narrow valley and hindered proper approaches of the TU–16 (Badgers) and SU24 (Fencer) bombers. The high altitude bombing was often way off the mark, permitting the *mujahedin* to make spoiling attacks from the flanks. Heliborne units, landing in side valleys, executed blocking actions, but several landed too far from aerial support and were decimated by *mujahedin* forces. In eight days, the Soviets advanced about 40 miles up to the village of Khenj, and by May 7 Dasht-i Ravat was occupied. Afghan garrisons were established in the valley and the Soviet/Kabul troops withdrew, permitting the *mujahedin* to move back into the valley by the end of June. Total Soviet casualties were said to have amounted to about 500, and some 200 *mujahedin* were killed. The Afghan garrisons found themselves isolated in hostile territory and eventually developed a *modus vivendi* in which they coexisted without causing much harm to each other. Masud was soon again free to attack Soviet convoys on the **Salang** Highway that provided much of the needs for the survival of the Kabul government. Eventually, the *mujahedin* captured isolated posts when the garrisons surrendered or defected. Since the fall of the Kabul regime in April 1992, Panjshir formed the heartland of Mas'ud's territory, to which he retreated when the *Taliban* captured Kabul.

PAPUTIN, LT. GEN. VICTOR S. First deputy minister of Internal Affairs, said to have been in command of the Soviet special forces' attempt to capture, or assassinate, President **Hafizullah Amin**. Paputin and Colonel Bayerenov, a KGB officer, were killed in the mission. According to another version, Paputin committed suicide because of the failure of his mission to capture Amin alive.

PARCHAM. A weekly newspaper founded in March 1968 by the *Parcham* (Banner) faction of the **PDPA**. It was published by **Sulaiman Layeq** and edited by him and Mir **Akbar Khaibar**, the faction's major ideologist. It carried articles in **Pashtu** and **Dari** and was openly critical of the Afghan government and was therefore closed in July 1969. One faction of the PDPA that supported **Babrak Karmal** in opposition to **Nur Muhammad Taraki** was subsequently named *Parcham* after this newspaper. *See* PEOPLES DEMOCRATIC PARTY OF AFGHAN ISTAN.

PAROPAMISUS (34-30' N, 63-30' E). Name given by Western writers to the **Safid Kuh** and **Band-i Baba**, the range bounding on the **Hari Rud** valley on the north.

PARSIWAN. *See* **FARSIWAN.**

PARWAN (35-15' N, 69-30' E). A province located north of Kabul with an area of 2,282 square miles and a population of about 418,000. Parwan now includes the former province of Kapisa (created in 1964 and subsequently made a sub-province, *loya woluswali*). The capital of Parwan is Charikar, a town with 22,500 inhabitants, located at the mouth of the Ghorband Valley about 49 miles north of Kabul. The province is famous for its grapes, some of which are dried and exported as raisins. The first cement plant in Afghanistan was started at Jabal-us-Siraj and a hydroelectric power plant provided electricity for Kabul. Subsequently a textile industry was developed at Gulbahar. The province is of great strategic importance as it is crossed by the **Salang** Highway, which leads from Kabul north over the **Hindu Kush**.

PASDARAN-I JIHAD-I ISLAM. A radical Islamist Shi'a group, inspired and supported by the Iranian *pasdaran* (Guardians of the Iranian Revolution), which established itself in the **Hazarajat** in 1983. Ustad **Akbari**, one of its leaders, collaborated with **Mir Husain Sadeqi** of **Nasr** and by 1984 succeeded in the expulsion of the **shura** commanded by **Sayyid Ali Beheshti** from most of the **Hazarajat**. The pasdaran were recruited with Iranian support from **Hazaras** resident in Iran and local militants in the Hazarajat who seceded from the **shura**. They are led by young members of the *ulama*, educated in Iran, and follow the "line" of Ayatollah Khomeini, professing hostility to the former Soviet Union and the United States ("neither East nor West") and look to Iran as a model for an Islamic state. The pasdaran seem to be moving away from close cooperation with their Iranian brothers and are part of the Hizb-i Wahdat. *See also* NASR and SADEQI.

PASHAI. A collective term for a Dardic language of an ethnic community of about 100,000 Sunni Muslims located primarily in Laghman and Kapisa Provinces. In 1981 the Kabul regime declared Pashai one of Afghanistan's national languages and began broadcasting in that language on Radio Kabul.

PASHTU. Or **PAKHTU.** Pashtu is the language of the largest Afghan ethnic group and of an equal number of people in parts of Baluchistan and the **North-West Frontier Province** of Pakistan. Until the early twentieth century in Afghanistan, only the Pashtu-speakers were called Afghans, while the rest of the population was called by their ethnic or tribal designation.

Pashtu is an Indo-Iranian language related to **Dari**, but the two languages are not mutually intelligible. Two main dialects are spoken, the "hard" or *Peshawari*, called *Pakhto*, and the "soft," or *Kandahari*, called *Pashtu*. The former is also called the "northern" or "eastern" dialect, the latter the "southern" or "western." The earliest Pashtu book is the *History of the Yusufzai* (1417), by Shaikh Mali, a Yusufzai chief. There is a considerable amount of native literature, consisting mainly of tribal and national histories and love poems. Most important of these are the *Divan* (Collection) of **Khushhal Khan Khatak** (1644–90); the *Makhzan-i Afghani* (Afghan Treasure), by Akhund Darwaza, a Tajik; the *Tarikh-i Murassa*, (History of Jewels) by Afzal Khan, Khatak, a grandson of Khushhal Khan (15th–16th c).

In Afghanistan, as in Central Asia and parts of India, Persian (or Dari) was the language of the royal court, but since the early twentieth century Afghan governments have promoted Pashtu as the national language. In 1923 a literary group, *Da Pashtu Maraka*, was formed for this purpose, followed by the Pashtu Academy (*see* AFGHAN ACADEMY), which conducted research in Pashtu literature and culture. But Dari remains the language of education in the greater part of Afghanistan, and virtually all educated Afghans speak and understand it. Many urban Pashtuns use Dari as their first language, and some

Pashtun nomads are now Dari-speakers. The Constitution of 1964 declared both Pashtu and Dari official languages.

PASHTU TOLANA. *See* **AFGHAN ACADEMY.**

PASHTUN(S). Also called Pakhtuns (and Pathans in India), the politically dominant group in Afghanistan, with a population estimated at from six to seven million concentrated largely in the west, south, and east, but also scattered throughout Afghanistan. Another seven million Pashtuns live in Pakistan across the **Durand** Line. Except for the **Turis** and a few groups in Pakistan, all Pashtuns are **Sunni** Muslims, and most were converted to Islam by the 10th century A.D. The Pashtuns are excellent soldiers, and many an invader of India chose to enlist them in his armies rather than force his way through their territory. Tribal society is organized along family, clan, sectional, and tribal lines. The tribe, *qabila*, or clan, *qaum*, (from the Arabic *qama*—those who rise together in war) are named after their eponymic ancestor and carry the suffix "zai," as in **Muhammadzai**, the "sons of Muhammad"; the clan or a group living in the same locality is called *khel*, like in Yahya Khel; and a kinship group is called the *kor*, or *kahol*. Alien affiliated groups, like hamsaya (dwellers under the same shade), are often attached to a tribe and enjoy its protection. Each section has its own chief, or *malik*, and the most powerful clan often provides the chief of the tribe. Although the tribal system has undergone changes, traditionally chiefs have to be successful leaders and exemplify Pashtun values; that is they have to be generous and brave. They are not absolute rulers of their fellow tribesmen. Each clan decides matters of its welfare by council, the *jirga*. Jirgas also arbitrate disputes.

The Pashtuns living in the inaccessible areas on both sides of the Durand Line adhere to their traditional code of behavior, the ***Pashtunwali***, which guides the jirgas in resolving disputes. The principal pillars of this code are *nanawati*, mediation or protection; *badal*, retaliation; and *mailmastia*, hospitality (*see* PASHTUNWALI). Urban Pashtuns still have a direct or emotional link to their tribes. The frontier Afghans are politically autonomous along the tribal belt on both sides of the Durand Line, but the rest have come increasingly under the control of the central governments.

Their dress consists of long shirts and wide pants that are gathered and tied around the waist. A turban (*lungi*) is wound in various styles over a skull cap, and open sandals (*chaplis*) are worn, regardless of the severity of the weather. A shawl of wool or cotton is wrapped around the body for protection from the cold. Frontier tribesmen also carry daggers and guns, which are usually manufactured in village workshops. Women wear long shirts, trousers, and a kerchief and adorn themselves with coins stitched to their shirts, as well as bracelets, necklaces, and earrings. Their long hair is usually kept in a braid. A Pashtun tribal dance, the *atan*, is performed by men; it has been adopted with some changes as the Afghan national dance (*see* ATAN).

About two million Pashtuns are still partially nomadic, most of them **Ghilzai** Pashtuns (called Kuchis in Afghanistan and **Powindahs** in India) who used to migrate each year far into British India (*see also* POWINDAHS). Afghanistan's relations with Pakistan since 1947 and the present war in Afghanistan have ended most of the seasonal transborder migrations, and many nomads from the frontier belt have remained in Pakistan.

Because secular education was largely in Dari, the Afghan government opened tribal boarding schools in Kabul and subsequently in the southern and eastern provinces where Pashtu is the language of education. Some of these schools prepared students for higher education in Kabul, Jalalabad, and Kandahar Provinces. Many opted for military careers, and Pashtu-speakers were drawn into the political mainstream of Kabul politics. *See also* TRIBES, PASHTUNS.

PASHTUNISTAN. "Land of the Afghans" (or Pashtuns), the name given by Afghan nationalists to the **North-West Frontier Province** and parts of Baluchistan in present Pakistan. It was part of Afghanistan when the state was founded in 1747 but soon came under the control of the **Sikh** ruler **Ranjit Singh** and subsequently the British-Indian government.

Direct rule of the area was difficult because it is mountainous and difficult to access; therefore the Pashtun tribes were allowed a considerable measure of autonomy. The British government cut the area from Afghanistan in 1893, drawing a border without regard to ethnic and cultural boundaries. Amir **Abdul Rahman** (r. 1880–1901) had scarcely consolidated his power and felt he had to accept "under duress" the Durand Line as his border (*see* DURAND AGREEMENT). In 1901, the British-Indian government created the North-West Frontier Province but left the tribal lands outside of the directly administered areas. Five Tribal Agencies (Malakand, Khaibar, Kurram, North Waziristan, and South Waziristan) were set up with autonomous *khans* (chiefs) and governed by tribal councils. A British agent protected the interests of the government. Tribesmen were engaged as militia to keep order in their own areas, and if a tribe conducted raids into the low lands, punitive campaigns were organized.

In 1947, when India was to be divided on the basis of a plebiscite, the Afghan government and Pashtun nationalists demanded that the Pashtuns be given an option to vote, if not for union with Afghanistan, then for the creation of an independent "Pashtunistan." This option was not given and, as a result of a boycott by members of the Frontier Congress, a Muslim party allied with the Hindu Congress party, 68 % of a low voter turnout agreed to union with Pakistan. Afghanistan protested the procedure and cast the only vote against Pakistan's admission to the United Nations. Afghanistan's relations with Pakistan were subsequently plagued by the Pashtunistan Question. The Afghan government supported the Pashtun nationalists. Pakistan retaliated by closing the border at times. This issue seems now to be dormant, if not dead; but just in case, the Pakistani government tended to support Islamist **mujahedin** groups, like **Gulbuddin Hekmatyar**'s *Hizb-i Islami*, to the exclusion of nationalist groups. Pashtun nationalists have protested the fact that the NWFP is the only province in Pakistan not named after its inhabitants and demanded the adoption of the name *Pakhtunkhwa* (P. for Pashtunistan). It remains to be seen whether the **Taliban**, which captured a large part of Afghanistan, will abandon nationalism for international Islamism, despite the fact that the *Taliban* area is largely Pashtun. *See also* AFGHAN FOREIGN RELATIONS and DURAND AGREEMENT.

PASHTUNWALI. Name of the Pashtun traditional code of behavior which can be summarized under the terms of *nanawati*, mediation or protection; *badal*, retaliation; and *melmastia*, hospitality.

Nanawati is the obligation to give protection to anyone seeking asylum, even at the risk of the protector's life, and to mediate for the weaker party seeking peace with someone he has injured. It is, therefore, a means of ending a feud.

Badal must be exacted for personal insults, damage to property, or blood feuds. *Badal* is exacted for the murder of a member of one's family or *hamsaya* (client) and for violation of safe conduct (*badragga*). Feuds may involve entire tribes and last for years until a *jirga* of elders, or **mullas**, succeeds in mediating a solution. *Khunbaha*, blood-money, has to be paid for murder, except in the case when an even number of feuding individuals were killed. Each injury has a price: at the turn of the century 180 to 300 rupees had to be paid for a life; the loss of an eye, ear, arm or leg carried a certain value (the British government in India codified tribal law, including the amounts of money to be paid). Anthropologists disagree as to the major cause of feuding, whether it is in defense of female honor, competition for land, or retaliation for personal insult.

Melmastia is considered a sacred duty, and every village has a guest house or uses its mosque as a shelter for visitors. A guest's person and property are protected, and a Pashtun is proud to "offer the guest or stranger what he can not even afford for himself."

In a sense, each Afghan tribe constitutes a nation, and no one may enter a tribe's territory without the permission of a tribe and the assurance of safe conduct, *badragga*. A traveler pays for an armed escort that will convey him through the territory of a tribe and hand him over to a *badragga* of the neighboring tribe.

Violation of the Pashtun code will bring dishonor and shame not just to an individual but to the entire tribe or the community. The process of "detribalization," sedentarization, and Islamization has led to a weakening of the of the practice of *Pashtunwali*.

PASHTU TOLANA. *See* **AFGHAN ACADEMY.**

PAYAM. Organ of the **Watan** party (new name for the **PDPA**) which succeeded the *Haqiqat-i Saur Inqilab*, the former party organ. *Payam* was under the editorship of **Bareq-Shafi'i**.

PAYAM-I IMRUZ. "Message of Today," a weekly newspaper published in **Dari** by Ghulam Nabi Khater and edited by Abdul Rauf Turkmani and Muhammad Tahir Muhsini. It was first published on February 9, 1966 and ceased publication on May 25 when the editors resigned. It was an opposition paper that demanded justice, equality, national unity, and the eradication of social vices. It favored the expansion of education and agricultural and industrial development.

PAZHWAK, ABDUL RAHMAN. A poet, scholar, and writer in **Pashtu** and **Dari** who served as president of the 21st General Assembly of the United Nations in 1966 and as ambassador to Bonn (1972), New Delhi (1973), and London (1976–78). Born in 1919 in Ghazni and educated in Nangarhar and at **Habibia School** in Kabul, he started a career as journalist. He was editor of *Islah* (1939), director general of the **Pashtu Tolana**, 1941, and was appointed press attache at the Afghan embassy in Washington in 1948 and London, 1946 and 1951. In 1955 he was appointed general director of political affairs in the ministry of Foreign

Affairs. In 1958 he became Afghan ambassador to the United Nations. During the **Taraki** regime he was under house arrest and left Afghanistan for medical treatment in 1982. He applied to the United Nations for political asylum and went to the United States but moved to Peshawar in April 1991 and died there in 1995.

PDPA. *See* **PEOPLES DEMOCRATIC PARTY OF AFGHANISTAN.**

PEOPLES DEMOCRATIC PARTY OF AFGHANISTAN (PDPA). Afghan Marxist party (after June 1990 called *Hizb-i Watan*, Fatherland Party) founded in 1965 and succeeded to power on April 27, 1978 in a coup called the Saur Revolution (named after Saur, the month of the revolt). The party was officially founded on January 1, 1965 at a meeting of 27 persons in **Nur Muhammad Taraki**'s house in Karte Char, Kabul. Taraki was chosen general secretary of the party and **Babrak Karmal** deputy secretary and secretary of a central committee, whose membership consisted of Taraki, Karmal, Ghulam Dastagir Panjshiri, Dr. Saleh Muhammad Zirai, Shahrullah(?) Shahpar, **Sultan Ali Keshtmand**, and **Taher Badakhshi**. Alternate members were Dr. Shah Wali, Karim Misaq, Dr. Muhammad Taher, and Abdul Wahhab Safi. The party drafted a manifesto which stated that it was a workers' party. It declared Afghanistan a feudal society that should be transformed into a socialist state and announced its intention of obtaining power by democratic means.

From the beginning there was rivalry between the two leading personalities, Karmal being urbane and known for his activities on the campus of **Kabul University** and as a member of parliament. He attracted followers among the Kabul intelligentsia, students, government officials, and some military officers of various ethnic backgrounds. Taraki, on the other hand, was more successful among the **Pashtuns**, military officers, and students and teachers of schools in which tribal Pashtuns predominated. The PDPA published a newspaper, called *Khalq* (Masses), which first appeared on April 11, 1966. Only six issues had appeared when it was banned on the recommendation of parliament for being "anti-Islamic" and opposed to the new constitution. By 1967 the party had split into two entities, subsequently called *Khalq* and *Parcham*, after their respective newspapers. *Parcham* (Banner) was founded in 1968, published by **Sulaiman Layeq** and edited by him and **Mir Akbar Khaibar**. Having been successful in winning a parliamentary seat, Babrak Karmal was willing to cooperate with Afghan governments, while the *Khalqis* remained aloof. In 1977 the two factions reunited in a tenuous coalition with the help of Soviet and Indian Communist Party mediation.

The Saur Revolt was precipitated when the *Parcham* ideologue Mir Akbar Khaibar was assassinated, according to some sources by *Khalqis* who resented his recruiting efforts in the army. The Marxists, however, accused the government of the deed, and the party followed up with a funeral procession that turned into a public demonstration by a crowd of about 15,000 against the Daud government. The government reacted with arrests of the leadership, but three days later, on April 27, 1978, Marxist officers in the armed forces staged their successful coup. The Democratic Republic of Afghanistan was proclaimed, and in early May the formation of a government was announced with Nur Muhammad Taraki as president and premier and Babrak Karmal as deputy premier. The majority of cabinet members were *Khalqis*. By July the *Khalqis* had purged members of the *Parcham* faction, including Babrak Karmal.

A number of decrees issued by the *Khalq* revolutionary council established Taraki as the "great leader" (No. 1), set up a government with Taraki as president of the revolutionary council and Karmal as vice president (No. 2), and abrogated the Daud constitution (No. 3). Subsequent decrees elevated the status of the Uzbeki, Turkmani, Baluchi, and Nuristani languages to the status of "national languages," to be promoted in the Afghan media (No. 4); deprived members of the royal family of their citizenship (No. 5); canceled mortgages (No. 6); gave equal rights to women (No. 7); and ordered land reforms (No. 8). Former government officials and political opponents were arrested, and thousands were assassinated.

Khalqi supremacy did, however, not end strife in the PDPA. **Hafiz-ullah Amin** had become vice premier and minister of foreign affairs and on July 8, 1978 was elected secretary of the secretariat of the central committee. By that time it became apparent that he was the dominant personality in the party. He became prime minister and minister of foreign affairs in April 1979 and president on September 16, 1979. Barely a month later, on October 9, Taraki was assassinated. A split occurred in the *Khalqi* faction between the "Red *Khalqis*" of Taraki and the "Black *Khalqis*" of Amin. A third faction, the followers of a Dr. Zarghun, already existed. They were called the "Paktia *Khalqis*." Increasing guerrilla activity of *mujahedin* forces prevented further strife in the *Khalqi* camp. Amin was said to have shown a tendency to develop into an "Afghan Tito" and demanded the recall of the Soviet ambassador, **Alexandr M. Puzanov**, who expected Amin to follow his bidding. Puzanov was reported to have been implicated in a plot to assassinate Amin.

Mass arrests and executions, blamed on the Taraki era, were not ended, as was apparent from a list published with about 12,000 names of killed or missing persons. Hafizullah Amin's intelligence service, **KAM**, replaced Taraki's **AGSA**, and new government and party positions were announced. About 5,000 Soviet advisers resided in Afghanistan when, on December 25, 1979, an airlift of Soviet troops began that eventually brought in some 115,000 troops. On December 27, a *Parchami* coup, with Soviet armed support, replaced Hafizullah Amin with Babrak Karmal.

Karmal announced a government that included the dreaded head of AGSA, **Asadullah Sarwari**, as deputy premier and two other *Khalqis*, Sayyid Muhammad Gulabzoi as minister of interior and Sherjan Mazduryar as minister of transport. KAM was purged and renamed KHAD, and the *Parchami* regime promised a new deal and an end to the excesses of the previous governments. Additional Soviet troops arrived in Afghanistan and established bases in various strategic locations. The government proclaimed a general amnesty and opened the doors of the feared **Pul-i-Charkhi** prison. Early *Khalqi* decrees of land reform (Nos. 6 and 8) and the emancipation of women (No. 7) were rescinded, and the tricolor replaced the red flag. But it was too late to overcome the "sins" of the past. The presence of Soviet forces in Afghanistan quickly transformed a civil war into a war of national liberation, and many of those freed from jail augmented the growing forces of the *mujahedin.*

Karmal's lack of success in destroying the *mujahedin* was the likely reason for his resignation (or ouster) on May 4, 1986 and his replacement by Dr. **Najibullah**, the one-time head of KHAD. Ideological evolution continued under Najibullah when the Kabul government initiated a policy of "national reconciliation" and changed the name of the PDPA to *hizb-i watan*, Fatherland Party. The early orthodoxy of adherence to Marxist-Leninism was gradually replaced by a general, socialist orientation and political liberalization, as the *Parchamis* attempted to survive in a national front coalition of "progressive" parties. Soviet troops withdrew from Afghanistan on February 15, 1989, but the party continued in power until President Najibullah announced his resignation in April 1992. After the *mujahedin* conquest of Kabul, the party ceased to exist, and many of its members joined opposing *mujahedin* groups. In fall 1994, it was reported that members of the communist party met in the Microrayon quarter of Kabul and elected **Mahmud Baryalai**, half brother of

Babrak Karmal, as its head. At the time of this writing, most of the Marxist leaders have found political exile abroad.

PESHAWAR, TREATY OF 1855–56. Opened diplomatic relations between Britain and Afghanistan. The treaty stipulated that "perpetual peace and friendship should be established between the two governments; that the British Government should respect the territories in possession of the Amir; that the Amir on his part should respect the territories of the British Government, and be the friend of its friends and the enemy of its enemies; and that the British should assist the Amir against his enemies, if they thought fit to do so" (MR, 28). Amir **Dost Muhammad** never knew whether the British "thought fit" to assist him against his enemies.

PIONEERS. *Sazman-i Peshahangan* was a youth movement of the **PDPA** patterned after the Soviet model. It recruited children between the ages of 10 and 15 and was led by adults. Most of the pioneers were the children of party members. Upon reaching the age of 15 the pioneers were enlisted into the Democratic Youth Organization of Afghanistan and upon reaching the age of 21 were recruited into the PDPA (later renamed Fatherland Party). Under *Parchami* rule the former ideological adherence to socialism and Marxism-Leninism gave way to a socialist-oriented, nationalist stage of political development. Like other innovations, the Pioneers disappeared after the victory of the **mujahedin**.

PIR. A religious leader; old man; title given to heads of Sufi orders.

POLLOCK, FIELD MARSHAL SIR GEORGE (1786–1872). Commander of the "Army of Retribution" after the British debacle in the **First Anglo-Afghan War**. Pollock gathered an army of about 8,000 men composed of eight infantry regiments, three cavalry corps, a troop and two batteries of artillery, and a mountain train. He entered the **Khaibar** Pass on April 5, 1842, where he overcame an **Afridi** attack, and after additional encounters on the way, rescued Jalalabad and a British garrison nearly starved to force surrender. Marching on the route of the British retreat, Pollock's army saw the remnants of the Army of the Indus, the wheels of the gun carriages crushing the bones of their comrades. He defeated **Akbar Khan** in the Battle of Tezin and entered Kabul on September 16, 1842. He destroyed the fortification of the **Bala Hisar** and the magnificent Kabul bazaar and permitted his troops to plunder, resulting in the nearly total destruction of the city. Many hundreds of Afghans were killed or executed (O'Ballance). In September he got the British hostages released after offering Saleh Muhammad, their guardian, a "reward" of 20,000 rupees and a pension of 12,000 rupees per year for life. Pollock's forces then moved against Istalif and Charikar and destroyed the towns before evacuating Afghanistan on October 12, 1842.

POLYTECHNIC INSTITUTE, KABUL. A technical institute for postsecondary education in Kabul, opened in February 1967 with Soviet assistance and staffed with Soviet and Afghan instructors. It awarded degrees in fields of engineering with special emphasis on geology, exploration, and extraction of mineral and natural gas resources. It was one sector of Afghan education where the Soviet Union was dominant and rivaled the American-supported engineering department of Kabul University. Many graduates of the institute went to the Soviet Union for advanced studies. After the **Saur Revolt** it was given a monopoly in engineering education, while the **Kabul University** engineering department was closed for reasons of "redundancy." *See also* EDUCATION and KABUL UNIVERSITY.

POPALZAI. A main division of the **Durranis**. The **Sadozai**, a chief branch of the Popalzai, produced the kings of modern Afghanistan from 1747 to the 1830s when the **Muhammadzai** branch of the Durranis succeeded to power. The Popalzai heartland lies to the north of Kandahar, but colonies of this branch exist also in Multan and Dera Ismael Khan on the Pakistani side of the **Durand** Line.

POTTINGER, MAJOR ELDRED (1811–43). Sent to explore Central Asia and came to Kabul disguised as a horse dealer. Reached Herat in 1837 and assisted in the defense of the city. **Auckland** called him the "Hero of Herat" responsible for the successful defense of Herat during the second Persian siege of the city from 1837–38. As a reward, he was appointed political officer to **Kamran**, the ruler of Herat. He was one of two Englishmen to survive the destruction of a British outpost at Charikar in November 1841, in which the Fourth (Gurka) Infantry was wiped out. As the senior surviving officer at Kabul, he negotiated the **Treaty of Capitulation** with Afghan *sardars* in December 1841. And as a hostage of **Sardar Muhammad Akbar**, he was instrumental in negotiating a deal for the release of the hostages in exchange for a monetary reward to their guardian, Saleh Muhammad Khan. The seemingly indestructible Pottinger returned to India, where a court of inquiry in 1842–43 accused him of drawing bills for 19 lakhs in favor of the Afghans and for signing a treaty without authorization. He was exonerated but did not get his back pay and was refused the award of a medal for his services. Died in Hong Kong of typhus.

POWINDAH. Or **KUCHI.** A term applied in India to **Pashtun** merchant-nomads who seasonally traveled far into India. There is disagreement as to the etymology of the name: one source derives the word from the Persian *parwinda*, a bale of merchandise, because of their occupation as merchant nomads. It is more likely from *pawidan*, to wander, or perhaps from the Pashtu word *powal*, to graze flocks. In Afghanistan Powindahs are called Kuchis.

The majority of the Powindah are Sulaiman Khel Pashtuns, one of the largest of the **Ghilzai** tribes. They lead a pastoral way of life, some as nomad shepherds, others as merchants and camel men, carrying on trade between Afghanistan and India. Individuals who left their families behind at times engaged in day labor, sold clothing, or lent money at interest. They were formerly scattered over northern India and would occasionally travel as far as Burma and Nepal.

In the Frontier Belt they were always heavily armed but upon entering India deposited their weapons, keeping only their daggers and swords. The Powindahs created an image of the Afghan, from their appearance in their "storm-stained Afghan clothing, reckless manners, and boisterous voices," as tall and haggard but proud and free. Their chiefs, *maliks*, were in charge only during migration and when crossing hostile tribal territory. They are Sunni Muslims of the Hanafi school and adhere to a Sufi fraternity but their law is a mixture of tribal code and the *Shari'a* (*see* ISLAMIC LAW).

After the British left India in 1947 and Pakistan was created, the Powindah were gradually limited in their migrations across international borders. As a result of the **Pashtunistan** dispute, Pakistan closed its borders to large-scale migration, and the Powindah were forced to redirect their routes of migrations. Afghan governments have tried to settle the nomads but have had only limited success. The nomads have been able to adapt to new ways by moving into the motorized transport business, and former nomads now control much of the transport from Afghanistan to the port of Karachi in Pakistan.

PRATAP, MAHENDRA. Hindu member of the **Hentig-Niedermayer Expedition** who formed a "Provisional Free India" government in

Kabul with **Maulawi Obaidullah** as "home minister" and **Barakat-ullah** as prime minister and himself as president. He was in touch with Indian revolutionaries and independence movements in India and frequently visited Germany and the Soviet Union to solicit support and political recognition. He eventually returned to India and wrote *My German Mission to High Asia*. He later founded the "Great School of Love," a religious, industrial arts school, and the Society of the "Servants of the Powerless," a syncretist religion combining aspects of Islam, Christianity, Judaism, and Buddhism.

PRESS AND JOURNALISM. According to undocumented claims, the first impetus for the establishment of journalism in Afghanistan came from the great Pan-Islamist and modernist **Jamaluddin Afghani**, who in the 1860s was said to have published the first newspaper, named *Kabul*. There is no evidence of the existence of a paper called *Kabul* nor of the fact that Afghani was instrumental in the publication of the *Shams al-Nahar* (The Morning Sun), which was published in the 1870s during the reign of Amir **Shir Ali**. An extant copy of this 16-page paper, published in January or February 1873, carried official announcements, "profitable and necessary information," and reports on events from London, America, Prussia, China, Russia, and Austria, in addition to domestic news from Badakhshan and Kabul. It appeared twice a month and cost 25 rupees a year, which was deducted from the salary of officials; chiefs, courtiers, and notables were invited to make a donation commensurate to their status. The paper ceased publication in the late 1870s as a result of the British invasion in the **Second Anglo-Afghan War**.

In 1906, Maulawi Abdul Rauf, head of the Royal Madrasa at Kabul, started a newspaper called *Seraj al-Akhbar-i Afghanistan* (Torch of News of Afghanistan) that appeared, however, only once in January 1906.

Journalism was permanently established by **Mahmud Tarzi**, the "Father of Afghan Journalism," with the publication of the *Seraj al-Akhbar-Afghaniya* (Beacon of Afghan News, 1911–18). Its name derived from Amir **Habibullah**'s title, "*seraj al-millat wa'd-din*" (Beacon of the Nation and Religion). In the first year of its existence the paper was lithographed from a handwritten copy by Muhammad Ja'far Kandahari and edited by Mahmud Tarzi. Subsequent issues were typeset and illustrated, and the paper soon became appreciated for its quality and relative independence. It served as a medium of information for a small circle of courtiers, government officials, and literate Kabulis, providing both domestic and foreign news. It adopted a Pan-Islamic, anti-British tone and advocated an Islamic modernist policy of reform. It continued with minor interruptions until 1918. Under King **Amanullah** the press experienced considerable growth. The weekly *Aman-i Afghan* (1919, Afghan Peace—derived from Amanullah's name) took over the tradition of the *Seraj al-Akhbar* with a reformist and decidedly nationalistic tone. Provincial newspapers appeared for the first time: *Ittihad-i Mashriqi* (1919, The Unity of the East) in Jalalabad, *Ittifaq-i Islam* (1920, The Concord of Islam) in Herat, and the weekly *Tulu-yi Afghan* (1921, The Rise of the Afghan) in Kandahar.

The first national newspaper that survived subsequent regimes was *Anis* (Companion), first published on May 5, 1927. *Islah* (Reform), published in late 1929 by Nadir Khan (the subsequent king), served as his organ to counter attacks in **Habibullah Kalakani**'s *Habib al-Islam*.

Beginning in the 1930s numerous journals and magazines appeared in both **Pashtu** and **Dari** as private individuals and government ministries published their house organs or specialized papers. The press experienced considerable growth with the increasing literacy resulting from the expansion of education after World War II. The *Kabul Times*, an English-language daily newspaper, was founded in 1962 under the auspices of the ministry of information and culture as a semiofficial medium with a measure of editorial autonomy. Article 31 of the Constitution of 1964 permitted freedom of the press, subject to respect for the fundamentals of Islam, the constitutional monarchy, and public morality. New, privately funded weeklies appeared in 1966: *Payam-i Imruz* (Message of Today), published by Ghulam Nabi Khater, demanding "justice, equality, national unity," and social and economic reforms; *Khalq* (The People) and *Parcham* (Banner), organs of the Marxist **PDPA**, published respectively by **Nur Muhammad Taraki** and **Sulaiman Layeq**; *Mardum* (People), an anti-Marxist paper published by Sayyid Moqadas Negah; *Wahdat* (Unity), published and edited by Maulana Khasta; *Afghan Millat* (The Afghan Nation), organ of the Afghan Social Democrats and a Pashtun nationalist paper, published by **Ghulam Muhammad Farhad**; and *Musawat* (Equality) published by Abdul Shukur Reshad, organ of the **Progressive Democratic Party** founded by **Muhammad Hashim Maiwandwal**. Most papers were banned soon after their first appearance on the grounds that they offended Islamic sentiments or constitutional provisions or on such technicalities as lacking an editor. Private newspapers were replete with ad hominem attacks and appealed only to small circles of the Kabul public. Therefore they were not economically viable. A publisher had to obtain a license from the ministry of information and culture and deposit from 10 to 15 thousand Afghanis as a security bond. *Khalq* and *Parcham* had the largest circulation of private newspapers, no doubt because they were secretly subsidized and espoused a Marxist line.

The relatively free press in Afghanistan ended in the period of President **Muhammad Daud** and the founding of *Jumhuriat* (1973, Republic) as the official organ. No independent papers were tolerated. After the **Saur Revolt** The *Kabul Times* was transformed for a few years into *The Kabul New Times*. *Anis* and *Haywad* continued under new editorship. The new party organ was the *Da Saur Inqilab*, renamed *Haqiqat-i-Saur Inqilab* under the *Parchami* regime (later called *Payam* of the Watan party). The contents of Kabuli newspapers was reproduced virtually unchanged in the provincial press, which now also included newspapers in Baluchi, Uzbek, Turkmani, Pashai, and Nuristani. The Kabul government censored the press, and when **Najibullah** became president the press had discarded a great deal of the Marxist rhetoric and appealed to the war-weary masses to win acceptance for the continuation of the regime. Since the fall of the Marxist regime no national newspaper exists. Numerous publications, mostly ephemeral, appeared in exile in many parts of the world, but it is beyond the scope of this article to discuss them here.

PROGRESSIVE DEMOCRATIC PARTY (PDP). Founded by Prime Minister **Maiwandwal** as a social democratic movement in support of parliamentary democracy and the principles of the 1965 constitution. Its organ was *Musawat* (Equality), a weekly that first appeared on June 24, 1966, with articles in **Dari** and **Pashtu**. It was published by Abdul Shakur Reshad and Muhammad Sharif Ayyubi and edited by Muhammad Rahim Elham and Abdul Ghani Maiwandi. *See also* MAIWANDWAL.

PROVINCES. *See* **ADMINISTRATIVE DIVISIONS.**

PUL-I CHARKHI (34-33'N, 69-21'E). A village on the Kabul River east of Kabul that is the site of a modern prison, built in the time of President Daud and heavily utilized since. The prison, built from a West German design, had a capacity of 5,000 prisoners, but during the *Khalqi* period it was said to have housed more than twice that amount. The prison has special wings for political prisoners, foreigners, and women. During the early years following the Saur Revolt, large numbers of prisoners at Pul-i Charkhi were executed. In 1979, the Amin government produced a list of approximately 12,000 Afghans who had been killed. When **Babrak Karmal** came to power in 1980 he disassociated himself from the *Khalqi* executions and amnestied most of the prisoners. The prison was partially destroyed during the subsequent civil war, but it served the **Rabbani** regime until it was captured by the *Taliban* in September 1996..

PUL-I KHUMRI (35-56' N, 68-43' E). An industrial town named after a bridge over the Surkhab/Kunduz River on the main highway from Kabul north to Baghlan and Kunduz. In 1938 the textile company *Nasaji* began construction of an electric power plant and a textile industry as well as a small town. At first the town only housed the industrial workers and staff, but it gradually grew with the addition of other industries engaged in the production of cement and briquettes and in mining nearby. In 1973 the town had about 20,000 inhabitants, mostly **Tajik** and **Pashtuns** but also about 20 % **Hazaras**. According to local tradition, the name Khumri comes from the name of Khumari, a young lady who lived in the area about four hundred years ago and had a bridge built to facilitate trade across the river.

PURDAH. See CHADARI.

PUSHTU. *See* **PASHTU.**

PUZANOV, ALEXANDR. Soviet ambassador accredited to Kabul in 1972, the final year of **Zahir Shah**, and an important figure during the republican and early Marxist periods. He was an active politician in Kabul and was therefore dubbed the "little czar." He was credited with helping to reunite the two factions of the **PDPA** in 1977 and was quoted saying that the **Saur Revolt** "came as a complete surprise to me." One expert describes him as "an alcoholic seventy-two-year-old castoff from Kremlin political struggles...[who] was trout fishing in the Hindu Kush" (Bradsher, 83) when the Saur Revolt occurred. He supported **Nur Muhammad Taraki** against **Hafizullah Amin** and was said to have lured Hafizullah Amin into an ambush. The "palace shoot-out" of September 14, 1979 misfired, and Amin demanded the recall of Puzanov; he left Kabul on November 19, 1979.

Q

QADHI. *See* **QAZI.**

QADIRI (QADIRIYYA). A Sufi order named after Shaikh Abdul Qadir al-Gailani (1088–1166), an ascetic preacher, acclaimed the most popular saint in the Islamic world. His tomb in Baghdad is a place of pilgrimage, maintained by the *Naqib,* custodian of the shrine, who is his descendant and the hereditary head of the Qadiri Sufi fraternity. **Sayyid Hasan Gailani,** younger brother of the Naqib al-Ashraf of Baghdad, came to Afghanistan in 1905 and established himself there. Upon the death of his brother, he was asked to return to Baghdad, but he stayed in Afghanistan. He was succeeded in Afghanistan by **Sayyid Ali Gailani,** who was succeeded by **Sayyid Ahmad Gailani,** who is also the head of the **National Islamic Front** of *mujahedin* forces. The Qadiri order is strong among the **Ghilzai** and Wardakis in southern Afghanistan.

QALAT. Or **QALAT-I GHILZAI** (32-7' N, 66-54' E). The administrative center of Zabul Province, located on the road from Kandahar to Ghazni and Kabul, about 87 miles northeast of Kandahar. Its celebrated 18th-century fort was occupied by the British in the **Second Anglo-Afghan War.** In 1973, the town had about 4,000 inhabitants, mostly from the **Ghilzai** tribe.

QANAT. *See* **KARIZ.**

QANDAHAR. *See* **KANDAHAR.**

QANUN. Statutory laws enacted after the 1965 Constitution.

QARAQUL. Or **KARAKUL.** A sheep bred originally in Russian Central Asia and introduced to Afghanistan at the time of World War I. **Uzbek** breeders began a lucrative industry in Afghanistan that soon became the major hard currency winner. Qaraqul skins became popular in Europe, and Afghan merchants were able to corner the market until the end of the 1940s, when the Soviet Union and South Africa became major competitors. In the face of increasing competition, the Afghan Qaraqul Institute was founded in 1966 to provide quality control and promote the export of the pelts. The skins come in various colors, most commonly grey and black but also brown and other colors, and are used in Afghanistan primarily to fashion the customary headgear for men, called *kula.*

QARI, ABDULLAH "MALIK AL-SHU'ARA." Proclaimed Afghan poet laureate in 1936. His *Diwan,* collection of poetry, was published in India and Kabul. Born in 1871 in Kabul and self-educated, he became an attendant of **Amir Habibullah** and tutor to his son Prince **Enayatullah.** He was a teacher at **Habibia School** and member of the Afghan Literary Society. He died in 1944.

QARLIQ. Or **QARLUQ.** A small ethnic community of **Sunni** Turks in Kunduz, Takhar, and Badakhshan Provinces. They migrated north from the Ghorband Valley (now Parwan Province) during the time of Amir **Abdul Rahman** (1880s). The Qarliq resemble the **Uzbek** but speak a different dialect.

QASIM-AFGHAN, USTAD MUHAMMAD. Ustad (Master), the best known singer and musician in Afghanistan in the first half of the 20th century. Born in 1881, the son of Ustad Sattar Kashmiri, he was court singer during the rule of Amir **Habibullah** and was responsible for creating an Afghan style of music that was akin to classical Indian music. He trained many Afghan singers. He died in 1957.

QATIL, SARDAR AZIZULLAH. Poet, diplomat, and honorary member of the Afghan Literary Society (*see* AFGHAN ACADEMY). Born in 1892 in Kabul, the son of Sardar **Nasrullah,** he served in the department of census during the reign of King **Amanullah** and was subsequently appointed ambassador at Tehran (1930). He died in 1935.

QAZI. Or **QADHI.** A judge with jurisdiction in cases of civil and criminal law. He usually is a graduate of a **madrasa** or theological college. *See* ISLAMIC LAW.

QIBLA. Prayer direction, the Ka'ba in the center of the Great Mosque of Mecca, which Muslims face when performing their daily prayers. In mosques and areas reserved for prayer the *qibla* is indicated either by the prayer niche, *mihrab,* or outdoors by a *sutra* (covering). *See* ISLAM.

QIRGHIZ (KIRGIZ). A Turkic *Sunni* community of about three million people in the Qirghiz Soviet Republic, of whom a small number lived in eastern Badakhshan Province. As a result of the Soviet intervention in Afghanistan in the 1980s, they fled first to Pakistan; later, most emigrated to Turkey. They visited Afghanistan seasonally in the early 19th century from Russian Central Asia and the Sinkiang Province of China and settled in the Afghan Pamirs in **Wakhan** Corridor during World War I. They lived in yurts and subsisted as herders of sheep, goats, and yaks. In the early 1970s the Afghan Qirghiz numbered about 1,900 persons.

QIZILBASH. Meaning "red heads" (T.), a people named after the color of pleats in their turbans. They were one of seven Turkic tribes who revered the Safavid ruler Ismail (r. 1499–1524) as both a spiritual and temporal ruler. The Persian ruler **Nadir Shah Afshar** stationed a rear guard (*chandawol*) of Qizilbash troops at Kabul on a campaign to India. They are **Shi'a** and were quartered in an area called Chandawol today. Estimated at about 30,000, they no longer speak their original Turkic dialect and live mainly in the cities of Herat, Kabul, and Kandahar. As an ethnic and religious minority, the Qizilbash have tended to be politically inactive to avoid discrimination but have held prominent positions in government service and commerce. They held military positions until the 1860s, the end of Amir **Dost Muhammad**'s reign (one of his wives was a Qizilbash). *See also* NADIR SHAH AFSHAR.

QOR'AN. Or **KORAN.** The sacred book of Muslims that is a collection of God's revelations through the medium of the Prophet Muhammad. Muslim orthodoxy considers the *Qor'an* literally the "Word of God." *Qor'an* means "reading" or "recitation." It is also called *al-Kitab* "The Book." It is divided into 114 chapters (*suras*), arranged roughly according to length and subdivided into sections (*aya*, pl. *ayat*). *See also* ISLAM and ISLAMIC LAW.

QUNDUZ. *See* **KUNDUZ.**

R

RABBANI, BURHANUDDIN (BURHAN AL-DIN). Leader of the *Jam'iat-i Islami-yi Afghanistan* (Islamic Society of Afghanistan), the

largely non-Pashtun group, and president of the Islamic Republic of
Afghanistan until 1996. Born in 1940 in Faizabad, Badakhshan
Province and educated in Islamic studies at **Kabul University** and
Al-Azhar University, Cairo, where he received an M.A. degree in 1968.
After returning to Afghanistan he taught at the faculty of theology at
Kabul University. He became editor of *Majallat-i Shari'at* (Journal of
Islamic Law) in 1970 and was a leading member of the **Islamist move-
ment** since the late 1950s. He organized university students to oppose
the secular trend in Afghanistan and to counteract the activities of leftist
students on campus. The 15-member high council of the *Jam'iat-i
Islami* selected him as its leader in 1971, and in 1974 he fled to
Pakistan where he sought the support of the Pakistan government and
the *Jama'at-i Islami*, a radical Islamist party. In 1975, the Jam'iat
carried out raids into Afghanistan, and failure of the armed attacks
revealed policy disagreements between Rabbani and **Gulbuddin
Hekmatyar**. Thereupon Hekmatyar founded his *Hizb-i Islami* in 1976.
Rabbani continued to lead the Jam'iat after the **Saur Revolt**. At the fall
of the **Najibullah** regime, Rabbani's forces, under Commander
Ahmad Shah Mas'ud, entered Kabul on April 25 and quickly expelled
members of Hekmatyar's forces from the presidential palace and the
interior ministry. The **Uzbek** forces of General **Dostum** also cooperated
with Jam'iat and other groups, including the **Shi'ite** *Hizb-i Wahdat*,
which occupied portions of Kabul and began the struggle for power
between the *mujahedin*. In March 1993, Rabbani succeeded
Sebghatullah Mujaddidi as president of the Islamic Republic of
Afghanistan, but he did not effectively control Kabul or the rest of
Afghanistan. His refusal to step down after a two-year term resulted in
considerable fighting and bombardment of Kabul, primarily by the
forces of Hekmatyar. The rise of the *Taliban* in 1994 posed a serious
threat to Rabbani but an attack on Kabul in February 1995 was
repulsed, and the *Taliban* and *Hizb-i Wahdat* were driven from the
greater Kabul area, leaving Rabbani in sole control of the capital.
Rabbani made peace with Hekmatyar, and a government was formed
with the latter as prime minister, but in September 1996 the *Taliban*
drove Rabbani from the capital.

RABI'A BALKHI. *See* **BALKHI, RABI'A** .

RADIO AFGHANISTAN. National Afghan radio station, first called
Radio Kabul, with daily mediumwave and shortwave domestic service

in **Pashtu** and **Dari** and, after the **Saur Revolt**, also in several minority languages. Its foreign broadcast program offered regular services in Arabic, English, Urdu, and Russian. Broadcasting began under King **Amanullah** in 1925 with the construction of a station in Kabul and was temporarily stopped at the end of his reign in 1929. In 1937 the Marconi company set up transmitters in Kabul, Khanabad, Khost, and Maimana, and experimental broadcasts resumed in 1939. A year later broadcasts reached a relatively wide public: 8,000 radio sets were owned by Afghans, most of them in Kabul, and loudspeakers were set up in bazaars and public places. In order to justify this innovation, the Afghan government stated its purpose as spreading the message of the *Qor'an*, promoting a spirit of nationalism, preserving Afghan culture and folklore, and advancing public education. The system soon expanded throughout the country with the establishment of stations in the provinces.

Radio Afghanistan contributed to the development of Afghan music. In 1964 more than half of the domestic programs consisted of native music. *Qor'an* and poetry readings were regularly featured, and plays were subsequently added. Programming was controlled by the government, and no private radio or television stations were permitted. In 1977 television was established in Kabul to give a new dimension to the cultural and political objectives of the Afghan government. After the *Taliban* captured Kabul in September 1996, they renamed the station Radio Shar'iat. It is rigorously censured and broadcasting of music is forbidden.

RAHMAN. *See* **ABDUL RAHMAN** and **HABIBURRAHMAN.**

RAHMAN BABA. Contemporary of the 17th-century **Pashtu** poet **Khushhal Khan Khatak** and mystical poet in the Pashtu language. Afghans call him the "Pashtun Hafiz" in reference to Shams al-Din Hafiz, the great Persian poet. A school in Kabul, originally intended to teach tribal students in Pashtu, is named after him.

RAHMAN QUL, HAJI. Chief of the Pamir **Qirghiz**. He fled from Sinkiang Province, China after the Communist takeover in 1949 and settled with about 2,000 followers in the **Wakhan** Corridor. After the Saur Revolt he fled to Pakistan with most of his followers then settled with them in eastern Anatolia, Turkey. *See also* QIRGHIZ.

RAMADHAN (RAMAZAN). Name of the ninth month of the Islamic (lunar) calendar and "the month in which the *Qor'an* was sent down," during which Muslims are enjoined to observe complete abstinence from food or drink during daylight hours. *See* ISLAM.

RANJIT SINGH. King (1780–1839) of the newly founded **Sikh** nation, a religio-political entity, who in 1820 controlled most of the northern **Panjab,** Kashmir, and Peshawar. He captured Lahore from its Afghan garrison in 1798, compelling **Shah Zaman** to appoint the Sikh chief as governor of the Panjab. Ranjit Singh was described as of small stature and blind in his right eye but quite fearless and a brilliant soldier. **Lord Auckland,** governor-general of India, sided with the Sikh ruler and concluded an alliance with Ranjit Singh and **Shah Shuja** for the purpose of restoring the latter to the Afghan throne (*see* SIMLA MANIFESTO; SIKH; and ANGLO-AFGHAN WARS). Ranjit Singh, at that time "an old man in an advanced state of decrepitude" was wise enough not to send his army into Afghanistan and therefore did not share the British disaster. Ranjit Singh died in 1839, and his empire was soon annexed by his former British allies.

RAWALPINDI PEACE CONFERENCE. *See* **ANGLO-AFGHAN PEACE TREATY OF 1919.**

RED SHIRTS. A Pashtun independence movement, also called *khuda-i khidmatgaran* (The Servants of God), founded in 1921 by **Khan Abdul Ghaffar Khan** in the **NWFP** of India. The movement was organized in cells and had members in most villages on the tribal belt. It was allied with the Indian Congress Party of Mahatma Gandhi and accepted his policy of peaceful resistance. Membership adhered to seven basic tenets: (1) admission open to all adults, (2) rejection of the Indian caste system, (3) wearing of national dress, (4) readiness to serve the people, (5) dedication of one's life to the interests of the people, (6) recognition of all members as brothers, and (7) obedience to the orders of the party.

The British government suspected them of being a Communist front because of their red uniforms and insistence not only on national autonomy but also on "freeing the oppressed, feeding the poor, and clothing the naked." Khan Abdul Ghaffar Khan and his supporters were frequently arrested, and the movement remained localized until 1947 when it espoused the cause of a "Free Pashtunistan." *See also* KHAN, KHAN ABDUL GHAFFAR and PASHTUNISTAN.

REGISTAN (31-0' N, 65-0' E). "The Country of Sand," a vast expanse of ridges and hillocks of loose red sand that covers the southern parts of Kandahar, Helmand, and Nimruz Provinces. This desert is sprinkled with bushes and vegetation, including alluvial soil in the hollows that are cultivated by **Baluch** and **Brahui** nomads. It has formed a natural boundary with India (now Pakistan) and has been an obstacle to penetration by conventional military forces.

RELIGION. *See* **ISLAM.**

REPUBLIC OF AFGHANISTAN. New name of the Democratic Republic of Afghanistan. *See* PEOPLES DEMOCRATIC PARTY OF AFGHANISTAN.

RESHTIA, SAYYID QASIM. Writer, historian, and diplomat. Born in 1913 and educated in Kabul, he embarked on a career in government service. He was editor of *Salnama* (Kabul Almanac) and of *Kabul Magazine*, 1934–38. In 1948 he was appointed president of the Department of Press (with cabinet rank), reappointed in 1957, and minister of press in 1963. He served as ambassador in Prague (1960), Cairo (1962), and Tokyo (1970). He was vice president of the committee for drafting of the constitution, 1963, and minister of Finance in 1964. He is the author of numerous publications on Afghan history.

ROBERTS, GEN. SIR ABRAHAM. Commander of Shah Shuja's **Army of the Indus** in the **First Anglo-Afghan War** (1838–42). He escaped the British debacle when he was recalled by **Lord Auckland**, governor general of the **East India Company**, who disliked Roberts's criticism of his policy. His son (below) was a British general in the **Second Anglo-Afghan War**.

ROBERTS, GEN. SIR FREDERICK (1832-1914). British general, the son of **Sir Abraham Roberts**, and commander of the Khurram Field Force in the **Second Anglo-Afghan War** (1878–80). He invaded Afghanistan through the Kurram Valley and reached Kabul on October 12, 1879, where he was the *de facto* ruler after the abdication of **Yaqub**

Khan Fought at Paiwar Kotal action on December 2, 1878. After **Cavagnari**'s assassination at Kabul, September 3, 1879, commanded the Kabul Field Force. Fought at Charasia, October 6. Received Amir Yaqub Khan's abdication and sent him to Indian exile. Engaged in operations around Sherpur, December 1879. After **Maiwand** marched from Kabul to Kandahar and defeated **Ayub Khan** at Kandahar, September 1. He was a legendary figure, called "Bobs" by his fellow generals and famous, or infamous, for ordering indiscriminate executions of Afghans. He arrested Yahya Khan, a nephew of Amir **Dost Muhammad**, for the purpose of looting his house. General Mac Gregor said of him: "Bobs is a cruel blood-thirsty little brute, he has shot some 6 men already in cold blood. I have saved three men from his clutches already" (Trousdale, 1985). Although Sir Frederick was able to defeat Ayub Khan, the Indian government agreed to withdraw from Afghanistan in April 1881 to avoid a repetition of the disaster of the **First Anglo-Afghan War**. Later created Earl Roberts and made Field Marshall, Sir Frederick died in 1914.

ROBERTS AND "RETRIBUTION." The London *Times* (February 18, 1879) reported that General F. S. Roberts had caused numerous villages to be looted and burned; that he ordered the cavalry to take no prisoners; and that some 90 prisoners, tied together, and were slaughtered. In response the general admitted that nine villages were looted and burned in retaliation for **Mangal** attacks after they were warned not to do it. He called it an "act of retributive justice." He ordered Major J. C. Steward, who with 40 sabres charged some 400 men running out of a village, to take no prisoners—but he said he merely meant to disperse them. Only 30 to 40 were killed, but "a 'nought' got added during its [official telegram] transmission" and the number appeared to be 300 to 400 killed. His force was too small, therefore he felt justified in giving the order to kill. He admitted that native officers tried to prevent the escape of prisoners and shot nine and wounded thirteen, mostly by bayonets but claimed that "every possible care was given to the wounded" (dated Camp Peiwar, April 1, 1879).

Roberts tried a number of Afghans before a military commission for participation in the attack on the British mission in Kabul. Four were executed "for dishonoring the bodies of the officers" in the embassy; four for possession of property belonging to the mission; six for being armed within five miles of the camp; four for attempting to free Afghan prisoners; and 69 for "murdering camp followers, participating in the attack on the Residency, inciting people to rise, carrying arms, traitorously firing and killing wounded soldiers."

ROKETI, MULLA ABDUL SALAM. A colorful individual of **Sayyaf**'s *Ittihad-i Islami* party who was robbed by Pakistanis of three **Stinger** missiles he wanted to sell. In retaliation he took ten Pakistani hostages, including the deputy commissioner of Ziarat and two Chinese engineers. He demanded his brother be freed from a Pakistani prison and the return of his Stingers but was eventually forced to give up his hostages when the Pakistan government threatened to close Sayyaf's offices in Pakistan. He was wounded by *Taliban* forces but has subsequently joined this movment.

ROSHAN (37-56' N, 71-35' E). A district in northern Badakhshan Province on the left bank of the Panja, or upper **Amu Daria**, with an area of 1,413 square miles and an agricultural population of about 6,500. The **Granville-Gorchakoff Agreement** of 1873 between Russia and Britain defined the Amu Daria as the northern boundary of Afghanistan; it was not known at the time that **Shignan** and Roshan included territory on both sides of the Amu Daria. In 1893 **Sir Henry Durand** (*see* DURAND AGREEMENT) succeeded in forging a compromise in which Afghanistan gained territory on the Afghan side for land lost across the river, thereby reducing the original size of Roshan.

The climate of Roshan is moderate in spite of the fact that the valley lies at an elevation of 6,000 feet. There are said to be considerable deposits of iron and copper in the area. Some mines are operated by the population, which consists largely of **Ghilzai Pashtuns, Tajiks,** and **Isma'ilis** (including Roshanis, Sanglichis, Wakhis, and Shignanis).

RULERS OF AFGHANISTAN. *See* **DURRANI DYNASTY.**

RUTSKOI, ALEXANDR. One of the Russian **Afgantsy**, he became vice president of Russia and head of the parliamentary opposition to President Yeltsin in October 1993. He spent five months in Leforto prison in Moscow as a result of his challenge to Yeltsin. Rutskoi is leader of the conservative Great Power Party. He served in Afghanistan from 1985–86 and again in 1988 and was a "Hero of the Soviet Union," having flown 428 combat missions and been shot down twice, once over Pakistan (Galeotti, 128). He became deputy commander of the 40th Army's air forces and with other Afgantsy is an important actor on the political scene in Russia.

S

SAADABAD PACT. A treaty of friendly relations and cooperation between Afghanistan, Iran, Iraq, and Turkey concluded in 1937 and renewed in 1943. The treaty, also dubbed the "Oriental Entente," was a gesture of solidarity rather than being of political importance. One Afghan diplomat commented on the nature of the agreement, posing the rhetorical question: "what do you get when you add zeros." Nevertheless, the Soviet government suspected some kind of British plot, in view of the fact that Iraq was still not emancipated from British control and could be seen as a *de facto* member. When Britain and the Soviet Union occupied Iran in World War II, none of the signatories of the pact protested.

SADEQI, HOJJAT AL-ISLAM MIR HUSAIN. One of the founders of *Sazman-i Nasr* (Victory Organization), a **Hazara** movement that fol-lows the line of Ayatollah Khomeini but appears to be free of Iranian political control. The movement was publicly proclaimed by Sadeqi and three other *ulama* (Shafaq and **Abdul Ali Mazari**) in 1980 in Meshed and soon controlled most of the **Hazarajat**. A Hazara, Sadeqi was born in the early 1930s in Nili in the Turkman Valley and studied Shi'ite theology in Kabul under Shaikh Muhammad Amin Afshar and in Najaf, Iraq. A book, entitled *Sayyid Gera'i*, was published under his name, questioning the political control of the *Sadat* (non-Hazara sayyids) of Hazara society. He is said to have advocated armed struggle against **Pashtuns** as well as against Soviet forces and broke with **Beheshti**, who supported the unity of the Afghan state. He fled to Iran in 1974 where he became active in the Islamist movement. Nasr is now part of the **Hizb-i Wahdat.**

SADO. Eponymic ancestor of the **Sadozai** dynasty, which ruled Afghanistan from 1747–1818. His place of birth is not known, but from the poetry he wrote Afghan historians assume that he belonged to the **Mohmand** tribe. He lived in Qal'a Bahadur near Peshawar and is buried in Hazar Khana, Peshawar. The line from Sado to **Ahmad Shah** extends over five generations. *See also* DURRANI DYNASTY and DURRANI TRIBE.

SADOZAI. *See* **DURRANI.**

SAFI. Or **QANDARI.** A tribe located northeast of Jalalabad, which is of **Nuristani** origin and speaks a Kohistani dialect in addition to **Pashtu** (some scholars count them as Pashtuns). They claim to be the descendants of the original Gandharis and among the last to convert to Islam when they adopted the name Safi as well as Qandari. They are divided into three sections—the Gurbuz, Masud, and the Wader. At the turn of the century they numbered about 3,000 fighting men. The Safis rebelled from 1947–49 and as a result were forcefully moved to areas in northern Afghanistan.

SAFID KUH. Or **SPIN GHAR** (33-58' N, 70-25' E). The "White Mountain," a high range on the Pakistan side of the border, forming part of the **Sulaiman Mountain** system that separates the basin of the Kabul River from Kurram. Its highest point is the Sikaram Peak, at a height of 15,620 feet. The Paiwar Kotal (Pass) is about five miles from the peak. Another range with this name is in the eastern part of the **Koh-i Baba**, which runs south of the Harirud valley into the vicinity of Herat.

SAFRONCHUK, VASILY S. Soviet economist and career diplomat who was in Kabul from May 25, 1979 to 1982. Officially, he was counselor-envoy of the USSR embassy, but unofficially he was an adviser to the Afghan foreign ministry. He unsuccessfully tried to prevent the rift between **Taraki** and **Amin** and was said to have recommended the establishment of a broad-based, national front government with the inclusion of non-communists. **Nur Ahmad Etemedi**, who was held in the Pul-i Charkhi prison at the time, was said to have been suggested for the position of prime minister. **Hafizullah Amin** refused, and Etemadi was executed in his prison cell (Cordovez and Harrison, 38). Safronchuk published two articles in *International Affairs* (Moscow, Jan. and Feb. 1991) in which he denied that he did more than advise Amin in matters relating to the United Nations and international relations. He characterized Amin as a "commonplace petty bourgeois and an extreme Pashtu nationalist."

SALANG. (35-12'N, 69-13'E) A village and district in Parwan Province located near the Salang Pass at an altitude of 13,350 feet. It is a choke point to north-south traffic on the 300-mile long Termez-Salang-Kabul Highway. The highway and a 1.7 mile long tunnel, located at an altitude of 11,000 feet, were built by Soviet experts and opened to general traffic in 1964. It was one of the routes of Soviet occupation in December 1978 and soon proved to be vulnerable to *mujahedin* attacks. In October 1984 an explosion in the tunnel was said to have led to the death of 1,000 people, including 700 Soviet troops. Commander **Mas'ud**, whose center of operations included the Panjshir Valley, staged numerous ambushes along the road, including one in March 1984, when he was reported to have destroyed 70 fuel tankers destined for Kabul. Repeated Soviet **Panjshir** campaigns could not secure safe passage through this vital link to Kabul. The area now separates Mas'ud from the *Taliban* forces.

SALE, GEN. SIR ROBERT HENRY (1782–1845). Controversial general, called "Fighting Bob" for his exploits in the Burmese War in 1823. When the **Army of the Indus** invaded Afghanistan during the **First Anglo-Afghan War**, Sale was in command of the First Brigade of the Infantry Division of the Bengal Column. Commanded advanced brigade to Kandahar, April 1839; at Girishk, Ghazni, Kabul and wintered in Jalalabad. Defeated Amir **Dost Muhammad** at Parwan Darra, November 2, 1840. He forced the **Khurd Kabul** and reached Jalalabad on November 12, 1841. Unable to return as ordered by **General Elphinstone**, he remained besieged in Jalalabad until April 7, 1842, when he sallied out of the city with almost his entire force of 1,430 men and six guns and defeated **Akbar Khan**. Was relieved by General **Pollock**'s "Army of Retribution" and went to Kabul, September 1842. A severe disciplinarian, he ordered hundreds of lashings for the least infringement by his soldiers. Made a Knight Commander of the Bath for the capture of Ghazni in spite of the fact that he "nearly muffed the whole operation" when he ordered the bugler to sound the retreat at the time a storming column had already effected a breach. He pursued Dost Muhammad into Bamian but was repulsed by his forces and failed to come to Elphinstone's aid at Kabul. "He would have surrendered Jalalabad without firing a shot if Havelock and Broadfoot [two of his officers] had not intervened. His victory over Akbar outside Jalalabad was only achieved because his officers forced him to attack against his own judgement" (Pottinger/Macrory, 153). Returned to India in September 1842. Many times wounded, Sale was killed in a battle with the Sikhs in 1845.

SALE, LADY FLORENTIA (1790–1853). Wife of Brigadier **Sir Robert Sale**, commander of the garrison at Jalalabad during the **First Anglo-Afghan War** (1838–42). Lady Sale was a hostage with other

British women and some of their officer husbands and thus escaped the general massacre of the British forces. She recorded her experience in a book, entitled *A Journal of the Disasters in Afghanistan, 1841-2*, which is an important source on the British misadventure. *See* ANGLO-AFGHAN WARS.

SALJUQI, FIKRI ABDUL RAUF. Poet, historian, and expert on the Herati school of miniature and Persian calligraphy. Born in 1900 in Herat. He was a cousin of **Ustad Salahuddin Saljuqi.**

SALJUQI, USTAD SALAHUDDIN. A philosopher, writer, and poet in Persian and Arabic, appointed president of the Department of Press (1953) and ambassador to Cairo (1955–62). Born in 1895 in Herat, the son of Sirajuddin Mufti, he received a traditional education and became a teacher of Persian and Arabic at **Habibia** and **Istiqlal** schools. Appointed director of the Herat newspaper *Ittifaq-i-Islam* (Consensus of Islam, 1923) and *Sarwat* (Wealth, Kabul, 1925), he became secretary to King **Amanullah** (1926). He served as consul general in Bombay (1931) and Delhi (1935). Participated in the Ariana encyclopedia project and was a member of the **Pashtu Tolana** (Academy). He died in the late 1960s.

SAMA. *See* **KALAKANI, ABDUL MAJID.**

SAMANGAN (36-15'N, 67-40'E). A province in northcentral Afghanistan with an area of 6,425 square miles and a population of 275,000. The administrative center of the province is Aibak, with about 8,000 inhabitants, which is an important archaeological site. The province is rich in mineral resources and is famous for its fruits, especially melons. The population is largely **Uzbek** who breed horses for the famous **Buzkashi** games. *See also* AIBAK and TASHQUR-GHAN.

SANA'I, HAKIM (1081–1150). A scholar, philosopher, physician, and mystical poet who wrote the first mystical epic in Persian. He is acclaimed as one of three great mystical poets in Persian. He was born and died in Ghazni in present Afghanistan.

SARAI. A resting place for travelers and their animals, surrounded by high walls for protection from marauding bandits or tribes. Before the advent of aerial warfare fortified sarais existed to garrison troops and ammunition. They were built at intervals of 12 miles along main roads and in major towns, accommodating as many as 300 men. The average sarai covered an area of 80 to 100 square yards with sun-dried brick walls 15 to 20 foot high and two to three feet thick. A covered gateway ten feet wide led to loopholed corner bastions, and firing platforms existed on top of the wall. Quarters for troops were located along the interior of the walls, and a well, often in the center of the yard, provided potable water of varying quality. Governors and high military officials would reside in sarais provided with a citadel for defense, and all officials of rank and distinguished visitors would be offered hospitality there. The use of heavy artillery has rendered the sarai obsolete as a fortification in modern military warfare, and it serves now primarily as a shelter for passing caravans where motor transport is not possible. In the frontier area tribal chiefs maintain sarais with watchtowers and fortifications that provide adequate protection in local skirmishes.

SARANDOY (TSARANDOY). The name of the Afghan Boy Scouts organization begun in 1932 and headed by the Afghan Crown Prince Muhammad Zahir (the subsequent king) and later by his son Ahmad Shah.

President **Muhammad Daud** organized a gendarmerie force called Sarandoy of some 20,000 men, which the *Khalqi* government continued and **Babrak Karmal** reorganized in 1981 into a defense force of six brigades, 20 battalions of 6,000 men, and various support units. The Sarandoy forces were stationed in major urban areas held by the Kabul government. The Sarandoy was under the direction of the ministry of interior and was a *Khalqi* stronghold under Col. Gen. Gulabzoy and his successors. It used to rival the power of *Parcham*-dominated **KHAD** until the **Tanai** coup of March 1990. After the fall of the Marxist regime the organization disintegrated, its members joining competing *mujahedin* groups.

SARDAR. Title of the heads of **Durrani** clans, meaning leader, general, or prince. The title was awarded by the king also to commoners but subsequently only referred to members of the Afghan royal family.

SAR-I KOL Or **ZOR QUL** (37-25'N, 73-42'E). A lake, called Lake Victoria by the British, located at the head of the Pamir branch of the **Amu Daria**. It is 12 miles long and one and one-half to two and one-half miles wide and lies at an altitude of 13,390 feet.

SAR-I PUL (36-13' N, 65-55' E). A town and a district in Jozjan Province that is the center of a new province formed by the Marxist government in April 1988. The town is located at an altitude of 2,155 feet and lies on the river of the same name. During the reign of **Ahmad Shah Durrani**, Sar-i Pul was a dependency of Maimana. It became independent in 1810 but was annexed by the Kabul government in 1875. A village with about 950 families in 1885, the town counted 12 to 16 thousand inhabitants in 1973, mostly **Uzbeks** and **Tajiks**. A new town on the northwest edge was started in 1963. A shrine, the Ziarat-i Hazrat-i Yahya, is a well-known place of pilgrimage that attracts many visitors, especially during *nau ruz*, New Year (March 21). The discovery of natural gas and oil nearby has led to the construction of buildings and workshops. An oil refinery was planned but never constructed.

SARWARI, ASADULLAH. Member of the *Khalq* faction of the **PDPA** and head of **AGSA**, the security service of **Nur Muhammad Taraki**. He was replaced by **Hafizullah Amin**'s nephew, Asadullah Amin, in October 1979. When Babrak Karmal succeeded to power in the last days of December 1979, Sarwari was appointed vice president and deputy prime minister; but he was soon afterward appointed ambassador to Ulan Bator, Mongolia (1980–86). He was stripped of membership in the Politburo in 1981 and expelled from the central committee in July 1986. Dr. **Najibullah** appointed him ambassador to Berlin until 1988 and to Aden, South Yemen, in 1989. He came to Delhi, India, at the time **Shahnawaz Tanai**, the commander in chief, attempted a coup against the Najibullah regime. Born about 1930 in Ghazni and educated in Afghanistan, he went to the Soviet Union to be trained as a helicopter pilot. He participated in the Daud Coup in 1973 and after the **Saur Revolt** became first deputy prime minister and vice president of the Revolutionary Council. He was reported to have been arrested in India, and the Najibullah government requested his extradition which was not carried out.

SAUR REVOLT (REVOLUTION). Marxist coup of April 27, 1978, named after the Afghan month (7. of Saur 1357), which initiated eleven years of rule by the PDPA. *See* PEOPLES DEMOCRATIC PARTY OF AFGHANISTAN.

SAYYAF, ABDUL RASUL (ABD AL-RABB AL-RASUL). Leader of the *Ittihad-i Islami Baraye Azadi-ye Afghanistan* (Islamic Union for the Liberation of Afghanistan), a radical Islamist movement that aims at the establishment of an Islamic State in Afghanistan (*See* ISLAMIST MOVEMENT). He was born in 1946 in Paghman and educated there, at Abu Hanifa Theological school, and at the faculty of theology of **Kabul University**. He went to Egypt and obtained an M.A. degree at Al-Azhar University. He was a member of the Islamist movement and in 1971 deputy of **Burhanuddin Rabbani**. In 1974, when he was about to leave for the United States for legal training, he was arrested at Kabul International Airport by intelligence officers and spent more than five years in prison. Freed by the *Parcham* regime in 1980, he went to Peshawar and joined the *mujahedin* as spokesman of the Alliance. Elected for a period of two years (1980–1981), he wanted to continue in this position but was forced to step down. He then formed his own group. He is an eloquent speaker in Arabic and has been able to receive financial support from Arabic Gulf states. He is ideologically close to the groups headed by **Hekmatyar** and **Khales** and allied himself with Arab *"Wahhabi" mujahedin* groups. During the present civil war he had frequent clashes with the *Hizb-i Wahdat* and has allied himself with the Jam'iat of Rabbani. Driven from his base in Paghman, he fled with his forces to Jalalabad and from there to Kabul. In May 1996, he was instrumental in achieving a reconciliation between Rabbani and Hekmatyar, which resulted in the establishment of a government with Hekmatyar as prime minister. But by September the rulers of Kabul were in flight when the *Taliban* captured Kabul. *See also* ISLAMIST MOVEMENT and ISLAMIC ALLIANCE FOR THE LIBERATION OF AFGHANISTAN.

SAYYID (SAIYID). Sayyid (pl. Sadat) means prince, lord, chief, or mister in Arabic and is applied as a title for the descendants of the Prophet Muhammad. In Afghanistan the name is also applied to healers and holy men. Communities of Sayyids exist in Kunar Province and the **Hazarajat**, where they constitute a hereditary clergy.

SAYYID HUSAIN. A **Tajik** of Charikar and minister of war in the government of Amir **Habibullah (Kalakani)**. He was born about 1895, the son of a wealthy landowner, and "quickly squandered" his inheritance and "never had any profession but highway robbery." As minister of war he made himself unpopular with his extortions and cruelty. He was executed together with Habibullah on November 1, 1929. *See also* HABIBULLAH KALAKANI, AMIR.

SAYYID-I KAYAN. Sayyid Nadir Shah Husain, commonly called Sayyid-i Kayan, was elected head of the **Isma'ili** community in Afghanistan by the Agha Khan and served for 45 years until his death in the 1960s at age 83. He was a scholar and writer who published a number of works on religious, literary, and historical topics. Before his death, he appointed his son Sayyid Shah Nasir Naderi as his successor.

Sayyid Shah Nasir Nadiri was born in 1933 in Darra-yi Kayan in Baghlan Province. He was elected to parliament in 1965 and in 1968 became vice president of the *wolesi jirga.* Six months after the republican coup of 1973, Sayyid Nadiri and his four brothers were imprisoned. Freed after two years, Sayyid Nadiri and his brothers were again jailed after the **Saur Revolt.** He was in Pul-i Charkhi prison until **Babrak Karmal** proclaimed an amnesty in 1980. Sayyid Shah Nasir Nadiri left Afghanistan in 1981 and now lives in England. His brothers Sayyid Nuruddin Raunaq, Sayyid Abdul Qadir, and Sayyid Gauhar Khan are missing and presumed dead. Raunaq was a noted Afghan poet. Sayyid Mansur is acting head of the community, seeking protection in tactical alliances, lately with General **Dostum** against *jam'iat* forces.

SAZMAN-I NASR. *See* **NASR, SAZMAN-I** and **SADEQI, HOJJAT AL-ISLAM MIR HUSAIN.**

SCHOOLS. *See* **EDUCATION.**

SECOND ANGLO-AFGHAN WAR (1878–79 [–81]). The "Signal Catastrophe" of the previous war inclined the British to pursue a policy of "masterly inactivity" that was to leave Afghanistan to the Afghans. But a generation later the advocates of a "forward policy" to counter Russian moves in Central Asia succeeded in being heard. Technology had advanced considerably since the **First Anglo-Afghan War,** and British conquests had extended across the Indus River and approached the passes leading into Afghanistan. British-Indian telegraph lines and rail terminals had reached the borders of Afghanistan. The Indian forces, now wearing khaki uniforms, were equipped with breech-loading Martini-Henry and Snider rifles that were faster to operate. The Afghan army still depended largely on the *jezail* and muzzle-loading rifles.

Amir **Shir Ali** (r. 1863–79), a son of Amir **Dost Muhammad**, had ascended the Afghan throne after eliminating a number of rivals. He gained British recognition in 1869 and was invited to meet Lord Mayo in **Ambala**, India. Shir Ali was worried about Russian advances in Central Asia and wanted British guarantees from Russian aggression and recognition of his son, Abdullah Jan, as crown prince and his successor; but the viceroy was not willing to make any such commitment and merely gave the Afghan king 600,000 rupees and a few pieces of artillery. Disappointed, Shir Ali was receptive when **General Kaufman**, the Russian governor-general at Tashkent, made overtures, promising what Britain was not willing to give. **General Stolietoff** arrived uninvited in Kabul on July 22, 1878, with the charge to draft a treaty of alliance with the Afghan ruler. Lord Lytton was now alarmed and sent General **Neville Chamberlain** to lead a British military mission to Kabul. Arrangements had been made with the independent tribes on the frontier for the mission's escort of one thousand troops, but when the British reached the border, they were prevented from entering Afghan territory. In response to this "insult," the Indian government issued an ultimatum and dispatched an army under General **Frederick Roberts** that entered Kabul on July 24, 1879. Shir Ali fled north in the hope of receiving Russian support. No help was forthcoming, and the amir died apparently of natural causes in Mazar-i Sharif on February 21, 1879.

The Indian government wanted the "Complete establishment of British influence in Afghanistan, and the rectification of the frontier." It did not want too much territory, "only the passes leading into India" (OA 2, 177).

Britain recognized Shir Ali's son **Yaqub Khan** as the Afghan ruler (Abdullah Jan had preceded his father in death) at the cost of his signing the **Treaty of Gandomak** on May 26, 1879. **Louis Cavagnari** was established as British envoy at Kabul, and history repeated itself when, on September 3, 1879, mutinous troops whose pay was in arrears stormed the British mission and assassinated the envoy and his staff. The incident encouraged attacks on British positions elsewhere, which grew, in spite of British attempts at pacification, culminating in the rout of General Burrows at the **Battle of Maiwand** (July 27, 1880). Fearing a repetition of the "Signal Catastrophe," the British Indian government recognized **Abdul Rahman** as "amir of Kabul and its dependencies" and thus facilitated an orderly exit from Afghanistan. *See also* SHIR ALI; ABDUL RAHMAN; and YAQUB KHAN.

For India the war was an economic disaster; instead of the original estimate of £5 million it cost £19.5 million, exclusive of 395,000 rupees paid to the Amir, and an additional sum of 50,000 rupees per month for six months. The exchequer bore its share of £5,000,000; the Indian revenues paid the rest (OA 2, 723).

The greatest number of troops employed in Afghanistan at any one date was about 20,000, with 72 guns in the main theater and 50,000 men with 74 guns on the lines of communication (MR, 65).

According to one source (Hanna), the British suffered 40,000 casualties which, if correct, must include camp followers. Almost 99,000 camels perished, a loss that was long felt in the areas from which they had been requisitioned.

O'Ballance says, "The real winners of this war were the breach-loading Martini and Snider rifles, and the disciplined direction under which they were employed" (49).

SECOND AFGHAN WAR, REASONS FOR ENDING. An interesting source as to the reasons for ending the Second Afghan war is a Memo by T. F. Wilson, a military official, dated July 10, 1880. It gave the "political and financial reasons why we should withdraw from Northern Afghanistan." It stated that for eighteen months the government had carried on a war at peace establishment. Not a petty war, but one involving 50,000 men and more. "This has denuded India to a great extent of troops, and left our garrisons weak, especially in European soldiers...." The majority of the viceroy's council had protested against the war, and Wilson quotes **Sir Henry Durand**, "Peace in India is but an armed truce." Our Asiatic subjects see "that we have met with considerable difficulty and opposition, while the persistent drain on the country for transport animals, such as bullocks, asses, mules, ponies, and camels, has brought the matter home in a convincing manner to even remote parts of India by the detrimental effect which it has more or less exercised on agricultural industry...." Members of the Native Army were away too long. He quotes the commander-in-chief, saying

> The position is very serious; we have to face extended operations in Afghanistan, and a more or less prolonged occupation of the country. Our cavalry regiments on service, instead of being 500 strong, have only 378 effectives, and our infantry corps, instead of 800, have only 587 effectives. Constant marching and fighting, and harassing fatigues, and the vicissitudes of a climate severe and trying beyond measure for natives of India, have reduced our numbers and impaired the health of

every Native regiment, while recruiting is at a standstill, the entire
Bengal Army having obtained only 46 recruits during the month of
January late.... Such is the picture of the Bengal Native Army in 1880,
painted by its own chief. Even in the darkest days of the mutiny of 1857
no difficulty existed in raising new regiments. Stories of First War seem
to discourage others. [We] Underestimated cost of war at 14 million,
add to this renewals required, pensions to Afghan collaborators –
altogether no less than 20 million.

It is now nine months since we occupied Cabool – after a resistance
just sufficient to throw the Commander of the army off his guard...
followed by the narrowest escape of his force from destruction; this last
resulting in a scare which has never been entirely shaken off.

In fact, the occupation of Cabool has been marked by three distinct
epochs; the first that of heedless audacity and misguided unnecessary
executions and severity; the second by surprise and defeat, followed by
timidity, want of enterprise, and a general condonation of all offenses;
and the third by aimless, costly, and weak attempts at diplomacy
resulting in fruitless efforts to win over influential people to our
interests.

Since early in January last, our force at Cabool has not been less than
from 8 to 9,000...yet it has never taken the initiative or ventured to do
much more than hold the position of Sherpore... fortifications continued
to be piled on each other, the army being allowed to grow into a belief
that it could only command the ground on which it stood behind its
defenses.

Seeing all this, and remembering how their foot soldiers captured our
horse artillery guns, drove us into Sherpore, and plundered the city at
their leisure under our eyes; is it to be wondered at that the Afghan
nation continue elated and defiant? Kabul is 190 miles from Peshawar,
19 marches, but 15,000 men are barely sufficient to keep the line open.

In short, our military position in Afghanistan is this. We have 11,500
men at Candahar, and on its line of communication with India; 20,000
at Cabool, or in its immediate vicinity; 15,000 holding the line through
Jellalabad and the Khyber to Peshawar; and 8,500 locked up in the
Kurram valley; or a total of 57,000 men in the field, yet we command
little more than the ground on which we stand.

The creation of 'the strong and friendly Government at Cabool,' and
our determination 'to have an English Ambassador at the Dooranee
Court,' are now but dreams of the past, from which Englishmen turn to
the thought of, How can we best get our army back to India? How can
we best disentangle ourselves from the false position we occupy?

We have recently based our hopes on Abdool Raheeman [**Abdul
Rahman**] as the best candidate for the vacant masnud...[but] we must
not forget that he has for years past been in receipt of a liberal pension,
and an honored guest in Russian dominions. This need not result in any

gratitude to the Russians for whatever he may now say or promise, he will in the future act only according to his own views and belief...if we can come to some patched up arrangement with this man that will enable us to quit the country without absolute discredit...

Whenever we withdraw care must be taken to avoid all appearance of precipitancy...the enemy should be prevented from following our troops. The last withdrawal awoke in India a belief that we had at last met with a nut we could not crack; and two legacies resulted—the long and severe struggle with the Punjab and the Mutiny.

In every Native Court it will be said 'the Feringhees could not hold Cabool.' [He did, however, recommend to keep Kandahar and demand some border adjustments.]

In the present temper of Parliament, and the people of England. . . whether we leave the 'strong and friendly Government' behind us or anarchy....Government or no Government, Ameer or no Ameer, *coute qu'il coute*, we shall withdraw early in the autumn.

Abdool Raheeman is playing with us....Evidently he is not such a fool as to come to Cabool and accept the throne from us.

And, indeed, the amir came with an army, possibly to make war with Britain, but he concluded an agreement that permitted the British forces to withdraw with a semblance of dignity.

SEPAH-I PASDARAN. *See* **PASDARAN-I JIHAD-I ISLAM.**

SERAJ AL-AKHBAR AFGHANIYA. A biweekly newspaper, published during the reign of Amir **Habibullah** from 1911 to 1918. It was edited by **Mahmud Tarzi** and propagated Pan-Islamic and modernist ideas. One of the staff members was **Abdul Hadi Dawai** who became president of the Afghan senate, 1966–73. During the first year of its existence the paper was lithographed, but subsequent editions were handsomely typeset and illustrated, occasionally with political cartoons. Although circulation was small (1,600 copies), the paper had a regular readership as far distant as Russian Central Asia, Iran, the Ottoman Empire, India, and even Japan. To make the paper economically feasible, Mahmud Tarzi requested that courtiers and government and military officials to subscribe. The newspaper was independent, but Amir Habibullah occasionally censored an issue when the British Indian government protested its hostile attitude. The paper ceased publication in December 1918, two months before the assassination of Amir Habibullah. *See also* PRESS AND JOURNALISM.

SERAJ AL-MILLAT WA'D DIN. "Torch of the Nation and Religion," the title adopted by Amir **Habibullah** upon being sworn in as amir in 1901. His descendants subsequently adopted Seraj as a family name.

SETAM-I MILLI. *See* **BADAKHSHI, TAHIR.**

SEWWUM-I-AQRAB. The Afghan date of a series of demonstrations (the third of Aqrab 1344, corresponding to October 25, 1965), when students under leftist leadership protested the secret session of parliament, which was to decide on a vote of confidence for the government of Prime Minister **Muhammad Yusuf.** Troops responding to stone-throwing students opened fire and killed three and wounded several others. As a result of the demonstrations the prime minister resigned, and the "Sewwum-i-Aqrab" subsequently became a rallying cry of the Afghan left. *See also* MUHAMMAD YUSUF.

SHAFIQ, MUHAMMAD MUSA. Afghan foreign minister (1971) and prime minister from October 1972 until the coup of Sardar **Muhammad Daud** in July 1973. Arrested by the Daud government and held from 1973–76, later under house arrest until the **Saur Revolt**, when he was executed during the **Taraki** regime. Born in 1930 in Kabul, he attended *Qor'an* school and the Islamic College (Dar al-Ulum-i Sharia) in Kabul, Al-Azhar in Cairo, Egypt, and studied Islamic and comparative law at Columbia University. He opened the first private law firm in Kabul in 1961 and had a major role in drafting the Constitution of 1964. Served as Afghan ambassador to Cairo from 1968 to 1971.

SHAH MAHMUD, GHAZI. *See* **GHAZI, SHAH MAHMUD.**

SHAHNAMA. *See* **FIRDAUSI, ABU'L QASEM MANSUR.**

SHAHR-I BARBAR. The remains of an ancient city on a hill between the Firuzbahar and Band-i Amir Streams in Bamian Province. It is said to have been the capital of a kingdom comprising the **Hazarajat** and inhabited by a people called Barbar, probably the ancestors of the Hazaras who were also known as Barbari.

SHAH SHUJA-UL-MULK (r. 1803–10 and 1839–42). Born about 1792, the seventh son of **Timur Shah**, he became governor of Peshawar in

1801 during the reign of his full brother **Shah Zaman**. In 1803 he captured Kabul, imprisoned his brother **Mahmud**, and proclaimed himself king. He accepted a British mission in 1809 under **Mountstuart Elphinstone** and concluded a treaty of alliance that states in Article 2

> If the French and Persians in pursuance of their confederacy should advance towards the King of Cabool's country in a hostile manner, the British State, endeavoring heartily to repel them, shall hold themselves liable to afford the expenses necessary for the above-mentioned service to the extent of their ability.

This treaty was to prevent a Franco-Persian invasion of India that never occurred; but it did not protect the amir from attack by Persia alone. At that time Mountstuart Elphinstone described the Afghan ruler as "a handsome man...his address princely," and he marveled "how much he had of the manners of a gentleman, or how well he preserved his dignity, while he seemed only anxious to please" (Macrory, 32).

Two years later Mahmud, who had managed to escape, captured Kabul and forced Shah Shuja to flee to Bukhara and later to India where he remained as an exile for almost 30 years. En route to India he had to pass through the territory of the **Sikh** ruler **Ranjit Singh** who took from him the **Koh-i Nur**, a prized diamond that is now part of the British crown jewels. The internecine fighting between the **Sadozai** princes brought **Dost Muhammad** to power and marked the end of the Sadozai dynasty. In 1839 Britain invaded Afghanistan and restored Shah Shuja to the throne in a campaign that became known as the **First Anglo-Afghan War**. At that time the amir was described as "elderly, stout, pompous and unheroic" (Macrory, 298). The Sadozai ruler was not able to govern without British protection; he remained ensconced in the protection of the **Bala Hisar** and was assassinated by a **Barakzai** *sardar* on April 25, 1842, only a few months after the British army was forced to a disastrous retreat. *See* ANGLO-AFGHAN WARS.

SHAH WALI, MARSHAL. Conqueror of Kabul from the forces of **Habibullah Kalakani** in October 1929. He was born in 1885, the son of Sardar Muhammad Yusuf Khan and brother of **Nadir Shah**. He headed Amir **Habibulla**'s bodyguard and commanded King **Amanullah**'s forces during the **Khost Rebellion** of 1924-25. He left for France in 1926 and remained there with Nadir Khan until they started their campaign against the **Tajik** king. Nadir Shah appointed him minister in London in 1930 and Paris 1932; **Zahir Shah** assigned him as ambassador to Karachi in 1947 and in London in 1949. During the later reign of Zahir Shah, he was an adviser to the king. He carried the title of Marshal. President **Muhammad Daud** placed him under house arrest. He left Afghanistan and died in Rome in 1976.

SHAH ZAMAN (r. 1793–1800). Born in 1772, one of 23 sons of **Timur Shah**, and his successor to the throne in 1793. During most of his reign he was engaged in intermittent warfare with his brothers **Mahmud** and Humayun. He wanted to win over the British for a concerted war against the **Maratha** confederacy in India. Instead the British concluded an alliance with Persia to keep the Afghans out of India (*See* AFGHAN FOREIGN RELATIONS). Shah Zaman appointed **Ranjit Singh** governor of Lahore, in spite of the fact that he had previously rebelled. He abolished the hereditary posts established by **Ahmad Shah Durrani** and carried out bloody executions, antagonizing many Afghans. While he was in the Panjab, Mahmud captured the Kabul throne. Shah Zaman was blinded and imprisoned but eventually escaped and lived in Indian exile until his death in 1844.

SHAIKH ALI HAZARAS. *See* **HAZARAS.**

SHAMS AL-NAHAR. The "Sun of the Day" was the first Afghan newspaper published during the reign of Amir **Shir Ali** at Kabul from 1873 to 1877. An extant copy in possession of this writer (dated the 15th *zi 'l-hijja* 1290, corresponding to February/March 1873) shows a masthead consisting of an emblem inscribed *Shams al-Nahar Kabul*, positioned between two lions who hold a dragon with one paw and a sword in the other. Around it are four couplets that state: "The work I have begun with your support, you, my Lord, complete with excellence." The price of a copy was ten annas, in cash or deducted from the creditor's account (salary?). Notables, courtiers, chiefs, and government officials paid "according to their glorious ranks and names." The 16-page paper featured public announcements, international and domestic news, and a weather report. Human interest stories discuss the manner of solving paternity suits in China and Kafir religious practices, as told by a recent convert to Islam. Only the name of the printer, one Mirza Abdul Ali, was given. *See also* PRESS AND JOURNALISM.

SHAMSI CALENDAR. The solar (*shams*, Ar., sun) year calendar introduced in Afghanistan under King **Amanullah**. *See* CALENDAR.

SHARI'A. *See* **ISLAMIC LAW.**

SHI'A. Or **SHI'ISM.** A Muslim sect that derives its name from *shi'at Ali*, the party of Ali, and holds that leadership of the Islamic community should be by dynastic succession from *Imam* Ali (cousin and son-in-law of the Prophet Muhammad) and his descendants. Their view conflicts with the *Sunni* principle that Muhammad's successor, *khalifa* (**caliph**), should be elected. *Shi'as* divide into three major sects according to which of their *imams* is believed to be the "Expected One," who will return on judgment day: the fifth, seventh, or twelfth. In Afghanistan the small **Qizilbash** and **Farsiwan** communities, and most of the **Hazara** population, are "Twelver" (*Ithna'ashariyya*, or *imami*) Shi'as, the same sect that predominates in Iran. There are also small groups of *Isma'ilis*, or "Seveners," who live in northeastern Afghanistan.

The Twelvers believe their *imam* is infallible and that their theologians, the *mujtahids*, may legislate in the absence of the imam. In addition to Mecca and Medina, their holy places are Najaf and Karbala in Iraq, as well as Mashshad and Qum in Iran. They accept the practice of temporary marriages, *mut'a* (called *sigha* in **Dari**), and *taqqiya*, prudent denial of their religion if in danger of persecution. They believe in an esoteric interpretation of the *Qor'an* but like the *Sunnis* accept the "Five Pillars of Islam" (*see* ISLAM) with only minor exceptions. In Afghanistan the *Shi'as* constitute about 15 % of the Afghan population and, in addition to being a sectarian minority, also are an ethnic minority. *See also* ISLAM and SHI'A MUJAHEDIN GROUPS.

SHI'A MUJAHEDIN GROUPS. The people of the **Hazarajat**, home to a large part of the Afghan *Shi'a* population, rebelled in February 1979 and by the end of the year had liberated their area from Marxist control. The Revolutionary Council of Islamic Unity of Afghanistan (*Shura-yi inqilab-i ittifaq-i islami-yi Afghanistan*) established a government headed by **Sayyid Ali Beheshti** with its administrative center at Waras in Bamian Province. It set up administrative offices, formed a defense force drafted from the local population, and collected taxes to defray the costs of running a state. Until about 1983, the Shura was the dominant movement; but radical Islamist parties emerged, which challenged the authority of the traditional Shura. The *Sazman-i Nasr* (Organization for Victory), headed by **Mir Husain Sadeqi** and the **Pasdaran**, (Guardians), modeled after the Iranian *Sepah-i Pasdaran* and following the "line" of Ayatollah Khomeini, gained strength and conquered much of the Hazarajat from the Shura. Smaller groups controlling enclaves in the Hazarajat were the *ittihad-i mujahedin-i Islami* (Union of Islamic Fighters), led by Abdul Husain Maqsudi and the *harakat-i Islami* (Islamic Movement) of **Muhammad Asef Muhsini**, headquartered in Quetta and subsequently allied with **Rabbani** at Kabul. Numerous groups, like *Ra'd* (Thunder), headed by Shaikhzada Khaza'i, and *Hizbullah* (The Party of God) of Shaikh Ali Wusuki, and others, Islamist or Marxist, published their manifestos but never succeeded in winning popular support. Unifying efforts were not successful. In 1987 they founded the Council of Islamic Alliance, which the Shura joined a year later. And during a meeting of commanders in Bamian on June 16, 1990, creation of the Party of Islamic Unity of Afghanistan (*Hizb-i wahdat-i Islami-yi Afghanistan*) was announced. **Abdul Ali Mazari** was appointed its leader, followed by **Karim Khalili** after Mazari's assassination. Ustad **Akbari**, who broke away from **Wahdat**, also joined the **Rabbani** government at Kabul. Major divisions exist between the traditional and Islamist groups and a multitude of notables and khans, **sayyids**, and the new elite of Islamists who are competing for leadership. **Wahdat** issued a declaration supporting the independence of an indivisible Afghanistan, demanding freedom for all nationalities and sects, and seeking security and social justice for all. It supports women's rights, including the right to vote.

The spectacular victory of the *Taliban* in September 1996 and their capture of Kabul left the *Hizb-i wahdat, jam'iat,* and General **Dostum**'s forces as the only remaining forces to fight the *Taliban* or join them in a national government.

SHIBERGHAN (36-41'N, 65-45'E). The capital of Jozjan Province, located some 80 miles west of Mazar-i Sharif. In 1970 the town was estimated to have 15,000 inhabitants. Afghan historians link the name to Asaburgan, a prosperous ninth-century town that was destroyed as a result of Turco-Mongolian invasions. The town was surrounded by a wall and the seat of an independent **Uzbek** khan (chief) until it was annexed in 1859 by Amir **Dost Muhammad**. In the late 1930s the Afghan government began construction of a new town, and further expansion resulted from the discovery of natural gas in the vicinity and the construction of a pipeline and complex of buildings for the needs of the rapidly growing oil industry. A World Bank study estimates that the fields at Yatimdagh, Khwaja Gugerdak, Jarquduq, and Khwaja Burhan, northeast and southeast of Shiberghan, contain a combined reserve of natural gas amounting to 140 billion cubic meters. In the 1970s Shiberghan was a modern town with wide open streets and avenues and flat roofed houses and a thriving handicraft industry in leather and wood. Because of the large Russian personnel involved in the oil industry, Shiberghan was popularly called the "Russian" town (**Lashkargah** being the "American" town). The Americans left in the late 1970s, and most Russians departed with the Soviet troops in 1989; the rest left after the fall of the Marxist regime in April 1992. General **Dostum** who, at the time of this writing, rules north central Afghanistan, has tried to negotiate a pipeline project.

SHIGHNAN (37-27' N, 71-27' E). A district in northern Badakhshan that until 1859 was an independent **Tajik** khanate. It came under the direct administration of the Kabul government in 1883. Britain and Russia in 1873 recognized the **Amu Daria** as Afghanistan's northern boundary and the limit of Russian influence. But the agreement (*see* GRANVILLE-GORCHAKOFF AGREEMENT) was concluded in ignorance of the fact that Shighnan extended across the river. The boundary question continued to be an issue until in 1893 Amir **Abdul Rahman** ceded the portions of Shighnan lying across the river in exchange for **Darwaz**, which was on the Afghan side of the river. The Shighnanis speak a language of their own and are **Isma'ili Shi'as**. *See also* ROSHAN.

SHINDAND (SABZAWAR) AIR BASE (33-18'N, 62-8'E). A town and district in Farah Province that was the location of the largest operational air base of Soviet forces in Afghanistan. It was one of the objectives in a pincer move into Afghanistan on December 27, 1978, when the 357th MRD advanced from Kushka to Herat and established its control at Shindand. The airfield was considerably expanded from 1980–82 to become the largest Soviet airbase in Afghanistan. It was the main base of Hind D helicopters and the 5th Guards MRD, as well as some 45 fighter and fighter bombers, which operated from the relative safety of the base. It was located in flat territory and surrounded by a three-ringed security belt, covering an area of 40 kilometers. Although it was well protected, *mujahedin* claim to have destroyed some 22 aircraft, two helicopters, and 18 oil tankers in a spectacular case of sabotage on June 8, 1985. After the fall of the Kabul regime, Shindand became the major air base of Muhammad Isma'il Khan until it was captured by the *Taliban* on September 2, 1995.

SHINWARI. The Shinwaris are **Pashtuns** who migrated in the 16th century into the area of Nangarhar. The tribe is divided into four divisions: the Mandezai, Sangu Khel, Sipah, and Alisher Khel who can muster a fighting force of 12,000 men. The Alisher Khel, on the Pakistani side of the **Durand** Line, have a reputation as excellent soldiers.

In the early 11th century the Shinwaris accompanied **Mahmud of Ghazni** on his invasions of India. They fought the British in **three Anglo-Afghan wars** and in the late 19th century repeatedly rose against Amir **Abdul Rahman**. The Shinwaris were members of a coalition of tribal forces that caused the downfall of King **Aman-ullah**. *See also* SHINWARI MANIFESTO.

SHINWARI MANIFESTO. A proclamation by the Shinwari leaders Muhammad Alam and Muhammad Afzal, in November 1928, listing their principal grievances against the government of King **Amanullah** and declaring war against the Afghan king. The manifesto objected to the king's legal and social reforms, such as the framing of legal codes, recommendation of monogamy, the removal of purdah, and the opening of theaters and cinemas in Kabul. They invested Dakka and Jalalabad and tied down Amanullah's forces, enabling **Habibullah Kalakani** to capture Kabul and install himself on the Kabul throne.

SHIR ALI, AMIR (r. 1863–66 and 1868–79). One of Amir **Dost Muhammad**'s 27 sons who became amir of Afghanistan in 1863 and spent much of his tenure trying to meet challenges from his brothers who governed various provinces. By 1869 he had consolidated his power and traveled to **Ambala**, India, in response to an invitation from the viceroy, Lord Mayo. He was willing to form an alliance with India in exchange for British protection from Russian attacks, assistance in weapons and money, and recognition of the succession of his favorite son Abdullah Jan. But the viceroy merely expressed his pleasure that the civil war among the princes had come to an end and, as a gesture of friendship, gave the Afghan ruler a present of 600,000 rupees and a few pieces of artillery.

Disappointed in his dealings with Britain, the amir decided to listen to Russian overtures. Russia sent **General Stolietoff** to Kabul on July 22, 1878 who promised what Britain was not willing to grant. Alarmed, the viceroy's government decided to send General **Neville Chamberlain** to Kabul, but he was not permitted to enter Afghanistan. Following an ultimatum, a British army invaded Afghanistan in a campaign known as the **Second Anglo-Afghan War**. Shir Ali left his son **Yaqub** in command at Kabul and went north to seek Russian support, but **General Kaufman**, the Russian governor-general of Turkistan province, merely advised Shir Ali to make peace with the British. Shir Ali died on February 21, 1879 in Mazar-i Sharif and was succeeded in Kabul by his son Yaqub.

Shir Ali was the first to initiate modern reforms: he established an advisory council to assist in the administration of the state and created an army organized on European lines. He abolished the feudal system of tax-farming, set up a postal system, and published the first Afghan newspaper, the *Shams al-Nahar* (Sun of the Day).

SHIR (SHER) DARWAZA. A hill on the outskirts of Kabul, overlooking the town and the location of the "noon cannon," which sounds noontime and the end of daylight fasting during the month of *Ramadhan* (*See* ISLAM).

SHIRKAT-I SAHAMI-YI MILLI. *See* **BANK-I MILLI** .

SHU'LA-YI JAVID. Name of a weekly Marxist newspaper with articles in **Dari** and **Pashtu**, published by Dr. **Rahim Mahmudi**. The newspaper was banned in July 1969, three months after its first appearance, because it advocated the violent overthrow of the Afghan government. It was the organ of the New Democratic Party (*Jam'iat-i Demukrati-yi Nawin*), popularly also called *Shu'la-yi Javid* (Eternal Flame), and vied with other leftist groups in organizing strikes and student demonstrations. The party opposed Pashtun nationalism and advocated the right of self-determination of all nationalities and therefore found supporters among ethnic and sectarian minorities. It appeared to be ideologically closer to China than the Soviet Union. Prominent leaders included Dr. **Abdul Hadi Mahmudi**, brother of Rahim, Professor Akram Yari, and Muhammad Osman. After the **Saur Revolt** the party opposed the *Khalqi* regime and set up a *mujahedin* group; it was soon decimated, and most of its members fled abroad or were killed.

SHURA. Council, a consultative body or parliament. Islamic political theory demands that rulers seek council, *Shura*. Islamic modernists base their demands for a representative government on this principle. After the downfall of the Marxist government in Kabul, local *mujahedin* groups, remnants of the Afghan army, and even some Marxist groups united in *Shuras* to maintain local control in various area of Afghanistan.

SHURA-I INQILAB-I ITTIFAQ. *See* **BEHESHTI.**

SIKH, SIKHISM. A religio-political community that rose in the **Panjab**, India in the 15th century, founding a state that reached its height under **Ranjit Singh** in the late 18th century. Sikhism began as a syncretist religion, combining Islamic and Hindu beliefs under Nanak, the first guru (sage). Subsequently, belief in ten gurus and the *Granth Sahib*, their sacred book, constituted the creed of the Sikhs. In constant conflict with Indian and Afghan rulers, the Sikhs became increasingly militant and under Ranjit Singh captured Multan in 1818, Kashmir in 1819, and Peshawar in 1834.

The Sikh nation supported the British invasion of Afghanistan in the **First Anglo-Afghan War**, but after the death of Ranjit Singh, the British ended Sikh rule when it annexed the Panjab in the "Sikh Wars" of 1845–46 and 1848–49. In the 1970s, there were about 10,000 Sikhs resident in Afghanistan.

SIMLA MANIFESTO. A document issued by the governor-general of India on October 1, 1838, which declared war on the Afghan Amir **Dost Muhammad**. It accused him of "a sudden and unprovoked attack" on its ally, **Ranjit Singh**, and announced Britain's intention of restoring to the Afghan throne **Shah Shuja** "whose popularity throughout Afghanistan had been proven to his Lordship [the governor-general] by the strong and unanimous testimony of the best authorities" (Sykes, 339). The result was the **First Anglo-Afghan War** (1839–42) and the British disaster in Afghanistan. *See* ANGLO-AFGHAN WARS and AFGHAN FOREIGN RELATIONS.

SINGH. *See* **RANJIT SINGH.**

SIRAJ. *See* **SERAJ.**

SIRR-I-MILLI. Name of a secret organization which in 1909 plotted a coup against Amir **Habibullah** and aimed at the establishment of a republican form of government (*mashruta*). Its reputed head was Maulawi Muhammad Sarwar Wasif, a native of Kandahar. Dr. **Abdul Ghani**, an Indian Muslim who was head of **Habibia School**, and some of his students were accused of membership in the *Sirr-i milli* (Secret of the Nation). The organization wrote increasingly threatening letters to Amir Habibullah, telling him to "mend his ways, or face the consequences." Abdul Ghani was arrested and jailed until 1919, when King **Amanullah** ascended the throne. *See also* ABDUL GHANI.

SOCIETY OF ULAMA. *See* **JAMI'AT-I 'ULAMA.**

SOVIET-AFGHAN RELATIONS. Formal diplomatic relations between Russia and Afghanistan began in June 1919, when the Soviet Union and Afghanistan announced their intention to establish legations in Kabul and Moscow. A cease-fire had just been declared in the **Third Anglo-Afghan War** and King **Amanullah** wanted to demonstrate Afghanistan's independence by establishing diplomatic relations with European powers. A mission, headed by **Muhammad Wali**, proceeded to Tashkent and Moscow, where it was given a rousing welcome. N. N. Nariman, a spokesman of the foreign ministry, announced that "Russian imperialism, striving to enslave and degrade small nationalities, has gone, never to return." Muhammad Wali expressed the hope that "with the assistance of Soviet Russia, we shall succeed in emancipating our Afghanistan and the rest of the East." He presented V. I. Lenin a letter from King Amanullah, which was received "with great pleasure." A Bolshevik diplomat, Michael K. Bravin (who subsequently defected and was killed by an Afghan), proceeded to Kabul to arrange for the arrival of a permanent representative, Z. Suritz, in January 1920. Suritz immediately set about negotiating the preliminaries for the Treaty of 1921, which recognized the "mutual independence" of both states and bound them not to "enter into any military or political agreement with a third State, which might prejudice one of the Contracting Parties." *See* ANGLO-AFGHAN TREATY OF 1921.

The Soviet Union agreed to permit free and untaxed transit of Afghan goods and recognized the independence and freedom of Khiva and Bokhara "in accordance with the wishes of the people." It provided for Soviet technical and financial aid of one million rubles in gold or silver and promised a return of the "frontier districts which belonged to the latter [Afghanistan] in the last century," a reference to the area of **Panjdeh**. Britain had held a monopoly in the supply of arms and war materiel, which could only be shipped to Afghanistan by way of India; the treaty now opened a new avenue for materiel purchased in Europe. King Amanullah was able to crush the **Khost Rebellion** in summer 1924, with the assistance of several aircraft from the Soviet Union and a number of foreign pilots, including several Russians. In spite of the friendly rhetoric, differences existed between the two countries: King Amanullah wanted Khiva and Bukhara to be free from Soviet control, possibly associated with Afghanistan in a Central Asian confederation, but the "Young Khivan and Bukharan" revolted and opted for membership in the Soviet Union. The Soviet Union saw this as an expression of the "wishes of the people" and retained the Tsarist possession of Central Asia. A more serious crisis in Soviet-Afghan relations occurred in December 1925 when Soviet troops occupied the island of Darqad (also called Urta Tagai and Yangi Qal'a) on the **Amu Daria**. At the turn of the century the course of the Amu Daria had changed from south of the island to the north and, since the main stream was designated as the Afghan boundary, Kabul considered the island Afghan territory. After the Bolshevik Revolution, refugees from the Soviet Union settled on the island, including some **Basmachi** counter-revolutionaries, who made it a base for raids into Soviet Central Asia. The matter threatened to develop into an international conflict, but the Soviets apparently wanted good relations with King Amanullah and evacuated their troops on February 28, 1926. Moscow paid the promised subsidy only irregularly, and by the mid-1920s the Kabul government had expanded its diplomatic base to the extent that it did not need to maintain a special relationship with the Soviet Union.

During the 1929 civil war the Soviet Union had maintained its embassy in Kabul and immediately recognized the government of **Nadir Shah**. The new king sent **Muhammad Aziz**, his half brother, as ambassador to Moscow, to indicate the importance of the post, but he was determined to end Soviet influence in Afghanistan. He renegotiated and signed on (June 24, 1931) the treaty of 1921, with the inclusion of an article calling for the prohibition in both territories of activities that "might cause political or military injury" to the other. Nadir Shah was thinking of the followers of ex-King Amanullah who might attempt a return to power, and the Soviets were concerned about the **Basmachi** threat. A commercial treaty had to wait until 1936, and the Afghan government did not renew a Soviet airline concession and eventually dismissed all Soviet airline pilots and mechanics. The Afghan government turned increasingly to Germany for its technological and developmental needs, and a special relationship developed which greatly disturbed Moscow and was accepted in London only as the lesser of two evils. The outbreak of World War II and the temporary alliance between Germany and the Soviet Union resulted in fears in London and Kabul that the Soviets might support a pro-Amanullah coup. And, indeed, these worries were not unwarranted. The German foreign ministry considered **Zahir Shah** pro-British and toyed with the idea of supporting a coup against the monarch. Count Schulenberg, the German ambassador in Moscow, queried Vyacheslav Molotov whether the Soviet Union would permit the transit of Afghan forces into northern Afghanistan. But Molotov was noncommittal, and the matter was dropped.

On June 22, 1941, Germany attacked the Soviet Union, and Moscow joined the Western alliance. The alliance of Britain and the Soviet Union caused considerable anxiety in Kabul because Afghan foreign policy had been based on the premise that its territorial security depended on the continued rivalry between its imperialist neighbors. Concerted Allied action was soon to follow: in October 1941, the Allies presented separate notes to the Afghan government demanding the expulsion of all Axis nationals. Kabul was forced to comply, and the Afghan king convened a **Loya Jirga**, Great Council, which gave retroactively its approval after the Axis nationals had left. The Afghan government insisted that they be given safe passage to a neutral country. From that time the Afghan government kept its northern border closed to non-diplomatic travelers, but trade continued between the two countries.

When India became independent in 1947 and the State of Pakistan was created, Afghanistan repudiated the treaties that accepted the **Durand** Line as international boundary and demanded that the Afghans of the **NWFP** be given the choice of independence. Afghanistan was the only country voting against the admission of Pakistan to the United Nations. The cold war had begun, and the Eisenhower administration sought to contain Moscow's expansionism by sponsoring alliances with states bordering on the Soviet Union. Washington supported creation of the Baghdad Pact (later renamed CENTO), which united Britain, Turkey, Iraq, Iran, and Pakistan in a defensive alliance. This alliance guaranteed international borders but ignored irredentist and nationalist aspirations in the Middle East. As a result, relations between Afghanistan and Pakistan, a Western ally, turned increasingly hostile.

The Afghan government "normalized" its relations with the Soviet Union and in 1946 agreed to accept the *thalweg* (middle) of the Amu Daria as the international boundary. A telegraph link was established with Tashkent in 1947, and in 1950 Afghanistan signed a four-year trade agreement with the USSR. The Soviet government praised Afghanistan's "positive" neutrality and, when in December 1955 Nikita Krushchev and Nikolai Bulganin came to Kabul, the stage was set for a major rapprochement. The two countries renewed the Treaty of 1931 for ten years, the Soviet Union granting Afghanistan a $100 million loan at two percent interest for projects selected by a joint USSR-Afghan committee. The Afghan national airline started flights from Kabul to Tashkent in 1965, which were subsequently extended to Moscow and other European countries.

The Afghan government wanted to purchase arms from the United States, and when it was unable to obtain what it wanted, Prime Minister **Muhammad Daud** turned to the Soviet Union for help. In 1956 the first shipments of East Bloc weapons arrived and the Afghan armed forces began to be Soviet-equipped. Thousands of Soviet advisers came to Afghanistan, and thousands of Afghan technicians and military officers went to the Soviet Union for training. The result was a growing cadre of military officers, students, and technocrats with leftist, if not pro-Russian, sympathies. When Muhammad Daud staged a coup with leftist support on July 17, 1973, the stage was set for the **Saur Revolt** that brought a Marxist government to power. The new Kabul government accepted Soviet advisers in virtually all its civilian and government branches and concluded a series of treaties that made the Soviet Union the dominant influence in Afghanistan. On December 5, 1978, the **Taraki** regime concluded a treaty of friendship, similar to one the Soviet Union concluded with Vietnam, that also provided for military assistance and that became the basis for military intervention a year later. Resistance was growing against the Marxist regime, resulting in a civil war that turned into a war of liberation when Soviet troops tried to prop up a faltering regime. The war turned out to be costly to Afghanistan: *mujahedin* sources claim that as many as one million Afghans perished, whereas the Kabul government claimed that 243,900 soldiers and civilians were killed. After Soviet troops evacuated Afghanistan in February 1989, Moscow announced it had suffered about

13,000 deaths and another 35,000 wounded. *See also* AFGHAN
FOREIGN RELATIONS.

SOVIET INTERVENTION/INVASION. The question as to the motive
for Soviet intervention in Afghanistan was a matter of conjecture. Some
saw it, as well as the Marxist coup in Afghanistan, as part of a master
plan with the objective of gaining access to the resources and the warm
water ports of the Persian/Arabian Gulf. But recent revelations of
politburo notes indicate that it was to be a temporary effort to rescue a
faltering Kabul regime from defeat by rebel forces. Recent disclosures
of minutes of politburo meetings in March 1979 indicate that requests
by **Nur Muhammad Taraki** for direct military assistance were at first
not granted. Yuri V. Andropov, chairman of the KGB, is quoted as
having said, "We can suppress a revolution in Afghanistan only with the
aid of our bayonets, but that is for us entirely inadmissible.... Thus our
army if it enters Afghanistan will be an aggressor." Prime Minister
Alexei N. Kosygin added "we cannot introduce troops.... There would
be huge minuses for us...and no pluses for us at all." In a meeting with
Taraki in which the Defense Minister Dimitri F. Ustinov also
participated, the Soviets pointed out that Vietnam never demanded
assistance of foreign troops. Taraki was told that he could expect
considerable assistance, "You have working for you 500 generals and
officers. If necessary we can send an additional number of party
workers, as well as 150–200 officers," but, he was told, the
introduction of Soviet forces would alarm the international community
and would involve the Soviets in a conflict with the Afghan people and
"a people does not forgive such things." By the end of 1979, these
prescient words were forgotten or the situation had deteriorated to such
a degree that the Kremlin agreed on intervention. Its legality was based
on the Soviet-Afghan treaty of friendship and cooperation of December
5, 1978, which stated in Article 4 that

> The high contracting parties...shall consult each other and take by
> agreement appropriate measures to ensure the security, inde-
> pendence, and territorial integrity of the two countries.

The "temporary occupation" was legalized under a Status of Armed
Forces Agreement signed in April 1980. The Kabul government
claimed that the rebels were supported by foreign powers and that the
Limited Contingent of Soviet Forces in Afghanistan (LCSFA)
would withdraw at the end of foreign interference.

The reconnaissance for the intervention was said to have been carried out by General Ivan Pavlovski, a Soviet deputy defense minister, who spent three months in Afghanistan prior to the invasion. The overall command was under Marshall Sergei Sokolov. By the time the Soviet 40th Army entered Afghanistan on December 27, 1979, two airborne assault brigades had already secured the **Bagram** air base, about 40 miles north of Kabul, and in 180 sorties of Antonov-12 and Antonov-22 transport aircraft, escorted by 100 combat aircraft, troops and munitions were brought in. The **Salang** Pass/Tunnel, and the Kabul airport were secured by paratrooper and *spetsnaz* units. Two motorized rifle divisions crossed the Amu Daria on pontoon bridges, and in a pincer movement the 357th proceeded from Kushka south to Herat and Shindand; and the 360th "Nevel-Polovsk" moved from Termez to Salang and to Kabul and Kandahar (Isby, 1989, 23. Urban [42] gives the route to Kandahar via Herat). The Soviet forces were equipped for conventional war, including an SA-4 anti-aircraft missile brigade and chemical warfare decontamination units. Within a week some 50,000 Soviet troops with some 350 tanks and 450 other armored vehicles had crossed the **Amu Daria**. (O'Ballance, 89) The objective was to secure the key cities and links of communication. The Soviet armed forces were intended for the protection of major towns and lines of communication, leaving counter-insurgency tasks to the Afghan army, but they were inevitable drawn into search-and-destroy missions that cost 80 % of its casualties. *See also* LIMITED CONTINGENT OF SOVIET FORCES IN AFGHANISTAN and AFGANTSY.

SPETSNAZ. Special Operations Forces (*Spetsnaz*) are an elite counter-insurgency force that, together with airborne, air assault/air mobile, and designated reconnaissance units, made up 10 to 20 % of the Soviet forces deployed in Afghanistan. The elite force was created in the years 1941–42 during World War II and in the 1960s expanded to battalion size. In December 1978, *spetsnaz* forces were said to have been employed in securing air fields, communications centers, and other key points in Afghanistan prior to the invasion. They constituted the commando unit that was responsible for the assassination of **Hafizullah Amin**. *Spetsnaz* operated as raiders, sabotage teams, and reconnaissance and intelligence commandos. According to McMichael (108), they operated disguised as shepherds, nomads, and itinerant traders. It is not clear how effective they could have been, since they were primarily of Slavic background, blond haired and blue eyed and not familiar with any Afghan languages. Altogether about nine battalions with 250 men each are said to have been active in Afghanistan. They were stationed at Asadabad, Baraki-Barak, Ghazni, Shahjoy (about midway between Ghazni and Kandahar), Lashkargah, Farah, Kandahar, and Jalalabad. Brigade headquarters were at Lashkargah and Jalalabad.

STINGER. An American infrared, heat-seeking missile, with high explosive warhead, capable of engaging low altitude aircraft, including high-speed jets, that has been credited in dipping the tactical balance in favor of the *mujahedin*. Long sought by the resistance, the first missiles were fired in September 1986 and became an immediate success. According to **General Yousaf**, head of the **ISI**, the American government trained Pakistanis who then trained Afghans. The first missiles were delivered to commanders of **Hekmatyar** and **Yunus Khales**, and possession of a stinger soon became the ultimate status symbol. The American government agreed to deliver 250 grip stocks with 1,000 to 2,000 missiles per year (Yousaf and Adkin, 182). The missiles had been deployed by American forces first in 1981, but had never been used in combat. According to Yousaf, the *mujahedin* achieved a hit-rate of 70 to 75 % (68 % according to Isby, 1989), much better than the rate of their Pakistani or American teachers. To reward success, *mujahedin* commanders were given two stingers for each hit (Rubin, 1995, 196) As was to be expected, a *spetsnaz* commando was able to capture a number of missiles in an ambush, and one commander, Mulla Malang, boasted of having sold, four launchers for one million dollars each with 16 missiles to Iran (Rubin, 1995, 336, n 45). Overby (115) claims that of 1,150 *stingers* originally sent only 863 reached the *mujahedin*. China obtained several stingers and was said to be copying them (*Les Nouvelles*, No. 63). In 1987 the Soviet/Kabul forces had 150 to 200 air losses, and the much-feared Hind D helicopter never recovered its tactical preeminence. Isby (114) quotes the Commander **Ahmad Shah Mas'ud**, saying "There are only two things Afghans must have: the Koran and Stingers." *See also* ROKETI, MULLA ABDUL SALAM.

STOLIETOFF, MAJ. GEN. Head of an uninvited Russian mission sent to the court of Amir **Shir Ali** by **General Kaufman** in 1878 to conclude an alliance against Britain. Stolietoff reached Kabul on July 22 at a time when General Kaufman was dispatching a force of 15,000 men to the upper reaches of the **Amu Daria**. Not being able to prevent the mission from reaching Kabul, the amir treated the Russian and his staff of six officers with courtesy. Stolietoff presented several "letters of friendship" in one of which Kaufman wrote

> I have deputed my agent, Major-General Stolietoff, an officer high in the favour of the Emperor. He will inform you of all that is hidden in my mind. I hope that you will pay great attention to what he says, and believe him as you would myself.... The advantage of a close alliance with the Russian Government will be permanently evident. (Sykes, vol. 2, 97)

The draft of a treaty promised what Britain was not willing to offer: protection from foreign aggression and recognition of Shir Ali's son Abdullah Jan as heir-apparent. Article 3 of the treaty stated that

> The Russian Government engages that if any foreign enemy attacks Afghanistan and the Amir is unable to drive him out, and asks for the assistance of the Russian Government, the Russian Government will repel the enemy either by means of advice or by such other means as it may consider proper. (Sykes, vol. 2, 107)

The fact that the type of Russian support was left to the discretion of the Russian government apparently did not occur to the amir. His refusal to permit a British mission under General **Sir Neville Chamberlain** to proceed to Kabul was taken as Lord Lytton's excuse to start the **Second Anglo-Afghan War**.

SUFISM. Islamic mysticism (A., *tasawwuf*), emerged in the eighth century A.D. and rapidly spread over most of the Islamic world. The generally accepted etymology derives the word Sufism from *suf*, wool, the robes of coarse wool worn by Muslim mystics. Sufism was long in conflict with Islamic orthodoxy, because it sought the personal experience (*ma'rifa*) of union with God, rather than rational knowledge (*'ilm*), the scholasticism of Sunni Islam. Al-Ghazzali (d. 1111), the great canonist and theologian, was largely instrumental in reconciling Sufism with orthodox Islam.

Sufi orders originated among the urban artisan classes and organized into brotherhoods (tariqa—way, path), following a particular spiritual leader or saint (*pir, shaikh*, or *murshid*). Sufi lodges (*khanaqah*) were founded at the residence or tomb of a venerated *pir* and supported with contributions of the disciples (*murid*). Members meet regularly in homes or public places to perform *zikr* (A., remembrance), ecstatic recitations of the names of Allah, or passages of the *Qor'an*, accompanied by rhythmical breathing and physical movement.

Sufism has experienced a revival in Turkey after orders were closed in the early 1920s in conformance with the Kemalist policy of secularization. The Hanbali school of Islamic jurisprudence prevalent in Saudi Arabia also does not accept Sufism as an orthodox practice.

Famous mystical poets which Afghanistan shares with the Islamic world are **Sana'i** of Ghazni, who wrote the first mystical epic in Persian in the early 12th century A.D.; **Jalaluddin Rumi [Balkhi]**, famous for the *maulawia*, whirling dervishes, who was born in 1207 in Balkh (therefore called Balkhi by Afghans); and **Jami** born in Jam, Khorasan who died in Herat in 1492. The most important contemporary Sufi orders in Afghanistan are the *Qadiri* and *Naqshbandi*. The Qadiri order is headed by **Pir Sayyid Ahmad Gailani** whose ancestor, Abd al-Qadir al-Jilani (d.1166), "the sultan of saints," founded the order. Gailani's devotees are primarily among the Pashtuns in southern and eastern Afghanistan. The Naqshbandi order originated in Bukhara in the 14th century and is found in parts of northern and southern Afghanistan. The **Mujaddidi** family is associated with devotees of the Naqshbandi order in southern Afghanistan. Of about 200 orders, 70 are still active in the Islamic world. *See also* QADIRI; NAQSHBANDI; GAILANI; AND MUJADDIDI.

SULAIMAN KHEL. A division of the Ghilzai tribe. *See* GHILZAI and POWINDAH.

SULAIMAN RANGE. The name given by Western geographers to the southern portion of the great watershed between the Helmand and the Indus Rivers. The range probably got its name from the Sulaiman Khel Ghilzais (*See* GHILZAI) through whose territory it passes. Starting from the Shutur Gardan Pass (11,200 feet) in Paktia Province, it runs in a south-southeasterly direction under the names of Mangal and Jadran hills where its peaks reach altitudes between 11,000 and 12,000 feet. The British-Indian general staff considered the route over the Shutur Gardan the best avenue for an attack on Kabul. There are two ranges with this name—one that extends along the Afghan border and the other, the eastern range, that runs along the Baluchistan-Panjab border in a generally north-south direction.

SUNNA. The tradition (A., trodden path), the deeds and sayings of the Prophet Muhammad that have become part of Islamic law. *See* ISLAMIC LAW.

SUNNI. Major branch of two Islamic sects, comprising about 80 % of Muslims, also called the orthodox branch in distinction to the *Shi'a* branch. *See* ISLAM and ISLAMIC LAW.

SUPREME COORDINATION COUNCIL OF THE ISLAMIC REVOLUTION IN AFGHANISTAN (SCCIRA). An alliance of four groups fighting the **Rabbani** government, comprising **Hekmatyar's Hizb-i Islami, Karim Khalili's Wahdat**, General **Dostum's Junbesh**, and **Mujaddidi's Jabha**. Mujaddidi was its leader, but he resigned and the organization broke up when Hekmatyar negotiated a separate deal with Rabbani that established him as prime minister in Kabul summer 1996.

T

TAIMANI. One of the Chahar Aimaq tribes (*see* AIMAQ) that numbers about 180,000 Farsi-speaking Sunni Muslims. They are the most numerous of the Chahar **Aimaq** and occupy the hilly country southeast of Herat between the district of Sabzawar (also called Shindand) in Farah Province on the west and the Hazarajat on the east. Their country is virtually barren of trees and bushes except for the upper course of the Farah Rud. The Taimanis are of Turco-Mongol origin.

TAIMURI (TIMURI). Also called Aimaq-i Digar (the other Aimaq) as distinguished from the Chahar **Aimaq**. They are **Sunnis**, number about 30,000, and inhabit the area of northwestern Herat, Farah, and southern Fariab Provinces. They claim Arab descent and derive their name from Sayyid Timur, Kurkhan, of Tirmiz in Bukhara. The Taimuris participated on various sides in the civil wars of the **Sadozai** princes, as a result of which a part of the tribe was compelled to move to Khorasan, Persia. In 1893 there were about 12,000 Taimuris each in the **Khorasan** Province of Iran and western Afghanistan.

TAJIK. A name, generally applied to Farsi/**Dari** speakers whose number has been estimated at about four to five million people. The term comes from the Persian *tazi* (running) or *taj*, (crown?) meaning "Arab," but the Turks applied it to non-Turks and eventually only to Farsi- speakers. They are largely **Sunni** Muslims, except for the "mountain Tajiks" who are **Isma'ilis** (*see* Shi'a) and inhabit various areas of Badakhshan Province.

The Tajik are the ancient population of **Khorasan** and Sistan who were sedentary and made a living as traders. They were also located in northern Afghanistan and predominated in Balkh and Bukhara, until they moved south as a result of Timurid invasions. Now they are scattered all over the country, but are concentrated in communities in western, northern, and northeastern Afghanistan. They are mainly agricultural, except in the towns where many are artisans or engage in commercial activities. They have been engaged as clerks and predominate in the government administration. As a community, the Tajik are relatively better educated and more modernized. Conscious of a great cultural tradition, the elite of the Tajiks have been the "men of the pen," whereas the **Pashtuns** have been the "men of the sword" of Afghanistan.

TAKHAR (36-30' N, 69-30' E). A province in northeastern Afghanistan with an area of 6,770 square miles and a population estimated at 528,000. The province borders on Tajikistan in the north, Badakhshan Province in the east, Parwan/Kapisa in the south, and Baghlan and Kunduz in the west. Since 1963 the administrative center of the province has been Taloqan, a town of about 20,000 inhabitants. Major agricultural products of the province include cotton, corn, and wheat; local industries include gold and silver mining and carpet production. Takhar provides two-thirds of the salt used in Afghanistan.

TALIBAN. A movement of "*Taliban*," students, who attended religious schools in Pakistan and suddenly emerged as a politico-military force in Afghanistan. Headed by **Maulawi Muhammad Omar**, a Nurzai from Oruzgan, and his deputy Maulawi Muhammad Hasan, the movement first came to public attention in November 1994 when it rescued a Pakistani truck convoy bound for Central Asia from *mujahedin* captors. The *Taliban* then captured the city of Kandahar and moved north against Kabul. On Monday, February 13, 1995, they captured Pul-i Alam and the next day Charasiab, the stronghold of *Hizb-i Islami* leader **Hekmatyar**. Hekmatyar was forced to flee to Sarobi, about 37 miles east of Kabul. In March 1995, the **Shi'a** *Hizb-i Wahdat* surrendered its enclave in Kabul to the *Taliban*, and **Abdul Ali Mazari**

was killed while in *Taliban* captivity. On September 3, the *Taliban* captured **Shindand,** an important airbase, and two days later the city of Herat. In September 1996 the *Taliban* renewed their offensive and captured Jalalabad, Sarobi, and by the end of the month they were installed as rulers in Kabul.

It is still unclear who supported the "students" and and their teachers and how they were able to quickly defeat the supposedly battle-hardened *mujahedin*. Most observers believe that financial support from sympathizers provided funds and the Pakistani **ISI** financed, armed, and otherwise supported the *Taliban*. Often they conquered without a fight as ex-army officers and *mujahedin* commanders defected. The *Taliban* claim not to be affiliated with any of the *mujahedin* groups and only desire to unite Afghanistan, end the power of the war lords, and create a "true" Islamic state. One can no longer speak of a "student" movement, because the ranks of the *Taliban* have been augmented by other **Pashtun mujahedin** groups, pitting them against the largely non-Pashtun forces of **Dostum, Rabbani**, and **Khalili**.

TALIBAN ORGANIZATION. According to an announcement on November 6, 1996, the following government was set up:

Maulawi Muhammad Omar	Amir
Mulla Muhammad Rabbani	Head, Kabul Governing Council
Mulla Muhammad Hasan	Deputy Head (was gov. Of Kandahar)
Mulla Muhammad Ghaus	Foreign Minister
Sher Muhammad Stanakzai	Deputy
Mullah Abdul Razzaq	Defense (captured by Masud)
Amir Khan Mutaqi	Information and Culture
Sayyid Ghiasuddin	Education
Shinwari	Depty. Religious Education
Maulawi Hafizullah	Planning
Qari Din Muhammad	Planning (Nov. 6,96)
Maulawi Isatullah	Deputy
Mulla Abdul Sattar	Refugee Repatriation
Maulawi Abdul Raqib	Refugee Repatriation
Maulawi Abdul Bakh	Martyrs and Disabled
Maulawi Muhammad Rustam	Urban Reconstruction
Maulawi Abdul Salam	Labor and Social Affairs
Mulla Mashar	Commerce

Abdul Sattar Paktis	Depty. Health
Mulla Hamdullah	Depty. Civil Aviation & Tourism
Maulawi Ihsanullah	Head, Administration
Maulawi Pasani	Chief Justice
Mulla Muhammad Fazal	Security

Governors

Maulawi Karamatullah	Paktia
Maulawi Shamsuddin	Paktika
Maulawi Abdul Salam	Oruzgan
Abdul Qayyum	Oruzgan
Maulawi Muhd. Hasan	Kandahar
Maulawi Abdul Muhammad	Helmand
Maulawi Yar Muhammad	Herat
Maulawi Shafiq	Herat, Director of Info & Culture
Maulawi Abdil Ghani	Zabul
Mulla Turabi	Wardak
Abdul Kabir	Nangarhar
Maulawi Muhammad Zahir	Commander, 4th Armored Div.
Maulawi Bor Jan	Commander, Kabul Front

TAMERLANE. *See* **TIMUR-I LANG.**

TANAI. Or **TANI.** A section of the Khostwal Pashtun tribe. They inhabit the southwest corner of the Khost valley.

TANAI COUP. *See* **TANAI, LT. GEN. SHAHNAWAZ.**

TANAI, LT. GEN. SHAHNAWAZ. Member of the *Khalq* faction of the **PDPA**, chief of general staff since 1986, and minister of defense from 1988 to 1990. A Pashtun born in Paktia Province of the small Tani tribe. A captain-major until the **Saur Revolt**, Tanai was considered a rising star in the PDPA, when on March 6, 1990, he and several *Khalqi* officers staged a coup against the **Najibullah** government from the **Bagram** air force base. They attacked the presidential palace and key government facilities in Kabul but were unable to topple the government. Tanai and some of his closest supporters escaped from Bagram air base in three military aircraft and a helicopter and landed in Parachinar, Pakistan. **Gulbuddin Hekmatyar**, leader of the most radical of mujahedin groups, gave the coup his support. This alliance of hard-line *Khalqis* and radical Islamists caused considerable consternation in Afghanistan. Tanai and Hekmatyar were seen as determined to win power, regardless of ideological considerations. Najibullah's control of the air force and scrambling of the communications network enabled him to rout the rebels. On March 16, Tanai made his appearance in the Hekmatyar camp in Logar Province, claiming to continue the campaign against Najibullah but remaining a loyal member of the PDPA. After the fall of Najibullah in April 1992, many *Khalqi* officers also joined Hekmatyar's forces. Tanai is said to have joined the *Taliban* in November 1995.

TANG-I GHARU (34-34'N, 69-30'E). A spectacular gorge through which pass the Kabul River and the road linking Kabul to Jalalabad. The gorge begins five miles below Pul-i Charkhi, about seven miles east of Kabul, and extends for about ten miles to the vicinity of the village of Gogamanda. It is an alternate route to the difficult Lataband Pass (alt. 7,950 feet) and replaced it in 1963 when the new paved highway to Tor Kham at the Afghan border was completed. At the top of the gorge one can see five or six levels of highway winding within a short distance of three miles. The gorge narrows in places to 20 yards with cliffs on both sides rising almost perpendicularly.

TARAKI. A section of the Burhan branch of the **Ghilzai** tribe, estimated in the early 19th century at about 12,000 families. They inhabit Mukur and the country to the south.

TARAKI, NUR MUHAMMAD. Member of the *Khalq* faction of the **PDPA** and, after the **Saur Revolt**, president of the Revolutionary Council and prime minister of the Democratic Republic of Afghanistan. Taraki was born of a **Ghilzai** nomad family on July 15, 1917 in Ghazni Province. After attending a village school in Nawa, Ghazni Province, he took night courses in Bombay and college credit in Kabul. He worked as a clerk for **Abdul Majid Zabuli** at the Pashtun Trading Company in Kandahar and at its office in Bombay. Because of his knowledge of English he was able to obtain employment in various Afghan ministries and at Bakhtar News Agency. In the 1950s he became known as an author and journalist, and in 1953 he served for a few months as press attache at the Afghan embassy in Washington. Subsequently he opened the "Nur Translation Bureau" in Kabul, which translated **Dari** and

Pashtu materials for various foreign missions in Kabul, including the American embassy.

His ideological transformation from social critic to Communist occurred in the early 1960s. Taraki convened the "founding congress" of the PDPA on January 1, 1965, which was attended by 27 persons. The members elected him secretary general in a split decision, some voting for his subsequent rival **Babrak Karmal**, who was elected secretary of the central committee. In April 1966, Taraki started publication of *Khalq*, the party organ, which became also the name of his faction of the PDPA. In 1967 the party split into two factions over tactical and leadership disputes, until ten years later they reunited and attained power in a coup in April 1978 (*see* PEOPLES DEMO-CRATIC PARTY OF AFGHANISTAN). After the Saur Revolt, Taraki became the "Great Leader," and a personality cult prepared the way to legitimize his rule as the "teacher and great guide" of the Communist movement. Leading *Parchamis* were purged from government positions and Taraki's *Khalqis* ruled until a new split developed among the *Khalqis*. **Hafizullah Amin** attacked his former teacher as unfit for leadership. The "red *khalqis*" of Taraki and "black *khalqis*" of Amin were pitted against each other and Hafizullah prevailed. On October 9, 1979, Taraki was secretly executed.

TARNAK (31-26' N, 65-31' E). A river that rises near Muqur in Ghazni Province and, flowing in a southwesterly direction, runs into the Dori River about 25 miles southwest of Kandahar.

TARZI, GHULAM MUHAMMAD (1830-1900). A calligrapher and poet who took the penname *Tarzi* (the stylist) and was the author of a large body of religious, mystic, and secular poetry. He was the son of Rahmdil Khan, a **Muhammadzai** from Kandahar. He received a yearly stipend from Amir **Dost Muhammad**, but Amir **Abdul Rahman** forced Tarzi and his family into Indian exile in December 1881. Tarzi traveled in 1885 to Baghdad and Istanbul and from there to Damascus, where he lived as a pensioner of the sultan/caliph, Abdul Hamid. Ghulam Muhammad had five daughters and six sons, one of whom, **Mahmud Tarzi**, returned to Afghanistan after the death of his father and held high offices at the courts of Abdul Rahman's successors.

TARZI, MAHMUD. Prominent Afghan nationalist, "Father of Afghan Journalism," and high government official during the reigns of Amir

Habibullah and King **Amanullah**. Born in Ghazni on August 23, 1865, the son of **Ghulam Muhammad Tarzi**, he accompanied his father into exile and was educated in India and in Damascus under the supervision of his father. He returned to Kabul after the death of Amir **Abdul Rahman** and became editor of the *Seraj al-Akhbar*. During the reign of King **Amanullah**, Tarzi served as foreign minister (1919–22) and headed the Afghan delegation at the peace conferences at **Mussoorie** (1920) and Kabul (1921). He was the first Afghan minister at Paris 1922–24, and again foreign minister 1924–27, and left Afghanistan with King Amanullah in January 1929. He was a great reformer but did not agree with some of King Amanullah's innovations. One of his daughters was married to King Amanullah and another to Sardar **Enayatullah**. He died in Istanbul in 1933.

TASAWWUF. *See* **SUFISM.**

TASHQURGHAN. Now **KHULM** (36-42'N, 67-41'E). A town, now called Khulm, with 28,000 inhabitants, which once was the principal market between Central Asia and Kabul. The town was founded on the site of an ancient town (destroyed as a result of Turco-Mongol invasions) in the early 19th century by Amir Kalich Ali Beg, Khan of Khulm, who built a citadel there and called it *Tashqurghan* (T., stone, or brick, fort). Ali Beg was able to expand his domains, creating the largest khanate in Afghan Turkistan. In 1850 Amir **Dost Muhammad** defeated the khan and brought Tashqurghan under the control of Kabul.

TATAR. An ethnic group of **Sunnis** claiming to be of Mongol descent. They number about 60,000 and inhabit the northern part of Bamian and parts of Samangan Province. Larger numbers of Tatars also live in Bukhara and Khiva in Uzbekistan. In the mid-nineteenth century their chief was Shah Pasand Khan. His son Dilawar Khan supported Amir **Shir Ali** (r. 1863–66 and 1868–79) in the wars of the princes, but in the early 1880s Amir **Abdul Rahman** took the khanate under Kabul control.

TAWANA, SAYYID MUSA. A founder of the **Islamist** movement in Afghanistan. Born in Takhar Province, he was educated at the Dar al-Ulum-i Shari'a (now Abu Hanifa) madrasa, **Kabul University**, and Cairo's Al-Azhar University. In the late 1950s he belonged to a small circle at Kabul University who perceived a "danger of apostasy among university students." The group designed a three-point program of action: 1) refute the claims of secularists on questions of Islam, 2) write and translate articles to propagate the teachings of Islamist scholars, and 3) study Communism and European history with a view of understanding the enemy. In 1961 he graduated from Kabul University and became lecturer at the faculty of theology of Kabul University until 1964, when he proceeded to Cairo to study at Al-Azhar University. After graduating with a Ph.D. degree in 1971 he returned to Kabul and in 1972 was appointed a professor at the faculty of shari'a of Kabul University. At that time the "professors" founded the *jami'at-i Islami* with **Rabbani** as head and **Sayyaf** his deputy. **Habiburrahman** was secretary, and in charge of military affairs. **Gulbuddin Hekmatyar** was in a Kabul jail at the time. As a result of the Daud coup on July 17, 1973, the Islamist movement had to go underground. *See* ISLAMIST MOVEMENT.

TAZI. *See* **AFGHAN HOUND.**

THIRD ANGLO-AFGHAN WAR (1919). A short war between Afghanistan and British-Indian forces which lasted from May 4 until conclusion of a cease-fire on June 3, 1919. Amir **Amanullah** had ascended the throne in February 1919, after the assassination of his father, Amir **Habibullah**. He was an ardent nationalist and reformer and was said to have been a member of the "war party" at the Afghan court, which favored an attack on India during World War I. Afghanistan had remained neutral in the "holy war" against Britain, and Amir Habibullah expected a generous financial reward and British recognition of Afghanistan's complete independence. But once the European conflict was ended, Britain showed no intention of freeing the country from its control.

Upon accession to power, Amir Amanullah demanded a treaty that would end Afghanistan's political dependence on Britain and establish normal, neighborly relations between the two states. Lord Chelmsford, the viceroy of India, however, suggested that no new treaty was required, despite the fact that previously India had held that the agreements with Afghan rulers were personal and therefore subject to renegotiation with each new ruler. He merely acknowledged Amanullah's election as amir "by the populace of Kabul and its surrounding," implying that Amanullah was not in complete control of his country. The subsidy paid to previous Afghan rulers was halted, and when Amanullah sent his new envoy to India he was asked "what amir" he represented.

On the occasion of a royal darbar on April 13, 1919, Amanullah showed himself belligerent, announcing to an assembly of dignitaries

> ... I have declared myself and my country entirely free, autonomous and independent both internally and externally. My country will hereafter be as independent a state as the other states and powers of the world are. No foreign power will be allowed to have a hair's breath of right to interfere internally and externally with the affairs of Afghanistan, and if any ever does I am ready to cut its throat with this sword.

He turned to the British agent and said, "Oh Safir, have you understood what I have said?" The British agent replied, "Yes I have" (Adamec, 1967, 110).

To emphasize his demands, Amanullah sent three of his generals to the border: Saleh Muhammad, the commander-in-chief, arrived at Dakka, the border town, on May 3; **Abdul Quddus**, the prime minister (*sadr-i a'zam*) moved to the area of Qalat-i Ghilzai on May 5; and a day later **Muhammad Nadir**, the commander-in-chief (and subsequent king of Afghanistan), moved to Khost with a tribal *lashkar* (army) of several thousand men in addition to his regular forces.

On May 5 the government of India stopped demobilization of all combatant forces in India and began to recall all British officers. India intended to confront the Afghans with an overwhelming force in the Khaibar to induce them to withdraw quietly.

Lt.-General G. N. Molesworth described the Afghan regular forces as ill-trained, ill-paid, and probably under strength. But the superiority of the British-Indian forces was to a certain extent matched by the power of the Pashtun tribal *lashkars* from both sides of the border. They were aggressive fighters and operated in an inaccessible terrain that was well-known to them. The Pashtun soldiers of the British Khaibar Rifles were not willing to fight their Afghan brothers and, given the choice, 600 men out of 700 elected to be discharged, making it necessary for the British to disband the units. (OA3, 22–23)

Lord Chelmsford was warned by the London government "that you will not have forgotten [the] lessons of history, that we have not so much to fear from [the] Afghan regular Army as from the irregular tribesmen and their constant attacks on our isolated camps and lines of communications" (Adamec, 1967, 116).

Hostilities began on May 4, 1919, when Afghan troops cut the water supply to Landi Kotal on the Indian side of the border, and Britain retaliated by closing the Khaibar pass. The Afghans wanted to make a concerted effort involving the frontier tribes and the people of Peshawar, but a Peshawar revolt was prevented when British forces cut the supplies of water, electricity, and food to the city. Saleh Muhammad's forces became prematurely engaged and had to give ground. It was primarily on the Waziristan front that the Afghans were able to break through the British defenses and lay siege to the British base at Thal. The entire North-West Frontier was in ferment and Indian tribesmen were ready to rally to support the Afghans.

John Maffey, the chief political officer with the field force, indicated in a letter that the "threat to Thal has delayed the Jalalabad move, as the motor transport available does not admit of two simultaneous offensives." He also was afraid that British forces would have to push so far that there would be nobody to settle up with (Adamec, 1967, 118).

Therefore the Indian government permitted the Afghan envoy in India to proceed to Kabul to persuade Amanullah to end his hostile activities. Amanullah agreed, and a cease-fire was concluded leading to peace and the establishment of normal neighborly relations after long and heated negotiations at **Rawalpindi**, **Mussoorie**, and **Kabul**. On the southern front British forces captured Spin Boldak but could not follow up on their conquest, and no major campaign occurred on the northern, Chitral, front. British casualties included 236 killed (49 British ranks) and 615 wounded (British ranks 133), as well as 566 deaths of cholera and 334 of other diseases and accidents. British "ration strength" reached 750,000 British and Indian, and animals involved, 450,000. (Molesworth, vii) No figures are available on Afghan casualties. *(See also* AFGHAN FOREIGN RELATIONS; MUSSOORIE CONFERENCE; and ANGLO-AFGHAN TREATY, 1919; and 1921)

TIMURIDS. *See* **TIMUR-I LANG.**

TIMUR-I LANG Or **TAMERLANE** (r. 1370–1405). "The Lame Timur" founded the Timurid dynasty and wreaked destruction on the towns he conquered but made Samarkand into a city of splendor. He was a warrior, not an empire builder, and could not hold his extensive territorial conquests. The "Lame Timur" was a Turk, born at Kesh, near Samarkand, who claimed Mongol descent and began his career as a raider for booty. Claiming to wage *jihad*, holy war, he fought Muslim rulers in Russia and India and subdued the Ottomans at the Battle of Ankara in 1404. He was preparing a campaign against China when he died in 1405. His son Shahrukh chose Herat as his capital and made it an important cultural center. Under **Husain Baiqara** (r. 1468–1506), the last of the great Timurid rulers, Herat experienced a cultural renaissance, and artists, poets, and scholars enjoyed the sponsorship of the Timurid court. Architectural remains from the Timurid period include the Musalla (minarets) and the mausoleum of Gauhar Shad, the wife of Shahrukh. Timurid rule ended when the Uzbek Shaibanid dynasty took Herat in the early 16th century. The government of Uzbekistan is presently celebrating Timur as a national hero, others remember him as destroyer of civilizations equal to Genghis Khan.

TIMUR SHAH (r. 1773–93). One of **Ahmad Shah**'s six surviving sons and governor of Herat at the time of the death of his father. He defeated his brother, Sulaiman Mirza, and quickly established himself as successor to the Afghan throne at Kandahar. To weaken the power of the **Durrani** chiefs he moved his capital to Kabul, where he continued his father's policy of forging an alliance with the **Barakzais**, granting hereditary offices, and maintaining a strong army. He made alliances by marriage and further strengthened his power by creating an elite bodyguard of non-Pashtun soldiers. However, he was unable to create a centralized state. Afghan historians describe him as "humane and generous but...more a scholar than a soldier." He appointed his sons Zaman, Humayun, **Mahmud**, Abbas, and Kohandil as governors of Afghan provinces, and upon his death in 1793 they started an internecine struggle for power that eventually cost the **Sadozai** rulers their throne.

TIRAHI (TIRA'I). A small ethnic group that was moved by **Timur-i Lang** from the area of Tehran to the Tirahi plateau. Later expelled from Tirah, they settled in the Nangarhar Valley, where they are engaged in agriculture. They were *Shi'as* at one time but became **Sunnis** and speak Pashtu, although some may still know their original language. The Tirahis are divided into three sections: the Shabadwani, Sipai, and Lartoi. At the turn of the century they numbered about 3,000.

TOKHI. A section of the Ghilzai tribe. *See* GHILZAI.

TREATIES. *See* under individual treaties, AFGHAN FOREIGN RELA-TIONS and ANGLO-AFGHAN WARS.

TREATY OF KABUL. *See* **ANGLO-AFGHAN TREATY OF 1921.**

TREATY OF PESHAWAR, 1855. A treaty of friendship and alliance between Amir **Dost Muhammad** and the government of India that stipulated perpetual peace and friendship, that the British government should respect the territories in possession of the amir, and the amir respect the territories of the British government. The Afghan ruler was to be the friend of Britain's friends and enemy of her enemies, and the British should assist the amir against his enemies.

TREATY OF SIMLA. *See* **TRIPARTITE AGREEMENT.**

TRIBES. *See* individual entries.

TRIBES, PASHTUNS. Pashtuns are tribally organized and derive their origin from an eponymic ancestor. Although almost all speak Pashtu, some may have been of Turkic or other ethnic background. Today, the Pashtuns are the dominant factor in Afghanistan and the **North-West Frontier Province** (NWFP) of Pakistan. Beyond these boundaries they can be found in considerable numbers in India and other neighboring countries.

The Pashtuns (Pathans) of the NWFP include the following tribes:

Afridis	Barbars	Bajauris (or Tarkanris)	
Bangash	Bannuchis	Batannis	
Bahramzais	Chamkannis	Daudzais	Daurs
Dilazaks	Gandapurs	Gaodarras	Gharbinas
Gigianis	Jajis	Khalils	Khasors
Khattaks	Khetrans	Kundis	Lohanis
Mahsuds	Makbals	Mangals	Marwats
Mishwanis	Mohmands	Mullagoris	Multanis
Muhammadzais	Niazis	Orakzais	Safis
Sam Ranizais	Shinwaris	Turis	Urmars
Ushtaranas	Utman Khel	Wazir (or Darwish Khel)	
Yusufzais	Zaimukhts		

Pashtuns in Baluchistan include the following:

Achakzais	Babis	Barech	Ja'fars
Kakars	Kansis	Lunis	Mando Khel
Panis	Shiranis	Tarins	Zmarais

Pashtuns in Afghanistan include the following:

Durranis	Ghilzais	Khostwals	Jadrans
Safis	Shinwaris	Utman Khel	Yusufzais

as well as others present in the NWFP. (Ridgway, 1910)

For information on the major Pashtun tribes, see individual entries. *See also* ETHNIC GROUPS for major non-Pashtun groups and PASHTU; PASHTUN; and PASHTUNISTAN.

TRIPARTITE AGREEMENT. An agreement, also called Treaty of Simla, signed on July 16, 1838 between **Ranjit Singh**, ruler of the **Sikh** nation of the **Panjab**, **Shah Shuja**, the exiled king of Afghanistan, and the British government. It stipulated relations between the future Afghan ruler and Ranjit Singh and allied the three powers in an attempt to restore Shah Shuja and the **Sadozai** dynasty to the Kabul throne. Ranjit Singh was not required to commit his army and wisely left the task of invading Afghanistan to the British **Army of the Indus**. He was thus spared the British defeat in the **First Anglo-Afghan War**. *See also* AFGHAN FOREIGN RELATIONS; ANGLO-AFGHAN WARS; and SIMLA MANIFESTO.

TSARANDOY. *See* **SARANDOY.**

TURI. A **Pashtun** tribe of the Ghurgusht branch. Babur Shah, founder of the Moghul dynasty of India (*see* BABUR), mentions the Turis as residing in 1506 in the Kurram Valley, where they are found today. Kurram was part of Afghanistan until 1880, when the Turis rebelled, coming under British "protection" in 1882. They are *Shi'as* and disciples of one of four Sayyid families: the Tirah, Ahmadzai, Kirman, and Maura. In the conflict between the *mujahedin* and the Kabul government, the Kurram Valley was an important supply route of *mujahedin* operating in the Kabul area. This resulted in friction between them and the local population of Turis.

TURKOMAN. A **Sunni** Turkic people, estimated at from 125 to 400 thousand. They inhabit the northwestern part of Afghanistan, where the majority of them had fled after the Bolshevik Revolution. They contributed greatly to the Afghan economy as breeders of **Qaraqul** sheep and weavers of Turkoman carpets. The Marxist government tried to win minority support, declaring Turkmani one of the national languages, and permitting the publication of newspapers and broadcasts in that language.

U

ULAMA. Doctors of Islamic sciences. The word comes from the Arabic word *'alim*, (pl. *ulama*) and denotes "one who possesses the quality of *'ilm*, knowledge, or learning, of the Islamic traditions and the resultant canon law and theology." Afghan rulers established a hierarchy of *ulama*, headed by the *khan-i 'ulum* (chief of the ulama) and including the *qazis* (judges), *muftis* (canon lawyers), and *mullas* (preachers) who, at the time of Amir **Abdul Rahman**, were members of his royal council, *darbar-i 'am*. They seldom enjoyed political power but were an influential factor in the mobilization of the masses against King **Amanullah** in 1929 and against the Marxist regime when it was in control of the Kabul government. There may, however, be a change as the victorious *Taliban* seem to be determined to establish a theocracy of *ulama* and their "students." *See also* ISLAMIC LAW.

ULFAT, GUL PACHA. One of the founders of *Wish Zalmayan*, president of the Pashtu Academy (1957, *see* AFGHAN ACADEMY), president of tribal affairs (1963–65), and popular Pashtu poet. He was born in 1909 in Laghman Province and educated in Islamic studies. In 1936 he became editor of the daily newspaper *Anis* and subsequently served as director of *Ziray* (1938), *Himanat* (1940), *Kabul Magazine* (1942), and *Ittihad-i Mashriqi* (1947). He was member of the **Loya Jirgas** of 1956 and 1964 and of the seventh and eighth parliaments. He was a social critic, political writer and **Pashtun** nationalist. He died on December 20, 1977. *See also* PRESS AND JOURNALISM.

UMAR. *See* **OMAR.**

UMMA. Name for the Islamic community; the Pan-Islamic concept that all Muslims belong to one community, or Islamic nation.

UNITED STATES-AFGHANISTAN RELATIONS. The United States was slow in establishing diplomatic relations with Afghanistan because of several factors. Afghanistan had achieved independence from Great Britain in the **Third Anglo-Afghan War**, but Washington still considered the country within the British sphere of influence. Afghanistan was not attractive as a market for American industrial products nor as a source of vital raw materials. Americans knew little about the country; and whatever the U.S. government wanted to know it learned from the British, and they were not eager to have American competition in Afghanistan. Therefore, it is not surprising that Washington did not establish a legation at Kabul. The mission of **Wali Muhammad**, which visited European capitals for the purpose of establishing diplomatic relations, arrived in Washington in July 1921 with high hopes. Faiz Muhammad, a member of the mission, later described the event as follows:

> After waiting for some weeks to present the letter from King Amanullah to the President of the United States the members of our delegation were very much humiliated to read in the newspapers that President Harding had entertained Princess Fatima [the Afghan "princess" was not known by any member of the mission] at luncheon. Some days later we were received briefly and informally, presented our letter and received in reply one in which the President expressed regret at the death of the King's illustrious father [Amir Habibullah] and congratulated His Majesty on his ascension to the throne. It was all very disappointing and heart-breaking (ADAMEC, 1974).

The Afghan government wanted to embark on a plan of development and modernization for which it needed the assistance of Western know-how. Both Britain and the Soviet Union were too close to permit a relationship of dependency. Kabul, therefore, hoped that the United States would become a "third power" that would balance the influences of Afghanistan's neighbors. Afghanistan offered incentives to American enterprises: In 1930-31 an American firm sold 68 trucks for 121,000 dollars to the Afghan government, but Britain made this an expensive deal, insisting that the trucks be transported on the Indian railroad rather than proceeding on their own power. In the same year the U.S. consul at Karachi came to Kabul, but when asked why the United States was not ready to establish diplomatic relations with Afghanistan, he could not give a satisfactory reply. The speaker of parliament reproached him, saying "Americans had always said kind things about Afghanistan but, despite the fine opinion of the country, they refused to recognize a friendly state." In May 1935, W. H. Hornibrook arrived from Tehran to arrange for accreditation of U.S. diplomats stationed in India. The Afghans were ready to offer an oil concession to the United States. The Afghan foreign minister explained: "For obvious reasons we cannot give the concessions to the British and for the same reasons we cannot give it to the Russians....We therefore look to your country to develop our oil resources." He added that this would require a permanent American legation in Kabul. An oil concession was signed and ratified with the Inland Oil Exploration Company in April 1937, but the company canceled the concession a year later "in view of the worsening of the international situation."

Finally, in 1942 the U.S. government established a permanent legation in Kabul because of geopolitical reasons. The German advance on Stalingrad threatened the Allied logistics link through western Iran. Eastern Iran or western Afghanistan were the only areas for an alternate route. An American presence in Kabul could help gain Afghan approval for construction of a railroad. Therefore, on June 6, 1942, **Cornelius van Engert** became the first resident minister. The German defeat at Stalingrad made it unnecessary to raise the question of a railroad project with Kabul.

In the post World War II era, the United States provided aid for the war-torn and impoverished world, and Afghanistan received loans in 1950 and 1954 to finance its Helmand Valley electrification and irrigation projects. The American Morrison-Knudsen Construction Company undertook the ambitious task, which consumed a considerable amount of Afghanistan's hard currency reserves and did not live up to expectations (*see* HELMAND VALLEY AUTHORITY). The beginning of the cold war further complicated American-Afghan relations.

The United States sought allies in its effort to contain Soviet expansionism and promised economic and military assistance to those states that were willing to join. The Afghan government was unable to obtain American guarantees of protection from Soviet aggression, but Pakistan did and became a member of the Baghdad Pact. The U.S. Department of State made the decision to defend the Indian sub-continent at the Khaibar rather than at Afghanistan's northern boundary. This was bound to exacerbate relations with Pakistan (*see* PASHTUNISTAN) and prompted the Afghan government to pursue a policy of "positive neutrality," which eventually led to dependence on the Soviet Union. The American government was willing to help, but Washington was not willing to match Soviet aid. Between 1950 and 1971, the total of American loans and grants amounted to about $286 million, as compared to $672 million from the Soviet Union. American policy was to foster cordial relations with Afghanistan, help expand its communications infrastructure, participate in certain sectors of education, and provide moral, but not military, support to strengthen Afghanistan's independence. In the late 1970s the U.S. Department of State downgraded the American embassy in Kabul to the category of missions of countries of least importance to the United States, and Afghanistan was tacitly left in the Soviet sphere of influence.

After the **Saur Revolt**, the United States recognized the Marxist government, but relations quickly deteriorated. The assassination of the American Ambassador, Adolf Dubs, in February 1979, in a botched rescue attempt from kidnapers by Kabul police, further worsened relations. The Soviet military intervention in December 1979 resulted in vital American support for the *mujahedin*, forcing the Soviet government to withdraw its forces by February 1989. Fearing a general massacre in Kabul and the quick defeat of the Kabul government, the United States closed its embassy for "security reasons" in January 1989 and prevailed on others to do likewise. As a result of the *Taliban* capture of Kabul in September 1996, the American government examined whether conditions permitted the establishment of diplomatic relations, but in view of the *Taliban*'s harsh regime, human rights violations, tolerance of continued poppy cultivation, decided against it.

URTA TAGAI (37-30' N, 69-30' E). A 160-square mile island in the Amu Daria, also called Yangi Qal'a and Darqad, which in the 1920s became an issue in Soviet-Afghan relations. *See* SOVIET-AFGHAN RELATIONS.

UZBEK (UZBAK). The largest Turkic-language group in Afghanistan, estimated to number about 1.3 million (Uzbekistan has a population of about 17.5 million, half of them Uzbeks). They inhabit northern Afghanistan from Fariab Province in the west to Badakhshan Province. The Uzbek trace their name to an eponymic ancestor or a major tribe that migrated from the area north of the Syr Daria to the area north of the Afghan border. In the 15th century the Uzbeks were clients of various Timurid princes but soon struck out independently and by the early 16th century had captured Bukhara, Samarkand, and Khiva. They expelled **Babur Shah** from Ferghana, were defeated by Shah Isma'il of Persia in 1510, and carved out a khanate in Transoxania. **Ahmad Shah Durrani** gave Balkh to Haji Khan, Uzbek, to protect the border from raids, but after the latter's death the khanate became a source of dispute between the Afghans and the amir of Bukhara. In 1869, Amir **Shir Ali** placed the khanate under the administration of the governor of Balkh.

The Uzbeks are distinguished from other Turkic groups in their dress. They wear long striped *chapans* (kaftans—still popular in Afghanistan), small turbans, rather than the Turkoman sheep-skin caps, and boots of soft leather that fit tightly over wool stockings and reach up to the knees. They are largely sedentary agriculturalists. The Marxist government tried to win their support and proclaimed Uzbek a national language, permitting the use of the language in education, the press, and the broadcasting media. Some Uzbek groups served the Marxist government in Kabul as militia units in **Pashtun** areas, and General **Dostum**, leader of the Uzbeks, controls six provinces in northcentral Afghanistan. The country is now divided along ethnic lines with the largely **Pashtun** *Taliban* facing the non-Pashtun forces of **Dostum**, **Rabbani**, and **Khalili**. *See also* JOZJANIS and ABDUL RASHID DOSTUM.

V

VICEROYS. And GOVERNOR-GENERALS OF INDIA.

Governors-General:

Hastings, Warren	1774–85
Lord Cornwallis	1786–93
Sir John Shore	1793–98
Lord Wellesley	1798–1805
Cornwallis, Charles C	1805
Lord Minto	1807–13
Lord Hastings	1813–23
Lord Amherst	1823–28
Lord Bentinck	1828–35
Lord Auckland	1836–42
Lord Ellenborough	1842–44
Lord Hardinge	1844–48
Lord Dalhousie	1848–56
Lord Canning	1856–58

Viceroys:

Lord Canning	1858–62
Lord Elgin	1862–63
Lord Lawrence	1864–69
Lord Mayo	1869–72
Lord Northbrook	1872–76
Lord Lytton	1876–80
Lord Ripon	1880–84
Lord Dufferin	1884–88
Lord Lansdowne	1888–94
Lord Elgin	1894–99
Lord Curzon	1899–1905
Lord Minto	1905–10
Lord Hardinge	1910–16
Lord Chelmsford	1916–21
Lord Reading	1921–25
Lord Irwin	1926–31
Lord Willingdon	1931–36
Lord Linlithgow	1936–43
Lord Wavell	1943–47
Lord Mountbatten	1947

VITKEVICH, CAPT. IVAN (VICKOVICH). A Russian agent, or adventurer, of Lithuanian descent who came to Kabul in December 1837 for the purpose of establishing commercial relations with Afghanistan. He had a letter from Count Simonich, the Russian ambassador to Tehran, and an unsigned letter purported to be from the Tsar. **Alexander Burnes** was also at Kabul on a similar assignment for the British-India Company. Consulted by the amir, Burnes told him to receive Vitkevich and inform the British of his objective. **Dost Muhammad** wanted to regain Peshawar from Sikh control, but Burnes told him that he must surrender all claims to Peshawar and should make his peace with the Sikh ruler. Having gotten no help from the British, Amir Dost Muhammad negotiated with Vitkevich for Russian support. Vitkevich was later repudiated by the Russian government and, upon his return to St. Petersburg, committed suicide. The mission aroused fears in Britain that Dost Muhammad would ally himself with Russia, and the decision was made to depose the Afghan ruler. *See*

ANGLO-AFGHAN WARS; ALEXANDER BURNES; and DOST MUHAMMAD.

W

WAHDAT. *See* **HIZB-I WAHDAT.**

WAHDAT. Name of a weekly newspaper in **Dari/Pashtu** that was published and edited by the poet and calligrapher **Khal Muhammad Khasta** in 1966. It was the organ of *wahdat-i milli* (National Unity Party), which was headed by the poet **Khalilullah Khalili**. The paper closed after six months because of financial difficulties. An issue, dated January 31, 1966 (11. Dalw 1344) published the party's manifesto. It demanded the rule of law, constitutionalism, nonalignment, struggle for human rights, and peaceful coexistence. It asked for agricultural development and Afghan cultural revival, the expansion of medical and educational facilities, and equal rights for women.

WAKHAN (37-00'N, 73-00'E). The extreme northeastern district of Badakhshan Province, extending from Ishkashim in the west to the borders of China in the east and separating Tajikistan from the Indo-Pakistani subcontinent. The Anglo-Russian Boundary Commission awarded this area in 1895-96 to Afghanistan to create a buffer between the two empires. Amir **Abdul Rahman** was reluctant to accept this gift, declaring he was not "going to stretch out a long arm along the **Hindu Kush** to have it shorn off." But eventually the amir accepted the award when the gift was sweetened with a special annual subsidy of 50,000 rupees. The Wakhan is inhabited by some 6,000 **Isma'ilis** (Wakhis) and fewer than 2,000 **Sunni Qirghiz**. The latter emigrated to Turkey as a result of the Soviet intervention in Afghanistan. The area was ruled by an independent *mir* (from A., amir, prince) until 1882 when it came under the administrative control of the governor of Badakhshan. The corridor consists of high valleys traversed by the Wakhan River, which flows into the Ab-i-Panj, as the upper **Amu Daria** is called there. The two-humped Bactrian camel and yak are the major beasts of burden. In the years before the Saur Revolt the Wakhan Corridor attracted hunters for Marco Polo sheep and alpinists who explored its peaks. The inhabitants of the Wakhan Corridor are **Uzbeks** and Wakhis. The Qirghiz herders lived in a symbiotic relationship with the agricultural Wakhis.

WALI MUHAMMAD. Afghan foreign minister 1922–24, minister of war 1924–25, and regent during King Amanullah's journey abroad (1927–28). He was a descendant of the royal family of Darwaz and became custodian of Amir **Habibullah**'s correspondence. He headed a mission to Moscow and major European capitals to establish diplomatic relations. In July 1922 the mission arrived in the United States but could not convince President Harding to establish relations with Afghanistan. After the downfall of King Amanullah, Muhammad Wali was imprisoned and, when **Nadir Shah** ascended the throne, he was sentenced to eight years imprisonment but was executed with a number of supporters of King Amanullah in September 1933. *See also* UNITED STATES-AFGHAN RELATIONS.

WARDAK. A community of **Sayyids** inhabiting a region that runs from the **Hazara** portion of the Ghazni Province to the western part of the Logar Valley. They are said to derive their name from an eponymic ancestor called Ward. In the late 19th century they numbered about 20,000 families.

WARDAK (34-15'N, 68-0'E). A province in eastcentral Afghanistan (formerly called Maidan) with an area of 3,745 square miles and a population of about 310,000 of whom about 23,000 lived as refugees in Pakistan. The administrative center is the newly constructed town Maidanshahr (replacing Kot-i Ashro), located a few miles west of the Kabul-Kandahar Highway. The province is mountainous and crossed by the Kabul-Kandahar Highway and the road west into the **Hazarajat** and northwest to Bamian Province. The inhabitants are **Ghilzai** and **Durrani** Pashtuns in the south and Hazara in the north and west. The province is 80 % pasture land. About 60 % of the farms comprise areas of less than five *jaribs* (one *jarib* = about 0.5 acre) The province has suffered considerably during the 1980s and has seen large-scale destruction of the infrastructure built during the 1970s.

WATAN. (Homeland) is a biweekly, liberal newspaper in Dari, published by **Mir Ghulam Muhammad Ghobar** and Mir Muhammad Siddiq Farhang from 1951-52. It was closed by the government after the appearance of 48 issues.

WATAN, HIZB-I. "Homeland (or Fatherland) Party" was the name of the PDPA after June 1990. *See* PEOPLES DEMOCRATIC PARTY OF AFGHANISTAN.

WATANJAR, MUHAMMAD ASLAM. Held positions as minister of Communications, Interior, and, finally, Defense in Prime Minister Khaliqyar's government of May 1990. A member of the *Khalq* faction of the **PDPA**, he had a leading role in the coup of **Muhammad Daud** (1973) and the subsequent **Saur Revolt** (1978). In both events he rode the lead tank in the assault on the palace, and his tank was placed on a pedestal in the square facing the presidential palace in commemoration of the 1978 coup. In April 1978 he and General **Abdul Qadir** headed the Revolutionary Council that formed the government until **Nur Muhammad Taraki** was installed as president. In September 1979 he was said to have been involved in a plot to remove **Hafizullah Amin** from power and fled to the protection of the Soviet embassy in Kabul until the *Parcham* takeover. After the revolt of **Shahnawaz Tanai** in March 1990, Dr. Najibullah appointed Watanjar minister of Defense, the position previously held by Tanai. Watanjar was born in 1946 in Paktia Province of an Andar **Ghilzai** family and was educated in military schools at Kabul and in the Soviet Union. He apparently fled abroad after the fall of the Marxist regime in April 1992.

WAZIRI. The Waziris (also called Darwish Khel) are Ghurghusht **Pashtuns** claiming descent from Wazir. Their original home was in Birmal (now Paktika Province) from where they gradually moved eastward in the 14th century and settled in the present Waziristan and across the border in Afghanistan. They are estimated to number about 250,000, most of them on the Pakistani side of the border. They are divided into two major branches: the Ahmadzai and Utmanzai. They supported **Nadir Khan** (the subsequent king) in his war against **Habibullah Kalakani** and, under the command of Marshal **Shah Wali** and their leader Allah Nawaz Khan, captured Kabul and the royal palace in October 1929.

WEAPONS BAZAAR. *See* **ARMS BAZAAR.**

WISH ZALMAYAN. A liberal political organization (Awakened Youth) founded in 1947 in Kandahar by writers and **Pashtun** nationalists. It included such individuals as Abdul Hai Aziz, **Gul Pacha Ulfat, Shams-**

uddin Majruh, Abdul Rauf Benawa, Mir Ghulam Muhammad Ghobar, Faiz Muhammad Angar, and **Nur Muhammad Taraki**. The organization wanted to reform Afghan society and aimed at the advancement of education, the eradication of corruption, the promotion of national welfare, understanding and respect among the people, and steadfastness in advancing toward their objectives. It was one of the earliest political groups in Afghanistan and subsequently divided on the issue of Pashtun nationalism. The nationalists supported the Red Shirt movement of **Khan Abdul Ghaffar Khan**.

WOLESI JIRGA. Literally "people's council," the name of the lower house (or House of the People) of Parliament, established by the Constitution of 1964. *See* CONSTITUTIONAL DEVELOPMENT.

Y

YANGI QAL'A. *See* **URTA TAGAI.**

YAQUBI, GEN. GHULAM FARUQ. Deputy president of State Security Services, **KHAD** (*see* AFGHAN SECURITY SERVICE), 1980–85. President of KHAD, succeeding Dr. **Najibullah** in December 1985. His position was upgraded to that of minister of State Security (WAD), a position he held in the 1988 and 1990 governments. He became a member of the **PDPA** politburo in 1986 and was said to be an important ally of Najibullah. Born in 1938 in Kabul, the son of Khan Muhammad, and educated at **Najat** school, the Kabul police academy, and in West Germany, he began his career as a lecturer at the police academy in 1961. Subsequently he served as director of operations and general director of the criminal department of the Ministry of Interior. He committed suicide on April 16, 1992 or, according to one source, was assassinated by a **Parchami** rival.

YAQUB KHAN, AMIR MUHAMMAD (r. February–October 1879). Born about 1849, Amir **Shir Ali**'s son and governor of Herat. Yaqub Khan also coveted Kandahar and was greatly disturbed when in 1868 the amir gave his favorite son Abdullah Jan that post. In 1871 Yaqub Khan rebelled and marched on Kabul but was forced to retreat to Herat. Amir Shir Ali forgave Yaqub Khan and reappointed him governor of Herat. Yaqub Khan came to Kabul under a promise of safe conduct, which the amir did not keep, holding him in confinement until

December 1878, when British troops invaded Afghanistan. Amir Shir Ali fled to northern Afghanistan and appointed Yaqub his regent. The latter proclaimed himself amir in February 1879, after he learned of the sudden death of his father. Hoping to save his throne, Yaqub concluded the **Treaty of Gandomak** with Britain and accepted a mission under **Sir Louis Cavagnari** at Kabul. When the latter was assassinated during an insurrection of troops, the British took control of government powers, and Yaqub was forced to abdicate in October 1879. He went to India and lived there until his death in 1923. *See also* ANGLO-AFGHAN WARS and GANDOMAK, TREATY OF.

YAR MUHAMMAD, WAZIR. Wazir, prime minister, of Prince **Kamran** (r. 1830–42) who ruled Herat as an independent principality. He is said to have been an able but cruel man who eventually became the virtual ruler of Herat. He ably withstood Persian attempts to capture Herat and led the defenses in two sieges in 1833 and 1837–38 in which the Russian General Berovski participated on the Persian side and **Eldred Pottinger** on the side of the defenders. Yar Muhammad had Prince Kamran assassinated in 1842 and embarked on an ambitious plan of conquest. He allied himself in marriage with **Akbar Khan**, son of Amir **Dost Muhammad**, and conquered the western Uzbek khanates of Afghan Turkistan. He died in 1851.

YAZDAN-BAKHSH, MIR. Born in 1790, the son of Mir Wali Beg, the chief of Behsud, **Hazarajat**. He expelled his older brother, Mir Muhammad Shah, who had become chief of Behsud after his father was assassinated by a minor chief. Mir Yazdan-bakhsh consolidated his power to become the undisputed chief of the Hazaras from 1843–63. Amir **Dost Muhammad** Khan called him to Kabul and had him imprisoned. He escaped and fled to Bamian where he was assassinated. *See also* HAZARA and HAZARAJAT.

YOUSAF, MOHAMMAD. (YUSUF, MUHAMMAD). Brigadier Muhammad Yusuf, head of the Afghan Bureau of the **Inter-Services Intelligence** of the Pakistan military from 1983 to 1987. He claims to have held a pivotal position in the war of the Afghan *mujahedin* against the Soviet and Kabul forces. In his book, *The Bear Trap: Afghanistan's Untold Story* (coauthored with Mark Adkin), this "commander in chief" of the *mujahedin* forces controlled the distribution of weapons bought with CIA and Saudi Arabian funds from the United States, Britain,

China, and Egypt. He organized the training of rebels and planned missions of sabotage, ambushes, and assassinations inside Afghanistan and the Soviet Union. He was succeeded in 1978 by General Hamid Gul, at a time when the Soviet government had decided to end its involvement in Afghanistan.

YUNUS KHALES. *See* **KHALES, MUHAMMAD YUNUS.**

YUSUF, DR. MUHAMMAD. *See* **MUHAMMAD YUSUF.**

YUSUFZAI. A **Pashtun** tribe, originally settled in Peshawar, which migrated to the Helmand Valley and the Kabul region in the fifth century A.D. and in the 16th century returned to the northeastern corner of the Peshawar Valley. They now inhabit the Pakistan districts of Peshawar, Mardan, and Swat. They divided into two great branches: the Yusufzai and the Mandanr. They are agriculturists and usually dress in white clothes and shave their heads, leaving "a pair of love locks" at their temples. They have been romanticized as the "Pashtuns of the Pashtuns" among whom the **Pashtunwali** is still a living code of behavior. **Khushhal Khan Khatak**, not himself a Yusufzai, extols their sense of honor, saying

> The nobles of the Afghans are the Yusufzai'is,
> Hard in battlefield and hospitable at home,
> All Pakhtuns possess the sense of honor (*nang*)
> None, however, can vie with them.

Z

ZABIHULLAH, ABDUL QADIR. A *mujahedin* commander affiliated with **Jam'iat** who was a member of the Islamist youth organization (*see* ISLAMIST MOVEMENT) and operated successfully in the Mazar-i Sharif area. He was said to have been trained by Commander Mas'ud in Panjshir and subsequently cooperated with him. He was killed on December 14, 1984 when his jeep hit a land mine. Born in 1951 and educated in Mazar-i Sharif, he worked as a teacher and became a member of the Islamic movement. After the **Saur Revolt**, he adopted the *nom de guerre* Zabihullah. He operated with **Ahmad Shah Mas'ud** in the Panjshir valley and later moved to Mazar-i Sharif where he coordinated the activities of commanders and administered the territory under his control. After his death, effective large-scale resistance collapsed in the Mazar-i Sharif area.

ZABUL (32-0' N, 67-15' E). A province in southcentral Afghanistan with an area of 6,590 square miles and a population of 181,000. The administrative center of the province is the town of Qalat, located about 87 miles northeast of Kandahar. The province is arid with almost perpetual winds, and agriculture is limited to the valleys of the Tarnak and Arghastan Rivers and a few areas that are irrigated by means of **Kariz**. The province, however, abounds in almond trees, one of the major items of export. The Zabulis are noted as good horsemen and perform a game, called "tent pegging" (*naiza bazi*), in which they spear pegs planted in the ground. The population is largely **Pashtun** in the south and b in the north. *See also* QALAT.

ZABULI, ABDUL MAJID. The most successful Afghan capitalist and financier, who in 1933 founded the Ashami Company that eventually developed into the **Bank-i Milli**. He became minister of national economy in 1936 and established industries in Pul-i Khumri, Kunduz, and Kabul. He was instrumental in charting the course of Afghan economic development in cooperation with German commercial and industrial enterprises. Zabuli resigned in 1951 and went abroad. He was born in 1896 and educated in Herat and later at Tashkent. In 1917 he headed his father's export-import company in Herat, trading with Iran and Russia. In 1922 he moved his firm's office to Tashkent and from there to Moscow to operate a textile mill under the Soviet "New Economic Policy." He moved to Germany in 1929 and devoted his activities to international investment. Invited by **Nadir Shah** to return to Afghanistan, he founded the Ashami Company in 1933 with 80 % private and 20 % government shares. He issued paper money and founded the **Da Afghanistan Bank**, Industrial Bank, and Bank-i Milli branches in Berlin, London, Bombay, Karachi, Peshawar, and later in New York (Afghan-American Trading Company). Zabuli was seen as having political ambitions: he favored a laissez-faire economy and cooperation with Germany in Afghan economic development. Disagreements with Prime Minister **Shah Mahmud Ghazi** led to his resignation, but members of his family continued to attend to family interests in Kabul. He retired and has been living in the United States since 1970. *See also* BANKING.

ZAHIR SHAH, MUHAMMAD. King of Afghanistan, 1933-73. Born on October 15, 1914, the only surviving son of **Nadir Shah**, he was educated at Kabul and in France. He was proclaimed king on November 8, 1933 a few hours after his father's assassination and adopted the title *al-Mutawakkil Ala'llah, Pairaw-i Din-i Matin-i Islam* (Confident in God, Follower of the Firm Religion of Islam). During the early period of his reign (1933–46), the young king reigned while his uncles **Muhammad Hashim** and **Shah Mahmud Ghazi** ruled, holding the powerful position of prime minister. His cousin, **Muhammad Daud**, succeeded as prime minister from 1953 until 1963, when Zahir Shah forced his resignation. In 1964 he promulgated a new constitution that excluded members of the royal family from certain government positions (*see* CONSTITUTIONAL DEVELOPMENT), provided for a bicameral parliament, free elections, a free press, and the formation of political parties. It ushered in a period of unprecedented political tolerance that was marred only by the intransigence of parliamentary repre-sentatives who could not establish a working coalition. The law on political parties was never ratified by the king, but parties were tolerated, although not legally permitted, and numerous groups published their manifestos in privately-published newspapers and periodicals. Members of parliament were elected as independents and not members of a party, but parliament was stymied with political infighting. Foreign aid from East and West kept flowing into the country, and Kabul experienced considerable growth. However, not all sectors of Afghan society benefitted from the economic development. Zahir Shah toured Afghanistan on several occasions and frequently traveled abroad. During one of his trips abroad, his cousin Muhammad Daud staged a coup and established a republican government with himself as president. Zahir Shah abdicated in August 1973 and has since lived in Italy. The impasse in the present war has led to demands by some that the ex-king return to serve as head of an interim government that would end the war and establish a representative government in Afghanistan.

ZAMAN SHAH. *See* **SHAH ZAMAN.**

ZHAWAR, BATTLE OF. Zhawar is a village in Khost Province south of Parachinar and about six miles from the Pakistan border. It was the major base along the ***mujahedin*** supply route for attacks on the Kabul garrison at Khost. The importance of the base can be seen from the fact that about 60 % of *mujahedin* supplies passed through Zhawar and Ali

Khel (Yousaf, 164). The base, built by a Pakistani construction company, had large underground facilities: seven tunnels housed living and medical quarters as well as depots of weapons and other facilities. Generators provided electricity and permitted radio communication. The base was defended by commanders of **Khales**, **Hekmatyar**, **Nabi**, and **Gailani**. **Jalaluddin Haqani** was one of the major commanders. Some 400 men provided close protection and administrative support, and some additional 10,000 *mujahedin* controlled positions between Zhawar and Ali Khel. Being close to the Pakistan border, reinforcements could quickly be obtained. The *mujahedin* had anti- aircraft protection, including British Blowpipe missiles, three Oerlikon guns, and shoulder-fired SA-7s. Anti-Tank mine fields, mortars, and other heavy artillery provided for a formidable defense. Destruction of the base and closure of the supply line had long been an object of the Kabul government, and in early 1986 it started a major offensive. Major-General **Tanai**, who was a native of this area, was in tactical command, and Brigadier Abdul Ghafur led the Soviet/Afghan contingent. The Soviets deployed one air assault regiment of the 103rd Guards Airborne Assault Division, and the Afghan forces included units of the seventh and eighth Division in Kabul, the 12th Division of Gardez, and the 14th Division at Ghazni and Khost, numbering altogether about 12,000 men. After a slow and fiercely disputed advance the Soviet/Kabul forces reached Zhawar on April 11 and during the coming week succeeded in isolating the base and destroyed the underground structures with laser-guided bombs. A Soviet heliborne commando brigade, landing in an open area, was destroyed to a man. The *mujahedin* fired 13 Blowpipe missiles, without destroying an aircraft (Yousaf, 171); nevertheless, at the end of the battle the *mujahedin* claimed to have downed 13 helicopters and aircrafts. The Kabul government captured the base but withdrew shortly thereafter, and the *mujahedin* returned within 48 hours. The Kabul government claimed to have killed 2,000 and wounded 4,000, and the *mujahedin* claimed to have captured 100 Afghan soldiers and killed or wounded about 1,500. A *mujahedin* spokesman said only 300 *mujahedin* were killed. The Kabul campaign did not achieve its objective.

CHRONOLOGY

ca. 2000-1000 B.C.	Arians move from northern Afghanistan to northern India.
522-486	Darius I rules and Afghan territory becomes part of the Achaemenid Empire.
330-327	Alexander the Great rules Bactria (Balkh) becomes province of empire.
305	The Seleucids are defeated and Maurians establish rule.
ca. 250	Maurian kingdom under Asoka.
250-128	Graeco-Bactrian kingdom at Balkh.
ca. 50 A.D.-250	Afghanistan area is part of Kushanid Empire.
ca. 225-600s	Sassanids establish control.
652-664	First Muslim-Arab conquests.
8th-10th cent.	Hindushahis rule Kabul and eastern part of Afghan territory.
871	Yaqub b. Laith, Saffarid, defeats Hindushahis.
997-ca. 1150	Ghaznavid rule.
1186	Ghorids succeed Ghaznavids.

1227-1350	Kurt dynasty in Balkh, Ghazni, and Sarakhs.
1370	Timur-i Lang crowned in Balkh.
1405-1506	Timurid rule in Herat and Balkh.
1504-1525	Babur invades; establishes capital in Kabul.
1600	British East India Company founded.
1648	Persians take Kandahar.
1713	Mir Wais revolt on Kandahar.
1716	Abdali revolt in Herat.
1709-38	Ghilzais establish a dynasty that also rules Iran.
1747	Ahmad Shah crowned, begins 26-year rule during which he united Afghan tribes under the Sadozai dynasty.
1748	Durranis move against Lahore. In November Ahmad Shah begins third invasion of India.
1757	January. Khutba read in name of Ahmad Shah at Delhi, India, and coins are struck in his name, making him suzerain ruler of India.
1761	Afghans defeat Maratha confederacy at Battle of Panipat, marking greatest extent of Ahmad Shah's empire, which included Kashmir, the Panjab, and parts of Baluchistan.
1769-70	Ahmad Shah moves into Khorasan.
1772	Oct. 16/17. Ahmad Shah dies at Toba Maruf.
1773	Timur Shah begins 20-year rule. Moves capital from Kandahar to Kabul. Campaigns in Sind and Bukhara.

1793	Zaman Shah begins six-year rule.
1798	Britain, fearing Afghan invasions of India, initiates policy of containment, enlisting Persia to keep Afghanistan in check.
1800	Mahmud Shah deposes Shah Shuja, rules for three years.
1803	Shah Shuja deposes Shah Mahmud.
1805	Persian attempt to take Herat fails.
1807	At Tilsit, Alexander II and Napoleon plan joint Russian-French invasion of India through Persia.
1809	British envoy Mountstuart Elphinstone and Shah Shuja sign defensive alliance in first official contact between Afghanistan and a European power. Shah Mahmud defeats Shah Shuja at Gandomak and rules until blinding of Fateh Khan, his Barakzai wazir, causes Barakzai revolt and Shah Mahmu's downfall in 1817.
1816	Persian attempt to capture Herat fails.
1818	Civil war results in division of Afghanistan into virtually independent states until 1835. Ranjit Singh seizes Peshawar.
1819	Ranjit Singh conquers Kashmir.
1826	Dost Muhammad, ruler of Ghazni, takes Kabul.
1833	Persians besiege Herat.
1834	Dost Muhammad defeats Shah Shuja and captures Kandahar.

1835	Dost Muhammad begins his first rule of Afghanistan.

1837   Lord Auckland appointed governor-general.
            Akbar Khan, son of Dost Muhammad, defeats Sikhs
            at Jamrud.
            August. Eldred Pottinger arrives at Herat.
            Sept. 20. Alexander Burnes arrives in Kabul on a
            diplomatic mission for British.
            Nov. 23. Commencement of second siege of Herat.
            Dec. 19. Ivan Vitkewich (Witkiwicz), emissary from
            Russia, arrives in Kabul.

1838   Apr. 26. Burnes leaves Kabul.
            June 26. Tripartite Treaty signed by Ranjit Singh, the
            British East India Company, and Shah Shuja to
            restore the latter to the Afghan throne.
            Sept. 9. Siege of Herat raised.
            Oct. 1. British break relations with Dost Muhammad.
            and declare war.

1839   **First Anglo-Afghan War**
            Apr. 25. Sir John Keane's force arrives at Kandahar.
            July 23. British capture Ghazni.
            Aug. 2. Amir Dost Muhammad flees.
            Aug. 7. Kabul occupied by the Army of the Indus.
            Oct. 15. Bengal troops begin return march to India.
            Oct. 18. Bombay troops begin return march to India.

1840   August. Dost Muhammad escapes from Bukhara.
            Nov. 2. Surrender of Amir Dost Muhammad.
            Nov. 12. Dost Muhammad leaves for India.

1841   Nov. 2. Assassination of Burnes.
            Nov. 7. Return of Akbar Khan to Bamian.
            Nov. 18. Macnaghten recommends holding out.
            Dec. 13. Evacuation of Bala Hisar.
            Dec. 22. Orders issued for the evacuation of Ghazni,
            Kandahar, and Jalalabad.
            Dec. 23. Assassination of Macnaghten.
            December. Mutiny at Kandahar.

1842	Treaty of Capitulation ratified.
	Jan. 6. Retreat from Kabul commences.
	Jan. 13. British last stand at Jagdalak. Arrival of Brydon at Jalalabad.
	Apr. 5. General Pollock forces the Khaibar Pass.
	Apr. 7. Battle at Jalalabad.
	Apr. 25. King Shah Shuja assassinated at Kabul.
	May. Pollock at Jalalabad. Relief of Kalat-i Ghilzai. Akbar Khan captures Bala Hisar.
	June-October. Fateh Jang becomes Amir.
	Aug. 7. Evacuation of Kandahar.
	Aug. 20. Pollock sets out from Jalalabad. Action near Gandomak.
	Sept. 5. British reenter Ghazni.
	Sept. 15. Pollock arrives at Kabul.
	Sept. 19. Nott arrives at Kabul.
	Oct. 12. British force leaves Kabul.
	End of First Anglo-Afghan War.
	Dec. Dost Muhammad returns to Kabul and rules for 21 years.
1855	Treaty of Peshawar reopens diplomatic relations between Britain and Afghanistan.
1856	Oct. Persians capture and hold Herat for a few months.
1857	Jan. Anglo-Afghan treaty signed in Peshawar. provides subsidy for Dost Muhammad.
1863	Dost Muhammad takes Herat and dies. Shir Ali ascends Afghan throne. During next two years Shir Ali put down revolts by half brothers, Azam and Afzal, and his brother, Muhammad Amin. Abdur Rahman and his uncle, Azam, attack Kabul, liberate Afzal, Abdur Rahman's father.
1866	Afzal becomes Amir. Shir Ali flees to Kandahar.
1867	Amir Afzal dies.

1868   Azam becomes Amir.

1869   Shir Ali defeats Azam. Abdur Rahman goes into exile
                          in Russia. British recognize Shir Ali as Amir but
                          refuse to recognize his son, Abdullah Jan, as succes-
                          sor.
                          March. Ambala Conference held between Amir Shir
                          Ali and Lord Mayo, viceroy of India.

1872   In Granville-Gorchakoff Agreement Russia assures
                          Britain that Afghanistan is outside Russia's sphere of
                          influence. British commission marks Sistan boundary.

1873   Abdullah Jan named heir to Afghan throne. Shir Ali's
                          oldest son, Yakub Khan, revolts, flees to Herat. Rus-
                          sia takes Khiva.

1874   Yakub Khan imprisoned in Kabul.

1876   British occupy Quetta.

1878   July 22. Russian mission under General Stolietoff
                          arrives in Kabul.
                          Second Anglo-Afghan War
                          Sept. 21. General Faiz Muhammad, commander of
                          Ali Masjid, denies the British envoy, General Sir
                          Neville Chamberlain, passage into Afghanistan. Amir
                          Shir Ali is given an ultimatum to apologize for this
                          "insult" and to meet certain conditions lest he be
                          treated as an enemy. Lord Lytton denounces alliance
                          with Amir Dost Muhammad.
                          Nov. Colonel Grodekoff arrives in Herat from
                          Samarkand.
                          Nov. 21. Sir Samuel Brown attacks the fort of Ali
                          Masjid, General Roberts crosses the frontier at Thal,
                          and an advance guard of General Donald Steward
                          marches from Quetta against Kandahar.
                          Nov. 22. Fort Ali Masjid is captured.
                          Dec. 20. General Brown occupies Jalalabad.

1878   Dec. 23. Amir Shir Ali leaves Kabul and appoints his son Yaqub Khan governor of Kabul.

1879   Jan. 12. General Steward occupies Kandahar and takes Qalat-i Ghilzai on January 21.
              Feb. 21. Amir Shir Ali dies at Mazar-i Sharif, Yaqub Khan proclaimed king.
              May 26. Treaty of Gandomak signed by Sir Louis Cavagnari and Amir Yaqub Khan.
              July 24. Cavagnari arrives in Kabul to assume post of British envoy to amir.
              Sept. 3. Cavagnari and his staff are killed.
              Oct. 6. General Roberts's Army of Retribution wins battle of Charasia.
              Oct. 12. General Roberts occupies Kabul.
              Oct. 28. Amir Yaqub abdicates, British take over the government of Kabul.
              Dec. 14. General Baker driven from Asmai hills with losses. General Roberts abandons the Bala Hisar and Kabul city and stations his forces at Sherpur.
              Dec. 15-22, Muhammad Jan cuts Roberts's communications and lays siege to Sherpur.
              Dec. 23. Muhammad Jan's forces are defeated and Roberts returns to Bala Hisar the next day.

1880   June 15. (about) Sardar Ayub Khan moves from Herat against Kandahar.
              July 10. A brigade under General Burrows moves against Ayub.
              July 22. Britain recognizes Sardar Abdur Rahman as Amir of Kabul and its Dependencies.
              July 27. General Burrows is totally defeated in Battle of Maiwand, and the remnant of his brigade forced to seek security in Kandahar.
              Aug. 6. Ayub Khan invests Kandahar.
              Aug. 8. General Roberts begins march from Kabul to Kandahar.
              Aug. 11. General Steward withdraws from Kabul and Amir Abdur Rahman moves in.

1880	Aug. 16. Sortie of the British garrison of Kandahar is repulsed with great losses. Aug. 31. Sir Roberts arrives at Kandahar. Sept. 1. Sir Roberts defeats Ayub Khan at Baba Wali Kotal. Sept. 9. British troops return to India from the Paiwar Kotal and the Kurram Valley and begin withdrawal from Jalalabad.
1881	Apr. 21. British troops withdraw from Kandahar. **End of Second Anglo-Afghan War**.
1882	Muslim agent appointed to represent British in Kabul.
1883	Russia occupies Tejend Oasis. Britain annexes Quetta district. Abdur Rahman occupies Shignan and Roshan. Britain grants Abdur Rahman subsidy of twelve lakhs (1,200,000 rupees).
1884	Britain and Russia open negotiations on northern boundary of Afghanistan. Sir Peter Lumsden leads British mission to Herat. British again start building Quetta railroad. Russians occupy Pul-i-Khatun.
1885	Russians occupy Zulfikar and Akrobat and take Panjdeh.
1886	British construct Bolan railway to Quetta. Oct. British boundary mission returns to India by way of Kabul.
1887	Russia occupies Karki. Britain and Russia make final settlement and demarcation of Afghan-Russian frontier. Ayub Khan escapes from Persia, but rebellion in Afghanistan fails; and he surrenders at Mashhad and is exiled to India.
1888	January. British extend Quetta Railway to Kila Abdullah.

1888	July. Ishaq Khan, son of Azam, revolts in Turkestan, retreats to Samarkand.
1891	Abdur Rahman introduces oath of allegiance on the Koran among his councillors.
1892	Uprising of Hazaras suppressed.
1893	Nov. 12. Afghanistan and Britain sign Durand Agreement that sets eastern and southern borders. British increase Amir Abdur Rahman's subsidy by six lakhs and permit Afghanistan to import munitions. British occupy New Chaman as railway terminus.
1895	Abdur Rahman abolishes slavery in Afghanistan. Abdur Rahman accepts oaths of allegiance from whole state of Afghanistan and adopts title of *Zia ul-Millat wa ud-Din.* Sardar Nasrullah, second son of Abdur Rahman, visits England. Russia and Britain agree on Wakhan border.
1896	Kafiristan brought under Afghan control by Amir Abdur Rahman; renamed Nuristan.
1900	Russia presses for direct Afghan-Russian relations along northern Afghan border in memorandum of February 6 to Britain.
1901	Oct. 1. Abdur Rahman dies. Oct. 3. Habibullah proclaimed Amir, rules 18 years.
1902	British envoy, Sir Henry Dobbs, supervises reerection of boundary pillars on Afghan-Russian border during 1902 and 1903.
1903	A. H. McMahon leads British mission in demarcating Sistan boundary. Habibia College, first secular high school, opened in Kabul. British begin construction of Quetta-Nushki railroad.

1905   British agreements of 1880 and 1893 with Abdur
                Rahman confirmed by treaty with Amir Habibullah.

1906   Shah of Iran rejects McMahon arbitration award.

1907   Jan. Amir Habibullah visits India.
                Aug. 31. Britain and Russia sign convention
                concerning spheres of influence in Afghanistan,
                Persia, and Tibet.

1909   Plot on Amir Habibullah's life fails.

1910   First telephone line in Afghanistan built between
                Kabul and Jalalabad.

1911   Mahmud Tarzi begins publishing the newspaper
                Seraj al- Akhbar.

1914   General   Muhammad   Nadir   Khan   named
                commander-in-chief of the Afghan Army. Habibullah
                declares Afghanistan's neutrality in World War I.

1915   Sept. Hentig-Niedermayer mission from Germany
                arrives in Kabul and remains nine months.

1918   Kabul Museum opened.

1919   Feb. 20. Amir Habibullah assassinated in Laghman.
                Nasrullah Khan named amir in Jalalabad.
                Feb. 25. Amanullah proclaimed amir in Kabul.
                Feb. 28. Nasrullah arrested.
                Mar. 3. Amanullah suggests new Anglo-Afghan
                agreement to viceroy of India.
                Apr. 13. Amanullah proclaims Afghanistan inde-
                pendent
                May 1. Saleh Muhammad Khan, the commander-in-
                chief, moves to the Indian border with two companies
                of infantry and two guns, for the ostensible purpose of
                inspecting the border.

1919	**Third Anglo-Afghan War**

May 3. An escort of British Khaibar Rifles accompanying a caravan is stopped in the disputed area between Landi Khana and Torkham.

May 4. Afghan uniformed troops occupy Bagh and begin to cut the water supply to Landi Kotal. A *fatwa* proclaimed *jihad*.

May 7. Afghan forces at Bagh strengthened, and Nadir Khan moves to Khost.

May 8. Peshawar uprising suppressed.

May 9. First Battle of Bagh, British forces stopped.

May 11. Second Battle of Bagh.

May 13. British occupy Dakka.

May 24. Kabul bombed by Royal Air Force.

May 21. General Nadir Khan crosses Indo-Afghan boundary, marches on Thal. Decision made to evacuate the militia posts on the Waziristan front.

May 27. Battle of Spin Buldak.

May 28. Wali Muhammad Khan arrives in Tashkent on way to Moscow and Europe as Amanullah's envoy.

June 2. Armistice.

Aug. 8. Preliminary Anglo-Afghan treaty signed at Rawalpindi peace conference.

End of Third Anglo-Afghan War.

September. Soviet envoy arrives in Kabul.

Oct. 10. Muhammad Wali Khan arrives in Moscow.

1920	Apr. 17. Mussoorie Conference opens. Mahmud Tarzi represents Afghanistan and Henry Dobbs, Britain.

July 18. Mussoorie Conference ends.

1921	Amir of Bukhara seeks asylum in Afghanistan.

Jan. 20. Kabul conference between Afghanistan and Britain opens.

Feb. 28. Treaty of friendship signed by Afghanistan and the Soviet Union.

Mar. 1. Treaty of friendship signed by Afghanistan and Turkey.

1921	May 30. Fundamental law of government of Afghanistan goes into force. June 3. Treaty of friendship signed by Afghanistan and Italy. June 22. Treaty of friendship signed by Afghanistan and Persia. Dec. 2. Kabul Conference ends. Britain recognizes Afghanistan as independent in internal and external relations. Diplomatic relations established between two states.
1922	Apr. 28. Treaty establishes diplomatic and commercial relations between France and Afghanistan. Sept. 9. Agreement gives France rights to conduct archaeological excavations in Afghanistan.
1923	Jan. Istiqlal high school founded. Apr. 10. First Constitution adopted. June 5. British-Afghan trade convention signed. Sept. French legation opened in Afghanistan. Oct. Criminal code adopted. Nov. Statute governing marriage issued. Dec. Statute on civil servants confirmed. Dec. German legation opens in Afghanistan.
1924	Jan. Amani (Najat) high school founded. First hospital for women and children opened in Kabul. Mar. Uprising of tribes in Khost.
1925	Jan. Khost rebellion defeated.
1926	Afghani introduced as new monetary unit. Ten afghanis equal eleven Kabuli *ropea*. Mar. 3. Treaty of friendship signed by Afghanistan and Germany. June 7. Amanullah adopts title of King. Aug. 15. Soviet Union agrees to cede Urta Tagai Islands in Amu River to Afghanistan.

1926	Aug. 31. Treaty of neutrality and mutual non-aggression signed by Afghanistan and Soviet Union.
1927	*Anis* founded as fortnightly, later major national daily newspaper. Nov. 27. Treaty of neutrality and mutual non-aggression signed by Afghanistan and Persia. Dec. King Amanullah visits India, Egypt, and Europe.
1928	May 25. Treaty of friendship and collaboration signed by Afghanistan and Turkey. July. King Amanullah returns to Afghanistan. July-Sept. Amanullah introduces reforms in dress. Nov. Uprising of Shinwari near Jalalabad. Dec. Habibullah Kalakani leads uprising in Kohistan.
1929	*Islah* newspaper founded. Jan. 14. Amanullah renounces throne. His brother, Enayatullah, abdicates after three days. Jan. 18. Habibullah Kalakani proclaimed amir. Oct. 14. Kabul seized by Nadir Khan's troops. Oct. 17. Nadir Khan proclaimed king. Nov. 3. Habibullah Kalakani caught and shot.
1930	May. Nadir Shah confirms validity of 1921 and 1923 Anglo-Afghan Agreements and other international treaties. Sept. 20. Nadir Shah confirms statute governing elections of members of National Assembly.
1931	June 24. New treaty of neutrality and mutual non-aggression signed by Afghanistan and Soviet Union. July. Nadir Shah opens National Assembly session. Literary Society founded. Oct. 31. New Constitution confirmed by Nadir Shah.
1932	Medical school founded; other schools closed by Habibullah Kalakani reopened.

1932	May 5. Treaty of friendship signed by Afghanistan and Saudi Arabia. Aug. 24. Statute setting up new administrative divisions issued. Five major and four minor provinces formed. Oct. Uprising begins in Khost. Nov. 8. Ghulam Nabi executed on charge of complicity in Dari Khel Ghilzai revolt.
1933	Road over Shibar Pass to north completed. June 6. Muhammad Aziz, Afghan minister to Germany, assassinated in Berlin. Nov. 8. Nadir Shah assassinated. His son, Muhammad Zahir, becomes king, and brother of Nadir Shah, Muhammad Hashim, prime minister. The cabinet is composed of the following:

Shah Mahmud	Minister of War
Faiz Muhammad	Foreign Affairs
Muhammad Gul Khan	Interior
Fazl Ahmad Mujaddidi	Justice
Mirza Muhd. Yaftali	Finance
Ahmad Ali Sulaiman	Education
Mirza Muhd. Yaftali	Commerce
Allah Nawaz	Public Works
Muhammad Akbar	Health
Rahimullah	PTT

1934	Feb. 16. Zahir Shah orders general election for National Assembly. Mar. State begins to control purchase and export of qaraqul skins. Bank-i Milli founded. Aug. 21. United States formally recognizes Afghanistan. Sept. 25. Afghanistan joins League of Nations.
1935	Apr.-May. W.H. Hornibrook accredited as non-resident American minister to Kabul. May. Turkish arbitrate Afghanistan's boundary dispute with Persia.

1935 June 8. National Assembly session opened by Zahir Shah.
Sept. Mohmand uprising.

1936 Pashtu proclaimed national language of Afghanistan.
Mar. Treaty on commerce and non-interference signed by Afghanistan and Soviet Union.
Mar. 26. Treaty of friendship signed by Afghanistan and United States.

1937 Lufthansa starts weekly service between Berlin and Kabul: first regular air link between Afghanistan and Europe.
Turkish military mission arrives at Kabul.
July 7. Treaty of Saadabad signed by Afghanistan, Iran, Iraq, and Turkey.

1938 May. Afghan Air Force expanded by purchase of planes from Italy and Britain. Officers sent to Britain, Soviet Union, and Italy for training. Arms bought from Britain and Czechoslovakia.

1939 Sept. 3. Beginning of World War II and Afghan armed forces mobilized as precautionary measure.

1940 Jan. 12. All men over 17 obliged to do national service. Special taxes imposed to pay for arms, build radio station. Radio Kabul gets 20 kilowatt medium wave transmitter.
May. Joint stock company founded to handle ginning, spinning, and weaving of cotton. Sugar beet raising to be encouraged.
July 29. Trade agreement by Afghanistan and Soviet Union signed.
Aug. 17. Zahir Shah declares Afghanistan's neutrality in World War II in statement to National Assembly.

1941 July 28. Afghanistan reaffirms its neutrality in World War II.

1941	Oct. 19. Afghanistan agrees to expel German and Italian residents at demand of Britain and the Soviet Union.
1942	Apr. 27. Cornelius van Engert, consul-general in Beirut, named resident U.S. minister to Afghanistan. Nov. 5. Afghanistan reaffirms neutrality in World War II.
1943	May 16. Afghan consulate opened in New York. June 5. Abdul Husain Aziz, first Afghan minister to United States, presents credentials. Dec. 28. Saadabad pact reported automatically renewed after five years.
1944	Mar. 5. Treaty of friendship signed by Afghanistan and China.
1946	Kabul University established by combining already existing faculties, such as medicine and law. Jan. 22. King Zahir orders election of deputies for session of National Assembly to meet April 21. May 9. Muhammad Hashem Khan resigns as prime minister, citing poor health as reason. Mahmud Khan, minister of defense, asked to form new government:

Ali Muhammad	Foreign Affairs
Muhammad Daud	War (Defense)
Ghulam Faruq Osman	Interior
Mir Ata Muhammad	Justice
Mir Mud. Haidar Husaini	Finance
Najibulla Torwayana	Education
Abdul Majid Zabuli	National Economy
Muhammad Kabir	Public Works
Ahmad Ali Sulaiman	Health
Abdullah Malikyar	Information
Ghulam Muhd. Sherzad	Mines
Muhd. Atiq Rafiq	Agriculture
Sayyid Qasim Reshtia	Press

1946
> June 13. Boundary treaty signed with Soviet Union. Soviet Union gets Kushka River water rights.
>
> Nov. 9. United Nations General Assembly approves entry of Afghanistan.
>
> Nov. 19. Abdul Husain Aziz, Afghanista's first representative to United Nations, takes seat.

1947
> Apr. 24. Afghan delegation arrives in Tashkent to start demarcation of Afghan-Soviet border.
>
> June 13. Afghanistan sends note to British and Indian governments saying that inhabitants of region between Afghan-Indian border and Indus River are Afghans and must decide themselves whether to join Afghanistan, Pakistan, or India or become independent.
>
> July 3. Britain replies it holds to Treaty of 1921 by which boundary was recognized by both nations and asks Afghanistan to abstain from any act of intervention   on northwest frontier at time of transfer of powers   to Indian government.
>
> July 10. Afghanistan reiterates views on Pashtuns in second note to Britain.
>
> July 26. Prime Minister Mahmud arrives in London.
>
> Aug. 3. Prime Minister Mahmud arrives in New York City.
>
> Sept. 18. Iran says diversion of Helmand waters in Afghanistan causes crop failures in Sistan.
>
> Sept. 30. Afghanistan casts only vote against admitting Pakistan to United Nations on grounds that Pashtuns have not had fair plebiscite.

1948
> Apr. 1. Muhammad Naim named Afghan ambassador to United States.
>
> Apr. 23. Sir Giles Squire named British ambassador to Afghanistan.
>
> May 6. Faiz Muhammad named Afghan ambassador to Britain.
>
> June 5. United States legation elevated to status of embassy. Ely E. Palmer presents credentials as first U.S. ambassador.

1948   June 16. Pakistan arrests Abdul Ghaffar Khan and
                other *Khuda-i Khetmatgar* leaders. Afghanistan 1948
                begins press and radio campaign for independent
                Pashtunistan.
                Sept. 29. Afghan-Soviet mission completes
                demarcation of border. Agreement signed fixing
                revised boundary.

1949   Mar. 24. Foreign Ministry says statement of Pakistani
                governor general that tribal territory is integral part of
                Pakistan is contrary to pledges of Jinnah in 1948.
                Apr. 2. Charge d'affaires in Karachi recalled after
                Pakistani bombing in Waziristan.
                Apr. 20. Louis G. Dryfus named U.S. ambassador to
                Afghanistan.
                June 4. Afghanistan restricts movement of vehicles
                along border with Pakistan.
                June 12. Pakistani plane bombs Moghalgai (inside
                Afghan territory), killing 23.
                June 20. Alfred Gardener named British ambassador
                to Afghanistan.
                June 30. Afghan National Assembly opens 7th
                Session, known as "Liberal Assembly."
                July 11. Pakistani foreign minister says Pakistan will
                discuss economic cooperation with Afghanistan but
                rejects Afghanistan's claims to tribal territory.
                July 26. Afghan National Assembly repudiates
                treaties with Britain regarding tribal territory.

1950   Jan. 4. Treaty of peace and friendship signed by
                Afghanistan and India.
                Jan. 13. Afghanistan recognizes Chinese People's
                Republic.
                Mar. 8. Zahir Shah begins visit to Europe.
                May 26. Recall of Pakistan embassy staff member for
                violating Afghan laws, requested by Afghanistan.
                July 18. Four-year trade agreement signed by Afghan-
                istan and Soviet Union.
                Oct. 14. New cabinet announced by Prime Minister
                Shah Mahmud:

1950	Muhammad Daud	Defense
	Ali Muhammad	Foreign Affairs
	Abdul Ahad Malikyar	Interior
	Muhammad Nauruz	Finance
	Mir Sayyid Kasim	Justice
	Abdul Majid	Education
	Mir Muhd. Haidar	National Economy
	Ghulam Faruq	Public Health
	Muhammad Akram	Public Works
	Muhd. Naim Ziai	Mines

Oct. Emigration of Afghan Jews to Israel authorized by Afghan government.

1951   Feb. 9. Agreement for technical assistance under Point Four program signed by Afghanistan and United States.
Mar. 19. George R. Merrell appointed U.S. ambassador to Afghanistan.
Apr. 25. Prime Minister Shah Mahmud arrives in United States.
May 28. United Nations assists in drilling exploratory oil wells in north.

1952   Jan. 15. United States suspends economic and technical aid to Afghanistan until bilateral agreement under Mutual Security Act signed.
Sept. 23. Soviet note expressing concern over activities of United Nations technical assistance experts in areas near Afghan-Soviet border rejected by Afghan government.

1953   Jan. 8. United States extends loan of $1.5 million for emergency purchase of wheat and flour from United States.
Mar. 18. Sultan Muhammad named foreign minister to succeed Ali Muhammad who remains deputy prime minister.
Sept. 6. Shah Mahmud resigns as prime minister, citing poor health. Zahir Shah asks cousin, Muham-

1953   mad Daud, present defense and interior minister, to
                           form new cabinet.
                           Sept. 20. Prime Minister Daud announces cabinet
                           members:

Ali Muhammad	Depty. Prime Minister
Muhammad Arif	Defense
Muhammad Naim	Foreign Affairs
Abdul Malik	Actg. Finance
Abdul Hakim	Public Works
Abdul Majid	Education
Ghulam Faruq	Health
Muhammad Yusuf	Mines
Shamsuddin Majruh	Tribal Affaires
Mir Muhd. Yusuf	Agriculture
Salahuddin Saljuqi	Press

                           Oct. 26. Muhammad Hashim, prime minister from
                           1929 to 1946, dies.
                           Nov. United States Export-Import Bank makes loan
                           of $18.5 million for development of Helmand Valley.
                           Dec. 30. Prime Minister Daud describes proposed
                           U.S. military aid to Pakistan as a "grave danger to
                           security and peace of Afghanistan."

1954   Jan. 27. Soviet Union makes loan of $3.5 million for
                           construction of two grain mills and two silos. Soviet
                           technicians to help carry out projects.
                           Feb. 8. Muhammad Atiq Rafiq named Afghan
                           ambassador to Pakistan. Abdul Husain Aziz named
                           Afghan ambassador to India.
                           Apr. 20. Afghanistan becomes member of United
                           Nations Economic Commission for Asia and the Far
                           East.
                           Sept. 17. Foreign Minister Naim arrives in Karachi to
                           continue talks begun in Kabul on improving relations
                           between Afghanistan and Pakistan.
                           Nov. 7. Foreign Minister Naim says Pashtunistan
                           issue is not question of territorial adjustment but of

1954

giving Pashtuns an opportunity to express their wishes.

1955

Jan. 14. Former Prime Minister Shah Mahmud meets Pakistan prime minister.

Jan. 19. Afghanistan and the Chinese People's Republic establish diplomatic relations at embassy level.

Jan. 25. Legislation strengthening armed forces approved by upper house of parliament.

Mar. 2. Fine arts college opened under A. G. Breshna.

Mar. 29. Prime Minister Daud warns Pakistan of "grave consequences" if Pashtun areas of the North-west-Frontier Province are included in unified West Pakistan.

Mar. 30. Demonstrators march on Pakistani embassy and ambassador's residence in Kabul.

Mar. 31. Demonstrators march on Pakistani consulate in Kandahar.

Apr. 1. Demonstrators march on Pakistani consulate in Jalalabad. Afghan consulate in Peshawar attacked.

Apr. 4. Britain, Turkey, and United States protest attack on Pakistan embassy in Kabul.

Apr. 12. Pakistan rejects Afghan replies to its protests, evacuates families of diplomats and nationals, closes Jalalabad consulate.

Apr. 18. Foreign Minister Naim goes to Bandung Conference.

Apr. 29. Col. Gamal Abdul Nasser, prime minister of Egypt, visits Afghanistan. Afghanistan says it is willing to apologize, pay compensation for damage, and make amends for the insult to Pakistani flag if similar amends are made for the insult to its flag.

May 1. Pakistan demands closing of all Afghan consulates in Pakistan, says it will close its consulates in Afghanistan.

May 4. Afghanistan mobilizes troops.

1955

May 13. Afghanistan and Pakistan accept Saudi Arabian offer of mediation.

June 21. Five-year agreement signed with Soviet Union allowing goods of each nation free transit across territory of other.

June 28. Saudi Arabian mediator announces his proposals have been rejected.

July 5. Thin Kuo Yu, ambassador to Afghanistan from Chinese People's Republic, presents credentials.

July 14. Afghanistan tells Pakistan it will be held responsible for any loss or damage to goods held up in transit to Kabul or Quetta.

July 14. Afghanistan becomes member of International Monetary Fund and International Bank.

July 28. State of emergency ended; Afghan army demobilized.

Aug. 14. Postal agreement signed by Afghanistan and Soviet Union.

Aug. 17. India agrees to export four Dakota planes to Afghanistan for internal service.

Sept. 9. Foreign Minister Naim and Pakistan ambassador negotiate agreement to stop hostile propaganda.

Sept. 13. Pakistan flag raised over Pakistani embassy in Kabul.

Sept. 15. Afghan flag raised over consulate in Peshawar.

Oct. 11. Afghan leaders request meeting with Pakistani leaders on condition one-unit act can be postponed. Pakistan says postponement impossible.

Oct. 17. Afghanistan recalls ambassador from Karachi.

Oct. 18. Pakistan recalls ambassador from Kabul.

Nov. 8. Afghanistan protests further restrictions by Pakistan on transit of goods to Afghanistan.

Nov. 20. During five-day session, Loya Jirgah gives its approval to resolutions calling for plebiscite to decide future of Pashtun area disputed with Pakistan, recommending government find means to reestablish balance of power upset by Pakistan's decision to

1955

accept arms from the United States, and refusing to recognize Pashtunistan as part of Pakistan.

Dec. 6. Defense Minister Muhammad Arif resigns.

Dec. 15-18. Soviet Prime Minister Bulganin and Soviet Communist Party Secretary Khrushchev make official visit to Kabul.

Dec. 16. Soviet Union backs Afghanistan in Pashtunistan dispute.

Dec. 18. Three agreements signed by Afghanistan and Soviet Union: a loan of $100 million, a protocol extending 1931 treaty of neutrality and non-aggression, a statement of foreign policy matters. Foreign Minister Naim says agreements do not weaken Afghan determination to remain neutral.

Dec. 21. United States confirms it has offered to mediate Pashtunistan dispute between Afghanistan and Pakistan.

1956

Jan. 8. Afghan consul in Quetta recalled at request of Pakistan. Pakistan military attaché requested to leave Afghanistan.

Jan. 24. Soviet economic delegation begins talks with Afghan government on use of $100 million loan.

The following cabinet changes are announced:

Abdul Hakim	Interior
Sayyid Abdullah	Actg. Justice
Abdul Zahir	Actg. Health
Muhammad Hashim	Depty. Foreign Affs.

Jan. 30. Soviet Union presents Ilyushin 14 to Zahir Shah.

Feb. 18. Technical cooperation agreement signed by Afghanistan and the United States for 1956.

Mar. 1. Technical assistance agreement signed by Afghanistan and the Soviet Union for building of hydroelectric plants, highway through Hindu Kush, air fields, motor repair shop, and reservoirs.

Mar. 6. SEATO powers declare region up to Durand Line is Pakistani territory and within treaty area.

1956

Mar. 21. Afghanistan formally protests SEATO decision to uphold Durand Line as Afghan-Pakistani border.

Mar. 26. United States International Cooperation Administration announces grant of $997,000 to Teachers College of Columbia University to set up English language program for Afghan secondary schools and train English teachers.

Mar. 31. Gift of 15 buses and equipment for 100-bed hospital to Kabul municipality from Soviet Union arrives.

Apr. 4-18. Afghan military mission visits Czechoslovakia.

May 7. Regular air service available to Europe through Karachi, after air agreement signed by Afghanistan and Pakistan.

June 27. Agreement for $14 million to develop Afghan civil aviation signed by Afghanistan and United States.

July 26. Soviet Union agrees to carry out Nangarhar irrigation project.

Aug. 7-11. Pakistan President Iskander Mirza visits Kabul.

Aug. 25. Prime Minister Daud announces military arms agreements with Czechoslovakia and Soviet Union.

Sept. 12. Pan American Airline to supervise pilot and ground crew training of Ariana Afghan Airlines. A $2.5 million contract to be part of $14 million program announced earlier which also includes $5.5 million for Kandahar airport.

Sept. 24. Air service to Iran inaugurated.

Sept. 27. First installment of arms from Soviet Union and Czechoslovakia arrives.

Oct. 17-30. Prime Minister Daud visits Soviet Union.

Oct. 28. Afghan Air Force receives 11 jet planes from Soviet Union.

Nov. 5. Afghans call attention of United Nations to Israeli-British-French attack on Suez as violation of Charter.

1956

Nov. 10. Gen. Muhammad Omar named Afghan ambassador to India.

Nov. 16. Afghanistan offers troops for United Nations police force in Suez.

Nov. 24. Prime Minister Daud discusses Pashtunistan question with Pakistani leaders during visit to Karachi.

1957

Jan. 8. Trade protocol signed with Soviet Union.

Jan. 19-23. Chou En-lai, prime minister of Chinese People's Republic, visits Afghanistan.

Jan. 27. M.C. Gillett named British ambassador to Afghanistan.

Feb. 10. Radio Moscow inaugurates Pashtu program.

Mar. 31-Apr. 3. United States Ambassador to the Middle East James P. Richards visits Kabul. Joint Afghan-U.S. statement says Afghanistan welcomes U.S. President Eisenhower's program of economic aid to the Middle East.

Apr. 14-May 19. Prime Minister Daud visits Turkey, Czechoslovakia, Poland, Austria, and Egypt.

Foreign Minister Naim visits Turkey and Pakistan.

Apr. 27. Agreement for increased aid from Czechoslovakia signed by Afghanistan.

June 8-11. Pakistani Prime Minister Suhrawardy visits Kabul. Afghanistan and Pakistan agree to restore diplomatic relations.

June 30. United States makes loan of $5,750,000 for Helmand Valley Authority and $2,860,000 for building roads and training personnel.

July 17-31. Communique says Soviet Union will aid Afghanistan in prospecting for oil, that a special commission to regulate boundary questions will be created, and that an agreement was reached regarding use of waterways crossing the two countries.

July 28. Trade agreement signed by Afghanistan and Chinese People's Republic.

Aug. 31. Foreign Minister Naim says Afghanistan to receive about $25 million in military assistance under arms agreement signed with Soviet Union in 1956.

1957   Oct. 22. Prime Minister Daud begins visit to Chinese
                       People's Republic.
                       Dec. 21. Andrei Gromyko, Soviet foreign minister,
                       meets Afghan mission in Moscow to negotiate new
                       frontier agreement.

1958   Jan. 8. Soviet Union agrees to survey oil deposits in
                       Afghanistan.
                       Jan. 18. Treaty regulating Afghan-Soviet border
                       signed by Afghanistan and Soviet Union.
                       Feb. 1-6. Zahir Shah visits Pakistan.
                       Feb. 11-27. Zahir Shah arrives in India for two-week
                       visit.
                       June 26. Cultural agreement signed by Afghanistan
                       and United States.
                       Protocol on utilization of Amu Darya signed by
                       Afghanistan and Soviet Union.
                       June 30. Prime Minister Daud begins U.S. visit.
                       United States agrees to help Afghanistan improve
                       highway from Spin Boldak to Kabul and makes
                       $7,708,000 grant to Pakistan to improve its transport
                       lines with Afghanistan.
                       July 17. Agreement on transport of goods by road
                       signed by Afghanistan and Pakistan.
                       Sept. 11. Czechoslovakian firm to install telephone
                       exchange in Kandahar.
                       Oct. 1-5. Marshal Voroshilov, president of the
                       Supreme Soviet of the Soviet Union, visits
                       Afghanistan.
                       Nov. 18. Foreign Investment Law promulgated.
                       Dec. 7. Governmnt puts afs. 2 and afs. 5 coins in
                       circulation.

1959   Jan. 1-6. Foreign Minister Naim visits Soviet Union.
                       Jan. 12. United States agrees to ship 50,000 tons of
                       wheat to Afghanistan.
                       Jan. 20. Henry A. Byroade named U.S. ambassador
                       to Afghanistan.
                       Feb. 5-13. Prime Minister Daud visits India.
                       Mar. 9. Prime Minister Daud calls Baghdad Pact
                       aggravation of international tension.

1959

Apr. 23. Afghanistan and Soviet Union sign protocol on exchange of goods.

May 18-22. Prime Minister Daud visits Soviet Union.

May 28. Afghanistan and Soviet Union sign agreement on building of 750 km. Kandahar-Herat-Kushka Highway.

July 15. Afghan military mission visits Turkey and United Arab Republic.

Aug. 23. Soviet Union agrees to provide assistance to complete Nangarhar irrigation project.

Aug. 31. Afghan women appear unveiled in public at Jashen celebration.

Sept. 5. Foreign Minister Naim begins visit to Chinese People's Republic.

Sept. 14. Indian Prime Minister Nehru visits Afghanistan. Afghan women appear without veils at dinner for Nehru. Henceforth veil no longer obligatory.

Oct. 28. Afghan-Soviet Friendship Society founded.

Dec. 1. Afghanistan and Soviet Union to begin joint survey of Amu Daria for construction of dam to provide electricity and water for irrigation.

Dec. 9. U.S. President Eisenhower spends six hours in Kabul. Assures Afghanistan of continued economic support.

Dec. 21. Police and army units suppress rioting in Kandahar. No official figure of casualties given. Radio Kabul blames element trying to evade payment of overdue taxes. Other reports say religious leaders oppose government measures of allowing women to remove veil and accepting Soviet assistance.

1960

Jan. 19. Afghanistan and Soviet Union sign agreement for construction of irrigation and power project on Kabul River.

Mar. 2-5. Soviet Prime Minister Khrushchev visits Kabul. Inspects Soviet aid projects, signs cultural cooperation agreement, assures Afghanistan support on Pashtun question.

1960

Mar. 6. Pakistan calls Soviet support of Afghanistan on Pashtun question interference in Pakistan's internal affairs.

Mar. 7. Prime Minister Daud says Pakistan is putting out propaganda against reforms in Afghanistan such as the emancipation of women. Says Afghan monarchy has decided to give Afghans complete freedom to choose form of government and to organize political parties.

Apr. 3. Construction work begins on Kandahar-Herat-Kushka Highway.

Apr. 26. Former King Amanullah dies in Switzerland.

May 13. Prime Minister Daud meets Soviet Prime Minister Khrushchev while in Moscow for medical treatment.

May 18. Foreign Minister Naim protests to Pakistan and United States the violation of Afghan airspace by U.S. U-2 plane.

July 15. Soviet prospecting team announces discovery of petroleum and natural gas deposits in northern Afghanistan.

Aug. 4. Czechoslovakia announces 100,000 pounds sterling technical assistance grant to Afghanistan.

Aug. 10. Two-year Afghan-Soviet barter agreement signed.

Aug. 13. Two Pakistani aircraft violate Afghan airspace, land at Kandahar. Pakistan says it was error. Planes and pilots were returned to Pakistan on September 17.

Aug. 18. Darunta Canal opened. Built with Soviet assistance.

Aug. 21-26. Chen Yi, foreign minister of Chinese People's Republic, visits Afghanistan.

Aug. 26. Treaty of friendship and nonaggression signed by Afghanistan and Chinese People's Republic. Commercial and payments agreement renewed.

Dec. 3. Agreements on trade and transit signed with Iran during visit of Iranian Prime Minister to Kabul.

1961

Apr. 5. Prime Minister Daud confers with Soviet Prime Minister Khrushchev in Moscow on return from Rome where Daud underwent a spinal operation. *Pravda* article says Pashtun situation is not a matter of indifference to Soviet Union.

Apr. 18. Cultural agreement signed by Afghanistan and Federal Republic of Germany.

May 19. Afghanistan denies Pakistani reports that Afghan soldiers are taking part in border fighting.

June 6. Prime Minister Daud says Pakistan has savagely bombarded Afghan populations with aid of arms furnished by United States and has confined more than 1,200 leaders of Pashtunistan in Peshawar in past five days. Denies that Afghanistan has pushed Pashtun tribes to revolt.

June 8. King Zahir opens National Assembly session with speech stressing economic development and self-determination for Pashtunistan. Dr. Abdul Zahir named president of the Assembly.

June 15. Pakistan protests acts of provocation and aggression in note to Afghan government.

June 22. Pakistan says nomads will no longer be allowed to enter Pakistan without valid passports, visas, and international health certificates.

June 23. Pakistan says friendlier atmosphere should exist between Afghanistan and Pakistan before any summit meeting held.

June 26. Prime Minister Daud confers with British Foreign Secretary Home and is received by Queen Elizabeth during visit to London.

June 28. Foreign Minister Naim tells news conference that Pashtun self-determination is only problem in Afghan-Pakistani relations that requires negotiation.

July 23. Muhammad Hashem Maiwandwal, ambassador to the United States, expresses his government's grave concern over Pakistan's use of American arms against Pashtun tribes during meeting with President Kennedy.

1961   Aug. 23. Pakistan announces it is closing Afghan
                       consulates and trade offices in Pakistan and is
                       considering prohibiting transit facilities given to
                       Afghanistan.

                       Aug. 30. In reply to Pakistani note of August 23,
                       Afghanistan says it considers decision to close
                       consulates an inimical act and threatens to break
                       diplomatic relations. Prime Minister Daud leaves for
                       Belgrade Conference of Nonaligned Nations.

                       Sept. 3. Afghanistan seals border. Transfer of
                       merchandise suspended between Afghanistan and
                       Pakistan.

                       Sept. 6. Afghanistan breaks diplomatic relations with
                       Pakistan.

                       Sept. 12. Islamic Congress of Jerusalem appeals to
                       Afghanistan and Pakistan to resolve their differences.

                       Sept. 16-20. Foreign Minister Naim visits Soviet
                       Union.

                       Sept. 18. Pakistan accepts Iranian offer of mediation
                       in dispute.

                       Sept. 19. Saudi Arabia agrees to look after Pakistani
                       interest in Afghanistan.

                       Sept. 21. United Arab Republic agrees to look after
                       Afghan interest in Pakistan.

                       Sept. 27. Foreign Minister Naim says Afghanistan
                       will not allow its transit trade to pass through
                       Pakistan unless its trade offices and consulates in
                       Pakistan are reopened.

                       Sept. 29. Pakistani President Ayub Khan rejects
                       possibility of reopening Afghan consulates and trade
                       offices, says they were used for subversive activities.

                       Oct. 4. U.S. President Kennedy sends message to
                       Zahir Shah and Pakistan President Ayub Khan,
                       suggesting the United States might make proposals to
                       help improve relations.

                       Oct. 11. Soviet Army delegation arrives in Kabul for
                       11-day visit.

                       Oct. 16. Afghan-Soviet technical and economic coop-
                       eration agreement signed.

1961   Oct. 24. Soviet deputy minister of Public Works
              arrives in Kabul to inspect projects carried out with
              Soviet assistance.
              Nov. 19. Supplementary transit agreement, providing
              expansion of facilities for Afghan foreign trade,
              signed with Soviet Union.

1962   Jan. 23. Four-year agreement signed with Soviet
              Union to develop Afghan meteorological services.
              Jan. 24. John M. Steeves named U.S. ambassador to
              Afghanistan.
              Jan. 29. Afghanistan opens border with Pakistan for
              eight weeks to allow entry of U.S. aid goods.
              Apr. 14. Prime Minister Daud announces Second
              Five Year Plan. Calls for spending Afs. 31.3 billion
              for economic development.
              Apr. 20. Five-year transit agreement signed by Iran
              and Afghanistan.
              May 6. Pul-i Khumri power station opened. Built
              with Soviet assistance.
              July 1. Pakistan accepts Shah of Iran's offer to
              mediate its dispute with Afghanistan.
              July 12. Afghanistan accepts Shah of Iran's offer to
              mediate its dispute with Pakistan.
              July 27-31. Formal talks held in Kabul between Shah
              of Iran and Zahir Shah and in Rawalpindi between the
              Shah and President Ayub Khan in effort to settle
              Afghan-Pakistani dispute.
              Aug. 6. During meeting in Quetta, Pakistani President
              Ayub Khan suggests a confederation of Afghanistan,
              Iran, and Pakistan.
              Aug. 6-15. Zahir Shah makes visit to Soviet Union.
              Oct. 24. Agreement signed by Afghanistan with
              Federal Republic of Germany for loan of DM 200
              million to finance construction of a power station and
              a sewage network, improve drinking water, and
              develop industry.

1963   Feb. 5. Cabinet approves establishment of nation's
                        second university—Nangarhar University, to be
                        started in Jalalabad with a medical school.
                        Feb. 12. United States decides to ship all its foreign
                        aid goods to Afghanistan via Iran because of the
                        continuing dispute between Afghanistan and
                        Pakistan.
                        Feb. 25. Trade and assistance agreement signed by
                        Afghanistan and Soviet Union.
                        Mar. 10. Resignation of Prime Minister Daud an-
                        nounced.
                        Mar. 14. King Zahir Shah asks Muhammad Yusuf,
                        former minister of mines and industries, to form new
                        government.
                        Prime Minister Yusuf's first cabinet includes:

Ali Ahmad Popal	Deputy Prime Minister and Minister of Education
Abdullah Malikyar	Deputy Prime Minister and Minister of Finance
Sayyid Abdullah	Interior
Gen. Khan Muhammad	Defense
Shamsuddin Majruh	Justice
Gul Pacha Ulfat	Tribal Affairs
Abdul Hai Aziz	Planning
Abdul Rahim	Health
Sayyid Qasim Reshtia	Press

                        Prime Minister Yusuf to serve as own foreign
                        minister.
                        Mar. 28. Constitutional Review Committee named,
                        headed by Minister of Justice Majruh.
                        Apr. 18. At press conference Prime Minister Yusuf
                        says introducing democracy and improving economic
                        conditions are major aims of the government.
                        He estimates that the United States has furnished
                        about $252 million and the Soviet Union an equi-
                        valent amount plus arms.
                        Apr. 26. United States grants loan of $2,635,000 for
                        purchase of a DC-6 and two convairs for Ariana
                        Afghan Airlines. Purchase will bring Ariana's fleet to
                        nine planes.

1963

Apr. 29. Cultural cooperation agreement signed by Afghanistan and Soviet Union.

May 11-15. Indian President Radhakrishnan visits Afghanistan.

May 25. Afghan and Pakistani representatives begin meetings in Tehran to resolve dispute over Pashtunistan.

May 28. Shah of Iran announces that Afghanistan and Pakistan have agreed to reestablish diplomatic and commercial relations.

May 29. Joint Afghan-Pakistani communique confirms reestablishment of relations.

June 14. Prime Minister Yusuf says at press conference that United States was asked to contribute $60 million to Second Plan, has promised $16 million.

July 18. Afghan delegation, led by Dr. Abdul Zahir, president of the National Assembly, visits United States. Dr. Zahir tells press conference that Afghanistan is planning a new form of government with distinct separation of legislative, executive, and judicial powers.

July 20. Afghan consuls reopen consulates in Peshawar and Quetta. Communication reestablished on Afghan-Pakistani border.

July 25. First trucks cross Afghan-Pakistani border in 22 months. Ariana Afghan Airlines resumes flights halted at same time.

Aug. 12. Afghanistan and Pakistan exchange ambassadors.

Aug. 15. Shah of Iran says confederation of Afghanistan, Iran, and Pakistan is good idea but cites many obstacles.

Sept. 2-19. Zahir Shah and Queen Homaira visit United States.

Sept. 6. Afghanistan and Soviet Union sign agreement for construction of atomic reactor in Afghanistan and training of specialists in peaceful use of atomic energy. United States grants $125,000 to Afghanistan for surveys of several industrial projects.

1963

Oct. 12-17. Soviet President Leonid Brezhnev visits Afghanistan; lays cornerstone for new polytechnic institute in Kabul.

Oct. 16. Agreement signed with Soviet Union for technical assistance in extraction and exploitation of natural gas in northern Afghanistan.

Dec. 2. Border treaty signed by Afghanistan and Chinese People's Republic.

1964

Feb. 29. Consultative Constitutional Commission, headed by Abdul Zahir, begins sessions which last through May 14.

May 31. Zahir Shah opens new Aliabad campus of Kabul University, built with United States assistance.

June 29-July 14. Afghan military delegation visits Soviet Union.

July 1. During one-day stay in Kabul, Pakistani President Ayub Khan discusses ways to improve Afghan-Pakistani relations with King Zahir Shah and Prime Minister Yusuf.

July 4-5. Anastas Mikoyan, deputy prime minister of Soviet Union, visits Kabul.

July 8. Dr. Muhammad Anas, ambassador to India, named minister of Education, replacing Ali Ahmad Popal who becomes ambassador to Federal Republic of Germany. Sayyid Qasim Reshtia named minister of finance, replacing Abdullah Malikyar.

July 13. Soviet Union makes loan of $25.2 million for Pul-i Khumri/Mazar-i Sharif/Shiberghan Highway.

July 21. Zahir Shah sets Loya Jirgah session for September 9. Its 450 members will include members of National Assembly, Cabinet, High Judicial Council, and Constitutional Commission, 173 specially elected representatives, and 27 members appointed by King.

July 26. Prime Minister Yusuf cautions students against engaging in political activity.

July 27. Cabinet approves new Constitution.

Aug. 4. Proposed content of new Constitution announced in press. It allows freedom of speech and

1964

press and formation of political parties, calls for two-house parliament and independent judiciary, and bars members of royal family from serving as prime minister, cabinet member, chief justice, or parliament members. King appoints prime minister and commands armed forces.

Sept. 3. Zahir Shah and Soviet Deputy Prime Minister Alexei Kosygin open Kabul-Doshi Highway over Salang Pass. Built with Soviet assistance.

Sept. 6. Delegation returns from demarcating 90 km. border with Chinese People's Republic.

Sept. 9-19. Loya Jirgah debates and approves Constitution after adding that members of royal family cannot become members of political parties nor renounce their titles to participate in politics.

Sept. 21. Federal Republic of Germany loans DM 400,000 for dental and maternity clinics in Afghanistan.

Sept. 22. Reception, given by embassy of Chinese People's Republic, marks founding of Afghan-Chinese Friendship Society.

Oct. 1. Zahir Shah endorses new Constitution. National Assembly dissolved. Transitional government to govern for a year.

Oct. 27. Soviet Union agrees to loan $6.2 million to build polytechnic institute in Kabul.

Oct. 29-Nov. 12. Zahir Shah, accompanied by Queen Homaira, makes first visit to Chinese People's Republic by any Afghan head of state.

Nov. 18. Discovery of first Greek city to be found in Afghanistan announced. French archaeological team says city at confluence of Kokcha and Amu Rivers was abandoned in 130 B.C. and never reoccupied. Site now known as Ai Khanum

Nov. 22-29. Walter Scheel, minister for economic cooperation in Federal Republic of Germany, visits Afghanistan, assures Afghanistan of expanding economic assistance particularly on Paktia regional project and urges protocol to improve atmosphere for foreign investment.

1964   Dec. 19. Muhammad Hashim Maiwandwal,
                ambassador to Pakistan, named minister of Press and
                Information.

1965   Jan. 1. Founding of the PDPA.
                Jan. 12. United States agrees to loan $7.7 million for
                construction of 121 km. Herat-Islam Kala Highway.
                Jan. 18. Soviet Union agrees to loan Afghanistan
                $11.1 million over three years for import of
                consumer goods.
                Jan. 20. United Nations Special Fund makes grant of
                $7,178,200 for soil and water surveys, Hazarajat
                highway survey, telecommunication and teacher
                training schools.
                Jan. 22. Water supply network to serve 110,000 of
                Kabul's residents completed with Japanese
                assistance.
                Feb. 15. Protocol on exchange of goods and prices for
                1965 signed by Afghanistan and Soviet Union.
                Increase of 20 % expected in reciprocal goods de-
                liveries.
                Feb. 18-28. Prime Minister Yusuf holds talks with
                Indian Prime Minister Shastri during visit to India.
                Feb. 24. Gen. Muhammad Aref named Afghan
                ambassador to Soviet Union.
                U.S. Ambassador-at Large Averell Harriman meets
                Zahir Shah and Prime Minister Yusuf during stop in
                Kabul.
                Mar. 2. New five-year trade transit agreement,
                replacing 1958 agreement, signed by Afghanistan and
                Pakistan.
                Mar. 11. Zahir Shah and Soviet Prime Minister
                Dimitri Polyansky open Nangarhar irrigation and
                power project, built with Soviet assistance.
                Mar. 22-25. Chen Yi, deputy prime minister and
                foreign minister of Chinese People's Republic, con-
                fers with Zahir Shah and Prime Minister Yusuf during
                a three-day visit. Boundary protocol, cultural
                agreement, and economic and technical cooperation
                agreement signed.

1965

Apr. 5. High schools start requiring entrance exams to give all students equal chance, avoid overcrowding, and keep educational standards high.

Apr. 18-20. Cultural agreement signed by Afghanistan and Britain during visit of Lord Walston, British parliamentary under secretary of state for foreign affairs.

Apr. 18. World Bank agrees to finance foreign exchange cost of $350,000 to survey Kunduz and Khanabad basins for possible irrigation and agriculture projects.

Apr. 21-30. Prime Minister Yusuf makes official visit to Soviet Union. Gets assurance of Soviet help with Third Plan.

Apr. 28. Kunduz airport completed. Built with U.S. assistance.

May 11. New electoral law, providing for universal, direct vote by secret ballot for all Afghan men and women over 20, goes into effect.

May 23. Ariana Airlines begins weekly flight to Tashkent, its first to Soviet Union.

June 5. Mazar-i Sharif airport completed. Built with U.S. assistance.

June 6. First of three regional appellate courts established in Kabul. Others to be in Mazar-i-Sharif and Kandahar.

June 22. Jangalak smelts its first iron ore mined in Afghanistan.

July 1. Land survey and statistics law goes into effect.

July 7. King Zahir Shah announces plan to rebuild old city of Kabul.

July 15. United States agrees to help increase wheat production and provide up to 150,000 tons of wheat; make $2 million credit for machinery purchase available; make long-term loan to build Kajakai power plant; provide credits up to $800,000 to import diesel generators; increase project planning in Helmand Valley to 20,000 acres a year, and make $5 million long-term loan to construction unit of Helmand Valley Authority.

1965   July 18. Prime Minister Yusuf lays cornerstone for
Jangalak technicum for 700 students being built with
Soviet assistance.

July 20. Cadastral survey of Kabul begins. Direct
telephone link between Kabul, Rawalpindi, and
Lahore inaugurated.

July 24. Soviet Union agrees to build 97 km. pipeline
from Shiberghan gas fields to Soviet border and 88
km. line from fields to fertilizer and power plants in
Balkh Province.

July 28. Soviet Union agrees to extend payment on
loans to Afghanistan by 30 years and provide teachers
for Polytechnic Institute.

Aug. 3-14. Zahir Shah and Queen Homaira visit
Soviet Union. Afghanistan and Soviet Union agree to
extend treaty on neutrality and mutual nonaggression
of 1931 for ten years.

Aug. 8. First census of Kabul finds population of
435,203.

Aug. 26-Sept. 28. Election of parliament members
held. Over 1,000 run for 216 seats in Wolesi Jirgah
(House of the People) and 100 for 28 elective seats in
Meshrano Jirgah (House of Elders). All run as
independents.

Sept. 9. New press law goes into effect allowing
Afghan citizens freedom of expression while
safeguarding the fundamental values of Islam and the
principles embodied in the Constitution.

Oct. 12. Dr. Abdul Zahir elected president of Wolesi
Jirgah. Zahir Shah names Abdul Hadi Dawai
president of Meshrano Jirgah.

Oct. 13. Zahir Shah's appointees to Meshrano Jirgah
announced.

Prime Minister Yusuf presents report of interim
government and offers resignation. King asks him to
form new government.

Oct. 14. Parliament officially opened by King Zahir
Shah.

1965

Oct. 19. Wolesi Jirgah decides proposed cabinet members should submit lists of property they hold before vote of confidence is taken.

Oct. 24. Prime Minister Yusuf's presentation of his cabinet to Wolesi Jirgah postponed when spectators crowd into deputies' seats and refuse to leave.

Oct. 25. Wolesi Jirgah decides 191-6 to hold vote of confidence in secret session.

Student demonstrations are dispersed by force by police and army; three persons are killed. Schools are closed and public meetings banned.

Wolesi Jirgah approves Prime Minister Yusuf's cabinet. Vote reported to be 198 in favor and 15 abstaining. Ministers are:

Sayyid Shamsuddin Majruh	Deputy Prime Minister and Minister of Foreign Affairs
Gen. Khan Muhammad	Defense
Muhd. Husain Masa	Interior
Abdullah Yaftali	Finance
Muhammad Anas	Education
Mir Muhd. Akbar Reza	Agriculture
Ghulam Dastagir Azizi	Public Works
Muhd. Hashem Waiwandwal	Press, Information
Nur Ali	Commerce
Abdul Samad Hamid	Planning
Abdul Majid	Health
Muhammad Haidar	Communications

Justice, Mines and Industries, and Tribal Affairs left to be filled later.

Oct. 27. King Zahir Shah receives cabinet.

Oct. 29. In wake of demonstrations, Prime Minister Yusuf resigns, giving poor health as reason. King Zahir Shah asks Muhammad Hashem Maiwandwal to form cabinet.

Nov. 2. Prime Minister Maiwandwal presents cabinet to Wolesi Jirgah and gets vote of confidence 190 to seven with three abstaining and 16 absent. Entire

1965   proceedings broadcast over Radio Afghanistan. Cabinet members are:

Nur Ahmad Etemadi	Foreign Affairs
Gen. Khan Muhammad	Defense
Abdul Satar Shalizi	Interior
Abdullah Yaftali	Finance
Abdul Hakim Tabibi	Justice
Mir Muhd. Akbar Reza	Agriculture
Ahmadullah	Public Works
Nur Ali	Commerce
Muhd. Osman Anwari	Health
Abdul Samad Salim	Communications

Maiwandwal is to act as his own minister of Education and Press and Information. Planning and Tribal
Affairs to be filled later.

Nov. 4. Prime Minister Maiwandwal makes
unexpected appearance at condolence ceremony on
Kabul University campus for those killed during Oct.
25 demonstrations. Brings king's message of sympathy and promises to consider student demands.
Toryalai Etemadi elected president of Kabul University by university senate.
Nov. 6. Ministry of Interior announces three people
died during demonstrations on October 25.
Nov. 7. List of property belonging to ministers
debated and accepted by Wolesi Jirgah members.
Nov. 27. Kabul University senate refuses to accept
student demands for a lower passing grade and
postponement of exams.
Dec. 1. Prime Minister Maiwandwal announces five
cabinet appointments:

Muhd. Osman Anwari	Education
Mis Kubra Nurzai	Health
Muhd. Osman Sidqi	Press, Information
Abdul Hakim Ziayi	Planning
Muhammad Khalid Roshan	Tribal Affairs

1965

Dec. 13. Kabul University's college of science closed because of continued disturbances.

Dec. 14. Ministry of Interior forbids public gatherings after two days of demonstrations.

1966

Jan. 1-2. President Ayub Khan of Pakistan makes stop in Kabul on way to Tashkent talks.

Jan. 14-15. Soviet Prime Minister Alexei Kosygin stops in Kabul for talks on way from Delhi to Moscow.

Jan. 17. Kabul University's college of education graduates its first 58 students.

Jan. 31. *Wahdat* publishes first edition. The Dari and Pashtu weekly edited by Khal Muhammad Khasta is the first privately owned newspaper published in Kabul in 14 years.

Feb. 1-10. Prime Minister Maiwandwal visits Soviet Union.

Feb. 10. Ghulam Muhammad Sulaiman named Afghan ambassador to Pakistan.

Feb. 11. *Payam-i Imruz*, a twice weekly newspaper published by Ghulam Nabi Khater, first issued.

Feb. 15. Dr. Muhammad Asif Sohail named Afghan ambassador to Chinese People's Republic.

Feb. 23. Nasir Zia named Afghan ambassador to India.

Mar. 2. New Kabul University constitution approved by cabinet.

Mar. 15. Khalilullah Khalili named Afghan ambassador to Saudi Arabia.

Apr. 4-9. Liu Shao-Chi, president of Chinese People's Republic, makes official visit to Kabul.

Apr. 5. *Afghan Millat*, a Pashtu newspaper owned by Ghulam Muhammad Farhad, starts publication.

Apr. 11. *Khalq*, a Pashtu and Dari newspaper published by Nur Muhammad Taraki, puts out first issue.

Apr. 13. Wolesi Jirgah begins consideration of political parties draft law.

1966

May 4. After debate on *Khalq*, Meshrano Jirgah passes resolution saying any publication against values of Islam should be halted.

May 22. Wolesi Jirgah passes resolution, asking government to take action against *Khalq* for not following values of constitution.

May 23. Government bans distribution of Khalq under Art. 48 of the press law.

May 25. *Payam-i Imruz* newspaper stops publication on instructions from Ministry of Information and Culture, which says that according to press law, it cannot publish again until it has an editor. Previous editor had resigned.

May 31. Sayyid Shamsuddin Majruh named Afghan ambassador to UAR.

June 20. Prime Minister Maiwandwal names Foreign Minister Etemadi and Interior Minister Shalizi first and second deputy ministers respectively.

July 19. Wolesi Jirgah approves political parties draft law.

Aug. 17. Prime Minister Maiwandwal appoints Muhammad Haidar minister of Justice and Abdul Karim Hakimi minister of Communications.

Aug. 20. Supreme judiciary committee set up as foundation of future supreme court.

Aug. 24. Prime Minister Maiwandwal gives speech on eve of *Jashen* on Radio Afghanistan in which he explains his philosophy of progressive democracy.

Aug. 28. Former Prime Minister Yusuf named Afghan ambassador to the Federal Republic of Germany.

Sept. 20. Abdul Rahman Pazhwak, Afghan representative to the United Nations, elected president of the UN general assembly.

1967

Jan. 25. Prime Minister Maiwandwal shuffles cabinet, names Abdullah Yaftali minister without portfolio, Abdul Karim Hakimi minister of Finance, and Muhammad Husain Masa minister of Interior.

1967

Feb. 12. Abdullah Malikyar named Afghan ambassador to United States. Abdul Majid named Afghan ambassador to Britain.

Mar. 25-Apr. 9. Prime Minister Maiwandwal visits United States.

Apr. 2. Abdul Hakim Tabibi named ambassador to Japan.

May 10. Protocol on export of natural gas signed by Afghanistan and Soviet Union. Afghanistan expected to earn over $320 million in next 18 years from export of gas which is to reach three bil. cu.m. a year by 1971.

May 30-June 2. Nikolai Podgorny, chairman of Presidium of Supreme Soviet of Soviet Union, visits Afghanistan.

June 13. Abdul Rauf Benawa named minister of Information and Culture. Muhammad Osman Sidqi named secretary general in Foreign Ministry.

July 27. Prime Minister Maiwandwal appoints Abdullah Yaftali minister of Planning, Dr. Muhammad Anas minister without portfolio, and Muhammad Ehsan Rostamel minister of Justice.

Aug. 20. Direct telephone link between Kabul and Herat completed.

Oct. 11. Prime Minister Maiwandwal resigns because of poor health. King Zahir Shah names Abdullah Yaftali acting prime minister.

Oct. 15. Zahir Shah inaugurates supreme court.

Nov. 1. Zahir Shah asks Nur Ahmad Etemadi to form new government.

Nov. 13. Etemadi submits cabinet to Wolesi Jirgah:

Ali Ahmad Popal	First Depty. P.M. and Education
Abdullah Yaftali	Second Depty. P.M.
Gen. Khan Muhammad	Defense
Muhd. Omar Wardak	Interior
Muhammad Asghar	Justice
Muhd. Anwar Ziayi	Finance
Nur Ali	Commerce

1967

Muhd. Husain Masa	Public Works
Muhammad Anas	Information
Muhd. Azim Gran	Communications
Mis Kubra Nurzai	Health
Abdul Samad Salim	Mines, Industries
Mir Muhd. Akbar Reza	Agriculture
Abdul Samad Hamid	Planning
Abdul Wahid Sorabi	Without Portfolio
Said Masud Pohanyar	Tribal Affairs

Nov. 15. Prime Minister Etemadi gets vote of confidence 173 to seven with six abstentions after three-day debate in which 183 deputies spoke. Entire proceedings broadcast over radio. Etemadi pledges to work against bribery and corruption.

1968

Jan 25. Education commission organized to decide national education policy for Afghanistan.
Jan. 31. Soviet Prime Minister Kosygin stops in Kabul to discuss economic questions.
Feb. 4. Chakhansur Province renamed Nimruz, name given to area in Pahlavi literature.
Feb. 20. Afghan Polytechnic Institute, built with Soviet assistance, completes first year of instruction. Has 224 students in first class.
Apr. 21. Indian Airlines introduces weekly jet airline service between Delhi and Kabul.
Apr. 22. Shiberghan gas pipelines officially opened by Second Deputy Prime Minister Yaftali and Skachkov, president of Soviet Union's council of ministers committee of external affairs.

1969

May 25. U.S. Secretary of State Rogers pays a brief visit to Kabul for talks with government leaders.
June 10. Indian Prime Minister Indira Gandhi ends a five day official visit.
June 22. Afghan government ordered closing of all primary and secondary schools in Kabul, after a wave

1969   of student unrest and a student boycott of the Kabul University.

July 17. A Soviet military delegation led by Marshal of the Soviet Union Ivan Bagramyan begins a visit.

Nov. 17. New cabinet announced as follows:

Nur Ahmad Etemadi	Prime Minister
Abdullah Yaftali	First Deputy
Abdul Qayyum	Second Deputy and Education
Khan Muhammad	Defense
Muhd. Bashir Lodin	Interior
Abdul Wahid Sorabi	Planning
Abdul Satar Sirat	Justice
Muhd. Akbar Omar	Commerce
Muhammad Aman	Finance
Mahmud Habibi	Information
Muhd. Azim Gran	Communication
Ibrahim Majid Siraj	Health
Amanullah Mansuri	Mines, Industries
Abdul Hakim	Agriculture

Ministers without portfolio are Shafiqa Ziayi and Ghulam Ali Ayin.

Dec. 25. A Soviet military delegation led by Defense Minister Grechko arrives for an official visit.

1970   Jan. 21. The USSR signs a protocol for the export of 2.5 billion cubic meters of Afghan natural gas in 1970.

Jan. 26. Defense Minister Khan Mohammed begins an official visit to the U.S.

1971   May 17. It announced that the government of Premier Nur Ahmad Etemadi has resigned. King Zahir Shah accepts the resignation and requests the premier stay in office until a new government can be formed.

June 8. Former ambassador to Italy, Abdul Zahir, is asked to form a new Cabinet:

1971	Dr. Abdul Zahir	Prime Minister
	Dr. Abdul Samad Hamid	First Deputy
	Gen. Khan Muhammad	Defense
	Muhammad Musa Shafiq	Foreign Affairs
	Amanullah Mansuri	Interior
	Muhd. Anwar Arghandiwal	Justice
	Dr. Ghulam Haidar Dawar	Finance
	Hamidullah Enayat Siraj	Education
	Muhd. Aref Ghausi	Commerce
	Khwazak Khan	Public Works
	Muhd. Ibrahim Abbasi	Information
	Eng. Nasratullah Malikyar	Communications
	Dr. Ibrahim Majid Siraj	Health
	Eng. Muhd. Yaqub Lali	Mines, Industries
	Abdul Hakim	Agric. & Irrigation
	Dr. Abdul Wahid Sorabi	Planning
	Mrs. Shafiqa Ziayee	Without Portfolio
	Dr. Abdul Wakil	Without Portfolio
	Abdul Satar Sirat	Without Portfolio
	Dr. Abdul Samad Hamid	Tribal Affairs

June 13. Muhammad Zahir Shah ends a ten-day visit to the USSR with a joint communique reaffirming their mutual allegiance to the principles of peaceful coexistence.

July 26. The National Assembly gives Abdul Zahir a vote of confidence after a 17-day debate, and he takes office along with his Cabinet.

Aug. 22. Afghanistan is suffering the worst drought in its recorded history.

1972   Jan. 3. The USSR signs an agreement for expanding natural gas refining and collection centers in the north.

Jan. 11. Pakistan President Zulfikar Ali Bhutto arrives in Kabul for official talks.

Apr. 3. Indian Foreign Affairs Minister Swaran Singh leaves after a three-day visit and talks on economic aid and cooperation.

1972

Apr. 15. It is announced that the Minister of Education Enayat Siraj has resigned for "health reasons."

May 16. Kabul Radio broadcasts a demand for Pashtunistan's independence from Pakistan.

July 21. U.S. special envoy John Connally tells the government that the U.S. can not make any further commitment of aid.

Aug. 25. A natural gas discovery at Jarquduq is estimated to be the second largest in the country.

Sept. 25. Premier Abdul Zahir tenders his resignation, but it is refused by the King.

Dec. 5. Muhammad Zahir Shah accepts the resignation of Premier Abdul Zahir who agrees to remain in office until a new premier can be appointed.

Dec. 9. Musa Shafiq was appointed to form a new government.

Dec. 11. A new cabinet is announced with Muhammad Musa Shafiq premier and foreign affairs minister. Members of cabinet includes the following:

Gen. Khan Muhammad	Defense
Nematullah Pazhwak	Interior
Muhammad Khan Jalalar	Finance
Khwazak Zalmai	Health
Sabahuddin Kushkaki	Information
Nasratullah Malikyar	Communications
Ghulam Dastagir Azizi	Mines, Industries
Abdul Wakil	Agriculture
Abdul Wahid Sorabi	Planning

1973

Jan. 17. It is announced that diplomatic relations will be established with East Germany.

Mar. 13. Iranian Prime Minister Amir Abbas Hoveyda and Prime Minister Muhammad Musa Shafiq of Afghanistan sign a formal settlement of the Helmand River dispute.

Apr. 21. A royal decree is issued setting general parliamentary election dates.

May 11. The border with Pakistan is ordered closed for two weeks for "administrative reasons."

1973   July 8. Zahir Shah arrives in Italy for a vacation.
                      July 17. **Sardar Muhammad Daud deposes his**
                      cousin, the king, and proclaimes a republic.
                      July 18. Muhammad Daud proclaimed president and
                      Defense minister.
                      July 19. The Soviet Union and India extend
                      diplomatic recognition of the new government.
                      July 27. President Daud abrogates the Constitution of
                      1964 and dissolves Parliament.
                      Aug. 2. New cabinet announced with Muhammad
                      Daud holding the portfolios of premier, Defense, and
                      Foreign Affairs:

Muhd. Hasan Sharq	Deputy Premier
Abdul Majid	Justice
Abdulillah	Finance
Faiz Muhammad	Interior
Nematullah Pazhwak	Education
Pacha Gul	Frontier Affairs
Abdul Qayyum	Mines, Industries
Abdul Hamid	Communications
Nazar Muhd. Sikandar	Health
Abdul Rahim Nawin	Information
Ghulam Jilani Bakhtari	Agriculture

                      Aug. 24. Deposed King, Muhammad Zahir,
                      announces his abdication.
                      Sept. 23. It is announced that a plot to overthrow the
                      government was discovered and a number of senior
                      army officers arrested. Pakistan is accused of sup-
                      porting the group.
                      Oct. 30. Indian Foreign Minister Swaran Singh
                      arrives for an official visit.

1974   Apr. 5. It is reported that a new trade and payments
                      agreement between Afghanistan and the Soviet Union
                      was concluded after a visit to Moscow by Minister of
                      Trade Muhammad Khan Jalallar.
                      July 7. A trade protocol is signed with India.

1974

July 19. Soviet assistance in the development of the Jarquduq natural gas field and in oil exploration is reported.

July 24. Iran and Afghanistan signs a protocol for cooperation in a large scale development program in the "joint region of the Helmand River."

Nov. 1. U.S. Secretary of State Henry Kissinger arrives and meets with Premier Muhammad Daud.

1975

Feb. 26. The government issues a statement protesting the U.S. decision to lift the arms ban on Pakistan.

Mar. 13. President Muhammad Daud concludes an official visit to India.

May 1. The government announces the nationalization of all banks and banking affairs.

July 11. Deputy Foreign Minister Wahid Abdallah flew to Saudi Arabia to attend the Islamic Foreign Ministers Conference.

July 28. Afghan security forces capture a "terrorist" group in Panjshir that was allegedly armed by Pakistan.

Oct. 17. Iran signs an agreement to provide aid and technical assistance to construct a railroad system and Kabul airport and to build a meat processing plant.

Nov. 21. New cabinet was appointed in October:

Muhammad Daud	President, Premier, Defense, and Foreign Affairs
Muhd. Hasan Sharq	First Deputy Premier
Sayyid Abdullah	Second Deputy Premier and Finance Minister
Abdul Qadir	Interior
Abdul Tawab Asefi	Mines, Industries
Azizullah Wasefi	Agriculture
Abdul Karim Atayi	Communications
Ali Ahmad Kurram	Planning
Nazar Muhd. Sikandar	Health
Abdul Majid	Justice
Abdul Rahim Nawin	Information

Faiz Muhammad   Frontier Affairs

Dec. 2. Afghanistan denies Pakistani charges that it has mobilized troops along its border with Pakistan.

1976

Jan. 2. An agreement is concluded with the Soviet Union for the development of the Jarquduq gas fields and the provision of gas production and processing facilities.

Apr. 23. The League of Red Cross Societies says that about 100,000 people in Afghanistan have been left homeless by earthquakes, torrential rains, and floods.

June 7. Pakistani President Zulfikar Ali Bhutto begins a visit to Afghanistan.

June 8. Pakistani President Bhutto meets with President Muhammad Daud.

July 4. Indian Premier Indira Gandhi arrives in Kabul for a three-day visit.

Aug. 8. U.S. Secretary of State Henry Kissinger meets with President Daud in Kabul.

Dec. 9. According to reports, more than 50 people have been arrested and accused of a plot to overthrow the government.

1977

Jan. 30. President Muhammad Daud convenes the Loyah Jirgah, or Grand Assembly, to approve the draft of a new constitution.

Feb. 14. The new constitution is approved by the Loyah Jirgah.

Feb. 15. Muhammad Daud is sworn in, and the Loyal Jirgah is dissolved.

Feb. 24. President Muhammad Daud promulgates a new constitution.

Feb. 26. President Daud disbands the cabinet and the central revolutionary committee.

Mar. 13. The Afghan government announces formation of new cabinet:

Ghulam Haidar Rasuli   Defense

1977		
	Sayyid Abdullah	Finance
	Abdul Majid	Without Portfolio
	Wafiyullah Sami'i	Justice
	Abdul Qadir	Interior
	Ghulam Siddiq Muhibi	Higher Education
	Ibrahim Majid Siraj	Education
	Muhd. Khan Jalalar	Commerce
	Azizullah Wasefi	Agriculture
	Abdul Tawab Asefi	Mines, Industries
	Ghausuddin Fayeq	Public Works
	Abdul Rahim Navin	Information
	Ali Ahmad Kurram	Planning
	Abdul Karim Atayi	Communications
	Abdullah Omar	Health
	Juma Muhd. Muhammadi	Water & Power
	Abdul Qayyum	Border Affairs
	Wahid Abdullah	Deputy Minister of Foreign Affairs

Mar. 23. A Soviet trade delegation begins a trip to Afghanistan to hold talks on bilateral trade.

Mar. 29. An agreement reached in Kabul to resume air links between Pakistan and Afghanistan.

June 22. Pakistani Premier Zulfikar Ali Bhutto arrives in Kabul for talks with President Muhammad Daud.

July 29. Afghanistan and the USSR concludes a six-year consumer goods agreement in Kabul.

Oct. 11. Pakistani Chief Martial Law Administrator Muhammad Zia-ul-Haq meets with President Daud at the Presidential Palace.

Nov. 7. President Daud appoints the following to the central council: Abdul Majid, State; Ghulam Haidar Rasuli, Defense; Sayyid Abdullah, Finance; and Abdul Qayyum, Border Affairs.

Nov. 16. Minister of Planning Ali Ahmad Khurram is assassinated in Kabul.

1978   Feb. 19. Sayyid Abdulillah is appointed vice president.

1978

Feb. 21. President Muhammad Daud leaves Kabul for Belgrade on an official visit to Yugoslavia.

Feb. 24. A trial of 25 people accused of plotting to assassinate President Daud begins in Kabul.

Mar. 4. President Daud meets with Indian Premier Morarji Desai in New Delhi.

Apr. 17. Mir Akbar Khaibar, one of the founders of the PDPA, is assassinated in Kabul.

Apr. 20. Thousands turn Khaibar's funeral into an anti-government demonstration.

Apr. 26. President Daud has PDPA leaders arrested.

Apr. 27. **Communist Coup**. Members of the PDPA gains power in a coup led by insurgents in the armed forces. The military revolutionary council formes a new government.

Apr. 29. The government radio reports that Defense Minister Ghulam Haidar Rasuli, Interior Minister Abdul Qadir Nuristani, and Vice President Sayyid Abdulillah have been killed in the coup along with President Daud and his brother Muhammad Naim.

Apr. 30. A "Revolutionary Council" is proclaimed. Nur Muhammad Taraki is named president and premier of the Democratic Republic of Afghanistan. The Revolutionary Council selects the following leading ministers:

Babrak Karmal	Deputy Premier
Hafizullah Amin	Deputy Premier and Foreign Minister
Muhd. Aslam Watanjar	Deputy Premier and Communications
Abdul Qadir	National Defense
Shah Wali	Health
Nur Ahmad Nur	Interior
Dastagir Panjshiri	Education
Sultan Ali Keshtmand	Planning
Sulaiman Layeq	Radio, Television
Saleh Muhd. Zirai	Agriculture
Abdul Karim Misaq	Finance
M. Hasan Bareq-Shafi'i	Information, Culture

1978

Abdul Hakim Shara'i	Justice, Attorney Gen.
Anahita Ratebzad	Social Affairs
Abdul Quddus Ghorbandi	Commerce
Muhd. Ismail Danesh	Mines, Industries
Muhammad Rafi'i	Public Works
Muhd. Mansur Hashimi	Water & Power
Mahmud Suma	Higher Education
Nizamuddin Tahzib	Tribal Affairs

May 1. Shah Muhammad Dost and Abdul Hadi Mokamel are named deputy ministers of Foreign Affairs.

May 6. Premier Taraki says Afghanistan is "nonaligned and independent."

May 18. Foreign Minister Hafizullah Amin leaves Kabul for Havana for a meeting of nonaligned countries.

May-June. First *mujahedin* camp set up in Pakistan.

July 5. Kabul Radio says that Interior Minister Nur Ahmad Nur has been named ambassador to Washington and that Vice President and Deputy Premier Babrak Karmal has been named ambassador to Czechoslovakia.

Aug. 17. The central committee of the Peoples Democratic Party decides that President of the Revolutionary Council Nur Muhammad Taraki will assume the duties of minister of Defense.

Aug. 18. Kabul Radio announces that a plot to overthrow the government has been foiled and Defense Minister Abdul Qadir has been arrested for his role in the plot.

Aug. 23. The politburo of the PDPA orders the arrest of Planning Minister Sultan Ali Keshtmand and Public Works Minister Muhammad Rafi'i for their parts in the conspiracy.

Aug. 28. The following appointments were announced:

Dastagir Panjshiri	Public Works
Abdul Rashid Jalili	Education
Sahibjan Sahrayi	Border Affairs

1978   Sept. 9. Pakistani Chief Martial Law Administrator
                              Muhammad Zia-ul-Haq meets with Chairman of the
                              Revolutionary Council Taraki at Paghman, near
                              Kabul.
                              Sept. 17. The government announces it is breaking
                              diplomatic relations with South Korea.
                              Sept. 19. Indian External Affairs Minister Anal Bihari
                              Vajpayee meets with Taraki in Kabul.
                              Sept. 22. Taraki dismisses six ambassadors who had
                              been appointed in July. All were members of the
                              Parcham section of the PDPA.
                              Oct. 19. Afghanistan adopts a red flag as its new
                              national emblem.
                              Dec. 3. President Nur Muhammad Taraki arrives in
                              Moscow for talks with Soviet leaders.
                              Dec. 5. Afghanistan and the Soviet Union signs a 20-
                              year treaty of friendship and cooperation in Moscow.

1979   Jan. 28. Guerrillas fight government troops in the
                              eastern provinces bordering Pakistan.
                              Feb. 2. It is reported that Afghan dissidents are
                              undergoing guerilla training at a Pakistan military
                              base north of Peshawar.
                              Feb. 14. U.S. Ambassador to Afghanistan Adolph
                              Dubs is taken hostage by terrorists in Kabul. Afghan
                              forces rush the building in which he is held, and he is
                              slain.
                              The U.S. protest the use of force by the Afghan
                              government to free the U.S. ambassador.
                              Feb. 19. Foreign Minister Hafizullah Amin rejects a
                              U.S. protest over the incident leading to the slaying of
                              the U.S. ambassador as "completely baseless."
                              Feb. 22. U.S. President Jimmy Carter orders U.S. aid
                              to Afghanistan to be reduced.
                              Mar. 16. Revolt and uprising in Herat with the
                              participation of the military garrison. Thousands are
                              said to have been killed in recapture of town by
                              government troops.
                              Mar. 23. A U.S. spokesman says the U.S. expects
                              that the "principle of noninterference" in Afghanistan

1979   will be respected by all parties in the area "including
                        the Soviet Union."
                        Mar. 27. Foreign Minister Hafizullah Amin is named
                        premier.
                        Apr. 1. The new Afghan government is announced:
                        Hafizullah Amin, premier and foreign affairs; Shah
                        Wali, deputy premier. Others included:

Saleh Muhd. Zirai	Agriculture
Dastagir Panjshiri	Public Works
Abdul Karim Misaq	Finance
Mahmud Suma	Higher Education
Aslam Watanjar	Defense
Abdul Rashid Jalili	Education
Abdul Hakim Shara'i	Justice, Attorney Gen.
Mahmud Hashemi	Water and Power
Khial M. Katawazi	Information, Culture
Muhd. Ismail Danesh	Mines, Industries
Abdul Quddus Ghorbandi	Commerce
Hasan Bareq-Shafi'i	Transport
Sahibjan Sahra'i	Frontier Affairs

Apr. 2. Washington denies Soviet charges that
America is arming Afghan guerrillas.
Apr. 8. Soviet Vice Minister of Defense Aleksey
Yepishev meets with President Nur Muhammad
Taraki in Kabul.
Apr. 30. Taraki says Pakistani President Muhammad
Zia-ul-Haq was "involved" with attacks on border
positions in eastern Afghanistan.
June 13. Afghanistan accuses Pakistan of involvement
in a rebellion against the Afghan government.
June 23. Kabul Radio reports that anti-government
demonstrators (Hazaras) in Kabul had been
"annihilated and arrested" during the day.
June. Soviet special forces occupy Bagram air force
base.
July. 28. The cabinet is reshuffled: Hafizullah Amin,
premier and vice president of the Revolutionary
Council; Shah Wali deputy prime and Foreign Affairs
minister. Others included:

1979

Muhammad Gulabzoi	PTT
Muhd. Aslam Watanjar	Interior
Abdul Rashid Jalili	Agriculture
Muhd. Siddiq Alemyar	Planning
Saleh Muhd. Zirai	Health
Muhd. Salim Masudi	Education
Abdul Quddus Ghorbandi	Commerce
Muhd. Hasan Bareq-Shafi'i	Transport
Dastagir Panjshiri	Public Works
Abdul Hakim Shara'i	Justice
Khial Muhd. Katawazi	Information, Culture
Sherjan Mazduryar	Border Affairs
Mahmud Suma	Higher Education
Muhd. Ismail Danesh	Mines, Industries
Abdul Karim Misaq	Finance
Mansur Hashemi	Water, Electricity

Aug. 5. Heavy fighting breaks out in Kabul between loyal troops and a rebellious army unit at the Bala Hissar Fort. The rebellion is crushed and a curfew imposed on the city.

Aug. 19. Premier Hafizullah Amin says there are "no more than 1,600 Soviet advisers" in Afghanistan.

Sept. 15. Kabul radio reports that Interior Minister Aslam Watanjar and Frontier Affairs Minister Sherjan Mazduryar have been removed from their posts.

It is reported that gunfire and explosions had occurred in Kabul following the announcement of the cabinet dismissals.

Sept. 16. Kabul Radio reports that President Taraki had asked to be relieved of his government positions because of "bad health and nervous weakness."

Premier Amin assumes the additional post of president. Other appointments include:

Faqir Muhd. Faqir	Interior
Sahibjan Sahra'i	Frontier Affairs

Sept. 23. President Amin says that former President Taraki is "alive but definitely sick."

1979   Oct. 8. Kabul announces that President Amin has
                        commuted death sentences of former Defense
                        Minister Abdul Qadir and former Planning Minister
                        Sultan Ali Keshtmand to 15 years imprisonment.
                        Rebel tribesmen say they have cut the road leading
                        from Kabul to Gardez during fighting with
                        government troops.
                        Oct. 9. Kabul radio announces that Taraki has died.
                        President Amin publishes a list of 12,000 killed by
                        Taraki regime.
                        Oct. 14. Heavy fighting takes place at Rishkhur
                        barracks southwest of Kabul.
                        Oct. 16. It is reported that the government has
                        crushed an army mutiny near Kabul.
                        Soviet forces take command of Shindand air force
                        base.
                        Nov. 9. It is reported that several ambush attacks
                        have been launched on government troops near
                        Kabul, killing 200 persons.
                        Dec. 21. U.S. officials say that the Soviet Union has
                        moved three army divisions to the border with
                        Afghanistan and has sent about 1,500 combat soldiers
                        to an air base near Kabul.
                        Dec. 26. A U.S. government spokesman says that in
                        the past 24 hours there has been "a large-scale Soviet
                        airlift" to Kabul, raising Soviet military involvement
                        in Afghanistan to "a new threshold."
                        Dec. 27. Fighting breaks out in Kabul and President
                        Hafizullah Amin is overthrown and assassinated.
                        Former Deputy Premier Babrak Karmal assumes the
                        post of president.
                        It is reported that Soviet troops have taken part in the
                        fighting in Kabul.
                        Dec. 28. President Karmal says the Soviet Union has
                        agreed to supply Afghanistan "urgent political, moral
                        and economic aid, including military aid."
                        U.S. President Jimmy Carter calls the Soviet military
                        intervention "a grave threat to the peace" and a
                        "blatant violation of accepted rules of international
                        behavior."
                        A Cabinet is formed as follows:

1979	Babrak Karmal - premier, chairman, Revolutionary Council, and secretary general, Central Committee;

Asadullah Sarwari	deputy premier
Sultan Ali Keshtmand	deputy premier and Planning
Rafi'i	National Defense
Sayyid Muhd. Gulabzoi	Interior
Shah Muhammad Dost	Foreign Minister
Anahita Ratebzad	Education
Abdul Wakil	Finance
Sherjan Mazduryar	Transport
Faiz Muhammad	Borders and Tribes
Muhammad Khan Jalalar	Trade.

1980

Jan. Carter administration requests about $30 million in covert aid to the Afghan guerrillas.

U.S. begins covertly channeling Soviet-made weapons including Kalashnikov AK-47 automatic rifles to the rebels in Pakistan.

Jan. 1. Afghanistan says it has invited Soviet troops into the country "in view of the present aggressive actions of the enemies of Afghanistan."

Jan. 2. Karmal addresses government leaders near Kabul and calls on the Afghan people to "come together and support our glorious revolution."

Jan. 5. The UN Security Council opens debate on Afghanistan.

Jan. 7. The Soviet Union vetoes a UN resolution that called for the immediate withdrawal of "all foreign troops in Afghanistan." The vote is 13 to two in favor of the resolution.

Jan. 9. The Security Council votes 12 by two with one abstention for a resolution to move the issue of Afghanistan to the General Assembly.

Jan. 10. The Afghan cabinet is expanded as follows:

Muhd. Aslam Watanjar	Communications
Abdul Majid Sarbuland	Information, Culture
Abdul Rashid Arian	Justice
Muhd. Ismail Danesh	Mines, Industries
Raz Muhd. Paktin	Water and Power

1980

Guldad	Higher Education
Nazar Muhammad	Public Works
Muhd. Ibrahim Azim	Health
Fazl Rahim Mohmand	Agriculture and Land Reform

Jan. 14. The General Assembly votes 104 to 18 with 18 abstentions for a resolution that "strongly deplored" the "recent armed intervention" in Afghanistan and called for the "total withdrawal of foreign troops" from the country.

Jan. 23. President Carter announces sanctions against the Soviet Union, including a grain embargo.

Jan. 27. A conference of Islamic Foreign Ministers opens in Islamabad to consider the situation in Afghanistan.

Jan. 29. The conference in Islamabad adopts a resolution that condemns "the Soviet military aggression against the Afghan people."

Feb. 13. Egyptian Defense Minister Kamal Hasan 'Ali says that Egypt is providing assistance to Afghan rebels and is "training some of them."

Feb. 14. The UN Human Rights Commission votes 27 to eight with six abstentions to condemn the Soviet intervention in Afghanistan as "an aggression against human rights."

Feb. 15. The *New York Times* cites "White House officials" as saying the U.S. had begun an operation to supply light infantry weapons to Afghan insurgent groups.

Feb. 19. Foreign ministers of the European Economic Community (EEC) proposes that Afghanistan be declared a neutral country under international guarantees if the Soviet Union withdraws its troops.

Feb. 22. Soviet President Leonid Brezhnev says that the Soviet Union will withdraw its troops from Afghanistan "as soon as all forms of outside interference" were "fully terminated."

Demonstrations and rioting against the government and the Soviet Union take place in Kabul.

Feb. 25. Shops remain closed in Kabul.

1980   Feb. 26. It is reported that mass arrests have been
made in Kabul during the day.

Feb. 28. Almost all shopkeepers open for business in
Kabul. It is reported that striking civil servants have
returned to work.

Mar. 3. The *Hizb-i Islami* of Hekmatyar, one of six
Afghan insurgent groups negotiating an alliance, says
it has withdrawn from the alliance.

Mar. 7. Soviet soldiers appeare on the streets of
Kabul. Soviet fighter planes and helicopter gun ships
fly over the city.

Mar. 10. Justice Minister Abdurrashid Arian says that
forty-two associates of former President Hafizullah
Amin are being held for trial.

Mar. 12. It is announced that the following ministers
have been appointed:

Muhd. Khan Jalalar	Commerce
Fazl Rahim Mohmand	Agriculture

Mar. 13. Foreign Minister Shah Muhammad Dost
arrives in Moscow on a "friendly visit."

Apr. Status of Soviet Armed Forces Agreement
signed.

May 18. Indian Foreign Secretary R.D. Satha meets
with President Babrak Karmal in Kabul.

May 22. A conference of Islamic foreign ministers,
meeting in Islamabad, adopts a resolution that
demands the "immediate, total and unconditional
withdrawal of all Soviet troops from Afghanistan" and
decides to establish a committee that will open
"appropriate consultations" to seek a solution to the
crisis in Afghanistan.

May 24. Demonstrators protesting the Soviet
presence in Afghanistan march in Kabul.

June 8. Kabul Radio announces that 10 supporters
and aides of slain former President Hafizullah Amin
have been executed.

June 14. Kabul news service reports that former
Communications Minister Muhammad Zarif, former
Frontier Affairs Minister Sahibjan Sahra'i, and former

1980   Planning Minister Muhammad Siddiq Alemyar have been executed.

July. Sixty countries boycott the Moscow Olympics in protest over the invasion of Afghanistan.

July 2. The Soviet Communist Party newspaper *Pravda* says that for a political settlement of the situation in Afghanistan to take place, armed incursions by the "mercenaries of the imperialist and reactionary forces from the territory of neighboring states" must first be ended.

Aug. 16. Kabul radio reports that Justice Minister Abdurrashid Arian has been named to the additional post of deputy premier.

Sept. 14. Frontier Affairs Minister Faiz Muhammad is killed earlier in the week while trying to enlist the support of Afghan tribes.

October. CIA provides some SAM-7 portable surface-to-air missiles to Ahmad Shah Mas'ud.

Oct. 15-Nov. 5. President Karmal and other high officials leave Kabul on a visit to the Soviet Union.

Nov. 13. President Karmal says that those who are not working for the good of the party will be expelled "even if they had been heroes in the past."

Nov. 20. The UN General Assembly votes by 111 to 22 with 12 abstentions for a resolution that calls for the "unconditional" pullout of "foreign troops" from Afghanistan.

Nov. 21. Foreign Affairs Minister Shah Muhammad Dost says the UN resolution is "a flagrant interference in Afghanistan's internal affairs."

Dec. 25. Egyptian President Anwar al-Sadat says that he has "sent weapons" and would "send more weapons" to Afghan insurgents.

Dec. 27. Deposed King Muhammad Zahir says in exile that he prays to God "to aid the Afghan people in its heroic struggle and its legitimate war for independence."

1981   Pakistan government declares that henceforth it will recognize only six Pakistan-based resistance organizations.

1981   Feb. 18. President Babrak Karmal arrives in Moscow for talks with Soviet leaders.

Mar. 9. U.S. President Ronald Reagan says that if Afghan "freedom fighters" who are fighting Soviet forces ask for weapons, it will be something "to be considered."

Apr. 7. Saudi Arabia announces it is severing diplomatic relations with "the current illegal regime" in Afghanistan.

May 9. Pakistani officials estimate the number of Afghan refugees in Pakistan at two million.

May 11. Sultan Ali Keshtmand becomes prime minister.

June 11. President of the Revolutionary Council Babrak Karmal turns the post of premier over to Sultan Ali Keshtmand and removes Abdul Rashid Arian as deputy premier.

June 13. The Revolutionary Council electes as its vice presidents Nur Ahmad Nur and Abdul Rashid Arian.

July 12. Member of the national committee of the National Fatherland Front Gen. Fateh Muhammad is killed by rebels.

July 22. Diplomatic sources in Kabul report heavy fighting between the rebels and Soviet forces in Paghman, 16 miles from the capital.

Aug. 6. Foreign Minister Shah Muhammad Dost meets with UN Representative Javier Perez de Cuellar.

Aug. 12. Kabul radio announces changes in the land distribution program that lift restrictions on acreage held by religious and tribal leaders.

Aug. 22. Five Afghan resistance groups form an alliance and create a 50-member advisory council.

Sept. 9. Foreign Minister Dost meets with Prime Minister Indira Gandhi in New Delhi.

Sept. 22. Egyptian President Anwar al-Sadat says in a U.S. television interview that the U.S. has been buying old Soviet-made arms from Egypt and sending them to rebels fighting Soviet forces in Afghanistan. U.S. officials have no comment.

1981   Nov. 18. By a vote of 116-23 with 12 abstentions the UN General Assembly votes for the third time that the Soviet Union must withdraw its troops from Afghanistan.

Dec. 15. President Babrak Karmal begins a visit to Moscow.

1982   Jan. 6. In Washington, military analysts say Soviet troops in Afghanistan have grown to 110-120,000.

Feb. 20. The Afghan government rejects the appointment of Archer K. Blood, designated U.S. charge d'affaires to Kabul. In response, the U.S. State Department imposes travel restrictions on Afghan diplomats in Washington.

Mar. 10. President Reagan proclaims March 21 "Afghanistan Day."

Apr. 1. The revolutionary council presidium announces new appointments:

Khalil Ahmad Abawi, vice chairman of council of ministers; Muhammad Yasin Sadiqi, director, local organizations committee and director, council of ministers; Mehrabuddin Paktiawal, director, central bank.

The UN World Food Program announces additional $18.5 m. in food aid to Afghan refugees in Pakistan.

June 8. Soviet and Afghan troops regain control of the key Panjshir Valley in a major offensive against *mujahedin* forces.

May 16. A two-day PDPA conference ends in Kabul with the 841 delegates endorsing resolutions aimed at purging dissidents and continuing a program of land reform.

June 16-25. The first United Nations-sponsored direct talks between Afghanistan and Pakistan begin in Geneva.

Aug. 2. The Afghan government amends the conscription law, lengthening the term of service.

Aug. 28. President Karmal approves four appointment changes:

Abdul Ghaffar Lakanwal   Agric. & Land Reform

1982   Abdul Samad Qayyumi   Local Government
                Fazl Rahim Mohmand   Central Statistics
                Najibullah Masud   Secretary, Council of
                                           Ministers

                Sept. 12. Minister of Education Guldad and Minister
                of Information and Culture Abdul Majid Sarbuland
                are removed from their posts but retain their positions
                as deputy prime ministers.
                Oct. 30. An explosion in the Salang Tunnel north of
                Kabul kills more than 1,000 people, including 700
                Soviet troops.
                November. The UN General Assembly approves a
                resolution demanding "the immediate withdrawal of
                foreign troops from Afghanistan" by a vote of 114 to
                21 with 13 abstentions.
                December. It is reported that the CIA was ordered to
                provide the Afghan insurgents with bazookas,
                mortars, grenade launchers, mines, and recoilless
                rifles.

1983   Jan. 19. UN Deputy Secretary General Diego
                Cordovez begins a peace mission to Geneva, Tehran,
                Islamabad, and Kabul to resolve the Afghan crisis.
                Feb. 16. The UN Human Rights Commission votes
                29 to seven with five abstentions for an immediate
                Soviet withdrawal from Afghanistan.
                June 15. The foreign ministers of Afghanistan and
                Pakistan arrives in Geneva for a third series of talks
                on the withdrawal of foreign troops.
                June 24. UN sponsored talks on Soviet troop
                withdrawal ends in Geneva without progress.
                Nov. 23. The UN General Assembly calls for the 1983
                immediate withdrawal of Soviet troops by a vote of
                116-20 with 16 abstentions.
                Dec. 27. The Afghan government says it will request
                the departure of 105,000 Soviet troops if it receives
                international guarantees that all opposition would end.

1984   Jan. 24. President Karmal has replaced his three top
                military advisers. Chief of Staff Gen. Baba Jan is

1984

replaced by Lt. Gen. Nazar Muhammad; Deputy Defense Minister Maj. Gen. Khalilullah by Maj. Gen. Muhammad Nabi Azami; and Chief of Operations Gen. Nuristani by Maj. Gen. Ghulam Qadir Miakhel.

Mar. 21. A bomb explodes in a Kabul mosque, killing four people and injuring seven.

Apr. 11. The Kabul government orders the expulsion of Third Secretary Richard S. Vandiver of the U.S. embassy in Kabul on charges of espionage. The U.S. denies the charge.

May 14. The National Olympic Committee announces that Afghanistan will boycott the 1984 Summer Olympics in Los Angeles.

May 17. U.S. Vice President George Bush visits theKhaiber Pass, where he condemned the Soviet invasion and expresses support for the Afghan resistance.

July 7. Radio Kabul announces nomination of Muhammad Kabir as minister of Finance.

July 26. The U.S. House of Representatives appropriations committee approves $50 million in covert aid to Afghan, according to intelligence sources.

Aug. 27. The foreign ministers of Afghanistan and Pakistan meet separately in Geneva with a UN intermediary in talks on a political settlement to the Afghan war.

Aug. 30. The third round of talks between Afghanistan and Pakistan adjourns in Geneva with no sign of progress.

Aug. 31. A bomb explosion occurs at the Kabul airport.

Nov. 4. Nine people are executed for the August 31 bomb explosion at Kabul airport.

Dec. 3. Radio Kabul reports that President Karmal has appointed Army Chief of Staff Brig. Gen. Nazar Muhammad to replace Lt. Gen. Abdul Qadir as defense minister.

1985

Jan. 18. The U.S. announces it will increase its aid to Afghan *mujahedin* in 1985 to approximately $280

1985
million. Saudi Arabia, Israel, and China are also reportedly assisting the rebels.

Jan. 26. The Afghan *mujahedin* leader, Khan Gul, is sentenced to death in Paktia Province.

Jan. 29. Zabiullah, a leader of the *Jam 'iat-i Islami*, is killed when his jeep hits a mine.

Mar. 3. According to reports from Iran, four Shi'a *mujahedin* groups have merged: the *Sazman-i Nasr*, the *Pasdaran*, Guards; the Islamic Movement of Afghanistan; and the United Front of the Islamic Revolution.

Apr. 8. Maulawi Abdul Wali is appointed minister of Islamic Affairs.

Apr. 23. President Karmal opens a grand tribal assembly (Loya Jirgah) in Kabul in an effort to gain popular support in the government's war against the *mujahedin*.

May 10. Leaders of three of the main *mujahedin* groups in Peshawar denounce the attempt by Abd al-Rasul Sayyaf to appoint himself for another term as head of the seven-member Alliance of Afghan Mujahedin.

June 17. U.S. and Soviet officials meet in Washington to discuss the war in Afghanistan.

June 20. UN-sponsored "proximity talks" begin in Geneva between Afghan and Pakistani governments regarding the war in Afghanistan.

June 25. Afghan-Pakistani talks end in Geneva, and are described as "intense and fruitful."

Aug. 30. UN mediator Diego Cordovez says progress had been made on three of four points in the UN plan for ending the Afghan war. The two sides remain divided on the question of withdrawing Soviet troops.

Oct. 23. Afghan authorities order all males of up to 40 years of age to enlist for three years of military service.

Afghan Foreign Minister Shah Muhammad Dost says Afghanistan could not reach agreement on the withdrawal of Soviet troops unless Pakistan enters direct negotiations.

1985   Nov. 2. Afghan troops ring the U.S. embassy in Kabul
                       in an effort to force the release of a Soviet soldier who
                       walked into the embassy Oct. 31, reportedly seeking
                       help to return to the USSR.

                       Nov. 13. By a vote of 122 to 19 with 12 abstentions,
                       the UN General Assembly adopts a Pakistani reso-
                       lution calling for the immediate withdrawal of Soviet
                       troops from Afghanistan.

                       Nov. 22. Three senior members of the PDPA are
                       removed from the politburo: Maj. Gen. Abdul Qadir,
                       Ghulam Dastagir Panjshiri, and Isma'il Danesh.

                       Nov. 30. Sayyid Muhammad Nasim Maihanparast is
                       appointed deputy chairman of the council of min-
                       isters.

                       Dec. 6. Radio Kabul announces that Ghulam Faruq
                       Yaqubi has been named director of the KHAD,
                       Afghanistan's secret police.

                       Dec. 13. The State Department notifies the UN that
                       the U.S. is ready to act as guarantor of a peace
                       settlement in Afghanistan that would involve a Soviet
                       troops withdrawal and an end to U.S. aid to the
                       mujahedin.

                       Dec. 19. In Geneva, Afghanistan and Pakistan
                       suspends their latest round of peace talks to study new
                       UN proposals for a timetable for Soviet withdrawal.

                       Dec. 26. The DRA council of ministers makes the
                       following new appointments:
                       Sayyid Amanuddin Amin vice chairman, council of
                       ministers; Sarjan Khan Zazai, Tribal and Nationalities
                       Affairs; Abdul Wahid Sorabi, Social and Cultural
                       Affairs; Abdul Ghaffar Baher, Islamic Affairs; Fazl
                       Haq Khaliqyar, Economic Affairs.

                       Dec. 31. The Afghan government presents an
                       informal timetable for the withdrawal of Soviet troops
                       as part of an overall accord, during UN-sponsored
                       Geneva talks Dec. 16 to 19, according to the State
                       Department.

1986   Jan. 11. President Babrak Karmal rejects the U.S.
                       offer to serve as guarantor of a peace settlement.

1986   Feb. 4. Guerrilla activity near Kandahar has report-
                        edly declined in recent days after former rebel leader
                        Asmatullah Achakzai Muslim and his militia decided
                        to back the Kabul government.

                        Feb. 20. The Revolutionary Council Presidium 1996
                        appoints a 74-member commission to draft a consti-
                        tution.

                        Mar. 17. The Foreign Ministry rejects a UN report on
                        human rights violations in Afghanistan as "a collec-
                        tion of groundless slanders and accusations."

                        Mar. 20. Pakistan lodges a "strong protest" over
                        Afghan attacks on a border post and refugee camp in
                        Khurram Agency that killed six people on March 16
                        and 18.

                        Apr. 2. The US reportedly agrees to supply hundreds
                        of Stinger missiles to Afghan *mujahedin*.

                        Apr. 6. Kabul Radio says that rebels detonated a car
                        bomb in Kabul that wounded 22 people.

                        Apr. 11. Soviet/Kabul forces start campaign against
                        Zhawar.

                        May 4. Babrak Karmal resigns as secretary general of
                        the PDPA because of "ill health," according to Kabul
                        Radio. He is replaced by Najibullah, former head of
                        KHAD, the secret police. Babrak retains the post of
                        chairman of the Revolutionary Council and a seat in
                        the seven-member politburo.

                        May 5. The seventh round of peace talks between the
                        foreign ministers of Afghanistan and Pakistan opens
                        at UN headquarters in Geneva.

                        May 15. Najibullah announces a collective leadership
                        including himself as party leader, Babrak as head of
                        the Revolutionary Council Presidium, and Prime
                        Minister Sultan Ali Keshtmand.

                        May 19. The seventh round of UN-sponsored indirect
                        talks between Afghanistan and Pakistan resume in
                        Geneva.

                        May 28. Najibullah announces that a bicameral
                        parliament will be established "within a few months,"
                        on the basis of "free and democratic elections."

1986

June 16. President Reagan meets with Afghan *mujahedin* in Washington and promises an "unshakable commitment" to their cause.

June 17. *Mujahedin* leaders Gulbuddin Hekmatyar and Rasul Sayyaf criticize the four other Peshawar leaders for the Washington visit.

1987

Feb. 18. Prime Minister Sultan Ali Keshtmand arrives in Moscow for talks.

Feb. 23. Pakistan's Foreign Minister Yaqub Khan meets with Soviet Foreign Minister Shevardnadze in Moscow to discuss Afghanistan.

Feb. 26. The tenth round of negotiations aimed at ending the war in Afghanistan opens in Geneva.

Mar. 4. *Mujahedin* stage rocket attacks into Soviet territory from Imam Sahib in Kunduz Province.

Mar. 24. Agriculture Minister Abdul Ghaffar Lakanwal and Public Health Minister Nabi Kamyar are replaced by Ghulam Faruq and Sher Bahadur.

July 20. Afghan leader Najibullah meets with Soviet leader Michail Gorbachev.

Aug. 11. Felix Ermacora, the UN special human rights investigator, is allowed to visit three Afghan prisons and interview political prisoners.

Oct. 10. Najibullah authorizes the purchase of weapons from mujahedin who put down their arms.

Oct. 13. Yunus Khales, leader of the *Hizb-i Islami*, denies reports that his commanders have sold Stinger missiles to Iranian Pasdaran.

Oct. 18. Maulawi Yunus Khales is elected spokesman of the seven-party *mujahedin* alliance.

Oct. 24. Shi'a groups headquartered in Iran announce a new coalition of *mujahedin* groups headquartered in Iran.

Oct. 30. The Revolutionary Council announces the appointment of Muhammad Ishaq Kawa as minister of Mines and Industries and Najibullah Masir as minister of Light Industries and Foodstuffs.

Nov. 10. Kabul Radio announces that the Revolutionary Council Presidium endorses a decree provi-

1987

ding for the formation and registration of political parties.

Nov. 22. Col. Muhammad Rasi is appointed minister of Technical and Vocational Education.

Nov. 24. Lt. Gen. Muhammad Nabi Azimi, first deputy of defense, is reported to have committed suicide after an offensive he led ended in failure.

Nov. 29. A Loya Jirga has been called to approve a new constitution.

Nov. 30. The Loya Jirga confirms Najibullah as president under the new "Islamized" constitution.

Dec. 6. *Mujahedin* leader Yunus Khales says the seven-party Alliance will not accept communist participation in any future Afghan government.

Dec. 10. UN envoy Diego Cordovez is reported to have opened negotiations between exiled King Muhammad Zahir and *mujahedin* leaders regarding forming a transitional coalition government.

1988

Jan. 4. Soviet Foreign Minister Shevardnadze arrives in Kabul for an "official working visit."

Jan. 6. In an interview with Afghan News Agency, Shevardnadze says the Soviet Union hopes to be out of Afghanistan by the end of 1988 regardless of the type of rule established there. He, however, links troop withdrawal to the cessation of U.S. aid to the *mujahedin.*

Jan. 12. Pakistani President Zia-ul-Haq and Prime Minister Muhammad Khan Junejo say in separate interviews that members of the pro-Moscow government must be allowed to participate in any future government as a condition for the withdrawal of Soviet troops from the country.

Jan. 17. *Mujahedin* leader Yunus Khales rejects statements by Pakistani leaders that the *mujahedin* would have to "coexist with remnants of a communist regime."

Jan. 20. At a press conference Najibullah states that his government will be committed to nonalignment, following the withdrawal of Soviet forces, and that

1988   Kabul is willing to accept aid from any country willing to give it.

Jan. 22. In Jalalabad at least 17 people are killed when two bombs explode at the public funeral of Khan Abd al-Ghaffar Khan, who died on Jan. 20.

Feb. 8. Soviet leader Michail Gorbachev says Soviet troops will begin pulling out of Afghanistan on May 15 if a settlement can be reached by mid-March.

Feb. 10. Reagan administration officials say a U.S. commitment was made in 1985 to end military aid to the *mujahedin* at the start of Soviet withdrawal. This commitment was made by Michael Armacost without the knowledge of the president. The official U.S. position is that the cutoff of aid will occur 60 days after a peace settlement and concurrent with a simultaneous withdrawal.

Feb. 11. Sayyid Bahauddin Majruh, head of the Afghan Information Office in Peshawar, is assassinated in Peshawar city.

Feb. 23. The *mujahedin* alliance announces the formation of an interim government.

Mar. 4. The Reagan administration says it will not halt aid to the *mujahedin* until Moscow stops its supply to the Afghan government.

Mar. 14. Gulbudin Hekmatyar is reported appointed spokesman of the *mujahedin* alliance.

Mar. 17. *Bakhtar* reports that Mines and Industries Minister Najibullah Masir was appointed deputy prime minister in charge of the administration of the northern provinces.

Mar. 23. Nikolai Egorchev (?) is reported to have replaced Pavel Mojayev as Soviet ambassador to Afghanistan after Mojayev suffers a heart attack.

Mar. 24. U.S. officials report that Pakistan withdrew its demand that an interim government be formed to oversee the Soviet withdrawal.

Mar. 26. The Reagan administration is reported ending its supply of Stinger missiles to the *mujahedin* in anticipation of a Geneva settlement.

Mar. 29. President Najibullah promises opposition

1988   groups 54 of the 229 lower house seats and 18 out of
                     62 in the senate if they will participate in the coming
                     parliamentary elections.
                     Mar. 30. The *mujahedin* reject President Najib-
                     ullah's offer to form a coalition government.
                     Apr. 3. The Kabul government creates Sar-i Pol
                     Province and appoints Gharib Husain as governor.
                     The new province is part of the Hazarajat.
                     Apr. 9. A *mujahedin* leader says that the *mujahedin*
                     "[will] not be bound by the outcome of the Geneva
                     agreements."
                     Apr. 14. Afghanistan, Pakistan, the Soviet Union, and
                     the United States sign the Geneva accords. Under
                     the agreement the Soviet Union will withdraw its
                     troops within nine months. The United States and the
                     Soviet Union will be the guarantors of the agreement,
                     which also provides for the return of Afghan refugees
                     and a halt to military aid by both sides.
                     Apr. 21. President Najibullah says that 1.55 million
                     voted in the Afghan elections.
                     Apr. 25. A UN "implementation assistance group,"
                     headed by the Finnish Maj. Gen. Rauli Helminen,
                     arrives in Islamabad to monitor the Geneva accord.
                     Minister of Defense Maj. Gen. Muhammad Rafi is
                     promoted to lieutenant general as is Armed Forces
                     Chief of Staff Shahnawaz Tanai. Minister of Commu-
                     nications Muhammad ASLAM Watanjar is promoted
                     to major general.
                     Apr. 28. President Najibullah says that Soviet military
                     advisors will remain after the Soviet troop with-
                     drawal.
                     May 4. President Najibullah arrives in New Delhi for
                     three days of talks.
                     May 11. The United Nations appoints Sadruddin
                     Agha Khan as coordinator for relief and resettlement
                     in Afghanistan.
                     May 15. The Soviet Union begins withdrawing troops
                     from Afghanistan.
                     May 19. Afghan army Maj. Gen. Fazil Ahmad Samadi
                     defects to the *mujahedin*.

1988   **May 25.** The Soviet Union announces the following casualties in the Afghan war: 13,310 dead, 35,478 wounded, and 311 missing.

May 26. Muhammad Hasan Sharq is appointed prime minister, replacing Sultan Ali Keshtmand who becomes secretary of the PDPA central committee.

May 27. Sayyid Muzaffaruddin Shah is elected temporary president of the House of Representatives.

May 31. A State Department official says U.S. aid to the *mujahidin* will continue because the Soviet Union plans to leave $1 billion worth of equipment in Afghanistan.

June 3. The National Assembly approves the appointment of four vice presidents by presidential decree: Abdul Hatef; Defense Minister Muhammad Rafi'i; Deputy Prime Minister Abdul Hamid Mohtat; and Minister of Higher and Vocational Education Abdul Wahid Sorabi.

June 7. President Najibullah addresses the UN General Assembly, complaining that Pakistan continues to violate the Geneva accords.

June 9. President Najibullah says, according to the Bakhtar news agency, that 243,900 soldiers and civilians have died in ten years of war.

June 15. Pir Sayyid Ahmad Gailani, Head of the National Islamic Front, becomes spokesman of the seven-member *mujahedin* alliance.

June 16. President Najibullah announces the formation of a new government:

Muhammad Hasan Sharq	Prime Minister
Abdul Wakil	Foreign Affairs
Sayyid Muhammad Gulabzoi	Interior
Ghulam Faruq Yaqubi	State Security
Hamidullah Tarzi	Finance
Muhammad Bashir Baghlani	Justice
Shah Muhammad Dost	UN Representative
Muhd. Aslam Watanjar	Communications
Muhd. Khan Jalallar	Commerce
Abdul Ghafur	Returnees Affairs

1988

Sulaiman Layeq	Tribal Affairs
Sultan Husain	Planning
Muhd. Asef Zaher	Rural Development
Muhammad Ghofran	Agric. & Land Reform
Abdul Fatah Najm	Public Health
Ghulam Rasul	Education
Nur Ahmad Barits	Higher Education
Muhd. Ishaq Kawa	Mines, Industries
Muhammad Aziz	Transportation
Nazar Muhammad	Construction
Pacha Gul Wafadar	Civil Aviation
Dost Muhd. Fazl	Light Industries and Foodstuffs
Raz Muhammad Paktin	Water and Power

Without Portfolio: Nematullah Pazhwak, Ghulam Faruq Yaqubi, Fazl Haq Khaliqyar, Shah Muhammad Dost, Sarjang Khan Jaji.

July 9. Ahmad Bashir Ruigar is appointed minister of Information and Culture.

July 18. Sebghatullah Mujaddidi's National Front for the Liberation of Afghanistan joins Sayyid Ahmad Gailani's National Islamic Front of Afghanistan in expressing support for UN envoy Diego Cordovez's peace plan to establish a neutral government.

July 21. President Najibullah approves the creation of Nuristan Province.

July 23. President Najibullah approves the formation of a political organization called the Self-Sacrificing Afghan People's Solidarity Movement (*Nahjat-i Hambastagi-yi Mardom-i Afghanistan Fedaiyan*).

July 27. The Kabul government announces the permission for formation of a new party, the Union of God's Helpers (*Ittehadia-ye Ansarullah*).

Aug. 1. The Constitution Council is set up to examine the constitutionality of laws and compliance of treaties and laws.

Aug. 8. Soviet troops begin the withdrawing from Kabul.

Aug. 17. Lt. Gen. Shahnawaz Tanai is appointed Defense Minister and Maj. Gen. Muhammad Asef

1988   Delawar is appointed chief of the Armed Forces
                  General Staff.
                  Aug. 29. Abdul Ahad Mohmand and two Soviet
                  cosmonauts lift off their Soyuz TM-6 spacecraft for a
                  six-day voyage that will threaten to strand them in
                  outer space.
                  Sept. 25. Edmund McWilliams, Jr. is appointed
                  special envoy to the *mujahedin*.
                  Oct. 5. Maulawi Zahir, a commander of Burhanuddin
                  Rabbani's forces is killed in Nejrab by Hekmatyar's
                  forces.
                  Oct. 13. Yuli Vorontsov, Soviet first deputy Foreign
                  Minister, is appointed ambassador to Kabul.
                  Oct. 17. Burhanuddin Rabbani, head of the *Jam'iat-i*
                  Islami, becomes spokesman of the seven-member
                  mujahedin alliance.
                  Oct. 21. Diego Cordovez, UN special representative
                  for Afghanistan, calls on ex-King Muhammad Zahir
                  to assist in establishing a national reconciliation
                  government.
                  Oct. 26. Herat Governor Khaliqyar is also appointed
                  governor of Badghis and Ghor Provinces.
                  Nov. 2. The Kabul government makes the following
                  new appointments:

                  Nizamuddin Tahzib   Chief Justice
                  Abdul Karim Shadan   Special   Court   of
                                             National Security.

                  Nov. 8. Kabul Radio reports Soviet acceptance of
                  Sayyid Muhammad Gulabzoi's appointment as
                  Afghanistan's ambassador to the Soviet Union.
                  Nov. 16. The appointment of Muhammad Aslam
                  Watanjar as interior minister is approved.
                  Nov. 17. Deputy Foreign Minister Abdul Ghafur
                  Lakanwal and Sayyid Kamaluddin, deputy director in
                  the Foreign Ministry are reported to have defected.
                  Nov. 19. Soviet military command in Afghanistan
                  warns if guerrillas escalate war, they will jeopardize
                  the withdrawal of Soviet troops.

1988   Nov. 28. Muhammad Gul, a KHAD brigadier general
                              and cousin of Najibullah, is reported to have defected.
                              Dec. 3. Alliance leaders, headed by Burhanuddin
                              Rabbani, meet in Ta'if, Saudi Arabia, for talks with
                              Soviet Deputy Minister Vorontsov.
                              Dec. 19. Mir Azimuddin is approved as minister of
                              Communications, and Khalilullah is appointed as
                              Transportation minister.
                              Dec. 25. Soviet Deputy Vorontsov meets with
                              ex-King Muhammad Zahir in Rome (at the request of
                              Moscow).

1989   Jan. 1. The newspaper *Haqiqat-i Saur Inqilab* (Truth
                              of the April Revolution) appears for the first time
                              under the new name *Payam*.
                              Jan. 2. Sebghatullah Mujaddidi succeeds Rabbani as
                              spokesman of the alliance.
                              Jan. 13. Soviet Foreign Minister Edward Shevard-
                              nadze arrives in Kabul.
                              Jan.18. Sebghatullah Mujaddidi returns from Iran
                              where he unsuccessfully tries to invite the Shi'a
                              mujahedin groups to join an interim government.
                              Jan. 21. West Germany's diplomatic staff leaves
                              Kabul.
                              Jan. 25. The United States decides to close its
                              embassy.
                              Jan. 26. A *mujahedin* delegation, headed by Gulbud-
                              din Hekmatyar, meets with Iranian Foreign Minister
                              Ali Akbar Velayati in Tehran.
                              Jan. 27. Britain, France, Japan, and Italy announce
                              their decision to withdraw their diplomats from
                              Kabul.
                              Jan.28. Soviet Defense Minister Dimitri Yazov ends
                              two days of talks with President Najibullah. He says
                              Moscow will "not abandon its friends."
                              Jan. 30. The United States formally closes its
                              embassy.
                              Feb. 2. President Najibullah denounces the closing of
                              Western embassies as "psychological war."
                              In Peshawar some 500 Afghans demonstrate for the
                              return of ex-King Muhammad Zahir.
                              Feb. 7. A *mujahedin* commander says that the "Pak-

istanis are pushing us now to do an all-out attack on Jalalabad," but the *mujahedin* want to wait to prevent a bloodbath.

Feb. 13. President Bush signs a National Security Directive pledging continued financial and military support.

Feb. 14. The last Soviet soldier leaves Kabul airport.

Feb. 15. The United States rejects a Soviet call for an end to arms shipments to Afghanistan.

Feb. 18. The government declares a nationwide state of emergency. President Najibullah appoints new cabinet members:

Burhanuddin Ghiasi	Commerce
Sherjan Mazduryar	Civil Aviation
Abdul Baher	Light Industries and Foodstuffs
Ismail Danesh	Higher and Vocational Education
Sayyid Amin Zara	Public Health
Sayyid Akram	Returnees' Affairs
Abdul Ghafur Baher	Islamic Affairs and Endowments
Nur Ahmad Barits	Without Portfolio

Muhammad Nabi Muhammadi becomes spokesman of the *mujahedin* alliance.

Feb. 20. Prime Minister Sharq resigns.

Feb. 21. Sultan Ali Keshtmand is appointed chairman of the executive committee of the council of ministers.

Feb. 23. *Mujahedin* leaders elect Abdul Rasul Sayyaf as acting prime minister and Sebghatullah Mujaddidi as acting president of the interim government. The portfolios are distributed as follows:

Muhd. Nabi Muhammadi	Defense
Muhd. Shah Fazli (Harakat)	Scientific Research
Maulawi Islamuddin (Harakat)	Agriculture
Gulbuddin Hekmatyar (Hizb)	Frontier Affairs
Ali Ansari (Hizb-H)	Frontier Affairs

1989

Qazi Najiulla (Hizb-H)	Justice
Yunus Khalis (Hizb-K)	Interior
Haji Din Muhd. (Hizb-K)	National Security
Maulawi Abdul Razzaq (H-K)	Religious Affairs
Burhanuddin Rabbani (Jam)	Reconstruction
Najibullah Lafra'i (Jam)	Islamic Guidance
Ishan Jan (Jam)	Mining, Industries
Ahmad Shah (Ittihad)	Communications
Sayyid Nadir Khurram (Jabha)	Health

Pir Sayyid Gailani challenges the legitimacy of the government.

Mar. 5. The *mujahedin* launch an offensive against Jalalabad.

Mar. 16. Afghan Army Chief of Staff Lt. Gen. Asef Delawar is reported in Jalalabad supervising its defense.

Mar. 20. *Mujahedin* attempt to capture Jalalabad fails.

Mar. 24. An 85-truck government convoy breaks through to Jalalabad.

Mar. 27. President Najibullah offers *mujahedin* commanders autonomy if they end the war. A council of 35 commanders rejects the offer.

Apr. 6. U.S. Secretary of State James Baker III recommends Peter Tomsen as special envoy to the *mujahedin* with the rank of ambassador.

Apr. 12. The *mujahedin* cabinet begin a three-day session in Afghan territory.

Apr. 23. The *New York Times* reports that the unsuccessful attack on Jalalabad was made by the Benazir government and U.S. Ambassador Robert Oakley against the advice of Gen. Hamid Gul, director of Inter-Services Intelligence. No Afghan representatives were present.

Apr. 24. Afghan Foreign Minister Abdul Wakil accuses Pakistan of aggression.

May 6. Valentin I. Varennikov, Soviet deputy minister of defense, ends a four-day visit to Kabul.

1989

May 9. Sayyid Ahmad Gailani challenges the legitimacy of the interim government.

May 16. KHAD chief Abdul Rahman is said to have defected to Yunis Khalis *mujahedin* group.

May 17. Government troops reopens Jalalabad-Kabul road.

May 21. President Najibullah invites *mujahedin* leaders and commanders to take part in the Loya Jirgah.

May 24. President Najibullah offers regional autonomy to *mujahedin* commanders if they agree to stop fighting.

May 24. A convoy of Soviet-made tanks and artillery arrives in Kabul.

June 24. President Najibullah appoints Mahmud Baryalai as first deputy prime minister.

July 5. Government troops recapture Tor Kham.

July 19. Units of Burhanuddin Rabbani and Muhd. Nabi Muhammadi are fighting over turf in Helmand Province.

July 24. Defense Minister Shahnawaz Tanai is said to be under house arrest.

July 26. Najmuddin Kawiani, head of foreign relations committee of the national assembly and politburo member, reports secret peace talks with the "opposition."

July 29. Nur Ahmad Nur is appointed ambassador and permanent representative to the United Nations.

Aug. 1. Defense Minister Tanai is reported to be implicated in coup attempt.

Aug. 7. Haji Abdul Latif, 76-year old commander with the National Islamic Front, dies from poisoning.

Aug. 8. Two bodyguards of Abdul Latif who confessed to killing him are executed.

Aug. 11. Abdul Rasul Sayyaf, prime minister, rejects Gulbuddin Hekmatyar's suggestion that the rebels should take control by backing an army coup.

Aug. 14. Government spokesman Muhammad Nabi Amani says 183 civilians were killed in Kabul by rockets in one week.

1989   Aug. 20. Maj. Gen. Muhammad Faruq Zarif, head of
              Najib's security force, announces his defection.

              Aug. 25. Jam'iat-i Islami Commander Mas'ud
              accuses *Hizb-i-Islami* of collusion with Kabul gov-
              ernment.

              Aug. 29. Fighters of Sayyaf and Muhammadi battle
              over control of a bridge in Helmand Province that
              produces lucrative tax and toll revenues.

              Aug. 30. Gulbuddin Hekmatyar's *Hizb-i Islami*
              withdraws from the *mujahedin* alliance.

              Oct. 11. Muhammad Asghar becomes president of the
              15-member National Salvation Society, which was
              formed to seek a peaceful solution to the war.

              Oct. 17. Boris Nikolayevich Pastukhov, Soviet
              ambassador, presents his credentials

              Nov. 7. Lt. Gen. Ali Akbar is killed in fighting in
              Kandahar.

              Nov. 14. *Mujahedin* launch a three-pronged attack on
              Jalalabad that is repulsed.

              Nov. 21. President Najibullah extends the state of
              emergency for another six months.

              Nov. 30. *Mujahedin* leaders Burhanuddin Rabbani
              and Gulbuddin Hekmatyar announce a cease-fire and
              exchange of prisoners and captured land.

              Dec. 2. The Kabul government arrests 127 people
              suspected of plotting a coup.

              Brig. Gen. Ghulam Haidar is killed in fighting at
              Jalalabad.

              Dec. 21. Jam'iat executes four members of *Hizb*,
              including Sayyid Jamal, who had ambushed Jam'iat
              commanders.

              Dec. 31. President Najibullah calls for PDPA to
              change its name.

1990   Jan. 24. President Najibullah says that he will step
              down if his government is defeated in UN-supervised
              elections.

              Feb. 2. Some 10,000 refugees demonstrate in favor of
              the return of Zahir Shah in Quetta.

1990

Feb. 12. Farid Ahmad Mazdak is appointed acting chairman of the National Front's central council, replacing Abdur Rahim Hatif.

Mar. 5. Trials begin of some 124 Afghans arrested in December and charged with plotting a coup.

Mar. 6. Defense Minister Shahnawaz Tanai launches a coup against President Najibullah.

Mar. 7. Gulbuddin Hekmatyar says his forces are supporting the Tanai coup.

Mar. 9. Government troops recapture the Bagram air base.

Other *Mujahedin* groups refuse to support the Tanai coup.

Mar. 18. The PDPA plenum expels twenty-four members for "treachery" against the party and country.

Apr. 6. Two generals and 11 other people are killed at a ceremony when a *Mujahedin* group that promised to surrender opens fire on Government troops. Fazl Haq Khaliqyar, governor of Herat, is wounded.

Apr. 14. The Kabul government accuses the United Nations of failing to monitor alleged violations of the Geneva accords.

May 21. Prime Minister Khaliqyar presents his new cabinet:

Mahmud Baryalai	First Deputy Premier
Abdul Wahid Sorabi	Deputy Premier
Nematullah Pazhwak	Deputy Premier
Abdul Qayyum Nurzai	Deputy Premier
Sarwar Mangal	Deputy Premier
Mahbubullah Kushani	Deputy Premier
Nur Ahmad Barits	Adviser
Faqir Muhd. Yaqubi	Adviser
Shah Wali	Adviser
Sayyid Akram Peigir	Adviser
Muhd. Aslam Watanjar	Defense
Raz Muhd. Paktin	Interior
Abdul Wakil	Foreign Affairs
Muhammad Hakim	Finance

1990	Abdul Wahid Sorabi	Planning
	Mas'uma Esmati Wardak	Education
	Anwar Shams	Higher and Vocational Education
	Faqir Muhd. Nikzad	Construction
	Zakim Shah	Commerce
	Bashir Ruigar	Information, Culture
	Mehr Muhd. Ejazi	Health
	Sayyid Nasim Alawi	Communications
	Anwar Dost	Light Industries and Foodstuffs
	Muhd. Siddiq Sailani	Islamic Affairs
	Khalilullah	Transport
	Hamidullah Tarzi	Civil Aviation
	Hayatullah Azizi	Reconstruction and Rural Development
	Ghulam Faruq Yaqubi	State Security
	Sarjang Zazai	Border Affairs
	Muhammad Ghufran	Agriculture and Land Reform
	Ghulam Muhyiuddin	Justice
	Shahbaz	Statistics
	Saleha Faruq Etemadi	Social Affairs
	Fath Muhammad Tarin	Repatriation
	Abdul Samad Saleh	Mines, Industries
	Abdul Ghafur Rahim	Water & Power

May 28. Kabul government convenes a Loya Jirga in preparation for amending the constitution.

June 11. Agreement of economic cooperation signed between the Kabul government and India.

June 16. Nine Shi'a *Mujahedin* parties unite in the *Hizb-i Wahdat*, Party of Unity.

June 22. Conference of *Mujahedin* commanders in Paktia Province.

June 27. Opening of the second party congress that reelects Dr. Najibullah and changes the name of the party to "Homeland Party" (*Hizb-i Watan*).

1990

June 30. Meeting of former prominent government officials at the invitation of President Mujaddidi. Members invited include:

Muhammad Yusuf, prime minister
Abdul Samad Hamed, minister
Rawan Farhadi, minister and diplomat
Sabbahuddin Kushkaki, minister and writer
Abdul Hakim Tabibi, minister and diplomat
Nangyalai Tarzi, diplomat
Humayun Asefi, diplomat
Agha Jan Barakzai
Sayyid Ishaq Gailani, *mujahedin* leader
Sayyid Makhdum Rahin, poet and writer
Abdul Ahad Karzai, member of parliament
Abdul Hai Tokhi (Tukhay)
Abdur Rahman Ulfat, adviser
Ihsanullah Mayar
Sayyid Asadullah Nuktadan
Abdul Aziz Firogh
Abdul Qadir Nurzai
Wali Ahmad Sherzai
Enayatullah Iblagh
Ishaq Akhlaqi
Muhammad Akram, scholar and diplomat
Muhammad Anwar Sherzai
Siddiq Rashid Saljuqi
Muhammad Gulab Nangarhari, minister and poet
Muhammad Hashim Mujaddidi, educator and senator
Muhammad Yahya Nauruz, general

Members of the Shi'a Wahdat alliance of *mujahedin* groups also participated.
July 9. Nizamuddin Tahzib, a Parjami, is relieved from his post as chief justice of the supreme court.
July 18. Italian embassy reopened in Kabul.
July 25. Beginning of UN-assisted repatriation of refugees from Pakistan.
July 29- Aug. 25. Najibullah visits the Soviet Union; Abdur Rahim Hatef is acting president.

1990

Aug. 3. Columbia establishes diplomatic relations with Afghanistan.

Aug. 29. Najibullah leaves for official visit to Delhi.

Sept. 4. *Jam'iat* and *Hizb* (H) clash in vicinity of Kabul in which 16 *mujahedin* fighters are killed.

Sept. 5. Kabul government removes unruly militias from the city.

Sept. 11. Najibullah decrees legalization of political parties.

Sept. 30. Alliance of democratic parties of the left dissolves itself.

Oct. 5. Tirin Kot, administrative center of Oruzgan Province, captured by *mujahedin* forces.

Oct. 15. Mas'ud, the *Jam'iat* commander, visits Islamabad where he meets the Pakistani head of state and Gulbuddin Hekmatyar.

Oct. 25. The U.S. congress reduces its aid to the Afghan resistance.

Nov. 19. President Najibullah arrives in Switzerland for discussions with Afghan personalities.

1991

Jan. 9. Afghan General Hashim is captured by the resistance and executed.

Jan. 22. Esmat Muslim, chief of the pro-government militia, dies.

Jan. 23. Prof. Rabbani opens embassy of the resistance in Khartum.

Feb. 5. Floods cause considerable damage in southwestern Afghanistan.

Feb. 7. President Najibullah appoints new ministers: Ghulam Muyiuddin Shahbaz, Planning; Muhammad Nazir Shahadi, Statistics; Wadir Safi, Civil Aviation and Tourism.

Feb. 8. Afghan resistance sends 300 *mujahedin* to Saudi Arabia in war with Iraq. Sayyaf and Hekmatyar protest.

Mar. 31. Khost captured by *mujahedin* forces headed by Commander Haqani, 2,200 prisoners taken and seven generals (including Col. Gen. Muhammad

1991

Zahir Solamal—deputy minister of Defense; Maj. Gen. Ghulam Mustafa—chief of political affaires of the armed force; Maj. Gen. Muhammad Qasim—commander of artillery, special guards; Major Muhammad Azam—an air force commander; Lt. Gen. Shirin—commander of the Khost militia units).

Apr. 2. Kabul government declares a "Day of Mourning."

Apr. 6. Muhammad Nurzad elected Mayor of Kabul to replace Abdul Karim Misaq who defected and moved to Germany.

Apr. 10. Vice President Sultan Ali Keshtmand is dismissed.

Apr. 16. President Najibullah offers a new amnesty to all Afghans living abroad who return to Afghanistan.

Apr. 20. Explosion at Jamilurrahman's Asadabad (Wahhabi) headquarters in Kunar province results in some 500 killed and 700 wounded. According to eyewitness accounts, the explosion occurred at the Dawa (formerly Asadabad Hotel), and a number of Arabs and 63 Pakistanis were among those killed. Some sources suspect a car bomb for the explosion, whereas the "Wahhabis" claim it was the result of a SCUD missile attack.

Apr. 22. Afghan Foreign Minister Abdul Wakil sets out on a trip to Moscow and New York.

Apr. 26. Representatives of the Pakistani military intelligence service (ISI) meet in Geneva with representatives of the Kabul government.

May 21. Javier Perez de Cuéllar, United Nations secretary general, issues a five-point proposal for a political settlement in Afghanistan.

May 27-28. Soviet-Pakistan talks in Moscow about Afghanistan.

May 31. Explosion of ammunition depot in Nowshera, Pakistan.

June 20. Babrak Karmal returns to Afghanistan from exile in the Soviet Union.

July 1. The Kabul regime omits all references to the Saur Revolution from official documents

1991   July 22. Ahmad Shah Mas'ud takes Ishkashem and
                       shortly thereafter the Wakhan Corridor.
                       Aug. 30. Assassination in Pakistan of Jamilur
                       Rahman, chief of the Kunar "Wahhabi" republic.
                       Sept. 13. The USSR and The United States agree to
                       end delivery of weapons to the Afghan combatants as
                       of January 1, 1992.
                       Oct. 14. The supreme justice of Kabul declares that
                       all legal decisions must conform to Islamic law.
                       Nov. 4. The former King Zahir is slightly wounded in
                       an assassination attempt.
                       Dec. 5. UN agrees on solution for transfer of
                       government.
                       Dec. 15. The Soviet Union stops arms deliveries to
                       Afghanistan.

1992   Jan. 14. Najibullah annuls decree 14, depriving the
                       royal family of its property.
                       Feb. 6. Gens. Dostum, Naderi, and Momen rebel
                       against Najib government.
                       Mar. 15. *Mujahedin* seize Samangan Province.
                       Mar. 18. President Najibullah agrees to resign as soon
                       as interim government is installed.
                       Mar. 29. *Wahdat* party takes Sar-i Pol.
                       Apr. 8. Gen. Dostum takes over Mazar-i Sharif.
                       Apr. 12. Masud takes control of Salang Tunnel.
                       Apr. 15. Dostum militia takes Kabul airport.
                       Apr. 16. Najibullah takes refuge in UN compound.
                       Ghazni and Gardez taken by the resistance.
                       Military junta holds Kabul, consisting of Baba Khan,
                       Asef Delawar, Abdul Momin, and Nabi Azimi,
                       supported by party people Abdul Wakil, Farid
                       Mazdak, and two other civilians.
                       The resistance controls Herat.
                       Apr. 18. Kunduz and Jalalabad fall to the resistance.
                       Rahim Hatef nominated as interim president.
                       Apr. 21. Pul-i Alam in Logar taken by *Hizb-i Islami*.
                       Apr. 22. Gardez taken by Jalaluddin Haqani.

1992

Apr. 24. Resistance leaders set up interim Islamic council of 51 members. Mujaddidi assumes provisional control.

Jalalabad taken by mujahedin.

Apr. 25. Resistance enters Kabul, partisans of Mas'ud and Hekmatyar fight.

Apr. 26. Mas'ud takes presidential palace and takes barracks from *Hizb-i Islami.*

Shi'a *Harakat-i Islami* takes missile base of Darul-aman.

Apr. 28. Mujaddidi arrives in Kabul, proclaims Islamic State of Afghanistan, and announces general amnesty.

Apr. 29. *Hizb-i Islami* fighters ejected from interior ministry. Ahmad Shah Masud arrives in Kabul.

May 3. Egypt recognizes Islamic State of Afghanistan. Hekmatyar threatens to attack if Dostum does not leave Kabul.

May 6. First session of the Jehad Council under the presidency of Prof. Rabbani.

May 10. Sayyid Ahmad Gailani arrives at Kabul.

May 21. Mas'ud and Hekmatyar conclude cease fire. Yunus Khales arrives at Kabul.

May 24. Mujaddidi nominates Dostum general (*setar genral*) and Naderi (*dagar genral*).

May 30. Dostum and Hekmatyar fight for control of Karte Nau district.

June 19. Dostum militia and Mas'ud's forces clash.

June 28. Mujaddidi surrenders presidency to Rabbani.

July 4. Violent artillery combat between forces of Dostum and Hekmatyar.

Aug. 2. Yunus Khales resigns from Jehad Council.

Aug. 15. Twenty-seven members of UN staff leave Afghanistan.

Aug. 27. Cease fire concluded between Rabbani and Hekmatyar.

Sept. 5. Uzbek militia quits Kabul.

Sept. 17. Agreement of Paghman between Rabbani and Hekmatyar, designation of an assembly for choosing the successor of Rabbani.

1993

Feb. 3. The United Nations suspends its aid shipments by way of south and eastern Afghanistan.

Feb. 5. India evacuates its diplomats from Kabul.

Feb. 6. General Dostum is nominated deputy minister of defense.

Feb. 7. Government forces and *Wahdat* fight in the Soviet embassy compound.

Feb. 8. Turkey closes its embassy at Kabul.

Feb. 11. The *imam* of al-Azhar University calls on the *mujahedin* to stop fighting and direct their efforts to areas where Muslims are still oppressed. Chinese diplomats leave Kabul.

Feb. 16. The firing in Kabul has stopped for the first time since January 19.

March 7. The Islamabad Accord between Afghan parties (except Khales and Dostum) nominates Rabbani president for 18 months and Hekmatyar prime minister. A defense council of all parties is to be in charge of the ministry of defense; all heavy weapons are to be removed from the capital; a council to be elected in eight months, and presidential and legislative elections to be held in mid-1995. The Organization of Islamic Conference, the Afghan parties, and Pakistan should supervise the cease fire.

Mar. 8. *Hizb-i Islami* and *Wahdat* fire 70 missiles on Kabul.

Mar. 11. The leaders assemble at Mecca to fix the details of the prerogatives of the prime minister, the control of the defense council, and the power of the Uzbek militia. The accord is countersigned by King Fahd.

Mar. 19 and 20. Reunion at Jalalabad failes to achieve agreement.

Mar. 22. Fighting between *Wahdat* and *Ittihad* continues in Kabul.

Mar. 23. *Hizb-i Islami* captures Naghlu dam from *Harakat-e Inqilab-i-Islami*. Pakistani militia seize Stinger missiles from Mulla Abdul Salam (Mulla Roketi), and the mulla takes 27 hostages in reprisal.

1993

Mar. 28. General Fauzi, a spokesman of Dostum, declares that there will not be any peace without representation of Dostum in the Kabul government.

Apr. 1. *Jam'iat* and *Hizb* form a committee to resolve their problems.

Apr. 2. *Jam'iat* and *Wahdat* agree to release prisoners and restore quiet.

Apr. 7. Afghan defense minister claims that Hekmatyar and Sayyaf supply weapons to Tajik Islamists.

Apr. 9. First break in the ceasefire between *Jam'ia*t and *Wahdat*.

Apr. 15. The governors of Herat and Khorasan, Iran, sign an accord of cooperation against the traffic in drugs.

Mar. 25. Kabul blockaded by the forces of Hekmatyar.

May 3. More than 50 Islamists are killed fighting in Tajikistan.

May 9 and 10. Heavy fighting between forces of *Ittihad* and *Wahdat* in Kabul.

May 11. Kabul Museum burns.

May 12. Bombardment of Kabul resumed.

May 13. Mas'ud gains help of Dostam against *Hizb-i Islami* forces.

May 19. Rabbani and Hekmatyar agree to a ceasefire.

May 20. Mas'ud resigns as Defense minister.

June 6. Hekmatyar presides at the first meeting of his government at Charasiab.

June 17. Government meets in Paghman.

June 21. Council of ministers meets in Darulaman.

June 23-28. Fighting between *Wahdat* and Mas'ud forces.

July 3. President Rabbani receives General Dostum.

July 12. Dostum and Hekmatyar meet and agree to a ceasefire.

July 15. Mas'ud and Hekmatyar forces fight near airport.

July 26. Mas'ud's forces take Bagram air base from *Ittihad*.

1993

Aug. 31. Ceasefire between *Ittihad* and *Wahdat*.

Sept. 14. *Hizb-i Islami* bombards eastern Kabul.

Sept. 15. The Afghan Communist party is said to have had a meeting in Microrayon and elected Mahmud Baryalai to head the party.

Oct. 2. A group of about 300 Tajik and *mujahedin* fighters carry an attack into Tajikistan.

Oct. 19. Kabul-Jalalabad Highway has been reopened for traffic.

Oct. 24. Afghanistan and Tajikistan sign an agreement to export natural gas to Tajikistan.

Nov. 2. A Russian plane bombards Badakhshan.

Nov. 9. Ms. Robin Raphel, American undersecretary of State for South Asia, visits Kabul regarding economic and humanitarian aid. She meets Rabbani, Hekmatyar, Mas'ud, and Dostum.

Nov. 21. Islamist ideologue Hasan Al-Turabi visits Kabul.

Nov. 28. Arrival at Kabul of French Charge d'Affaires M. Didier Leroy.

Dec. 3. Telephone connection with Kabul restored.

Dec. 23. Gen. Dostum regains Sher Khan Bandar without a fight.

1994

Jan. 1. Forces of Dostum and Hekmatyar attack Kabul forces.

Jan. 5. Rabbani forces take Kabul airport. General Momen killed in helicopter accident.

Jan. 6. Fighting around Bala Hisar and Microrayon. Mujaddidi supports Dostum-Hekmatyar alliance.

Jan. 10. Pul-i Khishti mosque destroyed.

Apr. 2. M. Mestiri, UN emissary, arrives in Kabul and meets with Rabbani, Mas'ud, and Hekmatyar.

Apr. 4. Mas'ud's forces attack Pul-i Khumri, held by Dostum and Isma'ili forces.

Apr. 6. Mestiri leaves Kabul without obtaining a cease fire between the belligerents.

Apr. 10. End of two-week ceasefire.

1994

Apr. 19. Rabbani announces his intention to prolong his mandate until December 1994, because his adversaries did not respect the accords of Jalalabad.

Apr. 24. Mulla Salam, also called Mulla Roketi, holds two Chinese engineers and ten Pakistanis and demands that Pakistan free his brother and return the three Stingers captured from him.

Apr. 27. According to Red Cross International, the civil war in Kabul has resulted in 2,500 deaths, 17,000 wounded, and 632,000 refugees from Kabul since January 1, 1994. At least 20,000 houses were destroyed.

May 1. Offensive of Hekmatyar forces against Kabul is stopped.

May 7. Grand reunion of Ghazni commanders; Haqani and Isma'il Khan participate.

May 9. Kabul air force bombards Mazar and Pul-i Khumri.

May 13-14. Dostum bombards the 10th Division at Qargha near Kabul.

May 17-18. Sayyaf takes Maidan Shahr from Hekmatyar forces.

May 21-22. General Dostum indicates having used six Stinger missiles to down two of Rabbani's aircraft. Dostum's head of the air force, Gen. Jalil, claims to have 32 operational planes, more than 22,000 bombs, and 100 pilots.

May 28. Conflict within *Wahdat* between supporters of Akbari and Mazari.

June 3. Dostum and Isma'il Khan forces clash in Shindand. Dostum bombs Herat.

June 8. Rabbani proposes that his successor be chosen by a Loya Jirga.

June 10. Fighting resumes in Kabul.

June 15. Rabbani extends his "mandate," which was to expire in June, for another six months.

June 19. Isma'il Khan escapes an assassination attempt.

June 25. *Harakat* recaptures control of Darulaman palace from *Hizb-i Islami*.

1994

June 26. Rabbani's forces expel Dostum's forces from the Bala Hisar and Maranjan hill.

June 17. Yunus Khales declares himself interim president.

July 8. The parties of Gailani, Hekmatyar, Mujaddidi, Muhammadi, Muhseni, Mazari, and Dostum form a commission to negotiate with Rabbani and Sayyaf.

July 14. The Pakistani minister of Foreign Affairs threatens to close the offices of Sayyaf's party, if Mulla Roketi does not liberate his hostages. They are freed on July 21.

July 20. Official opening of the Herat assembly in the presence of 700 participants.

July 24. Rabbani arrives at Herat, but does not participate in the assembly.

July 29. BBC Correspondent Mir Wais Jalil is killed in an area controlled by Hekmatyar.

Aug. 7. Rabbani receives Muhammadi, Muhseni, and Gailani at Kabul.

Aug. 16. Pakistani authorities prevent Ariana from flying over Pakistani territory, because it does not observe international rules.

Sept. 8. *Hizb-i Islami* takes control of Khenjan north of the Salang Pass.

Sept. 12. Fighting breaks out between *Wahdat* and *Harakat* for control of Darulaman. Akbari defects from *Wahdat*.

Sept. 25. Iranian intermediaries help in establishing a cease fire between the Shi'a parties.

Oct. 2. Pakistan holds goods destined for Afghanistan in Karachi.

Oct. 11. According to Red Cross International, 1,100 people were killed and 23,000 wounded in Kabul in September.

Nov. 2. A Pakistani convoy of goods destined for Turkmenistan is stopped by commanders between Spin Boldak and Kandahar. *Taliban* clash with commanders.

Nov. 5. The *Taliban* capture Kandahar; the commander of the Muslim group is hanged.

1994

Nov. 7. A spokesman of Rabbani accuses Uzbekistan of interference in Afghan internal affairs for having delivered 30 Russian tanks to Dostum.

Nov. 8. Visit to Kabul by a UN delegation for the first time in seven months.

Nov. 13. Having repelled the commanders Lalay (*Mahaz*) and Sarkateb (*Hizb-i-Hekmatyar*), the Taleban take control of Kandahar.

Nov. 17. The Pakistani minister of Interior announces that Pakistan will start to repair the route from Kandahar to Herat. Kabul calls this an invasion of Afghanistan.

Dec. 5. Arrival at Kabul of the first aid convoy in six months, 32 trucks for Rabbani and 32 for his opponents.

Dec. 6. Return to Pakistan of the convoy from Turkmenistan.

Dec. 12. Departure of Rabbani for Morocco to participate at a meeting of the Organization of the Islamic Conference.

Dec. 13. Arrival of a UN aid convoy in Kunduz, the first in two years.

Dec. 19. Arrival at Kabul of an Indian delegation to prepare reopening of the embassy.

Dec. 20. Dostum arrives in Islamabad.

Dec. 28. Mestiri arrives in Islamabad to restart his peace effort.

Dec. 30. Arrival in Afghanistan of a Sudanese delegation for talks with Hekmatyar.

1995

Jan. 1. M. Mestiri arrives in Kabul during an unofficial cease fire. Maulawi Yunus Khales returns to Jalalabad after an absence of 19 years.

Jan. 4. Mestiri opens a new UN office in Jalalabad and meets with Hekmatyar. The American ambassador to Pakistan meets Rabbani at Kabul.

Jan.. 17. Seven trucks with UN aid are plundered in Sarobi in the area controlled by Hekmatyar.

Jan. 22. The access roads to Kabul are again closed by the *Hizb* of Hekmatyar.

1995 Jan. 24. The *Taliban* take Ghazni.

Jan. 30. Dostum's forces capture Kunduz.

Feb. 4. The *Taliban* have deposed Qari Baba and replaced him with Maulawi Ihsanullah as head of Ghazni Province.

Feb. 10. *Taliban* capture Maidan Shahr. Mestiri announces a power transfer for February 20, at which Rabbani is to transfer power to a committee of 20 persons.

Feb. 11. The *Taliban* claim capture of Pul-i Alam and control of the entire Logar Province.

Feb. 14. Hekmatyar retires his forces from the Kabul area to Sarobi, abandoning his heavy weapons.

Feb. 15. The *Taliban* occupy Pul-i Charkhi and expel the *Hizb-i Islami* from Khost.

Feb. 16. Rabbani's forces have retaken Kunduz.

Feb. 17. Kabul airport reopens after being closed for more than a year.

Feb. 19. The *Taliban* take Sharan, center of Paktika, and Gardez, center of Paktia.

Feb. 20. *Jam'iat* forces fight *Wahdat*. Mestiri admits failure of his plan for transfer of power in Kabul.

Feb. 25. The *Taliban* threaten to attack Kabul if Rabbani does not lay down his arms.

Mar. 5. Mazari declares his readiness to recognize the Kabul government if the Hazara get 25% representation.

Mar. 6. *Jam'iat* forces attack the positions of *Wahdat* at Kabul.

Mar. 7. Mazari threatens to use SCUD missiles if Rabbani's forces will not stop their attacks.

Mar. 9. *Wahdat* surrenders its position south of Kabul to the *Taliban*. Qazi Humayun, the new Pakistani ambassador, arrives in Kabul.

Mar. 10. Nabi Muhammadi deserts Rabbani for the *Taliban*. Sayyaf sells his arms depot at the Pakistani border to a Trimangal tribal chief.

Mar. 11. Kabul forces capture all the territory held by *Wahdat*, including the SCUD base at Darulaman and Kabul Museum.

1995   Mar. 13. Mazari and a number of *Wahdat* leaders are
killed while in *Taliban* captivity.

Mar. 14. The *Taliban* claim conquest of Nimruz and
Ghor Provinces.

Mar. 19. Mas'ud's forces take Charasiab from the
Taliban.

Mar. 26. Mazari is buried in Mazar-i Sharif.

Mar. 30. A common grave of 22 executed Hazaras is
found at Charasiab.

Apr. 1. Mujaddidi replaces Hekmatyar as head of the
four-party opponents of Rabbani.

Apr. 4. *Taliban* attack the Shindand air base and
Herat. Also fight *Jam'iat* forces in Maidan Shahr.

Apr. 7. Iran prohibits commercial transit to Afghanistan.

Apr. 12. *Jam'iat* emissary Abdur Rahman meets
Dostam in Tashkent.

Apr. 13. *Taliban* demand that foreign states not
reopen their embassies in Kabul.

Apr. 19. The *Taliban* bloc the delivery of fuel to
Kabul. *Hizb* and *Taliban* establish contacts.

Apr. 27. The *Taliban* free 300 captives of Dostum's
forces.

Apr. 28. *Taliban* defeated in the Farah area.

May 3. India reopens its embassy in Kabul.

May 6. American diplomats visit Kabul University.

May 9. The Pakistani ambassador returns to Kabul.
Forces of Isma'il Khan take Farah.

May 14. Arrival at Kabul of delegations of the
government of Tajikistan and the opposition.

May 15. Forces of Rabbani capture Zaranj from the
Taliban.

May 17. M. Nuri and M. Rahmanov hold talks at
Kabul.

May 24. Continuation of stalled negotiation between
representatives of Dostam and Rabbani. Questions
raised are opening of the Salang route and lifting of
the *fatwa* proclaiming holy war against Dostum.

May 29. Arrival of Prince Turki al-Faisal, chief of the
Saudi secret service, at Kabul.

1995   June 20. *Jam'iat* forces take control of Bamian from
                the Shi'a *Wahdat*.
                June 29. Sardar Abdul Wali, son-in-law of ex-King
                Zahir Shah, arrives in Islamabad at invitation of
                Pakistan government.
                Aug. 20. Abdul Wali returns to Rome.
                Aug. 26. *Taliban* take Girishk.
                Aug. 31. *Taliban* take Delaram.
                Sept. 2. *Taliban* take Shindand
                Sept. 5. *Taliban* take Herat and Islam Qala.
                Sept. 6. Kabuli crowds attack Pakistan embassy, one
                is killed and 20 persons wounded, including the
                ambassador.
                Sept. 7. *Taliban* take Ghor Province.
                Sept. 15. Explosion in Herat by enemies of *Taliban*.
                Sept. 24. Another explosion and sabotage.
                Nov. 10. UNICEF suspends educational assistance to
                Taliban-controlled areas because of the closing of
                girls' schools.

1996   Apr. 3. About 1000 members of the *ulama* choose
                Taliban Mulla Muhammad Omar as *Amir al-Mu'
                minin*.
                May 24. Hekmatyar concludes an anti-*Taliban* treaty
                with Rabbani. Hekmatyar rejoins Kabul government
                as prime minister; upon arrival in Kabul orders all
                cinemas closed and forbids music to be broadcast on
                Kabul Radio and Television. He advises women to
                observe Islamic code of dress and orders government
                officials to perform their noon prayers in their places
                of work.
                June 1. *Taliban* take Chaghcharan, capital of Ghor
                Province.
                June 18. Taleban take a government base at Nimruz.
                July 6. Prime Minister Hekmatyar forms new cabinet:
                Wahidullah Sabawun (of *Hizb*) Defense; Abdul Hadi
                Arghandiwal (of *Hizb*) Finance; Muhammad Yunus
                Qanuni (of *Jam'iat*) Interior; Ahmad Shah Ahmadzai
                (of *Ittihad*) Education; Qayamullah Kashaf (of
                Ittihad) Information and Culture; Sayyid Ali Javid

1996

June 18. Taleban take a government base at Nimruz.

July 6. Prime Minister Hekmatyar forms new cabinet: Wahidullah Sabawun (of *Hizb*) Defense; Abdul Hadi Arghandiwal (of *Hizb*) Finance; Muhammad Yunus Qanuni (of *Jam'iat*) Interior; Ahmad Shah Ahmadzai (of *Ittihad*) Education; Qayamullah Kashaf (of *Ittihad*) Information and Culture; Sayyid Ali Javid (*Harakat* of Muhsini), Planning; Sayyid Husain Anwari (of *Harakat*) Work and social affairs; Maulawi Samiullah Najibi (of Kunar *Jama'at Tauhid*) Martyrs and Disabled; Sayyid Husain Alami (of Akbari *Wahdat*) Commerce; and Qutbuddin Helal (faction not known) deputy prime minister.

July 10. Norbert Holl, a German diplomat, is nominated as special representative of the UN for Afghanistan.

July 17. Sayyid Gailani announces creation of a new alliance, including Mujaddidi, Dostum, Khalili (*Wahdat*), Muhammad Nabi, and the Jalalabad *Shura*, headed by Haji Qadir.

July 27. Norbert Holl arrives at Kabul.

Sept. 11. *Taliban* capture Jalalabad from *Shura* and prepare for attack on Sarobi.

Sept. 12. *Taliban* capture Laghman Province and its capital, Mehterlam.

Sept. 22. *Taliban* capture Kunar Province.

Sept. 25. *Taliban* capture Sarobi.

Sept 27. *Taliban* capture Kabul, torture and execute ex-President Najibullah and his brother Shapur Ahmadzai. They also kill General Jaffar and M. Tokhi who shared UN shelter with Najibullah. *Taliban* announce establishment of an Islamic state. *Taliban* take Bagram and Charikar.

Sept. 28. Sebghatullah Mujaddidi announces his support for the *Taliban*.

Sept. 29. *Taliban* take Jabal-us-Siraj.

M. Holl, special UN envoy for Afghanistan arrives in Kabul.

1996   Nov. 5. General Tanai, minister of Defense under the
                              Najibullah regime, gives his support to the *Taliban*.
                              Nov. 24. *Taliban* take Kalakan village.
                              Nov. 27. *Taliban* take Istalif.

1997   Jan. 9. Forces of General Dostum attack Taliban
                              troops in Badghis.
                              Jan. 16. Taliban take Bagram and Charikar.
                              Jan. 17. Taliban move into Kapisa Province, take
                              Mahmud Raqi.
                              March 19. An explosion in Jalalabad police head-
                              quarter destroys ammunition depot and surrounding
                              homes. About 50 people are killed and hundreds
                              wounded. Cause is said to be an accident.
                              March 20. Afghan Taliban prohibit New Year
                              (*nauruz*) celebrations.
                              March. Taleban government declines to extradite
                              Osama bin Laden, a Saudi millionair who financed
                              Islamist movements and has threatened terrorist
                              attacks on Saudi Arabia and the United States.

BIBLIOGRAPHY

The sources presented in the following sections are a representative selection of books and articles, with special emphasis on materials in English. Because French and German scholars have been pioneering in certain fields (archaeology and the sciences) a number of sources in French and German are also listed.

The reader who desires a comprehensive survey may refer to the bibliographies listed below, especially the more up-to-date one by Keith McLachlan and William Whittaker (1983). An excellent, though dated, bibliography is the two-volume *Bibliographie der Afghanistan-Literatur* (1968 and 1969), which also lists sources in Dari and Pashtu. The most recent bibliographical compilation is the work by Muhammad Akram (1990), which is available on microfiche at the Bibliotheca Afghanica in Liestal, Switzerland.

Scholars may obtain access to the library of the Bibliotheca Afghanica, founded by Paul Bucherer-Dietsche, which is located in the founder's home. The Afghanistan Archiv of the Institut für Entwicklungsforschung und Entwicklungs-politik of the Ruhr University of Bochum has a considerable amount of material in the fields of economics and the sciences. Probably the best library for Dari/Pashtu sources in the United States is at the Center for Afghanistan Studies, at Omaha, Nebraska, headed by Thomas E. Gouttierre. The center published two catalogs of its sources in 1995, compiled by Shaista Wahab, entitled *Arthur Paul Afghanistan Collection Bibliography* Vol. 1, Pashto and Dari Titles; and *Bibliography of the Arthur Paul Afghanistan Collection at the University Library, University of Nebraska at Omaha.* Both are available from the center. The Centre de Recherches et d'Etudes Documentaires sur l'Afghanistan in Paris, France, published in 1994 a bibliography of its sources by Pette, Xavier, entitled *Afghanistan: Catalogue des Livres, Monographies, Périodiques de la Bibliothèque du CEREDAF.* Schuyler Jones published a bibliography in 1992 under the World Biographical Series, entitled *Afghanistan.*

The most important sources for archival materials are the National Archives of India at New Delhi, India; and the British Library Oriental and India Office Collection in London, England. German foreign ministry archives exist on microfilm from about 1867 to 1945. Catalogs of files and microfilms of the German foreign ministry archives are available in the United States at major university libraries. Microfilm copies of German sources may be obtained from the United States National Archives in Washington, D.C. The Washington archives also have American consular reports and studies by various American agencies. Most foreign political archives are closed for a period of 25 years; but with special permission a scholar may obtain access to closed materials.

CONTENTS

1. GENERAL

Bibliographies

Akram, Muhammad. *Bibliographie analytique de l'Afghanistan.* Paris: Centre de Documentation Universitaire, 1947. This has been updated to 1990 and is available on microfiche from the Bibliotheca Afghanica, Liestal, Switzerland.

Beaureceuil, Serge de L. *Manuscrits d'Afghanistan.* Cairo: Institut Français d'Archéologie Orientale, 1964.

————. "Les Publications de la Societe d'Histoire d'Afghanistan." Cairo: *Mélange de l'Institut Dominicain d'Etudes Orientales du Caire* 7 (1963). 236-240.

Deutsches Orient Institut. *Bibliographie der Afghanistan Literatur, 1945-1967.* Vol. 1, *Literatur in europäischen Sprachen.* Vol. 2, *Literature in orientalischen Sprachen.* Hamburg and Bochum: Institut für Entwicklungsforschung und Entwicklungspolitik der Ruhr-Universitaet Bochum, 1969.

Hall, Lesley A. *A Brief Guide to Sources for the Study of Afghanistan in the India Office Records.* London: British Library, Oriental and India Office Collection, 1981.

Jones, S. *An Annotated Bibliography of Nuristan (Kafiristan) and the Kalash Kafirs of Chitral: Selected Documents from the Secret and Political Records, 1885-1900.* Copenhagen: Royal Danish Academy of Sciences and Letters. Part 1 (1966); Part 2 (1969).

————. *Afghanistan.* World Bibliographical Service. Oxford: Clio Press, 1992.

Mayel-Harawi, Ghulam Reza. *Fehrest-i Kutub-i Matbu'-i Afghanistan az Sal-i 1330 ila 1344*. Kabul: Government Press, 1965.

McLachlan, Keith and William Whittaker. *A Bibliography of Afghanistan*. Cambridge, England: Menas Press, 1983.

Ovesen, J. "An Annotated Bibliography of Sources Relating to the Pashai People of Afghanistan." Afghanistan. 32/1 (1979): 87-98.

Pette, Xavier. *Afghanistan: Livres, Monographies, Périodiques*. Paris: Centre de Recherches et d'Etudes sur l'Afghanistan, 1994.

Pickett, L. C., Mayar, and Saleh. *Bibliography of Materials Dealing with Agriculture in Afghanistan*. Kabul: Kabul University, 1968.

Pourhadi, Ibrahim V. *Persian and Afghan Newspapers in the Library of Congress, 1871-1978*. Washington, D.C.: Library of Congress, 1979.

Rosenbaum, H. "Das Afghanistan Archiv des Instituts fuer Entwicklungsforschung und Entwicklungspolitik der Ruhr-Universitaet Bochum." *Afghanistan Journal* 2/4 (1975): 151.

Stwoda, M. Ibrahim and Ahmad Ziya Mudarresi. *Hutakian: Ketabshenasi-yi Tausifi*. (Bibliography of the Hotakis) Kabul: Government Press, 1357/1978.

United Nations. *Afghanistan, a Selected and Partially Annotated Bibliography*. Kabul: UNICEF, 1972.

Wahab, Shaista. *Arthur Paul Afghanistan Collection Bibliography*. Vol. 1, *Pashto and Dari Titles*. Lincoln, NE: Dageforde Publishing, 1995.

———. *Bibliography of the Arthur Paul Afghanistan Collection at the University Library*, University of Nebraska at Omaha. Omaha, NE: 1995.

Wilber, Donald N. *Annotated Bibliography of Afghanistan*. New Haven, CT: Human Relations Area Files, 1968.

Witherell, Julian W. *Afghanistan: An American Perspective: A Guide to U.S. Official Documents and Government-Sponsored Publications.* Washington, D.C. 1986.

Archival Works

Aitchison, C.U. A Collection of Treaties Engagements and Sanads Relating to India and Neighboring Countries. Vol. 13, *Persia and Afghanistan.* Calcutta: Superintendent of Government Printing, 1933.

Baluchistan Intelligence Bureau. *Notes on the Tribes of Afghan Descent in Baluchistan.* Quetta: Government of India, 1937.

Bruce, C. E. *The Tribes of Waziristan.* London: India Office, 1929.

Defense Mapping Agency. *Gazetteer of Afghanistan.* Washington, D.C.: 1983.

Dundas, A.D.F. *Precis on Afghan Affairs, 1927-1936.* New Delhi: Government of India, 1938.

General Staff, India. *Brief Gazetteer of the Most Important and Useful Place Names in the Waziristan District.* Dera Ismail Khan: General Staff, 1935. (Official use only.)

———. *A Dictionary of the Pathan Tribes on the North-West Frontier of India.* Calcutta: Government of India, 1910.

———. *Handbook of Kandahar Province, 1933.* Simla: Government of India, 1933. (Secret.)

———. *Military Report, Afghanistan.* Delhi: Government of India, 1925.

———. *Routes in Afghanistan, South-East.* Calcutta: Government of India, 1937.

Intelligence Branch, Army Headquarters, India. *The Second Afghan War, 1878-80.* Abridged Official Account, compiled by S.P. Oliver. London: 1908.

Johnson, H. H. *Notes on Mahsuds.* London: India Office, 1934.

Maconachie, R.R. *Precis on Afghan Affairs, 1919-1927.* Simla: Government of India, 1928.

Maitland, P. J. *A Note on the Movements of Turkoman Tribes.* Simla: Government of India, 1888.

Raverty, Henry G. *Notes on Afghanistan and Part of Baluchistan.* Reprint from 1888 edition. Quetta: Gosha-ye Adab, 1976

Ridgway, Major R.T.I. *Handbooks for the Indian Army: Pathans.* Calcutta: Government of India, 1910.

Robinson, J. A. *Notes on Nomad Tribes of Eastern Afghanistan.* Peshawar: Government of India, 1934. (Confidential.)

Wheeler, J. Talboys. *Memorandum on Afghanistan Affairs, from A. D. 1700.* Calcutta: Government of India, 1896.

Wynne, LePoer. *Narrative of Recent Events in Afghanistan from the Recovery of Candahar to the Conclusion of the Rebellion of Yacoob Khan.* Simla: Government of India, 1871. (Secret.)

Dictionaries and Grammars

Arayanpur-Kashani, Abbas. *The Concise English-Persian Dictionary.* Tehran: Amir Kabir, 1977.

———. *The Concise Persian-English Dictionary.* Tehran: Amir Kabir, 1976.

———. *The New Unabridged English-Persian Dictionary.* 6 vols. Tehran: Amir Kabir, 1963.

Badakhshi, Shah Abdullah. *A Dictionary of Some Languages and Dialects of Afghanistan*. Kabul: Government Press, 1960.

Chavarria-Aguilar, O. L. *Pashto Basic Course*. Ann Arbor, MI: University of Michigan, 1962.

Dulling, G. K. *The Hazaragi Dialect of Afghan Persian*. London: Central Asian Research Center, 1973.

Edelman, D. I. *The Dardic and Nuristani Languages*. Moscow: Nauka, 1983.

Farhadi, A. G. Rawan. *The Spoken Dari of Afghanistan*. Kabul: Peace Corps, 1975.

Gilbertson, George W. *The Pakkhto Idiom: A Dictionary*. 2 vols. Hertford, England: Austin & Sons, 1932.

Haim, S. *The Larger English-Persian Dictionary*. 2 vols. Tehran: Beroukhim, 1959, 1960.

———. *New Persian-English Dictionary*. 2 vols. Tehran: Beroukhim, 1960, 1962.

Lorentz, M. *Lehrbuch des Pashto/Afghanisch*. Leipzig: VEB Verlag, 1979.

Morgenstierne, Georg. *An Etymological Vocabulary of Pashtu*. Oslo: Det Norske Videnskaps-Academi, 1927.

Penzl, Herbert. *A Grammar of Pashto*. Washington, D.C.: American Council of Learned Societies, 1955.

———. *A Reader of Pashto*. Ann Arbor: University of Michigan, 1962.

Phillot, D.C. *Higher Persian Grammar*. Calcutta: Baptist Mission Press, 1919.

Pashto Academy. *English-Pushtu Dictionary*. Kabul: Pashtu Academy, 1975.

Raverty, H. G. *Dictionary of the Pukhto, Pushto, Language of the Afghans.* Karachi: Indus Publication, 1980.

Steingass, F. *A Comprehensive Persian-English Dictionary.* London: Routledge & Kegan Paul, 1957.

Yearbooks

Afghanistan Almanac. A yearbook, published in Dari and Pashtu by the Afghan government from 1311/1932 under the title *Salnama-yi Majalla-yi Kabul* until 1940 and then called in Pashtu *Da Kabul Kalanai* and finally *Da Afghanistan Kalanai.* Kabul: Government Press.

Baryalai, Mahmud. *Democratic Republic of Afghanistan Annual: Saur 7, 1358.* Kabul: Government Press, 1979.

———. *Republic of Afghanistan Annual.* Kabul: Government Press, 1978.

Danishyar, Abdul Aziz. *Afghanistan Republic Annual, 1975.* Kabul: Government Press, 1975.

———. *Afghanistan Republic Annual, 1976.* Kabul: Government Press, 1976.

———. *Afghanistan Republic Annual, 1977.* Kabul: Government Press, 1977.

Khalil, Sayyid. *The Kabul Times Annual, 1970.* Kabul: Government Press, 1970.

Rahimi, Nur M. *The Kabul Times Annual, 1967.* Kabul, Government Press, 1967.

Yusufzai, G.R. *Democratic Republic of Afghanistan Annual.* Kabul: Government Press, 1980.

Guides and Description

Abdul Rahim, Munshi. *Journey to Badakhshan, 1879-80.* Calcutta: Government of India, n.d.

Adamec, Ludwig. *Historical Dictionary of Afghanistan.* Metuchen, NJ: Scarecrow Press, 1991.

Ali, Muhammad. *A New Guide to Afghanistan.* Kabul: Afghan Historical Society, 1958.

Dupree, Nancy Hatch. *Bamian.* Kabul: Afghan Tourist Organization, 1967.

―――. *Herat: A Pictorial Guide.* Kabul: Afghan Tourist Organization, 1966.

―――. *An Historical Guide to Afghanistan.* Kabul: Afghan Tourist Organization, 1970.

―――. *An Historical Guide to Kabul.* Kabul: Afghan Tourist Organization, 1977.

―――. *The Road to Balkh, Kabul, Koh-i-Daman, Salang, Pul-i-Khumri, Surkh Kotal, Samangan, Tashkurghan, Mazar-i-Sharif, Qunduz.* Kabul: Government Press, 1967.

Dupaigne, Bernard, and Gilles Rossignol. *Guide de Afghanistan.* Lyon: Manufacture, 1989.

Fodor, Les Guides Modernes. *Afghanistan.* Paris: Edition Vilo, 1972.

Gharghasht, Muhammad Naser. *Rahnama-yi Kabul* (A Guide to Kabul). Kabul: Government Press, 1345/1966.

Hayat Khan, Muhammad. *Afghanistan and Its Inhabitants.* Translated by Henry Priestley. Lahore, Pakistan: Indian Public Opinion Press, 1874.

Kabul Times Publishing Agency. *Afghanistan at a Glance.* Kabul: 1967.

Klimburg, Max. *Afghanistan.* Wien: Austria Edition, 1966.

Kohzad, Ahmad Ali. *Bala Hesar-i Kabul*. Kabul: Government Press, 1340/1961.

Kraus, Willy. *Afghanistan*. Tübingen, Germany: Horst Erdmann Verlag, 1972.

Kushkaki, Maulawi Burhanuddin. *Rahnama-yi Qataghan wa Badakhshan*. Kabul: Ministry of War, 1302/1923. Translated from Dari into French by Marguerite Reut under the title *Qataghan et Badakhshan*. Paris: Sorbonne, 1979.

Michaud, Roland, and Sabrina Michaud. *Afghanistan*. Paris: Vendome Press, 1980.

ORBIS. *Afghanistan Yesterday and Today*. Prague: 1982.

Poulton, Michelle, and Robin Poulton. *Que Sais-je? L'Afghanistan*. Paris: Presses Universitaires de France, 1981.

United States Government. Government Printing Office. *Afghanistan: A Country Study*. Washington, D.C.: 1986.

Wolfe, Nancy Hatch (Dupree). *The Valley of Bamian*. Kabul: Afghan Tourist Organization, 1963.

Journals

AFGHANews. Peshawar, Pakistan: Jam'iat Islami Afghanistan.

Afghan Information Centre. Peshawar, Pakistan: Edited by Sayyid B. Majruh.

Afghanistan Forum. New York: Edited by Mary Ann Siegfried and Leonard Oppenheim.

Afghanistan Journal. Graz, Austria: Akademische Druck-u. Verlagsanstalt, 1974-1982.

The Afghanistan Studies Journal. Omaha, NE: Center for Afghanistan Studies

Afghanistan Tribune. Aachen, Germany: Afghanisches Nachrichtenmagazin in Deutscher Sprache.

American Universities Field Staff Reports: Afghanistan. New York: Louis Dupree.

The Asiatic Review. London.

Central Asia: Journal of Area Study Centre. Pakistan: University of Peshawar.

EFIS Afghans. Paris, France: The Bureau International Afghanistan (BIA).

The Firmest Bond. Islamic Unity Magazine. Geneva, Switzerland: Publisher and Editor-in-Chief, Dr. Abdul Hakim Tabibi.

Kultur. Bonn: Afghanisches Kulturzentrum.

Les Nouvelles d'Afghanistan. Paris, France: The Amitie Franco-Afghane (AFRANE).

Writers Union of Free Afghanistan (WUFA). Peshawar, Pakistan: Editor-in-Chief, Rasul A. Amin.

2. CULTURAL

Archaeology and Prehistory

Allchin, F. R., and N. Hammond. *The Archaeology of Afghanistan from the Earliest Times to the Timurid Period.* New York: Academic Press, 1978.

Ball, Warwick. *Archaeological Gazetteer of Afghanistan.* 2 vols. Paris: Editions Recherches sur les Civilisations, 1982.

Barthoux, J. *Les Fouille de Hadda: Figures et Figurines*. Paris: G. Van Oest, 1930.

Bernard, P. "Ai Khanum on the Oxus: A Hellenistic City in Central Asia." London: Proceedings of the British Academy, 1967.

―――. "La Campagne de Fouilles de 1970 a Ai Khanoun (Afghanistan)." Paris: Comptes Rendus de l'Academie des Inscriptions et Belles Lettres, 1971.

Berre, M. Le, D. Schlumberger, and B. Dagens. "Monuments Pre-Islamiques d'Afghanistan." Paris: Memoires de la Delegation Archeologique Francaise en Afghanistan 19, 1964.

Bombaci, A. "Ghazni" *East and West* 8 (1957): 247-260.

Courtois, J.C. "Summary of the History of Archaeological Research in Afghanistan." *Afghanistan* 16/2 (1961): 18-29.

Dor, R. "Lithoglyphes du Wakhan et du Pamir." *Afghanistan Journal* 3/4 (1976): 122-129.

Dupree, L. "An Archaeological Survey of N. Afghanistan." *Afghanistan* 15/3 (1960): 13-15.

―――. "Results of a Survey for Palaeolithic Sites in Dasht-i-Nawur." *Afghanistan* 29/2 (1976): 55-63.

Fischer, K. "Archaeological Field Surveys in Afghan Seistan, 1960-1970." Edited by N. Hammond. *South Asian Archaeology.* (1973): 131-155.

Foucher, A. "The French Archaeological Delegation in Afghanistan Oct. 1922-Nov. 1925." Paris: Comptes Rendus de l'Academie des Inscriptions 1927. 117-123.

Franz, H. G. "Der Buddhistishe Stupa in Afghanistan, Urspruenge und Entwicklung." *Afghanistan Journal* 4/4 (1977): 131-143 and 5/1 (1978): 26-38.

———. "Erste Monographie zur Archaeologie Afghanistans." *Afghanistan Journal* 6/4 (1979): 109-116.

Fussman, G. "Daniel Schlumberger, 1904-1972." *Bulletin de l'Ecole Francaise d'Extreme-Orient* 60 (1973): 411-422.

———. *Monuments Buddhiques de la Region de Caboul.* Paris: Boccard, 1976.

Ghirshman, R. "Die Franzosische Archaeologische Forschung in Iran und Afghanistan, 1940-1952." *Saeculum, Jahrbuch fuer Universal-Geschichte* 4/1 (1952).

Grenet, F., J. Lee, and R. Pinder-Wilson. "Les Monuments Anciens du Gorzivan (Afghanistan du Nord-Ouest)." *Afghanistan Quarterly* 33/3 (1980): 17-51.

Grousset, R. "Un Savant Francais: Joseph Hackin." *Revue de Paris* 52/1 (1945): 78-85; *Afghanistan* 5/4 (1950): 1-12.

Hackin, J. *Diverses Recherches Archeologiques en Afghanistan (1933-1940).* Paris: Presses Universitaire de France, 1959.

———. "The Recent Work of the French Archaeological Mission at Bamiyan." *Indian Art and Letters* 8/1 (1934): 36-42.

———. "Recherches Archeologiques en Afghanistan." *Revue de l'Art Ancien et Moderne* (1937): 302-304.

Jackson, A.V.W. "The Tomb of the Moghul Emperor Babar in Afghanistan." *Proceedings of the American Philosophical Society* 68/3 (1929): 195-207.

Jettmar, K. "Bronze Axes from the Karakoram." *Proceedings of the American Philosophical Society* 105/1 (1961): 98-104.

Knobloch, E. "Survey of Archaeology and Architecture in Afghanistan." *Afghanistan Journal* 8/1 (1981): 3-20.

Kohzad, A. A. "Archaeology in Afghanistan." *Afghanistan* (1956): 1-8.

Masson, C. "Notes on the Antiquities of Bamian." *Journal of the Asiatic Society of Bengal* (1836): 707.

Moline, J. "The Minaret of Jam." *Kunst des Orients* 9 (1973-1974): 131-148.

Motamedi, A. A. "Hada after the last Seasons of Excavation at Tepe Hotor." *Afghanistan* 32/3 (1979): 49-55.

Papadopoulos-Marigo, Véra. *Hadda au Royaaume de Nagarahara en Afghanistan. Lieu de Passages et de Rencontres. Une Recherche Historique.* Paris: Univ. Paris IV, 1995.

Pugachenkova, G. A. "A l'Etude des Monuments Timurides d'Afghanistan." *Afghanistan* 23/3 (1970): 24-49.

Schlumberger, Daniel. *Le Temple de Surkh Kotal en Bactriane.* Paris: Imprimerie Nationale, Journal Asiatique, II 1954, III 1955, and IV 1964.

———. "The Archaeological Exploration of Afghanistan." *Afghanistan* 2/4 (1947).

Trousdale, W. "The Homeland of Rustam." *Afghanistan* 29/2 (1976): 64-71.

Architecture

Anand, M. R. "The Development of Islamic Architecture in Afghanistan." *Marg* 24/1 (1970): 17-46.

Bechhoefer, W. B. "Architectural Education in Afghanistan." *Afghanistan Journal* 4/4 (1977): 147-148.

———. "Serai Lakon: Traditional Housing in the Old City of Kabul." *Afghanistan Journal* 3/1 (1976): 3-15.

Edelberg, Lennart. *Nuristani Buildings*. Aarhus, Denmark: Jutland Archaeological Society, 1984.

Etemadi, Goya. "The General Mosque of Herat." *Afghanistan* 8/2 (1953): 40-50.

Fischer, K. "Interrelations of Islamic Architecture in Afghanistan. The Remains of Afghan Seistan." *Marg* 24/1 (1970): 47-56.

Frye, R.N. "Notes on the History of Architecture in Afghanistan." *Ars Islamica* 11-12 (1946): 200-202.

————."Observations on Architecture in Afghanistan." *Gazette des Beaux-arts* 6/29 (1946): 129-138.

Hallet, S. I., and R. Samizay. *Traditional Architecture of Afghanistan*. New York and London: Garland, 1980.

Marigo, Alain. "Herat sous les Timourides 15-16eme Siecle." Paris: *Les Nouvelles d'Afghanistan*, 41-42 (March 1989).

Najimi, Abdul Wasay. *Herat: the Islamic City, A Study in Urban Conservation*. Kopenhagen: Scandinavian Institute of Asian Studies, 1988.

Stark, F. *The Minaret of Djam: an Excursion in Afghanistan*. London: J. Murray, 1970.

Linguistics and Literature

Ali, M. "Khushhal Khan Khattak, the Soldier Poet." *Afghanistan* 17/3 (1962): 1-6.

————. "Maulana Jalal-du-Din Balkhi, the Great Sufi Poet and Profound Philosopher." *Afghanistan* 18/1 (1963): 1-12.

Barret, P., and J. Ahmad. *A Collection of Afghan Legends*. Kabul: Education Press, 1970.

Beaureceuil, Serge de. "Abdullah Ansari, a Profile." *Afghanistan* 29/1 (1976): 88-90.

―――. "Studying Ansari of Herat." *Afghanistan* 29/1 (1976): 91-97.

Becka, Jiri. "Young Afghan Prose in Dari." *Afghanistan Journal* 5/3 (1978).

Benava, A.R. "Les Poetesses de l'Aryana." *Afghanistan* 9/3 (1954): 49-55.

Biddulph, C. E. *Afghan Poetry of the Seventeenth Century, Being Selections from the Poems of Khosh Hal Khan Khatak.* London: Paul Kegan, 1890.

Breshna, A. G. "Haji Mirwais Khan, an Historical Play." *Afghanistan* 23/2, 1970.

Dupree, L. "Ajmal Khattak, Revolutionary Pushtun Poet." *American Universities Field Staff Reports* 20/9 (1976).

Dvorjankov, N. A. "The Development of Pushtu as the National and Literary Language of Afghanistan." *Central Asian Review* 14/3 (1966): 210-220.

Farhadi, A. G. R. "The Meaning of Love According to Mawlana Jalaluddin of Balkh." *Afghanistan* 29/1 (1976): 1-7.

Fussman, G. *Atlas Linguistique des Parlers Dardes et Kafirs.* 2 vols. Paris: Ecole Francaise d'Extrême Orient, 1972.

Gilbertson, George W. *The Baluchi Language: A Grammar and Manual.* Hertford: Gilbertson, 1923.

Habibi, A. H. "Pashto Literature at a Glance." *Afghanistan* 20/4 (1968): 51-64; 21/1, 53-57.

Morgenstierne, G. *Indo-Iranian Frontier Languages.* 3 vols. Oslo: Instituttet for Sammenlignend Kulturforskning, 1929-1944.

―――. "The Languages of Afghanistan." *Afghanistan* 20/3 (1967): 81-90.

Weiers, M. "Die Sprache der Hazara und der Mongolen von Afghanistan in Lexikostatischer Sicht." *Afghanistan Journal* 2/3 (1975): 98-102.

3. ECONOMIC

General

Asian Development Bank. *Economic Report on Afghanistan*. Kabul: A.D.B., 1973.

Asiel, M. A., and G. Schmitt-Rink. *Aussenhandel und Terms of Trade' Afghanistans 1961-1975*. Bochum: Studienverlag, 1979.

Balland, D. "Une Nouvelle Generation d'Industries en Afghanistan. Contribution a l'Etude de l'Industrialisation du Tiers-monde." *Bulletin de la Societe Languedocienne de Geographie* 7/1 (1973).

Buescher, H., N. Assad , and H. Berger. "Betriebswirschaftiche Probleme in Afghanischen Industrieunternehmen." *Afghanische Studien*. Meisenheim: Anton Hain, 17, 1977.

Dorner, K. *Entwicklung und Entwicklungpolitik in Afghanistan*. Bochum, Germany: Ruhr-Universität Bochum, 1967.

Ekker, M. H. *Economic Aspects of Development in Afghanistan*. New York: United Nations, 1952.

Fry, M. J. *The Afghan Economy: Money, Finance and the Critical Constraints to Economic Development*. Kabul: USAID, 1973.

―――. *The Afghan Economy: Money, Finance and the Critical Constraints to Economic Development*. Leiden, Netherlands: E. J. Brill, 1974.

―――. *The Financial Institutions of Afghanistan: Description and Analysis*. Kabul: USAID, 1973.

———. *Kabul and Kandahar Money Bazaars: Their Role in Afghanistan Foreign Trade*. Kabul: USAID, 1973.

Guha, "Economic Development of Afghanistan, 1929-1961." *International Studies* 6 (1965): 421-439.

———. "The Rise of Capitalistic Enterprises in Afghanistan, 1929-45." *Indian Economic and Social History Review* 1 (1963): 145-176.

Hapgood, D. *Policies for Promoting Agricultural Development. Report of a Conference on Productivity and Innovation in Agriculture in the Underdeveloped Countries*. Cambridge: MIT, 1964.

Jensch, W. *Die Afghanischen Entwicklungsplane vom Ersten bis zum Dritten Plan*. Meisenheim, Germany: Verlag Anton Hain, 1973.

Kamrany, N. M. *Peaceful Competion in Afghanistan: American and Soviet Models for Economic Aid*. Washington, DC: Communication Service Corp., 1969.

Kanun, M. H. "The System of Taxation of Afghanistan in the Nineteenth Century." *Afghanistan* 30/3 (1977): 1-26.

McChesney, R. D. "The Economic Reforms of Amir Abdur Rahman Khan." *Afghanistan* 21/3 (1968): 11-34.

Monsawi, G. *Wirtschaftspolitische Chronik*. Köln, Germany: N. p., 1980.

Noorzoy, M. Siddieq. "Alternative Economic Systems for Afghanistan." *International Journal of Middle East Studies* 15 (1983).

———. "Planning and Growth in Afghanistan." *World Development* 4/9 (1976): 761-773.

Paul, A. "Constraints on Afghanistan's Economic Development and Prospects for the Future." *Asia* 29 (1973): 1-15.

Picard, P. *A Chief Social and Economic Survey of the Central Provinces*. Kabul: Ministry of Agriculture, 1968.

Stilz, D. *Entwicklung und Struktur der Afghanisschen Industrie.* Meisenheim, Germany: Verlag Anton Hain, 1974.

United States Agency for International Development. *Afghanistan—Financial Development Committee Reports 1973.* Kabul: 1973.

Agriculture

Allen, R.H. *Agricultural Development in Afghanistan.* Kabul: Nathan Associates, 1965.

Amin, H. *Agricultural Geography of Afghanistan.* Kabul: Kabul University, 1974.

Arez, G.J. *The Pattern of Agriculture in Afghanistan.* Kabul: Kabul University, n.d.

Burns, R. H. *Helmand Valley and Research Programs.* Kabul: Wyoming Team, 1957.

Coleman, J. C. *Afghanistan: Helmand-Argandab Valley Project Executive Management.* Bost, Afghanistan: USAID, 1967.

Democratic Republic of Afghanistan. *The Democratic Land Reforms in Afghanistan: Full Action to Uproot Feudalism.* Kabul, n.d.

Gul, Azam. et al. *An Agronomic Survey in Six Eastern Provinces of Afghanistan.* Kabul: No pub., 1966.

International Cooperation Administration, et al. *Development of Afghan Agriculture.* Kabul: ICA, 1960.

Janata, A. "Landwirtschaftliche Struktur Afghanistan." *Bustan* 3 (1963): 36-48.

Lateef, N. V. *Characteristics and Problems of Agriculture in Afghanistan.* Rome: Background Country Study No. 5, 1957.

Lewis, R.H. *General Description of Afghanistan and Its Agriculture.* Kabul: USAID, n.d.

Ministry of Agriculture and Irrigation (Afghanistan). *First Five Year Plan of Ministry of Agriculture.* Kabul: 1957.

————. *Summary of Five Year Plan of Ministry of Agriculture, 1961-1966.* Kabul: 1961.

Ministry of Planning (Afghanistan). *Afghan Agriculture in Figures.* Kabul: 1978.

Schah-Zeidi, M. "Die Afghanische Agrarverfassung." *Bustan* 8/3 (1967): 36-48.

Senzai, M. O., and R. K. Harlan. *Agri-facts: Report on Economic Survey of Agriculture in Nangarhar Province.* Kabul: Kabul University, 1965.

Stevens, I. M. and K. Tarzi. *Economics of Agricultural Production in Helmand Valley, Afghanistan.* Denver, CO: U.S. Department of Interior, Bureau of Reclamation, 1965.

Stiller, F. K. "Die Landwirtschaft Afghanistans." *Der Diplomlandwirt* 4 (1954): 76.

Swedish Committee for Afghanistan. *Agricultural Survey of Afghanistan: Repatriation and Rehabilitation of Afghan Refugees.* Peshawar: 1993.

————. *Farm Power.* Peshawar: 1989.

————. *Farming Systems in Afghanistan.* Peshawar: 1993.

————. *Farming Systems of Maydan Shahr District.* Wardak: 1992.

————. Farming Systems of Mehtelam, Laghman Province. Peshawar: 1992.

————. *Farming Systems of Nad Ali District, Helmand Province.* Peshawar: 1992.

———. *Farming Systems of Nejrab District. Kapisa Province.* Peshawar: 1992.

———. *Farming Systems of Qarabagh District, Ghazni Province.* Peshawar: 1992.

———. *Farming Systems of Shulgara District, Balkh.* Peshawar: 1992.

———. *Northern Afghanistan Food Deficit Survey.* Peshawar: 1990.

———. *Northern Afghanistan Insect Damage Survey.* Peshawar: 1990.

———. *Regional Farming Problems.* Peshawar: 1991.

———. *Repatriation and Rehabilitation of Afghan Refugees.* Peshawar: 1993.

———. *Repatriation and Rehabilitation Survey, Part III, Kandahar.* Peshawar: 1992.

———. *Repatriation and Rehabilitation Survey, Part V, Western Paktia.* Peshawar: 1992.

———. *Repatriation and Rehabilitation Survey, Part IV, Central Nangarhar.* Peshawar: 1992.

———. *Survey, 1991. Fourteenth Report.* Peshawar: 1992

Tkachev, N. D. *Survey of Land and Water Resources: Afghanistan, General Report.* Rome: FAO Reports, UN, 1965.

Mining and Minerals

"Afghanistan." *World Oil* 157/3 (1967): 188-189.

"Afghanistan." *World Petroleum Report* 1973, 1974, 1975.

Aurah, A. L., and A. Q. Majeed. "Case History of the Khwaja Gogerdak and Yatim Tagh Gas Fields of Northern Afghanistan." *3rd ECAFE Sympo-*

sium on the Development of Petrol Resources in Asia and the Far East
3/43, 1965.

"(Barite Reserves in) Afghanistan." *World Minerals* 29/8, 1976.

Bouladon J., and A. F. de Lapparent. "The Hajigak Iron Ore Deposit. Afghanistan Stratigraphic Position, Geological Environment and Paragenesis (Lower Paleozoic)." *Miner Deposita* 10/1 (1975): 13-25.

Bruckl, K. "Die Minerallagerstaetten von Ost-Afghanistan; Versuch Einer Gliederung Nach Genetischen Gesichtspunkten." *Neues Jahrbuch fuer Mineralogie, Abhandlungen.* 72/1 (1936): 1-97.

Clapp, F. G. "Explorations in Iran and Afghanistan." *Oil Weekly* 92/12 (1939): 71-72.

Fuchs, G., A. Matura, and O. Schermann. "Preliminary Report on Geological and Mineral Investigations in Nurestan, Afghanistan." *Verhandlungen der Geologischen Bundesanstalt* 1 (1974): 9-23.

Furon, R. "Les Resources Minieres de l'Afghanistan." *Revue Scientifique* 1924.

Hendrikson, K. H. *Industrial Survey, 1966/67-1969/70.* Kabul: Ministry of Mines and Industries, 1971.

Kinney, G. T., Ed. "Survey Finds Gas Prospects Good in N. Afghanistan." *Oil and Gas Journal* 75/15 (1977): 40.

Kulke, H. "Die Lapislazuli-Lagerstaette Sare Sang (Badakhshan). Geologie, Entstehung, Kulturgeschichte und Bergbau." *Afghanistan Journal* 3 (1976): 43-56.

Mazina, B. G. *Mineral Resources of Iran and Afghanistan.* Moscow: Gol Izdat, 1949.

McLean, P. "Time of Development of Processes of Oil-Gas Formation in Mesozoic and Paleogene Sediments of the Afghano-Tadzhik Oil-gas Region." *Petroleum Geology* 12/7 (1975): 362-363.

Rossovskiy, L. N., and V. M. Chmyrev. "Distribution Patterns of Rare-Metal Pegmatites in the Hindu Kush (Afghanistan)." *International Geological Review* 19/5 (1977): 511-520.

Rossovskiy, L. N., V. M. Chmyrev, and A.S. Salakh. "New Fields and Belts of Rare-Metal Pegmatites in the Hindu Kush (Eastern Afghanistan)." *International Geological Review* 18 (1976): 1339-1342.

Shroder, John F. Jr. *The USSR and Afghanistan Mineral Resources.* Omaha, NE: University of Nebraska at Omaha, n.d.

Smith, G.I. *Potash and Other Evaporite Resources of Afghanistan.* Washington, DC: U.S. Geological Survey 75/89, 1975.

Weber, G. "Afghanistan (Petroleum Production Statistics)." *International Petroleum Encyclopaedia.* 10, 1977.

Williams, L. "Afghanistan Coal (Development)." *Mining Magazine* 136/6 (1977): 509.

Woods, C.W. "Inland Exploration Co. Acquires all Afghanistan for Oil Search: Five Provinces to be Chosen Eventually. An Outline of the Concession Terms." *Petrol Times* 38/967 (July 24, 1937): 78-79 and 121-122.

Water

Auden, J. B., and A. E. Pallister. "Survey of Land and Water Resources." *Afghanistan* 2/1 and 2/2 (1965).

Bruns, W. *Analysis of Water.* Kabul: Kabul University, 1950.

Field, N. C. "The Amu Darya: A Study in Resource Geography." *Geographical Review* 44 (1954): 528-542.

Helmand River Delta Commission. *Report of the Helmand River Delta Commission; Afghanistan and Iran.* Kabul: 1951.

Jentsch, C. "Die Kareze in Afghanistan." *Erdkunde* 24/2 (1970): 112-120.

Latkovich, Vito J. *Activities of the Senior Field Engineer, Surface-Water Research Project, Afghanistan, 1964-68.* Washington, DC: U.S. Geological Survey, 1968.

Proctor and Redfern International Ltd. *Water Supply, Sewage Drainage and Solid Waste Systems for Greater Kabul.* 3 vols. Kabul: World Health Organization, n.d.

Rathjens, C. "Das Hilmend-Projekt in Afghanistan." *Petermanns Geographische Mitteilungen.* 100, 1956.

Rawlinson, H. C. "Monograph on the Oxus." *Journal of the Royal Geographical Society* 42 (1872).

Westfall, Arthur O. *Surface Water Investigations in Afghanistan, 1952-1969.* Washington, DC.: USAID, 1969.

Westfall, Arthur, and V.J. Latkovich. *Surface Water Resources Investigations Plan for Afghanistan.* Kabul: USAID, 1966.

World Health Organization. *Water Quality in Afghanistan.* WHO, 1972.

4. HISTORIC AND POLITICAL

Early Period to the End of the Monarchy

Abdul Ghani. *A Brief Political History of Afghanistan.* Edited by Abdul Jaleel Nafji. Lahore, Pakistan: Najaf Publishers, 1989.

———. *A Review of the Political Situation in Central Asia.* Author, 1921.

Adamec, Ludwig W. *Afghanistan 1900-1923: A Diplomatic History.* Berkeley, CA: University of California Press, 1967.

———. *Afghanistan's Foreign Affairs to the Mid-Twentieth Century: Relations with the USSR, Germany, and Britain.* Tucson, AZ: University of Arizona Press, 1974.

———. *Biographical Dictionary of Contemporary Afghanistan*. Graz, Austria: ADEVA, 1987.

———. *Historical and Political Who's Who of Afghanistan*. Graz, Austria: ADEVA, 1975.

———. *Les Dourranis aux 18e et 19e Siècle*. Paris: CEREDAF, 1995.

———. *Mission of an Afghan Prince to London: Nasrullah Khan's Visit to Britain as Reflected in the Press*. New York: Occasional Paper 33, Afghanistan Forum, 1995.

Alder, G. J. *British India's Northern Frontier 1865-95: A Study in Imperial Policy*. London: 1963.

Ali, Mohammed. *Afghanistan (The Mohammadzai Period). A Political History of the Country Since the Beginning of the Nineteenth Century with emphasis on its Foreign Relations*. Pakistan: Punjab Educational Press, 1959.

———. *Aryana or Ancient Afghanistan*. Kabul: Afghan Historical Society, 1957.

———. "The Battle of Maiwand." *Afghanistan* 10/2 (1955): 26-38.

———. *A Cultural History of Afghanistan*. Lahore, Pakistan: Punjab Educational Press, 1964.

Anderson, J. H. *The Afghan War: 1878-1880*. London: n.p., 1905.

Anwar Khan, M. *England, Russia and Central Asia: A Study in Diplomacy, 1857-1878*. Peshawar, Pakistan: 1963.

Bellew, Henry W. *Afghanistan and the Afghans*. London: Sampson Low Marston, 1979.

Beveridge, A. S. *The Babar Nama*. Leyden, Netherlands: Brill, 1905.

Bosworth, Clifford E. *The Gaznavids: Their Empire in Afghanistan and Eastern Iran, 994-1040*. Edinburgh: Edinburgh University Press, 1963.

———. *The Later Ghaznavids: Splendor and Decay.* Edinburgh: Edinburgh University Press, 1977.

Broxup, Marie. "Afghanistan: The Last Thirty Years." Paris: A special issue of CEREDAF Conference papers in *Central Asian Survey,* 1988.

Buescher, H. "Demokratisierung und Ansaetze zur Parteienbildung in Afghanistan." *Vierteljahresberichte* 3942 (1970): 1-32.

Bunbury, N. L. *A Brief History of the Hazara Pioneers.* London: N.p., 1949.

Burnes, Alexander. *Cabool being a Personaly Narrative of a Journey to and Residence in that City in the Years 1836, 1837 and 1838.* Graz, Austria: ADEVA, 1973.

Cardew, F. G. *The Second Afghan War 1878-80.* London: J. Murray, 1908.

Caroe, Olaf. *The Pathans, 550 BC-AD 1957.* London: Macmillan, 1958.

Castagne, Joseph A. "Notes sur la Politique Exterieure de l'Afghanistan Depuis 1919." *Revue du Monde Musulman* 48, (1921): 1-75.

Curzon, G.N. *Russia in Central Asia in 1889, and the Anglo-Russian Question.* New York: Barnes and Noble, 1967.

Diver, Maud. *The Hero of Herat.* London: John Murray, 1924.

———. *Kabul to Kandahar.* London: Peter Davies, 1935.

Dupree, Louis. *Afghanistan.* Princeton, NJ: Princeton University Press, 1980.

Dupree, Louis, and Linette Albert eds. *Afghanistan in the 1970s.* New York: Praeger, 1974.

Durand, Sir Henry M. *The First Afghan War and its Causes.* London: Longmans, Green & Co. 1879.

Edwardes, Michael. *Playing the Great Game*. London: Hamish Hamilton, 1975.

Elliot, H. M., and Dowson, J. *History of Ghazni*. Calcutta: Susil Gupta, Ltd. 1953.

Elphinstone, Mountstuart. *An Account of the Kingdom of Caubul, and its Dependencies in Persia, Tartary and India*. London: Longman, 1815.

Eyre, Vincet. *The Kabul Insurrection of 1841-42*. London: W. H. Allen, 1879.

————. *The Military Operations in Kabul*. London: W. H. Allen, 1843.

Ferrier, J. P. *History of the Afghans*. London: John Murray, 1858.

Fletcher, Arnold C. *Afghanistan: Highway of Conquest*. Ithaca, NY: Cornell University Press, 1965.

Forbes, A. *The Afghan Wars 1839-42 and 1878-80*. London: Seeley and Co. Limited, 1892.

Fraser-Tytler, W. Kerr. *Afghanistan: A Study of Political Developments in Central and Southern Asia*. London: Oxford University Press, 1953.

Ghaus, Abdul Samad. *The Fall of Afghanistan*. Washington, DC: Pergamon-Brassey, 1988.

Ghobar, G. *Afghanistan dar Masir-i Tarikh*. Kabul: Government Press, 1968.

Grassmuck, George, and Ludwig W. Adamec. *Afghanistan: Some New Approaches*. Ann Arbor, MI: University of Michigan, 1969.

Gray, John A. *My Residence at the Court of the Amir*. London: Bentley, 1901.

Gregorian, Vartan. *The Emergence of Modern Afghanistan: Politics of Reform and Modernization, 1880-1946*. Stanford, CA: Stanford University Press, 1969.

Grevemeyer, Jan-Heeren. *Afghanistan*. Berlin: Express Edition, 1986.

———. "Bericht ueber die Afghanische Historiographie." In *Neue Forschungen in Afghanistan*, by K. Rathjens. Opladen: N.p., 1981.

———. *Herrschaft, Raub und Gegenseitigkeit: Die Politische Geschichte Badakhschans*. Wiesbaden: Otto Harrassowitz, 1982.

Griffiths, John C. *Afghanistan*. London: Pall Mall Press, 1967.

Habberton, W. *Anglo-Russian Relations Concerning Afghanistan*. Urbana, IL: University of Illinois, 1937.

Habibullah, Amir. *My Life from Brigand to King*. London: Sampson Low, Marston & Co., n.d.

Hamilton, Angus. *Afghanistan*. New York: Charles Scribner's Sons, 1906.

Hanna, Henry B. *The Second Afghan War, 1878-79-80: Its Causes, Its Conduct, and Its Consequences*. 3 vols. London: Constable, 1910.

Harpviken, Krisitan Berg. *Political Mobilization among the Hazara of Afghanistan*. Oslo: Department of Sociology, University of Oslo, 1995.

Harrison, Selig S. *In Afghanistan's Shadow: Baluch Nationalism and Soviet Temptations*. New York: Carnegie Endowment for International Peace, 1981.

Hauner, M. "The Soviet Threat to Afghanistan and India, 1938-40." *Modern Asian Studies* 15/2 (1981): 287-309.

Heathcote, T. A. *The Afghan Wars, 1839-1919*. London: Osprey, 1980.

Hensman, Howard. *The Afghan War of 1879-80*. London: W. H. Allen, 1881.

Hold, F. L. *Alexander the Great and Bactria*. Mnemosyne, 1995.

Holdich, Thomas H. *The Gates of India*. London: Macmillan, 1910.

Jalalazai, Musa Khan. *Sectarianism and Ethnic Violence in Afghanistan.* Lahore: Vanguard Books, n.d.

Jansson, Erland. *India, Pakistan or Pakhtunistan?* Uppsala, Sweden: Almqvist, 1981.

Kakar, M. Hasan. *Afghanistan: A Study in Internal Political Developments, 1880-1896.* Lahore: Punjab Educational Press, 1971.

————. *Government and Society in Afghanistan: The Reign of Amir Abd al-Rahman Khan, 1880-1901.* Austin, TX: University of Texas Press, 1979.

————. *The Pacification of the Hazaras of Afghanistan.* New York: Afghanistan Council, 1973.

Kaye, J. *History of the War in Afghanistan.* 3 vols. London: W. H. Allen, 1890.

Khan, Sultan Mahomed. *The Life of Abdur Rahman: Amir of Afghanistan.* London: John Murray, 1901.

Kohzad, Ahmad Ali. *Men and Events Through 18th and 19th Century Afghanistan.* Kabul: Historical Society, n.d.

Lal, M.M. *Life of Amir Dost Mohammad Khan of Kabul.* 2 vols. Karachi: Oxford University Press, 1978.

Lockhart, L. *The Fall of the Safavi Dynasty and the Afghan Occupation of Persia.* Cambridge: Cambridge University Press, 1958.

————. *Nadir Shah: A Critical Study Based Mainly on Contemporary Sources.* London: Luzac, 1938.

Macrory, Patrick A. *The Fierce Pawns.* Philadelphia: J. B. Lippincott, 1966.

————. *Signal Catastrophe: The Story of the Disastrous Retreat from Kabul, 1842.* London: Hodder and Stoughton, 1966.

Malleson, George B. *History of Afghanistan from the Earliest Period to the Outbreak of the War of 1878*. London: W. H. Allen, 1879.

Manz, B. F. *Central Asia in Historical Perspective*. Boulder, CO: Westview Press, 1995.

Masson, Charles. *Narrative of Various Journeys in Blochistan, Afghanistan and the Panjab, Including a Residence in those Countries*. 2 vols. Graz: ADEVA, 1975.

Maxwell, Leigh. *My God—Maiwand!* London: Leo Cooper, 1979.

McChesney, R. D. *Waqf in Central Asia: Four Hundred Years in the History of a Muslim Shrine, 1480-1889*. Princeton, NJ: Princeton University Press, 1991.

McMunn, G. *Afghanistan from Darius to Amanullah*. London: G. Bell & Sons, 1929 and 1977.

Miller, Charles. *Khyber: British India's North West Frontier*. London: MacDonald & James, 1977.

Molesworth, George Noble. *Afghanistan 1919: An Account of Operations in the Third Afghan War*. London: Asia Publishing House, 1962.

Morison, John L. *From Alexander Burnes to Frederick Roberts; A Survey of Imperial Frontier Policy*. London: Proceedings of the British Academy, 1936.

Nawid, Senzil. "King Amanullah and the Afghan Ulama: Religious Response to Reform, 1919-1929." Ph.D. diss., University of Arizona, 1978.

Nazim, M. *The Life and Times of Sultan Mahmud of Ghazna*. Cambridge: Cambridge University Press, 1931.

Nematullah. *History of the Afghans*. Translated by Bernhard Dorn. London: Oriental Translation Committee, 1829.

Newell, Richard S. *The Politics of Afghanistan*. Ithaca, NY: Cornell University Press, 1972.

Noelle, Christine. "The Anti-Wahhabi Reaction in 19th Century Afghanistan." *The Muslim World* Jan.-Apr. 1995.

———. "The Interaction Between State and Tribe in 19th Century Afghanistan: The Reign of Amir Dost Muhammad Khan." Ph.D. diss., University of California at Berkeley: 1995.

Norris, James A. *The First Afghan War, 1838-42*. London: Cambridge University Press, 1967.

O'Ballance, Edgar. *Afghan Wars 1839-1992*. London: Brassey's, 1993.

Pazhwak, Abdur Rahman. *Afghanistan (Ancient Aryana)*. Hove, England: Key Press, 1954.

———. *Pakhtunistan*. Hove, England: Key Press, 1955.

Pennel, Theodore L. *Among the Wild Tribes of the Afghan Frontier*. London: Oxford University Press, 1927.

Poladi, Hassan. *The Hazaras*. Stockton, CA: Mughal Pub. Co., 1989.

Pottinger, George. *The Afghan Connection: The Extraordinary Adventures of Major Eldred Pottinger*. Edinburgh: Scottish Academic Press, 1983.

Poullada, Leon B. *Reform and Rebellion in Afghanistan, 1919-1929*. Ithaca, NY: Cornell University Press, 1973.

———. "Afghanistan and the United States: The Crucial Years" *Middle East Journal* 35 (1981).

Poulada, Leon B., and Leila, D. J. *The Kingdom of Afghanistan and the United States, 1828-1973*. Omaha, NE: University of Nebraska at Omaha, 1995.

Poulton, M., and R. Poulton. *L'Afghanistan*. Paris: Presses Universitaires de France, 1981.

Reshtia, Sayed Qassem. *Between two Giants: Political History of Afghanistan in the Nineteenth Century*. Peshawar: Afghan Jehad Works, 1990.

Rubinstein, Alan Z. *Soviet Policy Toward Turkey, Iran and Afghanistan*. New York: Praeger Special Studies, 1982.

Sale, F. *A Journal of the Disasters in Afghanistan, 1841-1842*. London: John Murray, 1843.

Shadbolt, Sydney H. *The Afghan Campaigns of 1878-80: Compiled from Official and Private Sources*. 2 vols. London: Sampson Low Marston, 1882.

Schinasi, M. *Afghanistan at the Beginning of the Twentieth Century. Nationalism and Journalism in Afghanistan. A Study of Seraj ul-Akhbar (1911-1918)*. Naples: Instituto Universario Orientali, 1979.

————. *Italie-Afghanistan: 1921-1941*. Annali. Napoli: Instituto Universitario Orientale, 1987.

Shah, Iqbal Ali. *Afghanistan of the Afghans*. London: The Diamond Press, 1928.

Shah Wali, Sadar. *My Memoirs*. Kabul: Education Press, 1970.

Singh, G. *Ahmad Shah Durrani, Father of Modern Afghanistan*. Bombay: Asia Publishing House, 1959.

Singhal, D. P. *India and Afghanistan 1876-1907. A Study in Diplomatic Relations*. Melbourne: University of Queensland Press, 1963.

Spain, James. *The Pathan Borderland*. Hague: Mouton and Co., 1963.

Stewart, Rhea Talley. *Fire in Afghanistan, 1914-1929*. New York: Doubleday, 1973.

Sykes, Sir P. *A History of Afghanistan*. New York: AMS Press, 1940.

Tabibi, Abdul H. *Reminiscences of my Four Decades of Diplomatic Life at the Service of Afghanistan and the World at Large*. Nicosia, Cyprus: Troodos Printing & Publishing, 1995.

Tarn, W. W. *The Greeks in Bactria and India*. Cambridge: Cambridge University Press, 1951.

Trousdale, William. *War in Afghanistan, 1879-80*. Detroit, MI: Wayne State University Press, 1985.

Van Dyk, Jere. *In Afghanistan: An American Odyssey*. New York: Coward, McCann & Geoghegan, 1983.

Viollis, Andree. *Tourmente sur l'Afghanistan*. Paris: Librairie Valois, 1930.

Volodarsky, Mikhail. *The Soviet Union and its Southern Neighbours: Iran and Afghanistan, 1917-1933*. Portland, OR: Frank Cass & Co, 1994.

Wheeler, S. *The Amir Abdur Rahman*. London: Bliss, Sands and Foster, 1895.

Wild, Roland. *Amanullah: Ex-King of Afghanistan*. London: Hurst & Blackett, 1933.

Yapp, Malcolm E. *Strategies of British India: Britain, Iran, and Afghanistan, 1798-1850*. New York: The Clarendon Press, 1980.

———. "Tribes and States in the Khyber, 1838-42." In *The Conflict of Tribe and State in Iran and Afghanistan*. London: Croom-Helm, 1983.

The Afghan Republic and War

Adamec, Ludwig. W. *Biographical Dictionary of Contemporary Afghanistan*. Graz, Austria: ADEVA, 1987.

———. *Historical Dictionary of Afghanistan*. Metuchen, NJ: Scarecrow Press, 1991.

Ahady, Anwar-ul-Haq. "Afghanistan: State Breakdown." In *Revolutions of the Twentieth Century,* edited by Jack A. Goldstone, et al. Boulder, CO: Westview, 1991.

———. "The Decline of the Pashtuns in Afghanistan." *Asian Survey* 7 (July 1995).

Amstutz, J. Bruce. *Afghanistan: The First Five Years of Soviet Occupation.* Washington, DC: National Defense University Press, 1986.

Anwar, Raja. *The Tragedy of Afghanistan: A First-Hand Account.* London: Verso, 1988.

Arnold, Anthony. *Afghanistan: The Soviet Invasion in Perspective.* Stanford, CA: Hoover Institution Press, 1981.

———. *Afghanistan's Two-Party Communism: Parcham and Khalq.* Stanford, CA: Hoover Institution Press, 1983.

———. *The Fateful Pebble: Afghanistan's Role in the Fall of the Soviet Empire.* Novato, CA: Presidio Press, 1993.

Ashraf, Abdur Rahman. *Muhammad Zahir Shah: Payam-ha, Musahebe-ha, wa Bayanayi-ha Ishan dar Dehat-i Jehad.* (Muhammad Zahir Shah: His Messages, Interviews, Statements in the Decade of the Jehad) Bonn: Author, 1990.

Banuazizi, Ali, and Myron Weiner. *The State, Religion and Ethinc Politics: Afghanistan, Iran, and Pakistan.* Syracuse, NY: Syracuse University Press, 1986.

Bennigsen, Alexandre. "Mullahs, Mujahidin and Soviet Muslims." *Problems of Communism* 33 (1984).

Bennigsen, Alexandre, et al. *Afghanistan: Dix Annees Terribles, 1977-1987.* Paris: Internationale de la Résistance. 1988.

Bennigsen, Alexandre, and Marie Broxup. *The Islamic Threat to the Soviet State.* New York: N.p. 1983.

Bernstein, Carl. "Arms for Afghanistan." *The New Republic* 18 July (1981): 8-10.

Bocharov, G. *Russian Roulette: Afghanistan through Russian Eyes.* New York: Hamish Hamilton, 1990.

Bonner, Arthur. *Among the Afghans.* Durham, NC: Duke University Press, 1987.

Bonosky, Phillip. *Washington's Secret War Against Afghanistan.* New York: International Publishers, 1985.

Bradsher, Henry S. *Afghanistan and the Soviet Union.* Durham, NC: Duke University Press, 1983.

———. "Afghanistan." *The Washington Quarterly* (1984).

Brigot, Andre, and Olivier Roy. *The War in Afghanistan.* New York: Harvester, 1988.

Broxup, J. M. "The Soviets in Afghanistan: The Anatomy of a Takeover." *Central Asian Survey* (1983).

Bucherer-Dietschi, Paul. *Afghanistan: Vom Koenigreich zur Sovietischen Invasion.* Liestal, Switzerland: 1985.

Centlivres, Pierre, et al. *Afghanistan: La Colonisation Impossible.* Paris: CERF, 1984.

Centlivres-Demont, Micheline. *The Politics of Social Transformation in Afghanistan, Iran and Pakistan.* Syracuse, NY: Syracuse University Press, 1994.

Central Asian Survey. *Children in War.* Geneva: n.d.

Chaliand, Gerard. *Report from Afghanistan.* New York: Viking Press, 1982.

Cogan, Charles. *Holy Blood: An Inside View of the Afghan War.* Westport, CT: Praeger, 1993.

Collins, Joseph J. *The Soviet Invasion of Afghanistan: A Study of the Use of Force in Soviet Foreign Policy.* Lexington, MA: Lexington Books, 1985.

―――. "The Soviet Invasion of Afghanistan: Methods, Motives and Ramifications." *Naval War College Review* (1980).

―――. "Soviet Military Performance in Afghanistan: A Preliminary Assessment." *Comparative Strategy* (1983).

Cordovez, Diego, and Selig S. Harrison. *Out of Afghanistan: The Inside Story of the Soviet Withdrawal.* Oxford: Oxford University Press, 1995.

Democratic Republic of Afghanistan. *Babrak Karmal's Speeches.* Kabul: Government Press, 1980.

―――. *Documents and Records of the National Conference of the Peoples Democratic Party of Afghanistan.* Kabul: Government Press, 1982.

―――. *Excerpts of Interviews and Speeches Delivered by Babrak Karmal.* Kabul: Gorvernment Press, 1981.

―――. *White Book: Foreign Policy Documents of the Democratic Republic of Afghanistan.* Kabul: Government Press, 1981.

Deutsches Orient-Institut. *Afghanistan Seit dem Sturz der Monarchie.* Hamburg: 1981.

Dupree, Louis. "Afghanistan under the Khalq." *Problems of Communism.* 28 (August 1979).

―――. "The Democratic Republic of Afghanistan, 1979." *American Universities Field Staff Reports. Asia* 32 (1979): 11.

___. "Red Flag over Hindu Kush, Part I: Leftist Movements in Afghanistan." *American Universities Field Staff Reports. Asia* 44 (1979).

___. "Red Flag over Hindu Kush, Part II: The Accidental Coup, or Taraki in Blunderland." *American Universities Field Staff Reports. Asia* 45 (1979).

————. "Red Flag over the Hindu Kush, Part III: Rhetoric and Reforms, or Promises!" *American Universities Field Staff Reports. Asia* 23 (1980).

————. "Red Flag over the Hindu Kush, Part IV: Foreign Policy and Economy." *American Universities Field Staff Reports. Asia* 27 (1980).

————. "Red Flag over the Hindu Kush, Part V and VI: Repressions, or Security Through Terror Purges." *American Universities Field Staff Reports. Asia* 28 (1980).

Duran, Khalid. *Islam und Politischer Extremismus.* Hamburg: Deutsches Orient Institut, 1985.

Emadi, Hafizullah. *State, Revolution, and Superpowers in Afghanistan.* New York: Praeger, 1990.

Es'haq, Mohammed. *Situation in the North of Afghanistan, 1987.* Peshawar, Pakistan: Jam'iat Political Office, n.d.

Farr, Grant M., and John G. Merriam. *Afghan Resistance: The Politics of Survival.* Boulder, CO: Westview Press, 1987.

Fazelly, Muhammad Kacem. "Hachem Waiwandwal, un Projet Politique Assassiné." *Les Nouvelles d'Afghanistan* 44 (October 1989).

Galeotti, Mark. *Afghanistan: The Soviet Union's Last War.* London: Frank Cass, 1995.

Gall, Sandy. *Afghanistan: Agony of a Nation.* London: The Bodley Head, Ltd., 1988.

————. *Behind Russian Lines: An Afghan Journal.* London: Sidgwick and Jackson, 1983.

Ghaus, Abdul Samad. *The Fall of Afghanistan.* Washington, DC: Pergamon-Brassey's, 1988.

Gibbs, David. "Does the USSR Have a Grand Strategy? Reinterpreting the Invasion of Afghanistan." *Journal of Peace Research* 21/4 (1987).

————. "The Peasant as Counterrevolutionary: The Rural Origins of the Afghan Insurgency." *Studies in Comparative International Development* 21/1 (1986).

Gille, Etienne. "Khalq et Partcham: 25 ans de Déchirements." *Les Nouvelles d'Afghanistan* 48 (July 1990).

————. "L'Accession au Pouvoir des Communistes ProSovietiques." In *Afghanistan: La Colonisation Impossible*. Paris: CERF, 1984.

Gille, Etienne, and Sylvie Heslot. *Letters d'Afghanistan de Serge de Beaurecueil*. Paris: CEREDAF, n.d.

Girardet, Edward R. *Afghanistan: The Soviet War*. London: Croom Helm, 1985.

Goldman, Minton F. "Soviet Military Intervention in Afghanistan: Roots and Causes." *Polity* Spring 1984.

Goodwin, Jan. *Caught in the Crossfire*. New York: Dutton, 1987.

Greussing, Kurt, and Jan-Heeren Grevemeyer, et al. *Revolution in Iran und Afghanistan*. Frankfurt am Main: 1980.

Grevemeyer, Jan-Heeren. "Religion, Ethnizitaet und Nationalismus im Afghanischen Widerstand." *Leviathan* 13/1 (1985).

Gupta, Bhabani Sen. *Afghanistan*. London: Francis Pinter, 1986.

Halliday, Fred. "Afghanistan: A Revolution Consumes Itself." *The Nation* 229 (November 1979).

————. "The Revolution in Afghanistan." *New Left Review* 112 (1978).

————. "War in Afghanistan." *New Left Review* 119 (1980).

Hammond, Thomas T. *Red Flag over Afghanistan: The Communist Coup, The Soviet Invasion, and The Consequences*. Boulder, CO: Westview Press, 1984.

Harrison, Selig S. "Rough Plan Emerging for Afghan Peace." *Washington Quarterly* 3 (Summer 1980).

Hauner, Milan. *The Soviet War in Afghanistan: Patterns of Russian Imperialism.* Lanham, MD: University Press of America, 1991.

Hauner, Milan, and Robert L. Canfield. *Afghanistan and the Soviet Union.* Boulder, CO: Westview Press, 1989.

Huldt, Bo, and Erland Jansen, eds. *The Tragedy of Afghanistan: the Social, Cultural, and Political Impact of the Soviet Invasion.* London: Croom Helm, 1988.

Hyman, Anthony. *Afghanistan under Soviet Occupation.* New York: St. Martin's Press, 1982.

Isby, David C. *Russia's War in Afghanistan.* London: Osprey, 1986.

———. *The War in Afghanistan 1979-1989: The Soviet Empire at High Tide.* Hong Kong, 1990.

Kakar, Hasan. *Afghanistan: The Soviet Invasion and the Afghan Response, 1979-1982.* Berkeley, CA: University of California Press, 1995.

———. "The Fall of the Afghan Monarchy in 1973." *International Journal of Middle Eastern Studies* 9/2 (1978): 195-224.

Kaplan, Robert D. *Soldiers of God: With the Mujahidin in Afghanistan.* Boston, MA: Houghton Mifflin, 1990.

Khalilzad, Zalmay. "Afghanistan in 1994: Civil War and Disintegration." *Asian Survey* 7 (July 1995).

———. "Moscow's Afghan War." *Problems of Communism* Jan-Feb. 1986.

———. "Soviet-Occupied Afghanistan." *Problems of Communism* 29/6 (1980): 23-40.

Khan, Riaz M. *Untying the Afghan Knot: Negotiating Soviet Withdrawal.* Durham, NC: Duke University Press, 1991.

Khurasani, Hamid. *Facts and Fiction: Human Rights in the Democratic Republic of Afghanistan*. Kabul: Kabul Peace Publishing House, 1986.

Klass, Rosanne T. *Afghanistan: The Great Game Revisited*. New York: Freedom House, 1987.

Laber, Jeri, and Barnett R. Rubin. *A Nation is Dying*. Evanston, IL: Northwestern University Press, 1988.

Lohbeck, Kurt. *Holy War, Unholy Victory*. Washington, DC: Regnery Gateway, 1993.

———. *Jihad: Holy War*. Washington, DC: 1984.

Magnus, Ralph H., Ed., *Afghan Alternatives: Issues, Options, and Policies*. New Brunswick, NJ: Transaction Books, 1985.

———. *Afghanistan: Marx, Mullah, and Mujahed*. Boulder, CO: Westview Press, 1985.

Magnus, Ralph, and Eden Nabi. "Afghanistan and Central Asia: Mirrors and Models." *Asian Survey* 25/7 (July 1995).

Majrooh, S.B., and S.M.Y. Elmi. *The Sovietization of Afghanistan*. Peshawar: Jihad Press, 1986.

Male, Beverley. *Revolutionary Afghanistan: A Reappraisal*. New York: St. Martin's Press, 1982.

Maley, William, and Fazl Haq Saikal. *Political Order in Post-Communist Afghanistan*. Boulder, CO and London: International Peace Academy, Occasional Papers Series. Lynne Riemer Publishers, 1992.

Malhuret, Claude. "Report from Afghanistan." *Foreign Affairs* Winter 1983-1984.

Maprayil, Cyriac. *The Soviets and Afghanistan*. London: Cosmic Press, 1982.

McMichael, Scott. *The Stumbling Bear: Soviet Military Performance*. London: Brassey's, 1991.

Misra, K. P. *Afghanistan in Crisis*. New Delhi: Vikas Publishing House, 1980.

Monks, Alfred L. *The Soviet Invasion in Afghanistan*. Washington, DC: American Enterprise Institute, 1981.

Moorcraft, Paul L. "Bloody Standoff in Afghanistan." *Army* April 1985.

Muhammad Daud, Sardar. *The Republic of Afghanistan: Statements, Messages, and Press Interviews of the National Leader and the Founder of the Republic*. Kabul: Government Press, 1973.

Naby, Eden. "The Changing Role of Islam as a Unifying Force in Afghanistan." In Ali Banuazizi, *The State, Religion, and Ethnic Politics*. Syracuse, NY: Syracuse University Press, 1986.

Nayar, Kuldip. *Report on Afghanistan*. New Delhi: Allied Publishers, 1980.

Newell, Nancy Peabody, and Richard S. Newell. *The Struggle for Afghanistan*. Ithaca, NY: Cornell University Press, 1981.

Nikolayev, Lev. *Afghanistan: Between the Past and the Future*. Moscow: Progress Publishers, 1986.

O'Ballance, Edgar. *Afghan Wars, 1939-1992*. London: Brassey's, 1993.

Olesen, Asta. *Islam and Politics in Afghanistan*. London: Curzon Press, 1995.

Overby, Paul. *Holy Blood: The Afghan War from the Inside*. Westport, CT: Praeger, 1993.

Picolyer. "Caravans on Moonless Nights: How the CIA Supports and Supplies the Anti-Soviet Guerrillas." *Time* 11 June 1984.

Reshtia, Sayed Qassem. *The Price of Liberty: The Tragedy of Afghanistan*. Rome: Bard Editore, 1984.

Rogers, Tom. *The Soviet Withdrawal from Afghanistan: Analysis and Chronology*. Westport, CT: Greenwood Press, 1992.

Roy, Olivier. *From Holy War to Civil War*. Princeton, NJ: Princeton University Press, 1994.

———. *Islam and Resisance in Afghanistan*. Cambridge: Cambridge University Press, 1986.

———. "The Origins of the Afghan Communist Party." In *Afghanistan in the Last Thirty Years*. Oxford: Pergamon Press, 1988.

———. "The Origins of the Islamist Movement in Afghanistan." Oxford: *Central Asian Survey* 3/2 (1984) 117-127.

Rubin, Barnett R. *The Fragmentation of Afghanistan: State Formation & Collapse in the International System*. New Haven, CT: Yale University Press, 1995.

———. *The Search for Peace in Afghanistan: From Buffer State to Failed State*. New Haven, CT: Yale University Press, 1995.

Ryan, Nigel. *A Hitch or Two in Afghanistan: A Journey Behind Russian Lines*. London: Weidenfeld & Nicolson, 1983.

Saikal, Amin. *Regime Change in Afghanistan: Foreign Intervention and the Politics of Legitimacy*. Boulder, CO: Westview Press, 1991.

———. "The Afghanistan Crisis: A Negotiated Settlement?" *The World Today* November 1984.

Saikal, Amin, and William Maley. *The Soviet Withdrawal from Afghanistan*. Melbourne: Cambridge University Press, 1989.

Samimy, S. M. *Hintergruende der Sovietischen Invasion in Afghanistan*. Bochum, Germany: Author, 1981.

Shahrani, M. Nazif, and Robert L. Canfield, eds. *Revolutions and Rebellions in Afghanistan*. Berkeley, CA: Institute of International Studies, University of California, 1984.

Shansab, Nasir. "The Struggle for Afghanistan." In *Combat on Communist Territory*. Lake Bluff, VA: 1985.

Simons, Lewis M. "Standoff in Afghanistan." *The New Republic* 187 (August 1982).

"Special Issue on Afghanistan." *World Affairs* 145/3 (1982-83).

Stahel, Albert A., and Paul Bucherer. *Afghanistan, 1984/85: Besetzung und Widerstand*. Liestal, Switzerland: Schweizerisches Afghan Archiv, 1985.
———. *Afghanistan, 1985/86: Besetzung und Kriegfuehrung der UdSSR*. Liestal, Switzerland: Schweizerisches Afghan Archiv, 1986.

———. *Afghanistan, 1986/87: Internationale Strategische Lage und Sovietisierung Afghanistans*. Liestal, Switzerland: Schweizerisches Afghan Archiv, 1987.

———. *Afghanistan: 5 Jahre Widerstand und Kleinkrieg*. Frauenfeld, Switzerland: Huber, 1984.

Tabibi, Abdul Hakim. *Afghanistan: A Nation in Love With Freedom*. Cedar Rapids, IA: Igram Press, 1985.

Tawana, Sayyed Musa. "Glimpses into the Historical Background of the Islamic Movement in Afghanistan." *AfghaNews*. Parts 1-8 (April-July, 1989).

Urban, Mark. *War In Afghanistan*. New York: St. Martin's Press, 1990.

Vertzberger, Yaacov. "Afghanistan in China's Policy." *Problems of Communism* 31 (June 1982).

Vogel, Claudia, and Michael Sagurna. *Der Freiheitskrieg in Afghanistan*. Bonn: Bonner Friedensforum, 1984.

Wiegandt, Winfried F. *Afghanistan: Nicht aus Heiterem Himmel*. Zurich, 1980.

Yousaf, Mohammad, and Mark Adkin. *The Bear Trap: Afghanistan's Untold Story*. Lahore: Jang Publishers, 1992.

Zeray, Muhammad Saleh. "Afghanistan: The Beginning of a New Era." *World Marxist Review* 22 January 1979.

5. JURIDICAL

Laws and Constitutions

Afghanistan. "The Flag Law in Afghanistan." *Afghanistan* 27/1 (1974): 1-8.

Asia Society. *The Constitution of the Republic of Afghanistan*. New York: Afghanistan Council, 1977.

————. "Afghanistan: Laws, Statutes, etc., English Translation of some of the New Laws Promulgated by the Republic of Afghanistan." New York: Afghanistan Council, 1975.

Beck, Sebastian. "Das Afghanische Strafgesetzbuch vom Jahre 1924 mit dem Zusatz vom Jahre 1925." *Die Welt des Islam* 2/1-2 (1928).

————. "Afghanistan: Das Hoechste Gericht." In *Die Hoechsten Gerichte der Welt*. By Julius Magnus Leipzig: 1929.

Brunner, Christopher. *New Afghan Laws Regarding Agriculture*. New York: Afghanistan Council, Occasional Paper 12 (1977).

Dari, Gholam M. *Huquq-i Famil dar Afghanistan* (Family Law in Afghanistan). Kabul: Government Press, 1971.

Dupree, Louis. "Constitutional Development and Cultural Change." *American Universities Field Staff Reports. Afghanistan* 9/1-10 (1965).

Fazelly, Muhammad Kacem. "L'Islam dans le Droit Afghan." *Les Nouvelles d'Afghanistan* 12/13 (March 1983).

————. *La Loya Djirga*. Paris: CEREDAF, 1989.

Franklin Book Programs. *Draft of the New Constitution of Afghanistan*. Kabul: Government Press, 1964.

Hager, P. "Compiled Translations of the Laws of Afghanistan." *United Nations Development Programme*. Kabul: Government Press, 1975.

Haqqani, Abdul Karim. *Rahnama-yi Mu'amilat* (Guide on Transactions). Kabul: Government Press, 1348/1969.

Huquqi, Walid A. *Judicial Organization in Afghanistan*. Kabul: Government Press, 1971.

Kamali, Muhammad H. *Law in Afghanistan*. Leiden, Netherland: E. J. Brill, 1985.

Karimi, Ahmadullah. "The Constitution of Afghanistan." *Afghanistan* 1/1 (1946).

Khan, Sultan Mahomed. *The Constitutions and Laws of Afghanistan*. London: John Murray, 1900.

Libesny, Herbert J. "Judicial Systems in the Near and Middle East: Evolutionary Development and Islamic Revival." *The Middle East Journal* 37/2 (1983).

Massoum, Gholam Sakhi. "Der Voelkerrechtliche Status von Afghanistan." Ph.D. diss., Hamburg University, 1960.

Parker, G. L. "Central Bank Law" (Preliminary Draft). Kabul: Nathan Associates. 1967.

Roy, Olivier. "Islam et Code Tribal." *Les Nouvelles d'Afghanistan*. 12/13 (March 1983).

Royal Government of Afghanistan, Ministry of Commerce. *Foreign and Domestic Private Investment Law*. Kabul: 1965.

United States Agency of International Development. *Commercial Law of Afghanistan*. Kabul: USAID, 1955.

United States Department of Labor. *Labor Law and Practice in Afghanistan*. Washington, DC: Bureau of Labor Statistics, 1969.

Weinbaum, Marvin G. "Legal Elites in Afghan Society." *IJMES* 12/1 (1980): 39-51.

――――. "The Legislator as Intermediary: Integration of the Center and Periphery in Afghanistan." In *Legislatures in Plural Societies: The Search for Cohesion in National Development*, edited by Albert F. Eldridge. Durham, NC: 1977.

Wilber, Donald N. "Commentary on the Constitution of Afghanistan of 1st October 1964." *Middle East Journal* Spring 1965.

Wiseman, H. Victor. "The New Constitution of Afghanistan: Some Observations." *Parliamentary Affairs* 18/4 (1965): 434-441.

Zhwand, Samiuddin. "The Judiciary." Kabul: *The Kabul Times Annual*, 1967.

6. SCIENTIFIC

Flora and Fauna

Aitchinson, J. F. T. "The Botany of the Afghan Delimitation Commission." *Transactions of the Linnean Society. Botany* III (1888): 1-139.

Akhtar, S. A. "Ab-Istadeh, a Breeding-place of the Flamingo in Afghanistan." *Journal of the Bombay Natural History Society* 47/2 (1947): 308-315.

Annandale, N. "Report on the Aquatic Fauna of Seistan." *Record of the Indian Museum* 18 (1919-21): 1-24.

Balthazar, V. "Neue Spheciden aus Afghanistan (Opuscula Hymenopteralogica)." *Mitteilungen der Munchner Entomologischen Gesellschaft* 47 (1957): 186-200.

Breckle, S. W., and W. Frey. "Die Vegetationsstufen in Zentralen Hindukusch." *Afghanistan Journal*. 1/3 (1974): 75-80.

———. "Afghanistanische Drogen und Ihre Stammpflanzen, 1. Seissholz." *Afghanistan Journal* 6/3 (1979): 87-91.

———. "Botanical Literature of Afghanistan." *Edinburgh Royal Botanical Garden Notes* 29/3 (1969): 357-372.

———. "Botanical Literature of Afghanistan: Supplement 1." *Edinburgh Royal Botanical Garden Notes* 33/3 (1975): 503-521.

Cumming, J.W.N. "Birds of Seistan, Being a List of the Birds Shot or Seen in Seistan by the Arbitration Commission, 1903-1905." *Journal of the Bombay Natural History Society* (1905): 686-699.

Dupree, L. "Note in the Distribution of the Indian Crested Porcupine." *Afghanistan Journal of Mammalogy* 37/2 (1956): 299-300.

Eshghy, N., and M. K. Nushine. "Insecticide Resistance of Anopheles Culicifacies in the Province of Helmand, Southwest Afghanistan, 1976." *Mosquito News* 38/1 (1978): 97-101.

Freitag, H. "Flora und Vegetation." *Afghanistan Laendermonographie*. Liestal, 1986.

Gaedike, R. "Austrian Entomological Expedition to Iran and Afghanistan, Contributions to the Lepidoptera Fauna." *Annalen de Naturhistorischen Musueums in Wien* 72 (1968): 529-533.

Hassanyar, A. S. "Environmental Problems in Afghanistan." *Geographical Review of Afghanistan* 12/2 (1973): 1, 9-17.

Hassinger, J. D. "A Survey of the Mammals of Afghanistan." *Feldiana Zoology* 60 (1973): 195.

Hoogstraal, H. "Biological Patterns in the Afghanistan Tick Fauna." *Proceedings of the 3rd International Congress of Acarology*. Prague: (1971). 511-514.

Kitamura, S. *Flora in Afghanistan, Results of the Kyoto University Scientific Expedition to the Karakorum and Hindu Kush, 1955.* Kyoto: Kyoto University Press, 1960.

————. *Plants of West Pakistan and Afghanistan, Committee of the Kyoto University Scientific Expedition to the Karakorum and Hindu Kush.* Kyoto: Kyoto University Press, 1964.

Kullmann, E. "The Mammals of Afghanistan." *Science Quarterly Journal* 3 (1965): 20.

Leviton, A. E. "Report on a Collection of Reptiles from Afghanistan." *Proceedings of the California Academy of Sciences* 29/12 (1959): 445-463.

Linchevsky, I. A., and A. V. Prozorovski. "The Basic Principles of the Distribution of the Vegetation of Afghanistan." *New Bulletin* 2 (1949): 179-214.

Meyer-Oehme, D. "Die Saugetiere Afghanistans 3. Chiroptera." *Science Quarterly Journal* 1965.

Millett, E. R. *Annual Reports, Regional Insect Control Project, Afghanistan.* Kabul: USAID/USDA/ARS, 1960.

————. *Annual Reports, Summary of Insect Conditions in Afghanistan.* Kabul: USAID, 1961.

————. "Insect Pests Identified from Afghanistan." In *USDA and USNM Taxonomists.* Kabul: USAID, 1961.

Paludan, Knud. *On the Birds of Afghanistan.* Copenhagen: C. A. Reitzel, 1959.

Papp, L. "New Species and Records of Sphaeroceridae (Diptera) from Afghanistan." *Acta Zoologica* 24/1-2 (1978): 149-168.

Rathjens, C. "Klimatische Jahreszeiten in Afghanistan." *Afghanistan Journal* 1/1 (1974): 13-18.

————. "Vegetation and Flora of the Central Hindu Kush, Afghanistan." *Geographische Zeitschrift* 69/2 (1981): 159.

Schneider, P. "Honigbienen und ihre Zucht in Afghanistan." *Afghanistan Journal* 3 (1976): 101-104.

Vaurie, C. "A Revision of the Bird Family Dicruridae: Afghanistan." *American Museum of Natural History* 93/4 (1949): 199-342.

Wendelbo, P., and J. Hedge. *Studies in the Flora of Afghanistan.* Bergen, Norway: Arbok University 18 (1963): 56.

Geography

Adamec, Ludwig W. *Historical and Political Gazetteer of Afghanistan.* 6 vols. Graz, Austria: ADEVA, 1972-1985.

Ali, Muhammad. "Afghanistan's Mountains." *Afghanistan* 8/1 (1953): 47-52.

———. *Guide to Afghanistan.* Lahore: Northern Pakistan Publishing Co., 1938.

Amin, Hamidullah, and Gordon B. Schiltz. *A Geography of Afghanistan.* Omaha, NE: Center for Afghanistan Studies, 1976.

Arez, G. J. "Geography of Afghanistan." *Kabul Times Annual* (1970): 19-28.

———. "The Urban Structure of Kabul." *Geographical Review of Afghanistan* 12/3 (1973): 1-19.

Balland, D. "Le Coton en Afghanistan: Essay d'Analyse Geographique et economique d'une Culture Industrielle dans une Pay Sous-Industrialise." *Revue Geographique de l'Est* 13/1-2 (1973): 17-75.

———. "Reflexions d'un Geograph sur une Decennie de Recherches Francaises en Afghanistan (1968-1978)." *Mission Scientifique, Afghanistan Bulletin* 8 (1979): 3-21.

Bellew, Henry W. *Journal of a Political Mission to Afghanistan, in 1857.* London: Smith, Elder & Co. 1862.

Brandenburg, D. *Herat: Eine Timuridische Hauptstadt.* Graz, Austria: ADEVA, 1977.

Burnes, A. *Kabool: Being a Personal Narrative of a Journey to, and Residence in that City, in the year 1836,7,8.* London: 1842 and Graz, Austria: ADEVA, 1975.

Dehmel, R. "Neue Stauseen in Afghanistan." *Geographische Rundschau* 1953.

Diemberger, A. "Begsteiger Erschliessen den Hindukush." *Jahrbuch des Deutschen Alpenvereins* 90 (1965).

Douglas, W. O. "West from the Khyber-Pass." *National Geographic Magazine* 114 (1958).

Dupree, Louis. "Aq Kupruk: A Town in North Afghanistan." Part I: "The People and their Cultural Patterns." Part II: "The Political Structure and Commercial Patterns." *Universities Field Staff, South Asia Series* X/9-10 (1966).

English, P. "The Traditional City of Herat, Afghanistan." In *From Madina to Metropolis* by L. C. Brown. Princeton, NJ: Princeton University Press, 1973.

Fairchild, Inc. "Making of Afghanistan." *Afghanistan* 3 (1960).

Field, Neil, C. "The Amu Daria: A Study in Resource Geography." *Geographical Review* 44 (1954): 528-542.

Fischer, K. "Zur Lage von Kandahar an Landverbindungen zwischen Iran und Indien." *Bonner Jahrbuecher* 167 (1967): 129-232.

Fischer, L. "Afghanistan eine Geographisch-Medizinische Landeskunde." In *Medizinische Laenderkunde.* Berlin: Springer Verlag, 1968.

Geokart. *National Atlas of the Democratic Republic of Afghanistan.* Warsaw: 1985.

Ghoubar, M. "Les Provinces Orientales de l'Afghanistan." *Afghanistan* 2 (1947).

Glicken, Milton. "Making a Map of Afghanistan." *Photogrammetric Engineering* 26/5 (1960).

Groetzbach, Erwin. *Afghanistan: eine Geographische Landeskunde.* Darmstadt: Wissenschaftliche Buchgesellschaft, 1990.

———. *Aktuelle Probleme der Regionalentwicklung und Stadtgeographie Afghanistans.* Meisenheim, Germany: Verlag Anton Hain, 1976.

———. *Kulturgeographische Wandel in Nordost-Afghanistan seit dem 19. Jahrhundert. Afghanische Studien.* Meisenheim, Germany: Verlag Anton Hain, 4 (1974).

———. *Staedte und Basare in Afghanistan.* Wiesbaden, Germany: Reichert, 1979.

Gysel, Alfred. "Afghanistan-Klima und Landschaft." *Mitteilungen der Naturerforschenden Gesellschaft in Bern* 9 (1952): 36-37.

Hahn, Helmut. "Geography in the Frame of the Social Sciences." *The Geographical Review of Afghanistan* 1/2, 9 (1962): 38-40.

———. "Die Stadt Kabul (Afghanistan) und ihr Umland." I: "Gestaltwandel einer Orientalischen Stadt." II: "Sozialstrukstur und Wirtschafliche Lage der Agrarbevoelkerung im Stadtumland." In *Bonner Geographische Abhandlung.* Bonn: 1964, 1965.

Hasse, D. "Hindukusch: Allgemeiner Uberblick sowie Vorschlag fuer eine Begrenzung und Gliederung." *Osterreichische Alpenzeitung* 83 (1965).

Humlum, J. *La Geographie de l'Afghanistan.* Kopenhagen: Scandinavian University Books, 1959.

Jentsch, Ch. *Das Nomadentum in Afghanistan. Afghanische Studien.* Meisenheim, Germany: Verlag Anton Hain, 9 (1973).

Kohzad, Ahmad Ali. "Nimruz ou le Bassin Inferieur de l'Hilmend." *Afghanistan* 8/4 (1953).

―――. "The Panjshir." *Afghanistan* 3/4 (1948)

Kohzad, Mohammad Nabi. "Kabul." *Afghanistan* 8/4-14/1 (1958-59): 1-15.

Kushkaki, Burhanuddin. *Kataghan o Badakhsan.* French translation by Marguerite Reut. Paris: Edition du Centre National de la Recherche Scientifique, 1979.

Masson, Ch. *Narrative of Various Journeys in Balochistan, Afghanistan, and the Panjab.* London, 1842. Reprint, Graz, Austria: ADEVA, 1975.

Mattai, James. *A Geographical Introduction to Herat Province.* Kabul: Faculty of Education, Kabul University, 1966.

Michaud, R., and S. Michaud. *Caravans to Tartary.* PARIS: Editions du Chene, 1978.

―――. "Winter Caravan to the Roof of the World." *National Geographic Magazine* (April 1972): 435-465.

Michel, Aloys A. "The Kabul, Kunduz, and Helmand Valleys and the National Economy of Afghanistan." *National Academy of Sciences* 1959.

Niedermayer, O. V. *Afghanistan.* Leipzig: W. Hiersmann, 1924.

Rathjens, Carl. "Afghanistan." *Die Weltwirtschaft* 2 (1957): 59-60.

―――. "Der Afghanische Hindukusch." *Jahrbuch des Deutschen Alpenvereins* 80 (1955).

―――. "Erschliessung des Hindukusch." *Mitteilungen des Deutschen Alpenvereins* 17 (1965): 8-10.

―――. "Kabul die Hauptstadt Afghanistan." *Leben und Umwelt* 13 (1957): 73-82.

————. "Landschaft und Mensch im Hindukusch." *The Geographical Review of Afghanistan* 2 (1963): 1-12.

Reshtya, Sayed Qasim. "L'Afghanistan du Point de Vue Geographique." *Afghanistan* 2/1 (1947): 16-22.

————. "The Rivers of Afghanistan." *Afghanistan* 2/2 (1943): 8-14.

Schurmann, H. F. *The Mongols of Western Afghanistan: An Ethnography of the Mongols and Related People of Afghanistan.* Berkeley, CA: University of California, 1957.

Snoy, Peter. "Die Bevoelkerung." In *Afghanistan.* Innsbruck: Penguin Verlag, 1985.

————. "Nuristan und Mungan." *Tribu* 14 (1965): 101-148.

Szabo, Albert, and Thomas J. Barfield. *Afghanistan: An Atlas of Indigenous Domestic Architecture.* Austin, TX: University of Texas Press, 1991.

Thesiger, Wilfred. "A Journey in Nuristan." *Geographical Journal* 123 (1957): 457-464.

Wiebe, D. "Die Raeumliche Gestalt der Alstadt von Kandahar: Ein Kultur-geographischer Beitrag zum Problem der Partiellen Modernisierung." *Afghanistan Journal* 4 (1976): 132-146.

Geology

Afghanistan Geological Survey. *South Afghanistan, Sedimentary Basin Structure.* Kabul University 1963. 198-200.

Clapp, F. G. "Geology of Afghanistan." *Bulletin of the Geological Society of America* 50/12 (1939): 1904.

Desio, A. *Geology of Central Badakhshan, North East Afghanistan and Surrounding Countries.* Leiden, Netherlands: E.J. Brill, 1975.

Fuchs, G., and A. Matura. "The Geology of the Nilaw Area in Central Nurestan, Afghanistan." *Jahrbuch der Geologischen Bundesanstalt* 119/2 (1976): 97-128.

Griesbach, C. L. "Afghan Field-Notes." *Records of the Geological Survey of India* 18/1 (1885): 57-64.

———. "Geologische Notizen aus Afghanistan." *Verhandlungen der K.K. Geologischen Reichsanstalt* 28 (1885): 314-315.

Hayden, H. H. "The Geology of Northern Afghanistan." *Memoirs of the Geological Survey of India* 29/1 (1911).

Hunger, J. P. *Geological Survey in Afghanistan*. Kabul: Government Press, 1964.

Lapparent, A. F. de. "La Montagne du Fer d'Hajigek en Afghanistan Central." *Afghanistan Journal* 2/1 (1975): 8-11.

Nasiri, A. "The History of Lapis Lazuli in Afghanistan." *Afghanistan* 17/4 and 18/1, 2 (1962).

Popal, S. A. "Geologie von Afghanistan." *Ariana* 1955.

Reed, F. R. C. "Upper Carboniferous Fossils from Afghanistan." *Palaeontologia Indica* (1931): 1-39.

Rosset, L. F. "Precious Stones in Afghanistan: The Diamond." *Afghanistan* 2/1 (1947).

Schwab, M. *Establishment of a Geological Survey Department in Afghanistan*. New York: UN Report, 1955.

Stenz, Edward. "Earthquakes in Afghanistan." *Afghanistan* 1/1 (1946).

Wolfart, R., and H. Wittekindt. *Geologie von Afghanistan*. Berlin: Borntraeger, 1980.

Geomorphology

Balland, V., and J. Lang. "Les Rapports Geomorphologique Quarternaises et Actuels du Bassin de Banyan et de Ses Bordures Montagneuses." *Revue de Geographie Physique et de Geologie Dynamique* 16/3 (1974): 327-350.

Burnes, A. "On the Reg-Ruwan or Moving Sand, a Singular Phenomenon of Sound Near Cabul." *Journal of the Asiatic Society of Bengal* 7 (1838): 324-325.

Taniwal, Z. "La Region de Band-i-Amir: Etude de Geographie Physique." *Afghanistan* 31/4 (1979): 29-60.

Meteorology

British Embassy. *Weather Records for Kabul, 1942 through 1953.* Kabul 1953.

Matthai, J. *Climate Statistics for Afghanistan.* Kabul: Faculty of Education, Kabul University, 1966.

Rathjens, C. "Hohe Tagessummen des Niederschlags in Afghanistan." *Afghanistan Journal* 5/1 (1978): 22-25.

Sivall, T. R. "The Problems of Meteorology in Afghanistan." *Geographical Review of Afghanistan* 1/2 (1962): 16-21.

Stenz, E. "Precipitation, Evaporation and Aridity in Afghanistan." *Acta Geophysica Polonica* 5 (1957): 245-266.

7. SOCIAL

Ethnography

Ali, Muhammad. *Manners and Customs of Afghans.* Lahore: Punjab Education Press, 1958.

Anderson, Jon. W., and Richard. F. Strand. *Ethnic Processes and Inter-group Relations in Contemporary Afghanistan.* The Afghanistan Council of the Asia Society. 1978.

Bacon, E. E. "The Inquiry into the History of the Hazara Mongols of Afghanistan." *Southwestern Journal of Anthropology* 7 (1951): 230-247.

Bellew, H.W. *An Enquiry Into the Ethnography of Afghanistan Prepared for and Presented to the Ninth International Congress of Orientalists.* London, 1891. Reprint, ADEVA, Graz 1973.

———. *A General Report on the Yusufzeis.* Lahore, India: Govern-ment Press, 1864.

Broguetti, Michele. *The Current Situation in Hazarajat.* Oxford, England: Oxford University Press, 1982.

Burnes, A. "On the Siah-posh Kafirs, With Specimens of their Language and Costume." *Journal of the Asiatic Society of Bengal* 7 (1838): 325-333.

Centlivres, P. "La Contribution Francaise et Suisse a l'Ethnographie de l'Afghanistan Depuis la Seconde Guerre Mondial." *Central Asiatic Journal* 16 (1972): 181-193.

Charpentier, C. J. *Bazaar-e Tashqurghan: Ethnographical Studies in an Afghan Traditional Bazaar.* Uppsala, Sweden: SEU, 1972.

Clifford, M. L. *The Land and People of Afghanistan.* Philadelphia, PA: Lippincott, 1973.

Dianous, H. J. de. "Hazaras and Mongols en Afghanistan." *Orient* 19 (1961): 71-98.

Dupree, L. "Nuristan: (The Land of Light) Seen Darkly." *American Universities Field Staff Reports* 15/16 (1971).

Edelberg, L., and S. Jones. *Nuristan.* Graz, Austria: ADEVA, 1979.

Ferdinand, K. "Ethnographical Notes on Chahar Aimaq, Hazara and Moghol." *Acta Orientalia* 28/3-4 (1964): 175-203.

Fischel, W. J. "The Rediscovery of the Medieval Jewish Community at Firuzkuh in Central Afghanistan." *Journal of the American Oriental Society* 85 (1965).

Janata, A. "Die Afghanischen Sammlungen des Museums fuer Völkerkunde in Wien." *Afghanistan Journal* 1/1 (1974): 5-12.

———. *Schmuck in Afghanistan.* Graz, Austria: ADEVA, 1980.

Kohzad, A. A. "The Panjsher." *Afghanistan* 3/4 (1948): 17-29.

Nabi, Eden. "The Uzbeks in Afghanistan." *Central Asian Survey* 3/1 (1984).

Olesen, Asta. *Afghan Craftsmen: The Culture of Three Itinerant Communities.* London: Thames & Hudson, 1994.

Orywal, Erwin. *Die Ethnischen Gruppen Afghanistans.* Wiesbaden: Ludwig Reichert Verlag, 1986.

Rao, A. "Qui Sont les Jat d'Afghanistan." *Afghanistan Journal* 8/2 (1981): 55-65.

Raverty, H. G. "Indian, Afghan and Pathan Tribes." *Asiatic Quarterly Review* 7 (1894).

———. "Kafiristan and the Kafiri Tribes." *Calcutta Review.* 1896.

Robertson, G. S. *The Kafirs of the Hindu Kush.* London: Oxford University Press, 1974.

Schurmann, H. F. *The Mongols of Western Afghanistan: An Ethnography of the Mongols and Related Peoples of Afghanistan.* Berkeley, CA: University of California Press, 1957.

Shahrani, M. N. M. *The Kirghiz and Wakhi of Afghanistan: Adaptation to Closed Frontiers.* Seattle, WA: University of Washington Press, 1979.

Snoy, Peter. *Ethnologie und Geschichte. Festschrift für Karl Jettmar.* Wiesbaden, Germany: Franz Steiner, 1983.

Wadud, A. *The Story of Swat.* Peshawar, Pakistan: N. p.., 1963.

Anthropology

Anderson, Jon. "Tribe and Community Among the Ghilzai Pashtun. Preliminary Notes on Ethnographic Distribution and Variation in Eastern Afghanistan." *Anthropos* 70 (1975): 575-601.

Bacon, Elizabeth E. "The Inquiry into the History of the Hazara Mongols of Afghanistan." *Southwestern Journal of Anthropology* 7 (1951).

Barfield, T. J. *The Central Asian Arabs of Afghanistan.* Austin, TX: University of Texas Press, 1981.

Bauer, W. P., and A. Janata. "Kosmetik, Schmuck und Symbolik in Afghanistan." *Archiv fuer Volkerkunde* 28 (1975): 1-43.

Bellew, Henry W. *The Races of Afghanistan, Being a Brief Account of the Principal Nations Inhabiting that Country.* Calcutta: Thacker, Spink, 1880.

Canfield, R. *Factions and Conversion: Study on the Hazara.* Ann Arbor, MI: University of Michigan Press, 1969.

———. *Hazara Integration into the Afghan Nation, some Changing Relations between Hazaras and Afghan Officials.* Asia Society. New York, 1973.

Jettmar, Karl. *Cultures of the Hindukush.* Wiesbaden, Germany: Franz Steiner, 1974.

Jones, S. *An Outline of the Political Organization of the Kam Kafirs.* Edinburgh: University of Edinburgh, 1965.

————. *Men of Influence in Nuristan: A Study of Social Control and Dispute Settlement in Waigal Valley, Afghanistan.* London: Seminar Press, 1974.

Katz, David J. "Kafir to Afghan." Ph.D. diss., UCLA Los Angeles, 1982.

Lentz, W. *Zeitrechnung in Nuristan und am Pamir.* Graz, Austria: ADEVA, 1978.

Ridgway, R. T. I. *Pathans.* Calcutta: Government Printing, 1910.

Schurmann, H. F. *The Mongols of Afghanistan.* Gravenhage, Netherlands: Mouton, 1962.

Shahrani, M. Nazif. *The Kirghiz and Wakhi of Afghanistan.* Seattle, WA: University of Washington, 1979.

Spain, J. W. *The Way of the Pathans.* London: Hale, 1962.

Zadran, A. S. "Kinship, Family and Kinship Terminology." *Afghanistan Quarterly* 33/2 (1960): 45-68.

Demography

American Universities Field Staff. *Population: Perspective 1973.* CA: Freeman, Cooper & Co., 1973.

Amerkhail, N. "Family Planning in Afghanistan." *Population Review* 1961.

Asia Society, Afghanistan Council. *Demographic Research in Afghanistan: A National Survey of the Settled Population.* New York: 1977.

Blanc, J. C. *L'Afghanistan et Ses Populations.* Paris: Presses Universitaires de France, 1976.

Dupree, L. "Population Review 1970: Afghanistan." *American Universities Field Staff Reports* 15/1 (1971): 20.

Government of Afghanistan and United States Agency for International Development. *National Demographic and Family Guidance Survey of the Settled Population of Afghanistan.* 3 vols. New York: USAID, 1975.

―――. *A Provisional Gazetteer of Afghanistan.* 3 vols. Kabul: Central Statistics Office, 1975.

Hendrick, P. *Infant and Early Childhood Mortality Survey: Protocol for Prospective Study in Kabul.* Kabul: Ministry of Public Health, 1973.

Institute of Social Studies. *Methodology of Population Censuses and Practical Problems in Afghanistan.* The Hague: 1970.

Langley, G. *Population: Family Planning.* Kabul: USAID, 1972.

Puffer, R.R. *Patterns of Mortality in Childhood. Report of the Inter-American Investigation of Mortality in Childhood.* Washington, DC: Pan American Health Organization, 1973.

Trussel, J., and E. Brown. "A Close Look at the Demography of Afghanistan." *Demography* 16/1 (1979): 137-156.

Education

Dupree, L. "The Afghan-American Education Commission." *American Universities Field Staff Reports* 18/2 (1973).

―――. "The Afghan-American Education Commission." *American Universities Field Staff Reports* 18/2 (1974).

―――. "Afghan Studies: An Overview, with Notes on Research, Institutional Activity and Bibliography." *American Universities Field Staff Reports* 20/4 (1976).

Harris, F. *Public School Education in Afghanistan.* Kabul: U.S. Operations Mission to Afghanistan, n.d.

Hoelgaard, S. *Plan for Operation for Improvement of Primary Education in Afghanistan.* Kabul: UNICEF, 1974.

Martin, R. T. *Kabul University, its Role in Education, Research, and Public Service in Afghanistan*. Kabul: Kabul University, 1959.

Ministry of Education (Afghanistan). *Education in Afghanistan During the Last Fifty Years*. Kabul: 1968.

———. *Education Statistics, Afghanistan: 1969, 1970, 1971, 1972*. Kabul: 1969-72.

Natik, G. N. *Engineering Education in Afghanistan*. Kabul: Kabul University, 1972.

Ordyniec, J. *Women's Education in Afghanistan: Mission Oct.1967-March 1970*. UNESCO, 1970.

Rahel, S. *Monograph on Cultural Policy in Afghanistan*. Paris: UNESCO, 1975.

Rishtya, Sayyid Q. "Education in Afghanistan." *Afghanistan* 1/1 (1946): 20-25.

Weinbaum, Marvin G. "Foreign Assistance to Afghan Higher Education." *Afghanistan Journal* 3/2 (1976).

Ziai, A. Hakim. "The Role of Education in Securing Human Rights." *Afghanistan Journal* 19/2 (1964).

Health

Care Medico. *Report on Afghanistan Nutrition Study Project*. Kabul: AID, 1970.

Clarke, J. A. K. *Nutritional Status in the Hazarajat*. Kabul: Medical Assistance Program, 1970.

Fischer, L. *Afghanistan: Eine Geographischmedizinische Landeskunde*. Berlin: Springer Verlag, 1968.

———. "Volksmedizin in Afghanistan." *Afghanistan Journal* 1/3 (1974): 15-64.

Gobar, A. H. "Drug Abuse in Afghanistan." *Bulletin on Narcotics* 28/2 (1976): 1-11.

Helfenbein, S., and M. Higgins. *Afghanistan Nutrition Study Project.* Kabul: Care Medico, Final Report, n.d.

O'Connor, R.W. *Managing Health Systems in Developing Areas: Experiences from Afghanistan.* Lexington, MA: Lexington Books, 1980.

Prowi, T. T. *Foods and Nutrition in Afghanistan.* Kabul: Kabul University, 1962.

United States Agency for International Development. *A Health Survey of Afghanistan.* Kabul: 1963.

Wakeham, P. *Annual Report of the Medical Assistance Program, Afghanistan Project.* Kabul: N.p., 1972-1973.

Refugees

Dadfar, Muhammad Azam. "Refugee Syndrome." *WUFA, Quarterly Journal of the Writers Union of Free Afghanistan* (1986).

Dupree, Nancy Hatch. "The Afghan Refugee Family Abroad: A Focus on Pakistan." *WUFA, Quarterly Journal of the Writers Union of Free Afghanistan* (1987).

Rogers, Tom. "Afghans in Exile: Refugees—a Threat to Stability?" *Conflict Studies* 202 (1987).

Shaharani, M. Nazif. "Afghanistan's Kirghiz in Turkey." *Cultural Survival Quarterly* 8/1 (1984).

Steul, Willi, and Wolfgang G. Beitz. *Hilfe Für Afghanistan.* Bonn: 1981.

United Nations High Commissioner for Refugees, UNHCR Background Reports. *Ghazni Province,* 1990; *Wardak Province,* 1990; *Laghman Province,* 1989; *Logar Province,* 1989; *Kandahar Province,* 1989;

Kunar Province, 1989; *Paktia Province*, 1989; *Paktika Province*, 1989.

Religion

Anderson, Jon W. "How Afghans Define Themselves in Relation to Islam." In *Revolutions and Rebellions in Afghanistan*. Berkeley, CA: Institute of International Studies, 1984.

Barry, M. "Afghanistan, Terre d'Islam." *Les Temps Modernes* 408-409 (1980): 29-52.

Canfield, R. L. *Faction and Conversion in a Plural Society: Religious Alignments in the Hindu Kush*. Ann Arbor, MI: Museum of Anthropology, University of Michigan, 1973.

————. *Suffering as a Religious Imperative in Afghanistan*. 9th International Congress of Anthropological and Ethnological Sciences, 1973.

Dupree, L. "Afghanistan, Islam in Politics: A Symposium." *Moslem World*. 56 (1966): 269-276.

————. "The Afghans Honor a Muslim Saint: Reprise." *American Universities Field Staff Reports* 20/7 (1976): 12.

————. "Militant Islam and Traditional Warfare in Islamic South Asia." *American Universities Field Staff Reports* 21 (1980): 12.

————. "Saint Cults in Afghanistan." *American Universities Field Staff Reports* 20/1 (1976): 26.

Edwards, D. B. "Print Islam: Media and Religious Revolution in Afghanistan." *Anthropological Quarterly* 3 (July 1995).

Einzmann, H. "Religious Folk Tradition in Afghanistan, Pilgrimage and Veneration of Saints." In *Islam in Southern Asia* 61-63. Heidelberg: Heidelberg University, 1975. 61-63.

Farhadi, A. G. R. "Ibn Sina und Sufism." *Afghanistan Quarterly* 33/2 (1980): 1-8.

Fazelly, Muhammad Kasem. "L'Islam Shi'ite en Afghanistan." Paris: *Les Nouvelles d'Afghanistan* 12/13 (March 1983).

Ghani, Ashraf. "Disputes in a Court of Shariaa, Kunar Valley, Afghanistan, 1885- 1890." *IJMES* 15 (1983).

————. "Islam and State-building in a Tribal Society, Afghanistan 1880-1901." *Modern Asian Studies* 12 (1978): 269-284.

Ghobar, M. "Le Role de l'Afghanistan Dans la Civilisation Islamique." *Afghanistan* 1/1 (1946): 27-34.

Jalalzai, Musa Khan. *Sectarianism and Ethnic Violence in Afghanistan.* Lahore: Vanguard Books, n.d.

Jettmar, K. *The Religions of the Hindukush.* Warminster, England: Aris & Phillips, 1986.

Kohzad, A. A. "L'Afghanistan au Point de Vue de la Religion." *Afghanistan* 8/3 (1953): 1-17.

Lafrance, Pierre, Gilles Rossignol and Pierre Centlivres, et al. "L'Islam en Afghanistan." *Les Nouvelles d'Afghanistan* 12/13 (March 1983).

Majrouh, S. B. "The Message of a Sufi for the Modern World." *Afghanistan* 29/3 (1976): 38-55.

Noelle, Christine. "Anti-Wahhabi Reaction in 19th Century Afghanistan." *The Muslim World* 1-2 (April 1995).

Olesen, Asta. "Islam and Politics in Afghanistan." In *Neue Beiträge zur Afghanistanforschung.* Liestal, Switzerland: Bibliotheca Afghanica, 1988.

Schimmel, A. "The Meaning of Prayer in Mawlana Jalaloddin Balkha's Work." *Afghanistan* 23/3 (1974): 33-45.

Tabibi, A. H. "The Great Mystics of Afghanistan." *Afghanistan* 30/2 (1977): 25-39.

———. *Sufism in Afghanistan.* Kabul: Author, 1977.

Utas, B. "Notes on Afghanistan. Sufi Orders and Khanaqahs." *Afghanistan Journal* 7/2 (1980): 60-67.

———. "Scholars, Saints and Sufis in Modern Afghanistan." In *The Tragedy of Afghanistan*, edited by Bo Hultdt, Erland Jansson, et al. London: Croom Helm, 1988.

Wiebe, D. "Die Heutigen Kultstaetten in Afghanistan un Ihre Inwertsetzung fuer den Fremdenverkehr." *Afghanistan Journal* 7/3 (1980): 97-108.

Wilber, D. N. "The Structure and Position of Islam in Afghanistan." *Middle East Journal* 6/1 (1952): 41-48.

Sociology

Ahmed, A. S. *Social and Economic Change in Tribal Areas.* Karachi: Oxford University Press, 1977.

Anderson, J. "Khan and Khel: Dialectics of Pakhtun Tribalism." In *The Conflict of Tribe and State in Iran and Afghanistan*, edited by R. Tapper. London: Croom-Helm, 1983.

———. "Social Structure and the Veil: Comportment and Interaction in Afghanistan." *Anthropos* 77 (1982).

———. "There are no Khans Anymore: Economic Development and Social Change in Tribal Afghanistan." *Middle East Journal* 32/2 (1978): 167-183.

Boesen, I. W. "Women, Honour and Love: Some Aspects of the Pashtun Woman's Life in Eastern Afghanistan." *Afghanistan Journal* 7/2 (1980): 50-59.

Buescher, H. *Die Industriearbeiter in Afghanistan: eine Studie zur Gesellschaftpolitischen Problematik Sozial Schwacher Bevolkerungsschichten in Entwicklungslaendern*. Meisenheim, Germany: Verlag Anton Hain, 1969.

Dupree, L. "The Green and the Black: Social and Economic Aspects of a Coal Mine in Afghanistan." *American Universities Field Staff Reports* 7/5 (1963): 30.

———. "Religion, Technology and Evolution: A Case Study of a Muslim Community." *Journal of Social Research* 4 (1961): 341-354.

———. "Tribalism, Religionism and National Oligarchy." In *Expectant Peoples*, edited by K. Silbert. New York: 1963, 41-76.

Ferdiand, Klaus. "Les Hazara." In *Peuples du Monde Entier*. Paris: Alpha, 1976.

Ghani, A. "Continuity and Change in the Function of Pashtun Intellectuals." *Afghanistan* 30/2 (1977): 40-53.

Harpviken, Kristian Berg. *Political Mobilization among the Hazara of Afghanistan, 1978-1992*. Oslo: Department of Sociology, 1995.

Jarring, G. "An Uzbek on his Native Town and its Circumstances." *Ethnos* 4 (1939): 73-80.

Knabe, E. *Frauenemanzipation in Afghanistan. Ein Empirischer Beitrag zur Untersuchung von Soziokulturellem Wandel und Sozio-Kultureller Beständigkeit*. Meisenheim, Germany: Verlag Anton Hain, 1977.

Mormann, H., and E. Ploger. *Buskaschi in Afghanistan*. Lucern and Frankfurt: Bucher, 1978.

Sarwari, M. S. *Afghanistan Zwischen Tradition und Modernisierung*. Bern and Frankfurt: H. Lang, 1974.

Shalinsky, A. *Central Asian Emigres in Afghanistan: Problems of Religious and Ethnic Identity*. New York: Afghanistan Council, Asia Society, 1979.

Strand, R. F. "The Changing Herding Economy of the Kom Nuristani."
Afghanistan Journal 2/4 (1975): 123-134.

Swinson, A. *North-West Frontier: People and Events, 1839-1947.* London: Hutchinson, 1967.

Nomads

Besters, H. H., and K. H. Kraus. "Nomadismus als Entwicklungproblem."
In *Bochumer Symposium.* Bielefeld, Germany: Np., 1969.

Centlivres, P., and M. Centlivres-Demont. "Chemins d'Ete, Chemins d'Hiver Entre Darwaz et Qataghan." *Afghanistan Journal* 4/4 (1977): 155-163.

Dakshieyger, G. F. *Settlement and Traditional Social Institutions of the Former Nomads (on the Example of the Kazakh People)*, 9th International Congress of Anthropological and Ethnological Sciences, 1973.

Ferdinand, K. *Aspects of the Relations Between Nomads and Settled Populations in Afghanistan.* Moscow: Seventh International Congress of Anthropological and Ethnological Studies, 1964.

――――. "Nomad Expansion in Central Afghanistan: A Sketch of Some Modern Trends." *Folk* 4 (1962): 123-159.

――――."Nomadism in Afghanistan with an Appendix on Milk Products."
Viehwirtschaft und Hirt Kultur, edited by L. Forder. Budpest: 1969, 127-160.

――――. "Ost-Afghanischer Nomadismusein Beitrag zur Anpassungsfahigkeit der Nomaden." *Nomadismus als Entwicklungsproblem* (1969): 107-128.

Glatzer, B. *Nomaden von Gharjistan: Aspekte der Wirtschaftlichen, Sozialen und Politischen Organisation Nomadischer Durrani-Paschtunen in Nordwest-afghanistan.* Wiesbaden: F. Steiner, 1977.

Jentsch, C. *Das Nomadentum in Afghanistan*. Meisenheim: Verlag Anton Hain, 1973.

―――. "Structural Changes of Nomadism in Afghanistan." *Geographical Review of Afghanistan* 7/2 (1969): 8-13.

―――. "Die Wirtschaftlichen und Politischen Aspekte des Nomadentums in Zentralasien. Besonders die Jungste Entwicklung Afghanistan." *National* Schweizerische UNESCO - Kommission. (Eds.), Seminar Uber das Nomadentum in Zentralasien (Afghanistan, Iran, USSR), Schlussbericht Bern, (1976): 45-57.

Kraus, R. W. H. "Siedlungsprojekte in der Provinz Helmand (Afghanistan) unter Besonderer Berucksichtigung Gesiedelter Nomaden." *Vierteljahresberichte* 46 (1971): 419-432.

Majruh, S. B. "Aktuelle Fragen des Nomadismus in Afghanistan." *Nomadismus als Entwicklungsproblem* (1969): 155-160.

Pedersen, G. *Afghan Nomads in Transition* . London: Thames & Hudson, 1994.

―――. "Socio-economic Change Among a Group of East Afghan Nomads." *Afghanistan Journal* 8/4 (1981): 115-122.

Renesse, E. A. von, and H. C. G. Sponeck. "Nomadismus in Afghanistan als soziookonomisches Problem." *Nomadismus als Entwicklungsproblem* (1969): 161-170.

―――. "Nomadism in Afghanistan." *Nomadismus als Entwicklungsproblem* (1969): 173-182.

Robinson, J. A. *Notes on Nomad Tribes of Eastern Afghanistan*. Quetta, Pakistan: Nisa Traders, 1978.

Shahrani, M. N. M. "Kirghiz Pastoral Nomads of the Afghan Pamirs: A Study in Ecological and Intra-Cultural Adaptation." M.A. thesis, University of Washington, 1976.

Singer, A. "Problems of Pastoralism in the Afghan Pamirs." *Asian Affairs* 63 (1976): 156-160.

Strand, R. F. "The Changing Herding Economy of the Kom Nuristani." *Afghanistan Journal* 2/4 (1975): 123-134.

Tapper, N. "Pashtun Nomad Women in Afghanistan." *Asian Affairs* 64/2 (1977): 163-170.

ABOUT THE AUTHOR

Ludwig W. Adamec (B.A., in political science; M.A., journalism; Ph.D. Islamic and Middle East studies, UCLA) is a professor of Middle Eastern studies at the University of Arizona and was director of its Near Eastern Center for ten years. Widely known as a leading authority on Afghanistan, he is the author of a number of reference works on Afghanistan and books on Afghan history, foreign policy, and international relations, including *Afghanistan 1900-1923: A Diplomatic History, Afghanistan's Foreign Affairs to the mid-Twentieth Century*, a six-volume *Political Gazetteer of Afghanistan*, and a *Dictionary of Afghan Wars, Revolutions, and Insurgencies*.

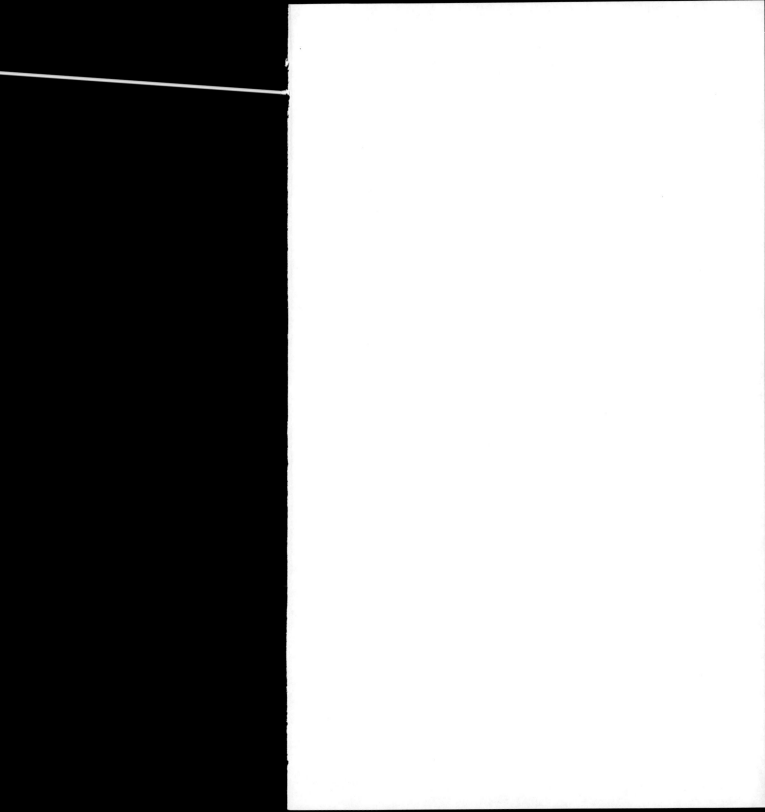